Start Your Own Business

Entrepreneur MAGAZINE'S

Start Your Own Business

The Only Start-Up Book You'll Ever Need

By Rieva Lesonsky, Editorial Director,
and the Staff of Entrepreneur Magazine

ENTREPRENEUR MEDIA INC.
2392 Morse Ave., Irvine, CA 92614

Forthcoming books from Entrepreneur Media Inc.:

Young Millionaires: Inspiring Stories to Ignite Your Entrepreneurial Dreams

303 Marketing Ideas: Guaranteed to Boost Your Business

Library of Congress Cataloging-in-Publication Data
Start your own business: the only start-up book you'll ever need
    p. cm.
    Includes index.
    ISBN 1-891984-00-4
    1. New business enterprises—Management.   2. Small business—Management.   I. Entrepreneur Media, Inc.
    HD62.5.S7373   1998
    658'.041—dc21   98-20898
                                        CIP

Printed in the United States of America

08 07 06 05 04 03 02 01 00 99   10 9 8 7 6 5 4 3 2

Editorial Director
Rieva Lesonsky

Managing Editor
Marla Markman

Project Editor
Karen Axelton

Proofreader
Julie Flick

Contributing Writers
Jill Amadio, Leanne Anderson, Jane Easter Bahls,
Stephen Barlas, Stephanie Barlow, Johanna Billings,
Bruce Blechman, J. Tol Broome, Andrew Caffey,
Carolyn Campbell, Melissa Caresosa, Cassandra Cavanah,
Janean Chun, Bob Coleman, Sandra Eddy, David Evanson,
Iris Lorenz-Fife, Lorayne Fiorillo, Jerry Fisher, Barbara Frantz,
Charles Fuller, Cheryl Goldberg, Kim Gordon, Cynthia Griffin,
Mark Henricks, Frances Huffman, Christopher Keanelly,
Danielle Kennedy, Erika Kotite, Jay Conrad Levinson,
David Lindo, Jacquelyn Lynn, Richard Maturi, Robert McGarvey,
Sean Melvin, Heather Page, Debra Phillips, Marcia Perkins-Reed,
Karen Roy, Edward Rybka, Bev Stehli, Gayle Sato Stodder,
Guen Sublette, Joan Szabo, Ed Tittel, Conrad Theodore,
Bob Weinstein, Glen Weisman, Linda Wroblewski

Production Design
Coghill Composition Company

Illustrations
John McKinley

Cover Design
Janice Olson & Associates

Indexer
Alta Indexing Service

Acknowledgments

Producing this book has been like giving birth. Even though the material within is second nature to us, the process of putting it together into a book, something that as magazine publishers we were unfamiliar with, was the tough part. We dedicated a lot of research, time and energy to the creation of this book.

Start Your Own Business is the culmination of *Entrepreneur's* decades of reporting on the world of small business, each year gaining more insight, knowledge and expertise into what makes and breaks successful business ownership. This product is the result of *Entrepreneur's* 21 years of covering the business of small business.

This book wouldn't have been possible without the hard work and dedication of many people. First and foremost, a heartfelt thank you goes out to Rieva Lesonsky, *Entrepreneur's* editorial director, and this division's mentor and guiding light. It was her vision, leadership and wealth of small-business knowledge (she is a small-business guru in her own right) that helped us make *Start Your Own Business* into a first-rate product we can all be proud to put the "Entrepreneur" name on.

Thanks also to project editor Karen Axelton, who took an intimidating, sky-high stack of *Entrepreneur* issues, added her own unique wit and wisdom, and delivered seamless, sparkling prose. A special appreciation goes to Maria Anton, *Entrepreneur's* senior managing editor, whose amazing memory helped me fulfill my book topic wish list and whose never-ending patience was also amazing as she instructed me in the fine art of navigating our database. And I can't forget the *Entrepreneur* staff as well.

Last, but certainly not least, thank you to the Business Products Division staff—Susan Stone Russell, director of marketing; Lori Gunnette, marketing project manager; and Sylvia Lee, production designer—whose support and creative energy were invaluable on this project.

—*Marla Markman*
Managing Editor

ON YOUR MARK... 1

GET SET. . . 211

Chapter 18: First Impressions:
Creating a professional image

Chapter 19: Taking Stock:
The lowdown on inventory

GO! ... 435

On Your Mark . . .

Why did you pick up this book? Perhaps you know you want to be an entrepreneur and take charge of your own life. You've already got a great idea for a business you're sure will be a hit. Or perhaps you think, somewhere in the back of your mind, that maybe you might like to start your own business . . . but you're not sure what venture to start, what entrepreneurship is really like and whether it's for you.

Whichever of these categories you fall into, you've come to the right place. In Part 1, "You Gotta Start Somewhere," we'll show you what it means to be an entrepreneur. Take our exclusive quiz, and find out if you've got what it takes. Don't have a business idea or not sure if your idea will fly? You'll learn the secrets to spotting trends before they happen and coming up with dozens of sure-fire business ideas. We'll also discuss various ways of going into business, including part- and full-time entrepreneurship. Finally, we'll show you the different options for start-up, such as starting from scratch, purchasing an existing business, or buying into a franchise or business opportunity system.

Planning is key to every thriving business, and in Part 2, "Building Blocks," you'll learn just what you need to do to lay the groundwork for success. Find out how to pinpoint your target market, plus dozens of ways to do market research—from hiring experts to money-saving do-it-yourself tips. Since the name you choose can make or break your business, we share plenty of techniques for coming up with the perfect moniker—one that will attract customers to your company in droves. And don't forget the nuts-and-bolts necessities, like getting licenses and permits to operate your business, plus choosing a legal structure—corporation, partnership, sole proprietorship and more. You'll discover all the information you need to guide you through these often confusing steps to start-up.

A business plan is your road map to success, guiding the growth of your business at every stage along the way. We'll show you how to craft a business plan that puts you on the fast track. Finally, find out why you need professional advisors to help you through your start-up, and how to select an accountant and attorney who can help you make money—without costing you a bundle.

Speaking of money, every entrepreneur knows that adequate start-up capital is essential to success. But just where do you find that crucial cash? In Part 3, "Where's The Money?" we give you the inside scoop on getting the money you need. Discover dozens of sources of capital. We show you secrets to financing your business yourself, how to tap into the most common source of start-up financing (family and friends), plus places you may never have thought of to look for money.

Do you stand a chance of getting venture capital, or attracting private investors? You'll find out in this section. And if you're looking for a loan, look no further for the secrets to finding the right bank. We show you what bankers look for when evaluating a loan application—and how to make sure yours makes the grade. Seeking money from Uncle Sam? You'll get all the details about dozens of loan programs from the government, including special assistance for women and minority entrepreneurs. Whatever your needs, you're sure to find a financing source that's right for you.

Part One:

You Gotta Start Somewhere

CHAPTER 1

INTRODUCTION

Buying this book may be the smartest thing you ever did. OK, I may be exaggerating some, but I am serious about the impact that *Start Your Own Business* can have on your life. As the editorial director of *Entrepreneur* magazine, I have been covering the business of entrepreneurship for a long time now, and I can honestly say I have met few entrepreneurs who are sorry they took the leap into business ownership. Most have succeeded (though not necessarily at the business they initially launched); some have returned to life as an employee. But few regret the journey.

Start Your Own Business is designed to help you navigate your own journey to business ownership. We're here to instruct and inspire, to tell you the things you don't know and remind you of the things you do. Some will tell you that the path you are about to embark on is a perilous one, but it's not. However, it is not without its curves, speed bumps and detours. *Start Your Own Business* helps prepare you as you go. You'll learn what to expect at each step along the way. Some wise person once said, "Forewarned is forearmed." So consider this book part of your arsenal.

I would never presume to tell anyone how to read a book. But the very first thing you might want to do is turn to the following "Pop Quiz" chapter and take our test to determine if you're cut out to be an entrepreneur. My guess is you are, or you wouldn't have bought this book. Some people mistakenly believe you have to be born an entrepreneur to succeed. You don't. You can learn what it takes. That's what this book is all about.

Start Your Own Business takes you step by step through the start-up journey, from how to get an idea for a business to finally opening the doors to your new venture. Along the way, we provide lots of forms, work sheets and checklists you can actually use in your business as well as to make sure you're on the right track. The book is also filled with four different types of helpful tip boxes:

Beware!

Heed the warnings in this box to avoid common mistakes and pitfalls.

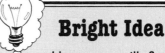

Bright Idea

Here you will find helpful information or ideas you may not have known or thought about before.

Dollar Stretcher

This box provides valuable tips on ways you can save money during start-up.

Smart Tip

Look for this box to reveal ideas on how to do something better or more efficiently or a method of working smarter.

Finally, at the end of the book, there are three appendices chock-full of business resources that list contact addresses and phone numbers:

1. In "**Business Resources**," we list business associations, books, and magazines and publications in areas ranging from advertising and marketing to accounting and taxes. We even provide Internet resources and equipment manufacturers.

2. Our "**Government Listings**" appendix provides contact information for Small Business Development Centers, Small Business Administration district offices and state economic development departments across the country.

3. Lastly, if you need financing, you'll definitely want to check out our listing of "**Small-Business-Friendly Banks**."

Starting your own business is not as mysterious as some would have you believe (for more on this, see the "What's The Big Idea?" chapter) nor as frightening or risky as legend would have it. But it is a journey that is better not taken alone. With *Start Your Own Business* as your companion, you will be a wiser traveler on the road to business ownership. So what are you waiting for? As an ancient Chinese philosopher once sagely said, "Every journey . . . must begin with a single step."

CHAPTER 2

POP QUIZ

Are you ready to be an entrepreneur?

Do you have what it takes to be an entrepreneur? Only you can answer that question, but this chapter will help you figure it out. You'll learn about the qualities of successful entrepreneurs (as well as the qualities that can hinder your business), plus ways to determine if you're really meant to run your own business. There's even a test you can take to assess your entrepreneurial potential. So what are you waiting for? Read on . . . and find out if you've got what it takes.

THE ENTREPRENEURIAL PERSONALITY

Every year, hundreds of thousands of people make the transition from employee to entrepreneur. But while some succeed, others fail. Many of those who fail do so because they simply weren't ready to make the change.

Quitting a full-time job to start a business isn't something to be taken lightly. Anyone considering striking out on his or her own should carefully assess the proposition before doing so. How do you know if the entrepreneurial life is for you? Self-assessment tests such as the one in this chapter can be used to measure your potential success. But even if a test indicates you've got the right personality for entrepreneurial success, that doesn't necessarily mean you're ready to become one at this point in time. Many questions remain: Do I have enough money? Is my family ready for this? Do people need a product or service like mine? Parts 1, 2 and 3 of this book will help you answer those questions. If the answers are yes, congratulations: You may be on your way to becoming a business owner.

Taking The Plunge

Most successful entrepreneurs recall a sense of urgency that made starting their own business not just a desire but a necessity. One entrepreneur says you'll know the time is right when "you can honestly say 'I'll put my house, jewelry and other personal collateral on the line to attain the start-up capital I need for the long-term rewards I deserve.'" Once you're ready to commit your own personal assets, you've probably crossed the line.

But what motivates potential entrepreneurs to stop daydreaming about business ownership and actually do something about it? While many people think one single incident—such as getting fired or being passed over for a promotion—is the impetus for becoming your own boss, most experts agree it's usually a series of frustrations that leads to entrepreneurship.

A fundamental need to control their own destiny ranks very high on most entrepreneurs' list of reasons for starting their own businesses. This need is so strong that entrepreneurs will risk family, future and careers to be their own boss. Unable to feel truly fulfilled working for someone else, these individuals cannot be happy taking orders from a higher-up.

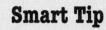

Smart Tip

According to many experts, the final element that determines whether you are ready to become an entrepreneur is if you are able to raise significant amounts of money from investors. If you can make other people believe in your dream and share your goals so that they are willing to invest hard-earned cash in your venture, chances are you have what it takes.

Joe R. Mancuso, president of the Center for Entrepreneurial Management, says, "It's a lot of little incidents, maybe a series of four or five little things coming together at the precise time, that creates the start of a new business." It might be that potential customers start calling you, or perhaps a business in the area goes under and you see an opportunity. Maybe you feel as if you're underemployed (working below your potential salary level or your skill level) or not putting your talents to their best use. Or perhaps you're experiencing all these sentiments at once.

Reality Check

Once you've made the decision to break away, there are a number of things you should do before taking the big step. You need to do thorough market research, make sure you have enough cash and discuss the decision with your family. (You'll find out more about all these steps in Parts 1, 2 and 3 of this book.)

It's important to understand that the rewards of small-business ownership are not instantaneous. You must be ready to defer gratification and make substantial sacrifices to ensure the rewards eventually do come.

Beware!

If you've felt unfulfilled at your job for a long time, chances are you'll harbor resentment toward your past employer after you start your own business. But if you leave a job because you're angry, be sure not to transfer this anger to your new business, or failure is almost certain. Once you start your own business, you must leave behind any bad feelings about your former job or boss.

You must also make sure you're really ready for the responsibility that comes with being a business owner. When things go wrong, the buck stops with you. You will no longer have the luxury of going home at 5:00 while the company president stays all night to fix a chaotic situation. Someone whose only desire is to make a lot of money fast probably won't last long owning his or her own business.

Through surveys and research, experts have found that entrepreneurs share some common personality traits, the most important of which is confidence. They possess confidence not only in themselves but also in their ability to sell their ideas, set up a business and trust their intuition along the way. Small business is fiercely competitive, and it's the business owners with confidence who will survive. If you can combine this all-important quality with the other characteristics mentioned, then the time is probably right for you.

YOUR STRENGTHS AND WEAKNESSES

It's rare that one person has all the qualities needed to be successful in business. Everyone has strong suits and weak points, and the same is true of business owners. What's important is to understand those strengths and weaknesses. To do this, you need to evaluate the major achievements in your personal and professional life and the skills you used to accomplish them. The following steps will help:

1. **Create a personal resume.** Compose a resume that lists your professional and personal experiences as well as your expertise. For each job you've had, describe the duties you were responsible for and the degree of your success. Include professional skills, your educational background, hobbies and personal accomplishments that required expertise or special knowledge.

    When complete, this resume will give you a better idea of the kind of business that best suits your interests and experience. It will also serve as a warning flag if you are planning to start a business that falls outside your talents and strengths.

2. **Analyze your personal attributes**. Are you friendly and self-motivated? Are you a hard worker? Do you have common sense? Are you good with numbers? Are you well-organized?

   Evaluating your personal attributes reveals your likes and dislikes as well as strengths and weaknesses. Obviously, if you don't feel comfortable around other people, especially strangers, then a business that requires a lot of customer interaction might not be right for you. Or you may want to hire a "people person" to handle customer service, while you concentrate on the tasks you do best.

FROM THE HORSE'S MOUTH

One of the best ways to determine whether you are just daydreaming about becoming an entrepreneur or actually ready for it is to meet with other entrepreneurs and see what they do. Looking at their lifestyles and talking about entrepreneurship can help you figure out whether you are really suited for life as a business owner.

"Usually when you talk to someone who's done it, they'll tell you all the bad things about owning a business, like the time they had to work a 24-hour day or when the power went out. Those are the things you need to learn about beforehand," says one entrepreneur who used this technique. Once you realize that entrepreneurship isn't a 9-to-5 job with a secure income, you may have to re-evaluate your interest.

In addition to meeting with successful entrepreneurs, you might want to talk to a few who weren't so successful. Find out what went wrong with their ventures so you can avoid the same problems. Did they fail to conduct market research before forging ahead? Were they unwilling to work long hours? Were they undercapitalized? Did they have misconceptions about what the entrepreneurial lifestyle is really like?

Many potential business owners find it useful to attend seminars or classes in entrepreneurship. You can often find such courses at community colleges or continuing education programs near you. Others seek assistance from consulting firms that specialize in helping small businesses get off the ground. All these methods can give you a taste of reality—and help you decide if you're prepared to take the plunge.

3. **Analyze your professional attributes.** Small-business owners wear many different hats, but that doesn't mean you have to be a jack-of-all-trades. Just be aware of the areas where you are competent and the areas where you need help, such as sales, marketing, advertising and administration. Next to each function, record your competency level—excellent, good, fair or poor.

GO FOR THE GOAL

In addition to evaluating your strengths and weaknesses, it's important to define your business goals. For some people, the goal is the freedom to do what they want when they want, without anyone telling them otherwise. For others, the goal is financial security.

Setting goals is an integral part of choosing the business that's right for you. After all, if your business doesn't meet your personal goals, you probably won't be happy waking up each morning and trying to make the business a success. Sooner or later you'll stop putting forth the effort needed to make the concept work.

When setting goals, aim for the following qualities:

1. **Specificity:** You stand a better chance of achieving a goal if it is specific. "Raising capital" isn't a specific goal; "raising $10,000 by July 1" is.

2. **Optimism:** Be positive when you set goals. "Being able to pay the bills" is not exactly an inspirational goal. "Achieving financial security" phrases your goal in a more positive manner, thus firing up your energy to attain it.

3. **Realism:** If you set a goal to earn $100,000 a month when you've never earned that much in a year, that goal is unrealistic. Begin with small steps, such as increasing your monthly income by 25 percent. Once your first goal is met, you can reach for larger ones.

4. **Thinking short and long term.** Short-term goals are attainable in a period of weeks to a year. Long-term goals can be for five, 10 or even 20 years from now; they should be substantially greater than short-term goals but should still be realistic.

There are several factors to consider when setting goals:

1. **Income:** Many entrepreneurs go into business to achieve financial security. Consider how much money you want to make during your first year of operation and each year thereafter, up to five years.

2. **Lifestyle:** This includes areas such as travel, hours of work, investment of personal assets and geographic location. Are you willing to travel extensively or to move? How many hours are you willing to work? Which assets are you willing to risk?

3. **Type of work:** When setting goals for type of work, you need to determine whether you like working outdoors, in an office, with computers, on the phone, with lots of people, with children and so on.

4. **Ego gratification:** Face it, many people go into business to satisfy their egos. Owning a business can be very ego-gratifying, especially if you're in a business that's considered glamorous or exciting. You need to decide how important ego gratification is to you and what business best fills that need.

> **Beware!**
>
> If you have a family, make sure they understand the emotional and financial sacrifices business success requires. When your family doesn't support your business, if they're always saying "Can't you leave that alone and come to dinner?" it's going to be tough to make your business work. Unless your family is ready for you to become an entrepreneur, chances are this isn't the right time to do it.

The most important rule of self-evaluation and goal-setting is honesty. Going into business with your eyes wide open about your strengths and weaknesses, your likes and dislikes and your ultimate goals lets you confront the decisions you'll face with greater confidence and a greater chance of success.

WHAT'S YOUR EQ?

Common characteristics in areas such as family background, childhood experiences, core values, personalities and more turn up time and time again in studies of entrepreneurs. Find out how you fit the mold by determining your Entrepreneurial Quotient, or EQ.

The following test is no measure of your future success, but it may show you where you excel and where you need to improve to help make your business soar. Answer the following questions with a "yes" or "no," and total your score at the end to find out your EQ.

1. Did your parents immigrate to the United States? ___ Yes ___No
2. Were you a top student in school? ___ Yes ___No

3. Did you enjoy participating in group activities
    in school, such as clubs, team sports or
    double dates? ___ Yes ___No

4. Did you prefer to be alone as a youngster? ___ Yes ___No

5. Did you run for office at school or initiate
    enterprises at an early age, such as lemonade
    stands, family newspapers or greeting card sales? ___ Yes ___No

6. Were you a stubborn child? ___ Yes ___No

7. Were you cautious as a youngster? ___ Yes ___No

8. Were you daring or adventurous? ___ Yes ___No

9. Do the opinions of others matter a lot to you? ___ Yes ___No

10. Would changing your daily routine be an
    important motivator for starting your own
    enterprise? ___ Yes ___No

11. You might really enjoy work, but are you
    willing to work overnight? ___ Yes ___No

12. Are you willing to work as long as it takes
    with little or no sleep to finish a job? ___ Yes ___No

13. When you complete a project successfully,
    do you immediately start another? ___ Yes ___No

14. Are you willing to commit your savings to
    start a business? ___ Yes ___No

15. Would you also be willing to borrow from
    others? ___ Yes ___No

16. If your business should fail, would you
    immediately work on starting another? ___ Yes ___No

17. Or would you immediately start looking for
    a job with a regular paycheck? ___ Yes ___No

18. Do you believe being an entrepreneur is risky? ___ Yes ___No

19. Do you put your long- and short-term goals
    in writing? ___ Yes ___No

20. Do you believe you have the ability to deal with
    cash flow in a professional manner? ___ Yes ___No

21. Are you easily bored? ___ Yes ___No

22. Are you an optimist? ___ Yes ___No

What's The Score?

1. If yes, score one point; if no, subtract one. Significantly high numbers of entrepreneurs are children of first-generation Americans.
2. If yes, subtract four points; if no, add four. Successful entrepreneurs are not, as a rule, top achievers in school.
3. If yes, subtract one point; if no, add one. Entrepreneurs are not especially enthusiastic about participating in group activities in school.
4. If yes, add one point; if no, subtract one. Studies of entrepreneurs show that, as youngsters, they often preferred to be alone.
5. If yes, add two points; if no, subtract two. Enterprise usually can be traced to an early age.
6. If yes, add one point; if no, subtract one. Stubbornness as a child seems to translate into determination to do things your own way—a hallmark of successful entrepreneurs.
7. If yes, subtract four points; if no, add four. Caution may involve an unwillingness to take risks, a handicap for those embarking on previously uncharted territory.
8. If yes, add four points.
9. If yes, subtract one point; if no, add one. Entrepreneurs often have the faith to pursue different paths despite the opinions of others.
10. If yes, add two points; if not, subtract two. Being tired of a daily routine often precipitates an entrepreneur's decision to start an enterprise.
11. If yes, add two; if no, subtract six.
12. If yes, add four points.
13. If yes, add two points; if no, subtract two. Entrepreneurs generally enjoy their type of work so much, they move from one project to another—nonstop.
14. If yes, add two points; if no, subtract two. Successful entrepreneurs are willing to use their savings to finance a project.
15. If yes, add two points; if no, subtract two.
16. If yes, add four points; if no, subtract four.
17. If yes, subtract one point.

> ### Smart Tip
>
> Once you understand your own strengths and weaknesses, there are two ways to deal with them: You can either improve your abilities in the areas where you're weak (by taking a class in bookkeeping, for example) or hire an employee to handle these aspects of business (for instance, hiring a bookkeeper).

18.   If yes, subtract two points; if no, add two.
19.   If yes, add one point; if no, subtract one. Many entrepreneurs make a habit of putting their goals in writing.
20.   If yes, add two points; if no, subtract two. Handling cash flow can be critical to entrepreneurial success.
21.   If yes, add two points; if no, subtract two. Entrepreneurial personalities seem to be easily bored.
22.   If yes, add two points; if no, subtract two. Optimism can fuel the drive to press for success in uncharted waters.

Determining Your EQ

A score of 35 or more: You have everything going for you. You have the potential to achieve spectacular entrepreneurial success.

A score of 15 to 34: Your background, skills and talents give you excellent chances for success in your own business. You should go far.

A score of zero to 14: You have a head start of ability and/or experience in running a business and should be successful in opening an enterprise of your own if you apply yourself and learn the necessary skills to make it happen.

A score of -1 to -15: You might be able to make a go of it if you ventured on your own, but you would have to work extra hard to compensate for a lack of built-in advantages and skills that give others a leg up in beginning their own businesses.

A score of -16 to -43: Your talents probably lie elsewhere. You should consider whether building your own business is what you really want to do because you may find yourself swimming against the tide. Working for a company or for someone else, or developing a career in a profession or an area of technical expertise may be far more congenial to you and allow you to enjoy a lifestyle appropriate to your abilities and interests.

—Quiz provided by Northwestern Mutual Life Insurance Co.

Personal Goals And
Objectives Work Sheet

Setting goals not only gives you an ongoing road map for success, but it shows you the best alternates should you need or desire a change along the way. You should review your goals on a regular basis. Many do this daily as it helps them assess their progress and gives them the ability to make faster and more informed decisions. Take a few minutes to fill out the following questionnaire. You will find this very helpful in setting and resetting your goals.

1. The most important reason to me for being in business for myself is:

2. What I like best about being in business for myself is:

3. Within five years I would like my business to be:

4. When I look back over the past five years of my career I feel:

5. My financial condition as of today is:

6. I feel the next best thing I must do about my business is:

7. The most important part of my business to me is (or will be):

8. The area of my business I really excel in is:

CHAPTER 3

WHAT'S THE BIG IDEA?

How to get an idea for your business

Many people think it's "oh so mysterious" to start a business. So often I hear "I can't do it" or "I have no idea what to do." Nonsense! In this chapter, you're going to find out how to get an idea for a business—how you figure out exactly what it is that you want to do and then how to take action on it.

But before we get started, I want you to know that this is a great time to launch a business. When I started with *Entrepreneur* in 1978, it wasn't such a great time to be on your own. People who were entrepreneurs were often thought to be unemployable, people who couldn't get along with their fellow employees or their bosses. Since they couldn't hold a job (or so many people thought), they decided to start their own businesses.

A lot has happened since then: Today, there are about 23 million small businesses in the United States. Estimates vary, but generally more than 1 million businesses are started every year in the United States. Yet for every American who actually starts a business, there's likely millions more who start each year saying "OK, this is the year I am going to start a business," and then nothing happens.

Everybody has his or her own roadblock, something that keeps them from taking that first crucial step. Most people are afraid to start; they may fear the unknown or failure or even success. Others are just overwhelmed by the belief they have to start from scratch. They think they have to start with an empty slate and figure out "OK, what product can I invent? What service can I start? What can I do that no one has ever done before?" In other words, they think that they have to reinvent the wheel.

But unless you are a technological genius, trying to reinvent the wheel is a big waste of time. If you are another Bill Gates or Steve Jobs, then this is the way to go. But for most people starting a business, the issue should not be coming up with something so unique that no one has ever heard of it.

It's answering the question: "How can I do something better?" or "How can I do it differently than the other guy doing it over there?"

Get The Juices Flowing

How do you start the idea process? First, take out a sheet of paper, and across the top write "Things About Me." List five to seven things about yourself—things you like to do or that you are really good at. Your list might include: I am really good with people, I love kids, I love to read, I love computers, I love numbers, I am good at coming up with marketing concepts. Just write down whatever comes to your mind; it doesn't need to make▾ sense. Once you have your list, number them down one side of the paper.

On the other side of the paper, list things that you don't think you are good at or you don't like to do. Maybe you are really good at marketing concepts, but you don't like to meet people, or you're really not that fond of kids, or you don't like to do public speaking or you don't want to travel. Don't over-think it; just write down your thoughts.

When you are finished, draw a line underneath both lists, then ask yourself: "If there were three to five products or services that would make my personal life better, what would they be?" This is your personal life as a man, woman, father, husband, mother, wife, whatever your situation may be. Determine what products or services would make your life easier or happier, make you more productive or efficient, or simply give you more time. Next, ask yourself the same question about your business life.

Also examine what you like and dislike about your work life as well as what traits people like and dislike about you. Finally, ask yourself why you're seeking to start a business in the first place. Then, when you are done, look for a pattern to emerge (i.e., is

Bright Idea

Experts agree, the best place to look for ideas is to start with what you know.

there a need for a business doing one of the things you like or are good at?). To make the process a bit easier, we've provided a "Things About Me" work sheet in this chapter for you to complete in this chapter.

They Delivered

Let me give you an example. I live and work in Irvine, California, a planned community. Most of the fast-food restaurants are located where the neighborhoods are. So in the office areas there are not many easily accessible places to go on a lunch hour. Several years ago, two young men in Irvine found this lunch situation very frustrating. There weren't many affordable choices. Sure, there were some food courts located in strip

THINKING IT THROUGH

Before you start a business, you have to look at what the potential is, what your product or service is, and if there is a lot of opportunity to make a good deal of money over the long run. Or is it a "hit and run" product, where you're going to get in, make a lot of money, and then get out? That's not necessarily a bad thing; fads have made some entrepreneurs incredibly successful. But remember, once you're in business, one of the hardest things to do is to know when it's time to get out, to let go. And if you guess wrong, if you try to make a classic out of a fad, you are going to start losing all the money you have earned. And no one wants to do that.

centers, but the parking lots were really small and the wait was horrendous.

One day, as they were lamenting their lunch problem, one of them said "Wouldn't it be great if we could get some good food delivered?" The proverbial light bulb goes on—what a concept! Then they did what too many people don't do: They did something about their idea. Coincidentally, they purchased one of *Entrepreneur* business start-up guides and started a restaurant delivery business.

Today, they're not even 30, yet their business boasts $5.4 million in sales. It's not a complicated business nor an original one. Their competition has gotten stiffer, and yet they are doing phenomenally well. And it all began because they listened to their frustrations and decided to do something about them. Recently, I read that one of the biggest complaints by American workers was the shrinking lunch hour. Some only get 30 minutes, making it nearly impossible to get out, get lunch and get back in that time. So while these young entrepreneurs initially thought they were responding to a personal need, in our area, they actually struck a universal chord.

That's one way to get ideas, listening to your own (or your neighbors', family's or co-workers') frustrations. The opportunities are all there; you just need to search them out a bit. If your

Smart Tip

Need a business idea? Don't forget those solid standbys. New communities always need dry-cleaning shops, ice cream stores, cleaning services (think carpet cleaners, janitorial services), etc. Remember the new creed the American consumer lives by: value and convenience.

brain is always set in idea mode, then many ideas may come from just looking around or reading. For instance, if you read the article about the shrinking lunch hour, and if you were thinking entrepreneurially, you would say "Wow, maybe there is an opportunity there for me to do something."

Smart Tip

Don't overlook publications in your search for ideas. Books, newspapers and magazines all contain a wealth of ideas. Your reading list should include—but not be limited to—the latest business periodicals.

Inspiring Moments

Inspiration can be anywhere. Let me share one of my favorite entrepreneurial success stories. Remember the TopsyTail? It is a small plastic device with a loop on the end that you stick in your hair to create a ponytail with a French twist. Tomima Edmark, the woman who invented this product, was a marketing representative for IBM. One night, she went to see the movie "When Harry Met Sally" and somebody in the audience was sporting this unique hairstyle. When she got home, she tried to replicate the hairstyle, but her efforts led to frustration rather than fruition.

She started running around her house trying to find something that would make her hair do this. Finally, she came up with an idea. She pulled out a pair of circular knitting needles, cut them in half, and taped them together. She stuck it in—and it worked.

Now why (and sometimes you don't question this) she thought that anybody else would care is beyond me. But she did. So she placed mail order ads in magazines. And she began a public relations campaign, which paid off when *Glamour* magazine ran an article about the TopsyTail. That article generated more than $100,000 worth of orders in just three weeks.

Edmark realized she could get even more orders if she had an instructional video demonstrating how to use her product. So she sent her product to several infomercial production companies. She hired one of the companies, and an infomercial was born. The infomercial demonstrated how to use her product and offered the TopsyTail and an instructional booklet for $12.95. When sales started booming, the TopsyTail went retail and sold for $9.95 without the instruction booklet. Her take from the infomercial, after just three months of airing, was $30 million in sales. Now, that's amazing!

Inspiration struck Edmark in a movie theater. For entrepreneur Bill Zanker, inspiration hit while enjoying a different leisurely pursuit. If you think a walk in the park is merely a way to get away from it all, ask Zanker. He had already made his first fortune by founding and later selling The

THINGS ABOUT ME WORK SHEET

Complete the following self-assessment work sheet as honestly as you can. Just write down whatever comes to mind; don't over-think the exercise. Most likely, your first response will be your best. Once you've finished the exercises, look for patterns (i.e., is there a need for a business doing one of the things you like or are good at?).

1. List at least five to seven things you like to do or are good at.

2. List five to seven things you are not good at or you don't like to do.

3. "If there were three to five products or services that would make my personal life better, what would they be?"

4. "If there were three to five products or services that would make my business life better, what would they be?"

5. When people ask what you do, what's your answer (list one occupation or whatever mainly occupies your week)?

6. List five things you enjoy about your work.

THINGS ABOUT ME WORK SHEET, CONT'D.

7. List five things you dislike about your work.

8. "When people tell me what they like most about me, their response is":

9. "Some people dislike the fact that I":

10. Other than your main occupation, list any other skills you possess, whether you excel at them or not:

11. In addition to becoming more financially independent, I would also like to be more:

12. Write down three things you want to see changed or improved in your community.

Learning Annex, an adult education company. One day, he was strolling through a San Francisco park when he had a brainstorm. Zanker spotted a man on a park bench selling back massages for a dollar a minute. Even though the guy wasn't massaging people correctly and had dirty hands, folks were lined up waiting for their turn. Zanker knew he could do it better—and he did. He returned home to New York City and in 1993 opened the first The Great American Backrub, where licensed massage therapists gave nine-minute backrubs for $7.95. Zanker later added back-related merchandise to his stores, devised a mobile "Backrubs-to-Go" service and expanded nationwide through franchising. Just last year, he sold the successful company to focus on new opportunities.

Made To Order

Getting an idea can be as simple as keeping your eyes peeled for the latest "hot" business; they crop up all the time. One recent trend were those paint-your-own-ceramic studios. They started in the bigger cities like Seattle, San Francisco and New York City. And in the urban areas they became very popular with young, single people. Some entrepreneurs paired the concept with other entertainment businesses, like wine bars.

> ## Bright Idea
>
> Is there a household chore that drives you up the wall? (One shudders to think of life before vacuum cleaners.) Common sources of frustration or irritation are great idea generators.

When these stores hit Irvine, a suburban family community, entrepreneurs aimed them at kids instead of the singles scene. On the weekend, these places were occupied by dozens of little 10-year-old girls painting. They have birthday parties at these stores; they attract Girl Scout troops.

My point: You can take any idea and customize it to your community. Add your own creativity to any concept. In fact, customizing a concept is not a choice; it's something you have to do if you want your business to be successful.

You can't just take an idea, plop it down, and say "OK, this is it, and it's gonna fit." Outside of a McDonald's or some other major franchise concepts, there are very few businesses that will work with a one-size-fits-all approach.

One of the best ways to determine if your idea will work in your community is to talk to people who know. If it's a business idea, talk to co-workers and colleagues. Run personal ideas by your family or your neighbors. Don't be afraid your friends will steal your idea; it's just not likely. All you have to do is ask.

NEVER SAY DIE

Once you get an idea for a business, what is the most important trait you need as an entrepreneur? Perseverance. When you set out to launch your business, you will be told "no" more times in your life than you have ever been before. And you can't take it personally; you've got to get beyond it and just move on to the next person because eventually, you're going to get to a "yes."

Princeton Checklist
For Evaluating Ideas

Princeton Creative Research has developed an excellent criteria checklist for evaluating ideas that is particularly well-suited to the entrepreneur. Ask yourself the following questions when evaluating an idea for a business or a product.

❏ Have you considered all the advantages or benefits of the idea? Is there a real need for it?

❏ Have you pinpointed the exact problems or difficulties your idea is expected to solve?

❏ Is your idea an original, new concept, or is it a new combination or adaptation?

❏ What immediate or short-range gains or results can be anticipated? Are the projected returns adequate? Are the risk factors acceptable?

❏ What long-range benefits can be anticipated?

❏ Have you checked the idea for faults or limitations?

❏ Are there any problems the idea might create? What are the changes involved?

❏ How simple or complex will the idea's execution or implementation be?

❏ Could you work out several variations of the idea? Could you offer alternative ideas?

❏ Does your idea have a natural sales appeal? Is the market ready for it? Can customers afford it? Will they buy it? Is there a timing factor?

❏ What, if anything, is your competition doing in this area? Can your company be competitive?

❏ Have you considered the possibility of user resistance or difficulties?

❏ Does your idea fill a real need, or does the need have to be created through promotional and advertising efforts?

❏ How soon could the idea be put into operation?

As you can see by the examples above, there are many methods available with which to evaluate your idea. You should pick and choose the criteria that best suit your needs, depending on the type of company and/or the type of product you seek to evaluate.

Source: Princeton Creative Research, Princeton, New Jersey. Reprinted with permission.

FIT TO A "T"

Every December in *Entrepreneur*, we profile the hottest businesses for the coming year. We do a lot of research and a lot of homework, and what we say is absolutely true. But that doesn't mean that it is true for everyone. After all, you may not be good at any of these businesses. Or you could live in an area where the business is already saturated or is not a viable option. Or they simply may not suit you and you'd end up hating your business. Just because you own a business doesn't mean you are going to like being there everyday, and, if this is true, then chances are you are going to fail.

Owning a business you hate is the same thing as having a job you hate. It's still hard to get out of bed in the morning, and you are just not going to do it as well. What all this means is that you need to come up with your ideas first, and then assess your traits to see which ideas best suit you.

Another one of my favorite success stories illustrates this point. It goes back to when we published *Entrepreneurial Woman* magazine; that's about nine years ago. A woman wrote to us and said "I just have to share this with you." She had been to Washington, DC, and went into a bookstore chain there called Kramer Books. This chain was like Barnes & Noble is today; it sold pastries and coffee with the books. This woman loved the concept so much that she returned home to Cleveland, Ohio, vowing to open the same type of bookstore.

There was just one problem: She had no bookstore or food experience. But she got an idea. She thought: "I am in the Midwest, but I am in a pretty big city; what's another city similar to mine?" She went to the library, picked up the Chicago Yellow Pages, turned to the bookstore section, and started calling people, looking for a bookstore that was comparable to the one in Washington. She figured in Chicago, there'd be a good chance of finding someone.

And she did. One by one, she called and told the owners that she wanted to start a similar store in Cleveland. She said, "I am no threat to you; can you tell me what to do?" A lot of them said no, but she kept on calling. Eventually, she reached a woman who said, "Pay your own way here, and I will tell you everything I know."

So she went to Chicago for two weeks, paid her own way, stayed in a cheap hotel, and actually went in every day as if she worked for this woman. This woman told her how to order books; what kind of food, coffee and cups she needed; how you do it; how you set it up; and what you need to look for—everything she would need to know to run this business.

After two weeks, she went home to Cleveland and opened a store. She wrote to us right after she opened. Her point was that you have to just keep trying. She kept going, and, finally, she got to the "yes." And that "yes" enabled her to start her business.

Just Do It!

Hopefully, by now I've at least somewhat demystified the process of determining what business is right for you. Understand business start-up is not rocket science. No, I'm not saying it's easy to begin a business; it certainly is not. But it is not as complicated nor as scary as many people think, either. It is a step-by-step common-sense procedure. So take it a step at a time. First step: Figure out what you want to do. Once you have the idea, talk to people to find out what they think. Ask "Would you buy and/or use this, and how much would you pay?"

Understand that many around you will not encourage you (indeed, some will discourage you) to become an entrepreneur. Some will tell you they have your best interests at heart; they just want you to see the reality of the situation. Some will envy your courage; others will resent you for having the guts to actually do something. You cannot allow these naysayers to dissuade you, to stop your journey before it even begins.

One of the most common warnings you will hear is about the risk. Everyone will tell you it's a risk to start your own business. And, sure, starting a business is risky, but what in life isn't? Plus, there's a difference between foolish risks and calculated ones. If you carefully consider what you're doing, get help when you need it and never stop asking questions, you can mitigate your risk. You cannot allow the specter of risk to stop you from going forward. Ask yourself "What am I really risking?" And assess the risk. What are you giving up? What will you lose if things don't work out? Don't risk what you can't afford. Don't risk your home, your family or your health. Ask yourself "If this doesn't work, will I be worse off than I am now?" If all you have to lose is some time, energy and money, then the risk is probably worth it.

Bright Idea

Your hobbies may lead you to business ideas. If tennis is your game, perhaps you can think of a product that makes serving a snap. If that sounds too technical, look around the courts and see if there's a service players would pay for.

BUSINESS COMPARISON WORK SHEET

This form helps you determine the compatibility of prospective businesses with your personal objectives, experience and lifestyle. Assign each business a column number. Answer each question along the left-hand side of the form assigning a rating of 1-3 for each question, with 3 being the strongest. Total each column after you're finished. The opportunities with the highest scores are the ones most suitable for you.

	Business 1	Business 2	Business 3	Business 4
Rate your experience and background in relation to the proposed business.				
Are you familiar with the operations of this type of business?				
Does the business meet your investment goals?				
Does the business meet your income goals?				
Does the business generate sufficient profits?				
Do you feel comfortable with the business?				
Does your family feel comfortable with the business?				
Does the business satisfy your sense of status?				
Is the business compatible with your people skills?				
Is there good growth projected for the overall industry of the business?				
Is the risk factor acceptable?				
Does the business require long hours?				
Is the business location-sensitive?				
Does the business fit your personal goals and objectives?				
Does this business fit your professional skills?				
Totals				

Determining what you want to do is only the first step. You've still got a lot of homework to do, a lot of research in front of you. Buying this book is a smart first step. Most important: Do something. Don't sit back year after year and say "This is the year I'm going to start my business." So turn the page, and make this the year you really start it!

CHAPTER 4

TIME IS ON YOUR SIDE . . . OR IS IT?

Should you launch your business part time or full time?

Should you start your business part time or full time? Even if you ultimately plan to go full time, many entrepreneurs and experts say starting part time can be a good idea.

Starting part time offers several advantages. It reduces your risk because you can rely on a regular income and benefits from your full-time job while you get your business off the ground. By starting part time, you also allow your business the opportunity to grow gradually.

"Starting part time is simply the best way," contends Philip Holland, author of *How to Start a Business Without Quitting Your Job* (Ten Speed Press). "You find out what running a business requires, while limiting your liability if it fails."

Yet the part-time path is not without its own dangers and disadvantages. Starting part time leaves you with less time to market your business, strategize and build a clientele. Since you won't be available to answer calls or solve customers' problems for most of the day, clients may become frustrated and feel you're not offering adequate customer service or responding quickly enough to their needs. Part-time entrepreneurs may also find that prospective customers, suppliers or investors don't take them seriously. Perhaps the most serious problem is the risk of burnout. Holding down a full-time job while running a part-time business leaves you with little, if any, leisure time; as a result, your personal and family life may suffer.

"Working by day and running a business by night creates a host of potential conflicts and adds a tremendous amount of stress," cautions Arnold Sanow, author of *You Can Start Your Own Business* (Washington Publications). Sanow says conflicts between a day job and a sideline business are common, as are family problems: "I've seen a lot of divorces as a result of working full time and having a business on the side."

That's not to say a part-time business can't work. It can, Sanow says—if

Beware!

Don't bite the hand that feeds you. Starting a business that directly competes with your current employer is foolish and may even get you in legal hot water by violating noncompete clauses in your employment contract. If you must start a business in the same industry, focus on a small niche your employer has overlooked.

you have excellent time-management skills, strong self-discipline, and support from family and friends. Also crucial, he says, is your own commitment: "Don't think that since you already have a job, you don't really have to work hard at your business. You must have a plan of attack."

Market Matters

As with any business, your plan of attack should start with a thorough assessment of your idea's market potential. Often, this step alone will be enough to tell you whether you should start part time or full time.

"You can't become so caught up in your love for what you're doing that you overlook the business realities," cautions homebased business consultant Sylvia Landman. If you find there is a huge unmet need for your idea, no major competition and a ready supply of eager customers, then by all means go ahead and start full time. If, on the other hand, you find that the market won't support a full-time business, but might someday with proper marketing and business development, then it's probably better to start part time at first.

To make sure there's a market for your product or service, Landman advises you to investigate factors such as the competition in your industry, the economy in your area, the demographic breakdown of your client base, and the availability of potential customers. If you're considering opening an upscale beauty salon, for example, evaluate the number of similar shops in operation, as well as the number of affluent women in the area and the fees they are willing to pay.

Once you've determined there is a need for your business, outline your goals and strategies in a comprehensive business plan. You should always conduct extensive research, make market projections for your business, and set goals for yourself based on these findings, Landman explains. "It gives [you] a tremendous view of the long-range possibilities and keeps the business on the right track," she says. Don't neglect writing a business plan even if you're starting part time: A well-written business plan will help you take your business full time later on.

Certain businesses lend themselves well to part-time operation: Holland cites mail order, food products, direct marketing and service businesses as examples. Doing your market research and business plan will give you a more realistic idea of whether your business can work part time. (For specifics on conducting market research and writing a business plan, see Part 2 Chapters 6, 7 and 10.)

If you've got your heart set on a business that traditionally requires a full-

Part-Time Pointers

Balancing a full-time job with a part-time business isn't easy—but it can be done. Arnold Sanow, author of *You Can Start Your Own Business* (Washington Publications), suggests these tips to help make your part-time business a success:

♦ *Involve your family in the business whenever possible.* Whether it's answering the phone, stuffing envelopes or putting together orders, giving your family the chance to help out is a great way to get more accomplished in less time—while also making your family feel part of your business.

♦ *Be ready to give up personal time.* You won't have much time for television, reading or hobbies you used to enjoy. Be sure the sacrifice is worth it, or both your job and your business will suffer.

♦ *Focus on the task in front of you.* When you're at work, focus on work; don't let thoughts of your business distract you.

♦ *Make the most of every minute.* Use lunch hours or early morning hours to make phone calls; use commuting time on the train to catch up on paperwork.

♦ *Take advantage of time zone differences and technology.* If you do business with people in other states or countries, make time differences work to your advantage by calling early in the morning or after work. Use faxes and e-mail to communicate with clients at any time of day or night.

♦ *Don't overstep your boundaries.* Making business calls on company time or using your employer's supplies or equipment for business purposes is a serious no-no.

♦ *Be honest.* Only you can assess your situation, but in many cases it's best to be upfront with your boss about your sideline business. As long as it doesn't interfere with your job, many bosses won't mind—and you'll gain by being honest rather than making them feel you have something to hide.

time commitment, think creatively: There may be ways to make it work on a part-time basis. For instance, instead of a restaurant, consider a catering business. You'll still get to create menus and interact with customers, but your work can all be done during evenings and weekends.

Financial Plan

One major factor in the decision to start part time or full time is your financial situation. Before launching a full-time business, most experts recommend putting aside enough to live on for at least six months to a year. (That amount may vary; completing your business plan will show you in more detail how long you can expect to wait before your business begins earning a profit.)

Basic factors to consider include the amount of your existing savings, whether you have assets that could be sold for cash, friends or family members who might offer you financing or loans, and whether your spouse or other family members' salary could be enough to support your family while you launch a business full time.

Bright Idea

If keeping a full-time job and a part-time business going at the same time sounds too difficult, but taking the full-time plunge into entrepreneurship sounds too scary, consider another option: taking a part-time or temporary job while you start a full-time business. This can be a good way to ensure you have some salary (and, in some cases, even benefits) coming in, while giving you more time to work on your business. Bonus: Part-time jobs often offer flexible evening or weekend hours—a big plus if you're starting a business where you need to be accessible to clients during regular weekday business hours.

If, like many people, you lack the financial resources to start full time, beginning part time is often a good alternative. However, even if you do start part time, you'll want to keep some figures in mind: Specifically, how do you know when your business is making enough money that you can say goodbye to your day job?

A good rule of thumb, according to Sanow, is to wait until your part-time business is bringing in income equivalent to at least 30 percent of your current salary from your full-time job. "With 30 percent of their income, plus all the extra time during the day to promote their business, [entrepreneurs] should be able to make [the transition at that point]," he says.

Another good idea: Start putting more money aside while you still have your day job. That way, when you take the full-time plunge, you'll have a financial cushion to supplement the income from your business.

Family Affairs

The emotional and psychological side of starting a business is less cut-and-dried than financial and market aspects, but it's just as important in your decision to start part time or full time.

Begin by discussing the situation with your spouse, significant other or family. Do they support your decision to start a business? Do they understand the sacrifices both full-time and part-time businesses will require—from you, from them and from the whole family? Make sure your loved ones feel free to bring any objections or worries out in the open. The time to do this is now—not three months after you've committed to your business, and it's too late to back out.

Then, work together to come up with practical solutions to the problems you foresee (could your spouse take over some of the household chores

Bright Idea

If you're a part-time entrepreneur seeking a full-time professional image, check out business incubators. For a small fee, business incubators typically provide office space, services such as answering phones, and access to equipment like copiers and fax machines. The biggest plus: Incubators also provide start-up help such as marketing and accounting assistance.

TAKE IT EASY

Does all work and no play make entrepreneurship no fun? Some entrepreneurs who run part-time businesses based on hobbies, such as crafts or cooking, find that going full time takes all the fun out of the venture. "Going full time turns an adventure into a job," as business expert Arnold Sanow puts it.

"Some entrepreneurs have trouble grasping the fact that their businesses aren't just pastimes anymore," says homebased business consultant Sylvia Landman. "They can't work at their leisure any longer, and their ventures may require them to develop talents they didn't know they had and perform tasks they'd rather leave to someone else."

Don't get so caught up in the creative aspects of the venture, Landman warns, that you lose sight of the business responsibilities you must assume to make your start-up succeed. Take a realistic look at what going full time will require. Perhaps you can hire people to handle the business aspects you dislike, such as sales or operations.

Smart Tip

What do you do if you can't afford to start your business full time but need to be available full time to answer client and customer calls? Consider teaming up with a partner whose available hours complement yours.

you currently handle, for example?). Lay some ground rules for the part-time business—for instance, no work on Sunday afternoons, or no discussing business at the dinner table.

To make your part-time business a success and keep your family happy, "time management is key," says Landman. "Balance the hours you have available. Get up early, and don't spend valuable time on frivolous phone calls and other time wasters."

Getting Personal

Besides the effect business ownership will have on your family, equally important to consider is the toll it might take on you. If the idea of taking the full-time business plunge and giving up your comfy salary and cushy benefits keeps you awake at night biting your nails, then perhaps a part-time business is best. On the other hand, if your current full-time job requires long hours, you commute 60 miles round trip and you have 2-year-old triplets, piling a part-time business on top of all those commitments could be the straw that breaks the camel's back.

Of course, a full-time business does require long, long hours, but a part-time business combined with a full-time job can be even more stressful. If this is the route you're considering, carefully assess the effects on your life. You'll be using evenings, weekends and lunch hours—and, most likely, your holidays, sick days and vacation time—to take care of business. You will probably have to give up leisure activities such as going to the movies, watching television, reading or going to the gym. How will you feel the next time you drag yourself home, exhausted after a late night at the office . . . then have to sit right down and spend four hours working on a project that a client needs the next morning? This is the kind of commitment you'll need to make if you expect your part-time business to succeed. Carefully consider whether you have the mental and physical stamina to give your best effort to both your job and your business.

Decisions, Decisions

Whether to start part time or full time is a decision only you can make. Whichever route you take, the secret to success is an honest assessment of your resources, your commitment level and the support systems you have in place. With those factors firmly in mind, you'll be able to make the right choice.

CHAPTER 5

MADE FROM SCRATCH OR STORE-BOUGHT?

Starting a business vs. buying one

When most people think of starting a business, they think of beginning from scratch—developing your own idea and building the company from the ground up. But starting from scratch presents some distinct disadvantages, including the difficulty of building a customer base, marketing the new business, hiring employees and establishing cash flow—all without a track record or reputation to go on.

Some people know they want to own their own businesses but aren't sure exactly what type of business to choose. If you fall into this category, or if you are worried about the difficulties involved in starting a business from the ground up, the good news is that there are other options: buying an existing business, buying a franchise, or buying a business opportunity. Depending on your personality, skills and resources, these three methods of getting into business may offer significant advantages over starting from scratch.

BUYING AN EXISTING BUSINESS

In most cases, buying an existing business is less risky than starting from scratch. When you buy a business, you take over an operation that's already generating cash flow and profits. You have an established customer base and reputation, as well as employees who are familiar with all aspects of the business. And you don't have to reinvent the wheel—setting up new procedures, systems and policies—since a successful formula for running the business has already been put in place.

On the downside, buying a business is often more costly than starting from scratch. However, it's often easier to get financing to buy an existing business than to start a new one. Bankers and investors generally feel more comfortable dealing with a business that already has a proven track record.

Beware!

You're investigating a business you like, and the seller hands you income tax forms that show a $50,000 profit. "Of course," he says with a wink and a nudge, "I really made $150,000." What do you do?

There may be perfectly legal reasons for the lower reported income. For instance, if the seller gave his nephew a nonessential job for $25,000 a year, you can just eliminate the job and keep the cash. Same goes for a fancy leased car. One-time costs of construction or equipment may have legitimately lowered net profits, too.

What to watch for: a situation where a seller claims he or she made money, but just didn't report it to the IRS. If this happens, either walk away from the deal . . . or make an offer based on the proven income.

In addition, buying a business may give you valuable legal rights, such as patents or copyrights, which can prove very profitable.

Of course, there's no such thing as a sure thing—and buying an existing business is no exception. If you're not careful, you could get stuck with obsolete inventory, uncooperative employees or outdated distribution methods. To make sure you get the best deal when buying an existing business, take the following steps.

The Right Choice

Buying the perfect business starts with choosing the right type of business for you. The best place to start is by looking in an industry you are familiar with and understand. Think long and hard about the types of businesses you are interested in and which are the best match with your skills and experience. Also consider the size of business you are looking for, in terms of employees, number of locations and sales.

Next, pinpoint the geographical area where you want to own a business. Assess the labor pool and costs of doing business in that area, including wages and taxes, to make sure they're acceptable to you.

Once you've chosen a region and an industry to focus on, investigate every business in the area that meets your requirements. Start by looking in the local newspaper's classified ad section under "Business Opportunities" or "Businesses for Sale." You can also run your own "Wanted to Buy" ad describing what you are looking for in a business.

Remember, just because a business isn't listed doesn't mean it isn't for sale. Talk to business owners in the industry; many of them might not have their businesses up for sale but would consider selling if you made them an offer. Put your networking abilities and business contacts to use, and you're likely to hear of other businesses that might be good prospects.

Contacting a business broker is another way to find businesses for sale. Most brokers are hired by sellers to find buyers and help negotiate deals. If you hire your own broker, he or she will charge you a commission—typically 5 percent to 10 percent of the purchase price. The assistance brokers can offer, especially for first-time buyers, is often worth the cost. However, if you are really trying to save money, consider hiring a broker only when you are near the final negotiating phase.

Brokers can offer assistance in several ways:

◆ **Pre-screening businesses for you.** Good brokers turn down many of the businesses they are asked to sell, either because the seller won't provide full financial disclosure or because the business is overpriced. Going through a broker helps you avoid these bad risks.

◆ **Helping you pinpoint your interests.** A good broker starts by finding out about your skills and interests, then helps you select the right business for you. With the help of a broker, you may discover that an industry you had never considered is the ideal one for you.

◆ **Negotiating.** During the negotiating process is when brokers really earn their keep. They help both parties stay focused on the ultimate goal and smooth over tempers and problems.

◆ **Assisting with paperwork.** Brokers know the latest laws and regulations affecting everything from licenses and permits to financing and escrow. They also know the most efficient ways to cut through red tape, which can slash months off the purchase process. Working with a broker reduces the risk that you'll neglect some crucial form, fee or step in the process.

A Closer Look

Whether you use a broker or go it alone, you'll definitely want to put together an "acquisition team"—your banker, accountant and attorney—to help you. (For more on choosing these advisors, see Part 2 Chapter 12.) These advisors are essential to what is called "due diligence," which means reviewing and verifying all the relevant information about the business you are considering. When due diligence is done, you will know just what you are buying and from whom.

The preliminary analysis starts with some basic questions. Why is this business for sale? What is the general perception of the industry and the particular business, and what is the outlook for the future? Does—or can— the business control enough market share to stay profitable? How have the company's product or service lines changed over time? Are the raw materials needed in abundant supply?

You also need to assess the company's reputation and the strength of its business relationships. Talk to existing customers, suppliers and vendors about their relationships with the business. Contact the Better Business Bureau, industry associations, licensing and credit-reporting agencies to make sure there are no complaints against the business.

If the business still looks promising after your preliminary analysis, your acquisition team should start examining the business's potential returns and its asking price.

Whatever method you use to determine the fair market price of the business, your assessment of the business's value should take into account such issues as the business's financial health, its earnings history and growth potential, and its intangible assets (for example, brand name and market position). To get an idea of the company's anticipated returns and future financial needs, ask the business owner and/or accountant to show you projected financial statements.

Balance sheets, income statements, cash flow statements, footnotes and tax returns for the past three years are all key indicators of a business's health. These documents will help you do some financial analyses that will spotlight any underlying problem and also provide a closer look at a wide range of less tangible information.

Among other issues, you should focus on the following:

◆ **Excessive or insufficient inventory:** If the business is based on a product rather than a service, take careful stock of its inventory. First-time business buyers are often seduced by inventory, but it can be a trap. Excessive inventory may be obsolete, or may soon become so; it also costs money to store and insure. Finally, excess inventory can mean there are a lot of dissatisfied customers who are experiencing lags between their orders and final delivery, or are returning items they aren't happy with.

   Try to determine the lowest level of inventory the business can carry, and have the seller agree to reduce stock to that level by the date you take over the company. Also add a clause to the purchase agreement specifying that you are buying only the inventory that is current and saleable.

◆ **Accounts receivable:** Uncollected receivables stunt a business's growth and could require unanticipated bank loans. Look carefully at indicators such as accounts receivable turnover, credit policies, cash collection schedules and the aging of receivables.

LET'S MAKE A DEAL

Short on cash? Try these alternatives for financing your purchase of an existing business:

◆ **Use the seller's assets.** As soon as you buy the business, you'll own the assets—so why not use them to get financing now? Make a list of all the assets you're buying (along with any attached liabilities), and use it to approach banks, finance companies and factors (companies that buy your accounts receivables).

Some investors will lend money based on purchase orders. Factors, finance companies and banks will lend money on receivables. Finance companies and banks will lend money on inventory. Equipment can also be sold, then leased back from equipment leasing companies.

◆ **Buy co-op.** If you can't afford the business yourself, try going co-op—buying with someone else, that is. To find a likely co-op buyer, ask the seller for a list of people who were interested in the business but didn't have enough money to buy. (Be sure to have your lawyer write up a partnership agreement, including a buyout clause, before entering into any partnership arrangement.)

◆ **Use an Employee Stock Ownership Plan (ESOP).** ESOPs offer you a way to get capital immediately by selling stock in the business to employees. If you sell only nonvoting shares of stock, you still retain control. By offering to set up an ESOP plan, you may be able to get a business for as little as 10 percent of the purchase price.

◆ **Lease with an option to buy.** Some sellers will let you lease a business with an option to buy. You make a down payment, become a minority stockholder and operate the business as if it were your own.

◆ **Assume liabilities or decline receivables.** Reduce the sales price by either assuming the business's liabilities or having the seller keep the receivables.

◆ **Net income:** Use a series of net income ratios to gain a better look at a business's bottom line. For instance, the ratio of gross profit to net sales can be used to determine whether the company's profit margin is in line with that of similar businesses. Likewise, the ratio of net income to net worth, when considered together with projected increases in interest costs, total purchase price and similar factors, can show whether you would earn a reasonable return on your investment. Finally, the ratio of net income to total assets is a strong indicator of whether the company is getting a favorable rate of return on assets.

Your accountant can help you assess all these ratios. As he or she does so, be sure to determine whether the profit figures have been disclosed before or after taxes and the amount of returns the current owner is getting from the business. Also assess how much of the expenses would stay the same, increase or decrease under your management.

◆ **Working capital:** Working capital is defined as current assets less current liabilities. Without sufficient working capital, a business can't stay afloat—so one key computation is the ratio of net sales to net working capital. This measures how efficiently the working capital is being used to achieve business objectives.

◆ **Sales activity:** Sales figures may appear more rosy than they really are. When studying the rate of growth in sales and earnings, read between the lines to tell whether the growth rate is due to increased sales volume or higher prices. Also examine the overall marketplace. If the market seems to be mature, sales may be static—and that might be why the seller is trying to unload the company.

◆ **Fixed assets:** If your analysis suggests the business has invested too much money in fixed assets such as the plant property and equipment, make sure you know why. Unused equipment could indicate that demand is declining or that the business owner miscalculated manufacturing requirements.

◆ **Operating environment:** Take the time to understand the business's operating environment and corporate culture. If the business depends on overseas clients or suppliers, for example, examine the short- and long-term political environment of the countries involved. Look at the business in light of consumer or economic trends; for example, if you are considering a clothing store that caters to the "Generation X" lifestyle, will that client base still be intact five or 10 years from now? If the company you are considering relies on just a few major clients for all its business, can you be sure those customers will stay with you after the deal is closed? ·

Law And Order

While you and your accountant review key financial ratios and performance figures, you and your attorney should investigate the business's legal status. Look for liens against the property, pending lawsuits, guarantees, new or proposed industry regulations or restrictions, potential zoning changes, labor disputes, and new or pending patents; all these factors can seriously affect your business. Be sure to:

◆ conduct a uniform commercial code search to uncover any recorded liens (start with city hall and check with the department of public records).

◆ ask the business's attorneys for a legal history of the company, and read all old and new contracts.

◆ review related pending state and federal legislation, local zoning regulations and patent histories.

Legal liabilities in a business take many forms and may be hidden so deeply that even the seller honestly doesn't know they exist. How to protect yourself? First, have your lawyer add a "hold harmless and indemnify" clause to the contract. This assures you are protected from the consequences of the seller's previous actions as owner.

Second, make sure your deal allows you to take over the seller's existing insurance policies on an interim basis. This gives you time to review your insurance needs at greater leisure while still making sure you have basic coverage from the minute you take over.

The cost of having a lawyer evaluate a business varies depending on your relationship with the lawyer, the complexity of the business and the stage at which the lawyer gets involved. Generally, costs range from about $1,500 up to $10,000 or more.

If you're considering buying a business that has valuable intellectual property, such as a patent, trade secret or brand name, you may want an intellectual property attorney to evaluate it. Generally, this will cost from 0.5 percent to 3 percent of the business's total selling cost.

The Art Of The Deal

If your financial and legal assessments show that the business is a good buy, don't be the first person to bring up the subject of price. Let the seller name the figure first, and proceed from there.

Deciding on a price, however, is just the first step in negotiating the sale.

More important is how the deal is structured. David H. Troob, chairman of the Geneva Companies, a national mergers and acquisitions services firm, suggests you should be ready to pay 30 percent to 50 percent of the price in cash and finance the remaining amount.

You can finance through a traditional lender, or sellers may agree to "hold a note," which means they accept payments over a period of time, just as a lender would. Many sellers like this method because it assures them of future income. Other sellers may agree to different terms—for example, accepting benefits such as a company car for a period of time after the deal is completed. These methods can cut down the amount of upfront cash you need; Troob advises, however, that you should always have an attorney review any arrangements for legality and liability issues. (For more ideas on financing your purchase, see "Let's Make A Deal" in this chapter.)

An individual purchasing a business has two options for structuring the deal (assuming the transaction is not a merger). The first is asset acquisition, in which you purchase only those assets you want. On the plus side, asset acquisition protects you from unwanted legal liabilities since instead of buying the corporation (and all its legal risks), you are buying only its assets. On the downside, an asset acquisition can be very expensive. The asset-by-asset purchasing process is complicated and also opens the possibility that the seller may raise the price of desirable assets to offset losses from undesirable ones.

The other option is stock acquisition, in which you purchase stock. Among other things, this means you must be willing to purchase all the business's assets—and assume all its liabilities.

The final purchase contract should be structured with the help of your acquisition team to reflect very precisely your understanding and intentions regarding the purchase from a financial, tax and legal standpoint. The contract must be all-inclusive and should allow you to rescind the deal if you find at any time that the owner intentionally misrepresented the company or failed to report essential information. It's also a good idea to include a noncompete clause in the contract to ensure the seller doesn't open a competing operation down the street.

Remember, you can walk away from a negotiation at any point in the process if you don't like the way things are going. "If you don't like the deal, don't buy," says Troob. "Just because you spent a month looking at something doesn't mean you have to buy it. You have no obligation."

Transition Time

The transition to new ownership is a big change for employees of a small business. To ensure a smooth transition, start the process before the deal is done. Make sure the owner feels good about what is going to happen to the business after he or she leaves. Spend some time talking to the key employees, customers and suppliers before you take over; tell them about your plans and ideas for the business's future. Getting these key players involved and on your side makes running the business a lot easier.

Most sellers will be happy to help you in a transition period during which they train you in operating the business. This period can range from a few weeks to six months or longer. After the one-on-one training period, many sellers will agree to be available for phone consultation for another period of time. Make sure you and the seller come to an agreement on how this training will be handled, and write it into your contract.

If you buy the business lock, stock and barrel, simply putting your name on the door and running it as before, your transition is likely to be fairly smooth. On the other hand, if you buy only part of the business's assets, such as its client list or employees, then make a lot of changes in how things are done, you'll probably face a more difficult transition period.

Many new business owners have unrealistically high expectations that they can immediately make a business more profitable. Of course, you need a positive attitude to run a successful business, but if your attitude is "I'm better than you," you'll soon face resentment from the employees you've acquired.

Instead, look at the employees as valuable assets. Initially, they'll know far more about the business than you will; use that knowledge to get yourself up to speed, and treat them with respect and appreciation.

Employees inevitably feel worried about job security when a new owner takes over. That uncertainty is multiplied if you don't tell them what your plans are. Many new bosses are so eager to start running the show, they slash staff, change prices or make other radical changes without giving employees any warning. Involve the staff in your planning, and keep communication open so they know what is happening at all times.

Taking on an existing business isn't always easy, but with a little patience, honesty and hard work, you'll soon be running things like a pro.

BUYING A FRANCHISE

If buying an existing business doesn't sound right for you but starting from scratch sounds a bit intimidating, you could be suited for franchise ownership. What is a franchise—and how do you know if you're right for one? Essentially, a franchisee pays an initial fee and ongoing royalties to a franchisor. In return, the franchisee gains the use of a trademark, ongoing support from the franchisor, and the right to use the franchisor's system of doing business and sell its products or services.

McDonald's, perhaps the best-known franchise company in the world, illustrates the benefits of franchising: Customers know they will always get the same type of food, prepared the same way, whether they visit a McDonald's in Moscow or Michigan. Customers feel confident in McDonald's, and as a result, a new McDonald's location has a head start on success compared to an independent hamburger stand.

In addition to a well-known brand name, buying a franchise offers many other advantages that are not available to the entrepreneur starting a business from scratch. Perhaps the most significant is that you get a proven system of operation and training in how to use it. New franchisees can avoid a lot of the mistakes start-up entrepreneurs typically make because the franchisor has already perfected daily operations through trial and error.

Beware!

Is a franchise or business opportunity seller doing the hustle? Watch out for a salesperson who says things like "Territories are going fast," "Act now or you'll be shut out" or "I'm leaving town on Monday, so make your decision now." Legitimate sellers will not pressure you to rush into such a big decision. If someone gives you the hustle, give their opportunity the thumbs-down.

Reputable franchisors conduct market research before selling a new outlet, so you can feel greater confidence that there is a demand for the product or service. Failing to do adequate market research is one of the biggest mistakes independent entrepreneurs typically make; as a franchisee, it's done for you. The franchisor also provides you a clear picture of the competition and how to differentiate yourself from them.

Finally, franchisees enjoy the benefit of strength in numbers. You gain from economies of scale in buying materials, supplies and services, such as advertising, as well as in negotiating for locations and lease terms. By comparison, independent operators have to negotiate on their own, usually getting less favorable terms. Some suppliers won't deal with new businesses or will reject your business because your account isn't big enough.

Is Franchising Right For You?

An oft-quoted saying about franchising is that it puts you in business "for yourself, but not by yourself." While that support can be helpful, for some entrepreneurs, it can be too restricting. Most franchisors impose strict rules on franchisees, specifying everything from how you should greet customers to how to prepare the product or service.

That's not to say you will be a mindless drone—many franchisors welcome franchisees' ideas and suggestions on how to improve the way business is done—but, for the most part, you will need to adhere to the basic systems and rules set by the franchisor. If you are fiercely independent, hate interference and want to design every aspect of your new business, you may be better off starting your own company from scratch or buying a business opportunity (see the "Buying A Business Opportunity" section in this chapter for more details).

More and more former corporate employees are buying franchises these days. For many of them, a franchise is an excellent way to make the transition to business ownership. As a corporate employee, you were probably used to delegating tasks like ordering supplies, word processing and answering phones. The transition to being an entrepreneur and doing everything for yourself can be jarring. Buying a franchise could offer the support you need in making the switch to entrepreneurship.

Smart Tip

For more information when investigating a franchise or business opportunity, try these sources:

◆ The Federal Trade Commission (FTC) provides a free package of information about the FTC Franchise and Business Opportunity Rule. Write to: Public Reference Branch, Federal Trade Commission, Washington, DC 20580, or call (202) 326-8128.

◆ The American Business Opportunity Institute Inc. is a national clearinghouse and seminar company specializing in business opportunity and franchise investment. For information, send a self-addressed, stamped, business-sized envelope to American Business Opportunity Institute Inc., c/o Andrew Caffey, #700, 3 Bethesda Metro Center, Bethesda, MD 20814.

Do Your Homework

Once you've decided a franchise is the right route for you, how do you choose the right franchise? With so many franchise systems to choose from, the options can be dizzying. Start by investigating various industries that interest you to find those with growth potential. Narrow the choices down to a few industries you are most interested in, then analyze your geographic area to see if there is a market for that type of business. If so, contact all the franchise companies in those fields and ask them for information. Any reputable company will be happy to send you information at no cost.

Of course, don't rely solely on these promotional materials to make your decision. You also need to do your own detective work. Start by visiting your library or going online to look up all the magazine and newspaper articles

It's Show Time

Franchise and business opportunity trade shows can be a great opportunity. Attending a show is exciting—*and* overwhelming. Prepare carefully, and you will get a lot more out of the experience.

BEFORE THE SHOW:

◆ *Think about what you are seeking from a franchise or business opportunity.* Part time or full time? What type of business would you enjoy? Consider your hobbies and passions.

◆ *Figure out your financial resources.* What is liquid, what can you borrow from family and friends, and how much do you need to live on? What are your financial goals for the business?

◆ *Get serious.* Dress conservatively, carry a briefcase, leave the kids at home, and take business cards if you have them. Show the representatives you meet that you are a serious prospect.

AT THE SHOW:

◆ *When you arrive, study the floor plan of the exhibitors listed.* Circle the businesses you recognize or that look interesting to you. Make sure you stop by these booths during your visit.

◆ *Don't waste time.* Pass by the sellers who are out of your price range or do not meet your personal goals. Have a short list of questions ready to ask the others:

 1. What is the total investment?

 2. Tell me about a franchisee's typical day.

 3. What arrangements are made for product supply?

 4. Is financing available from the franchisor?

 5. Ask for a copy of the company's UFOC. Not all franchisors will give you a copy of the UFOC at the show. This is perfectly acceptable, but if you are serious about investigating an opportunity, insist on a copy as soon as possible.

◆ *Collect handout information from all the companies that interest you.* Also gather business cards.

AFTER THE SHOW:

◆ *Organize the materials you collected into file folders.* Then read through the information more closely.

◆ *Follow up.* Call the representatives you met.

you can find about the companies you are considering. Is the company depicted favorably? Does it seem to be well-managed and growing?

Check with the consumer or franchise regulators in your state to see if there are any serious problems with the company you are considering. If the company or its principals have been involved in lawsuits or bankruptcies, try to determine the nature of the lawsuits: Did they involve fraud or violations of Federal Trade Commission (FTC) regulatory laws? To find out, call the court that handled the case and request a copy of the petition or judgment.

If you live in one of the 14 states (California, Hawaii, Illinois, Indiana, Maryland, Michigan, Minnesota, North Dakota, New York, Rhode Island, South Dakota, Virginia, Washington and Wisconsin) that regulate the sale of franchises, contact the state franchise authority, which can tell you if the company has complied with state registration requirements. If the company is registered with Dun & Bradstreet, request a D&B report, which will give you details on the company's financial standing, payment promptness and other information. And, of course, it never hurts to check with your local office of the Better Business Bureau for complaints against the company.

Does the company still sound good? That means your investigation is just beginning. If you haven't already received one, contact the franchisor again and ask for a copy of its Uniform Franchise Offering Circular (UFOC). This disclosure document must, by law, be given to all prospective franchisees within 10 days after the first personal meeting or 10 days before any agreement is signed or money changes hands (whichever is earlier). If a company says it is a franchise but won't give you a UFOC, contact the Federal Trade Commission—and take your business elsewhere.

The UFOC is a treasure trove of information for those who are serious about franchising. It contains an extensive written description of the company, the investment amount and fees required, any litigation and/or bankruptcy history of the franchisor and its officers, the trademark you will be licensed to use, the products you are required to purchase, the advertising program, and the contractual obligations of both franchisor and franchisee. It specifies how much working capital

Beware!

Exaggerated profit claims are common in franchise and business opportunity sales. Is a company promising you'll make $10,000 a month in your spare time? If it is a franchise, any statement about earnings (regarding others in the system or your potential earnings) must appear in the Uniform Franchise Offering Circular. Read the UFOC and talk to five franchise owners who have attained the earnings claimed.

is required, equipment needs and ongoing royalties. It also contains a sample copy of the franchise agreement you will be asked to sign should you buy into the system, as well as three years' worth of the franchisor's audited financial statements.

The UFOC has recently been revamped by the industry to make it less "legalistic" and more readable, so there is no excuse for failing to read yours carefully. You should take the UFOC to your attorney and accountant and have them read it as well before you make any serious decisions about purchasing the franchise.

From The Horse's Mouth

One of the most important parts of the UFOC is a listing of existing franchisees as well as of franchisees who have been terminated or have chosen not to renew. Both lists include addresses and phone numbers. If the list of terminated franchisees seems unusually long, it could indicate some trouble with the franchisor. Call the former franchisees and ask why the agree-

ON THE LEVEL

Multilevel marketing (MLM, also known as network marketing) is a type of business opportunity that is very popular with people looking for part-time, flexible businesses. Some of the best-known companies in America, including Avon, Tupperware and Mary Kay Cosmetics, fall under the MLM umbrella.

MLM programs feature a low upfront investment—usually only a few hundred dollars for the purchase of a product sample kit—and the opportunity to sell a product line directly to friends, family and other personal contacts. Most multilevel programs also ask participants to recruit other sales representatives. These recruits constitute a rep's "downline," and their sales generate income for those above them in the program.

Things get sticky when an MLM network compensates participants primarily for recruiting others rather than for selling the company's products or services. An MLM system where most of the revenues come from recruitment may be considered an illegal pyramid scheme.

Since multilevel programs are generally exempt from business opportunity regulation and are not defined as franchises under state and federal franchise laws, you will need to do your own investigation before investing any money.

ment was terminated—whether the franchisee wasn't making the grade or whether he or she had a grievance with the franchisor.

Next, choose a random sample of current franchisees to interview in person. This is perhaps the most important step in your research. Don't rely on a few carefully selected names the franchisor gives you; pick your own candidates to talk to.

Visit current franchisees at their locations. Talking to existing franchisees is often the best way to find out how much money individual stores actually make. You will also find out what their typical day is like, whether they enjoy what they do, and whether the business is challenging enough. Most will be relatively open about revealing their earnings and their satisfaction with the franchisor; however, the key to getting all the information you need before buying is asking the right questions. Some ideas to get you started:

◆ Was the training the franchisor offered helpful in getting the business off the ground?

◆ Is the franchisor responsive to your needs?

◆ Tell me about a typical day for you.

◆ Have there been problems you did not anticipate?

◆ Has your experience proved that the investment and cost information in the UFOC was realistic?

◆ Is the business seasonal? If so, what do you do to make ends meet in the off-season?

◆ Have your sales and profits met your expectations? Tell me about the numbers in the business.

◆ Are there expansion opportunities for additional franchise ownership in this system?

◆ Knowing what you know now, would you make this investment again?

Since running a franchise involves an ongoing relationship with the franchisor, be sure to get the details on the purchasing process—everything that happened from the day the franchisee signed the agreement to the end of the first year in business. Did the parent company follow through on its promises?

Talk to as many franchisees as you can—a broader perspective will give you a more accurate picture of the company. Take careful notes of the conversations so you can refer to them later.

Don't hesitate to ask about sensitive topics. One of the most important questions a prospective franchisee should ask, but rarely does, is "What conflicts do you have with the franchisor?" Even established, successful

FRANCHISE EVALUATION WORK SHEET

This work sheet helps you determine the attractiveness of each franchise you are consider-ing. Assign each franchise a column number. Answer each question along the left-hand side of the work sheet by assigning a rating of 1-3, with 3 being the strongest. Total each column after you've finished. The franchise with the highest score is the most attractive.

	Franchises			
The Franchise Organization	1	2	3	4
Does the franchisor have a good track record?				
Do the principals of the franchise have expertise in the industry?				
Rate the franchisor's financial condition.				
How thoroughly does the franchisor check its prospective franchises?				
Rate the profitability of the franchisor and its franchisees.				
The Product Or Service				
Is there demand for the product or service?				
Can the product or service be offered year-round?				
Are industry sales strong?				
Rate the product or service in comparison to the competition.				
Is the product or service competitively priced?				
What is the potential for industry growth?				
The Market Area				
Are exclusive territories offered?				
Rate the sales potential of the territory you are considering.				
Is the competition strong in this area?				
How successful are franchises in close proximity to this area?				
The Contract				
Are the fees and royalties associated with the franchise reasonable?				
How attractive are the renewal, termination and transfer conditions?				
If the franchisor requires you to purchase proprietary inventory, how useful is it?				
If the franchisor requires you to meet annual sales quotas, are they reasonable?				
Franchisor Support				
Does the franchisor help with site selection, lease negotiations and store layout?				
Does the franchisor provide ongoing training?				
Does the franchisor provide financing to qualified individuals?				
Are manuals, sales kits, accounting systems and purchasing guides supplied?				
Does the franchisor sponsor an advertising fund to which franchisees contribute?				
How strong are the franchisor's advertising and promotion programs?				
Does the franchisor have favorable national supplier contracts?				
Totals				

companies have conflicts. What you need to find out is how widespread and common those conflicts are.

Talking to franchisees can also give you something you won't get anywhere else: a feeling for what it's like to run this business day to day. Thinking solely in economic terms is a mistake if you end up with a franchise that doesn't suit your lifestyle or self-image. When you envision running a restaurant franchise, for instance, you may be thinking of all the money you're going to make. Talking to franchisees can bring you back to reality—which is a lot more likely to involve manning a fry station, disciplining teenage employees and working late hours than cruising around in your Ferrari. Talking to franchisees in a variety of industries can help you make a choice that fits your lifestyle.

Many franchisees and franchising experts say there's no better way to cap off your research than by spending time in a franchisee location to see what your life will be like if you buy. Buyers should spend at least one week working in a unit. This is the best way for the franchisor and franchisee to evaluate each other. Offer to work for free. If the franchisor doesn't want you to, you should be skeptical about the investment.

When all your research is completed, the choice between two equally sound franchises often comes down to your gut instinct. That's why talking to franchisees and visiting locations is so important in the selection process.

Proven Purchase

Buying a franchise can be a good way to lessen the risk of business ownership. Some entrepreneurs cut that risk still further by purchasing an existing franchise—one that's already up and running. Not only does an existing franchise have a customer base, but it also has a management system in place and ongoing revenues. In short, it already has a foundation—something that's very attractive to a lot of prospective entrepreneurs.

Finding existing franchisees who are willing to sell is simply a matter of asking the parent company what's available; you can also check local classified ads to find businesses for sale.

Once you've found some likely candidates, the investigation process combines the same steps used in buying an existing business with those used in buying a franchise. The good news, however, is that you'll get far more detailed financial information than you typically would when assessing a franchise company. Where other potential franchisees just get vague suggestions of potential earnings, you'll get hard facts.

Of course, there's a price to pay for all the advantages of buying an existing franchise: It's generally much more costly. In fact, the purchase price of an existing location can be two to four times more than you'd pay for a new franchise from the same company. Because you are investing more money, it's even more important to make sure you have audited financial statements and review them with your CPA.

Once in a while, you'll find a franchise that isn't doing well. Perhaps the current owner isn't good at marketing, isn't putting forth enough effort or isn't following the system correctly. In this case, you may be able to get the existing franchise for what it would cost to buy a new franchise—or even less. It's crucial, however, to make sure the problem is something you can correct and that you'll be able to get the location up to speed fast. After all, you're going to have immediate overhead expenses—for employees, royalties and operating costs—so you need some immediate income as well.

Also be aware that even if a particular franchise location is thriving, it doesn't mean the parent company is equally successful. In fact, sometimes franchisees who know the parent company is in trouble try to unload their franchises before the franchisor goes under. Carefully assess the franchisor's strength, accessibility and the level of assistance they provide. Don't settle for anything less than you would when buying a new franchise.

BUYING A BUSINESS OPPORTUNITY

If a franchise sounds too restrictive for you but the idea of coming up with your own business idea, systems and procedures sounds intimidating, there is a middle ground: business opportunities.

A business opportunity, in the simplest terms, is a packaged business investment that allows the buyer to begin a business. (Technically, all franchises are business opportunities, but not all business opportunities are franchises.)

Unlike a franchise, however, the business opportunity seller typically exercises no control over the buyer's business operations. In fact, in most business opportunity programs there is no continuing relationship between the seller and the buyer after the sale is made.

Although business opportunities offer less support than franchises, this could be an advantage if you thrive on freedom. Typically, you will not be obligated to follow the strict specifications and detailed programs that franchisees must follow. With most business opportunities, you simply buy a set of equipment or materials and can then operate the business any way and under any name you want. There are no ongoing royalties in most cases, and no trademark rights are sold.

However, this same lack of long-term commitment is also a business opportunity's chief disadvantage. Because there is no continuing relationship, the world of business opportunities does have its share of con artists who promise buyers instant success, then take their money and run. While increased regulation of business opportunities has lessened the likelihood of rip-offs dramatically, it is still important to investigate an opportunity thoroughly before you invest any money.

Legal Matters

In general, a business opportunity refers to one of a number of ways to get into business. These include:

◆ **Dealers/distributors** are individuals or businesses who purchase the right to sell ABC Corp.'s products but not the right to use ABC's trade name. For example, an authorized dealer of Minolta products might have a Minolta sign in his window, but he can't call his business Minolta. Often, the words "dealers" and "distributors" are used interchangeably, but there is a difference: A distributor may sell to several dealers, while a dealer usually sells direct to retailers or consumers.

◆ **Licensees** have the right to use the seller's trade name and certain methods, equipment, technology or product lines. If Business Opportunity XYZ has a special technique for reglazing porcelain, for instance, it will teach you the method and sell you the supplies and machinery needed to open your own business. You can call your business XYZ, but you are an independent licensee.

◆ **Vending machines** are provided by the seller, who may also help you find locations for them. You restock your own machines and collect the money.

◆ **Cooperatives** allow an existing business to affiliate with a network of similar businesses, usually for advertising and promotional purposes.

◆ **Multilevel marketing** (see "On The Level" in this chapter).

Legal definitions of business opportunities vary, particularly since not all states regulate business opportunities. (The 25 that do are Arizona, California, Connecticut, Florida, Georgia, Illinois, Indiana, Iowa, Kentucky, Louisiana, Maine, Maryland, Michigan, Minnesota, Nebraska, New Hampshire, North Carolina, Ohio, Oklahoma, South Carolina, South Dakota, Texas, Utah, Virginia and Washington.) Even among these, different states have different definitions of what constitutes a business opportunity. Most definitions contain the following:

◆ The investor purchases goods or services that allow him or her to begin a business.

◆ The purchase involves a certain amount of money. In 15 states and under FTC regulations, the minimum investment is $500; in the other 10 states, that figure drops to as little as $100.

◆ The seller makes any one of the following statements during the course of the sale:

1. The seller will assist in securing locations for display racks or vending devices;
2. The seller will return the money if the buyer is "unsatisfied" with the investment;
3. The seller will buy back the products assembled or produced by the buyer;
4. The seller guarantees (or, in some states, merely implies) that the buyer will be able to generate revenues in excess of the amount of the investment; or
5. The seller will provide a marketing plan or a sales plan to the buyer.

If a seller meets the definition of a business opportunity in states that regulate them, it generally means he or she must register the offering with state authorities and deliver a disclosure document to prospective buyers at least 10 business days before the sale is made. (For more information on specific states' regulations, check with consumer protection agencies—often a part of the attorney general's office–in your state.)

Checking It Out

Researching a business is a more challenging task than investigating a franchise. Particularly if the business opportunity you are considering doesn't provide buyers with a disclosure document, you get a lot less information, so you have to do a lot more legwork on your own.

Whenever possible, follow the same steps you would for investigating a franchise. Contact the Better Business Bureau to see if there have been complaints against the company. If the company is registered with Dun & Bradstreet, a financial report will give you details on its financial standing and other information.

Also check with the state regulatory agency—either the Commission of Securities or the Commission of Financial Institutions—in the state where the business opportunity has its headquarters. This will tell you if the company is complying with all state regulations. If you discover the company or its principals have been involved in lawsuits or bankruptcies, try to find out more details. Did the suits involve fraud or violations of regulatory laws? A copy of the petition or judgement, which you can get from the court that handled the case, will give you the answers to these questions.

Finally, see if the business opportunity seller will provide you with a list of people who have purchased the opportunity in the past. Don't let the

BUSINESS EVALUATION CHECKLIST

If you find a business that you would like to buy, you will need to consider a number of points before you decide whether or not to purchase it. Take a good, close look at the business and answer the following questions. They will help you determine whether the business is a sound investment.

❏ Why does the current owner want to sell the business?

❏ Does the business have great potential for future growth, or will its sales decline?

❏ If the business is in decline, will you be able to save it and make it successful?

❏ Is the business in sound financial condition? Have you seen audited year-end financial statements for the business? Have you reviewed the most recent statements? Have you reviewed the business's tax returns for the last five years?

❏ Have you seen copies of all of the business's current contracts?

❏ Is the business now, or has it ever been, under investigation by any governmental agency? If so, what is the status of any current investigation? What were the results of any past investigation?

❏ Is the business currently involved in a lawsuit, or has it ever been involved in one? If so, what is the status or result?

❏ Does the business have any debts or liens against it? If so, what are they for and in what amounts?

❏ What percentage of the business's accounts are past due? How much does the business write off each year for bad debts? How many customers does the business serve on a regular basis?

❏ Who makes up the market for this business? Where are your customers located? (Do they all come from your community or from across the state, or are they spread across the globe?)

❏ Does the amount of business vary from season to season?

❏ Does any single customer account for a large portion of the sales volume? If so, would the business be able to survive without this customer? (The larger your customer base is, the more easily you will be able to survive the loss of any customers. If, on the other hand, you exist mainly to serve a single client, the loss of that client could finish your business.)

BUSINESS EVALUATION CHECKLIST, CONT'D.

❏ How does the business market its products or services? Does its competition use the same methods? If not, what methods does the competition use? How successful are they?

❏ Does the business have exclusive rights to market any particular products or services? If so, how has it obtained this exclusivity? Is it making the best possible use of this exclusivity? Do you have written proof that the current business owner can transfer this exclusivity to you?

❏ Does the business hold patents for any of its products? Which ones? What percentage of gross sales do they represent? Would the sale of the business include the sale of any patents?

❏ Are the business's supplies, merchandise, and other materials available from several suppliers, or are there only a handful who can meet your needs? If you lost the business's current supplier, what impact would that loss have on your business? Would you be able to find substitute goods of the appropriate quality and price?

❏ Are any of the business's products in danger of becoming obsolete or of going out of style? Is this a "fad" business?

❏ What is the business's market share?

❏ What competition does the business face? How can the business compete successfully? Have the business's competitors changed recently? Have any of them gone out of business, for instance?

❏ Does the business have all of the equipment you think is necessary? Will you need to add or update any equipment?

❏ What is the business's current inventory worth? Will you be able to use any of this inventory, or is it inconsistent with your intended product line?

seller give you a few handpicked names; ask for a full list of buyers in your state. Try to track them down, and talk to as many as you can. Were they satisfied with the opportunity? Would they recommend it to friends?

The path to buying a business opportunity is not as clearly defined as the road leading to franchise ownership. The good news, however, is that you have more freedom to make your business opportunity work. More so than with a franchise, the success or failure of your business opportunity depends on you, your commitment and your level of effort. Put that same effort into finding the right business opportunity program, and your chances of success increase exponentially.

GLOSSARY

Accounts receivable: money due in to a business from clients and customers; outstanding invoices

Asset acquisition: a method of buying a business in which the buyer purchases only those assets of the business he or she wants

Business broker: a person who helps buy and sell businesses, similar to a real estate broker

Business opportunity: legal definitions vary; in its simplest terms, a business opportunity is a packaged business investment that allows the buyer to begin a business

Downline: the group of sales representatives that a given sales rep has recruited to join a multilevel marketing system; he or she receives a percentage of their sales

Due diligence: the process of investigating legal, financial and other aspects of any business deal (such as buying a business) before the deal is completed

Employee Stock Ownership Plan (ESOP): a plan that gives employees shares of stock in a company

Factors: companies that buy businesses' accounts receivable

Franchisee: the person who buys a system of doing business from a franchisor

Franchisor: a company or person that sells a system of doing business to franchisees and provides them with ongoing training and support

Hold harmless and indemnify: a clause in a contract that protects one party to a business purchase from being held responsible for results of the other party's actions prior to the purchase

Intellectual property: a nontangible property, such as a trade secret, patent or trade name, to which one has legal rights

Licensing: system of doing business where a buyer receives the right to use a business' specific methods, equipment, technology or products

Multilevel marketing (MLM): system of doing business in which participants recruit other sales representatives as part of their "downline" and receive a commission based on sales of their downline as well as on their own sales

Network marketing: see "multilevel marketing"

Pyramid scheme: an illegal type of multilevel marketing in which participants receive revenues primarily based on their downline's sales rather than on their own sales

Stock acquisition: a method of buying a business in which the buyer purchases the actual stock of the business

Uniform Franchise Offering Circular (UFOC): a disclosure document franchisors are legally required to provide to prospective franchisees

Part Two:
Building Blocks

CHAPTER 6

WHO IS YOUR CUSTOMER, ANYWAY?

Defining your market

You've come up with a great idea for a business . . . but you're not ready to roll yet. Before you go any further, the next step is figuring out who your market is.

There are two basic markets you can sell to: consumer and business. These divisions are fairly obvious. For example, if you're selling women's clothing from a retail store, your target market is consumers; if you're selling office supplies, your target market is businesses (this is referred to as "business-to-business" sales). In some cases—for example, if you run a printing business—you may be marketing to both businesses and individual consumers.

No business—particularly a small one—can be all things to all people. The more narrowly you can define your target market, the better. This process is known as creating a niche and is key to success for even the biggest companies. Wal-Mart and Tiffany's are both retailers but with very different niches: Wal-Mart caters to bargain-minded shoppers, while Tiffany's appeals to upscale jewelry consumers.

"Many people talk about 'finding' a niche as if it were something under a rock or at the end of the rainbow, ready-made. That's nonsense," says Lynda C. Falkenstein, author of *Nichecraft: The Art of Being Special* and *Starting Your Own Business: How to Make Niches That Increase Profits* (both Niche Press). Good niches don't just fall into your lap; they must be carefully crafted.

Rather than creating a niche, many entrepreneurs make the mistake of falling into the "all over the map" trap, claiming they can do many things and be good at all of them. These people quickly learn a tough lesson, Falkenstein warns: "Smaller is bigger in business, and smaller is not all over the map; it's highly focused."

Practicing Nichecraft

Creating a good niche, advises Falkenstein, involves following a seven-step process.

1. **Make a wish list.** With whom do you want to do business? Be specific: Identify your geographical range and the types of businesses or customers you want to target. If you don't know whom you want to do business with, you can't make contact. "You must recognize that you can't do business with everybody," cautions Falkenstein. Otherwise, you risk exhausting yourself and confusing your customers.

   These days, the trend is toward ever smaller niches (see "Direct Hit" in this chapter). Targeting teenagers isn't specific enough; targeting male, African-American urban teenagers with family incomes of $40,000 and up is. Aiming at companies that sell software is too broad; aiming at Northern California-based companies that provide Internet software sales and training, and have sales of $15 million or more is a better goal.

2. **Focus.** Clarify what you want to sell, remembering: a) you can't be all things to all people and b) "smaller is bigger." Your niche is not the same as the field in which you work. For example, a retail clothing business is not a niche but a field. A more specific niche may be selling maternity clothes to executive women.

   To begin this focusing process, Falkenstein suggests these techniques to help you:

   ◆ Make a list of the things you do best and the skills implicit in each of them.

   ◆ List your achievements and accomplishments.

   ◆ Identify the most important lessons you have learned in life.

   ◆ Look for patterns that reveal your style or approach to resolving problems.

Beware!

Even though many baby boomers are now over 50, don't make the mistake of marketing to them the same way you would seniors. "If you're dealing with a 50-year-old boomer, you're dealing with a person who doesn't see himself as 50 years old," says Phil Goodman, founder of the Boomer Marketing & Research Center. The moral? The same marketing approaches that appealed to boomers when they were 30 will appeal to them when they're 50, 60 and 70.

DIRECT HIT

Once upon a time, business owners thought it was enough to market their products or services to "18-to-49-year-olds." Those days are a thing of the past. "The consumer marketplace has become so differentiated, it's a misconception to talk about the marketplace in any kind of general, grand way," says Ross E. Goldstein, president of Generation Insights, a consulting firm that tracks trends. "You can market to socioeconomic status or to gender or to region or to lifestyle or to technological sophistication. There's no end to the number of different ways you can slice the pie."

Further complicating matters, age no longer means what it used to. Fifty-year-old baby boomers prefer rock 'n' roll to Geritol; 30-year-olds may still be living with their parents. "People now repeat stages and recycle their lives," says Goldstein. "You can have two men who are 64 years old, and one is retired and driving around in a Winnebago, and the other is just remarried with a toddler in his house."

Generational marketing, which defines consumers not just by age but by social, economic, demographic and psychological factors, has been used since the early '80s to give a more accurate picture of the target consumer.

A newer twist is **cohort marketing**, which studies groups of people who underwent the same experiences during their formative years. This leads them to form a bond and behave differently from people in different cohorts, even when they are similar in age. For instance, people who were young adults in the Depression era behave differently from people who came of age during World War II, even though they are close in age.

To get an even narrower reading, some entrepreneurs combine cohort or generational marketing with **life stages**, or what people are doing at a certain time in life (getting married, having children, retiring), and **physiographics**, or physical conditions related to age (nearsightedness, arthritis, menopause).

Today's consumers are more marketing-savvy than ever before and don't like to be "lumped" with others—so be sure you understand your niche. While pinpointing your market so narrowly takes a little extra effort, small-business owners who aim at a smaller target are far more likely to make a direct hit.

Your niche should arise naturally from your interests and experience. For example, if you spent 10 years working in a consulting firm, but also spent 10 years working for a small, family-owned business, you may decide to start a consulting business that specializes in small, family-owned companies.

Beware!

Marketing to ethnic consumers? Don't make these common mistakes: Sticking a few ethnic faces in the background of your marketing materials; "lumping" (for example, treating Japanese-, Chinese- and Korean-Americans as one big mass of "Asians"); relying on stereotypes such as slang or overtly ethnic approaches. Subtlety and sensitivity are keys to success when approaching these markets.

3. **Describe the customer's world view.** A successful business uses what Falkenstein calls the Platinum Rule: "Do unto others as they would do unto themselves." By looking at the world from your prospective customers' perspective, you can identify their needs or wants. The best way to do this is to talk to prospective customers and identify their main concerns. (Part 2 Chapter 7 will give you more ideas for ways to get inside customers' heads.)

4. **Synthesize.** At this stage, your niche should begin to take shape as your ideas and the client's needs and wants coalesce to create something totally new. A good niche has five qualities:

    ♦ it takes you where you want to go—in other words, it conforms to your long-term vision of your business;

    ♦ somebody else wants it—namely, customers;

    ♦ it's carefully planned;

    ♦ it's one-of-a-kind, the "only game in town"; and

    ♦ it evolves, allowing you to develop different profit centers while still retaining the core business, thus ensuring long-term success.

5. **Evaluation.** Now it's time to evaluate your proposed product or service against the five criteria in the previous step. Perhaps you'll find that the niche you had in mind requires more business travel than you're ready for. That means it doesn't fulfill one of the above criteria—it won't take you where you want to go. So scrap it, and move on to the next idea.

6. **Test.** Once you have a match between niche and product, test-market it. "Give people an opportunity to buy your product or service—not just theoretically but actually putting it out there," suggests Falkenstein. This can be done by offering samples of your services, such as a free miniseminar or a sample copy of your newsletter. The test shouldn't cost you a lot of money: "If you spend huge amounts of money on the initial market test, you're probably doing it wrong."

7. **Go for it!** It's time to implement your idea. For many entrepreneurs, this is the most difficult stage. But fear not: If you did your homework, entering the market will be a calculated risk, not just a gamble.

Keep It Fresh

Once your niche is established and well-received by your market, you may be tempted to rest on your laurels. Not a good idea, says Falkenstein: "[You must] keep growing by re-niching. This doesn't mean totally changing your focus but rather further adapting it to the environment around you."

TARGET MARKET WORK SHEET

Use the following exercise to identify where and who is your target market. Once you're done, you'll have an audience to aim for and hone in on rather than using a shotgun approach, which is a time and money waster.

1. Describe the idea:

2. What will the concept be used for?

3. Where are similar concepts used and sold?

4. What places do my prospects go to for recreation?

PROFITING FROM PROCUREMENT

Looking for a niche? One market many small-business owners ignore is the lucrative procurement pie. Although the federal government is by far the biggest customer in this arena, local governments, colleges and universities, school districts, nonprofit organizations, public utilities and corporations also have plenty of procurement opportunities available. The federal government's civilian agencies alone buy products in more than 4,000 categories, ranging from air brakes to zippers.

Contrary to what you might imagine, small businesses often have an edge in competing for procurement dollars. Government rules and regulations are designed to promote fair competition and a level playing field. And government agencies and large contractors are often required by law to give a certain amount of business to small, disadvantaged, women-owned or minority-owned businesses.

How to get started?

◆ To sell to the federal government, begin by registering with the SBA's Procurement Automated Source System (PASS). Government agencies search this online directory when they need suppliers.

◆ Agencies like the U.S. Postal Service, Department of Interior and the Army, as well as many others, send out solicitations to businesses that are on their mailing lists. To find out how to get on the lists, contact the agency you're interested in or check the Small Business Administration's (SBA) annual U.S. Government Purchasing and Sales Directory.

◆ Regularly scan the *Commerce Business Daily*, which lists available contracts; it can be found at many libraries. You can also approach agencies or prime contractors directly and market your services to them.

If you are a woman or member of a minority group, you will need to be certified as a woman- or minority-owned business to work with government agencies and many large contractors. This can be done several ways. Many cities have their own certification programs or can direct you to the certification programs that they accept. A good general place to start is with the SBA; you can reach them at 409 Third St. SW, Washington, DC 20416-6001, or call (800) 8-ASK-SBA.

Ask yourself the following questions when you think you have found your niche—and ask them again every six months or so to make sure your niche is still on target:

◆ Who are your target clients?

◆ Who aren't your target clients?

◆ Do you turn down certain kinds of business if it falls outside your niche?

◆ What do clients think you stand for?

◆ Is your niche in a constant state of evolution?

◆ Does your niche offer what prospective customers want?

◆ Do you have a plan and delivery system that effectively conveys the need for your niche to the right market?

◆ Can you confidently predict the life cycle of your niche?

◆ How can your niche be expanded into a variety of products or services that act as profit centers?

◆ Do you have a sense of passion and focused energy with respect to your niche?

◆ Does your niche feel comfortable and natural?

◆ How will pursuing your niche contribute to achieving the goals you have set for business?

According to Falkenstein, "Creating a niche is the difference between being in business and not being in business. It's the difference between surviving and thriving, between simply liking what you do and the joy of success."

ON A MISSION

Once you have designed a niche for your business, you're ready to create a mission statement. A key tool that can be as important as your business plan, a mission statement captures, in a few succinct sentences, the essence of your business's goals and the philosophies underlying them. Equally important, the mission statement signals what your business is all about to customers, employees, suppliers and the community.

The mission statement reflects every facet of your business: the range and nature of the products you offer, pricing, quality, service, marketplace position, growth potential, use of technology, and your relationships with your customers, employees, suppliers, competitors and the community.

"Mission statements help clarify what business you're in, your goals and your objectives," says Rhonda Abrams, author of *The Successful Business Plan: Secrets and Strategies* (Oasis Press).

Your mission statement should reflect your business' special niche. However, studying other companies' statements can fuel your creativity. One sample mission statement Abrams developed:

"AAA Inc. is a spunky, imaginative food products and service company aimed at offering high-quality, moderately priced, occasionally unusual foods using only natural ingredients. We view ourselves as partners with our customers, our employees, our community and our environment. We aim to become a regionally recognized brand name, capitalizing on the sustained interest in Southwestern and Mexican food. Our goal is moderate growth, annual profitability, and maintaining our sense of humor."

Or consider the statement one entrepreneur developed for her consulting business: "ABC Enterprises is a company devoted to developing human potential. Our mission is to help people create innovative solutions and make informed choices to improve their lives. We motivate and encourage others to achieve personal and professional fulfillment. Our motto is: Together, we believe that the best in each of us enriches all of us."

The Write Words

To come up with a statement that encompasses all the major elements of your business, start with the right questions. David Tucker, whose consulting business helps companies create mission statements and business plans, says the most important question is, What business are you in? Since you have already gone through the steps of creating your niche, answering this question should be easy for you.

Answering the following questions will help you to create a verbal picture of your business's mission:

◆ **Why are you in business?** What do you want for yourself, your family and your customers? Think about the spark that ignited your decision to start a business. What will keep it burning?

◆ **Who are your customers?** What can you do for them that will enrich their lives and contribute to their success—now and in the future?

◆ **What image of your business do you want to convey?** Customers, suppliers, employees and the public will all have perceptions of your company. How will you create the desired picture?

◆ **What is the nature of your products and services?** What factors determine pricing and quality? Consider how these relate to the reasons for your business's existence. How will all this change over time?

◆ **What level of service do you provide?** Most companies believe they offer "the best service available," but do your customers agree? Don't be vague; define what makes your service so extra ordinary.

◆ **What roles do you and your employees play?** Wise captains develop a leadership style that organizes, challenges and recognizes employees.

◆ **What kind of relationships will you maintain with suppliers?** Every business is in partnership with its suppliers. When you succeed, so do they.

◆ **How do you differ from competitors?** Many entrepreneurs forget they are pursuing the same dollars as their competitors. What do you do better, cheaper or faster than others? How can you use those competitors' weaknesses to your advantage?

◆ **How will you use technology, capital, processes, products and services to reach your goals?** A succinct description of your strategy will keep your energies focused on your goals.

◆ **What underlying philosophies or values guided your responses to the previous questions?** Some businesses choose to list these separately. Writing them down clarifies the "why" behind your mission.

Putting It All Together

Like anything with lasting value, crafting a mission statement requires time, thought and planning. However, the effort is well worth it. In fact, most start-up entrepreneurs discover that the process of crafting the mission statement is as beneficial as the final statement itself. Going through the process will help you solidify the reason for what you are doing and clarify the motivations behind your business.

Here are some tips to make your mission statement the best it can be:

1. **Involve those connected to your business.** Even if you are a sole proprietor, it helps to get at least one other person's ideas for

your mission statement. Other people can help you see strengths, weaknesses and voids in the marketplace you might miss. If you have no partners or investors to include, consider knowledgeable family members, close friends, accountants or employees. Be sure, however, to choose only positive, supportive people who truly want you to succeed.

2. **Set aside several hours—a full day, if possible—to work on your statement.** Mission statements are short—typically more than one sentence but rarely exceeding a page. Still, writing one is not a short process. It takes time to come up with language that simultaneously describes an organization's heart and soul and serves as an inspirational beacon to everyone involved in the business. Large corporations often spend an entire weekend crafting a statement.

3. **Plan a date.** Set aside time to meet with the people who'll be helping you. Write a list of topics to discuss or think about. Find a quiet, comfortable place away from phones and interruptions.

4. **Be prepared.** If you have several people involved, come equipped with refreshments, extra lists of topics, paper and pencils. Because not everyone understands what a mission statement is all about, explain its meaning and purpose before you begin.

5. **Brainstorm.** Consider every idea, no matter how silly it sounds. Stimulate ideas by looking at sample mission statements and thinking about or discussing the 10 questions above. If you're working with a group, use a flip chart to record responses so everyone can see them. Once you've finished brainstorming, ask everyone to write individual mission statements for your business. Read the statements, select the best bits and pieces, and fit them together.

6. **Use "radiant words."** Once you have the basic idea in writing, polish the language of your mission statement. "Every word counts," says Abrams. The statement should create dynamic, visual images and inspire action. Use offbeat, colorful verbs and adjectives to spice up your statement. Don't hesitate to drop in words like "kaleidoscope," "sizzle," "cheer," "outrageous" and "marvel" to add zest to the statement. If you want customers to "boast" about your goods and services, say so—along with the reasons why. Some businesses include a glossary that defines the terms used in the statement.

Once your mission statement is complete, start spreading the word! You need to convey your mission statement to others inside and outside the business to tell everyone you know where you are going and why. Post it in your office, where you, employees and visitors can see it every day. Print it on company materials, such as your brochures and your business plan or even on the back of your business cards.

When you're launching a new business, you can't afford to lose sight of your objectives. By keeping your mission statement always in front of you, you'll keep your goals in mind—and ensure smooth sailing.

GLOSSARY

Business-to-business sales: marketing your products and services to other businesses, as opposed to individual consumers

Cohort marketing: marketing to people based on the groups or "cohorts" they were part of during their formative years; for example, the World War II cohort, the Depression-era cohort

Consumer: individual who purchases services or products from a business

Generational marketing: marketing to consumers based on social, economic, demographic and psychological factors

Mission statement: a short written statement of your business goals and philosophies

Life stage marketing: marketing to consumers based on what they are doing at a given period in life, such as having children, buying a home or retiring

Physiographics: physical conditions related to aging, such as arthritis or near-sightedness

Target market: the specific group of consumers or businesses you want to sell to

CHAPTER 7

IF I BUILD IT, WILL THEY COME?

Conducting market research

So you've got a great idea for a product—something that's bound to capture the hearts and minds (and wallets) of consumers everywhere. Or perhaps you've stumbled upon a service that isn't being offered by anyone else; one that, as far as you can tell, is desperately needed. This is your opportunity! Don't hesitate . . . don't look back . . . jump right into it and . . .

Wait! Before you shift into high gear, you must determine whether there really is a market for your product or service. Not only that, you need to ascertain what—if any—fine-tuning is needed. Quite simply, you must conduct market research.

Many business owners neglect this crucial step in product development for the sole reason that they don't want to hear any negative feedback. They are convinced their product or service is perfect just the way it is, and they don't want to risk tampering with it.

Other entrepreneurs bypass market research because they fear it will be too expensive. With all the other start-up costs you're facing, it's not easy to justify spending money on research that will only prove what you knew all along: Your product is a winner.

Regardless of the reason, failing to do market research can amount to a death sentence for your product. "A lot of companies skim over the important background information because they're so interested in getting their product to market," says Donna Barson, president and owner of Barson Marketing Inc., a marketing, advertising and public relations consulting firm. "But the companies that do the best are the ones that do their homework."

Consider market research an investment in your future. If you make the necessary adjustments to your product or service now, you'll save money in the long run.

WHAT IT IS; WHAT IT DOES

What exactly is market research? Simply put, it's a way of collecting information you can use to solve or avoid marketing problems. Good market research gives you the data you need to develop a marketing plan that works. It enables you to identify the specific segments within a market that you want to target and to create an identity for your product or service that separates it from your competitors. Market research can also help you choose the best geographic location for your new business.

Before you start your market research, it's a good idea to meet with a consultant, talk to a business or mar-

Bright Idea

Small fries have big ideas that could help your business grow. If you're thinking about starting a child-related business, consider using children as marketing consultants. Kids think creatively—a big asset for entrepreneurs trying to reach this profitable market. Big companies like Microsoft and MTV hire kids to learn their views. But you don't need to be so formal: Just try polling the kids you know. Get their responses to your product, ask them for suggestions and brainstorm new ideas.

GOOD QUESTION

Whether you hire a professional market research firm or take on the task yourself, your market research should clearly answer the following questions:

◆ Who will buy my product or service?

◆ Why will they buy it?

◆ Where will they buy it—specialty shops, department stores, mail order?

◆ What do I need to charge to make a healthy profit?

◆ What products or services will mine be competing with?

◆ Am I positioning my product or service correctly? (In other words, if there's a lot of competition, look for a specialized market niche.)

◆ What government regulations will my product or service be subject to?

GENERAL MARKET QUESTIONNAIRE

1. Are you: ❑ Male   ❑ Female

2. What is your age?

❑ 18-24   ❑ 25-34

❑ 35-44   ❑ 45-54

❑ 55-64   ❑ 65 or over

3. What is the highest level of formal education you have completed to date? (Please check only one.)

❑ Attended High School   ❑ Graduated High School

❑ Attended College   ❑ Graduated College

❑ Post-Graduate Study Without   ❑ Post-Graduate Degree
   Degree

4. Please tell us your marital status.

❑ Married   ❑ Single, Never Married

❑ Separated or Divorced   ❑ Widowed

5. How many children under the age of 18 are currently living in your household?

Number of children under 18: _____

6. Please indicate your total 1998 personal income. (Include income from all sources—salary, bonuses, investment income, rents, royalties, etc. Please check only one.)

❑ Less than $30,000   ❑ $30,000-$39,999

❑ $40,000-$49,999   ❑ $50,000-$59,999

❑ $60,000-$74,999   ❑ $75,000-$99,999

❑ $100,000-$149,000   ❑ $150,000-$249,999

❑ $250,000-$499,999   ❑ $500,000-$999,999

❑ $1,000,000 or more

7. Please indicate your total 1998 household income. (Include income from all family members and include all sources—salary, bonuses, investment income, rents, royalties, etc. Please check only one.)

❑ Less than $30,000   ❑ $30,000-$39,999

❑ $40,000-$49,999   ❑ $50,000-$59,999

GENERAL MARKET QUESTIONNAIRE, CONT'D.

❏ $60,000-$74,999   ❏ $75,000-$99,999

❏ $100,000-$149,000   ❏ $150,000-$249,999

❏ $250,000-$499,999   ❏ $500,000-$999,999

❏ $1,000,000 or more

8a. Do you own a home, condominium or co-op as your primary residence?
   ❏ Yes   ❏ No

8b. If "Yes," what is the present market value of your primary residence?

❏ Under $100,000   ❏ $100,000-$199,999

❏ $200,000-$299,999   ❏ $300,000-$499,999

❏ $500,000-$749,999   ❏ $750,000-$999,999

❏ $1,000,000-$1,999,999   ❏ $2,000,000 or more

If $2,000,000 or more, please estimate value: _____

9. Do you own a second home, condominium or co-op?
   ❏ Yes   ❏ No

10. What is the current total net worth of yourself and all members of your household residing with you? (Please include the estimated market value of your business if you own one, all real estate including primary residence, cars, all household possessions, bank accounts, stocks, bonds and other investments, and assets. Please check only one.)

❏ Less than $50,000   ❏ $50,000-$99,999

❏ $100,000-$249,999   ❏ $250,000-$499,999

❏ $500,000-$749,999   ❏ $750,000-$999,999

❏ $1,000,000-$1,499,999   ❏ $1,500,000-$1,999,999

❏ $2,000,000-$4,999,999   ❏ $5,000,000-$9,999,999

❏ $10,000,000 and over

11. In which state and ZIP code area is your main residence?

State: _____   ZIP code: _____

The general market questionnaire is one example of how to compose a direct mail questionnaire to gather primary research regarding a targeted audience.

Smart Tip

When doing any type of consumer survey, whether it's a focus group, a questionnaire or a phone survey, pay particular attention to customers who complain or give you negative feedback. You don't need to worry about the customers who love your product or service, but the ones who tell you where you're going wrong provide valuable information to help you improve.

Beware!

Do you know what your competition is up to? If not, you could be headed for trouble. A recent study by professors at UCLA and Stanford University showed most business owners are clueless about the competition. Almost 80 percent were blind to their opponents' actions—which can lead to lost customers and market share.

The answer? Role-play. Put yourself in the competition's shoes and analyze their strategies. Visit their stores. Use the Internet to dig up as much information as you can about them, their tactics and their goals. In any battle, it pays to know thy enemy.

keting professor at a local college or university, or contact your local Small Business Administration (SBA) district office. These sources can offer guidance and help you with the first step in market research: deciding exactly what information you need to gather.

As a rule of thumb, market research should provide you with information about three critical areas: the customer, the industry and the competition.

1. **Industry information:** In researching the industry, look for the latest trends. Compare statistics and growth in the industry. What areas of the industry appear to be expanding, and what areas are declining? Is the industry catering to new types of customers? What technological developments are affecting the industry? How can you use them to your advantage? A thriving, stable industry is key; you don't want to start a new business in a field that is on the decline.

2. **Consumer close-up:** On the consumer side, your market research should begin with a market survey. A thorough market survey will help you make a reasonable sales forecast for your new business. To do a market survey, you first need to determine the market limits or physical boundaries of the area within which your business sells.

   Next, study the spending characteristics of the population within this area. Estimate the area's purchasing power based on its per-capita income, its median income level, the unemployment rate, population and other demographic factors. Determine the current sales volume in the area for the type of product or service you will sell. Finally, estimate how much of the total sales volume you can reasonably obtain. (This last step is extremely important. Opening your new business in a given community won't necessarily generate additional business volume; it may simply redistribute the business that's already there.)

3. **Know the competition:** Based on a combination of industry research and customer research, a clearer picture of your competition will emerge. Don't underestimate the number of competitors out there. Keep an eye out for potential future competitors as well as current ones.

KNOW THY ENEMY

There are two ways to define competitors. One is by strategic groups—competitors who use similar marketing strategies, sell similar products or have similar skills. Under this definition, you might group Toyota and Nissan as competitors within the car industry.

The second, less obvious way to group competitors is by customer—how strongly do they compete for the same customers' dollars? Using this method gives you a wider view of your competition and the challenges they could pose to your new business.

Suppose you're considering opening a family entertainment center. If there are no other family entertainment centers in the area, you might think you have no competitors. Wrong! Any type of business that competes for customers' leisure time and entertainment dollars is a competitor. That means children's play centers, amusement parks and arcades are all your competitors. So are businesses that, on the surface, don't appear similar, like movie theaters, bookstores or shopping malls. You could even face competition from nonprofit entities, like public parks, libraries or beaches. In short, anything that families might do in their leisure time is your competition.

Don't limit yourself to the obvious definitions of competition. Start thinking out of the box ... and you'll be less likely to get sideswiped by an unexpected competitor.

MARKET QUESTIONNAIRE

1. In what type of business, industry or profession are you primarily engaged? (Please check only one.)

❑ Agriculture/forestry/ construction/mining

❑ Data processing/computers

❑ Finance/banking/insurance

❑ Health care (medical, dental, etc.)

❑ Real estate

❑ Wholesale trade

❑ Personal/business services (consultant, CPA, lawyer, etc.)

❑ Communications/publishing/ advertising

❑ Education

❑ Government/public administration

❑ Manufacturing

❑ Transportation/public utilities

❑ Retail trade

❑ Other: _____ (please specify)

2. What is your title, position or rank? (Please check only one.)

❑ Chairman of the Board

❑ Owner/Partner

❑ Other Company Officer (V.P., Treasurer, etc.)

❑ Manager

❑ Scientist or Engineer

❑ Sales

❑ Clerical

❑ Retired

❑ President/CEO

❑ Director

❑ Department Head

❑ Supervisor/Foreman

❑ Other Administrative Position not mentioned

❑ Technical Specialist

❑ Military

❑ Other: _____ (please specify)

3. Approximately how many people, including yourself, are employed by your company, including branches, international offices and plants? (Please check only one.)

❑ Under 10

❑ 25-49

❑ 75-99

❑ 250-499

❑ 1,000-4,999

❑ 10,000 or more

❑ 10-24

❑ 50-74

❑ 100-249

❑ 500-999

❑ 5,000-9,999

MARKET QUESTIONNAIRE, CONT'D.

4a. Please indicate your company's gross sales or revenues in 1998 (include all plants, branches, divisions and subsidiaries).

❑ Less than $250,000   ❑ $250,000-$499,999

❑ $500,000 to $999,999   ❑ $1,000,000 to $4,999,999

❑ $5,000,000 to $9,999,999   ❑ $10,000,000 to $24,999,999

❑ $25,000,000 to $99,999,999   ❑ $100,000,000 or over

4b. In what year was your business started? _____

5. Do you serve on your company's board of directors?
   ❑ Yes   ❑ No

6. Do you serve on the board of directors of any other company?
   ❑ Yes   ❑ No

7a. Are you currently an owner or a partner of a business?
   ❑ Yes   ❑ No

7b. If you are currently an owner or partner of a business, in what industry or profession were you employed and what was your job title **before** you became an owner or partner? Industry or Profession: _____
   Job Title: _____

7c. Are you considering starting/buying a new or additional business?
   ❑ Yes   ❑ No

7d. If you are planning to start/buy a new business, approximately when would this be?

❑ In the next 6 months   ❑ In about 7 to 12 months

❑ In about 13 to 24 months   ❑ More than 24 months from

❑ Not sure   now

8. In your present position, have you in the last 12 months been directly involved in initiating, recommending, ordering or approving the purchase of any of the following products or services for your firm? (Please check all that apply.)

❑ Accounting services   ❑ Advertising media/PR/sales

❑ Answering/paging systems   promotion

❑ Building materials/equipment   ❑ Banking and financial services

❑ Travel services

Market Questionnaire, cont'd.

- ❏ Insurance
- ❏ Credit cards
- ❏ Real estate and/or office or plant location
- ❏ Temporary office help/employee recruitment
- ❏ Express mail/courier, package delivery, overnight delivery
- ❏ Computer software
- ❏ Computers and computer accessories and/or related computer equipment (including word processors and time sharing)

- ❏ Car/truck/van purchase or leasing for company
- ❏ Telecommunications equipment/services
- ❏ Copiers
- ❏ Fax machines
- ❏ Office furniture and fixtures
- ❏ Office supplies (including office paper)
- ❏ Other office machines (calculators, typewriters, postage meters, etc.)
- ❏ None of these

9. Which of the following express mail/package delivery services do you use? (Please check all that apply.)

- ❏ Federal Express
- ❏ United Parcel Service (UPS)
- ❏ Emery/Purolator

- ❏ U.S. Postal Service/Express Mail
- ❏ Other: _____ (please specify)

Similar to the general market questionnaire, the market questionnaire is used to further define a specific market segment. In this case, the questionnaire concentrates on capturing specific business information to gauge the businesses surveyed by the company.

Examine the number of competitors on a local and, if relevant, national scale. Study their strategies and operations. Your analysis should supply a clear picture of potential threats, opportunities, and the weaknesses and strengths of the competition facing your new business.

When looking at the competition, try to see what trends have been established in the industry and whether there's an opportunity or advantage for your business. Use the library, the Internet and other secondary research sources described below to research competitors. Read as many articles as you can on the companies you'll be competing with.

If you're researching publicly owned companies, contact them and obtain copies of their annual reports. These often show not only how successful a company is but also what products or services it plans to emphasize in the future.

MARKET RESEARCH METHODS

In conducting your market research, you will gather two types of data: primary and secondary. *Primary research* is information that comes directly from the source—that is, potential customers. You can either compile this information yourself or hire someone else to gather the data for you via surveys, focus groups and other methods. *Secondary research* involves gathering statistics, reports, studies and other data from organizations such as government agencies, trade associations or your local chamber of commerce.

SECONDARY RESEARCH

The vast majority of research you gather will be secondary research. While larger companies spend huge amounts of money on market research, the good news is that plenty of information is available for free to entrepreneurs on a tight budget. The best place to start? Your local library.

Reference librarians at public and university libraries will be happy to point you in the right direction. Become familiar with the business reference section— you'll be spending a lot of time there. One good source to look for: *Business Information Sources* (University of California Press) by Lorna M. Daniels lists industry statistics and trade associations throughout the United States by geographic region.

Other good books are *The Thomas Directory of Manufacturers* and *The Harris Industrial Directories*. Both can help you target businesses in a particular industry, read up on competitors or find manufacturers for your product.

To get insights into consumer markets, check out the *U.S. Statistical Abstract,* which you can find at most libraries. It contains a wealth of social,

Smart Tip

In addition to surveys conducted by trade organizations, businesses and Dun & Bradstreet, there's another crucial source of survey data you can tap. Universities are an excellent source of objective survey information. Another place to look for survey data: Many large newspapers and radio stations do surveys to learn about their markets. These surveys are usually easy to obtain and packed with up-to-date information about demographics and potential customers.

MOTIVATION QUESTIONNAIRE

1. How knowledgeable are you about computers?

❏ Very knowledgeable ❏ Somewhat knowledgeable
❏ Slightly knowledgeable ❏ Not knowledgeable at all

2. Which of the following functions are extremely important to you when evaluating a computer equipment purchase? (Please check all that apply.)

❏ After-sales support ❏ Attractive product
❏ Best price for features ❏ Brand name
❏ Easy to use ❏ Hardware compatibility
❏ Lowest price available ❏ Most features/functions
❏ Newest technology available ❏ Product quality
❏ Reputation of vendor ❏ Compact size
❏ Warranty ❏ Other: _____
(please specify)

3. Please indicate which of the following sources of information you use to make decisions about what computer or software products to purchase. (Please check all that apply.)

❏ Business publications ❏ Catalogs
❏ Colleagues ❏ Consultants
❏ In-store displays ❏ Manufacturer's reps
❏ PC publications ❏ Personal experience/knowledge
❏ Radio ❏ Television
❏ Trade shows ❏ Newspapers
❏ Other: _____
(please specify)

4. Please indicate which of the following publications you rely on for information in your business or your plans to start a business. (Please check all that apply.)

❏ *Business Week* ❏ *Business Start-Ups*
❏ *Byte* ❏ *Computer Shopper*
❏ *Computer World* ❏ *Entrepreneur*
❏ *Forbes* ❏ *Fortune*
❏ *Home Office Computing* ❏ *Inc.*

MOTIVATION QUESTIONNAIRE, CONT'D.

❑ *Nation's Business* ❑ *Macworld*

❑ *MacWeek* ❑ *PC Magazine*

❑ *PC Computing* ❑ *PC World*

❑ *PC Week* ❑ None of these

❑ *Windows Magazine*

5. As a small-business owner, please check the topics below in *Entrepreneur* magazine that you consider useful. (Please check all that apply.)

❑ Tax information ❑ Company profiles

❑ Financial (raising money, etc.) ❑ Management tips

❑ Marketing strategies ❑ Latest small-business trends and statistics

❑ Latest office equipment

❑ Franchise information ❑ All of the above

❑ New ideas for business ❑ None of these

❑ Computer technology

6. Are you:
   ❑ Male ❑ Female

7. Please indicate your total 1998 household income. (Please include income from all family members and all sources—salary, bonuses, investment income, rents, royalties, etc.)

❑ Less than $30,000 ❑ $30,000-$39,999

❑ $40,000-$49,999 ❑ $50,000-$59,999

❑ $60,000-$74,999 ❑ $75,000-$99,999

❑ $100,000-$149,999 ❑ $150,000-$249,999

❑ $250,000-$499,999 ❑ $500,000-$999,999

❑ $1,000,000 or more

Motivation questionnaires are designed to identify competing companies or products and the factors that influence the purchase decision. They can also be used to determine what needs aren't being addressed that are important to customers.

NETTING INFORMATION

If your market research budget is limited, try CenStats. A fee-based subscription service from the Census Bureau that's available on the Internet, CenStat gives you a lot for a little, letting you access the bureau's most popular databases and information sold via CD-ROM.

Search by county under County Business Patterns or ZIP code under ZIP Business Patterns, and you'll get business profiles for an area that include payroll information and business size by industry. Click on USA Counties to get counties' economic and demographic information, including personal income per capita, population size and more.

Test CenStats out by visiting the Census Bureau's Web page (www.census.com), clicking on the CenStats icon and hitting "Test Drive." If you like it, you can sign up online or call (301) 457-4100. Single-user subscriptions cost $40 for three months or $125 for a full year.

political and economic data. Another good source for consumer information is *American Demographics* magazine. Ask reference librarians for other resources targeted at your specific business.

Associations

Your industry trade association can offer a wealth of information such as market statistics; lists of members; and books and reference materials. Talking to others in your association can be one of the most valuable ways of gaining informal data about a region or customer base.

Look in the *Encyclopedia of Associations* (Gale Research) found in most libraries to find associations relevant to your industry. You may also want to investigate your customers' trade associations for information that can help you market to them. Most trade associations provide information free of charge.

Read your trade associations' publications, as well as those aimed at your target customers, to get an idea of current and future trends and buying patterns. And keep an eye out for more: New magazines and newsletters are launched every year. If you're not following all of them, you could be missing out on valuable information about new products and your competitors.

Government Guidance

Government agencies are an invaluable source of market research, most of it free. Almost every county government publishes population density and distribution figures in widely available census tracts. These will show you the number of people living in specific areas, such as precincts, water districts or even 10-block neighborhoods. Some counties publish reports on population trends that show the population 10 years ago, five years ago and currently. Watch out for a static, declining or small population; ideally, you want to locate where there is an expanding population that wants your products and services.

The U.S. Census Bureau turns out reams of inexpensive or free business information:

◆ The Census Bureau's *State and Metropolitan Area Data Book* offers statistics for metropolitan areas, central cities and counties.

◆ The *Monthly Product Announcement* lists all Census Bureau products released in the past month.

◆ *County Business Patterns* is an excellent Census product that reports the number of a given type of business in a county by Standard Industrial Classification code (four-digit codes for all industries in the United States).

◆ For breakdowns by cities, look to the *Economic Census*, which is published every five years.

Most of these products should be available at your local library. If not, contact your nearest Census office for a list of publications and ordering information, or write to the Bureau of the Census, Attn: Customer Service, Washington, DC 20233, or call (301) 457-4100. Most Census Bureau reports are also available on CD-ROM or the Internet free.

The Department of Commerce is another good source of information. If you're trying to estimate the size of a potential market, the Commerce Department's *"Case Studies in Using Data for Better Business Decisions"* identifies income and age statistics in specific regions throughout the country. If you were the head of a clothing company planning on introducing a teen line, for example, you could identify gross numbers of teens in a specific region. You could then go one step further to find out which counties have the highest number of teens and compare each county's household income. These numbers would tell you whether you would do better with a modestly priced or a designer line. This reference source is available on CD-ROM.

The *"U.S. Industrial Outlook,"* also available on CD-ROM and produced by the Department of Commerce, traces the growth of 200 different indus-

COST ANALYSIS OF PRIMARY RESEARCH METHODS

Mail Surveys	Cost
Printing questionnaires	
Envelopes	
Postage for mailing questionnaire and return postage	
Incentives for questionnaire response	
Staff time and cost for analysis and presentation of results	
Independent researcher cost if any	
Other costs—itemize	
TOTAL MAIL SURVEY COSTS	

Phone Surveys	Cost
Preparation of the questionnaire	
Interviewer's fee	
Phone charges	
Staff time and cost for analysis and presentation of results	
Independent researcher cost if any	
Other costs—itemize	
TOTAL PHONE SURVEY COSTS	

Personal Interviews	Cost
Printing of questionnaires and prompt cards	
Interviewer's fee and expenses	
Incentives for questionnaire response	
Staff time and cost for analysis and presentation of results	
Independent researcher cost if any	
Other costs—itemize	
TOTAL PERSONAL INTERVIEWS SURVEY COSTS	

Group Discussions	Cost
Interviewer's fee and expenses in recruiting and assembling the groups	
Renting the conference room or other facility and cost of recording media such as tapes if used	
Incentives for group participation	
Staff time and cost for analysis and presentation of results	
Independent researcher cost if any	
Other costs–itemize	
TOTAL GROUP DISCUSSION COSTS	

Before you begin your market research, decide what research method will be most effective. One way to do this is to choose the method that will produce the best responses. Another way is to choose the most cost-effective method, and you can use this cost analysis to do so.

tries and gives five-year forecasts for each. You can obtain sales and revenue information on just about any industry by state, county and standard metropolitan area.

If you're planning to get into exporting, contact the Department of Commerce's International Trade Administration (ITA). The ITA publishes several thousand reports and statistical surveys, not to mention hundreds of books on everything American entrepreneurs need to know about exporting. Most of the reports and books are available on CD-ROM. For information or to order the ITA's 50-page catalog *Export Programs Guide*, call the Trade Information Center at (800) 872-8723.

Maps

Maps of major trading areas in counties and states are available from chambers of commerce, industrial development boards, trade development commissions and local newspaper offices. These maps show the major areas of commerce and can also help you judge the accessibility of various sites. Access is an important consideration in determining the limits of your market area.

Colleges And Universities

Local colleges and universities are valuable sources of information. Many college business departments have students who are eager to work in the "real world," gathering information and doing research at little or no cost.

Finally, nearby business schools are a great source of experts. Many business professors do consulting on the side, and some will even be happy to offer you marketing, sales, strategic planning or financial information for free. Call professors who specialize in these areas; if they can't help you, they'll be able to put you in touch with someone who can.

Community Organizations

Your local chamber of commerce or business development agency can supply useful information, usually free of charge, including demographic reports, assistance with site selection and directories of local businesses. They may also offer seminars on marketing and related topics that can help you do better research.

Dun & Bradstreet

Financial and business services firm Dun & Bradstreet offers a range of reference sources that can help start-ups, including D&B's Regional Business Directories, D&B's family of CD-ROM products and many others:

- ◆ To help identify new prospects and assess market potential, detailed information can be found in *D&B's Regional Business Direc-*

tories. Besides basic information (telephone number, address and company description), the directories also tell you when the company was started, sales volume, number of employees, parent company (if any) and, if it's a public company, on which exchange it's traded.

◆ *D&B's Million Dollar Disc* family, which includes three CD-ROM disks, can help you develop a targeted marketing campaign for business-to-business sales. The first disk lists the 200,000 businesses in the United States that do more than $25 million in sales annually, employ 250 or more people, or have a net worth of $500,000 or more. The second disk lists 150,000 middle-market companies, and the third covers 200,000 public administration and service businesses, including nonmanufacturing enterprises such as government agencies, police and fire departments, doctors, lawyers and other consultants. This CD-ROM series also includes biographical information on company owners or officers, giving you insight into their background and business experience.

◆ For a wider view of your potential marketplace, *D&B's Census of American Business* is a directory that lists business characteristics in each state, providing statistics on industries and the number of workers by region of the country. This is valuable if you want to pinpoint potential markets for your products or potential labor sources.

Going Online

These days, entrepreneurs can conduct much of their market research without ever leaving their computers, thanks to the universe of online services and information. Start with the major consumer online services, which offer access to business databases. You can find everything from headline and business news to industry trends and company-specific business information, such as a firm's address, telephone number, field of business and the name of the CEO. This information is critical for identifying prospects, developing mailing lists and planning sales calls.

All of the sources mentioned above (trade associations, government agencies) should also have Web sites you can go to to get information quickly. For additional online sources, see "Appendix A."

If you don't have time to investigate online services yourself, consider hiring an information broker to find the information you need. Information brokers are an excellent way to gather information quickly. They can act as a small company's research arm, identifying the most accurate and cost-effective information sources.

To find information brokers, look in the Yellow Pages or ask the research librarian at your local public library. Many research librarians deal with information brokers and will be able to give you good recommendations.

Primary Research

The secondary research you conduct should help you focus your niche and get a better idea of the challenges facing your business. To get a complete picture of your target market, however, you'll need to do some primary research as well.

A market research firm can help you if you feel that primary research is too complicated to do on your own. These firms will charge a few thousand dollars or more, but depending on the complexity of the information you need, you may feel this is money well-spent. Your local chamber of commerce can recommend firms or individuals who can conduct market research for smaller businesses on a budget.

If you need assistance but don't want to spend that kind of cash, consider visiting your nearest Small Business Administration (SBA) district office for guidance. Counselors can assist you in figuring out what types of questions you need to ask your target market. As with secondary research, the SBA, Small Business Development Centers, and local colleges and universities are also good sources of help with primary research.

20 Questions

Whether you use students, get help from the SBA or go it alone, there are several simple ways you can get the primary research information you're looking for.

1. **Focus groups:** A focus group consists of five to 12 potential customers who are asked their opinions in a one-on-one interview.

   Focus group participants should fit your target market—for example, single men aged 18 to 25, or working mothers. To find participants, just go to your local mall or college campus and ask people fitting your customer profile if they would be willing to answer a few questions. Typically, companies pay participants $30 or more to serve on a focus group.

   Although focus group interviews are informal in nature, you should always have a list of questions in mind to help you direct the discussion. What should you ask? Start by asking whether your product or service is one the participants would buy or use. If so, what is the highest price they would pay for it? Where would they probably shop for such a product? Do they like or dislike the product's packaging? Your questions should center around specific predetermined objectives, such as finding out how high you can price your product or service or what to name your business.

If you're going the do-it-yourself route, you will probably act as the focus group moderator. Encourage an open-ended flow of conversation; be sure to solicit comments from quieter members of the group, or you may end up getting all your information from one or two talkative participants.

2. **Telephone interviews:** This is an inexpensive, fast way to get information from potential customers. Prepare a script before you make the calls to ensure you cover all your objectives. Since most people don't like to spend a lot of time on the phone, keep your questions simple, clearly worded and brief. If you don't have time to make the calls yourself, hire local college students to do it for you.

3. **Direct mail interviews:** If you want to survey a wider audience, direct mail can be just the ticket. Your survey can be as simple as a postcard or as elaborate as a cover letter, questionnaire and reply envelope. Keep questionnaires to a maximum of one page, and ask no more than 15 questions. Like phone interviews, direct mail surveys should be simple and structured with "yes/no" or "agree/disagree" check-off boxes so respondents can answer quickly and easily. Only ask for one or two write-in answers at most.

4. **Fax/e-mail interviews:** Many of the same principles used in direct mail interviews also apply to these types of surveys. One exception: Never send an unsolicited fax that is more than one page long. Give clear instructions on how to respond, and be appreciative in advance for the data you get back.

Making A List . . .

How do you get the names of potential customers to call or mail questionnaires to? You can get a list from many places, including your suppliers, trade associations or a list-rental company. List-rental companies can give you access to a mailing list of a specific group of people who fit into your desired market.

Refer to your local Yellow Pages for the names of list-rental companies in your area. If none are listed, contact the Direct Marketing Association in New York City. (For more information on mailing lists, see Chapter 32, "To Market, To Market.")

A less sophisticated approach to finding potential customer names is to pick them at random from the telephone book. If you've developed a latex glove for doctors, for example, you can get doctors' names out of the Yellow Pages.

Whatever method you use to gather your information, the key to market research is using what you learn. The most sophisticated survey in the world does you no good if you ignore the feedback customers provide.

GLOSSARY

Focus group: type of primary market research in which a group of potential customers (typically five to 12 of them) come together in an informal environment, under the guidance of a moderator, to discuss a product or service

List-rental company: company that rents mailing lists of consumer or business names and addresses

Market research: research into the characteristics, spending habits, location and needs of your target market; the industry as a whole; and the particular competitors you face

Market survey: study of the spending characteristics and purchasing power of the consumers within your business's geographic area of operation

Primary research: information you gain directly from the source, such as potential consumers

Secondary research: information that has already been gathered by other agencies or organizations and compiled into statistics, reports or studies

---

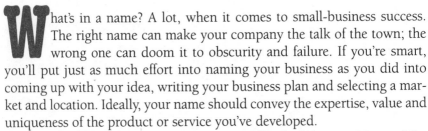

CHAPTER 8

WHAT'S IN A NAME?

Naming your business

What's in a name? A lot, when it comes to small-business success. The right name can make your company the talk of the town; the wrong one can doom it to obscurity and failure. If you're smart, you'll put just as much effort into naming your business as you did into coming up with your idea, writing your business plan and selecting a market and location. Ideally, your name should convey the expertise, value and uniqueness of the product or service you've developed.

Finding a good business name is more difficult than ever. Many of the best names have already been trademarked. But with advertising costs and competition on the rise, a good name is crucial to creating a memorable business image. In short, the name you choose can make or break your business.

There's a lot of controversy over what makes a good business name. Some experts believe that the best names are abstract, a blank slate upon which to create an image. Others think that names should be informative, so customers know immediately what your business is. Some believe that coined names (names that come from made-up words) are more memorable than names that use real words. Others think most coined names are eminently forgettable. In reality, any type of name can be effective if it's backed by the appropriate marketing strategy.

Do It Yourself?

Given all the considerations that go into a good company name, shouldn't you consult an expert, especially if you're in a field in which your company name will be visible and may influence the success of your business? And isn't it easier to enlist the help of a naming professional?

Yes. Just as an accountant will do a better job with your taxes and an ad agency will do a better job with your ad campaign, a naming firm will be more adept at naming your firm than you will. Naming firms have elaborate systems for creating new names, and they know their way around the trademark laws. They have the expertise to advise you against bad name choices and explain why others are good. A name consultant will take this perplexing task off your hands—and do a fabulous job for you in the process.

The downside is cost. A professional naming firm may charge anywhere from a few thousand dollars to $35,000 or more to develop a name. The benefit, however, is that spending this money now can save you money in the end. Professional namers may be able to find a better name—one that is so recognizable and memorable, it will cut down your costs in the long run. They have the expertise to help you avoid legal hassles with trademarks and registration—problems that can cost you plenty if you end up choosing a name that already belongs to someone else. And they are familiar with design elements, such as how a potential name might work on a sign or stationery.

If you can spare the money from your start-up budget, professional help could be a solid investment. After all, the name you choose now will affect your marketing plans for the duration of your business. If you're like most small-business owners, though, the responsibility for thinking up a name will be all your own. The good news: By following the same basic steps professional namers use, you can come up with a meaningful moniker that works . . . without breaking the bank.

What's In Your Name?

Start by deciding what you want your name to communicate. To be most effective, your company name should reinforce the key elements of your business. Your work in developing a niche and a mission statement (see Part 2 Chapter 6) will help you pinpoint the elements you want to emphasize in your name.

Gerald Lewis, whose consulting firm, CDI Designs, specializes in helping retail food businesses, uses retail as an example. "In retailing," Lewis explains, "the market is so segmented that [a name must] convey very quickly what the customer is going after. For example, if it's a warehouse

Smart Tip

Where to get ideas for your new business's name? Get your creative juices flowing by paying attention to all the business names you run across in your daily life—whether the businesses are similar to yours or not. Which names do you like, and why? What makes them effective? Which ones don't you like, and why are they unappealing? Soon you'll have a clearer idea of what makes a good (and bad) business name.

Beware!

One common naming error that can be fatal to a new business: choosing a name that's difficult to pronounce. If people don't know how to pronounce your business name, they'll be hesitant to say it. That means they're less likely to tell friends about your company or to ask for your product by name.

store, it has to convey that impression. If it's an upscale store selling high-quality foods, it has to convey that impression. The name combined with the logo is very important in doing that." So the first and most important step in choosing a name is deciding what your business is.

Should your name be meaningful? Most experts say yes. The more your name communicates to consumers, the less effort you must exert to explain it. Alan Siegel, chairman and CEO of Siegel & Gale, an international communications firm, believes name developers should give priority to real words or combinations of words over fabricated words. He explains that people prefer words they can relate to and understand. That's why professional namers universally condemn strings of numbers or initials as a bad choice.

On the other hand, it is possible for a name to be too meaningful. Naming consultant S.B. Master cautions business owners need to beware of names that are too narrowly defined. Common pitfalls are geographic names or generic names. Take the name "San Pablo Disk Drives" as a hypothetical example. What if the company wants to expand beyond the city of San Pablo, California? What meaning will that name have for consumers in Chicago or Pittsburgh? And what if the company diversifies beyond disk drives into software or computer instruction manuals?

Specific names make sense if you intend to stay in a narrow niche forever. If you have any ambitions of growing or expanding, however, you should find a name that is broad enough to accommodate your growth.

How can a name be both meaningful and broad? Master makes a distinction between *descriptive* names (like San Pablo Disk Drives) and *suggestive* names. Descriptive names tell something concrete about a business—what it does, where it's located and so on. Suggestive names are more abstract. They focus on what the business is about. Would you like to convey quality? Convenience? Novelty? These are the kinds of qualities that a suggestive name can express.

For example, Master came up with the name "Italiatour" to help promote package tours to Italy. Though it's not a real word, the name "Italiatour" is meaningful. Right away, you recognize what's being offered. But even better, the name "Italiatour" evokes the excitement of foreign travel. "It would have been a very different name if we had called it 'Italytour,'" says Master.

"But we took a foreign word, 'Italia,' but one that was very familiar and emotional and exciting to English speakers, and combined it with the English word 'tour.' It's easy to say, it's unique, it's unintimidating, but it still has an Italian flavor."

Before you start thinking up names for your new business, try to define the qualities that you want your business to be identified with. If you're starting a hearth-baked bread shop, for example, you might want a name that conveys freshness, warmth, and a homespun atmosphere. Immediately, you can see that names like "Kathy's Bread Shop" or "Arlington Breads" would communicate none of these qualities. But consider the name "Open Hearth Breads." The bread sounds homemade, hot, and just out of the oven. Moreover, if you diversified your product line, you could alter the name to "Open Hearth Bakery." This change would enable you to hold onto your suggestive name without totally mystifying your established clientele.

Making It Up

At a time when almost every existing word in the language has been trademarked, the option of coining a name is becoming more popular. Perhaps the best coined names come from professional naming firms. Some examples are Acura, a division of Honda Motor Co. coined by NameLab, and Flixx, a name CDI coined for a chain of video rental stores.

Since the beginnings of NameLab, founder Ira Bachrach has been a particular champion of the coined name. He believes that properly formulated coined names can be even more meaningful than existing words. Take, for example, the name "Acura." Although it has no dictionary definition, it actually suggests precision engineering, just as the company intended. How can that be? Bachrach and his staff created the name "Acura" from "Acu," a word segment that means "precise" in many languages. By working with meaningful word segments (what linguists call *morphemes*) like "Acu," Bachrach claims to produce new words that are both meaningful and unique.

"One of the reasons a new company is formed is that it has new value; it has a new idea," Bachrach contends. "If

Beware!

Make sure your business name clearly conveys what you do. A flower shop named Stargazers, for example, probably won't be the first place customers think of when buying flowers, since they'll probably expect you to sell telescopes or New Age products. Your name can even affect your ability to recruit employees. Someone interested in working at a flower shop wouldn't call Stargazers to ask about jobs since they wouldn't expect it to be a florist.

you adopt a conventional word, it's hard to express the newness of your idea. But as long as it's comprehensible, a new word will express that newness." Bachrach also admits, however, that new words aren't always the best solution. A new word is complex and implies that the service or product you're offering is complex, which may not be what you want to say. Plus, naming beginners might find this type of coining beyond their capabilities.

An easier solution is to use new spellings of existing words. For instance, CDI's creation: "Flixx." "Flixx" draws upon the slang term "flicks," meaning movies. But the unusual spelling makes it interesting, while the double "X" at the end makes it visually appealing. Just as important, "Flixx" is more likely to be available for trademarking than "Flicks," a factor that's especially important to a chain operation interested in national expansion.

Making A Name

Begin brainstorming, looking in dictionaries, books and magazines to generate ideas. Get friends and relatives to help if you like; the more minds, the merrier. Think of as many workable names as you can during this creative phase. Professional naming firms start out with a raw base of 800 to 1,000 names and work from there. You probably don't have time to think of that many, but try to come up with at least 10 names that you feel good about. By the time you examine them from all angles, you'll eliminate at least half.

The trials you put your names through will vary depending on your concerns. Some considerations are fairly universal. For instance, your name should be easy to pronounce, especially if you plan to rely heavily on print ads or signs. If people can't pronounce your name, they will avoid saying it. It's that simple. And nothing could be more counterproductive to a young company than to strangle its potential for word-of-mouth advertising.

Other considerations depend on more individual factors. For instance, if you're thinking about marketing your business globally or if you're located in a multilingual area, you should make sure that your new name has no negative connotations in other languages. On another note, Master points out, if your primary means of advertising will be in the telephone directory, you might favor names that are closer to the beginning of the alphabet. Finally, make sure that your name is in no way embarrassing. Put on the mind of a child and tinker with the letters a little. If none of your doodlings make you snicker, it's probably OK.

Chuck Brymer, president of naming firm Interbrand U.S.A., advises name seekers to take a close look at their competition. "The major function of a name is to distinguish your business from others," Brymer observes. "You have to weigh who's out there already, what type of branding approaches they have taken, and how you can use a name to separate yourself."

Testing, Testing

After you've narrowed the field to, say, four or five names that are memorable, expressive and can be read by the average kindergartner, you are ready to do a trademark search.

Must every name be trademarked? No. Many small businesses don't register their business names. As long as your state government gives you the go-ahead, you may operate under an unregistered business name for as long as you like—assuming, of course, that you aren't infringing on anyone else's trade name.

But what if you are? Imagine either of these two scenarios: You are a brand-new manufacturing business just about to ship your first orders. An obscure company in Ogunquit, Maine, considers your name an infringement on their trademark and engages you in a legal battle that bankrupts your company. Or, envision your business in five years. It's a thriving, growing concern, and you are contemplating expansion. But just as you are about to launch your franchise program, you learn that a small competitor in Modesto, California, has the same name, rendering your name unusable.

Do's And Don'ts

When choosing a business name, keep the following tips in mind:

♦ Choose a name that appeals not only to you, but also to the kind of customers you are trying to attract.

♦ To get customers to respond to your business on an emotional level, choose a comforting or familiar name that conjures up pleasant memories.

♦ Don't pick a name that is long or confusing.

♦ Stay away from cute puns that only you understand.

♦ Don't use the word "Inc." after your name unless your company is actually incorporated.

♦ Don't use the word "Enterprises" after your name; this term is often used by amateurs.

Smart Tip

After you have thought of potential names, compile a list of your competitors' names. If some of your name ideas are too similar to your competitors', remove them from your list.

To illustrate the risk you run of treading on an existing trademark with your new name, consider this: When NameLab took on the task of renaming a chain of auto parts stores, they uncovered no fewer than 87,000 names already in existence for stores of this kind.

That's why even the smallest businesses should at least consider having their business names screened. "You never know where your corner store is going to lead," CDI's Lewis notes. "If running a corner store is all a person is going to do, then no, he doesn't need to do a trademark search. But that local business may become a big business someday if that person has any ambition."

Master agrees. "Ensuring that your name is going to be federally registerable is important," she stresses. "And make sure that the individual states that you want to do business in will let you do business under that name."

Enlisting the help of a trademark attorney or at least a trademark search firm before you decide on a name is highly advisable. The extra money you spend now could save you countless hassles and expenses further down the road. Master also warns that business owners should try to contain their excitement about any one name until it has cleared the trademark search: "It can be very demoralizing to lose a name you've been fantasizing about."

Final Analysis

If you're lucky, you'll end up with three to five names that pass all your tests. How do you make your final decision?

Recall all your initial criteria. Which name best fits your objectives? Which name most accurately describes the company you have in mind? Which name do you like the best?

Master says each company arrives at a final decision in its own way. Some entrepreneurs go with their gut or use personal reasons for choosing one name over another. Others are more scientific. Some companies do consumer research or testing with focus groups to see how the names are perceived. Others might decide that their name is going to be most important seen on the back of a truck, so they have a graphic designer turn the various names into logos to see which works best as a design element.

Use any or all of these criteria. You can do it informally: Ask other people's opinions. Doodle an idea of what each name will look like on a sign or

on your business stationery. Read each name aloud, paying special attention to the way it sounds if you foresee radio advertising or telemarketing
in your future.

Say It Loud

Professional naming firms devote anywhere from six weeks to six
months to the naming process. You probably won't have that much time,
but plan to spend at least a few weeks on selecting a name.

Once your decision is made, start building your enthusiasm for the new
name immediately. Your name is your first step toward building a strong
company identity, one that should last you as long as you're in business.

CHAPTER 9

TO INC. OR NOT TO INC.

Choosing a business structure

Of all the decisions you make when starting a business, probably the most important one relating to taxes is the type of legal structure you select for your company.

Not only will this decision have an impact on how much you pay in taxes, but it will affect the amount of paperwork your business is required to do, the personal liability you face, and your ability to raise money.

There are esentially five business forms to choose from: sole proprietorship, partnership, corporation, S corporation, and limited liability company or LLC. Because each comes with different tax consequences, you'll want to make your selection wisely and choose the one that most closely matches your business's needs.

If you start as a sole proprietor but later decide to take on partners, you can reorganize as a partnership or other entity. If you do, be sure to notify the IRS and your state tax agency.

SOLE PROPRIETORSHIP

The simplest structure is the sole proprietorship, which usually involves just one individual who owns and operates the enterprise. If you intend to work alone, this may be the way to go.

The tax aspects of a sole proprietorship are especially appealing because income and expenses from the business are included on your personal income tax return, Form 1040. Your profits and losses are first recorded on a tax form called Schedule C, which is filed along with your 1040. Then the "bottom-line amount" from Schedule C is transferred to your personal tax return. This aspect is especially attractive because business losses you suffer may offset income earned from other sources.

As a sole proprietor, you must also file a Schedule SE with Form 1040.

You use Schedule SE to calculate how much self-employment tax you owe. In addition to paying annual self-employment taxes, you must also make quarterly estimated tax payments on your income. Currently, self-employed individuals with net earnings of $400 or more must make estimated tax payments to cover their tax liability. If your prior year's adjusted gross income is less than $150,000, your estimated tax payments must be at least 90 percent of your current year's tax liability or 100 percent of the prior year's liability, whichever is less. The federal government permits you to pay estimated taxes in four equal amounts throughout the year on the 15th of April, June, September and January.

Smart Tip

If you operate as a sole proprietor, be sure you keep your business income and records separate from your personal finances. It helps to establish a business checking account, and get a credit card to use only for business expenses.

With a sole proprietorship, your business earnings are taxed only once, unlike other business structures. Another big plus is that you have complete control of your business—you make all the decisions.

There are a few disadvantages to consider, however. Selecting the sole proprietorship business structure means you are personally liable for your company's liabilities. As a result, you are placing your own assets at risk, and they could be seized to satisfy a business debt or legal claim filed against you.

Raising money for a sole proprietorship can also be difficult. Banks and other financing sources are reluctant to make business loans to sole proprietorships. In most cases, you will have to depend on your own financing sources, such as savings, home equity or family loans.

Dollar Stretcher

To help sort through the business structure maze, you can order free IRS publications—*Partnerships* (Publication No. 541), *Corporations* (Publication No. 542), *Self-Employment Tax* (Publication No. 533)—by calling (800) TAX-FORM or by downloading them from the IRS Web site at irs.ustreas.gov.

PARTNERSHIP

If your business will be owned and operated by several individuals, you'll want to take a look at structuring your business as a partnership. Partnerships come in two varieties: general partnerships and limited partnerships. In a general partnership, the partners manage the company and assume responsibility for the partnership's debts and

PARTNERSHIP AGREEMENT

DATE _____

COMMENCES _____

EXPIRES_____

LOCATION _____

THIS PARTNERSHIP AGREEMENT is made on this _____ day of _____ , 19____ . between the individuals listed below:

_____

_____

_____

The partners listed above hereby agree that they shall be considered partners in business upon the commencement date of this **PARTNERSHIP AGREEMENT** for the following purpose:

_____

_____

The terms and conditions of this partnership are as follows:

1. The **NAME** of the partnership shall be: _____

2. The **PRINCIPAL PLACE OF BUSINESS** of the partnership shall be: _____

_____

3. The **CAPITAL CONTRIBUTION** of each partner to the partnership shall consist of the following property, services, or cash, which each partner agrees to contribute:

Name of Partner	Capital Contribution	Agreed-Upon Cash Value	% Share

Furthermore, the **PROFITS AND LOSSES** of the partnership shall be divided by the partners according to a mutually agreeable schedule and at the end of each calendar year according to the proportions listed above.

4. Each partner shall have equal rights to **MANAGE AND CONTROL** the partnership and its business. Should there be differences between the partners concerning ordinary business matters, a decision shall be made by unanimous vote. It is understood that the partners may elect one of the partners to conduct day-to-day business of the partnership; however, no partner shall be able to bind the partnership by act or contract to any liability exceeding $_____ without the prior written consent of each partner.

5. In the event a partner **WITHDRAWS** from the partnership for any reason, including death, the remaining partners may continue to operate the partnership using the same name. The withdrawing partner shall be obligated to sell their interest in the partnership. No partner shall **TRANSFER** interest in the partnership to any other party without the written consent of each partner.

6. Should the partnership be **TERMINATED** by unanimous vote, the assets and cash of the partnership shall be used to pay all creditors with the remaining amounts to be distributed to the partners according to their proportionate share.

7. Any **DISPUTES** arising between the partners as a result of this agreement shall be settled by voluntary mediation. Should mediation fail to resolve the dispute, it shall be settled by binding arbitration.

In witness whereof, this **PARTNERSHIP AGREEMENT** has been signed by the partners on the day and year listed above.

_____   _____
PARTNER   PARTNER

_____
PARTNER

This partnership agreement serves only as a sample. Consult an attorney before you draw up or sign any partnership agreements.

Howdy, Partner

If you decide to organize your business as a partnership, be sure you draft a partnership agreement that details how business decisions are made, how disputes are resolved, and how to handle a buyout. You'll be glad you have this agreement if for some reason you run into difficulties with one of the partners or if someone wants out of the arrangement.

The agreement should address the purpose of the business and the authority and responsibility of each partner. It's a good idea to consult an attorney experienced with small businesses for help in drafting the agreement. Here are some other issues you'll want the agreement to address:

1. **How will the ownership interest be shared?** It's not necessary, for example, for two owners to equally share ownership and authority. However you decide to do it, make sure the proportion is stated clearly in the agreement.

2. **How will decisions be made?** It's a good idea to establish voting rights in case a major disagreement arises. When just two partners own the business 50-50, there's the possibility of a deadlock. To avoid a deadlock, some businesses provide in advance for a third partner, a trusted associate who may own only 1 percent of the business but whose vote can break a tie.

3. **When one partner withdraws, how will the purchase price be determined?** One possibility is to agree on a neutral third party, such as your banker or accountant, to find an appraiser to determine the price of the partnership interest.

4. **If a partner withdraws from the partnership, when will the money be paid?** Depending on the partnership agreement, you can agree that the money be paid over three, five or 10 years, with interest. You don't want to be hit with a cash flow crisis if the entire price has to be paid on the spot in one lump sum.

other obligations. A limited partnership has both general and limited partners. In a limited partnership, the general partners own and operate the business and assume liability for the partnership, while the limited partners serve as investors only; they have no control over the company and are not subject to the same liabilities as the general partners.

Dollar Stretcher

If limited liability is not a concern for your business, you could begin your venture as a sole proprietorship or partnership so that monetary losses in the early years of the company can shelter your other income. These "passed through" losses can offset other income you may have. Then when the business becomes profitable, you can incorporate.

Unless you expect to have many passive investors, limited partnerships are generally not the best choice for a new business because of all the required filings and administrative complexities. If you have two or more partners who want to be actively involved, a general partnership would be much easier to form.

One of the major advantages of a partnership is the tax treatment it enjoys. A partnership does not pay tax on its income but "passes through" any profits or losses to the individual partners. At tax time, each partner files a Schedule K-1 form, which indicates his or her share of partnership income, deductions and tax credits. In addition, each partner is required to report profits from the partnership on his or her individual tax return. Even though the partnership pays no income tax, it must compute its income and report it on a separate informational return, Form 1065.

Personal liability is a major concern if you use a general partnership to structure your business. Similar to a sole proprietorship, general partners are personally liable for the partnership's obligations and debt.

In addition, each general partner can act on behalf of the partnership, take out loans and make business decisions that will affect and be binding on all the partners (if the general partnership agreement permits). Keep in mind that partnerships are also more expensive to establish than sole proprietorships because they require more extensive legal and accounting services.

CORPORATION

Using the corporate structure is more complex and expensive than most other business structures. A corporation is an independent legal entity, separate from its owners, and as such, it requires complying with more regulations and tax requirements.

The biggest benefit for a small-business owner who decides to incorporate is the liability protection he or she receives. A corporation's debt is not considered that of its owners, so if you organize your business as a corporation, you are not putting your personal assets at risk. A corporation also can retain some of its profits, without the owner paying tax on them.

Another plus is the ability of a corporation to raise money. A corporation

CORPORATE CHECKLIST

To make sure your corporation stays on the right side of the law, heed the following guidelines:

1. Call the secretary of state each year to check your corporate status.

2. Put the annual meetings (shareholders' and directors') on tickler cards.

3. Check all contracts to ensure the proper name is used in each. The signature line should read "John Doe, President, XYZ Corp.," never just "John Doe."

4. Never use your name followed by "dba" on a contract. Renegotiate any old ones that do.

5. Before undertaking any activity out of the normal course of business—like purchasing major assets—write a corporate resolution permitting it. Keep all completed forms in the corporate book.

6. Never use corporate checks for personal debts and vice versa.

7. Get professional advice about continued retained earnings not needed for immediate operating expenses.

8. Know in advance what franchise fees are due.

can sell stock, either common or preferred, to raise funds. Corporations also continue indefinitely, even if one of the shareholders dies, sells the shares or becomes disabled.

The corporate structure, however, comes with a number of downsides as well. A major one is higher costs. Corporations are formed under the laws of each state with their own set of regulations. You'll probably need the assistance of an attorney to guide you through the maze. In addition, because a corporation must follow more complex rules and regulations than a partnership or sole proprietorship, it requires more accounting and tax preparation services.

Another drawback: Owners of the corporation pay a double tax on the business's earnings. Not only are corporations subject to corporate income tax at both the federal and state levels, but any earnings distributed to shareholders in the form of dividends are taxed at individual tax rates on their personal income tax returns.

PRE-INCORPORATION AGREEMENT

AGREEMENT made this _____ day of _____ , 19 ___ , between _____ , _____ , and _____ .

WHEREAS the parties hereto wish to organize a corporation upon the terms and conditions hereinafter set forth; and

WHEREAS the parties wish to establish their mutual rights and responsibilities in relation to their organizational activities;

NOW, THEREFORE, in consideration of the premises and mutual covenants contained herein, it is agreed by and between the parties as follows:

FIRST: The parties will forthwith cause a corporation to be formed and organized under the laws of _____ .

SECOND: The proposed Articles of Incorporation shall be attached hereto as Exhibit A.

THIRD: Within seven days after the issuance of the corporation's certificate of incorporation, the parties agree that the corporation's authorized stock shall be distributed, and consideration paid, as follows:

1. _____shares of _____ (insert common, preferred) stock shall be issued to _____ in consideration of his/her payment to the corporation of $_____ cash.

2. _____shares of stock shall be issued to _____ in consideration of his/her transfer to the corporation of _____ (list property, real or personal, to be transferred).

3. _____shares of stock shall be issued to _____ in consideration of his transfer to the corporation of _____ .

4. . . . etc . . .

FOURTH: The corporation shall employ _____ as its manager for a term of _____ years and at a salary of $ _____ per annum, such employment not to be terminated without cause and such salary not to be increased or decreased without the approval of _____ % of the directors.

FIFTH: The parties agree not to transfer, sell, assign, pledge, or otherwise dispose of their shares until they have first offered them for sale to the corporation, and then, should the corporation refuse such offer, to the other shareholders on a pro rata basis. The shares shall be offered at their book value to the corporation, and in the event the corporation refuses, the other shareholders shall have thirty (30) days to purchase the shares. If the corporation or other shareholders do not purchase all the offered shares, the remaining shares may be freely transferred by their owner without price restrictions.

SIXTH: The parties to this agreement promise to use their best efforts to incorporate the organization and to commence its business.

_____

_____

_____

Pre-incorporation agreements spell out the roles various parties will play in the formation and operation of a corporation.

To avoid double taxation, you could pay the money out as salaries to you and any other corporate shareholders. A corporation is not required to pay tax on earnings paid as reasonable compensation, and it can deduct the payments as a business expense. Keep in mind, however, that the IRS has limits on what it believes to be reasonable compensation.

S Corporation

The S corporation is more attractive to small-business owners than a standard (or C) corporation. That's because an S corporation has some appealing tax benefits and still provides business owners with the liability protection of a corporation. With an S corporation, income and losses are passed through to shareholders and included on their individual tax returns. As a result, there's just one level of federal tax to pay.

> ## Beware!
> Keep in mind that any money you've invested in a corporation is at risk. Despite the liability protection of a corporation, in practice, most banks and many suppliers require business owners to sign a personal guarantee so they know corporate owners will make good on any debt if for some reason the corporation can't. In addition, it is still possible for the business owner to be brought into a lawsuit if a customer or client suffers a loss.

In addition, owners of S corporations who don't have inventory can use the cash method of accounting, which is simpler than the accrual method. Under this method, income is taxable when received and expenses are deductible when paid (see the "Bean-Counting 101" chapter).

Some relatively recent tax law changes brought about by the Small Business Job Protection Act of 1996 have made S corporations even more attractive for small-business owners. In the past, S corporations were limited to 35 shareholders. The 1996 law increased the number of shareholders to 75. Expanding the shareholder number makes it possible to have more investors and thus attract more capital, tax experts maintain.

S corporations do come with some downsides. For example, S corporations are subject to many of the same requirements corporations must follow, and that means higher legal and tax service costs. They also must file articles of incorporation, hold directors and shareholders meetings, keep corporate minutes, and allow shareholders to vote on major corporate decisions. The legal and accounting costs of setting up an S corporation are also similar to those for a standard corporation.

Another major difference between a standard corporation and an S corporation is that S corporations can only issue common stock. Experts say this can hamper the company's ability to raise capital.

Bright Idea

If you anticipate several years of losses in your business, keep in mind you cannot deduct corporate losses on your personal tax return. Other business structures, such as partnerships, sole proprietorships and S corporations, allow you to take those deductions.

In addition, unlike a standard corporation, S corporation stock can only be owned by individuals, estates and certain types of trusts. The 1996 Small Business Job Protection Act law also added tax-exempt organizations such as qualified pension plans to this list starting in January 1998. Tax experts believe this change should help provide S corporations with even greater access to capital because a number of pension plans are willing to invest in closely held small-business stock.

Putting Inc. To Paper

To start the process of incorporating, contact the secretary of state or the state office that is responsible for registering corporations in your state. Ask for instructions, forms and fee schedules on business incorporation.

It is possible to file for incorporation without the help of an attorney by using books and software to guide you along. Your expense will be the cost of these resources, the filing fees, and other costs associated with incorporating in your state.

If you do file for incorporation yourself, you'll save the expense of using a lawyer, which can cost from $500 to $1,000. The disadvantage of going this route is that the process may take you some time to accomplish. There's also a chance you could miss some small but important detail in your state's law.

One of the first steps you must take in the incorporation process is to prepare a certificate or articles of incorporation. Some states will provide you with a printed form for this, which either you or your attorney can complete. The information requested includes the proposed name of the corporation, the purpose of the corporation, the names and addresses of the parties incorporating, and the location of the principal office of the corporation.

The corporation will also need a set of bylaws that describe in greater detail than the articles how the corporation will run, including the responsibilities of the shareholders, directors and officers; when stockholder meetings will be held; and other details important to running the company. Once your articles of incorporation are accepted, the secretary of state's office will send you a certificate of incorporation.

Rules Of The Road

Once you're incorporated, be sure to follow the rules of incorporation. If you don't, a court can pierce the corporate veil and hold you and the other owners personally liable for the business's debts.

It is important to follow all the rules required by state law. You should keep accurate financial records for the corporation, showing a separation between the corporation's income and expenses and that of the owners'.

The corporation should also issue stock, file annual reports and hold yearly meetings to elect officers and directors, even if they're the same people as the shareholders. Be sure to keep minutes of these meetings. On all references to your business, make certain to identify it as a corporation, using Inc. or Corp., whichever your state requires. You also want to make sure that whomever you deal with, such as your banker or clients, knows that you are an officer of a corporation. (For more corporate guidelines, see "Corporate Checklist" in this chapter.)

LAYING THE FOUNDATION

When making a decision about which business structure to use, answering the following questions should help you narrow down which entity is right for you:

♦ How many owners will your company have, and what will their roles be?

♦ Are you concerned about the tax consequences of your business structure?

♦ How much paperwork are you prepared to deal with?

♦ Do you want to make all the decisions in the company?

♦ Can you deal with the added costs that come with selecting a complicated business structure?

♦ Are you planning to go public?

♦ Do you want to protect your personal resources from debts or other claims against your company?

♦ Are family succession issues a concern?

♦ Do you want to consider having employees become owners in the company?

LIMITED LIABILITY COMPANY

Limited liability companies, often referred to as "LLCs," have been around since 1977, but their popularity among small-business owners is a relatively recent phenomenon.

An LLC is a hybrid entity, bringing together some of the best features of partnerships and corporations. "An LLC is a much better entity for tax purposes than any other entity," says Ralph Anderson, a CPA and small-business tax specialist with accounting firm M. R. Weiser.

LLCs were created to provide business owners with the liability protection that corporations enjoy without the double taxation. Earnings and losses pass through to the owners and are included on their personal tax returns.

Sound similar to an S corporation? It is, except an LLC offers small-business owners even more attractions than an S corporation. For example, there is no limitation on the number of shareholders an LLC can have, unlike an S corporation, which has a limit of 75. In addition, any member or owner of the LLC is allowed a full participatory role in the business's operation; in a limited partnership, on the other hand, partners are not permitted any say in the operation.

To set up an LLC, you must file articles of organization with the secretary of state in the state where you intend to do business. Some states also require you to file an operating agreement, which is similar to a partnership agreement.

Like partnerships, LLCs do not have perpetual life. Some state statutes stipulate that the company must dissolve after 30 or 40 years. Technically, the company dissolves when a member dies, quits or retires.

Despite the attractions, LLCs also have their disadvantages. Since an LLC is relatively new, its tax treatment varies by state. If you plan to operate in several states, you must determine how a state will treat an LLC formed in another state. If you decide on an LLC structure, be sure to use the services of an experienced accountant who is familiar with the various rules and regulations of LLCs.

Even after you settle on a business structure, remember that the circumstances that make one type of business organization favorable are always subject to changes in the laws. It makes sense to reassess your form of business from time to time to make sure you are using the one that provides the most benefits.

CHOOSING A LEGAL FORM FOR YOUR BUSINESS

This chapter provides an overview of the various legal forms under which you might choose to operate your business. This table summarizes the characteristics of six different forms of business: sole proprietorships, general partnerships, limited partnerships, limited liability companies (LLCs), corporations in general, and S corporations. We list four characteristics for each legal form:

Control: Who holds authority in a business operating under this form?

Liability: Who is legally liable for any losses the business experiences?

Tax: How will business income and expenses be reported?

Continuity: If a business owner dies or wants to leave the business, does the business continue?

Sole Proprietorship

Control	Liability	Tax	Continuity
Owner maintains complete control over the business.	Owner is solely liable. His or her personal assets are open to attack in any legal case.	Owner reports all income and expenses on personal tax return.	Business terminates upon the owner's death or withdrawal. Owner can sell the business but will no longer remain the proprietor.

General Partnership

Control	Liability	Tax	Continuity
Each partner has the authority to enter contracts and make other business decisions, unless the partnership agreement stipulates otherwise.	Each partner is liable for all business debts.	Each partner reports partnership income on individual tax return. The business does not pay any taxes as its own entity.	Unless the partnership agreement makes other provisions, a partnership dissolves upon the death or withdrawal of a partner.

Choosing A Legal Form For Your Business, cont'd.

Limited Partnership

Control	Liability	Tax	Continuity
General partners control the business.	General partners are personally responsible for partnership liabilities. Limited partners are liable for the amount of their investment.	Partnership files annual taxes. Limited and general partners report their share of partnership income or loss on their individual returns.	Death of a limited partner does not dissolve business, but death of general partner might, unless the partnership agreement makes other provisions.

Limited Liability Company

Control	Liability	Tax	Continuity
Owner or partners have authority.	Partners are not liable for business debts.	The partners report income and income tax on their individual tax returns.	Different states have different laws regarding the continuity of LLCs.

Corporation

Control	Liability	Tax	Continuity
Shareholders appoint the board of directors, which appoints officers, who hold the highest authority.	Shareholders generally are responsible for the amount of their investment in corporate stock.	Corporation pays its own taxes. Shareholders pay tax on their dividends.	The corporation is its own legal entity and can survive the deaths of owners, partners and shareholders.

S Corporation

Control	Liability	Tax	Continuity
See entry for corporations.	See entry for corporations.	Shareholders report their shares of corporate profit or loss in their individual tax returns.	See entry for corporations.

GLOSSARY

Corporation: a business structure organized under state law and generally treated as a separate tax entity

Deductions: business and other expenses that directly reduce your income

Limited liability company (LLC): a hybrid business structure that combines the tax advantages of a partnership with the liability protection of a corporation

Partnership: a business that is unincorporated and organized by two or more individuals

S corporation: a type of corporation that provides its owners with tax treatment that is similar to a partnership

Self-employment tax: tax paid by a self-employed person to help finance Social Security and Medicare

Sole proprietorship: a business entity that usually involves just one individual who owns and operates the enterprise

CHAPTER 10

GET WITH
THE PLAN

Creating a winning
business plan

Tell friends you're starting a business, and you'll get as many different pieces of advice as you have friends. One piece of wisdom, however, that transcends all others is this: Write a business plan.

Some people think you don't need a business plan unless you're trying to borrow money. Of course, it's true that you do need a good plan if you intend to approach a lender—whether a banker, a venture capitalist or any number of other sources—for start-up capital. But a business plan is more than a pitch for financing; it's a guide to help you define and meet your business goals.

Just as you wouldn't start off on a cross-country drive without a road map, you shouldn't embark on your new business without a business plan to guide you. A business plan won't automatically make you a success, but it will help you avoid some common causes of business failure, such as under-capitalization or lack of an adequate market. As you research and prepare your business plan, you'll find weak spots in your business idea that you'll be able to repair. You'll also discover areas with potential you may not have thought about before—and ways to profit from them. Only by putting together a business plan can you decide whether your great idea is really worth your time and investment.

What is a business plan, and how do you put one together? Simply stated, a business plan conveys your business goals, the strategies you'll use to meet them, potential problems that may confront your business and ways to solve them, the organizational structure of your business (including titles and responsibilities), and, finally, the amount of capital required to finance your venture and keep it going until it breaks even.

Sound impressive? It can be, if put together properly. A good business plan follows generally accepted guidelines for both form and content. There are three primary parts to a business plan.

The first is the *business concept*, where you discuss the industry, your business structure, your particular product or service and how you plan to make your business a success.

The second is the *marketplace section*, in which you describe and analyze potential customers: who and where they are, what makes them buy and so on. Here, you also describe the competition and how you will position yourself to beat it.

Finally, the *financial section* contains your income and cash flow statement, balance sheet and other financial ratios, such as break-even analyses. This part may require help from your accountant and a good spreadsheet software program.

Breaking these three major sections down further, a business plan consists of seven major components:

1. Executive summary

2. Business description

3. Market strategies

4. Competitive analysis

5. Design and development plan

6. Operations and management plan

7. Financial factors

In addition to these sections, a business plan should also have a cover, title page and table of contents.

The Executive Summary

Anyone looking at your business plan will first want to know what kind of business you are starting. So the business concept section should start with an executive summary, which outlines and describes the product or service you will sell.

The executive summary is the first thing the reader sees. Therefore, it must make an immediate impact by clearly stating the nature of the business and, if you are seeking capital, the type of financing you want.

The executive summary describes the business, its legal form of operation

Smart Tip

Although it's the first part of the plan to be read, the executive summary is most effective if it's the last part you write. By waiting until you have finished the rest of your business plan, you ensure you have all the relevant information in front of you. This allows you to create an executive summary that hits all the crucial points of your plan.

SAMPLE EXECUTIVE SUMMARY

The business will provide ecology-minded consumers with an environmentally safe disposable diaper that will feature all the elements that are popular among users of disposable diapers but will include the added benefit of biodegradability. The product, which is patent pending, will target current users of disposable diapers who are deeply concerned about the environment as well as those consumers using cloth diapers and diaper services. The product will be distributed to wholesalers who will, in turn, sell to major supermarkets, specialty stores, department stores and major toy stores.

The company was incorporated in 1989 in the state of California under the name of Softie Baby Care. The company's CEO, president and vice president have more than 30 years of combined experience in the diaper industry.

With projected net sales of $871 million in its third year, the business will generate pretax net profits of 8 percent. Given this return, investment in the company is very attractive. Softie Baby Care Inc. will require a total of $26 million over three stages to start the business.

◆ The first stage will require $8 million for product and market development.

◆ The second stage of financing will consist of $12 million for implementation.

◆ The third stage will demand $6 million for working capital until break-even is reached.

First-stage capital will be used to purchase needed equipment and materials to develop the product and market it initially. To obtain its capital requirements, the company is willing to relinquish 25 percent equity to first-stage investors.

The company has applied for a patent on the primary technology that the business is built around, which allows the plastic within a disposable diaper to break down upon extended exposure to sunlight. Lease agreements are also in place for a 20,000-square-foot facility in a light industrial area of Los Angeles, as well as for major equipment needed to begin production. Currently, the company is being funded by $3 million from the three principals, with purchase orders for 500,000 units already in hand.

(sole proprietorship, partnership, corporation or limited liability company), the amount and purpose of the loan requested, the repayment schedule, the borrower's equity share, and the debt-to-equity ratio after the loan, security or collateral is offered. Also listed are the market value, estimated value or price quotes for any equipment you plan to purchase with the loan proceeds.

Your executive summary should be short and businesslike—generally between half a page and one page, depending on how complicated the use of funds is.

The Business Description

This section expands on the executive summary, describing your business in much greater detail. It generally starts with a description of your industry. Is the business wholesale, retail, food service, manufacturing or service-oriented? How big is the industry? Why has it become so popular? What trends are responsible for the industry's growth? Prove, with statistics and anecdotal information, how much opportunity there is in the industry.

Explain the target market for your product or service, how the product will be distributed, and the business' support systems—that is, its advertising, promotions and customer service strategies.

Next, describe your product or service. Discuss the product's applications and end users. Emphasize any unique features or variations that set your product or service apart from others in your industry.

If you're using your business plan for financing purposes, explain why the money you seek will make your business more profitable. Will you use the money to expand, to create a new product or to buy new equipment?

Market Strategies

Here's where you define your market—its size, structure, growth prospects, trends and sales potential. Based on research, interviews and sales analysis, the marketplace section should focus on your customers and your competition. How much of the market will your product or service be able to capture?

The answer is tricky since so many variables influence it. Think of it as a combination of words and numbers. Write down the who, what, when, where and why of your customers. (You know all this because you researched it in Part 2 Chapter 7.) The answers are critical in determining how you'll develop pricing strategies and distribution channels.

Be sure to document how and from what sources you compiled your market information. Describe how your business fits into the overall market picture. Emphasize your unique selling proposition (USP) —in other words, what makes you different? Explain why your approach is ideal for your market.

Once you've clearly defined your market and established your sales goals, present the strategies you'll use to fulfill those objectives.

<table><tr><td>

Smart Tip

There are many books, manuals and software programs that can help you write a business plan. Visit a bookstore or, for free information, look in your local library's business section. Also check out Entrepreneur's business start-up guide No. 1800, *Creating a Successful Business Plan.* Call (800) 421-2300 for ordering information.</td></tr></table>

◆ **Price:** Thoroughly explain your pricing strategy and how it will affect the success of your product or service. Describe your projected costs, then determine pricing based on the profit percentage you expect. Costs include materials, distribution, advertising and overhead. Many experts recommend adding 25 percent to 50 percent to each of your cost estimates, especially overhead, to ensure you don't underestimate anything.

◆ **Distribution:** This includes the entire process of moving the product from the factory to the end user. The type of distribution network you choose depends on your industry and the size of the market. How much will it cost to reach your target market? Are they upscale customers who will pay extra for a premium product or service, or budget-conscious consumers looking for a good deal? Study your competitors to see what channels they use. Will you use the same channels or try a different method that may give you a strategic advantage?

◆ **Sales:** Explain how your sales force (if you have one) will meet its goals, including elements such as pricing flexibility, sales presentations, lead generation and compensation policies.

Competitive Analysis

How does your business relate to the competition? The competitive analysis section answers this question.

Using what you've learned from your market research, detail the strengths and weaknesses of your competitors, the strategies that give you a distinct advantage, any barriers you can develop to prevent new competition from entering the market, and any weaknesses in your competitors' service or product development cycle that you can take advantage of.

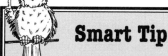

The competitive analysis is an important part of your business plan. Often, start-up entrepreneurs mistakenly believe their product or service is the first of its kind and fail to recognize that competition exists. In reality, every business has competition, whether direct or indirect. Your plan must show that you recognize this and have a strategy to deal with the competition.

Design And Development Plan

This section describes a product's design and charts its development within the context of production, marketing and the company itself. If you have an idea but have not yet developed the product or service, if you plan to improve an existing product or service, or if you own an existing company and plan to introduce a new product or service, this section is extremely important. (If your product is already completely designed and developed, you don't need to complete this section. If you are offering a service, you will need to concentrate only on the development half of the section.)

The design section should thoroughly describe the product's design and the materials used; include any diagrams if applicable. The development plan generally covers three areas: 1) product development, 2) market development and 3) organizational development. If you're offering a service, cover only the last two.

Create a schedule that shows how the product, marketing strategies and organization will develop over time. The schedule should be tied to a development budget so expenses can be tracked throughout the design and development process.

Operations And Management Plan

Here, you describe how your business will function on a daily basis. This section explains logistics such as the responsibilities of each member of the management team, the tasks assigned to each division of the company (if applicable), and the capital and expense requirements for operating the business.

Describe the business's managers and their qualifications, and specify what type of support staff will be needed for the business to run efficiently. Any potential benefits or pitfalls to the community should also be presented, such as new job creation, economic growth, and possible effects on the environment from manufacturing and how they will be handled to conform with local, state and federal regulations.

Financial Factors

The financial statements are the backbone of your business plan. They show how profitable your business will be in the short and long term, and should include the following:

The *income statement* details the business's cash-generating ability. It projects such items as revenue, expenses, capital (in the form of depreciation) and cost of goods. You should generate a monthly income statement for the business's first year, quarterly statements for the second year, and annual statements for each year thereafter (usually for three, five or 10 years, with five being the most common).

The *cash flow statement* details the amount of money coming into and going out of the business—monthly for the first year and quarterly for each year thereafter. The result is a profit or loss at the end of the period represented by each column. Both profits and losses carry over to the last column to show a cumulative amount. If your cash flow statement shows you consistently operating at a loss, you will probably need additional cash to meet expenses. Most businesses have some seasonal variations in their budgets, so re-examine your cash flow calculations if they look identical every month.

The *balance sheet* paints a picture of the business's financial strength in terms of assets, liabilities and equity over a set period. You should generate a balance sheet for each year profiled in the development of the business.

Bright Idea

Still need another reason to write a business plan? Consider this: If you decide to sell your business in the future, or if you become disabled or die and someone else takes over, a written business plan will help make the transition a smooth one.

After these essential financial documents, include any relevant summary information that's not included elsewhere in the plan but will significantly affect the business. This could include ratios such as return on investment, break-even point or return on assets. Your accountant can help you decide what information is best to include.

Many people consider the financial section of a business plan the most difficult to write. If you haven't started your business yet, how do you know what your income will be? You have a few op-

FINDING FUNDING

One of the primary purposes of a business plan is to help you obtain financing for your business. When writing your plan, however, it's important to remember who those financing sources are likely to be.

Bankers, investors, venture capitalists and investment advisors are sophisticated in business and financial matters. How can you ensure your plan makes the right impression? Three tips are key:

1. *Avoid hype.* While many entrepreneurs tend to be gamblers who believe in relying on their gut feelings, financial types are likely to go by the book. If your business plan praises your idea with superlatives like "one-of-a-kind," "unique" or "unprecedented," your readers are likely to be turned off. Wild, unsubstantiated promises or unfounded conclusions tell financial sources you are inexperienced, naive and reckless.

2. *Polish the executive summary.* Potential investors receive so many business plans, they cannot afford to spend more than a few minutes evaluating each one. If at first glance your proposal looks dull, poorly written or confusing, investors will toss it aside without a second thought. In other words, if your executive summary doesn't grab them, you won't get a second chance.

3. *Make sure your plan is complete.* Even if your executive summary sparkles, you need to make sure the rest of your plan is just as good and that all the necessary information is included. Some entrepreneurs are in such a hurry to get financing, they submit a condensed or preliminary business plan, promising to provide more information if the recipient is interested. This approach usually backfires for two reasons: First, if you don't provide information upfront, investors will assume the information doesn't exist yet and that you are stalling for time. Second, even if investors are interested in your preliminary plan, their interest may cool in the time it takes you to compile the rest of the information.

When presenting a business plan, you are starting from a position of weakness. And if potential investors find any flaws in your plan, they gain an even greater bargaining advantage. A well-written and complete plan gives you greater negotiating power and boosts your chances of getting financing on your own terms.

tions. The first is to enlist your accountant's help. An accountant can take your raw data and organize it into categories that will satisfy all the requirements of a financial section, including monthly and yearly sales projections. Or, if you are familiar with accounting procedures, you can do it yourself with the help of a good spreadsheet program. (For more information on developing financial statements, see the "Making A Statement" chapter.)

A Living Document

You've put a lot of time and effort into your business plan. What happens when it's done? A good business plan shouldn't gather dust in a drawer. Think of it as a living document, and refer to it often. A well-written plan helps you define activities and responsibilities within your business, as well as identify and achieve your goals.

To ensure your business plan continues to serve you well, make it a habit to update yours annually. Set aside a block of time near the beginning of the calendar year, fiscal year or whenever is convenient for you. Meet with your accountant or financial advisor, if necessary, to go over and update financial figures. Is your business heading in the right direction . . . or has it wandered off course?

Making it a practice to review your business plan annually is a great way to start the year fresh and reinvigorated. It lets you catch any problems before they become too large to solve. It also ensures that if the possibility of getting financing, participating in a joint venture or other such occasion arises, you'll have an updated plan ready to go so you don't miss out on a good opportunity.

Whether you're writing it for the first time or updating it for the 15th, creating a good business plan doesn't mean penning a 200-page novel or adding lots of fancy clip art and footnotes. It means proving to yourself and others that you understand your business and you know what's required to make it grow and prosper.

GLOSSARY

Balance sheet: paints a picture of the business's financial strength in terms of assets, liabilities and equity over a set period

Cash flow statement: details the amount of money coming into and going out of the business—monthly for the first year and quarterly for each year thereafter

Competitive analysis: section of a business plan that assesses the competition's strengths and weaknesses

Design and development plan: section of a business plan that describes the product's design and charts its development within the context of production, marketing and the company itself

Distribution: means of getting product to the end user; describes entire process of moving product from factory to end user

Executive summary: the opening section of a business plan; describes the business, product or service in brief

Income statement: projects such items as revenue, expenses, capital (in the form of depreciation) and cost of goods

Operations and management plan: section of a business plan that describes how the business will function on a day-to-day basis

Unique selling proposition (USP): what differentiates your product or service from others of a similar type; what makes it unique

CHAPTER 11

MOTHER, MAY I?

Don't forget business licenses and permits

When you're embroiled in the excitement of starting a new business, it's easy to ignore the need for licenses and permits. "Oh, that's just bureaucratic mumbo-jumbo," you think. "I'll take care of those little details later, when things settle down."

Sure, getting licenses and permits is about as much fun as visiting the dentist. But failing to do it—right from the beginning—is one of the most common mistakes new entrepreneurs make.

Some licenses or permits are costly and hard to get, and you need to figure them into your start-up budget. Your grand plan for founding a fancy nightclub could grind to a screeching halt if you can't get (or can't afford) the liquor license. It's better to find that out in the beginning than after you've redecorated the building and hired the waitresses.

Or what if your business becomes a success beyond your wildest dreams . . . then, a few years from now, gets shut down by the county when they discover you don't have the proper license or permits? Short of a shutdown, lack of a license could lead to hefty fines, restrictions on your operations, lawsuits from suppliers or employees, problems with the IRS . . . what a headache! This is one situation where an ounce of prevention really pays off.

Following are some of the most common licenses and permits small-business owners may need and where to go for more information.

FICTITIOUS NAME (DBA)

If you are structuring your company as a sole proprietorship or a partnership, you have the option of choosing a business name or *dba* ("doing business as") for your business. This is known as a *fictitious business name*. If you want to operate your business under a name other than your own

GARY L. GRANVILLE
COUNTY CLERK-RECORDER
12 CIVIC CENTER PLAZA, ROOM 106
POST OFFICE BOX 238
SANTA ANA, CA 92702-0238

FICTITIOUS BUSINESS NAME STATEMENT
Print legibly or type all information and DO NOT ABBREVIATE.

THE FOLLOWING PERSON(S) IS (ARE) DOING BUSINESS AS:

1.	Fictitious Business Name(s) — Business Phone No. (____) _____
1A.	☐ New Statement ☐ Refile—List Previous No._____ ☐ Change
2.	Street Address, City & State of Principal place of Business (Do NOT use a P.O. Box) State Zip Code
3.	Full name of Registrant (If Corporation, enter corporation name) — If Corporation/L.L.C. State of Incorporation or organization
	Res./Corp. Address (Do NOT use a P.O. Box) City State Zip Code
	Full name of Registrant (If Corporation, enter corporation name) — If Corporation/L.L.C. State of Incorporation or organization
	Res./Corp. Address (Do NOT use a P.O. Box) City State Zip Code
	Full name of Registrant (If Corporation, enter corporation name) — If Corporation/L.L.C. State of Incorporation or organization
	Res./Corp. Address (Do NOT use a P.O. Box) City State Zip Code
4.	(CHECK ONE ONLY) This business is conducted by ( ) an individual ( ) a general partnership ( ) a limited partnership ( ) an unincorporated association other than a partnership ( ) a corporation ( ) a business trust ( ) co-partners ( ) husband and wife ( ) joint venture ( ) Limited Liability Co. ( ) Other–Specify ____
5.	Have you started doing business yet? Yes_____ Insert the date you started: _____ No_____ NOTICE: THIS FICTITIOUS NAME STATEMENT EXPIRES FIVE YEARS FROM THE DATE IT WAS FILED IN THE OFFICE OF THE COUNTY CLERK-RECORDER. A NEW FICTITIOUS BUSINESS NAME STATEMENT MUST BE FILED BEFORE THAT DATE. THE FILING OF THIS STATEMENT DOES NOT OF ITSELF AUTHORIZE THE USE IN THIS STATE OF A FICTITIOUS BUSINESS NAME IN VIOLATION OF THE RIGHTS OF ANOTHER UNDER FEDERAL, STATE, OR COMMON LAW (SEE SECTION 14400 ET SEQ., BUSINESS AND PROFESSIONS CODE).
6.	If Registrant is NOT a corporation, sign below: (See instructions on the reverse side of this form.) Signature _____ (Type or Print Name) If Registrant is a corporation, an officer of the corporation signs below: If Registrant is a limited liability company, a manager or an officer signs below. Limited Liability Company Name/Corporation Name Signature and Title of Officer or Manager Print or Type Officer's/Manager's Name and Title

(THIS FEE APPLIES AT THE TIME OF FILING)
FILING FEE $31.00 FOR ONE BUSINESS NAME.
$7.00 FOR EACH ADDITIONAL BUSINESS NAME.
$7.00 FOR EACH ADDITIONAL PARTNER AFTER FIRST TWO.
PROVIDE RETURN STAMPED ENVELOPE IF MAILED.
➡ F059-FictitiousBus.Stmt. (R8/97)   WHITE – CLERK-RECORDER'S COPY, PINK – BANK, NEWSPAPER AND REGISTRANT

(for instance, Carol Axelrod doing business as "Darling Donut Shoppe"), you may be required by the county, city or state to register your fictitious name.

Procedures for doing this vary among states. In many states, all you have to do is go to the county offices and pay a registration fee to the county clerk. In other states, you also have to place a fictitious name ad in a local newspaper for a certain amount of time. The cost of filing a fictitious name notice ranges from $10 to $100. Your local bank may require a fictitious name certificate to open a business account for you; if so, they can tell you where to go to register.

Smart Tip

In most cases, the newspaper that prints your fictitious name ad will also file the necessary papers with the county for a small fee.

In most states, corporations don't have to file fictitious business names unless the corporations do business under names other than their own. Incorporation documents have the same effect for corporate businesses as fictitious name filings do for sole proprietorships and partnerships. (For more on incorporating, see Part 2 Chapter 9.)

BUSINESS LICENSE

Contact your city's business license department to find out about getting a business license, which essentially grants you the right (after you pay a fee, of course) to operate in that city. When you file your license application, the city planning or zoning department will check to make sure your area is zoned for the purpose you want to use it for and that there are enough parking spaces to meet the codes. If you are opening your business in a building that previously housed a similar business, you're not likely to run into any problems.

You can't operate in an area that is not zoned for your type of business unless you first get a variance or conditional-use permit. To get a variance, you'll need to present your case before the planning commission in your city. In many cases, variances are quite easy to get, as long as you can show that your business won't disrupt the character of the neighborhood where you plan to locate.

HEALTH DEPARTMENT PERMIT

If you plan to sell food, either directly to customers as in a restaurant or as a wholesaler to other retailers, you'll need a county health department permit. This costs about $25 and varies

Beware!

Investigate zoning ordinances especially carefully if you plan to start a business in your home. Residential neighborhoods tend to have strict zoning regulations preventing business use of the home. Even so, it is possible to get a variance or conditional-use permit; and in many areas, attitudes toward homebased businesses are becoming more supportive. See *Entrepreneur's* business start-up guide No. 1815, *Starting & Running a Homebased Business.*

BUSINESS LICENSE APPLICATION

Please return to: City of Irvine - Business License
One Civic Center Plaza ● P.O. Box 19575
Irvine, California 92623-9575 ● (714) 724-6310

Business Name _____

Business Name (other) _____

Street Address _____ Suite _____
(May not be a P.O. Box)

City _____ State _____ Zip _____

Mailing Address _____ City _____ State _____ Zip _____

Business Phone ( ) _____ State Employer ID (SEIN) _____

State Sales Tax No.(RESALE) _____ Federal Employer ID (FEIN) _____

Business Fax ( ) _____

Please describe the exact nature of business activity to be conducted _____

Indicate ownership type   ☐Sole proprietorship   ☐Partnership   ☐Corporation   ☐Trust   ☐Ltd liability Co.

Indicate type of business   ☐Retail   ☐Wholesale   ☐Manufacturing   ☐Service

How many people including owners are working in Irvine for your business?_____

State Professional License No._____ Class _____ Expiration _____

State Contractor License No. _____ Class _____ Expiration _____

I declare under penalty of perjury that I am licensed by the State Contractors License Board _____
(Contractors only)   Signature

* THE NAME OF THE FIRST PERSON LISTED WILL BE PRINTED ON THE BUSINESS LICENSE CERTIFICATE
List residence, address, phone, title and driver's license number of Owner, President, Partner, CEO, CFO, etc.

1. _____
    name   residence address   city   state   zip

( ) _____
    phone   title   driver's license #   soc. security #

2. _____
    name   residence address   city   state   zip

( ) _____
    phone   title   driver's license #   soc. security #

On what date will/did your business begin operating in Irvine?   _____

ANNUAL GROSS RECEIPTS $ _____

---

depending on the size of the business and the amount and type of equipment you have. The health department will want to inspect your facilities before issuing the permit.

LIQUOR, WINE AND BEER LICENSES

In most states, you'll need to get one type of license to serve wine and beer and another to serve hard liquor. A liquor license is more difficult to

---

Business License Application, cont'd.

Do you sell taxable merchandise or provide a taxable service such as renting merchandise or fabrication labor from you location in Irvine?   ❏No   ❏Yes

If Yes: What type of goods are sold? _____

Are sales of your product made at the "Business Address" on this application?   ❏No   ❏Yes

Are sales made at other locations in this city?   ❏No   ❏Yes

Please list the other sales locations, if applicable. _____

Are you a sales AGENT for another company?   ❏No   ❏Yes

Please list the name(s) of the person or company. _____

Is this application made to move an existing business from another location?   ❏No   ❏Yes

If yes, please list the former address _____

Please indicate who the City should contact in the event of an emergency:

1. _____   _____   ( ) _____
    name   title   phone

2. _____   _____   ( ) _____
    name   title   phone

Please list other business locations in Irvine:

1. _____   _____   ( ) _____
    name   address   phone

2. _____   _____   ( ) _____
    name   address   phone

Is this business conducted from your home?   ❏No ❏Yes (If yes, complete a Home Occupancy Form)

Did you purchase this business?   ❏No ❏Yes If yes, enter the date of purchase? _____

Building Permit is required prior to making any physical modifications to the premises. If you have questions about building modifications, contact the Building & Safety Division at (714) 724-6524.

Does your business create, store, generate, or use hazardous substances or any products that are considered to be corrosive, reactive, ignitable, toxic, and / or ozone depleters?   ❏No ❏Yes

---

It is the responsibility of the applicant / licensee to ensure that his/her business complies with all applicable City Codes and the City Zoning Ordinance. In the event it is determined that the business does not comply, the business license may be revoked by the City. I hereby certify, under penalty of perjury, the information provided on this application is true and correct.

_____   _____   _____
Applicant signature   Print applicant's name and title   Date

FORM 22-05, REV 05/97[PM]

---

obtain than a beer-and-wine license. In some areas, no new liquor licenses are being issued at all; you can only obtain one by buying it from an existing license holder. As a result, although the original licenses may have cost less than $100, competition has forced the going price from $2,000 to tens of thousands, depending on the location. One advantage of buying out an existing restaurant is that if it served liquor, you may be able to acquire the license as part of the deal.

If your area is still issuing liquor licenses, in most cases you will have

Smart Tip

It's generally much easier to get a beer-and-wine license than a liquor license. Beer-and-wine licenses are usually issued for an annual period and are easy to renew if you haven't committed any offenses, such as selling alcoholic drinks to minors.

to file an application with the state beverage control board, then post a notice on the premises of your intent to sell liquor. In some states, the beverage control board requires holders of liquor licenses to keep all purchase records for a certain number of years. During that time, they are subject to inspection by the beverage control board and/or the IRS.

The White Pages of your telephone directory will have the number for the nearest beverage control agency, which can give you all the information you need about both types of licenses.

FIRE DEPARTMENT PERMIT

You may need to get a permit from your fire department if your business uses any flammable materials or if your premises will be open to the public. In some cities, you have to get this permit before you open for business. Other areas don't require permits but simply schedule periodic inspections of your

Beware!

Businesses such as theaters, restaurants, nightclubs, bars, retirement homes, day-care centers and anywhere else where lots of people congregate are subject to especially close and frequent scrutiny by the fire department.

business to see if you meet fire safety regulations. If you don't, they will issue a citation.

AIR AND WATER POLLUTION CONTROL PERMIT

Many cities now have departments that work to control air and water pollution. If you burn any materials, discharge anything into the sewers or waterways, or use products that produce gas (such as paint sprayers), you may have to get a special permit from this department in your city or county.

Environmental protection regulations may also require you to get approval before doing any construction or beginning operation. Check with

License No. _____

CITY OF IRVINE
APPLICATION FOR HOME OCCUPATION LICENSE*

BUSINESS NAME: _____

APPLICANT NAME: _____ BUSINESS PHONE: _____

HOME ADDRESS: _____

SPECIFIC TYPE OF BUSINESS/PRODUCT(S): _____

_____

Regulations for Home Occupation Permits are provided so that certain incidental and accessory uses may be established in residential developments under conditions which will ensure their compatibility with the neighborhood. They are intended to protect the rights of the residents to engage in certain home occupations that are harmonious with a residential environment.

Please check with your homeowner's association, or rental property management company for any Conditions, Covenants & Restrictions that may restrict business uses at your property.

In order to be issued a Home Occupation Permit, you must ensure the City of Irvine that the proposed use complies with City requirements as identified in Section V.E-209 of the Zoning Ordinance. By reading and understanding the regulations listed below, as well as signing this application form, you are certifying that your home occupation will conform to all applicable City of Irvine Ordinances:

It is the responsibility of the applicant/licensee to ensure that his/her business complies with all applicable city codes and the city zoning ordinance. In the event it is determined that the business does not comply, the business license may be revoked by the city.

1. My home occupation is an incidental and accessory use and does not change the residential character of my residence;
2. My residence is not the point of customer pick-up or delivery, and my home occupation does not cause an increase in vehicular traffic in the neighborhood;
3. My home occupation is conducted only within an enclosed structure (not in my yard or driveway);
4. There will not at any time be any signs or other exterior evidence relating to my home occupation;
5. My home occupation may be conducted in the garage, but will not, under any circumstances, utilize any space required for off-street parking (as identified in the City of Irvine Zoning Ordinance, Section V.E-400 et. seq.);
6. I understand the only employees who may work at my home-based business are residents of my home;
7. I will not utilize or use any electrical or mechanical equipment which may create visible or audible interference in radio, television or telephone service or may cause fluctuations in line voltage outside the residence; and
8. My home occupation does not now, nor will in the future create noise odors or use Hazardous Materials, in excess of that normally associated with a residential use.

My Home Occupation does not comply with Item _____, above. *Please contact the Development Assistance Center: (714) 724-6308 to discuss you situation, prior to submitting this application.*

I do hereby certify that, under penalty of perjury, to the best of my knowledge and belief, the information contained herein is true and correct:

Signed: _____ Date: _____

If you have any questions, please contact the Development Assistance Center at (714) 724-6308. If we are unable to approve you request for a home-based business you will be invited to attend a hearing pursuant to City Council Ordinance 93-06, Sections II.M-217 and II.M-218, prior to denying your business license. If you are not satisfied with the decision made following your hearing, you may file a Notice of Appeal with the City Clerk within thirty (30) days of receipt of the written decision to deny the license.

* This application must be filed with the completed Business License application.

(For City of Irvine Staff Use Only)

Community Development Department Planning Recommendation:

_____   _____
APPROVE   *DENY*

_____   _____
(Signature of Community Development Department Representative)   *Date*
Form 40-27, Rev. 12/96[word]

CITY OF IRVINE ● ONE CIVIC CENTER PLAZA ● P.O. BOX 19575, IRVINE, CALIFORNIA 92623-9575 ● (714) 724-6000

your state environmental protection agency regarding federal or state regulations that may apply to your business.

SIGN PERMIT

Some cities and suburbs have sign ordinances that restrict the size, location and sometimes the lighting and type of sign you can use outside your business. Landlords may also impose their own restrictions; they are likely to be most stringent in a mall. To avoid costly mistakes, check regulations and secure the written approval of your landlord before you go to the expense of having a sign designed and installed.

COUNTY PERMITS

County governments often require essentially the same types of permits and licenses as cities. If your business is outside of any city or town's jurisdiction, these permits apply to you. The good news: County regulations are usually not as strict as those of adjoining cities.

Smart Tip

You can find out which licenses and permits are required for your business by calling the state and local government offices in the area in which you are going to operate. Ask them to send you information and any forms that may be required.

STATE LICENSES

In many states, people in certain occupations must have licenses or occupational permits. Often, they have to pass state examinations before they can get these permits and conduct business. States usually require licensing for auto mechanics, plumbers, electricians, building contractors, collection agents, insurance agents, real estate brokers, repossessors, and anyone who provides personal services (i.e., barbers, cosmetologists, doctors and nurses). Contact your state government offices to get a complete list of occupations that require licensing.

FEDERAL LICENSES

In most cases, you won't have to worry about this. However, a few types of businesses do require federal licensing, including meat processors, radio and TV stations, and investment advisory services. The Federal Trade Commission can tell you if your business requires a federal license.

GLOSSARY

Air and water pollution control permit: may be required by your city or county if your business burns materials, discharges anything into the sewers or waterways, or uses products that produce gas

Beer-and-wine license: required by most states to sell beer and wine; does not allow holder to sell hard liquor

County permits: businesses operating outside a city or town may be required by the county to obtain certain permits

DBA (doing business as): see fictitious business name

Fictitious business name: a name other than your own under which you are doing business (i.e., Joe Smith doing business as Joe's Auto Body Shop); must typically be registered with the county, state or city

Fire department permit: may be required if your business uses flammable materials or is open to the public

Health department permit: permit required by the county health department if you plan to sell food

Liquor license: license required by most states to sell hard liquor

Sign permit: permit required by some cities and suburbs to erect a sign outside your business

State licenses: licenses required by many states for people in certain occupations, such as cosmetology, mechanics, plumbers, electricians and other fields

CHAPTER 12

YOU NEED PROFESSIONAL HELP

Hiring a lawyer and an accountant

As you start off on your business journey, there are two professionals you'll soon come to rely on to guide you along the path: Your lawyer and your accountant. It's hard to navigate the maze of tax and legal issues facing entrepreneurs these days unless these professionals are an integral part of your team.

HIRING A LAWYER

When do you need a lawyer? Although the answer depends on your business and your particular circumstances, it's generally worthwhile to consult an attorney before making any decision that could have legal ramifications. These include setting up a partnership or corporation, checking for compliance with regulations, negotiating loans, obtaining trademarks or patents, preparing buy-sell agreements, assisting with tax planning, drawing up pension plans, reviewing business forms, negotiating and drawing up documents to buy and sell real estate, reviewing employee contracts, exporting or selling products in other states, and collecting bad debts.

If something goes wrong, you may need an attorney to stand up for your trademark rights, go to court on an employee dispute or defend you in a product liability lawsuit. Some entrepreneurs wait until something goes wrong to consult an attorney, but in today's litigious society, that isn't the smartest idea. "Almost every business, whatever its size, requires a lawyer's advice," says James Blythe Hodge of the law firm Sheppard, Mullin, Richter & Hampton. "Even the smallest business has tax concerns that need to be addressed as early as the planning stages."

In a crisis situation—such as a lawsuit or trademark wrangle—you may not have time to thoroughly research different legal options. More likely, you'll end up flipping through the Yellow Pages in haste . . . and getting stuck with a second-rate lawyer. Better to start off on the right foot from the beginning by choosing a good lawyer now. Many entrepreneurs say their relationship with a lawyer is like a marriage—it takes time to develop. That's why it's important to lay the groundwork for a good partnership early.

Choosing An Attorney

How do you find the right attorney? Ask for recommendations from business owners in your industry or from professionals such as bankers or accountants you trust. Don't just get names; ask them for the specific strengths and weaknesses of the attorneys they recommend. Then take the process one step further: Ask your business associates' attorneys whom they recommend and why. (Attorneys are more likely to be helpful if you phrase the request as "If for some reason I couldn't use you, who would you recommend and why?") If you still need more prospects, contact your local Bar Association; many of them have referral services.

Next, set up an interview with the top five attorneys you're considering. Tell them you're interested in building a long-term relationship, and find out which ones are willing to meet with you for an initial consultation without charging a fee. Cover the following areas in your interviews of each attorney:

◆ **Experience:** Although it's not essential to find an expert in your particular field, it makes sense to look for someone who specializes in small-business problems as opposed to, say, maritime law. "Find someone who understands the different business structures and their tax implications," says Hodge. Make sure the lawyer is willing to take on small problems; if you're trying to collect on a relatively small invoice, for example, will the lawyer think it's worth his or her time?

◆ **Understanding:** Be sure the attorney is willing to learn about your business's goals. You're looking for someone who will be a long-term partner in your business's growth. Sure, you're a start-up today, but does the lawyer understand where you want to be tomorrow and share your vision for the future?

> ### Bright Idea
>
> When you're starting a business, you're short of money for just about everything—including legal services. Realizing this, many law firms offer a "start-up package" of legal services for a set fee. This typically includes drawing up initial documents, attending corporate board meetings, preparing minutes, drafting ownership agreements and stock certificates, and offering routine legal advice.

◆ **Ability to communicate:** If the lawyer speaks in legalese and doesn't bother to explain the terms he or she uses, look for someone else.

◆ **Availability:** Will the attorney be available for conferences at your convenience, not his or hers? How quickly can you expect emergency phone calls to be returned?

◆ **Rapport:** Is this someone you can get along with? You will be discussing matters close to your heart with this person, so make sure you feel comfortable doing so. Good chemistry will ensure a better relationship and more positive results for your business.

Smart Tip

When a client refuses to pay you, do you hand the case over to a lawyer? Some entrepreneurs do, but others handle small legal matters on their own by using their attorney as a coach. Lawyers can be very effective in coaching you to file lawsuits in small claims court, drafting employment manuals and completing other routine legal tasks.

◆ **Reasonable fees:** Attorneys charge anywhere from $90 to $300 or more per hour, depending on the location, size and prestige of the firm as well as the lawyer's reputation. Shop around and get quotes from several firms before making your decision. However, beware of comparing one attorney with another on the basis of fees alone. The lowest hourly fees may not indicate the best value in legal work because an inexperienced attorney may take twice as long to complete a project as an experienced one will.

◆ **References:** Don't be afraid to ask for references. What types of businesses or cases has the attorney worked with in the past? Get a list of clients or other attorneys you can contact to discuss competence, service and fees.

Cost Cutters

For many entrepreneurs, the idea of consulting a lawyer conjures up frightening visions of skyrocketing legal bills. While there's no denying that lawyers are expensive, the good news is there are more ways than ever to keep a lid on costs. Start by learning about the various ways lawyers bill their time:

◆ **Hourly or per diem rate:** Most attorneys bill by the hour. If travel is involved, they may bill by the day.

DIFFERENT STROKES

When you're hit with a lawsuit, the costs can be mind-boggling—even if you win. That's why more and more small businesses are using alternative dispute resolution (ADR), a concept that includes mediation, arbitration and other ways of resolving disputes without resorting to litigation. Both in contracts between businesses or in agreements between employers and employees, people are consenting ahead of time to submit future disputes to ADR. Here are the most common forms of ADR:

◆ **Negotiation:** In this simplest form, the two parties (or their lawyers) discuss their differences and agree on a settlement.

◆ **Mediation:** When the two parties need more help in working out a solution, they can hire a neutral third party (a mediator) skilled in asking questions, listening and helping make decisions. The result is a written agreement to settle the dispute; both parties share the mediation costs.

◆ **Arbitration:** An arbitrator hears a case much like a judge, then issues a decision. The parties have control over who hears the case—often, an expert in their field. In nonbinding arbitration, the arbitrator makes a recommendation that parties can accept or reject. In binding arbitration, the arbitrator's decision is legally binding.

◆ **Mini-trial:** Less common, this gives both parties a sense of how their disagreement might resolve in court. They watch their lawyers argue the case as if they were at trial. Generally, the parties are better able to see the other side and end up settling.

◆ **Summary jury trial:** Here, a jury of citizens hears a shortened trial and makes a nonbinding decision. Again, this usually helps the parties agree on a settlement.

Any time two parties enter a contract, they can include an agreement to submit any disputes to a specified type of ADR. Your attorney can help you draft a clause specifying how the situation will be handled. If you have employees sign an ADR agreement, make sure they understand that they will lose the option of a jury trial.

Even if you don't have an ADR clause in your contracts, it's still possible to suggest using ADR after a dispute arises. Once they understand how much money, time and aggravation ADR can save, the other side may agree to use it.

◆ **Flat fee:** Some attorneys suggest a flat fee for certain routine matters, such as reviewing a contract or closing a loan.

◆ **Monthly retainer:** If you anticipate a lot of routine questions, one option is a monthly fee that entitles you to all the routine legal advice you need.

◆ **Contingent fee:** For lawsuits or other complex matters, lawyers often work on a contingency basis. This means that if they succeed, they receive a percentage of the proceeds—usually between 25 percent and 40 percent. If they fail, they receive only out-of-pocket expenses.

◆ **Value billing:** Some law firms bill at a higher rate on business matters if the attorneys obtain a favorable result, such as negotiating a contract that saves the client thousands of dollars. Try to avoid lawyers who use this method, which is also sometimes called "partial contingency."

If you think one method will work better for you than another, don't hesitate to bring it up with the attorney; many will offer flexible arrangements to meet your needs.

When you hire an attorney, draw up an agreement (called an "engagement letter") detailing the billing method. If more than one attorney works on your file, make sure you specify the hourly rate for each individual so you aren't charged $200 an hour for legal work done by an associate who only charges $75. This agreement should also specify what expenses you're expected to reimburse. Some attorneys expect to be reimbursed for meals, secretarial overtime, postage and photocopies, which many people consider the costs of doing business. If an unexpected charge comes up, will your attorney call you for authorization? Agree to reimburse only reasonable and necessary out-of-pocket expenses.

No matter what type of billing method your attorney uses, here are some steps you can take to control legal costs:

◆ **Have the attorney estimate the cost of each matter in writing, so you can decide whether it's worth pursuing.** If the bill comes in over the estimate, ask why. Some attorneys also offer

Dollar Stretcher

Using paralegals as part of your legal team can be a good way to cut costs. Certain legal tasks—preparing a simple document, for instance—are straightforward enough that a paralegal may be able to handle them instead of a higher-priced lawyer. Don't assume your lawyer will suggest this route; ask him or her about it. And always make sure the paralegal is supervised by a business lawyer.

"caps," guaranteeing in writing the maximum cost of a particular service. This helps you budget and gives you more certainty than just getting an estimate.

◆ **Learn what increments of time the firm uses to calculate its bill.** Attorneys keep track of their time in increments as short as six minutes or as long as half an hour. Will a five-minute phone call cost you $50?

◆ **Request monthly, itemized bills.** Some lawyers wait until a bill gets large before sending an invoice. Ask for monthly invoices instead, and review them. The most obvious red flag is excessive fees; this means too many people—or the wrong people—are working on your file. It's also possible you may be mistakenly billed for work done for another client, so review your invoices carefully.

◆ **See if you can negotiate prompt-payment discounts.** Request that your bill be discounted if you pay within 30 days of your invoice date. Even a 5 percent discount on legal fees can add thousands of dollars to your yearly bottom line.

◆ **Be prepared.** Before you meet with or call your lawyer, have the necessary documents with you and know exactly what you want to discuss. Fax needed documents ahead of time so your attorney doesn't have to read them during the conference and can instead get right down to business. And refrain from calling your attorney 100 times a day.

◆ **Meet with your lawyer regularly.** At first glance, this may not seem like a good way to keep costs down, but you'll be amazed at how much it reduces the endless rounds of phone tag that plague busy entrepreneurs and attorneys. More important, a monthly five- or 10-minute meeting (even by phone) can save you substantial sums by nipping small legal problems in the bud before they have a chance to grow.

Making The Most Of Your Lawyer

Once your relationship with your lawyer is established, keep the lines of communication open. In addition to brief regular meetings, sit down with your attorney once annually to discuss the past year's progress and your goals for the coming year. Meet at your place of business so the attorney can get to know your operation.

How can you tell if your attorney is doing a good job? According to attorney Jerry Friedland, the quickest measure is how many legal difficulties

PAY NOW, NOT LATER

A new method has arisen to take charge of skyrocketing legal fees. It's called the prepaid legal plan, and more and more small business are using it.

Prepaid legal plans have been compared to HMOs because they offer certain basic services for a monthly fee. Prices range from as little as $10 a month to $70 or more; in return, an entrepreneur gets a package of services such as, say, unlimited phone consultation with a lawyer, review of three contracts per month, up to 10 debt collections per month and discounts on other legal services.

"Our experience shows 73 percent of all legal problems [members bring] can be resolved with a single telephone call," says Crystal Virtue of Caldwell Legal, U.S.A.

Typically, prepaid legal services contract with one law firm in each state to handle routine matters. Because the service is usually that firm's biggest client, small-business owners using the service receive a warmer welcome than they might at a big law firm. Specialists are usually available at reduced rates.

When considering a prepaid legal service, here are some factors to consider:

◆ What is included? Check the plan to make sure they've got what you need. The number of services offered at a reduced rate may be limited; what do they charge for other services?

◆ Consider whether you'd prefer to build a relationship with one attorney rather than talk to a different lawyer every time you call.

◆ Ask other entrepreneurs who have used such services about the quality of work. Also ask how the company handles conflicts of interest in case you have a dispute against a business that uses the same prepaid firm.

With these caveats in mind, a prepaid legal service firm could be just what a business on a budget needs. For more information, contact the National Resource Center for Consumers of Legal Services at P.O. Box 340, Gloucester, VA 23061, or call (804) 693-9330.

you're having. Lawyers should be fending off legal problems. A good attorney identifies potential problems in advance.

Like any competent professional, a good lawyer also returns phone calls

The Size Of It

Are you dithering over the choice between that large, fancy law or accounting firm, or that humble, one-person legal or accounting office down the street? Before you bust your budget to retain Squelch, Withers & Ream, know this: Bigger isn't always better.

A big law or accounting firm may boast impressive credentials on your first meeting with them. The problem is that they usually boast an impressive price. What's more, the hotshot you meet on your initial conference may not be the person who will work on your legal cases. That task is likely to fall to a less experienced junior partner. This isn't necessarily bad, but make sure you don't get charged $300 an hour for something a paralegal did.

Only you can decide what is right for you, but make sure you're not being swayed by a big name or fancy office. While a big law or accounting firm may be right for some needs, the reality is that your company will make up a much smaller share of such a firm's client list. As such, you may not get the attention they're devoting to bigger clients. In other words, if Standard Oil has a sudden tax emergency, your file is likely to get put on the back burner. This is one situation where it's better to be a big fish in a small pond.

promptly, meets deadlines and follows through on promises. A good lawyer is thorough in asking for information and discerning your goals. And good lawyers either research what they don't know and explain your options, or refer you to someone who can help.

In evaluating the attorney's performance on any matter, consider whether you've been able to meet your goals. If you've met your goals without undue costs, the attorney is probably doing a good job.

Once you've found a lawyer who understands your business and does a good job for you, you've found a valuable asset.

Hiring An Accountant

Don't assume only big companies need the services of an accountant. Accountants can help you keep an eye on major costs as early as the start-up stage, a time when you're probably preoccupied with counting every paper clip and postage stamp. Accountants help you look at the big picture.

Even after the start-up stage, many business owners have no idea how well they're doing financially until the end of the year, when they file their tax returns. Meanwhile, they equate their cash flow with profits, which is wrong. Every dollar counts for small-business owners, so if you don't know exactly where you stand on a monthly basis, you may not be around at the end of the year.

While do-it-yourself accounting software is plentiful and easy to use, it's not the sole answer. Just as having WordPerfect doesn't make you a writer, having accounting software doesn't make you an accountant. Software can only do what you tell it to do—and a good accountant's skills go far beyond crunching numbers.

In fact, perhaps no other business relationship has such potential to pay off. Today's accountants are more than just bean counters. A good accountant can be your company's financial partner for life—with intimate knowledge of everything from how you're going to finance your next forklift to how you're going to finance your daughter's college education.

While many people think of accountants strictly as tax preparers, in reality,

ALL THE RIGHT QUESTIONS

Here are 10 questions to ask when interviewing a potential accountant:

1. Are you a CPA? (Don't assume every accountant is.)
2. Are you licensed to practice in your state?
3. When and where did you receive a license to practice?
4. Where did you go to school, and what degrees did you earn?
5. Who are some of your clients? (Call them.)
6. In what area do you specialize?
7. How big or small are your clients, and what size were they when you began your relationship with them?
8. How accessible are you? (Some accountants are only available during business hours; others will give you their home or pager number.)
9. To what professional organizations do you belong? How active are you in those groups?
10. What are your fees? (Ask to see some current invoices.)

accountants have a wide knowledge base that can be an invaluable asset to a business. A general accounting practice covers four basic areas of expertise:

1. business advisory services,

2. accounting and record-keeping,

3. taxes, and

4. auditing.

These four disciplines often overlap. For instance, if your accountant is helping you prepare the financial statements you need for a loan and he or she gives you some insights into how certain estimates could be recalculated to get a more favorable review, the accountant is crossing the line from auditing into business advisory services. And perhaps, after preparing your midyear financial statements, he or she might suggest how your performance year-to-date will influence your year-end tax liability.

Here's a closer look at the four areas:

◆ **Business advisory services:** This is where accountants can really earn their keep. Since the accountant is knowledgeable about your business environment, your tax situation and your financial statements, it makes sense to ask him or her to pull all the pieces together and help you come up with a business plan and personal financial plan you can really achieve. Accountants can offer advice on everything from insurance (do you really need business interruption insurance, or would it be cheaper to lease a second site?) to expansion (how will additional capacity affect your operating costs?). "Accountants can bring a new level of insight to the picture, simply by virtue of their perspective," says David Lifson, a New York City CPA.

◆ **Accounting and record-keeping:** Accounting and record-keeping are perhaps the most basic accounting discipline. However, most business owners keep their own books and records instead of having their accountant do it. The reason is simple: If these records are examined by lenders or the IRS,

Bright Idea

If you're looking to master accounting for your new business—or simply don't want to be left in the dark when talking to your accountant—check out *Accounting for the New Business* (Adams Media) by Christopher R. Malburg. Offering a complete accounting course in one volume, this book features easy techniques you can use, simple solutions to common problems, and everything you need to gain an overall understanding of the accounting process.

Smart Tip

Find out how well-connected the CPA and his/her firm are before making a final decision. CPAs are often valuable resources for small businesses needing to borrow money or to raise capital from other sources. A well-connected CPA might help you get a foot in the door with a bank or investor.

the business owner is responsible for their accuracy; therefore, it makes more sense for the owner to maintain them.

Where accountants can offer help is in initially setting up bookkeeping and accounting systems and showing the business owner how to use them. A good system allows you to evaluate your profitability at any given point in time and modify prices accordingly. It also lets you track expenses to see if any particular areas are getting out of hand. A good system also lets you establish and track a budget, spot trends in sales and expenses, and reduce accounting fees required to produce financial statements and tax returns.

◆ **Taxes:** Tax advice from accountants comes in two forms: tax compliance and tax planning. Planning refers to reducing your overall tax burden; compliance refers to obeying the tax laws.

◆ **Auditing:** Auditing services are required for many purposes, most commonly by banks as a condition of a loan. There are many levels of auditing, ranging from simply preparing financial statements from figures that the entrepreneur supplies all the way up to an audit, where the accountant or third party gives assurances that a company's financial information is accurate.

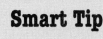

Smart Tip

The American Institute of Certified Public Accountants (AICPA) has a Web site that provides links to new updates, upcoming activities, accounting-related software and state CPA societies—whose Web sites provide links to more related sites and frequently asked tax questions. Visit www.aicpa.org.

Today, more and more accountants are moving into a fifth area: personal financial planning. For many, this is a natural extension of their familiarity with their clients' financial affairs.

Choosing An Accountant

The best way to find a good accountant is to get a referral from your attorney, your banker or a business colleague in the same industry. If you need more possibilities, almost every state has a Society of Certified Public Accountants that will make a referral.

Don't underestimate the importance of a CPA (certified public accountant). Those three letters are awarded only to those who have passed a rigorous two-day, nationally standardized exam. Most states require CPAs to have at least a college degree or its equivalent, and several also require postgraduate work.

Accountants generally work for large companies; CPAs, on the other hand, work for a variety of businesses, large and small. When you're dealing with an accountant, you can only hope he or she is well-educated and well-versed in your business's needs. Passing the CPA exam, on the other hand, is a guarantee of a certain level of abilities. Once you've come up with some good candidates, a little preparation is in order before you interview them. The first step in setting the stage for a successful search, says Lifson, is to take an inventory of what you need. It's important to determine beforehand just how much of the work your company will do and how much of it will be done by the accountant.

Accounting services can be broken down into three broad categories: recording transactions, assembling them, and generating returns and financial statements. Typically, the reporting part—that is, the generation of returns and financial statements—requires the highest level of expertise. But though the other activities require a lower skill level, many firms still charge the same hourly rate for them. Given the level of fees you are prepared to pay, you must decide where your responsibility stops and where the accountant's begins.

Once you've compiled your documentation and given some thought to your expectations, you're ready to interview your referrals. Five candidates is a good number to start with. For each candidate, plan on two meetings before making your decision. One of these meetings should be at your site; one at theirs. "Both parties need to know the environment the other works in," explains Lifson, who warns you should never hire an accountant without seeing his or her office.

During the ensuing interviews, your principal goal is to find out about three things: services, personality and fees.

Smart Tip

Entrepreneur's *Guide to Professional Services* (John Wiley & Sons) by Leonard Bisk helps you find, hire and manage a winning team of advisors and service providers, from lawyers, accountants and bankers to consultants, real estate brokers and ad agencies.

1. **Services:** Most accounting firms offer tax and auditing services. But what about bookkeeping? Management consulting? Pension fund accounting? Estate planning? Will the accountant help you design and implement financial information systems? Other services a CPA may offer include analyzing transactions for business loans and financing; preparing, auditing, reviewing and compiling financial statements; managing investments; and even representing you before tax authorities.

    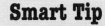

    Smart Tip

    If you are starting a retail or service business involving a lot of cash, make sure the CPA has expertise in providing input on controlling your cash. As you grow, this becomes an increasingly more vital issue, and a good CPA should be able to advise you in this area.

    Although smaller accounting firms are generally a better bet for entrepreneurs (see "The Size of It" in this chapter), they may not offer all these services. Make sure the firm has what you need. If it can't offer specialized services, such as estate planning, it may have relationships with other firms it can refer you to to handle these matters.

    In addition to services, make sure the firm has experience with small business and with your industry in particular. Someone who is already familiar with the financial issues facing your field of business won't have to waste time getting up to speed.

2. **Personality:** Is the accountant's style compatible with yours? Be sure the people you are meeting with are the same ones who will be handling your business. At many accounting firms, some partners handle sales and new business, then pass the actual account work on to others.

    When evaluating competency and compatibility, ask candidates how they would handle situations relevant to you. For example: How would you handle a change in corporation status from S to C? How would you handle an IRS office audit seeking verification of automobile expenses? Listen to the answers and decide if that's how you would like your affairs to be handled.

    Realize, too, that having an accountant who takes a different approach can be a good thing. "If you are superconservative, it's not a bad thing to have an accountant who exposes you to the aggressive side of life," Lifson says. "Likewise, if you are aggressive, it's often helpful to have someone who can show you the conservative approach." Be sure, however, that the accountant won't pressure you into doing things you aren't comfortable with. It's your money, and you need to be able to sleep at night.

3. **Fees:** Ask about fees upfront. Most accounting firms charge by the hour; fees range widely, from as low as $75 per hour to as much as $275. However, there are some accountants who work on a monthly retainer. Figure out what services you are likely to need and which option will be more cost-effective for you.

   Get a range of quotes from different accountants. Also try to get an estimate of the total annual charges based on the services you've discussed. Don't base your decision solely on cost, however: An accountant who charges more by the hour is likely to be more experienced and thus able to work faster than a novice who charges less.

At the end of the interview, ask for references—particularly from clients in the same industry as you. A good accountant should be happy to provide you with referrals; call them and ask how satisfied they were with the accountant's fees, services and availability.

Good Relations

After you've made your choice, spell out the terms of the agreement in an engagement letter that details the returns and statements to be prepared and the fees to be charged. This ensures you and your accountant have the same expectations and helps prevent misunderstandings and hard feelings.

Make the most of the accounting relationship by doing your part. Don't hand your accountant a shoebox full of jumbled receipts at the end of the year. Write down details of all the checks in your check register—whether they are for utilities, supplies and so on. Likewise, identify sources of income on your bank deposit slips. The better you maintain your records, the less time your accountant has to spend on your business—and the lower your fees will be.

It's a good idea to meet with your accountant every month. Review financial statements and go over any problem areas so you know exactly where your money is going. This is where your accountant should go beyond number-crunching to suggest alternative ways of cutting costs and act as a sounding board for any ideas or questions you have about your finances.

A good accountant can help your business in ways you never dreamed possible. Spending the time to find the right accountant—and taking advantage of the advice he or she has to offer—is one of the best things you can do to help your business soar.

GLOSSARY

Alternative dispute resolution (ADR): a way of resolving disputes without resorting to litigation

Binding arbitration: form of ADR in which the arbitrator's decision is legally binding

CPA (certified public accountant): accountant who has passed a nationally standardized exam in accounting; additional qualifications may be required in some states

Commissioned financial planner: Financial planner who receives commission on products he or she sells to clients

Engagement letter: letter of agreement between a lawyer or accountant and his/her client that spells out the terms of the agreement, such as services to be rendered and billing structure

Fee-for-service planner: financial planner who charges a fee for making recommendations about what you should do to achieve your financial goals

Nonbinding arbitration: form of ADR in which the arbitrator makes a recommendation that parties can accept or reject

Prepaid legal plan: payment structure in which a client pays a prepaid legal service a set monthly fee in return for a fixed amount of legal services per month (differs from monthly retainer in that legal services are typically more limited and relationship is not with one individual law firm, but with a prepaid legal service firm, which has relationships with many different law firms)

Part Three:

Where's The Money?

CHAPTER 13

CHARITY BEGINS AT HOME

Financing starts with yourself and friends and relatives

O nce you've decided on the type of business you want to start, the next step is figuring out where that money will come from to fund it. Where to start?

Begin by looking in the mirror. Self-financing is the number-one form of financing used by most small-business owners. In addition, when you approach other financing sources such as bankers or venture capitalists, they will want to know exactly how much of your own money you are putting into the venture. After all, if you don't have enough faith in your business to risk your own money, why should anyone else risk theirs?

DO IT YOURSELF

Begin by doing a thorough inventory of your assets. You're likely to uncover resources you didn't even know you had. Assets could include savings accounts, equity in real estate, retirement accounts, vehicles, recreational equipment and collections. You may decide to sell some assets for cash or to use them as collateral for a loan.

If you have investments, you may be able to use them as a resource. Low-interest margin loans against stocks and securities can be arranged through your brokerage accounts.

"The downside here is that if the market should fall and your securities are your loan collateral, you'll get a margin call from your broker requesting you to supply more collateral," says Vickie Hampton, a certified financial planner in Austin, Texas. "If you can't do that within a certain time, you'll be asked to sell some of your securities to shore up the collateral."

Also take a look at your personal line of credit. Some businesses have successfully been started on credit cards, although this is one of the most

GOOD BENEFITS

If you have been laid off or lost your job, another source of start-up capital may be available to you. Some states have instituted self-employment programs as part of their unemployment insurance systems.

People who are receiving unemployment benefits and meet certain requirements are recruited into entrepreneurial training programs that show them how to start businesses. This gives them an opportunity to use their unemployment funds for start-up, while boosting their chances of success.

Contact the department in your state that handles unemployment benefits to see if such a program is available to you.

expensive ways to finance yourself (see Part 3 Chapter 15 for more on credit card financing).

If you own a home, consider getting a home-equity loan on the part of the mortgage that you have already paid off. The bank will either provide a lump-sum loan payment or extend a line of credit based on the equity in your home. "Depending on the value of your home, a home-equity loan could become a substantial line of credit," Hampton says. "If you have $50,000 in equity, you could possibly set up a line of credit of up to $40,000."

A home-equity loan has many positive aspects as a potential cash source, Hampton says. Home-equity loans carry relatively low interest rates, and all interest paid on a loan of up to $100,000 is tax-deductible. But be sure you can repay the loan—you can lose your home if you don't.

Consider borrowing against cash-value life insurance. Hampton says you can use the value built up in a cash-value life-insurance policy as a ready source of cash. The interest rates are reasonable because the insurance companies always get their money back. You don't even have to make payments if you don't want to. Neither the amount you borrow nor the interest that accrues has to be repaid. "The only loss is that if you die and the debt hasn't been repaid," Hampton explains, "that money is deducted from the amount your beneficiary will receive."

If you have a 401(k) retirement plan through your employer and are starting a part-time business while you keep your full-time job, consider borrowing against the plan. "It's very common for such plans to allow you to borrow a percentage of your money that doesn't exceed $50,000," says Hampton. "The interest rate is usually about 6 percent with a specified re-

Personal Balance Sheet

ASSETS		TOTALS
Cash and Checking		
Savings Accounts		
Real Estate/Home		
Automobiles		
Bonds		
Securities		
Insurance Cash Values		
Other		
Total Assets	**A**	

LIABILITIES		TOTALS
Current Monthly Bills		
Credit Card/Charge Account Bills		
Mortgage		
Auto Loans		
Finance Company Loans		
Personal Debts		
Other		
Total Liabilities	**B**	
Net Worth (A-B=C)	**C**	

DEGREE OF INDEBTEDNESS

Note:
If total liabilities exceed total assets, subtract assets from liabilities to determine degree of indebtedness

(B-A=D)

Total Liabilities	**B**	
Total Assets	**A**	
Degree of Indebtedness	**D**	

By filling out a personal balance sheet, you will be able to determine your net worth. Finding out your net worth is an important early step in the process of becoming a business owner because you need to find out what assets are available to you for investment in your business.

payment schedule. The downside of borrowing from your 401(k) is that if you lose your job, the loan has to be repaid in a short period of time—often 30 days." Consult the plan's documentation to see if this is an option.

Another option is to use the funds in your individual retirement account (IRA). Within the laws governing IRAs, you can actually withdraw money from an IRA as long as you replace it within 60 days. "This is not a loan, so you don't pay interest," Hampton says. "This is a withdrawal that you're allowed to keep for 60 days." She says it would be possible for a highly organized entrepreneur to juggle funds among several IRAs. "But if you're one day late—for any reason—you'll be hit with a 10 percent premature-withdrawal fee, and the money you haven't returned becomes taxable."

If you are employed, another way to finance your business is by squirreling away money from your current salary until you have enough to launch the business. If you don't want to wait, consider moonlighting or cutting your full-time job back to part time. This ensures you'll have some steady funds rolling in until your business starts to soar.

One final method may be to apply for a grant. "As cushy as they sound, grants are the hardest kind of money to get," says Alona Sussman, a certified financial planner in Chicago. "They're highly competitive, and you have to answer many questions to prove the validity of your business. Also, the application process is long."

People generally have more assets than they realize. Use as much of your own money as possible to get started; remember, the larger your own investment, the easier it will be for you to acquire capital from other sources.

FRIENDS AND FAMILY

Your own resources may not be enough to give you the capital you need. "Most businesses are started with money from four or five different sources," says Mike McKeever, author of *How to Write a Business Plan* (Nolo Press). After self-financing, the second most popular source for business start-up money is comprised of friends, relatives and business associates.

"Family and friends are great sources of financing," says Tonia Papke, owner of small-business consulting firm Management Development International. "These people know you have integrity

Dollar Stretcher

You don't necessarily need a lawyer to write your loan agreement. You can find examples of loan agreements in many business books; just write up the same information, complete it and sign it. If you do decide to get legal advice, you can save money by drawing up the loan agreement yourself and then giving it to an attorney to redraft.

and will grant you a loan based on the strength of your character."

It makes sense. People with whom you have close relationships know you're reliable and competent, so there should be no problem in asking for a loan, right?

Keep in mind, however, that asking for financial help isn't quite the same as borrowing the family car. While squeezing money out of family and friends may seem an easy alternative to dealing with uptight bankers, it can actually be a much more delicate situation. Papke warns that your family members or friends may think lending you money gives them license to meddle. "And if the business fails," she says, "the issue of paying the money back can be a problem, putting the whole relationship in jeopardy."

Beware!

Watch out for the relative or friend who agrees to lend you money even though he or she can't really afford to. "There will always be people who want to do anything they can to help you, who will give you funds that are critical to their future just because you ask for it," says Mike McKeever, author of *How to Write a Business Plan* (Nolo Press). "These relatives will not tell you they really can't afford it, so you must be extra perceptive."

The bottom line, says McKeever, is that "whenever you put money into a relationship that involves either friendship or love, it gets very complicated." Fortunately, there are ways to work out the details and make the business relationship advantageous for all parties involved. If you handle the situation correctly and tactfully, you may gain more than finances for your business— you may end up strengthening the personal relationship as well.

The Right Source

The first step in getting financing from friends or family is finding the right person to borrow money from. As you search for potential lenders or investors, don't enlist people with ulterior motives. "It's not a good idea to take money from a person if it's given with emotional strings," says McKeever. "For example, avoid borrowing from relatives or friends who have the attitude of 'I'll give you the money, but I want you to pay extra attention to me.' "

Once you determine whom you'd like to borrow money from, approach the person initially in an informal situation. Simply let the person know a little about your business and gauge his or her interest.

If the person seems interested and says he or she would like more information about the business, make an appointment to meet with them in a professional atmosphere. "This makes it clear that the subject of discussion will be your business and their interest in it," says McKeever. "You may secure their initial interest in a casual setting, but to go beyond that, you have to make an extra effort. You should do a formal sales presentation, and make sure the person has all the facts."

A large part of informing this person is compiling a business plan, which you should bring to your meeting. Explain the plan in detail and do the presentation just as you would in front of a banker or other investor. Your goal is to get the other person on your side and make him or her as excited as you are about the possibilities of your business.

During your meeting—and, in fact, whenever you discuss a loan—try to separate the personal from the business as much as possible. Difficult as this may sound, it's critical to the health of your relationship. "It's important to treat the lender formally, explaining your business plan in detail rather than casually passing it off with an 'if you love me, you'll give me the money' attitude," says McKeever.

Be prepared to accept rejection gracefully. "Don't pile on the emotional pressure—emphasize that you'd like this to be strictly a business decision for them," says McKeever. "If relatives or friends feel they can turn you down without offending you, they're more likely to invest. Give them an out."

Putting It On Paper

Now it's time to put the loan in motion. First, you must state exactly how much money you need, what you'll use it for and how you'll pay it back. Next, draw up the legal papers—an agreement stating that the person will indeed put money into the business.

Too frequently, small-business owners fail to take the time to figure out exactly what kind of paperwork should be completed when they borrow from family or friends. "Often small-business owners put more thought into figuring out what type of car to buy than how to structure this type of lending arrangement," says Steven I. Levey of the accounting firm Gelfond, Hochstadt, Pangburn & Co. Unfortunately, once you've made an error in this area, it's difficult to correct it.

Your loan agreement needs to specify whether the loan is secured (that is, the lender holds title to part of your property) or unsecured, what the payments will be, when they're due and what the

> **Bright Idea**
>
> While not many grants are available to start-ups, community development grants are worth a look. If you believe your future business could contribute to community development or empower a group of economically disadvantaged people, visit your state economic development office to find out what types of grants may be available.

START-UP COSTS WORK SHEETS

The following two work sheets will help you to compute your initial cash require-ments for your business. They list the things you need to consider when deter-mining your start-up costs and include both the one-time initial costs needed to open your doors and the ongoing costs you'll face each month for the first 90 days.

Start-up Capital Requirements

One-time Start-up Expenses

Start-up Expenses	Amount	Description
Advertising		Promotion for opening the business
Starting inventory		The amount of inventory required to open
Building construction		The amount per contractor bid and other costs
Cash		Amount needed for the cash register
Decorating		Estimate based on bid if appropriate
Deposits		Check with utility companies
Fixtures and equipment		Use actual bids
Insurance		Bid from insurance agent
Lease payments		Fee to be paid before opening
Licenses and permits		Check with city or state offices
Miscellaneous		All other costs
Professional fees		Include CPA, attorney, etc.
Remodeling		Use contractor bids
Rent		Fee to be paid before opening
Services		Cleaning, accounting, etc.
Signs		Use contractor bids
Supplies		Office, cleaning, supplies, etc.
Unanticipated expenses		Include an amount for the unexpected
Other		
Other		
Other		
Total Start-up Costs		**Total amount of costs before opening**

Start-up Capital Requirements

Repeating Monthly Expenses*

Expenses	Amount	Description
Advertising		
Bank service fees		
Credit card charges		
Delivery fees		
Dues and subscriptions		
Health insurance		Exclude the amount shown on preceding page
Insurance		Exclude the amount shown on preceding page
Interest		
Inventory		See **, below
Lease payments		Exclude the amount shown on preceding page
Loan payments		Principal and interest payments
Miscellaneous		
Office expenses		
Payroll other than owner		
Payroll taxes		
Professional fees		
Rent		Exclude the amount shown on preceding page
Repairs and maintenance		
Sales tax		
Supplies		
Telephone		
Utilities		
Your salary		Only if applicable during the first three months
Other		
Total Repeating Costs		
Total Start-up Costs (*from preceding page*)		
Total Cash Needed		

* Include the first three months' cash needs unless otherwise noted.
** Include the amount required for inventory expansion. If inventory is to be replaced from cash sales, do not include here. Assume that sales will generate enough cash for the replacements.

interest is. If the money is in the form of an investment, you have to establish whether the business is a partnership or corporation and exactly what role, if any, the investor will play in the business. To be sure you and your family and friends have a clear idea of what financial obligations are being created, you have a mutual responsibility to make sure everyone is informed about each step of the process and decide *together* how best to proceed.

Most important, says McKeever, "outline the legal responsibilities of both parties and when and how the money should be paid back." If your loan agreement is complex, it's a good idea to consult your accountant about the best ways to structure the loan (see "Taxing Matters," below).

Whichever route you take, make sure the agreement is in writing if you expect the agreement to be binding. "Any time you take money into a business, the law is very explicit: You must have all agreements written down and documented," says McKeever. If you don't, emotional and legal difficulties could result in squabbles that end up in court. And if the loan isn't documented, you may find yourself with no legal recourse.

Taxing Matters

Putting the agreement on paper also protects both you and your lender come tax time. Relying on informal and verbal agreements is when tax quagmires arise. "In these cases, you have a burden of proof to show the IRS that [the money] was not a gift," says Tom Ochsenschlager, a partner with the accounting firm Grant Thornton LLP. If the IRS views it as a gift, then the lender becomes subject to the federal gift tax rules and will have to pay taxes on the money if it is more than $10,000. Also make sure the person providing the money charges an interest rate that reflects a fair market value.

If your friend or family member wants to give you a no-interest loan, make sure the loan is not more than $100,000. If you borrow more, the IRS will slap on what it considers to be market-rate interest, better known as "imputed interest." That means that while your friend or relative may not be receiving any interest on the money you borrowed, the IRS will tax them as if they were.

Imputed interest also kicks in if the loan is for more than $10,000 when the business owner has more than $1,000 in annual net investment income, such as interest, dividends and, in some cases, capital gains. To determine the interest rate on these transactions, the IRS uses what it calls the applicable federal rate, which it sets on a regular basis.

Keep in mind that if you don't put all the details of the loan in writing, it will be very difficult for you to deduct the interest you pay on it. Additionally, the relative who lent the money won't be able to take a tax deduction on the loss if you find you can't repay the loan.

Monthly Budget

Before you begin planning for the cash needs of your business, you must figure out how much money you will need to live on for the first six to 12 months of your business's operation. The best way to accomplish this is to create a budget that shows where you spent your money in the last 12 months. Make sure you look over the whole 12-month period because expenses often change a lot from month to month. When creating the schedule, be on the lookout for expenses that could be reduced or eliminated if necessary. Use the following form to create your own budget.

	JAN	FEB	MAR	APR	MAY	JUN	JUL	AUG	SEP	OCT	NOV	DEC	TOTAL
Income:													
Wages (take-home)—partner 1													
Wages (take-home)—partner 2													
Interest and dividends													
Other													
Total Income													
Expenses:													
Auto expenses													
Auto insurance													
Auto payment													
Beauty shop and barber													
Cable TV													
Charity													
Child Care													
Clothing													
Credit card payments													

Monthly Budget, cont'd.

	JAN	FEB	MAR	APR	MAY	JUN	JUL	AUG	SEP	OCT	NOV	DEC	TOTAL
Dues and subscriptions													
Entertainment and recreation													
Gifts													
Groceries and dining out													
Health insurance													
Home repairs													
Household													
Income tax (additional)													
Laundry and dry cleaning													
Life insurance													
Medical and dental													
Mortgage payment or rent													
Other debt payments													
Telephone bill													
Tuition													
Utilities													
Vacations													
Other													
Total Expenses													
Cash (Shortfall) Extra													

To play it really safe, Ochsenschlager recommends that you make the friend or relative who is providing the money one of the business' shareholders. This effectively makes the transaction an investment in your company and also makes it easier from a tax standpoint for your friend or relative to write off the transaction as an ordinary loss if the business fails. (This applies only if the total amount your company received for its stock, including the relative's investment, does not exceed $1 million.)

In addition, "if your company is wildly successful, your relative will have an equity interest in the business, and his or her original investment will be worth quite a bit more," Ochsenschlager points out. In contrast, if your relative simply gives you a loan and your company goes under, the relative's loss would generally be considered a personal bad debt. This creates more of a tax disadvantage because personal bad debts can be claimed as capital losses only to offset capital gains. If the capital loss exceeds the capital gains, only $3,000 of the loss can be used against ordinary income in any given year. Thus, an individual making a large loan that isn't repaid may have to wait several years to realize the tax benefits from the loss.

If the loan that can't be repaid is a business loan, however, the lender receives a deduction against ordinary income and can begin taking deductions even before the loan becomes totally worthless. (One catch: The IRS takes a very narrow view of what qualifies as a business loan. Generally, to qualify as a business loan, the loan would have to be connected to the lender's business.) Because this can be tricky, consult your accountant about the best way to structure the loan for maximum tax benefits to both parties.

Making your relative a shareholder doesn't mean you'll have to put up with Mom or Pop in the business. Depending on your company's organizational structure, your friend or relative can be a silent partner if your company is set up as a partnership, or a silent shareholder if you are organized as an S corporation or limited liability company.

Keep 'Em Happy

Even with every detail documented, your responsibilities are far from over. Don't make assumptions or take anyone for granted just because they're friends or family members. Communication is key.

If your relative or friend is not actively involved in the business, make sure you contact them once every month or two to explain how the business is going. "When people invest in small businesses, it often becomes sort of their pet project," says McKeever. "It's important to take the time to keep them informed."

And, of course, there are the payments. Though friends or relatives who invest in your business understand the risks, you must never take the loan for granted. "Don't be cavalier about paying the money back," McKeever says. "That kind of attitude could ruin the relationship."

CHAPTER 14

NOTHING VENTURED, NOTHING GAINED

How to find and attract investors

No matter what type of financing source you approach—a bank, a venture capitalist or your cousin Lenny—there are two basic ways to finance a business: debt financing or equity financing. In debt financing, you receive capital in the form of a loan which must be paid back. In equity financing, you receive capital in exchange for part ownership of the company. This chapter explains various types of equity financing; the following chapter explains debt financing.

EQUITY BASICS

Equity financing can come from various sources, including venture capital firms and private investors. Whichever source you choose, there are some basics you should understand before you try to get equity capital.

An investor's share in your company comes in various forms. If your company is incorporated, the investor might bargain for shares of stock. Or an investor who wants to be involved in the management of the company could come in as a partner.

Keeping control of your company can be more difficult when you're working with outside investors who provide equity financing. Before seeking outside investment, make the most of your own resources to build the company. "The more value you can add before you go to the well, the better," says John R. Thorne, a professor of entrepreneurship. If all you bring to the table is a good idea and some talent, an investor may not be willing to provide a large chunk of capital without receiving a controlling share of the ownership in return. As a result, you could end up losing control of the business you started. "The more of your own money you can put in," Thorne says, "the more likely you are to exercise control."

Don't assume the first investor to express interest in your business is a godsend. Even someone who seems to share your vision for the company may be bad news. "It pays to know your investor," Thorne says. An investor who doesn't understand your business may pull the plug at the wrong time—and destroy the company.

How It Works

Because equity financing involves trading partial ownership interest for capital, the more capital a company takes in from equity investors, the more diluted the founder's control. "The question is how much management you're willing to give up," says Jerry Friedland, an attorney with Galanas, Friedland & Pollack.

Friedland emphasizes the importance of voting control in the company. Investors may be willing to accept a majority of the *preferred* (nonvoting) stock rather than *common* (voting) stock. Another possibility is to give the investor a majority of the profits by granting dividends to the preferred stockholders first. Or, holders of nonvoting stock can get liquidation preference, meaning they're first in line to recover their investment if the company goes under.

Even if they're willing to accept a minority position, financiers generally insist on contract provisions that permit them to make management changes under certain conditions. These might include covenants permitting the investor to take control of the company if the corporation fails to meet a certain income level or makes changes without the investor's permission.

Investors may ask that their preferred stock be redeemable either for common stock or for cash at a specified multiple several years later. That gives the entrepreneur a chance to buy the company back if possible but also may allow the investor to convert to common stock and gain control of the company.

Some experts contend that retaining voting control is not as important as commonly believed. In a typical high-growth company, the founder only

Smart Tip

Make sure you ask any venture capitalist you are considering these five questions:

1. How do you plan to participate in my company?

2. What can you contribute to the success of my company?

3. How do you view the board of directors' role and management's role?

4. Can you tell me about other venture capitalists with whom you have discussed my company?

5. Do you or any of the other venture capitalists have any investment in our competitors?

owns 10 percent of the business by the time it goes public. That's not necessarily bad because 10 percent of $100 million is better than 100 percent of nothing. The key is how valuable the founder is to the success of the company. If you can't easily be replaced, you've got a lot of leverage even though you may not control the business.

Beware!

Remember, the ultimate goal of most venture capitalists is to take your company public. If that doesn't interest you, consider other sources of financing.

"If the entrepreneur is good enough, the investors may find their best alternative is to let the entrepreneur run the company," says Thorne. He advises against getting hung up on the precise percentage of ownership: "If it's a successful business, most people will leave you alone even if they own 80 percent." To protect yourself, however, you should always seek financial and legal advice before involving outside investors in your business.

Venture Capital

When most people think of equity financing, they think of venture capital. Once seen as a renegade source of financing for start-up businesses, venture capital—like most kinds of capital—is no longer so easy to come by. Still, it *can* be obtained—even if your business isn't yet off the ground.

Venture capital investing gained momentum in the late '70s and early '80s, fueled by emerging high-potential technology companies. Billions of dollars were invested in software, silicon chips, circuit boards, graphics accelerators and biotechnology instruments. But by the late '80s, economic stagnation and high losses caused smaller venture capital firms to either retrench or consolidate with other firms.

Though venture capital investment has rebounded, the face of the industry has changed. According to Steven Galante, publisher of the financial newsletter *Private Equity Analyst*, "The venture capital industry has matured."

Expecting Returns

Today, there are fewer venture capital firms, but they have much larger investment pools. Many are institutional investors; they manage a fund consisting of money from pension funds and other sources, and have to answer to their clients regarding the investments they make. As the amount of money in the fund climbs, the venture capital company's minimum investment rises correspondingly. According to investment research firm VentureOne, the average amount of capital raised for a company in its product development phase is $4 million.

KNOW YOUR STUFF

Just as you wouldn't start a business without planning, you shouldn't approach a venture capitalist without preparation. Before meeting with investors, be sure you can answer these questions:

1. Why did you start your company?
2. Where do you see your company going?
3. What problems do you see your company encountering?
4. What do you see as the company's main markets?
5. How do you plan to capitalize on those markets?
6. Who is your competition?
7. How do you plan to handle your competition?
8. What have you invested in the company?
9. How did you arrive at your financial projections?
10. When do you expect to meet the projections?
11. What type of financial controls do you have to prevent disorganization or embezzling and to handle accounts receivable and payable?
12. Who does your accounting?
13. Who does your marketing and advertising?
14. What is your company's short- and long-term business plan? Where do you see the company going in five years? In 10 years?
15. What are your criteria for site selection?
16. Who is your customer?
17. How many employees do you have? What do they do?
18. What additional personnel will need to be hired and when?
19. What is your overhead?
20. Do you have long-term contracts with suppliers?
21. How does the company plan to use the funds from our firm?
22. When do you think your company will next need financing?
23. How does your company's system differ from your competitors'?
24. Who is in charge of research and development?
25. How is research and development conducted?
26. What is the seasonability of the company's business?
27. What type of growth have you seen in your industry?

Fortunately, there are also venture capital firms that specialize in funding start-ups. These are more likely to invest smaller amounts—less than $1 million, and sometimes less than $500,000. Although these "seed money" venture capitalists have gotten harder to find, they still exist. The key to finding them is to look harder—and not to waste time trying to get money from firms that aren't interested in start-up companies.

Lower interest rates are prompting private investors to look for alternative, albeit riskier, ways to achieve better returns on their investment dollar. The downside, of course, is that start-up investors require more equity to compensate for their higher risk. The equity varies in proportion to the investment and amount of risk, but generally ranges from 20 percent to 80 percent. To ensure the company achieves the desired growth, the venture capital firm may send in its own management team.

Since venture capitalists make (or lose) money depending on how fast and how big the company grows, they invest in companies they feel have the best potential to make a large return. "We try to make five times the amount we invest," says Pat Hopf, managing general partner of St. Paul Venture Capital Inc. Venture capitalists will also expect to see results in three to five years.

Where The Money Is

While high-tech is still the most prevalent industry in which venture capital companies invest their dollars, nearly any kind of business has the potential to receive venture capital. In fact, according to The Entrepreneurial Advisory Service of Coopers & Lybrand LLP, a growing number of venture capital firms are going after low-tech or no-tech businesses.

The key is finding a venture capital firm that matches your business. A venture capital firm with partners experienced in real estate and commercial development, for example, will likely invest in companies involved in home building or property management. Some venture capital firms have more than one target industry or accept inquiries and proposals from all industries.

A close match between your business and the venture capital firm makes sense for both camps. A knowledge of the industry enables the venture capitalist to lessen risk by making smart decisions; it also assures you that the management team

Beware!

Looking for an investor through classified ads? Be aware there are legal implications when you solicit money through the newspaper. Always get legal advice before placing an ad.

WHERE TO GO

Finding a venture capital firm in your area isn't as easy as going to the neighborhood bank. Here are some resources to help:

◆ *National Venture Capital Association,* 1655 N. Ft. Meyer Dr., #850, Arlington, VA 22209, (703) 524-2549. Provides member directory listing names, addresses, phone and fax numbers, and contacts. Costs for services vary.

◆ *The International Venture Capital Institute,* P.O. Box 1333, Stamford, CT 06904, (203) 323-3143. A liaison of venture networking organizations and small businesses worldwide, providing a forum for entrepreneurs and investors to meet. Call for information about directory.

◆ *Small Business Investment Companies,* c/o Associate Administrator for Investment, U.S. Small Business Administration, 409 Third St. SW, Washington, DC 20416, (202) 205-7589. Provides a free directory of firms licensed by the SBA to supply equity/venture capital to qualifying businesses.

◆ *The National Association of Investment Companies,* 1111 14th St. NW, #700, Washington, DC 20005, (202) 289-4336. Member companies invest in businesses with socially or economically disadvantaged owners. Offers member directory.

◆ *Pratt's Guide to Venture Capital Sources,* SDC Publishing, 40 W. 57th St., #802, New York, NY 10019, (212) 765-5311. Annual reference guide lists hundreds of venture capital firms by state and alphabetically by company. Also includes foreign listing and index by industry preferences.

◆ *Technology Capital Network,* Massachusetts Institute of Technology, 201 Vassar St., Bldg. W59, Cambridge, MA 02139, (617) 253-7163. Maintains database of investors and entrepreneurs seeking capital. Makes matches according to industry, amount of capital needed and other factors.

assuming partial control of your company brings valuable experience and ideas to the table. (For sources of venture capital, see "Where To Go" in this chapter.)

For some new entrepreneurs, a good management team is more valuable than money. An entrepreneur often lacks the experience, contacts or manpower to help the company succeed.

If you already have a solid management team in place, look for a venture capital firm willing to act primarily as an advisory board and a backup in case of problems. Find out just how much hands-on management you'll be able to keep. Check references from other companies that have worked with the venture capital firm; ask them how the board of directors and management work together.

What They Want

What does a venture capital firm look for in a company? Opinions vary, and much depends on the type of investments the firm makes. For example, a firm specializing in financing start-ups generally makes high-risk investments in companies with little more than a good idea. Second-stage financing happens when management is in place; at this stage, a firm will look closely at the team's experience and qualifications. Third-stage financing involves the least risk of all: The entrepreneurial company is well-established, has tested its product extensively in the marketplace and is ready for mass distribution. Companies at this stage command a higher dollar value for an equity stake.

Whatever stage you're in, venture capitalists look for an idea that is well formulated, documented and protected. Patents, contracts with suppliers, and exclusive distribution territories all indicate an assured market presence and at least a limited period of product uniqueness. Your business plan should be serious and to the point. Good research and compelling arguments will win venture capitalists over; being cute, with colored graphs and fancy folders, won't.

"Do you have a concept that applies to a large market share? Will it be hard for competitors to reproduce? How far ahead of the marketplace is the product?" asks Sidney Andrews, a partner with accounting firm Coopers & Lybrand. These are all factors to consider before seeking venture capital. (For other things venture capitalists will want to know, see "Know Your Stuff" in this chapter.)

While getting financing from a venture capital firm can be done, it's not easy—especially for a start-up. To see whether your business is among the small minority of firms that professional venture capitalists will finance, run it through the following tests suggested by John Martinson, managing partner of Edison Venture Fund:

1. Are you capable of being a market leader? "We rarely finance a company that is going up against a market leader with a similar product," says Martinson.

2. Can the company be built inexpensively? "Venture capitalists like to build companies on the cheap to limit downside risk," says Martinson.

3. Is there a clear distribution channel? Many entrepreneurs come up with great products, but there's no clear or easy way to sell them, says Martinson. Venture capitalists also want a distribution channel that can be accessed fairly inexpensively.

4. Does the product require significant support? Complex products or services—say, a home security system—require customer support organizations that are expensive and difficult to establish and maintain. This is less appealing to venture capitalists because of the higher costs.

5. Can the product or service generate gross margins of more than 50 percent?

6. Can the company grow to $25 million in five years? "If there's no possibility you're going to hit the $25 million mark in five years," Martinson says, "it's simply a waste of time to pursue institutional venture capital."

    The key word here is "institutional." The vast majority of venture capital comes from individual investors, not professional venture capitalists. For more on those investors, keep reading.

Earth Angels

The unpleasant reality is that getting financing from venture capital firms is a long shot. The pleasant reality is that there are plenty of other sources you can tap for equity financing—typically with far fewer strings attached than an institutional venture capital deal. One source of private capital is an investment angel.

Originally a term used to describe investors in Broadway shows, "angel" now refers to anyone who invests his or her own money in an entrepreneurial company (unlike institutional venture capitalists, who invest other people's money). Angel investing has soared in recent years as a growing number of individuals seek better returns on their money than they can get from traditional investment vehicles.

Contrary to popular belief, most angels are not millionaires. Typically, they earn between $60,000 and $100,000 a year. This means there are likely to be plenty of them right in your own backyard.

Where Angels Fly

Angels can be classified into two groups: affiliated and nonaffiliated. An affiliated angel is someone who has some sort of contact with you or your business but is not necessarily related to or acquainted with you. A non-affiliated angel has no connection with either you or your business.

It makes sense to start your investor search by seeking an affiliated angel since he or she is already familiar with you or your business and has a vested interest in the relationship. Begin by jotting down names of people who might fit the category of affiliated angel.

◆ **Professionals:** These include professional providers of services you now use—doctors, dentists, lawyers, accountants and so on. You know these people, so an appointment should be easy to arrange. Professionals usually have discretionary income available to invest in outside projects, and if they're not interested, they may be able to recommend a colleague who is.

NETTING ANGELS

Looking for angels? Now there's a simple way for them to find you—online. The Angel Capital Electronic Network (ACE:Net), launched by the Small Business Administration, helps accredited angel investors find entrepreneurs in need of capital.

Angels can access ACE:Net's online listings of entrepreneurial companies using a search engine that lets them find out a company's product or service, financing desired and other criteria. Angels can also place search criteria on the network and get e-mailed whenever a company meeting those criteria appears on the network.

Access is limited to accredited investors—those with a net income in excess of $200,000 and meet other criteria. Entrepreneurs must also meet certain criteria to be listed. For more information, visit www.sbaonline.sba.gov or http://acenet.unh.edu, or contact the SBA's Office of Advocacy at (202) 205-6533.

- **Business associates:** These are people you come in contact with during the normal course of your business day. They can be divided into four subgroups:

- **Suppliers/Vendors:** The owners of companies who supply your inventory and other needs have a vital interest in your company's success and make excellent angels. A supplier's investment may not come in the form of cash but in the form of better payment terms or cheaper prices. Suppliers might even use their credit to help you get a loan.

> **Smart Tip**
>
> Keep this in mind when crafting your pitch to investor angels: When angels reject a potential investment, it's typically because: 1) they don't know the key people well enough or 2) they don't believe the owner and management has the experience and talent to succeed.

- **Customers:** These are especially good contacts if they use your product or service to make or sell their own goods. List all the customers with whom you have this sort of business relationship.

- **Employees:** Some of your key employees might be sitting on unused equity in their homes that would make excellent collateral for a loan to your business. There is no greater incentive to an employee than to share ownership in the company for which he or she works.

- **Competitors:** These include owners of similar companies you don't directly compete with. If a competitor is doing business in another part of the country and does not infringe upon your territory, he or she may be an empathetic investor and may share not only capital but information as well.

The nonaffiliated angels category includes:

1. **Professionals:** This can include lawyers, accountants, consultants and brokers whom you don't know personally or do business with.

2. **Middle managers:** Angels in middle-management positions start investing in small businesses for two major reasons—either they're bored with their jobs and are looking for outside interests or they are nearing retirement or fear they're being phased out.

3. **Entrepreneurs**: These angels are (or have been) successful in their own businesses and like investing in other entrepreneurial ventures. Entrepreneurs who are familiar with your industry make excellent investors.

Make The Connection

Approaching affiliated angels is simply a matter of calling to make an appointment. To find nonaffiliated angels, try these methods:

1. **Advertising**: The business opportunity section of your local newspaper or *The Wall Street Journal* is an excellent place to advertise for investors. Classified advertising is inexpensive, simple, quick and effective.

2. **Business brokers**: Business brokers know hundreds of people with money who are interested in buying businesses. Even though you don't want to sell your business, you might be willing to sell part of it. Since many brokers are not open to the idea of their clients buying just part of a business, you might have to use some persuasion to get the broker to give you contact names. You'll find a list of local business brokers in the Yellow Pages under "Business Brokers."

3. **Telemarketing**: This approach has been called "dialing for dollars." First, you get a list of wealthy individuals in your area. Then, you begin calling. Obviously, you have to be highly motivated to try this approach, and a good list is your most important tool. Look up mailing list brokers in the Yellow Pages. If you don't feel comfortable making cold calls yourself, you can always hire someone to do it for you.

4. **Networking**: Attending local venture capital group meetings and other business associations to make contacts is a time-consuming approach but can be effective. Most newspapers contain an events calendar that lists when and where these types of meetings take place.

5. **Intermediaries**: These are firms that find angels for entrepreneurial companies. They

---

> ### Bright Idea
>
> One entrepreneur who wanted to open a restaurant got a list of potential investors by attending all the grand openings of restaurants in the area where he wanted to locate. By asking for the names of people who invested in those restaurants, he soon had enough contact names to finance his own business.

are usually called "boutique investment bankers." This means they are small firms that focus primarily on small financing deals. These firms typically charge a percentage of the amount of money they raise for you. Ask your lawyer or accountant for the name of a reputable firm in your area.

Angels tend to find most of their investment opportunities through their friends and business associates, so whatever method you use to search for angels, it's also important to spread the word. Tell your professional advisors, people you meet at networking events, or anyone who could be a good source of referrals that you are looking for investment capital. You never know who they might know.

Getting The Money

Once you've found potential angels, how do you win them over? Angels look for many of the same things professional venture capitalists look for:

◆ **Strong management:** Does your management team have a track record of success and experience?

◆ **Proprietary strength:** Proprietary doesn't necessarily mean you must have patents, copyrights or trademarks on all your products. It just means that your product or service should be unusual enough to grab consumers' attention.

◆ **Window of opportunity:** Investors look for a window of opportunity when your company can be the first in a market and grab the lion's share of business before imitators come along.

◆ **Market potential:** Investors prefer businesses with strong market potential. That means a restaurateur with plans to franchise stands a better chance than one who simply wants to open one local site.

◆ **Return on investment:** Most angels expect a return of 20 percent to 25 percent over five years. However, they may accept a lower rate of return if your business has a lower risk.

If angels consider the same factors as venture capital companies, what is the difference between them? You have an edge with angels because many are not motivated solely by profit. Particularly if your angel is a current or former entrepreneur, he or she may be motivated as much by the enjoyment of helping a young business succeed as by the money he or she stands to gain. Angels are more likely than venture capitalists to be persuaded by an entrepreneur's drive to succeed, persistence and mental discipline.

That's why it's important that your business plan convey a good sense of your background, experience and drive. Your business plan should also address the concerns above and spell out the financing you expect to need from start-up to maturity. What if your plan is rejected? Ask the angel if he or she knows someone else your business might appeal to.

If your plan is accepted, you've got some negotiating to do. Be sure to spell out all the terms of the investment in a written agreement; get your lawyer's assistance here. How long will the investment last? How will return be calculated? How will the investment be cashed out? Detail the amount of involvement each angel will have in the business, and how the investment will be legalized.

Examine the deal carefully for the possibility of the investor parlaying current equity or future loans to your business into controlling interest. Such a deal is not made in heaven and could indicate you are working with a devil in angel's garb.

GLOSSARY

Angel investor: describes a private individual who invests money in a business

Common stock: stock representing equity ownership in a company; it entitles holder to elect corporate directors and collect dividends

Debt financing: capital in the form of a loan, which must be paid back

Equity financing: capital received in exchange for part ownership of the company

Liquidation preference: stockholders with liquidation preference are first in line to recover their investment if the company goes under

Nonvoting stock: see preferred stock

Preferred stock: stock that pays a fixed dividend and is given preference ahead of common stockholders in the event of liquidation of assets

Venture capital: generally refers to institutional venture capital firms that invest other people's money and manage it for them; venture capitalists typically seek a high degree of involvement and expect a high rate of return in a short time

Voting stock: see common stock

CHAPTER 15

CAN YOU BANK ON IT?

The ins and outs of debt financing

Unlike equity financing, where you sell part of your business to an investor, debt financing simply means receiving money in the form of a loan, which you will have to repay. There are many sources you can turn to for debt financing, including banks, commercial lenders and even your personal credit cards.

TYPES OF LOANS

You don't need to pinpoint the exact type of loan you need before you approach a lender; he or she will help you decide what type of financing is best for your needs. However, you should have some general idea of the different types of loans available so you will understand what your lender is offering.

There are a mind-boggling variety of loans available, complicated by the fact that the same type of loan may have different terms at different banks. For instance, a commercial loan at one bank might be written with equal installments of principal and interest, while at another bank the loan is written with monthly interest payments and a balloon payment of the principal.

Here is a look at how lenders generally structure loans, with common variations.

◆ **Line-of-credit loans:** The most useful type of loan for the small business is the line-of-credit loan. In fact, it's probably the one permanent loan arrangement every business owner should have with his or her banker since it protects the business from emergencies and stalled cash flow. Line-of-credit loans are intended for purchases of inventory and payment of operating costs for working capital and business cycle needs. They are not intended for purchases of equipment or real estate.

A line-of-credit loan is a short-term loan that extends the cash available in your business's checking account to the upper limit of the loan contract. Every bank has its own method of funding, but, essentially, an amount is transferred to the business's checking account to cover checks. The business pays interest on the actual amount advanced, from the time it is advanced until it is paid back.

Line-of-credit loans usually carry the lowest interest rate a bank offers since they are seen as fairly low-risk. Some banks even include a clause that gives them the right to cancel the loan if they think your business is in jeopardy. Interest payments are made monthly, and the principal is paid off at your convenience. It is wise to make payments on the principal often. Bankers may also call this a *revolving line of credit*, and they see it as an indication that your business is earning enough income.

Most line-of-credit loans are written for periods of one year and may be renewed almost automatically for an annual fee. Some banks require that your credit line be fully paid off for between seven and 30 days each contract year. This period is probably the best time to negotiate.

Even if you don't need a line-of-credit loan now, talk to your banker about how to get one. To negotiate a credit line, your banker will want to see current financial statements, the latest tax returns and a projected cash flow statement.

◆ **Installment loans:** These loans are paid back with equal monthly payments covering both principal and interest. Installment loans may be written to meet all types of business needs. You receive the full amount when the contract is signed, and interest is calculated from that date to the final day of the loan. If you repay an installment loan before its final date, there will be no penalty and an appropriate adjustment of interest.

The term of an installment loan will always be correlated to its use. A business cycle loan

Smart Tip

Loan officers at your bank may also be a valuable resource in identifying state, local, and agency assistance to the new businessperson. They may have gone through the steps with other new businesses in your area.

may be written as a four-month installment loan from, say, September 1 until December 31, and would carry the lowest interest rate since the risk to the lender is from one to seven years. Real estate and renovation loans may be written up to 21 years. An installment loan is occasionally written with quarterly, half-yearly or annual payments when monthly payments are inappropriate.

◆ **Balloon loans:** Though these loans are usually written under another name, you can identify them by the fact that the full amount is received when the contract assigned, but only the interest is paid off during the life of the loan, with a "balloon" payment of the principal due on the final day.

Occasionally, a lender will offer a loan in which both interest and principal are paid with a single "balloon" payment. Balloon loans are usually reserved for situations when a business has to wait until a specific date before receiving payment from a client for its products or services. In all other ways, they are the same as installment loans.

◆ **Interim loans:** When considering interim loans, bankers are concerned with who will be paying off the loan and whether that commitment is reliable. Interim loans are used to make periodic payments to contractors building new facilities when a mortgage on the building will be used to pay off the interim loan.

◆ **Secured and unsecured loans:** Loans can come in one of two forms: secured or unsecured. When your lender knows you well and is convinced that your business is sound and that the loan will be repaid on time, he or she may be willing to write an unsecured loan. Such a loan, in any of the above forms, has no collateral pledged as a secondary payment source should you default on the loan. The lender provides you with an unsecured loan because it considers you a low risk. As a new business, you are highly unlikely to qualify for an unsecured loan; it generally requires a track record of profitability and success.

A secured loan, on the other hand, requires some kind of collateral but generally has a lower interest rate than an unsecured loan. When a loan is written for more than 12 months, is used to purchase equipment or does not seem risk-free, the lender will ask that the loan be secured by collateral. The collateral used, whether real estate or inventory, is expected to outlast the loan and is usually related to the purpose of the loan.

Since lenders expect to use the collateral to pay off the loan if the borrower defaults, they will value it appropriately. A $20,000 piece of new equipment will probably secure a loan of up to $15,000, receivables are usually valued for loans up to 75 percent of the amount due, and inventory is usually valued at up to 50 percent of its sale price.

◆ **Letter of credit:** Typically used in international trade, this document allows entrepreneurs to guarantee payment to suppliers in other countries. The document substitutes the bank's credit for the entrepreneur's up to a set amount for a specified period of time.

Bright Idea

The Foundation for International Community Assistance (FINCA) helps entrepreneurs form their own "income-generating groups." Through a loan from FINCA, these groups offer members access to a series of short-term loans that provide working capital for small businesses. Based in Washington, DC, the foundation has locations in several states; call (202) 682-1510 for more information.

◆ **Other loans:** Banks all over the country write loans, especially installment and balloon loans, under a myriad of names. They include:

◆ Term loans, both short and long term according to the number of years they are written for

◆ Second mortgages, where real estate is used to secure a loan; usually long term, they are also known as equity loans

◆ Inventory loans and equipment loans for the purchase of, and secured by, either inventory or equipment

◆ Accounts receivable loans secured by your outstanding accounts

◆ Personal loans in which your signature and personal collateral guarantee the loan, which you, in turn, lend to your business

◆ Guaranteed loans, in which a third party—an inventory, spouse, or even the Small Business Administration—guarantees repayment (for more on SBA-guaranteed loans, see the following chapter)

◆ Commercial loans, in which the bank offers its standard loan for small businesses

Once you have an understanding of the different types of loans available, you're better equipped for the next step: "selling" a lender on your business.

Bright Idea

If you are a woman or a member of a minority group looking to purchase a franchise, you may be eligible for special financial incentives or assistance from the franchisor. Ask franchisors you are considering whether they have such programs and what the requirements are.

Sources Of Financing

When seeking debt financing, where do you begin? Carefully choosing the lenders you target can increase your odds of success. Here is a look at various loan sources and what you should know about each.

Bank On It

Traditionally, the paperwork and processing costs involved in making and servicing loans have made the small loans most entrepreneurs seek too costly for big banks to administer. Put plainly, a loan under $25,000—the type many start-ups are looking for—may not be worth a big bank's time.

In recent years, however, the relationship between banks and small business has been improving as more and more banks realize the strength and importance of this growing market. With corporations and real estate developers no longer spurring so much of banks' business, lenders are looking to entrepreneurs to take up the slack.

Many major banks have added special services and programs for small business; others are streamlining their loan paperwork and approval process to get loans to entrepreneurs faster. On the plus side, banks are marketing to small business like never before. On the downside, however, the streamlining process often means that, more than ever, loan approval is based solely on numbers and scores on standardized rating systems rather than on an entrepreneur's character or drive.

Given the challenges of working with a big bank, many entrepreneurs are taking a different tack. Instead of wooing big commercial institutions, they're courting community banks, where relationship banking is the rule, not the exception.

Even given today's banking climate, it's easier to get a start-up loan from a community bank, according to the Independent Bankers Association of America. They can be a little more flexible, don't have a bureaucracy to deal with, and are more apt to make character loans.

Don't get the idea that obtaining a loan from a community bank is a snap, however. You'll still have to meet credit and collateral requirements just as you would at a larger institution. The difference: "We give more weight to personal attributes," says James R. Lauffer, CEO of The First Na-

READ THE FINE PRINT . . .

Hallelujah and yippee! You can almost hear the choirs of angels singing as your banker smiles and hands you the loan document. You got the loan!

Not so fast. Before you sign that piece of paper, take a good look at what you're getting into. Many entrepreneurs are so excited about having their loans approved, they fail to read the fine print on their loan agreements. That can lead to trouble later on.

It's a good idea to get the loan documents ahead of time so you have a chance to review them for a couple of days before you sign, according to the American Bankers Association. Bankers won't have a problem sending advance copies of the documents but will generally do so only if they're specifically asked.

Most bankers will be happy to help you understand the fine print, but it's also a good idea to have your accountant and lawyer review the documents, too.

Although it varies slightly from bank to bank, a small-business loan package usually consists of several documents, typically including a loan agreement, a promissory note and some form of guarantee and surety agreement.

1. *Loan agreement:* This specifies, in essence, the promises you are making to the bank and asks you to affirm that you are authorized to bind your business to the terms of the loan.

2. *Promissory note:* This details the principal and interest owed and when payments are due. It also outlines the events that would allow the bank to declare your loan in default. Knowing these events ahead of time can help you protect your credit record. Look for "cure" language in the default section. A cure provision allows you a certain amount of time (usually 10 days) to remedy the default after you've been notified by the bank. If such a provision isn't included, ask if it can be added to prevent you from defaulting accidentally (in case a payment is lost in the mail, for example). Also make sure you understand what the bank can and can't do after declaring default.

3. *Guarantee and surety agreement:* Because start-ups generally have insufficient operating history or assets on which to base a loan, banks usually require the loan to be guaranteed with your personal assets.

tional Bank of Herminie. "If the business is located in town, the banker already knows the entrepreneur, and the family has lived in the area for years, these things count more in a community bank."

Whether the bank you target is big or small, perhaps what matters most is developing relationships. If you've done your personal banking at the same place for 20 years and know people with authority there, it makes sense to target that bank as a potential lender. If you don't have that kind of relationship, start getting to know bankers now. Visit chamber of commerce meetings; go to networking events; take part in community functions that local bankers or other movers and shakers are part of. A banker with a personal interest in you is more likely to look favorably on your loan application.

Boost your chances of getting a loan by finding a lender whose experience matches your needs. Talk to friends, lawyers or accountants, and other entrepreneurs in the same industry for leads on banks that have

FRANCHISE FOCUS

Financing is any start-up entrepreneur's biggest challenge—and it's no different for franchisees. The good news is franchisors may offer a little extra help in getting the capital you need.

Some franchisors offer direct financing to help franchisees with all or part of the costs of start-up. This may take the form of equipment, real estate or inventory financing. The goal is to free up money so franchisees have more working capital.

Many franchisors are not directly involved in lending but have established preferred relationships with banks and commercial finance companies. Because these lenders have processed loans for other franchisees, they are more familiar with new franchisees' needs.

The franchisor you're interested in can tell you about any direct financing or preferred lender programs available. The Uniform Franchise Offering Circular should also include this information.

If your franchisor doesn't have a preferred lender, you can often find financing by approaching banks that have made loans to other franchisees in the system. Talk to franchisees and see how they financed their businesses.

Once you've found a lender to target, you'll need to provide the same information and follow the same steps as you would with any type of business loan.

helped others in your business. Pound the pavement and talk to banks about the type and size of loans they specialize in. Put in the work to find the right lender, and you'll find it pays off.

Commercial Finance Companies

Banks aren't your only option when seeking a loan. Nonbank commercial lenders, or commercial finance companies, have expanded their focus on small business in recent years as more and more small banks, which traditionally made loans to entrepreneurs, have been swallowed up in mergers. The advantage of approaching commercial finance companies is that, like community banks, they may be more willing to look beyond numbers and assets. "Commercial finance companies give opportunities to start-ups and a lot of other companies banks will not lend to," says Bruce A. Jones of the Commercial Finance Association (CFA). Here are some commercial finance companies to get you started:

> **Bright Idea**
>
> Looking for financing? Consider an unexpected source—your vendors. Vendors may be willing to give you the capital you need, either through a delayed financing agreement or a leasing program. Vendors have a vested interest in your success and belief in your stability, or they wouldn't be doing business with you. Before entering any agreement, however, compare long-term leasing costs with short-term loan costs; leasing could be more costly.

- Princeton, New Jersey-based Business Alliance Capital Corp., for instance, offers loans of $150,000 to $1.5 million to entrepreneurs in manufacturing, distribution and service industries who cannot get loans from traditional sources.

- AT&T Capital Corp. in Morristown, New Jersey, offers loans for working capital in conjunction with equipment financing, business acquisition, leasehold improvements and other such expenditures. It also offers SBA-guaranteed loans and will finance franchises from certain established franchisors.

- Princeton Capital Finance Co. in Princeton Junction, New Jersey, specializes in loans for firms with contracts from government agencies and major corporations. Loans are from $50,000 to $10 million, typically short term (45 to 60 days).

- Sacramento, California-based The Money Store will finance from $200,000 to $3 million. The Money Store has a policy of lending to start-ups and often requires smaller down payments than other lenders. Most loans close within 60 days or less; the company specializes in franchise financing.

◆ At Hartford, Connecticut-based Business Lenders, loan evaluators look beyond traditional lending criteria to consider management ability and character. "Somebody with bad credit could still be a good credit risk," says founder Penn Ritter. "It depends on why they had the credit problem."

Commercial lenders require a business plan, personal financial statements and cash flow projections, and will usually expect you to come up with 25 percent of the needed capital yourself. For more information about commercial finance companies, call the CFA at (212) 594-3490.

Give Yourself Credit

One potentially risky way to finance your business is to use your personal credit cards. The obvious drawback is the high interest rate; if you use the card for cash advances rather than to buy equipment, the rates are even higher.

Some entrepreneurs take advantage of low-interest credit card offers they receive in the mail, transferring balances from one card to another as soon as interest rates rise (typically after six months). If you use this strategy, keep a close eye on when the rate will increase. Sometimes you can get the bank to extend the low introductory rate over the phone.

Experts advise using credit card financing as a last resort because interest rates are higher than any other type of financing. However, if you are good at juggling payments, your start-up needs are low, and you are confident you'll be able to pay the money back fairly quickly, this could be the route to take.

APPLYING FOR A LOAN

Once you've chosen the lender(s) you wish to approach, the next step is applying for the loan. It's important to know what you will need to provide and what lenders are looking for.

The Loan Application

Think of your loan application as a sales tool, just like your brochures or ads. When you put together the right combination of facts and figures, your application will sell your lender on the short- and long-term profit potential of lending money to your business. To do that, the application must convince your lender that you will pay back the loan as promised and that your managerial ability (and future loans) will result in a profit-making partnership.

"Banks are in the money-lending business," says banker Jon P. Goodman. "To lend money, they need evidence of security and stability. It's that simple."

How can you provide this evidence when your business hasn't even gotten off the ground? Begin by making sure your loan application is both realistic and optimistic. If you predict an increase in sales of between 8 percent and 12 percent, base your income projections on an increase of 10 percent, and then specify what you intend to do to ensure the additional sales.

Also make sure your application is complete. When a piece of an application is missing, bankers instantly suspect that either something is being hidden or the applicant doesn't know his or her business well enough to pull the information together.

There are 12 separate items that should be included in every loan application. The importance of each one varies with the size of your business, your industry and the amount you are requesting.

Bright Idea

Buying a franchise? Many municipalities and states have financing programs that can underwrite the cost of a franchise. Be aware, however, that the focus of these programs is job creation. To find programs in your area, call the nearest Small Business Development Center or economic development program. It takes a bit of investigating to find the programs, but the results could be well worth the effort.

- ◆ Cover sheet
- ◆ Cover letter
- ◆ Table of contents
- ◆ Amount and use of the loan
- ◆ History and description of your business
- ◆ Functions and background of your management team
- ◆ Market information on your product or service
- ◆ Financial history and current status
- ◆ Financial projections to demonstrate that the loan will be repaid
- ◆ A list of possible collateral
- ◆ Personal financial statements
- ◆ Additional documents to support the projections

Many of these items are already part of your business plan; a few of them will have to be added. Here's a closer look at each section:

PERSONAL FINANCIAL STATEMENT

Statement of financial condition as of _____ , 19 _____

INDIVIDUAL INFORMATION	CO-APPLICANT INFORMATION
Name	Name
Home Address	Home Address
City, State & ZIP	City, State & ZIP
Name of Employer	Name of Employer
Title/Position	Title/Position
No. of Years with Employer	No. of Years with Employer
Employer Address	Employer Address
City, State & ZIP	City, State & Zip
Home Phone Business Phone	Home Phone Business Phone

SOURCE OF INCOME	TOTALS	CONTINGENT LIABILITIES	TOTALS
Salary (applicant)		If guarantor, co-maker, or endorser	
Salary (co-applicant)		If you have any legal claims	
Bonuses & commissions (applicant)		If you have liability for a lease or contract	
Bonuses & commissions (co-applicant)		If you have outstanding letters of credit	
Income from rental property		If you have outstanding surety bonds	
Investment income		If you have any contested tax liens	
Other income*		If you listed an amount for any of the above, give details:	
TOTAL INCOME			

*Income from alimony, child support, or separate maintenance income need not be revealed if you do not wish to have it considered as a basis for repaying this obligation.

ASSETS	TOTALS	LIABILITIES	TOTALS
Cash, checking & savings		Secured loans	
Marketable securities		Unsecured loans	
Nonmarketable securities		Charge account bills	
Real estate owned/home		Personal debts	
Partial interest in real estate equities		Monthly bills	
Automobiles		Real estate mortgages	
Personal property		Unpaid income tax	
Personal loans		Other unpaid taxes and interest	
Cash value—life insurance		Other debts—itemize	
Other assets—itemize			
		TOTAL LIABILITIES	
		TOTAL ASSETS	
TOTAL ASSETS		NET WORTH (ASSETS −LIABILITIES)	

Entrepreneurs in search of start-up financing use personal financial statements as proof of their ability to manage money and be financially responsible.

1. **Cover sheet:** This is the title page to your "book." All it needs to say is "Loan application submitted by John Smith, Sunday's Ice Cream Parlor, to Big Bucks Bank, Main Street, Anytown." It should also include the date and your business telephone number.

2. **Cover letter:** The cover letter is a personal business letter to your banker requesting consideration of your application for a line of credit or installment loan.

    The second paragraph should describe your business. "Our company is a sole proprietorship, partnership or corporation in manufacturing, retailing, and distributing X type of goods."

    The third paragraph is best kept to just one or two sentences that "sell" your application by indicating what your future plans are.

3. **Table of contents:** This page makes it easy for your banker to see that all the documents are included.

4. **Amount and use of the loan:** This page documents how much you want to borrow and how you will use the loan. If you are buying a new piece of equipment, for instance, it should show the contract price, add the cost of freight and installation, deduct the amount you will be contributing, and show the balance to be borrowed.

5. **History and description of the business:** This is often the most difficult one or two pages to write. The key is to stay with the facts and assume the reader knows nothing about your business. Describe more fully than in the cover letter the legal form of your business and its location. Tell why you believe the business is going to succeed. Conclude with a paragraph on your future plans.

6. **Management team:** Bankers know that it's people who make things happen. Your management team might consist of every employee, if they oversee an important part of your operation, or it might be just you and one key person. It also includes any outside consultants you plan to use regularly, such as your accountant or banker.

    In one or two pages, list each person's name and responsibilities. Where appropriate, describe the background that makes this person the right choice for that job.

7. **Market information:** Start these pages with a complete description of your product line or service, and the market it is directed toward. Next, describe how you have targeted your market niche

and how successful you have been. Finally, detail your future plans to add new products or services.

8. **Financial history:** Most bankers want to see balance sheets and income (profit and loss) statements. As a start-up, you'll need to use projections. Bankers will compare these to norms in your industry.

9. **Financial projections:** This set of three documents—a projected income statement, balance sheet and cash flow statement—should show how the business, with the use of the loan, will generate sufficient profits to pay off the loan. Your accountant can help you prepare these documents.

10. **Collateral:** Listing your available collateral—cash reserves, stocks and bonds, equipment, home equity, inventory and receivables—demonstrates your understanding that your banker will normally look for a backup repayment source. Each piece of collateral listed should be described with its cost and current fair market value.

11. **Personal financial statements:** As a start-up, you will need to add your personal guarantee to any loan the bank makes. The banker will want to see your most recent tax return and balance sheets showing personal net worth. Most banks have pre-printed forms that make pulling these figures together relatively easy.

12. **Additional documents:** In this section, you can include whatever documents you feel will enhance your loan package. This might include a copy of the sales contract on a new piece of equipment, a lease and photograph of a new location, blueprints or legal documents. If you are introducing a new product or service, include a product brochure and additional market research information.

    This section can help a new business overcome the lack of a track record. While glowing letters won't make a banker overlook weak financials, an assurance from your largest customer that your services are valued can help your banker see your full potential.

What Lenders Look For

Your application is complete, with every "I" dotted and every "T" crossed. But is it enough to get you the cold, hard cash? What are lenders really looking for when they pore over your application? Lenders (particularly bankers) typically base their decisions on four criteria, often called the "Four C's of Credit":

1. **Credit:** The lender will examine your personal credit history to see how well you've managed your past obligations. If you have some black marks on your credit record, the banker will want to hear the details and see proof that you repaid what you legitimately owed. A couple of late payments are not a big deal, but two or more consecutive missed payments are.

   It's a good idea to get a copy of your credit history before you turn in your loan application. This way, you can find out about any problems and will be able to explain them before your banker brings them up.

Smart Tip

HUD (the federal Department of Housing and Urban Development) provides job and other grants to start-ups and small businesses for job creation (i.e., $10,000 per job created) in the form of low-interest loans, often in conjunction with the SBA. HUD will be able to provide the names and phone numbers of local city, county, and state organizations in your area that represent HUD for development of targeted geographic urban areas.

2. **Character:** Character is hard to measure, but lenders will use your credit history to assess this as well. They take lawsuits, bankruptcies and tax liens particularly seriously in evaluating your character. They will also do a background check and evaluate your previous work experience.

3. **Capacity:** What happens if your business slumps? Do you have the capacity to convert other assets to cash, either by selling them or borrowing against them? Your secondary repayment sources may include real estate, stocks and other savings. The lender will look at your business balance sheet and your personal financial statement to determine your capacity.

4. **Collateral:** As a start-up, you will most likely be seeking a secured loan. This means you must put up collateral—either personal assets, such as certificates of deposit or stocks, or business assets like real estate, inventory or equipment.

A Loan At Last

A good relationship with your banker is just as important after you get that precious loan as it is in getting one in the first place. The key word is "communication." Simply put, the bank wants to be told all the good news—and bad news—about your business as soon as it occurs.

Most small-business owners fear telling bankers bad news, but keeping problems hidden is one of the biggest mistakes you can make. Like any relationship, yours with your banker is built on trust. Keep him or her apprised of your business's progress on a regular basis. Invite your banker to visit your business and see how the proceeds of the loan are being put to good use.

Once you've established a relationship with a banker, it's simple to expand your circle of friends at the bank. Every time you visit, spend some time meeting and talking to people, especially those further up the ladder. Often, the bankers will be the ones to initiate contact. Take advantage of this opportunity. The more people you know at the bank, the easier it will be to get the next round of financing you need as your business grows.

GLOSSARY

Collateral: anything of value that can be pledged against a loan, including stocks and bonds, equipment, home equity, inventory, and receivables; if you cannot repay the loan, the lender will look to your collateral as a backup source of repayment

Cure provision: part of the default section of a promissory note, the cure provision allows you a certain amount of time (usually 10 days) to remedy a default after you've been notified by the bank

Guarantee and surety agreement: for businesses with insufficient operating history or assets on which to base a loan, banks will typically require the loan to be guaranteed with your personal assets, such as the equity in your home, in a guarantee and surety agreement

Loan agreement: written contract specifying terms of a loan

Promissory note: details the principal and interest owed on a loan and when payments are due; it also outlines the events that would allow the bank to declare your loan in default

CHAPTER 16

ASK YOUR FAVORITE UNCLE

How to get government loans

Where can you go when private financing sources turn you down? For many start-up entrepreneurs, the answer is the U.S. Small Business Administration (SBA). The federal government has a vested interest in encouraging the growth of small business. As a result, some SBA loans have less stringent requirements for owner's equity and collateral than do commercial loans, making the SBA an excellent financing source for start-ups. In addition, many SBA loans are for smaller sums than most banks are willing to lend.

Of course, that doesn't mean the SBA is giving money away. In fact, the SBA does not actually make direct loans; instead, it provides loan guarantees to entrepreneurs, promising the bank to pay back a certain percentage of your loan if you are unable to.

Banks participate in the SBA program as regular, certified or preferred lenders. The SBA can help you prepare your loan package, which you then submit to banks. If the bank approves you, it submits your loan package to the SBA. Applications submitted by regular lenders are reviewed by the SBA in an average of two weeks, certified lender applications are reviewed in three days, and approval through preferred lenders is even faster.

The most basic eligibility requirement for SBA loans is the ability to repay the loan from cash flow, but the SBA also looks at personal credit history, industry experience or other evidence of management ability, collateral and owner's equity contributions. If you own 20 percent or more equity in the business, the SBA asks that you personally guarantee the loan. After all, you can't ask the government to back you if you're not willing to back yourself.

The SBA offers a wide variety of loan programs for businesses at various stages of development. Here's a closer look:

The 7(a) Loan Guaranty Program

The biggest and most popular SBA loan program is the 7(a) Loan Guaranty Program. The SBA guarantees up to $750,000 or 75 percent of the total loan amount, whichever is less. For loans of less than $100,000, the guarantee usually tops out at 80 percent of the total loan.

SBA policy prohibits lenders from charging many of the usual fees associated with commercial loans. Still, you can expect to pay a one-time guarantee fee and a yearly servicing fee, which the agency charges the lender and allows the lender to pass on to you.

A 7(a) loan can be used for many business purposes, including real estate, expansion, equipment, working capital or inventory. The money can be paid back over as long as 25 years for real estate and 10 years for equipment and working capital. Interest rates are a maximum of 2.25 percent over prime if the loan term is less than seven years and 2.75 percent if more than seven years.

The LowDoc Program

A general 7(a) loan may suit your business's needs best, but the 7(a) program also offers several specialized loans. One of them, the LowDoc Program, promises quick processing for amounts less than $100,000. "LowDoc" stands for "low documentation," and approval relies heavily on your personal credit rating and your business's cash flow.

"The LowDoc is probably the closest you'll get these days to a good, old-

INFORMATION, PLEASE

Dealing with the federal government has gotten easier thanks to the U.S. Business Advisor—an online clearinghouse for small business. Instead of contacting dozens of agencies and departments for information on laws and regulations, you can use this one-stop shop to access government forms, business development software and business information from the SBA.

You can download application forms for the SBA's LowDoc, Export Working Capital and Pre-qualification programs. There's information on women- and minority-owned business development, international trade, government contracting and more. Select "News" from the main menu and get the latest news releases from government agencies. Hit "Search" and find government regulations at your fingertips. The U.S. Business Advisor's address is www.business.com.

SBA Form 4-L (6/94)

U.S. SMALL BUSINESS ADMINISTRATION
APPLICATION FOR BUSINESS LOAN (UP TO $100,000)
Maximum amount of loan $100,000, including existing SBA loans

OMB Approval No. 3245-0016
Expiration Date: 9/30/97

Corporate Name (If any)

Trade Name & Street Address _____ Corporate Structure: Proprietorship ___ Partnership___ Corp.___ LLC___

City _____ County _____ State ____ Zip ____ Phone (___)_____ TaxID#_____

Mailing Address (if different) _____

Type of Business _____ Date Established _____ Time as Owner _____ No. of Employees:_____

MANAGEMENT (Proprietor, partners, officers, directors owning 20% or more of the company)--Must account for 100% of the business

Name	Address		City	State	Zip		
Social Security #	*Veteran		*Gender	*Race	US Citizen		Alien Reg. #
Name	Address		City	State	Zip		
Social Security #	*Veteran		*Gender	*Race	US Citizen		Alien Reg. #

*This data is collected for statistical purposes only. It has no bearing on the credit decision to approve or decline this application. Disclosure is voluntary.

Are any of the above individuals (a) presently under indictment, on parole or probation or have they ever been (b) charged for any criminal offense other than a minor vehicle violation, or (c) convicted, placed on pretrial diversion, or placed on any form of probatio n including adjudication withheld pending probation for any criminal offense other than a minor vehicle violation? Yes __ No __ If yes, loan request must be submitted under regular 7(a) loan program.

Have you employed anyone to prepare this application? Yes __ No __ If yes, how much have you paid? $_____ How much do you owe? $_____

Have you or any officer of your company ever been involved in bankruptcy or insolvency proceedings? Yes __ No __ If yes, provide details to bank.
Are you or your business involved in any pending lawsuits? Yes ___ No ___ If yes, provide details to bank.

DESCRIBE YOUR BUSINESS OPERATION:

IS BUSINESS ENGAGED IN EXPORT TRADE? Yes ___ No ___ DO YOU INTEND TO BEGIN EXPORTING AS A RESULT OF THIS LOAN? Yes ___ No ___

SUMMARY OF MANAGEMENT'S BUSINESS EXPERIENCE, EDUCATION, AND TRAINING:

LOAN REQUEST: HOW MUCH, FOR WHAT, WHY IT IS NEEDED

INDEBTEDNESS: Furnish information on ALL BUSINESS debts, contracts, notes, and mortgages payable. Indicate by an (*) items to be paid with loan proceeds.

To Whom Payable	Original Amount	Original Date	Present Balance	Rate of Interest	Maturity Date	Monthly Payment	Collateral	Current or Past Due
	$		$			$		
	$		$			$		
	$		$			$		
	$		$			$		

PREVIOUS SBA OR OTHER GOVERNMENT FINANCING : If you or any principals or affiliates have ever requested Government Financing complete the following:

Name of Agency	Loan Number	Date Approved	$ Amount	Loan Balance	Status

If you knowingly make a false statement or overvalue a security to obtain a guaranteed loan from SBA you can be fined up to $10,000 or imprisoned for not more than five years or both under 18 USC 1001.

I hereby certify that all information contained in this document and any attachments is true and correct to the best of my knowledge.

If applicant is a proprietor or general partner, sign here: By: _____ Title _____ Date _____

If corporation sign below: Corporate Name _____

By: _____   Date: _____   Attested By: _____
  Signature of President   Signature of Corporate Secretary

LowDoc application for loans up to $100,000

fashioned character loan," says Al Stubblefield of the SBA. That fact, combined with the favorable interest rates, fees and maturity terms offered by the SBA, makes the LowDoc an unusually good deal in today's loan marketplace.

LowDoc loan proceeds can be used for many purposes. Applicants seeking less than $50,000 are required to complete only a one-page SBA form. Those seeking up to $100,000 submit the same short form, plus supply copies of individual income tax returns for the previous three years and financial statements from all guarantors and co-owners.

The reduced paperwork makes the application process easier for banks, too; consequently, banks are more willing to make the small loans. The SBA aims for a two-day turnaround on these loan requests.

The FA$TRAK Program

The FA$TRAK Program is a close cousin of the LowDoc, also offering loans of up to $100,000. However, FA$TRAK gets you an answer even more quickly because approved FA$TRAK lenders can use their own documentation and procedures to attach an SBA guarantee to an approved loan without having to wait for SBA approval.

The SBA guarantees up to 50 percent of FA$TRAK loans. Though it's still a pilot program, you will find that FA$TRAK is up and running in many regions across the country.

> ## Bright Idea
>
> Check out the SBA's Women's Business Center, a Web site for women who want to start or expand their businesses. There's free online counseling and a world of information about business practices, management techniques, technology training, market research and SBA services. Visit the site at www.onlinewbc.org.

CAPLines

For businesses that need working capital on a short-term or cyclical basis, the SBA has a collection of revolving and nonrevolving lines of credit called CAPLines. A revolving loan is similar to a credit card, where you carry a balance that goes up or down, depending on payments and amounts borrowed. With nonrevolving lines of credit, you borrow a flat amount and pay it off over a set period of time.

CAPLine loans are guaranteed by the SBA up to $750,000 or 75 percent of the total loan amount, whichever is less. There are five loan and line-of-credit programs that operate under the CAPLine umbrella:

1. **Seasonal line of credit:** designed to help businesses during peak seasons, when they face increases in inventory, accounts receivable and labor costs

2. **Contract line of credit:** used to finance labor and material costs involved in carrying out contracts

3. **Standard asset-based line of credit (formerly the GreenLine Loan Program):** helps businesses unable to meet credit qualifications associated with long-term credit; provides financing for cyclical, growth, recurring or short-term needs

4. **Small asset-based revolving line of credit:** provides smaller, asset-based lines of credit (up to $200,000), with less strict requirements than the standard asset-based program

---

OMB Approval No. 3245-0091
Expiration Date: 7/31/95

U.S. SMALL BUSINESS ADMINISTRATION

REQUEST FOR COUNSELING

A. NAME OF COMPANY	B. YOUR NAME (Last, First, Middle)	C. SOCIAL SECURITY NO.	D. TELEPHONE (H) (B)

E. STREET	F. CITY	G. STATE	H. COUNTY	I. ZIP	J. TAX IDENTIFICATION NO.

K. TYPE OF BUSINESS (Check one)
1. ☐ Retail   4. ☐ Manufacturing
2. ☐ Service   5. ☐ Construction
3. ☐ Wholesale 6. ☐ Not in Business

L. BUS. OWNSHP./GENDER
1. ☐ Male
2. ☐ Female
3. ☐ Male/Female

M. VETERAN STATUS
1. ☐ Veteran
2. ☐ Vietnam-Era Veteran
3. ☐ Disabled Veteran

N.
- INDICATE PREFERRED DATE AND TIME FOR APPOINTMENT
  DATE_____ TIME_____
- ARE YOU CURRENTLY IN BUSINESS? YES___ NO___
- IF YES, HOW LONG?_____
- TYPE OF BUSINESS (USE THREE TO FIVE WORDS)
  _____

O. ETHNIC BACKGROUND
a. Race:
1.☐ American Indian or Alaskan Native
2.☐ Asian or Pacific Islander
3.☐ Black
4.☐ White

b. Ethnicity:
1.☐ Hispanic Origin
2.☐ Not of Hispanic Origin

P. INDICATE, BRIEFLY, THE NATURE OF SERVICE AND/OR COUNSELING YOU ARE SEEKING
_____
_____

Q.
- IT HAS BEEN EXPLAINED TO ME THAT I MAY USE FURTHER SERVICES SPONSORED BY THE U.S. SMALL BUSINESS ADMINISTRATION   YES ___   NO___
- I HAVE ATTENDED A SMALL BUSINESS WORKSHOP   YES ___   NO___
- CONDUCTED BY_____

R. HOW DID YOU LEARN OF THESE COUNSELING SERVICES?
1. ☐ Yellow Pages   3. ☐ Radio   5. ☐ Bank   7. ☐ Word-of-Mouth
2. ☐ Television   4. ☐ Newspapers 6. ☐ Chamber of Commerce 8. ☐ Other____

S. SBA CLIENT (To Be Filled Out By Counselor)
1. ☐ Borrower   2. ☐ Applicant   3. ☐ 8(a) Client   4. ☐ COC   5. ☐ Surety Bond

T. AREA OF COUNSELING PROVIDED (To Be Filled Out By Counselor)   ☐
1. Bus. Start-Up/Acquisition   5. Accounting & Records   9. Personnel   13. Technology
2. Source of Capital   6. Finan. Analysis/Cost Control 10. Computer Systems
3. Marketing/Sales   7. Inventory Control   11. Internat'l Trade
4. Government Procurement   8. Engineering R&D   12. Business Liq./Sale

I request business management counseling from the Small Business Administration. I agree to cooperate should I be selected to participate in surveys designed to evaluate SBA assistance services. I authorize SBA to furnish relevant information to the assigned management counselor(s) although I expect that information to be held in strict confidence by him/her.

I further understand that any counselor has agreed not to: (1) recommend goods or services from sources in which he/she has an interest and (2) accept fees or commissions developing from this counseling relationship. In consideration of SBA's furnishing management or technical assistance, I waive all claims against SBA personnel, SCORE, SBDC and its host organizations, SBI, and other SBA Resource Counselors arising from this assistance.

SIGNATURE AND TITLE OF REQUESTER	DATE

FOR USE OF THE SMALL BUSINESS ADMINISTRATION

RESOURCE	DISTRICT	REGION

SBA FORM 641 (10-92) PREVIOUS EDITION IS OBSOLETE   WHITE: COUNSELOR

This form helps the Small Business Administration determine what area the applicant needs consulting in. It also serves as feedback for the SBA so it can find out how people heard about its services and how they are used.

5. **Builder's line of credit:** used to finance labor and materials costs for small general contractors and builders constructing or renovating commercial or residential buildings

OMB Approval No.:3245-0178
Expiration Date: 2-28-97

Return Executed Copies 1, 2, and 3 to SBA

United States of America

SMALL BUSINESS ADMINISTRATION

STATEMENT OF PERSONAL HISTORY

Please Read Carefully - Print or Type

Each member of the small business concern or the development company requesting assistance must submit this form in TRIPLICATE for filing with the SBA application. This form must be filled out and submitted by:

1. If a sole proprietorship by the proprietor.
2. If a partnership by each partner.
3. If a corporation or a development company, by each officer, director, and additionally by each holder of 20% or more of the voting stock.
4. Any other person including a hired manager, who has authority to speak for and commit the borrower in the management of the business.

Name and Address of Applicant (Firm Name)(Street, City, State, and ZIP Code)

SBA District/Disaster Area Office

Amount Applied for:

Loan Case No.

1. Personal Statement of: (State name in full, if no middle name, state (NMN), or if initial only, indicate initial.) List all former names used, and dates each name was used. Use separate sheet if necessary.

First   Middle   Last

Name and Address of participating bank (when applicable)

2. Date of Birth: (Month, day, and year)

3. Place of Birth: (City & State or Foreign Country)

4. Give the percentage of ownership or stock owned or to be owned in the small business concern or the Development Company

Social Security No.

U.S. Citizen ? ☐ YES ☐ NO
If no, give alien registration number:

5. Present residence address:

From: To: Address: City   State

Home Telephone No. (Include A/C):

Business Telephone No. (Include A/C):

Immediate past residence address:

From: To: Address:

BE SURE TO ANSWER THE NEXT 3 QUESTIONS CORRECTLY BECAUSE THEY ARE IMPORTANT.

THE FACT THAT YOU HAVE AN ARREST OR CONVICTION RECORD WILL NOT NECESSARILY DISQUALIFY YOU. BUT AN INCORRECT ANSWER WILL PROBABLY CAUSE YOUR APPLICATION TO BE TURNED DOWN.

IF YOU ANSWER "YES" TO 6, 7, OR 8, FURNISH DETAILS IN A SEPARATE EXHIBIT. INCLUDE DATES; LOCATION; FINES, SENTENCES, ETC.; WHETHER MISDEMEANOR OR FELONY; DATES OF PAROLE/PROBATION; UNPAID FINES OR PENALTIES; NAMES UNDER WHICH CHARGED; AND ANY OTHER PERTINENT INFORMATION.

6. Are you presently under indictment, on parole or probation?
☐ Yes ☐ No   (If yes, indicate date parole or probation is to expire.)

7. Have you ever been charged with or arrested for any criminal offense other than a minor motor vehicle violation? Include offenses which have been dismissed, discharged, or nolle prosequi (All arrests and charges must be disclosed and explained on an attached sheet.)
☐ Yes ☐ No

8. Have you ever been convicted, placed on pretrial diversion, or placed on any form of probation, including adjudication withheld pending probation, for any criminal offense other than a minor motor vehicle violation?
☐ Yes ☐ No

9.
☐ Fingerprints Waived   Date   Approving Authority
☐ Fingerprints Required
☐ Date Sent to FBI   Date   Approving Authority

10.
☐ Cleared for Processing   Date   Approving Authority
☐ Request a Character Evaluation   Date   Approving Authority

The information on this form will be used in connection with an investigation of your character. Any information you wish to submit that you feel will expedite this investigation should be set forth.

CAUTION: Knowingly making a false statement on this form is a violation of Federal law and could result in criminal prosecution, significant civil penalties, and a denial of your loan. A false statement is punishable under 18 USC 1001 by imprisonment of not more than five years and/or a fine of not more than $10,000; under 15 USC 645 by imprisonment of not more than two years and/or a fine of not more than $5,000; and, if submitted to a Federally insured institution, under 18 USC 1014 by imprisonment of not more than twenty years and/or a fine of not more than $1,000,000.

Signature   Title   Date

It is against SBA's policy to provide assistance to persons not of good character and therefore consideration is given to the qualities and personality traits of a person, favorable and unfavorable, relating thereto, including behavior, integrity, candor and disposition toward criminal actions. It is also against SBA's policy to provide assistance not in the best interests of the United States, for example, if there is reason to believe that the effect of such assistance will be to encourage or support, directly or indirectly, activities inimical to the Security of the United States. Anyone concerned with the collection of this information, as to its voluntariness, disclosure of routine uses may contact the FOIA Office, 409 3rd St. S.W., and a copy of 9"Agency Collection of Information" from SOP 40 04 will be provided.

SBA FORM 912 (12-93) SOP 9020 USE 5-87 EDITION UNTIL EXHAUSTED   Copy 1 - SBA File Copy

Please Note: The estimated burden hours for completion of this form is 15 minutes per response. If you have any questions or comments concerning this estimate or any other aspect of this information collection please contact, Chief Administrative Information Branch, U.S. Small Business Administration 409 Third Street, S.W. Washington, D.C. 20416 or Gary Waxman, Clearance Officer, Paperwork Reduction Project (3245-0178), Office of Management and Budget, Washington, D.C. 20503.

♻ PRINTED ON RECYCLED PAPER

* U.S. GPO: 1994-366-367

The Statement of Personal History is an essential document for determining the quality of the person applying for any Small Business Administration loan. It is filled out by the sole proprietor, each partner in a partnership, each member of a board of directors, or a manager authorized to act in the best interests of the company.

Each of the five credit lines has a five-year maturity but can be tailored to the borrower's needs. Also, with each credit line, the cash that is generated as a result of receiving the line of credit serves as the primary form of collateral.

Women And Minority Pre-qualification Programs

The SBA's Minority and Women's Pre-qualification Loan Programs help women and minority entrepreneurs pre-qualify for loans. Under the women's program, entrepreneurs can apply for loans of up to $250,000; under the minority program, you can get up to $250,000 or more on a case-by-case basis (this program is still in the pilot stage but is being expanded to more states). Working with the help of private intermediary organizations chosen by the SBA, eligible entrepreneurs prepare a business plan and complete a loan application. The intermediary submits the application to the SBA.

If the application is approved, the SBA issues you a pre-qualification letter, which you can then take, along with your loan package, to a commercial bank. With the SBA's guarantee attached, the bank is more likely to approve the loan.

THE CAPITAL STOPS HERE

In conjunction with the federal government's Empowerment Zone/Enterprise Community program, the SBA plans to open at least 12 One-Stop Capital Shops nationwide. The shops, which will be managed by nonprofit community development organizations, will serve as a regional and national distribution point for loans and investments within the targeted zones and communities.

The One-Stop Capital Shops will also offer access to a wide variety of SBA programs and resources for small-business development, including the SBA's Service Corps of Retired Executives, a counseling and mentorship program; and Small Business Development Centers.

Each shop will also contain a Business Information Center (BIC), which provides the latest in high-tech hardware, software and telecommunications to assist small business. Using computers, CD-ROMs and interactive videos, entrepreneurs will have access to market research databases, planning and spreadsheet software, and libraries of information to build a business. For more information on the One-Stop Capital Shops, contact the SBA at (202) 205-6657.

OMB Approval No. 3245-0188

PERSONAL FINANCIAL STATEMENT

U. S. SMALL BUSINESS ADMINISTRATION

As of _____ , 19 _____

Complete this form for: (1) each proprietor, or (2) each limited partner who owns 20% or more interest and each general partner, or (3) each stockholder owning 20% or more of voting stock, or (4) any person or entity providing a guaranty on the loan.

Name _____ Business Phone ( )

Residence Address _____ Residence Phone ( )

City, State, & Zip Code _____

Business Name of Applicant/Borrower _____

ASSETS	(Omit Cents)
Cash on hands & in Banks . . . . $	
Savings Accounts . . . . $	
IRA or Other Retirement Account . . . . . $	
Accounts & Notes Receivable . . . . . . $	
Life Insurance-Cash Surrender Value Only $	
(Complete Section 8)	
Stocks and Bonds . . . . $	
(Describe in Section 3)	
Real Estate . . . . $	
(Describe in Section 4)	
Automobile-Present Value . . . . $	
Other Personal Property . . . . $	
(Describe in Section 5)	
Other Assets . . . . $	
(Describe in Section 5)	
Total . . $	

LIABILITIES	(Omit Cents)
Accounts Payable . . . . $	
Notes Payable to Banks and Others . . . . $	
(Describe in Section 2)	
Installment Account (Auto) . . . . $	
Mo. Payments $	
Installment Account (other) . . . . $	
Mo. Payments $	
Loan on Life Insurance . . . . $	
Mortgages on Real Estate . . . . $	
(Describe in Section 4)	
Unpaid Taxes . . . . $	
(Describe in Section 6)	
Other Liabilities . . . . $	
(Describe in Section 7)	
Total Liabilities . . . . $	
Net Worth . . . . $	
Total . . $	

Section 1. Source of Income	
Salary . . . . $	
Net Investment Income . . . . $	
Real Estate Income . . . . $	
Other Income (Decribe below)* . . . . . $	

Description of Other Income in Section 1.

Contingent Liabilities	
As Endorser or Co-Maker. . . . . $	
Legal Claims & Judgments . . . . $	
Provision for Federal Income Tax . . . . $	
Other Special Debt . . . . $	

*Alimony or child support payments need not be disclosed in "Other Income" unless it is desired to have such payments counted toward total income.

Section 2. Notes Payable to Bank and Others. (Use attachments if necessary. Each attachment must be identified as a part of this statement and signed.).

Name and Address of Noteholder(s)	Original Balance	Current Balance	Payment Amount	Frequency (monthly,etc.)	How Secured or Endorsed Type of Collateral

SBA Form 413 (2-94) Use 5-91 Edition until stock is exhausted. Ref: SOP 50-10 and 50-30

(tumble)

The Personal Financial Statement shows a Small Business Administration loan officer the assets and liabilities, including source of income, from any business or business owner. It also indicates notes payable to banks and other lending institutions.

Section 3. Stocks and Bonds. (Use attachments if necessary. Each attachment must be identified as a part of this statement and signed).

Number of Shares	Name of Securities	Cost	Market Value Quotation/Exchange	Date of Quotation/Exchange	Total Value

Section 4. Real Estate Owned. (List each parcel separately. Use attachments if necessary. Each attachment must be identified as a part of this statement and signed).

	Property A	Property B	Property C
Type of Property			
Address			
Date Purchased			
Original Cost			
Present Market Value			
Name & Address of Mortgage Holder			
Mortgage Account Number			
Mortgage Balance			
Amount of Payment per Month/Year			
Status of Mortgage			

Section 5. Other Personal Property and Other Assets. (Describe, and if any is pledged as security, state name and address of lien holder, amount of lien, terms of payment, and if delinquent, describe delinquency).

Section 6. Unpaid Taxes. (Describe in detail, as to type, to whom payable, when due, amount, and to what property, if any, a tax lien attaches).

Section 7. Other Liabilities. (Describe in detail).

Section 8. Life Insurance Held. (Give face amount and cash surrender value of policies – name of insurance company and beneficiaries).

I authorize SBA/Lender to make inquiries as necessary to verify the accuracy of the statements made and to determine my creditworthiness. I certify the above and the statements contained in the attachments are true and accurate as of the stated date(s). These statements are made for the purpose of either obtaining a loan or guaranteeing a loan. I understand FALSE statements may result in forfeiture of benefits and possible prosecution by the U.S. Attorney General (Reference 18 U.S.C. 1001).

Signature:	Date:	Social Security Number:
Signature:	Date:	Social Security Number:

PLEASE NOTE: The estimated average burden hours for the completion of this form is 1.5 hours per response. If you have questions or comments concerning this estimate or any other aspect of this information, please contact Chief, Administrative Branch, U.S. Small Business Administration, Washington, D.C. 20416, and Clearance Office, Paper Reduction Project (3245-0188), Office of Management and Budget, Washington, D.C. 20503.

*U.S. Government Printing Office: 1994 — 301-368/14187   Federal Recycling Program   Printed on Recycled Paper

Small Business Administration Personal Financial Statement, con't.

The MicroLoan Program

SBA financing isn't limited to the 7(a) group of loans. The MicroLoan Program helps entrepreneurs get very small loans, ranging from under $100 up to $25,000. The loans can be used for machinery and equipment, furniture and fixtures, inventory, supplies and working capital, but not to pay existing debts. This program is unique because it assists borrowers who generally do not meet traditional lenders' credit standards.

MicroLoans are administered through nonprofit intermediaries. These organizations receive loans from the SBA and then turn around and make loans to entrepreneurs. The intermediaries will often walk you through writing your business plan and taking inventory of your business skills.

Maturity terms and interest rates for MicroLoans vary, although terms are usually short; the loans typically take less than a week to process. The only downside: The MicroLoan program is still not available in all regions of the country.

The 504 Loan Program

On the opposite end of the loan size spectrum is the 504 Loan Program, which provides long-term, fixed-rate loans for financing fixed assets, usually real estate and equipment. Loans are most often used for growth and expansion.

504 Loans are made through Certified Development Companies (CDCs)—nonprofit intermediaries that work with the SBA, banks and businesses looking for financing. There are CDCs throughout the country, each covering an assigned region.

If you're seeking funds up to $750,000 to buy or renovate a building or put in some major equipment, consider bringing your business plan and financial statements to a CDC. Typical percentages for this type of package are

Bright Idea

Women business owners have a friend in Washington: the Office of Women's Business Ownership (OWBO), part of the SBA. The OWBO coordinates federal efforts that support women entrepreneurs and produces publications for women business owners.

The OWBO also manages the Women's Network for Entrepreneurial Training, a mentor program that matches seasoned women entrepreneurs with start-up business owners. In addition, the office directs the Demonstration Project Program, a network of business training and counseling centers. For information about OWBO services, contact the OWBO at 409 Third St. SW, 6th Fl., Washington, DC 20416, (202) 205-6673 or visit your SBA district office.

EXPORT EXPERTISE

If exporting is part of your business game plan, the Export-Import Bank of the United States (Ex-Im Bank) can be your biggest ally. The bank makes working capital guarantees to small and medium-sized companies to cover up to 90 percent of the principal and interest on commercial loans. The guarantee can apply to a single loan or a revolving line of credit, and generally must be repaid in one year.

Entrepreneurs must have been in business at least one year in order to be eligible. Loans of up to $5 million are available, and can be used for raw materials or finished products for export; to pay for materials, labor and overhead used to produce goods for export; or to cover standby letters of credit, bid and performance bonds. Business owners can apply directly to Ex-Im Bank for a preliminary guarantee and then shop around for up to six months for the best loan package.

Business owners can approach Ex-Im Bank directly (202-565-3946) or through any commercial bank that deals with the agency.

In addition to working capital guarantees, Ex-Im Bank offers insurance programs, which insure transactions in case a foreign buyer fails to pay an entrepreneur. The Ex-Im Bank's Small Business and Umbrella Insurance programs are geared to small companies new to exporting.

Based in Washington, DC, Ex-Im Bank also has five regional offices in Chicago, New York City, Miami, Houston, and El Segundo, California. Ex-Im Bank also offers other resources for entrepreneurs, including an information hotline (800-424-5201) and briefing seminars and discussions; call (202) 566-4490 for a schedule.

50 percent financed by the bank, 40 percent by the CDC and 10 percent by the business.

In exchange for this below-market, fixed-rate financing, the SBA expects the small business to create or retain jobs or to meet certain public policy goals. Businesses that meet these public policy goals are those whose expansion will contribute to a business district revitalization, such as an Enterprise/Empowerment Zone; a minority-owned business; an

SBA PRE-QUALIFICATION LOAN APPLICATION

SBA OFFICE USE ONLY: DATE RECEIVED: **CID NUMBER:**

Legal Name of Business:	**Tax ID #:**
Address of Business:	
Business Phone #:	**Date Business Established:**
Legal Structure: ___ Proprietorship ___ Partnership ___ Corporation	
Standard Industrial Classification #:	**Numbers of Existing Employees:**

Describe History of Business: (If NEW business, submit copy of Business Plan)

Describe Business Operations:

Is Business engaged in export trade? Yes___ No___   **Do you intend to begin exporting as result of this loan? Yes___ No___**

OWNERS/MANAGEMENT (proprietors, partners and shareholders)							
Name	SS No.	% Owned	Sex	Military Service Y/N:	From	To:	Race
TOTAL		100.0%					

* Personal financial statements must be submitted by all owners of 20% or more.

a. Do any above individuals or groups of above individuals who hold ownership or management control of the applicant firm also have ownership or management control of any other business operations? _____Yes*___No
*If yes, please list each entity _____

b. Do any of the above individuals have personal unpledged liquid assets in excess of $50,000 or 25% of the requested loan amount (whichever is greater)(excluding IRA's, CV Life Insurance, savings for education)? _____Yes*___No
*If yes, list each individual: _____

c. Are any of the above individuals (a) presently under indictment, on parole or probation or (b) have they ever been charged with or arrested or convicted of any criminal offense other than a vehicle violation? _____Yes*___No
*If yes, the loan request must be submitted under the regular 7(a) loan program.

d. Have any above individuals, the applicant firm or affiliates (a) been involved in bankruptcy or insolvency proceedings or (b) have pending personal or business judgements, unsettled lawsuits or major disputes? __Yes*___No
*If yes, the loan request must be submitted under the 7(a) regular loan program.

e. Do you or any member of your household, or anyone who owns, manages, or directs your business or members of their households work for the Small Business Administration, Small Business Advisory Council, SCORE or ACE, any Federal Agency, or the participating lender? ___Yes* ___No
*If yes, the loan request must be submitted under the 7 (a) regular loan program.

f. U.S. Citizen? __Yes __No*
*If no, include a copy of Alien Registration Card (Form I 151 or 551). Alien Registration #: _____

11/21/94   Page 1

Loan application for the Women and Minority Pre-qualification Programs

export or manufacturing company; or a company whose expansion will contribute to rural development.

SBICs And SSBICs

Another source of financing: Small Business Investment Companies (SBICs). SBICs are privately owned venture capital firms, licensed by

PREVIOUS SBA OR OTHER GOVERNMENT FINANCING (Requested or obtained by principals, applicant firm or affiliates)						
Name of Agency	Declined or Approved	Date of Request	$ Amount	Loan Balance		Current or Past Due
			$	$		
			$	$		
			$	$		

CREDIT HISTORY				
Credit Reports Obtained For:	Type of Report	Credit Rating	Comments:	
Applicant				
Principal:				
Principal:				
Principal:				
Other:				

PROPOSED USES AND SOURCES OF FUNDS				
USES		SOURCES		
Working Capital	$	**SBA/Bank (requested loan amount)**	$	
Inventory	$	**Equity/Injection**[4]	$	
Machinery & Equipment	$			
Furniture & Fixtures	$	**Seller Financing**	$	
Real Estate[1] (purchase, construction, etc.)	$			
		Other:	$	
Purchase an Existing Business[2]	$	Other:	$	
Debt Refinance[3] (incl. in listing, below)	$	Other:	$	
TOTAL USES:	$	**TOTAL SOURCES:**	$	
Proposed SBA/Bank Maturity		**Proposed SBA/Bank Interest Rate**		

1   If financing Real Estate, who or what entity will hold title:_____

     If other than the applicant firm, list ownership of real estate:_____

2   Purchase price = $_____; Stock or asset purchase:_____; Why is seller selling?:_____

3   If refinancing debts, state benefit to applicant firm:_____

4.   State the source of the injection:_____

BUSINESS INDEBTEDNESS: on all existing business debts, contracts, notes and mortgages payable: (Indicate by an (*) items to be paid w/loan proceeds.)							
To Whom Payable	Original Amount	Original Date	Present Balance	Rate of Interest	Maturity Date	Secured By	Current or Past Due
	$		$			$	
	$		$			$	
	$		$			$	
	$		$			$	
	$		$			$	
	Total	$			Total	$	

11/21/94

Page 2

Loan application for the Women and Minority Pre-qualification Programs, con't.

the SBA, that invest their own capital along with money they've borrowed at favorable rates from the government. If you think working with venture capital investors will get your business off the ground—and you don't mind giving up some equity—it pays to investigate SBICs.

In addition to helping you finance your business, some SBICs also offer

Financial statements are: ___ Internal ___ Acc't. Compiled ___ Reviewed ___ Audited

BALANCE SHEET INFORMATION (Dollars in Thousands)	Last FYE Date:	Interim Date:	Debit	Credit	Proforma
ASSETS:					
Cash	$	$			$
Accounts Rec.	$	$			$
Inventory	$	$			$
Other	$	$			$
TOTAL CURRENT ASSETS	$	$			$
FIXED ASSETS	$	$			$
OTHER ASSETS	$	$			$
TOTAL ASSETS	$	$			$
LIABILITIES & NET WORTH:					
Accounts Payable	$	$			$
Notes Payable	$	$			$
Taxes	$	$			$
Other	$	$			$
SBA	$	$			$
TOTAL CURRENT LIABILITIES:					
Notes Payable	$	$			$
SBA	$	$			$
Other					
TOTAL LIABILITIES	$	$			$
NET WORTH	$	$			$
TOTAL LIABILITIES AND NET WORTH	$	$			$

PROFORMA RATIO INFORMATION:	Applicant	RMA
Proforma Working Capital	$	XXXXXXXXXXX
Proforma Current Ratio		
Proforma Quick Ratio		
Accounts Receivable Turnover (in days)		
Inventory Turnover (in days)		
Proforma Debt to Worth Ratio		

HISTORICAL & PROJECTED CASH FLOW FOR REPAYMENT INFORMATION

(Dollars in Thousands)	Prior Fiscal Year 19		Prior Fiscal Year 19		Most Recent Fiscal Year 19		Interium months		RMA 100%	Projection	
a Revenues	$	100%	$	100%	$	100%	$	100%	100%	$	100%
b Gross Profit	$	%	$	%	$	%	$	%		$	%
c Interest Expense	$	%	$	%	$	%	$	%		$	%
d Owner Withdraw	$	%	$	%	$	%	$	%		$	%
e Net Income (Aftr w/d, dvds, txs)	$	%	$	%	$	%	$	%		$	%
f Depreciation	$	%	$	%	$	%	$	%		$	%
g Cash Flow (c+e+f)	$		$		$		$		XXX	$	
h Rent Expense Saved (if applicable)	$		$		$		$		XXX	$	
i Other Expense Saved (explain)	$		$		$		$		XXX	$	
j Cashflow for Debt Service (g+h+i)	$		$		$		$		XXX	$	
k Existing Debt Service (Prin.& Int.)	$		$		$		$		XXX	$	
l New Debt Service (Prin. & Int.)	$		$		$		$		XXX	$	
m Total Debt Service (k+l)	$		$		$		$		XXX	$	
n Debt Coverage Ratio (j÷m)											

Combined Household Income:$_____

Number in Household:_____

Other Sources of Income:$_____

Withdrawals:$_____

11/21/94

Page 3

Loan application for the Women and Minority Pre-qualification Programs, con't.

management services. Because they take a vested interest in companies they invest in, they look at everything from inventory to cost control, hiring practices and location. Some SBICs only lend in industries they know; others will lend across the board.

Closely related to SBICs are Specialized Small Business Investment Companies (SSBICs), which serve socially and economically disadvantaged en-

COLLATERAL SUMMARY	Cost	Market Value	Prior Liens
Land and Buildings			
Machinery & Equipment			
Furniture and Fixtures			
Accounts Receivable			
Inventory			
Other:			
TOTAL			

Evaluation by:	Date:	
Total Cost or Appraised Value	XXXXXX	
Less: Prior Liens	XXXXXX	
= Net Collateral Value	XXXXXX	
COVERAGE RATIO: (net collateral value ÷ loan amount)	XXXXXX	

Is firm considered a frequently polluting industry?   Yes*   No
*If yes, Phase I must be completed and submitted in the private sector lender's loan package.

OTHER PERTINENT INFORMATION:

MANAGEMENT EXPERIENCE/BACKGROUND
(Describe key management/owner's education & business experience)

CERTIFICATIONS OF APPLICANT AND NON-PROFIT INTERMEDIARY

I hereby certify that all information contained in this document and attachments is true and correct to the best of my knowledge.   If you knowingly make a false statement or overvalue a security to obtain a guaranteed loan from SBA you can be fined up to $10,000 or imprisoned for not more than five years or both under 18 USC 1001.

IF A PROPRIETOR OR GENERAL PARTNER, SIGN HERE:

By: _____   Title: _____   Date: _____

Address: _____

IF A CORPORATION, SIGN HERE:

Corporate Name:_____

By: _____   Title: _____   Date: _____

Attested by: _____
Signature of Corporate Secretary

NON-PROFIT INTERMEDIARY: _____

By: _____   Title: _____   Date: _____

11/21/94   Page 4

Loan application for the Women and Minority Pre-qualification Programs, con't.

trepreneurs by investing in companies in economically depressed areas and those owned by women and minorities.

Enterprise/Empowerment Zones

Since 1980, more than 35 states have established programs to designate enterprise zones, offering tax breaks and other incentives to businesses that locate in certain economically disadvantaged areas. States vary widely in the number of zones designated, incentives offered and success of the programs. In some areas, businesses may also qualify for lower utility rates or low-interest financing from eligible government jurisdictions. To be eligible for any of these incentives, businesses must generally meet certain criteria such as creating new jobs in a community.

In 1993, President Clinton unveiled an Empowerment Zone/Enterprise Communities initiative, a 10-year plan to provide tax incentives and stimulate community investment and development. Specified urban and rural communities will receive grants and tax breaks for businesses in the area. The federal government's involvement means entrepreneurs in those areas can get federal tax breaks, not just state. In addition, the SBA plans to establish One-Stop Capital Shops in all the empowerment zones to provide loans, loan guarantees and equity investments (see "The Capital Stops Here" in this chapter).

If you choose to locate in an enterprise or empowerment zone, look beyond the tax breaks to consider long-term concerns such as availability of

---

SBA LOAN DOCUMENT CHECKLIST

Documents To Prepare For A New Business

❑ Loan request statement, describing loan amount and the type of business you are starting

❑ Your resume and the resumes of key managers you plan to employ

❑ Statement of your investment capabilities

❑ Current financial statement of all personal liabilities and assets

❑ Projection of revenue statement

❑ Collateral list

Documents To Prepare For An Existing Business

❑ Balance sheet

❑ Income statement of previous and current year-to-date incomes

❑ Personal financial statement, with each owner itemized

❑ Collateral list

❑ Loan request statement, describing loan amount and purpose

Bright Idea

Looking into exporting? Then look into the U.S. Export Assistance Centers. These one-stop shops combine the trade promotion and export finance resources of the SBA, the U.S. Department of Commerce and the Export-Import Bank, and are designed to deliver services to small and medium-sized businesses.

a work force and accessibility of your target market. Make sure the zone offers other business support services, such as streamlined licensing and permitting procedures. Most zones that succeed have high development potential to begin with, with good highway access, a solid infrastructure and a trainable labor force.

For more information on enterprise and empowerment zones, contact your local SBA district office, your state's economic development department, or see "Appendix B."

The 8(a) Program

The SBA's 8(a) Program is a small-business set-aside program that gives certified MBEs (Minority Business Enterprises) access to government contracts, as well as management and technical assistance to help them develop their businesses. The 8(a) Program is envisioned as a starter program for minority businesses, which must leave the program after nine years.

Entrepreneurs who participate in the 8(a) Program are eligible for the 7(a) Loan Guaranty and Minority Pre-qualification programs. The 8(a) Program has faced challenges in recent years as federal courts are increasingly questioning the legality of affirmative action and set-aside programs. This may mean new avenues for the program.

Export Working Capital Program

If you are planning to export, you should investigate the Export Working Capital Program (EWCP). This allows up to an 80 percent guarantee on private-sector loans of up to $750,000 for working capital. Loan maturities are typically 12 months, and include two 12-month renewal options. Loans can be for single or multiple export sales and can be used for pre-shipment working capital or post-shipment exposure coverage; however, they cannot be used to buy fixed assets.

Making The Most Of The SBA

The SBA is more than a source of fi-

Smart Tip

When seeking a SBA loan, choose your bank carefully. Not all bankers are versed in SBA loans, so look for one who is experienced.

FINANCIAL PLAN

	JAN	FEB	MAR	APR	MAY	JUN	JUL	AUG	SEP	OCT	NOV	DEC	TOTAL
Sales													
Cost of Sales													
Gross Profit													
Expenses													
Advertising													
Automobile													
Bank Discounts													
Depreciation													
Dues/Subscriptions													
Insurance													
Interest													
Office Supplies													
Payroll Taxes													
Professional Services													
Rent													
Repairs/Maintenance													
Salaries													
Supplies													
Taxes/Licenses													
Utilities/Phone													
Miscellaneous													
Total Expenses													
Profit Before Taxes													

This sample financial plan highlights specific expenses such as advertising, rent and supplies in comparison to the amount of profit accrued. This plan can be implemented in your start-up phase as a projection of your first 12 months of growth.

nancing. It can help you with many aspects of business start-up and growth. In particular, the SBA is an excellent place to "get your ducks in a row" before seeking financing. SBA services include many free resources to help you with such tasks as writing a business plan and improving your presentation skills—all of which boosts your chances of getting a loan.

For more information on specific SBA programs, visit the SBA's Web site at www.sbaonline.sba.gov, call the SBA's Answer Desk at (800) 8-ASK-SBA, or contact your local SBA district office. Each state has at least one district office, which can mail you a start-up booklet and a list of lenders, inform you about specialized loans tailored to your industry, and tell you where to go for help in polishing your business plan or putting together financial statements.

GLOSSARY

Certified Development Companies (CDCs): nonprofit intermediaries that work with the Small Business Administration and banks to make 504 Loans available to entrepreneurs

Enterprise zones/empowerment zones: designated economically disadvantaged zones that offer state and/or federal tax breaks and other incentives to businesses that locate there

Minority Business Enterprise (MBE): a business that is certified owned by a minority entrepreneur; certification can be obtained from a variety of organizations and is generally required to participate in government set-aside programs

Small Business Investment Companies (SBICs): privately owned venture capital firms, licensed by the SBA, that invest their own capital along with money they've borrowed at favorable rates from the government; SBICs may offer management services in addition to money

Specialized Small Business Investment Companies (SSBICs): privately owned venture capital firms that serve socially and economically disadvantaged entrepreneurs by investing in companies in economically depressed areas, and those owned by women and minorities

Get Set . . .

You've got a great idea, a perfect plan and the money to make it all happen. What's the next step? Get set for business with Part 4, "Setting The Stage." Here, we take you step-by-step through setting up your office. Learn how to select a prime location that will get customers to come in . . . and come back. We'll show you little-known operating options, such as kiosks and carts, plus how to negotiate the lease you want. Once you've found the right site, we share secrets for giving it a professional image with furniture, business cards and stationery that all spell "success." Next, stock your shelves with inventory: You'll learn how to choose, track and maintain your product supply, and discover the best sources for getting what you need.

Getting paid is the most important part of business ownership; in this section, we'll reveal how to give your customers credit without getting taken, plus tips for accepting credit cards, debit cards and checks, and collecting on slow-paying accounts. Since every business needs to use the mail, you won't want to miss our guide to setting up mailing and shipping accounts. Discover how to choose the right carriers, get the best rates and get your packages delivered on time. If employees are part of your game plan, you'll find all the information you need to hire smart. Learn the secrets of a good job interview, low-cost hiring options, and the laws you must know to stay out of hot water. Finally, protect the business you've worked so hard to start by checking out our chapter on insurance. We show you the basic insurance no business owner should be without, plus how to put together the perfect insurance package for your needs.

Now, get geared up for business with Part 5, "You'd Better Shop Around." In today's high-tech times, there's a dizzying array of equipment options out there. We guide you through the maze of machines to choose just what you need . . . without breaking the bank. Learn low-cost ways to get equipped, from superstores and mail order to leasing and buying used. Calling all entrepreneurs: Check out our chapter on phones to figure out the best system for your needs. We give you the lowdown on voice mail, and show how pagers and cellular phones can keep you in touch with customers no matter where you are. Before you hit the road, be sure to read our chapter on company vehicles. From leasing tips to purchasing plans, we give you all the details on getting the best buy for your business—whether you're looking for one car or a fleet of delivery vehicles.

If you're planning to buy a computer for business—or upgrade the one you already have—we show you how to put together the perfect system. You'll learn the bare-bones hardware and software requirements, plus ways to ensure your computer can be upgraded to meet future needs. We take a look at the latest developments, from notebooks and palmtops to personal information managers and more. Since surfing the Net is a big part of business these days, you won't want to miss our chapter on making the most of the Internet. Discover how fast your modem really needs to be, how to find the best Internet service provider and more. Last but not least, we share low-cost ways to give your small business all the amenities of a big office: copiers, fax machines and multifunctional devices that let you work faster, smarter and more efficiently.

Part Four:
Setting The Stage

CHAPTER 17

LOCATION, LOCATION, LOCATION

Choosing a location for your business

Where should you locate your business? One expert will tell you location is absolutely vital to your company's success; another will argue that it really doesn't matter where you are—and they're both right. How important location is for your new company depends on the type of business, the facilities and other resources you need, as well as where your customers are.

If you're in retailing or if you manufacture a product and distribution is a critical element of your overall operation, then geographical location is extremely important. If your business is information- or service-related, the actual location takes a back seat to whether or not the facility itself can meet your needs.

Regardless of the nature of your business, before you start shopping for space, you need to have a clear picture of what you must have, what you'd like to have, what you absolutely won't tolerate and how much you're able to pay. Developing that picture can be a time-consuming process that is both exciting and tedious, but it's essential that you give it the attention it deserves. While many start-up mistakes can be corrected later on, a poor choice of location is difficult—and sometimes impossible—to repair.

TYPES OF LOCATIONS

The type of location you choose depends largely on the type of business you're in, but there are enough mixed-use areas and creative applications of space that you should give some thought to each type before making a final decision. For example, business parks and office buildings typically have retail space so they can attract the restaurants and stores that business tenants want nearby. Shopping centers are often home to an assortment of professional services—medical, legal, accounting, insurance, etc.—as well as retailers. It's entirely possible some version of nontraditional space will work for you, so use your imagination.

1. **Homebased:** This is perhaps the trendiest location for a business these days, and many entrepreneurs start at home, then move into commercial space as their business grows. Others start at home with no thought or intention of ever moving. You can run a home-based business from an office in a spare bedroom, the base-ment, the attic—even the kitch-en table. On the plus side, you don't need to worry about ne-gotiating leases, coming up with substantial deposits or commuting. On the downside, your room for physical growth is limited and you may find accommodating employees or meet-ings with clients a challenge. (For more detailed information about locating a business in your home, see Entrepreneur's busi-ness start-up guide No. 1815, *Starting & Running a Homebased Business.*)

Dollar Stretcher

To keep costs down, con-sider sharing space with an-other company that does not compete with your business, one that might even comple-ment your own operation. In the franchise world, this is known as co-branding, such as when a sandwich chain places a unit in a convenience store. Be sure to put your space-sharing agreement in writing, com-pletely detailing each party's rights and responsibilities, and give yourself an out if you need it.

2. **Retail:** Retail space comes in a variety of shapes and sizes and may be located in enclosed malls, strip shopping centers, free-standing buildings, downtown shopping districts or mixed-use facilities. You'll also find retail space in airports and other trans-portation facilities, hotel lobbies, sports stadiums, and a variety of temporary or special event venues.

3. **Mobile:** Whether you're selling to the general public or other businesses, if you have a product or service that you take to your customers, your ideal location may be a car, van or truck.

4. **Commercial:** Commercial space includes even more options than retail. Commercial office buildings and business parks offer traditional office space geared to businesses that do not require a significant amount of pedestrian or automobile traffic for sales. You'll find commercial office space in downtown business dis-

LOCATION WORK SHEET

Answer the following questions by indicating whether it is a strength (S) or weakness (W) of the potential site as it relates to your business. Once you have completed a work sheet for each prospective location, compare the relative strengths and weaknesses of each site to determine the value of each to the success of your business.

	S	W
Is the facility large enough for your business?		
Does it meet your layout requirements well?		
Does the building need any repairs?		
Will you have to make any leasehold improvements?		
Do the existing utilities meet your needs, or will you have to do any rewiring or plumbing work? Is ventilation adequate?		
Is the facility easily accessible to your potential clients or customers?		
Can you find a number of qualified employees in the area in which the facility is located?		
Is the facility consistent with the image you would like to maintain?		
Is the facility located in a safe neighborhood with a low crime rate?		
Are neighboring businesses likely to attract customers who will also patronize your business?		
Are there any competitors located close to the facility? If so, can you compete with them successfully?		
Can suppliers make deliveries conveniently at this location?		
If your business expands in the future, will the facility be able to accommodate this growth?		
Are the lease terms and rent favorable?		
Is the facility located in an area zoned for your type of business?		

tricts, business parks, and sometimes interspersed among suburban retail facilities.

One office option to consider is an executive suite, where the landlord provides receptionist and secretarial services, faxing, photocopying, conference rooms and other support services as part of the space package. Executive suites help you project the image of a professional operation at a more affordable cost than a traditional office and can be found in most commercial office areas. Some executive suites even rent their facilities by the hour to homebased businesses or out-of-towners who need temporary office space.

5. **Industrial:** If your business involves manufacturing or heavy distribution, you'll need a plant or warehouse facility. Light industrial parks typically attract smaller manufacturers in nonpolluting indus-

---

Agent Avenues

Unless you have a significant amount of experience in shopping for commercial real estate, it's a good idea to use a qualified real estate agent. Whether you are buying or leasing, an agent can help by pre-screening properties, which saves you time, and by negotiating on your behalf, which can save you money.

Typically the seller or landlord pays the agent's commission, which may raise some questions in your mind about loyalty of the agent. However, keep in mind that the agent doesn't get paid until a deal that satisfies you both is negotiated.

You may opt to use a tenant's or buyer's agent that you pay yourself. In the real estate world, that's called tenant (or buyer) representation, a real estate specialty that is growing in popularity. Especially in tight market situations, it may be to your advantage to invest in an advocate who will negotiate on your behalf. For more information about tenant representation and for help in finding someone to assist you, contact the Society of Industrial and Office Realtors in Washington, DC.

Shop for a real estate agent as you would any professional service provider: Ask for referrals from friends and associates; interview several agents; be sure the agent you choose has expertise in the type of property or facility you need; check out the agent's track record, professional history and reputation; clarify how the agent will be compensated and by whom; and draw up a written agreement that outlines your mutual expectations.

tries as well as companies that need showrooms in addition to manufacturing facilities. Heavy industrial areas tend to be older and poorly planned and usually offer rail and/or water port access. Though industrial parks are generally newer and often have better infrastructures, you may also want to consider any free-standing commercial building that meets your needs and is adequately zoned.

ISSUES TO CONSIDER

With an overview of what's available, you now need to decide what's most appropriate for your business. Julien J. Studley, president and CEO of Julien J. Studley Inc., a real estate firm that represents commercial tenants nationwide, says the major things tenants are looking for is the best possible deal on the space and an available work force. He says the trend has shifted away from highly visible luxuries to utilitarian, practical buildings.

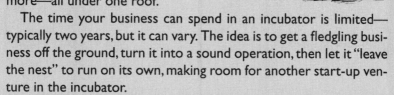

GROWING PLACES

Incubators are organizations sponsored by public and private investors that assist start-up and young companies in their critical early days with a variety of well-orchestrated business assistance programs. Incubators provide hands-on management assistance, access to financing, shared office services, access to equipment, flexible leases, expandable space, and more—all under one roof.

The time your business can spend in an incubator is limited—typically two years, but it can vary. The idea is to get a fledgling business off the ground, turn it into a sound operation, then let it "leave the nest" to run on its own, making room for another start-up venture in the incubator.

Incubators generally fall into the following categories: technology, industrial, mixed-use, economic empowerment, and industry-specific. For more information about incubators and for help finding one appropriate for your business, contact the National Business Incubation Association (NBIA) at (614) 593-4331. For a listing of incubators in your state, send a self-addressed, stamped envelope indicating the information you want to the NBIA at 20 E. Circle Dr., #190, Athens, OH 45701-3751.

MANUFACTURER'S SITE PLANNING CHECKLIST

When planning the layout of your manufacturing site, you want to be able to efficiently get raw material into the plant and move it through the manufacturing process as efficiently as possible. With this in mind, you should ask yourself the following questions.

❏ Is your receiving area in a location with easy access to large trucks?

❏ Is there suitable equipment on hand in the receiving area to unload incoming shipments efficiently?

❏ Do you have enough space to adequately warehouse your inventory of raw materials?

❏ Are your raw materials properly labeled in the warehouse area for easy retrieval?

❏ Is your warehouse space for raw material in close proximity to the first station used in the manufacturing process?

❏ Is there enough space on the manufacturing floor for the necessary equipment so the product can be taken through each step without having to backtrack to other stations on the floor?

❏ Have you analyzed each station in the manufacturing process to assure equipment is arranged in the most efficient manner?

❏ Are you maximizing the potential of each station in the manufacturing process by having as many tasks as possible performed in that area without creating a bottleneck?

❏ Is your finished product warehouse area located in close proximity to the last station in the manufacturing process?

❏ Are there proper storage materials and equipment such as floor racks, slip sheets, and pallets to handle the finished product?

❏ Is there appropriate materials-handling equipment to move the finished product into storage and out once it is ready to ship?

❏ Is your shipping area in close proximity to the warehouse area for the finished product?

❏ Is your shipping area easily accessible to large trucks?

Also, he says, there is much more emphasis on communications and computer-support needs today than in the past. Of course, your business may or may not follow the trends. Be systematic and realistic as you consider the following points.

Style Of Operation

Is your operation going to be formal and elegant? Or kicked-back and casual? Your location should be consistent with your particular style and image. If your business is retailing, do you want a traditional store, or would you like to try operating from a kiosk (or booth) in a mall or a cart that you can move to various locations? If you're in a traditional mall or shopping center, will the property permit you to have a sidewalk sale if you want to? Can you decorate your windows for special events the way you want to?

Smart Tip

If you're buying an existing business, look at the location as though you were starting from scratch. Ask questions like: Does the site meet your business's present and future needs? Have there been any significant changes regarding the location in recent years that could have a positive or negative impact on your business's future? Will you be taking over the seller's lease? If so, are you satisfied with the terms—and if you're not, can they be renegotiated?

Demographics

There are two important angles to the issue of demographics. One is your customers; the other is your employees.

First, consider who your customers are and how important their proximity to your location is. For a retailer and some service providers, this is critical; for other types of businesses, it may not be as important. The demographic profile you've developed of your target market will help you make this decision (see Chapter 7 for more on developing your target market).

Then, take a close look at the community. If your customer base is local, is the population large enough or does a sufficient percentage of that population match your customer profile to support your business? Does the community have a stable economic base that will provide a healthy environment for your business? Be cautious when considering communities that are largely dependent on a particular industry for their economy; a downturn could be a death knell for your company.

Now think about your work force. What skills do you need, and are people with those talents available? Does the community have the resources to serve their needs? Is there sufficient housing in the appropriate price range?

Bright Idea

If you're in a technology-related business, choose a location near a university that can help you with research, provide a resource for further education for your staff, and serve as a breeding ground for future employees.

Will your employees find the schools, recreational opportunities, culture and other aspects of the community satisfactory?

Especially when the economy is strong and unemployment figures are low, you may be concerned about the availability of good workers. Keep in mind that in many areas, few people may be unemployed, but many may be underemployed. If you're offering attractive jobs at competitive wages, you may find staffing your company easier than you thought. Look beyond the basic employment statistics to find out what the job market is really like. Consider placing a blind test ad (the local economic development agency may do this for you) to see what type of response you'll get in the way of applicants before making a final location decision.

Demographic information is available through a variety of resources. You could do the research yourself by visiting the local library or calling the U.S. Census Bureau and gathering a bunch of statistics and try to figure out what they mean, but chances are you probably don't have the time or statistical expertise to do that. So let other people do it for you—people who know how to gather the data and translate it into information you can understand and use. Contact your state, regional or local economic development agency (see "To The Rescue" in this chapter) or commercial real estate companies and use the data they've already collected, analyzed and processed.

Foot Traffic

For most retail businesses, foot traffic is extremely important. You don't want to be tucked away in a corner where shoppers are likely to bypass you, and even the best retail areas have dead spots. By contrast, if your business requires confidentiality, you may not want to be located in a high-traffic area. Monitor the traffic outside a potential location at different times of the day and on different days of the week to make sure the volume of pedestrian traffic meets your needs.

Accessibility And Parking

Consider how accessible the facility will be for everyone who must use it—customers, employees and suppliers. If you're on a busy street, how easy is it for cars to get in and out of your parking lot? Is the facility accessible to people with disabilities? What sort of deliveries are you likely to receive, and will your suppliers be able to easily and efficiently get materials to you? Small package couriers need to get in and out quickly; trucking companies need adequate roads and loading docks if you're going to be receiving freight on pallets.

Find out about the days and hours of service and access to locations you're considering. Are the heating and cooling systems left on or turned off at night and on weekends? If you're inside an office building, are there periods when exterior doors are locked and, if so, can you have keys? A beautiful office building at a great price is a lousy deal if you plan to work weekends but the building is closed on Saturdays and Sundays—or they allow you access, but the air conditioning is turned off so you roast in the summer and freeze in the winter.

Be sure, too, that there's ample convenient parking for both customers and employees. As with foot traffic, take the time to monitor the facility at various times and days to see how the demand for parking fluctuates. Also, consider safety issues: The parking lot should be well-maintained and adequately lighted.

CART BLANCHE

Carts and kiosks have become familiar sights in American malls, selling everything from inexpensive gift items to pricey jewelry and artwork. They make mall space affordable for the small-business owner, and the mall operators benefit from extra rent and a wider variety of merchandise.

Carts and kiosks have contributed to one of the hottest trends in retailing—temporary tenants. Most often these are seasonal businesses that only need to be open for a limited time. For example, a specialty candy shop may open just before Christmas, remain open through Valentine's Day, Easter and Mother's Day, then close for the remainder of the year. Some temporary tenants occupy traditional storefront space, but most opt for carts or kiosks. The most popular site for a temporary operation is a busy mall, but many operators are also finding success in airports and other transportation facilities, at sporting events, and at other creative venues limited only by their imagination and ability to strike a deal with the property manager.

Consider using carts and kiosks to test your product in a retail setting before making the larger investment in a traditional store. Styles range from simple to elaborate; whatever you choose, be sure it's attractive, well-lighted and functional.

Business Lease Checklist

After you have chosen a site, check the following points before you sign the lease:

❏ Is there sufficient electrical power?

❏ Are there enough electrical outlets?

❏ Is there enough parking spaces for customers and employees?

❏ Is there sufficient lighting? Heating? Air conditioning?

❏ Do you know how large a sign and what type you can erect at your facility?

❏ Will your city's building and zoning departments allow your business to operate in the facility?

❏ Will the landlord allow the alterations that you deem necessary for your business?

❏ Must you pay for returning the building to its original condition when you move?

❏ Is there any indication of roof leaks? (A heavy rain could damage stored goods.)

❏ Is the cost of burglary insurance high in the area? (This varies tremendously.)

❏ Can you secure the building at a low cost against the threat of burglary?

❏ Will the health department approve your business at this location?

❏ Will the fire department approve the operation of your business at this location?

❏ Have you included a written description of the property?

❏ Have you attached drawings of the property to the lease document?

❏ Do you have written guidelines for renewal terms?

❏ Do you know when your lease payment begins?

❏ Have you bargained for one to three months' free rent?

❏ Do you know your date of possession?

❏ Have you listed the owner's responsibility for improvements?

❏ Do you pay the taxes?

❏ Do you pay the insurance?

❏ Do you pay the maintenance fees?

❏ Do you pay the utilities?

❏ Do you pay the sewer fees?

❏ Have you asked your landlord for a cap of 5 percent on your rent increases?

❏ Have you included penalty clauses in case the project is late and you're denied occupancy?

❏ Have you retained the right to obtain your own bids for signage?

❏ Can you leave if the center is never more than 70 percent leased?

❏ Has a real estate attorney reviewed your contract?

Competition

Are competing companies located near your business? Sometimes competition can be good, such as in industries where comparison shopping is popular. (That's why competing retail businesses, such as fast-food restaurants, antique shops and clothing stores tend to cluster together.) You may also catch the overflow from existing businesses, particularly if your company is located in a restaurant and entertainment area. But if a nearby competitor is only going to make your marketing job tougher, look elsewhere.

DEMOGRAPHIC COMPARISON WORK SHEET

To see if the community you are considering offers a population with the demographic traits you need to support your business, fill out the following form.

Population	Market A	Market B	Market C
Within one mile of your business			
Within five miles of your business			
Within 25 miles of your business			

Income	Market A	Market B	Market C
Under $15,000			
$15,000–$25,000			
$25,000–$35,000			
$35,000–$50,000			
$50,000+			

Age	Market A	Market B	Market C
Preteen			
Teens			
20–29			
30–39			
40–49			
50–59			
60–69			
70+			

Density	Market A	Market B	Market C
Homeowners			
Renters			
Urban			

LEASE LOGIC

1. *Flat lease:* The oldest and simplest type of lease, the flat lease sets a single price for a definite period of time. It generally is the best deal for the tenant but is becoming increasingly hard to find. (Caution: Avoid a flat lease if the term is too short; a series of short-term flat leases could cost you more in the long run than a longer-term lease with reasonable escalation clauses.)

2. *Step lease:* The step lease attempts to cover the landlord's expected increases in expenses by increasing the rent on an annual basis over the life of the agreement. The problem with step leases is that they are based on estimates rather than actual costs, and there's no way for either party to be sure in advance that the proposed increases are fair and equitable.

3. *Net lease:* Similar to a step lease, the net lease increases the rent to cover increases in the landlord's costs but does so at the time they occur rather than on estimates. This may be more equitable than a step lease, but it's less predictable.

4. *Cost of living lease:* Rather than tying rent increases to specific expenses, this type of lease bases increases on the rises in the cost of living. Your rent will go up with general inflation. Of course, the prices for your products and services will also likely rise with inflation and that should cover your rent increases, so this type of lease can be very appealing.

5. *Percentage lease:* This lease lets the landlord benefit from your success. The rent is based on either a minimum or base amount, or a percentage of your business's gross revenue, whichever is higher. Percentages typically range from 3 percent to 12 percent. With this type of lease, you'll be required to periodically furnish proof of gross sales; to do this, you may have to allow the landlord to examine your books or sales tax records, or provide a copy of the appropriate section of your tax return. Percentage leases are common for retail space.

Proximity To Other Businesses

Take a look at what other businesses and services are in the vicinity from two key perspectives. First, consider whether you can benefit from nearby businesses, either by the customer traffic they generate, or because those companies and their employees could become your customers, or because it may be convenient and efficient for you to be their customer.

Second, think about how they will enrich the quality of your company as a workplace. Is there an adequate selection of restaurants so your employees have places to go for lunch? Is there a nearby day-care center for employees with children? Are other shops and services you and your employees might want conveniently located?

Smart Tip

Keep your long-range plan in mind, even when short-term advantages make a location look extremely attractive. A great deal on a place you're likely to outgrow in a few years may not really be such a great deal. Similarly, if the area shows evidence of pending decline, think about whether you really want to be located there in five years.

Image And History Of The Site

What does this address say about your company? Particularly if you're targeting a local market, be sure your location accurately reflects the image you want to project. It's also a good idea to check out the history of the site. Consider how it has changed and evolved over the years.

Ask about previous tenants. If you're opening a restaurant where five restaurants have failed in as many years, you may be starting off with an insurmountable handicap—either because there's something wrong with the location or because the public will assume that your business will go the way of the previous tenants. If several types of businesses have been there and failed, do some research to find out why—you need to confirm whether the problem was in the businesses or in the location. That previous occupants have been wildly successful is certainly a good sign, but temper that with information on what type of businesses they were.

Bright Idea

Consider stockpiling space. If you're reasonably sure you're going to need additional space within a few years, it might be wise to lease a facility of that size now and sublease the extra space until you need it. That way, you'll know the space will be available later on, and you won't be faced with moving.

Another historical point you'll want to know is whether a serious crime, tragedy or other notable event occurred on the property. If so, will the public's memory reflect on your operation, and is that reflection likely to be positive or negative?

Ordinances

Find out if any ordinances or zoning restrictions could affect your business in any way. Check for the specific location you're considering as well as neighboring properties—you probably don't want a night club opening up next to your day-care center.

The Building's Infrastructure

Many older buildings do not have the necessary infrastructure to support the high-tech needs of contemporary operations. Be sure the building you're considering has adequate electrical, air conditioning and telecommunications service to meet your business's present and future needs. It's a good idea to hire an independent engineer to check this out for you, so you're sure to have an objective evaluation.

To The Rescue

One of the best sources of information and assistance for start-up and expanding businesses is state, regional and local economic development agencies. According to Ted M. Levine, chairman of Development Counsellors International, a consulting firm specializing in economic development marketing and analysis, there are nearly 12,000 economic development groups across the United States that charge nothing for their services and assistance. These agencies are either public or private, or most often a public/private partnership, and their purpose is to promote economic growth and development in the areas they serve. They accomplish that by encouraging new businesses to locate in their area, and to do that, they've gathered all the statistics and information you'll need to make a decision.

Levine says economic development agencies will help any new business, regardless of size, in four primary ways:

1. Market demographics

2   Real estate costs and availability; zoning and regulatory issues

3. Work-force demographics

4. Referrals to similar companies and other resources

For the best overview, start with your state agency. The state agency can then guide you to regional and local groups for expanded information. (For a complete listing of state economic development agencies, see "Appendix B.")

Beware!

Be wary of incentives. Often incentives—such as free rent or tax breaks—may be masking serious problems. There's usually a good reason why any location offers incentives, and you need to be sure what it is before you sign up. You should be able to start a profitable business in that location without any incentives—and then let the incentives be a bonus.

Utilities And Other Costs

Rent is certainly the major portion of your ongoing facilities expense, but it's not all. Consider extras such as utilities—they're included in some leases, but not in others. If they're not included, ask the utility company for a summary of the previous year's usage and billing for the site. Also, find out what kind of security deposits the various utility providers require so you can develop an accurate move-in budget; however, you may not need a deposit if you have an established payment record with the company.

If you have to provide your own janitorial service, what will it cost? What are insurance rates for the area? Do you have to pay extra for parking? Make sure you consider all your location-related expenses, and factor them into your decision.

Room For Growth

Look at the facility with an eye to the future. It's generally unwise to begin with more space than you need, but if you anticipate growth, be sure the facility you choose can accommodate you.

WHAT CAN YOU EXPECT TO PAY?

Real estate costs vary tremendously based on the type of facility, the region, the specific location and the market. A commercial real estate broker will be able to give you an overview of costs in your area. You may want to look at historical data—how has the rate for your type of facility fluctuated over the years? Also ask for forecasts so you know what to expect in the future. Understanding the overall market will be a tremendous help when you begin negotiating your lease.

COMMERCIAL LEASES

If you've never been involved in renting commercial space, your first glimpse of a commercial lease may be overwhelming. They are lengthy, full of jargon and unfamiliar terms, and always written to the landlord's advantage. But they *are* negotiable. Whether you're working on the deal yourself or using an agent, the key to successful lease negotiations is knowing what you want, understanding what the lease document says, and being reasonable in your demands.

Especially for retail space, be sure your lease includes a *bail-out clause*, which lets you out of the lease if your sales don't reach an agreed-on amount, and a *co-tenancy clause* so you can break the lease if an anchor store closes or moves. If you're going to have to do a substantial amount of work to get the space ready for occupancy, consider negotiating a *construction allowance*—generally $5 to $25 per square foot—to help offset the costs.

Be sure you clearly understand the difference between *rentable* and what is *usable* space. Rentable space is what you pay for; usable is what you can actually use to run your business and typically doesn't include hallways, restrooms, lobbies, elevator shafts, stairwells and so forth.

You may be expected to pay a pro-rated portion of common area maintenance costs. This is not unusual, but be sure the fees are reasonable and that the landlord isn't making a profit on these charges. Also, check for clauses that allow the landlord the right to remodel at the tenants' expense without prior approval and insist on language that limits your financial liability.

Leasehold Improvements

Leasehold improvements are the nonremovable installations—either original or the results of remodeling—that you make to the facility to accommodate your business needs. Such improvements are typically more substantial when renting new space, which may consist of only concrete walls and flooring. Often existing space will include at least some fixtures you can use. Get estimates on the improvements you'll need to make before signing the lease, so you'll know what your total move-in costs will be and so you can make a fair construction allowance request.

Negotiating The Lease

The first lease the landlord presents is usually just the starting point. You may be surprised at what you can get in the way of concessions and extras simply by asking. Of course, you need to be reasonable and keep your demands in line with acceptable business practices and current market conditions. A good commercial real estate agent can be invaluable in this area. Avoid issuing ultimatums; they almost always close doors—and if you fail to follow through, your next "ultimatum" won't mean much. Consider beginning the process with something that's close to your "best and final offer." That way, your negotiations won't be lengthy and protracted, and you can either reach a mutually acceptable deal or move on to a different property. The longer negotiations take, the more potential there is for things to go wrong.

Essentially, everything in the lease is subject to negotiation, including financial terms, the starting rent, rent increases, tenant leasehold improvements, options for lease renewal, the tenant's rights and responsibilities, and other general terms and conditions. You or your agent can negotiate the lease, but then it should be drawn up by an attorney. Typically, the landlord or his attorney will draft the lease, and an attorney you hire who specializes in real estate should review it for you before you sign.

It Still Comes Down To You

Technology and statistics are important elements of your site-selection decision, but nothing beats your personal involvement in the process. Real estate brokers and economic development agencies can give you plenty of numbers, but remember their job is to get you to choose their location. To get a balanced picture, take the time to visit the sites yourself, talk to people who own or work in nearby businesses, and verify the facts and what they really mean to the potential success of your business.

GLOSSARY

Absolute net lease: a lease in which the tenant agrees to pay a basic rent and be responsible and separately pay for all maintenance, operating and other expenses of the building or office.

Amenities: any material goods, services or intangible items that increase the comfort, attractiveness, desirability, and value of an office suite or building

Assemblage: the combining of two or more contiguous properties into one large property. An assemblage will often make the one large property more valuable than the separate parts

Assessment: the determination or setting of a tax or other charge based on a building's estimated value

Attornment: a lease provision whereby the tenant agrees, in advance, to accept and pay rent or other required payments to a new landlord or legal owner of the property

Available office space: describes office space that is vacant and available for lease but that may or may not be ready for occupancy as it may be under construction, needs to be built-out to a tenant's specifications, or requires remodeling

Binding letter of intent: a letter of intent would be upheld in a court of law as an actual lease by the tenant from the landlord and by the landlord to the tenant regardless of whether an actual lease document was agreed to or signed

Broker: an individual who acts on behalf of another person as an agent to locate, negotiate for, lease, purchase, or sell office space, buildings, land or any other real estate

Building standard workletter: a list and/or detail specifications of the construction items (both quantity and quality) that will be provided by the developer to be used in building-out a tenant's office space

Commission: the fee earned by a real estate agent (broker, leasing agent, etc.) for matching a lessee and lessor and/or purchaser and seller of real estate, and for being the catalyst that makes a real estate transaction happen (a commission is typically a percentage of the total value of the transaction; however, it can also be any fee paid for brokerage services and, therefore, can be a fixed amount or even an equity or ownership position in the transaction)

Common areas: those areas or portions of a building used by more than one tenant, such as hallways, elevator lobby areas, janitorial and maintenance closets/rooms and restrooms

Comparables: the terms of executed leases that are used both as examples for the kinds and types of lease terms available in the marketplace for potential office users and for comparing the overall value of a proposed lease to executed leases for similar-sized office users, to leases in the same or nearby buildings, and to leases by a particular landlord

Contiguous office space: office suites adjacent to each other or having a common demising wall

Contingent agreement: an agreement between two parties in which a lease, sale, or purchase of property, or the payment of monies, is dependent on a special condition or contractual obligation (usually involving a third-party involvement or commitment)

Demising walls: the walls that designate the perimeter of an office suite and/or partition or separate one office suite from another; is typically constructed slab-to-slab and is both sound-conditioned and fire-resistant

Easement: the right of an individual or entity to use the land of another individual or entity, usually for a specific purpose

Escalator(s): term used to describe how a tenant's payment for rent or service shall increase

Holdover rent: an extremely high rent intended as a penalty to a tenant who continues to use or remain in possession of a leased premises beyond the lease term

Holding over: the period a tenant remains in possession of the leased premises beyond the expiration or termination date of the lease document; holding over can occur with or without the landlord's consent or permission

Lease: a contract whereby an individual or entity grants occupancy or use of property to another individual or entity for a specified time period, rent payment and other conditions

Lease clause: a paragraph or provision describing mutual agreement, business principles, performance criteria, or other arrangements, the sum of which make up a lease document

Leasehold improvements: the construction, fixtures, attachments, and any and all physical changes and additions made to lease premises either made by the tenant (with or without the landlord's permission) or on the tenant's behalf by the landlord or a representative (e.g., subcontractor) of the tenant

Lease term: the length of time a lease is in full force and effect

Leasing agent: an individual who specializes in leasing commercial real estate including office, retail and industrial space; a leasing agent must work for a principal broker and be licensed

Lessee: the individual or entity paying rent for, using and/or taking possession of office space; also known as the tenant

Lessor: the individual or entity receiving the rent for and/or granting permission to use or take possession of office space; also known as the landlord

Letter of intent: a signed agreement by both tenant and landlord prior to the lease that sets forth primary terms, conditions and considerations that are to form the basis of the lease

Liability of landlord provision: a lease clause severely limiting the landlord's liability for use of the building and office space by tenants, guests, employees, visitors, etc

Market rent: the current rental rates paid by tenants for like use (office space) in buildings of comparable size with similar qualities of construction and building amenities, and comparable surrounding neighborhood characteristics and environment; term is often used in renewal clauses as the rent that will be paid if lease renewal occurs

Pre-leasing: the leasing of office space before a building is constructed or during the construction phase

Rent abatement: a concession offered by a landlord as an inducement to tenants to lease office space; provides for a reduction of monthly rent by omitting a required payment for a specific number of months

Rentable area: a number expressed in terms of square feet, specified in the lease document as the amount of space the tenant has leased and for which the tenant shall be assessed rent

Sublease: a lease document subordinated to another lease document; a sublease is the document that covers sublet space

Sublet space: space that is being offered for lease by a tenant rather than a landlord

Tenancy: the possession or occupancy of land, a building, an office suite, a room, or other real estate by title, under a lease, or on payment of rent with or without a written lease; also refers to the period of time a tenant has occupancy or possession

Tenant: an individual or entity, such as a corporation, who holds or possesses property by any kind of right or title for a specified time period; also an individual or entity who pays rent to use or occupy land, a building, an office suite, a room, or other property owned by another individual or entity

Tenant construction workletter: an addendum or attachment to the lease document that details the responsibilities of both the tenant and the landlord as they relate to the construction of the tenant's office space

Tenant improvements: the construction, fixtures, attachments, and any and all physical changes and additions made to a tenant's office space for the benefit of the tenant, by the tenant (usually with the landlord's permission), or on the tenant's behalf by the landlord or a representative (subcontractor) of the tenant

Tenant occupancy: when a tenant has control or possession or actually uses the demised premises as defined in a lease

Usable area: the floor space on a given building's floor that can be used by a tenant and/or is enclosed as an office suite

Zoning: the mandate of local government through laws and ordinances as to the use and purpose of real property in specified areas or districts as well as any associated limitations or other requirements

CHAPTER 18

FIRST IMPRESSIONS

Creating a professional image

hese days, it's just not enough to create a terrific product, offer super service, and have a solid business plan to back you up. Your company image is equally important to the overall success of your business.

Think about it. Every time you hand out your business card, send a letter or welcome a client into your office or store, you're selling someone on your company. Your business card, letterhead and signage—just like traditional print, radio or TV ads—are valuable selling tools. The look of your office also helps "sell" your business by conveying an image, whether it's that of a funky, creative ad agency or a staid, respectable accounting firm.

Fortunately, just because you're a start-up company doesn't mean you have to look like one. Your logo, business card, signage and style are all part of a cohesive image program known as corporate identity. And with the right corporate identity, your company can appear highly professional and give the impression of having been in business for years. In this chapter, we'll discuss how to create a corporate image that works.

OFFICE SPACE

When you are a start-up with limited capital, it may be tempting to put all your money into advertising and equipment and skimp on office furniture. How you furnish your office might not seem to matter, especially if your customers won't see it. And if your office is located at home, the dining room table might look like the most logical choice.

But a nicely furnished office is not just a matter of aesthetics. Grabbing whatever furniture is at hand and plunking it down without a thought to organization can put you at a major disadvantage in terms of productivity.

Everything In Its Place

Improving your own and your employees' performance involves a lot more than finding comfortable chairs. It involves placement of offices or cubicles within the building, proximity to equipment, lighting, desk space, meeting areas, privacy and more. People spend most of their waking hours at the office, so its design has a tremendous effect on morale, according to *Office Access*, a guide to designing high-performance offices.

Smart Tip

If you do a lot of computer work, consider investing in an "L"-shaped desk, with your computer and keyboard tray on the small side of the "L." This gets your computer out of the way and ensures you have plenty of work space when you need it.

How can you create a high-performance office? The first step is addressing organizational issues of who sits where. According to *Office Access*, the days of big "power desks" and hierarchical corner offices are over. More businesses are turning to flexible environments ideal for small companies where the business owner probably doubles as salesperson.

With today's emphasis on team building, office design is moving away from compartmentalized offices and toward large spaces where teams of employees can work. When setting up your space, think about who needs to work with whom and which employees share what resources. By grouping those people together, you enhance their productivity.

ON THE OUTSIDE

The inside of your office may look great, but don't stop there. What about the outside? If the first impression a potential customer has of your business is a shabby door or an unkempt parking lot, you're not sending the right message . . . and all your hard work in designing an attractive, efficient office could be going to waste.

Step outside your place of business and take a long, hard look at the parking lot, sidewalks, windows, outside lighting, landscaping and the outside of the building itself. A well-maintained building projects an industrious, professional image. Weeds, trash, broken sidewalks, tattered awnings, dirty windows, dead plants and overflowing trash containers send the message "We don't care."

Whether you're in a retail location or an office building, take the time to check the property from outside, and make sure it's inviting and appealing every day.

In addition to maximizing your and your employees' productivity, your office may also function as a marketing tool if clients or customers visit. Think about what visitors will see when they come by. Will they be bombarded with noise from one department near the entrance? Or will they see a series of closed doors with seemingly no activity taking place? Visitors shouldn't be overwhelmed by chaos as they walk through your building, but they should see signs of life and get glimpses of the daily activities going on at your company.

Putting It All Together

Once considered some trendy European way to make business owners spend a lot of money, ergonomics has gained respect in recent years. Simply put, this term refers to designing and arranging furnishings and space to fit the natural movements of the human body. Ergonomics can help you and your employees avoid repetitive stress injuries from typing or bending, and can prevent common problems like back pain, which often sideline entrepreneurs and their employees.

WHAT'S IN STORE?

Got a retail location? Ask yourself these questions to make sure your store has the "eye appeal" it needs to keep customers coming back:

◆ Are your shelves clean and neat? Is merchandise displayed so people can see it easily?

◆ Is the area around your cash registers or terminals clean and orderly?

◆ Can you find the forms, packaging and related materials you need quickly and easily?

◆ Are light fixtures clean, bright and working properly?

◆ Is there plenty of room between counters and shelves so that aisles are wide and free of barriers?

◆ Are glass surfaces clean, and are floors vacuumed or swept and scrubbed regularly?

Noise pollution is one of the biggest problems in many offices. One good way to decrease noise is to cover computer printers with sound shields. Covering a printer can cut noise by more than 90 percent . . . and increases concentration accordingly.

Buy adjustable chairs. A good chair allows the user to adjust the seat height and the tension of the backrest. The seat should angle forward slightly to keep from cutting off your circulation. Boost the benefits of a good chair by providing footrests. Elevating the feet slightly while typing or sitting at a desk reduces lower back strain and improves circulation, keeping you more alert.

Make sure the desk and chair arrangement you choose allows you to keep the tops of your knuckles and tops of your wrists, and your forearms all in a straight line as you work on your computer. Your computer monitor should be at or below eye level. Use under-desk keyboard trays and monitor stands, if necessary, to get everything in line.

Another often-ignored problem in offices is lighting. Too much or too little lighting causes eye strain and tiredness, decreasing productivity. To cut down on glare, put filters on computer screens. Use individual lamps to illuminate desk work and help eyes adjust from overlit computer screens to underlit paper. Install miniblinds to let each employee control the amount of light to match the task at hand and time of day.

You can find office furniture touted as ergonomic at a variety of sources, from office supply superstores to traditional office furniture retailers. Just because something claims to be ergonomic, however, doesn't mean it's right for you. Always test furnishings before you buy. Sit in the chair and make sure it's comfortable; sit at the desk and make sure it's the right height. Make sure your desk and chair work together and that there is plenty of legroom under the desk.

When buying furniture, look for solid construction, particularly in desks. The ready-to-assemble desks available at home or office superstores are often poor quality. Most are made of particleboard, which won't stand up to heavy use. A better option for those on a budget is to buy used office furniture.

More and more furniture dealers these days sell used (also called "reconditioned") office furniture. You can find everything from a single desk and chair to a full fleet of cubicles for your staff. Typically, furniture has been repaired and repainted where necessary. In some cases, savings can be up to 70 percent over the cost of the same items new.

You can find used furniture sources in the Yellow Pages, or look in your local newspaper's classified ad section for individuals selling used pieces. Flea markets, auctions and estate sales can be other sources of used items.

DESIGNING A LOGO

Before you start designing a business card or picking colors for your letterhead, you need a logo. Featuring your company name and embellished with a little color and perhaps a few graphic touches here and there, your logo is the most important design element because it is the basis for all your other materials: stationery, packaging, promotional materials and signage.

"Through the use of color and graphics, your logo should reflect the overall image you want your company to convey," says Richard Gerstman, founder of Gerstman + Meyers, a brand identity and marketing consulting firm. "It should give people a feel for what your company is all about."

For example, say your product is an organic facial cream you'll be marketing to health-conscious consumers. Your logo should represent your product's best benefits—being all-natural and environmentally sound. Creating a simple, no-nonsense logo using earth tones and a plain typeface will give the impression of a product that is "back to basics," which is exactly what you want to achieve. Take that same product and give it a slick, high-tech look with neon colors, however, and people won't associate your logo with the down-to-earth product you're selling.

Logos come in two basic forms: abstract symbols (like the apple in Apple Computer) or logotypes, a stylized rendition of your company's name. You can also use a combination of both. Alan Siegel, chairman and CEO of Siegel & Gale, a design firm specializing in corporate identity, warns that promoting an abstract symbol can prove very costly for a small business on a budget. In addition, he says, such logos are harder to remember. "A logotype or word mark is much easier to recall," Siegel says. If you do use an abstract symbol, Siegel advises, always use it in connection with your business name.

Trying to create a logo on your own may seem like the best way to avoid the high costs of going to a professional design firm, which will charge anywhere from $4,000 to $15,000 for a logo alone. However, be aware that there are thousands of independent designers around who charge much less. According to Stan Evenson, founder of Evenson Design Group, entrepreneurs on a tight budget should shop around for a designer. "There are a lot of [freelance] design-

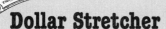

Dollar Stretcher

Creating your image can be costly, but you don't have to splurge on the whole works at once. To save money, start with the key items the public will see immediately. If you expect to attract most of your clients through sales calls, for instance, put more money into your business cards; if you expect to lure people with your sign, put the money there.

ers who charge rates ranging from $15 to $150 per hour, based on their experience," he says.

But don't hire someone just because of their bargain price. Find a designer who's familiar with your field . . . and with your competition. If the cost still seems exorbitant, Evenson says, "remember that a good logo should last at least 10 years. If you look at the amortization of that cost over a 10-year period, it doesn't seem so bad."

Even if you have a good eye for color and a sense of what you want your logo to look like, you should still consult a professional designer. Why? They know whether or not a logo design will transfer easily into print or onto a sign, while you might come up with a beautiful design that can't be transferred or would cost too much money to be printed. Your logo is the foundation for all your promotional materials, so this is one area where spending a little more now really pays off later.

Business Cards

Once you have your logo, it's time to apply it to the marketing items you'll use most, such as business cards. A good business card should convey the overall image of your business—not easy, considering the card mea-

In The Cards

Business cards don't have to be boring. If your industry allows for a little creative flair, here are some ideas to try:

◆ Use 4-by-7-inch cards that fold over (like a minibrochure), cards made of plastic or cards with photos on them. If your business relies on a lot of phone contact, consider cards that are prepunched to fit in a Rolodex.

◆ Although they're expensive, cards in nontraditional shapes get attention. Try a teddy bear shape for a day-care service, for example, or a birthday cake for a party planner.

◆ Textured paper can add to a card's interest (make sure it doesn't detract from readability, though), as can colored paper. In general, stay with lighter shades that enhance readability.

◆ Thermography, a process that creates raised, shiny print, adds interest to a card. Embossing and foil stamping are two other imprinting processes that can give your card visual appeal.

Beware!

Evaluate business card designs with three criteria in mind:

◆ Is the card easy to read?

◆ Does the design catch your eye? (A good designer can make even an all-type card appealing.)

◆ Is your name or the business's name immediately identifiable?

sures only 2 inches by 3½ inches. How can you possibly get a message across in such a small amount of space?

You can't expect your business card to tell the whole story about your company. What you should expect it to do is present a professional image people will remember. "A business card can make or break a client's first impression of your company," Evenson claims. That little card makes as much of an impression as your personal appearance—the suit you wear or the briefcase you carry.

The color, wording and texture of your business card have a lot to do with its appeal and its ability to convey your company image. Use common sense when designing your card. If your business markets children's games, you might try a card with bright, primary colors and words written in a child's script. On the other hand, if you run a financial consulting service, your card should convey professionalism and reliability, so stick to traditional looks such as black printing on a gray, beige or white background.

Of course, professional designers claim entrepreneurs shouldn't attempt a business card design on their own, but many cash-strapped business owners have no choice. Looking at all the business cards you receive and emulating the cards you like is a good idea. You've got more leeway if you're in a creative business, such as party planning or retailing, but in general, keep the following tips in mind:

◆ Use your logo as the basis. Make it the largest element on the card.

◆ Don't make the card an unusual shape.

◆ Keep it simple. Don't cram too much information on the card.

◆ Do include the essentials— your name, title, company

Smart Tip

Once you've got business cards, make the most of them:

◆ Always give people more than one card (so they can give them to others).

◆ Include your card in all correspondence.

◆ Carry cards with you at all times, in a card case so they're clean and neat.

name, address, phone and fax numbers and e-mail address.

◆ Make sure the typeface is easily readable.

◆ Stick to one or two colors.

SELECTING STATIONERY

Every time you mail a letter to a prospective client or to an existing customer, the missive leaves a long-lasting impression of your company. In a service business, your written materials are among your company's most important marketing items. And if you run a homebased business that doesn't have a commercial location or sign, introducing your company to clients through the mail can be one of your most effective marketing techniques.

The paper stock you choose, as well as the colors and graphics embellishing it, plays an important role in the image your stationery presents. A hot, neon-pink stock may work well for a new suntan cream manufacturer, but not for an accounting service. Your stationery should tie in with your business cards, featuring the same color scheme and overall look.

Don't get so caught up in the design elements of your business stationery that you forget the obvious. Every piece of stationery should include the basics: your company name or logo, address, phone and fax numbers, and e-mail address. Make it as easy as possible for your clients to respond to your offer by making all the information they need readily available. And attach your business card to each letter as well, so clients can put it in their Rolodexes for future reference.

DESIGNING YOUR SIGN

Retailers and restaurateurs alike realize the power of a good sign. Some companies rely on drive-by or walk-by traffic for customers, and if that's the case with your company, your sign may be the most important element of your entire corporate identity.

A good sign must do more than just attract attention; it also has to be readable from a good distance. That's why your original logo is so important—one that looks great on a tiny business card may not transfer well to a huge sign above your store. Clearly, going to a professional in the first

> ### Bright Idea
>
> Ask owners of non-competing but related businesses if you can display some of your business cards on their counters. A pet-sitter, for example, could leave her business cards on the counter at a pet store. Offer to do the same for them.

stages of developing your image is essential. If you find out your great logo can't be reproduced on a sign, you'll have to go back to square one and rethink your logo, which will end up costing you more in the long run.

In recent years, a whole host of new signage materials has emerged to provide more variety and individuality. This also means it's harder to choose among all the possibilities, which include neon, plastic, metal, wood and more. Do some investigating before making your final decision; there is a wide discrepancy in prices for various materials. Depending on your location, sign placement can make a big difference, too. Options include a free-standing sign, a wall sign, a projecting sign or a roof sign.

Since you probably don't have the know-how or the equipment necessary to make a sign yourself, you'll have to go to an outside manufacturer. Don't expect manufacturers to offer suggestions or point out any problems with your design if you've come up with one on your own. That's not their job. Before you head to the manufacturer with your design specifications, check your local zoning laws. You may find that the design you've come up with for your fried chicken restaurant—a 30-foot neon number in the shape of a chicken—isn't allowed in your area. If you are planning to move into a shopping center, the developer may have additional regulations governing signage that can be used in the facility.

Most entrepreneurs need professional assistance with signage since they don't have experience in this area. You probably won't know how big the letters should be to be visible from down the block, and you may not know which materials fare best in inclement weather. For this reason, you should visit a professional—either a designer or a sign fabricator.

A good designer knows when fabricators are cutting corners and not using the material requested or doing a shoddy job. A designer will also be present at the installation to make sure the sign is put in place properly.

The cost of a sign varies greatly depending on the materials and type of sign. Buying directly from a fabricator can cost as little as $500, but you run the risk of not meeting zoning requirements. If you hire a designer, you'll pay a design fee in addition to fabrication costs, but you have a better guarantee that the finished product will work for you.

CHAPTER 19

TAKING
STOCK

The lowdown
on inventory

Where would an apparel company be without clothing? An auto supply store without auto parts? A computer company without computers? Nowhere, of course. Understanding and managing your inventory is one of the most critical factors in business success.

Yet, many entrepreneurs fail to answer such basic questions as "What items are the winners and losers?" and "How often does inventory turn over?" Don't make this mistake.

"Companies can increase their profitability 20 to 50 percent through prudent inventory management," says John Newman, a professor of entrepreneurship. "Some companies have more than doubled their profitability."

INVENTORY CONTROL

There is more to inventory control than simply buying new products. You have to know what to buy, when to buy it and how much to buy. You also need to track your inventory—whether manually or by computer— and use that knowledge to hone your purchasing process.

Start-up entrepreneurs are at a disadvantage when it comes to inventory control. "Many of them don't know how to set realistic inventory levels," says Newman, "so they wind up buying too much or too little."

Maintaining Enough Inventory

Your business's basic stock should provide a reasonable assortment of products and should be big enough to cover the normal sales demands of your business. Since you won't have actual sales and stocking figures from previous years to guide you during start-up, you must project your first year's sales based on your business plan.

When calculating basic stock, you must also factor in lead time—the length of time between reordering and receiving a product. For instance, if your lead time is four weeks and a particular product line sells 10 units a week, then you must reorder before the basic inventory level falls below 40 units. If you do not reorder until you actually need the stock, you'll have to wait four weeks without the product.

Beware!

Inventory control doesn't just mean counting. Take physical control of your inventory, too. Lock it up or restrict access. Remember that inventory is money.

Insufficient inventory means lost sales and costly, time-consuming back orders. Running out of raw materials or parts that are crucial to your production process means increased operating costs, too. Your employees will be getting paid to sit around because there's no work for them to do; when the inventory does come in, they'll be paid for working overtime to make up for lost production time. In some situations, you could even end up buying emergency inventory at high prices.

One way to protect yourself from such shortfalls is by building a safety margin into basic inventory figures. To figure out the right safety margin for your business, try to think of all the outside factors that could contribute to delays, such as suppliers who tend to be late or goods being shipped in from overseas. Once you have been in business a while, you'll have a better "feel" for delivery times and will find it fairly easy to calculate your safety margin.

Avoiding Excess Inventory

Avoiding excess inventory is especially important for owners of companies with seasonal product lines, such as clothing, home accessories or holiday and gift items. These products have a short shelf life and are hard to sell once they are no longer in fashion. Entrepreneurs who sell more timeless products, such as plumbing equipment, office supplies or auto products, have more leeway because it takes longer for these items to become obsolete.

No matter what your business, however, excess inventory is something to be avoided. It costs you money in extra overhead, debt service on loans to purchase the excess inventory, additional personal property tax on unsold inventory and increased insurance costs. In fact, one merchandise consultant estimates that it costs the average retailer anywhere from 20 percent to 30 percent of the original inventory investment just to maintain it. Buying excess inventory also reduces your liquidity—something to be avoided. Consider the example of an auto supply retailer who finds himself with the opportunity to buy 1,000 gallons of antifreeze at a huge discount.

Smart Tip

In addition to counting inventory weekly, monthly or annually, some experts recommend checking a few items each day to see if your actual amount is the same as what you have in your records. This is a good way to troubleshoot and nip inventory problems in the bud.

If he buys the antifreeze and it turns out to be a mild winter, he'll be sitting on 1,000 gallons of antifreeze. Even though he knows he can sell the antifreeze during the next cold winter, it's still taking up space in his warehouse for an entire year—space that could be devoted to more profitable products.

When you find yourself with excess inventory, your natural reaction will probably be to reduce the price and sell it quickly. Although this solves the overstocking problem, it also reduces your return on investment. All your financial projections assume that you will receive the full price for your goods. If you slash your prices by 15 percent to 25 percent just to get rid of the excess inventory, you're losing money you had counted on in your business plan.

Other novice entrepreneurs will react to excess inventory by being overly cautious the next time they order stock. However, this puts you at risk of having an inventory shortage and continuing a costly cycle of errors. To avoid accumulating excess inventory, establish a realistic safety margin and order only what you're sure you can sell.

Inventory And Cash Flow

Cash flow problems are some of the most common difficulties small businesses encounter, and they are usually the first signs of serious financial trouble ahead. According to Resource Evaluation Inc., a management consulting firm, tying money up in inventory can severely damage a small company's cash flow.

To control inventory effectively, prioritize your inventory needs. It might seem at first glance that the most expensive items in your inventory should receive the most attention. But in reality, less expensive items with higher turnover ratios have a greater effect on your business than more costly items. If you focus only on the high dollar-value items, you run the risk of running out of the lower-priced products that actually contribute more to your bottom line.

Divide materials into groups A, B and C depending on the dollar impact they have on the company (not their actual price). You can then stock more of the vital A items while keeping the B and C items at more manageable levels. This is known as the ABC approach.

Often, as much as 80 percent of a company's revenues come from only

20 percent of the products. Companies that respect this "80-20 rule" concentrate their efforts on that key 20 percent of items. "It's a major mistake to try to manage all products the same way," says Kay Roscoe Davis, a professor of production management.

Once you understand which items are most important, you'll be able to balance needs with costs, carrying only as much as you need of a given item. It's also a good idea to lower your inventory holding levels, keeping smaller quantities of an item in inventory for a short time rather than keeping large amounts for a long time. Consider ordering fewer items, but doing so more often.

Tracking Inventory

A good inventory tracking system will tell you what merchandise is in stock, what is on order, when it will arrive and what you've sold. With such a system, you can plan purchases intelligently and quickly recognize the fast-moving items you need to reorder and the slow-moving items you should mark down or specially promote.

You can create your own inventory tracking system or ask your accountant to set one up for you. Systems vary according to the amount of inventory displayed, the amount of backup stock required, the diversity of merchandise and the number of items that are routinely reordered compared to new items or one-time purchases.

Some retailers track inventory using a *manual tag system*, which can be updated daily, weekly or even monthly. In a manual tag system, you remove price tags from the product at the point of purchase. You then cross-check the tags against physical inventory to figure out what you have sold.

For example, a shoe-store retailer could use the tag system to produce a monthly chart showing sales according to product line, brand name and style. Along the top of the chart, he would list the various product lines (pumps, sneakers, loafers), and down the left margin, the various brand names and different styles. At the intersecting spaces down the column, he would mark how many of each brand were sold, in what style and color, whether the shoes were on sale or discounted, and any other relevant information.

Smart Tip

As your business expands and becomes more complex, you'll need more complex inventory techniques to keep up. Tap outside sources to beef up your and your employees' inventory management expertise. Inexpensive seminars held by banks, consultants and management associations offer a quick but thorough introduction to inventory management techniques.

Dollar-control systems show the cost and gross profit margin on individual inventory items. A basic method of dollar control begins at the cash register with sales receipts listing the product, quantity sold and price. You can compare sales receipts with delivery receipts to determine your gross profit margin on a given item. You can also use software programs to track inventory by type, cost, volume and profit. (For more on computerized inventory tracking, see the following section on "Computerized Inventory Control.")

Unit-control systems use methods ranging from simply eyeballing shelves to using sophisticated bin tickets—tiny cards kept with each type of product that list a stock number, description, maximum and minimum quantities stocked, cost (in code), selling price and any other information you want to include. Bin tickets correspond to office file cards that list a stock number, selling price, cost, number of items to a case, supply source and alternative source, order dates, quantities and delivery time. Retailers make physical inventory checks daily, weekly, or as often as practical—once a year at the minimum. Sometimes a store owner will assign each employee responsibility for keeping track of a certain group of items or, if the store is large enough, hire stock personnel just to organize and count stock.

PHONE PHONIES

Watch out! As an entrepreneur, you're a target for one of the most common—and potentially most costly—business scams: telemarketing con artists selling overpriced, poor-quality office supplies. Here are some tips to protect your business:

◆ The Federal Trade Commission requires telemarketers to disclose that it's a sales call, who they are and the total cost of what they are selling—so don't be afraid to ask.

◆ Make sure your employees are scam-aware, and establish a procedure for handling such calls.

◆ Keep track of all orders, and limit the number of staff who are allowed to order.

◆ If you receive merchandise you didn't order—and the seller cannot prove you did—you can keep the materials and are not obligated to pay.

Computerized Inventory Control

While manual methods may have their place, most entrepreneurs these days find that computerizing gives them a far wider range of information with far less effort. Inventory software programs now on the market let you track usage, monitor changes in unit dollar costs, calculate when you need to reorder, and analyze inventory levels on an item-by-item basis. You can even expand your earlier ABC analysis to include the profit margin per item.

In fact, many experts say that current computer programs are changing the rules of the ABC analysis. By speeding up the process of inventory control, computers give you more time so you can devote as much attention to the B and C items as to the A's.

You can even control inventory right at the cash register with point-of-sale (POS) software systems. POS software records each sale when it happens, so your inventory records are always up to date. Better still, you get much more information about the sale than you could gather with a manual system. By running reports based on this information, you can make better decisions about ordering and merchandising.

With a POS system:

◆ you can analyze sales data, figure out how well all the items on your shelves sell, and adjust purchasing levels accordingly.

◆ you can maintain a sales history to help adjust your buying decisions for seasonal purchasing trends.

◆ you can improve pricing accuracy by integrating bar-code scanners and credit card authorization ability with the POS system.

There are plenty of popular POS software systems that enable you to use add-on devices at your checkout stations, including electronic cash drawers, bar-code scanners, credit card readers, and receipt or invoice printers. POS packages frequently come with integrated accounting modules, including general ledger, accounts receivable, accounts payable, purchasing and inventory control systems. In essence, a POS system is an all-in-one way to keep track of your business's cash flow.

Features to consider in a POS system include the following:

◆ **Ease of use:** Look for software with a user-friendly graphical interface.

◆ **Entry of sales information:** Most systems allow you to enter inventory codes either manually or automatically via a bar-code scanner. Once the inventory code is entered, the systems call up the standard or sales price, compute the price at multiple quantities and provide a running total. Many systems make it easy to enter sales manually when needed by letting you search for inventory codes based on a partial merchandise number, description, manufacturing code or vendor.

◆ **Pricing:** POS systems generally offer a variety of ways to keep track of pricing, including add-on amounts, percentage of cost, margin percentage and custom formulas. For example, if you provide volume discounts, you can set up multiple prices for each item.

> **Bright Idea**
>
> APICS can provide expert advice on inventory management and suggest software programs to use; contact them at (703) 237-8344. In addition, many computer and software vendors sponsor free seminars to introduce new lines of inventory control products to prospective buyers.

◆ **Updating product information:** Once a sale is entered, these systems automatically update inventory and accounts receivable records.

◆ **Sales tracking options:** Different businesses get paid in different ways. For example, repair or service shops often keep invoices open until the work is completed, so they need a system that allows them to put sales on hold. If you sell expensive consumer goods and allow installment purchases, you might appreciate a loan calculator that tabulates monthly payments. And if you offer rent-to-own items, you'll want a system that can handle rentals as well as sales.

◆ **Security:** In retail, it's important to keep tight control over cash receipts to prevent theft. Most of these systems provide audit trails so you can trace any problems.

◆ **Taxes:** Many POS systems can support numerous tax rates—useful if you run a mail order business and need to deal with taxes for more than one state.

Perhaps the most valuable way POS systems help you gain better control of your business is through their reporting features. You can slice and dice sales data in a variety of ways to determine what products are selling best at what time, and to figure out everything from the optimal ways to arrange shelves and displays to what promotions are working best and when to change seasonal promotions.

Reporting capabilities available in POS programs include sales, costs, and profits by individual inventory items, by salesperson, or by category for the day, month and year to date. Special reports can include sales for each hour of the day for any time period. You can also create multiple formats for invoices, accounting statements and price tags. Additional reports include day-end cash reconciliation work sheets and inventory management. Examine a variety of POS packages to see which comes closest to meeting your needs.

Every business is unique; you may find that none of the available off-the-shelf systems meet all your requirements. Industry-specific POS packages are available—for auto repair shops, beauty and nail salons, video rental stores, dry cleaners and more. In addition, some POS system manufacturers will tailor their software to your needs.

Inventory Turnover

When you have replaced 100 percent of your original inventory, you have "turned over" your inventory. If you have, on the average, a 12-week supply of inventory and turn it over four times a year, the count cycle plus the order cycle plus the delivery cycle add up to your needs period. Expressed as an equation, it would read:

$$\text{Count Cycle} + \text{Order Cycle} + \text{Delivery Cycle} = \text{Needs Period}$$

For instance, suppose you decided to count inventory once every four weeks (the count cycle). Processing paperwork and placing orders with your vendors take two weeks (the order cycle). The order takes six weeks to get to you (delivery cycle). Therefore, you need 12 weeks' worth of inventory from the first day of the count cycle to stay in operation until your merchandise arrives.

You can improve your inventory turnover, however, if you count inventory more often—every two weeks instead of every four—and work with your suppliers to improve delivery efficiency. Alternate ways of distributing goods to the store could cut the delivery cycle down to three weeks, which would cut inventory needs to six weeks. As a result, inventory turnover could increase from four times a year to eight times.

Another way to look at turnover is by measuring sales per square foot. Taking the average retail value of inventory and dividing it by the number of square feet devoted to a particular product will give you your average sales per square foot.

You should know how many sales per square foot per year you need to survive. Calculate your sales per square foot once a month to make sure they are in line with your expectations.

ON WITH THE SHOW

Trade shows are the primary way for new businesses to find suppliers. All major suppliers in an industry display their products at seasonal trade shows, where retailers go to buy and look at new items.

Although retailers buy from various sources year-round, trade shows are an important event in every store owner's buying cycle. Most retailers attend at least one trade show per year. Smart buyers come prepared with a seasonal budget calculated either in dollar amounts or in quantities of various merchandise.

Practically every major city hosts one or more trade shows relevant to specific retailers. Contact your local chamber of commerce or convention and visitor's bureau for upcoming shows in your city or state. Your industry's trade publications should also list relevant trade shows. The *Tradeshow Week Data Book*, published annually, lists important data on all U.S. trade shows. Look for it at the library.

INVENTORY ACCOUNTING

If you spend a few minutes considering inventory, how you account for that inventory, and the taxes you must pay on it, you'll never again question the need for an accountant. However, it's important for every entrepreneur to have a basic understanding of inventory accounting, even if you rely on your accountant to do the actual numbers. There are two methods used for inventory valuation:

The *Last In, First Out* (LIFO) method assumes that you will sell the most recently purchased inventory first. For instance, suppose you bought 10 ceiling fans a year ago at $30 each. A week ago, you purchased a second lot of 10 ceiling fans, but now the price has gone up to $50 each. By using the LIFO method, you sell your customers the $50 ceiling fans first, which allows you to keep the less expensive units (in terms of your inventory cost) in inventory. Then, when you have to calculate inventory value for tax purposes, LIFO allows you to value your remaining inventory (the $30 fans) at substantially less than the $50 fans, so you pay less in taxes.

First In, First Out (FIFO) was the traditional method used by most businesses before inflation became common. Under FIFO, the goods you receive first are the goods you sell first. Under this method, you value inventory at its most recent price. FIFO is usually used during periods of relatively low inflation since high inflation and increasing replacement costs tend to skew inventory accounting figures.

LIFO establishes the value of your inventory based on the most recent quantity received, while FIFO establishes the value of your inventory based on the oldest item in it. You can use either dollar control or unit control with these methods. Match your system to your needs, based on your accountant's recommendations.

Buying Inventory

Your inventory control system will tell you when to buy replacement inventory, what to buy (and what not to buy), and how much to buy.

The *open-to-buy* is the dollar amount budgeted for inventory purchases for a given period, usually one, three, or four months. Since you are a start-up without past performance to guide you, you must calculate the open-to-buy by determining the gross sales you need to pay store overhead and cover your other costs.

Your business plan should give you an idea of the basic stock levels and monthly or seasonal sales volume you need to have during start-up. After your business has been up and running for several months to a year, your inventory control system will provide this information.

Figure out your open-to-buy using the following formula:

Planned inventory	$25,000
Planned sales	+$25,000
equals	$50,000
less actual inventory	-$27,000
less stock on order	-$13,000
equals open-to-buy	**$10,000**

Most seasonal retailers calculate their open-to-buy seasonally to accommodate variations in the type of merchandise they sell and seasonal sales fluctuations. Instead of figuring open-to-buy in dollars, some retailers approach trade shows and other merchandise sources with a list of what they need to fill out their inventories and meet sales projections. But whether they work with dollars or by unit, experienced retailers recommend that the owner of a seasonal business should feel free to go beyond the budget or use less than the entire open-to-buy amount. In fact, you should leave room in the open-to-buy for unanticipated items.

SUPPLIERS

Suppliers are essential to any retail business. Depending on your inventory selection, you may need a few or dozens. Sometimes suppliers will contact you through their sales representatives, but more often, particularly when you're starting out, you'll need to locate them yourself—either at trade shows, wholesale showrooms and conventions, or through buyers directories, industry contacts, the Business-to-Business Yellow Pages and trade journals.

Suppliers can be divided into four general categories.

1. **Manufacturers:** Most retailers buy through company salespeople or independent representatives who handle the wares of

---

THE ONE AND ONLY

For decades, conventional wisdom warned that depending on a sole supplier could sink your business. After all, such a situation could spell doom if there was any interruption in your supply of products.

However, there are some situations where relying on a sole supplier makes sense. For example, if you're a specialty clothing retailer and most of your sales come from a certain product line, you may find yourself with a sole supplier. In some cases, there is only one supplier who can deliver the raw materials you need to make a product. In other cases, a company strikes an agreement with a sole supplier in return for special pricing deals.

The key to making a sole supplier relationship work is to make sure all the right safeguards are in place. Protect yourself by asking suppliers about backup product sources. Find out how many manufacturing plants and distribution centers exist in their product pipeline. Ask what contingency plans they have to supply you in case of emergency. What are their obligations to you in the event of a shortage? Will their top one or two customers get all the products they need, while your small business has to wait in line?

Keep up-to-date on alternative supply sources that could help your business survive temporary shutdowns from your sole supplier. Use your trade association directory and industry networking contacts to help expand your supplier pipeline. Above all, make sure you feel comfortable entering into a sole supplier relationship before you sign on the dotted line.

several different companies. Prices from these sources are usually lowest, unless the retailer's location makes shipping freight costly.

2. **Distributors:** Also known as wholesalers, brokers or jobbers, distributors buy in quantity from several manufacturers and warehouse the goods for sale to retailers. Although their prices are higher than a manufacturer's, they can supply retailers with small orders from a variety of manufacturers. (Some manufacturers refuse to fill

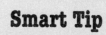

Smart Tip

While it is almost impossible to get exclusive rights to a manufacturer's goods, you can ask that a sales representative not sell identical merchandise to another store in the immediate vicinity. Be aware, however, that you may be expected to buy large amounts of the product to make up for lost sales to other stores in your area.

small orders.) A lower freight bill and quick delivery time from a nearby distributor often compensates for the higher per-item cost.

3. **Independent craftspeople:** Exclusive distribution of unique creations is frequently offered by independent craftspeople, who sell through reps or at trade shows.

4. **Import sources:** Many retailers buy foreign goods from a domestic importer, who operates much like a domestic wholesaler. Or, depending on your familiarity with overseas sources, you may want to travel abroad to buy goods.

Dealing With Suppliers

Reliability is the key factor to look for in suppliers. Good suppliers will steer you toward hot-selling items, increasing your sales. If you build a good relationship and your business is profitable for them, suppliers may be willing to bail you out when your customers make difficult demands.

Remember, though, that suppliers are in business to make money. If you go to the mat with them on every bill, ask them to shave prices on everything they sell to you, or fail to pay your bills promptly, don't be surprised when they stop calling.

As a new business owner, you can't expect to receive the same kind of attention a long-standing customer gets right off the bat. Over time, however, you can develop excellent working relationships that will be profitable for both you and your suppliers.

Once you have compiled a list of possible suppliers, ask for quotes or proposals, complete with prices, available discounts, delivery terms and other important factors. Don't just consider the terms; investigate the potential supplier's financial condition, too. Ask for customer references; call them and find out how well the supplier has performed. If there have been any problems, ask for details about how they were reconciled. Every supplier relationship hits bumps now and then; the key is to know how the rough spots were handled. Was the supplier prompt and helpful in resolving the problem, or defensive and uncooperative?

Be open, courteous and firm with your suppliers, and they will respond in kind. Tell them what you need and when you need it. Have a specific understanding about the total cost, and expect delivery on schedule. Keep in constant communication with your suppliers about possible delays, potential substitutions for materials or product lines, production quality, product improvements or new product introductions and potential savings.

Suppliers often establish a minimum order for merchandise, and this minimum may be higher for first orders to cover the cost of setting up a new store account. Some suppliers also demand a minimum number of items per order.

Payment Plans

While most service providers bill you automatically without requiring credit references, equipment and merchandise suppliers are more cautious. Since you are just getting started, you will not be able to give them trade references, and your bank probably will not give you a credit rating if your account has just opened.

If your supplier is small, the manner in which you present yourself is important in establishing credit. You may find the going tougher when dealing with a large supplier. A personal visit will accelerate your acceptance.

Present your financial statements and a description of your prospects for success in your new business. Don't even think of inflating your financial statements to cover a lack of references. This is a felony and is easily detected by most credit managers.

Some suppliers will put you on a c.o.d. basis for a few months, knowing that if you are under-financed, you will soon have problems with this payment method. Once you pass that test, they will issue you a line of credit. This creates a valid credit reference you can present to new suppliers until credit agencies accumulate enough data on your business to approve you for suppliers.

Most suppliers operate on a trade credit basis when dealing with other businesses. This basically means that when you're billed for a product or service, you have a certain grace period before the payment is due (typi-

Bright Idea

A *letter of credit* from a major customer can be used as a form of security in establishing relationships with suppliers. For instance, if you're starting a business manufacturing garden hoses, you could get a letter of credit from your biggest customer when the order is placed, showing that the customer has contracted to buy the finished hoses. The material to make the hoses is then purchased using the letter of credit as security . . . and you don't have to put up a penny to buy the material.

cally 30 days). During this time, the supplier will not charge interest. It's similar to buying a product with a credit card.

Carefully consider all costs, discounts and allowances before deciding whether to buy an item. Always take into account what the final shelf cost of any item will be. The most common discounts are given for prompt payment; many suppliers also give discounts for payment in cash. When you can, specify on all orders how the goods are to be shipped so they will be sent in the least expensive way.

Occasionally, suppliers grant customers discounts for buying in quantity, usually as a freight allowance for a specific amount of merchandise purchased. Some suppliers pay an increasing percentage of the freight bill as the retailer's purchase orders increases; others simply cover the entire freight cost for purchases over a minimum amount.

If you order merchandise from distant suppliers, freight charges can equal as much as 10 percent of your merchandise cost. Ask what a manufacturer's or supplier's freight policy is before ordering, and make sure the order is large enough to warrant the delivery charges. If the manufacturer does not pay freight on back orders, you might consider canceling a back order and adding it to the next regular shipment.

Become familiar with each of your suppliers' order-filling priorities. Some suppliers fill orders on a first-in, first-out basis; others give priority to the larger orders while customers with smaller orders wait. Consequently, most retailers specify a cancellation date on their orders. In other words, any goods shipped after that date will be returned to the suppliers. By specifying a cutoff date, you increase the chances that your orders will be shipped promptly and arrive in time.

Give careful attention to shipments when they arrive. Check to make sure you've received the correct amount and type of merchandise, and make sure the quality matches the samples you were shown.

GLOSSARY

80-20 rule: principle of inventory control that says 80 percent of a business' sales typically come from 20 percent of its inventory; as a result, most attention should be focused on that 20 percent that generates the most profit

ABC method: method of inventory control that divides items into A, B and C groups based on their importance to the business; most attention is then devoted to the A, or essential, items

Count cycle: the period at which you count your inventory; a four-week count cycle means you count inventory every four weeks

Delivery cycle: the time it takes for inventory to be delivered; a 10-week delivery cycle means inventory takes 10 weeks to arrive

Dollar-control system: system of inventory tracking in which the sales receipts are compared with the delivery receipts to determine the cost and gross profit margin on individual inventory items

First In, First Out (FIFO): method of inventory accounting that assumes items purchased first are sold first; typically used during times of low inflation

Last In, First Out (LIFO): method of inventory accounting that assumes most recently purchased items are sold first; allows business owner to value inventory at the less expensive cost of the older inventory; typically used during times of high inflation

Letter of credit: a letter from a major customer showing that the customer has contracted to buy from you; can be used as a form of security in establishing relationships with other suppliers

Manual tag system: system of inventory tracking in which tags are removed from products at the time of the sale and then cross-checked against physical inventory later to figure out what was sold

Open-to-buy: the dollar amount budgeted for inventory purchases for a given period, usually one, three or four months

Order cycle: the time it takes to process paperwork and place orders with your vendors for inventory

Needs period: the sum of the count cycle, delivery cycle and order cycle

Point-of-sale (POS): software that records information about inventory, sales and profits at the point of sale

Trade credit: practice of billing a business for products or services with a grace period (typically 30 days) before payment is due

Turnover: turning over your inventory means that 100 percent of original inventory has been sold

Unit-control system: system of inventory tracking in which bin tickets are kept with each product type, listing stock number, description, maximum and minimum quantities stocked, cost (in code) and selling price; these correspond to office file cards that list a stock number, selling price, cost, number of items to a case, supply source, order dates, quantities and delivery time

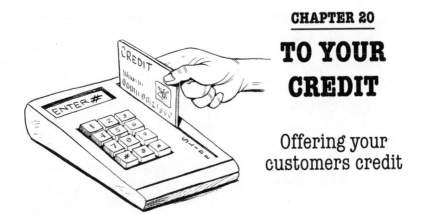

CHAPTER 20

TO YOUR CREDIT

Offering your
customers credit

Getting paid for your products or services is what business is all about. These days, there are more options than ever for accepting payment. Whether you are in a business-to-business or consumer-oriented industry, your choices can include extending credit, taking checks, and accepting credit or debit cards.

With so many options, it's easy for a new business owner to get caught up in the excitement of making sales and to forget the necessity for a well-thought-out credit policy. Deciding what forms of payment you will accept, how you will handle them and what collection methods you'll use to ensure debts are paid is essential to any small business' success.

ESTABLISHING A CREDIT POLICY

Credit can make or break a small business. A too-lenient credit policy can set the stage for collection and cash flow problems later, while a creatively and carefully designed policy can attract customers and boost your business's cash flow.

Many small businesses are reluctant to establish a firm credit policy for fear of losing customers. What they don't realize is that a consistent credit policy not only strengthens your company but also creates a more professional image in your customers' eyes.

A well-thought-out credit policy accomplishes four things:

◆ Avoids both bad debts and hard feelings

◆ Standardizes credit procedures, providing employees with clear and consistent directions

◆ Demonstrates to employees and customers that the company is serious about managing credit

♦ Helps the business owner define how credit fits into the overall sales and marketing plan

To establish a smart credit policy, start by investigating the way your competition handles credit. Your goal is to make it easy to buy your products. If your competition offers better terms, they have an advantage. You must meet your competitors' credit terms to attract customers.

At the same time, be cautious not to go too far. Novice entrepreneurs are often tempted to offer lower prices and longer payment terms to take business away from competitors. Credit is a double-edged sword. You want to attract customers with your credit policy, but you don't want to attract customers who aren't credit-worthy. Be aware that some troubled companies routinely switch suppliers whenever they reach their credit limit with one. Others are outright con artists who take advantage of new and naive entrepreneurs.

Beware!

Even the best customers can suddenly become deadbeats. Watch for these warning signs that a customer may be in financial trouble:

♦ Changes in personnel, especially buyers or management

♦ Changes in buying patterns, such as purchasing much larger amounts than usual or buying significant amounts off-season

♦ Failure to return calls with the usual promptness

How to protect yourself? One good way to start is to write a short, simple statement that sums up the intent and spirit of your company's credit policy. For example, a liberal policy might read: "Our credit policy is to make every reasonable effort to extend credit to all customers recommended by sales management, providing a suitable credit basis can be developed."

A conservative policy might say: "Our company has a strict credit policy, and credit lines will be extended only to the most credit-worthy accounts. New customers who fail to meet our credit criteria will need to purchase using cash-on-delivery terms until they establish their ability and willingness to pay on our terms."

Base your policy selection—conservative or liberal—on your industry, the size and experience of your staff, the dollar amount of your transactions, your profit margins and your appetite for risk. Also consider the industry to which you're selling. If your customers are in "soft" industries such as construction or computers, for example, you would do well to use a conservative policy.

If you do adopt a liberal credit policy, make sure you are prepared to handle the collection calls. Liberal policies will require you to be aggressive when customers don't pay on time.

Give 'Em Credit

The simplest customer credit policy has two basic points: 1) limiting credit risk and 2) diligently investigating each company's credit-worthiness.

Smart Tip

When dealing with a new client, it's a good idea to protect yourself by asking for part of your payment upfront. This is an especially good policy if the client is a new or fledgling business.

No matter how credit-worthy a customer is, never extend credit beyond your profit margin. This policy ensures that if you aren't paid, at least your expenses will be. For example, if you mark up your product or service 100 percent of costs, you can then safely risk that amount without jeopardizing your company's cash flow.

To gauge a company's credit-worthiness, draft a comprehensive credit application that contains the following:

◆ Name of business, address, phone and fax number

◆ Names, addresses, Social Security numbers of principals

◆ Type of business (corporation, partnership, proprietorship)

◆ Industry

◆ Number of employees

◆ Bank references

◆ Trade payment references

◆ Business/personal bankruptcy history

◆ Any other names under which the company does business

◆ A personal guarantee that the business owners promise to pay you if their corporation is unable to

Your credit application should also specify what your credit terms are and the consequences of failing to meet them. Indicate what late fees you'll charge, if any; that the customer is responsible for any attorney fees or collection costs incurred at any time, either during or prior to a lawsuit; and the venue where such a suit would be filed. Have your credit application form reviewed by an attorney specializing in creditors' rights to make sure it is in line with your state's regulations.

Once a potential customer has completed the application, how do you investigate the information? One way to verify the facts and assess the company's credit histories is to call credit-reporting agencies. Some companies' payment histories will also be available through Dun & Bradstreet. Because credit agencies' reporting can be unreliable, however, it's also a good idea to call others in the industry and try to determine that company's payment record and reputation. Most industries have associations that trade credit information.

Also ask the customer how much credit they think they will need. This will help you estimate the volume of credit and the potential risk to your business. Finally, as one entrepreneur says, "Use your intuition. If someone doesn't look you straight in the eye, chances are they won't let you see what's in their wallet, either."

Payment Due

Once you've set your credit policy, it's important to stick to it and do your part to ensure prompt payment. The cornerstone of collecting accounts receivable on time is making sure invoices go out promptly and accurately. If you sell a product, get the invoice out to the customer the same time the shipment goes out. If you're in a service industry, track your billable hours daily or weekly, and bill as often as your contract or agreement with the client permits. The sooner the invoice is in the mail, the sooner you get paid.

To eliminate any possibility of confusion, your invoice should contain several key pieces of information. First, make sure you date it accurately, and clearly state when payment is due, as well as any penalties for late payment. Also specify any discounts, such as discounts for payment in 15 days or for payment in cash.

Each invoice should give a clear and accurate description of the goods or services the customer received. Inventory code numbers may make sense to your computer system, but they don't mean much to the customer unless they are accompanied by an item description.

It's also important to use sequentially numbered invoices. This helps make things easier when you need to discuss a particular invoice with a customer and also makes it easier for your employees to keep track of invoices.

Before sending out an invoice, call the customer to ensure the price is correct, and check to make sure prices on invoices match those on purchase orders and/or contracts.

Smart Tip

Try this proactive approach to prompt a customer to pay faster: About 10 days before payment is due, call to ask if the customer received the bill. Make sure they are satisfied with the product; then politely ask "Do you anticipate any problems paying your bill on time?"

COLLECT CALL

Having trouble collecting on a bill? Your Better Business Bureau (BBB) may be able to help. Many BBBs now assist with business-to-business disputes regarding payment as part of their dispute resolution service. BBBs do not operate as collection agencies, and there is no charge beyond standard membership dues.

When the BBB gets involved, there can be three possible outcomes. First, the account may be paid; second, the BBB can serve as a forum for arbitration; third, if the company refuses to pay or arbitrate, the complaint is logged in the BBB's files for three years.

Most businesses find a call from the BBB a powerful motivator to pay up. If the debtor belongs to the BBB and refuses to pay, its membership could be revoked.

To find out if the BBB in your area offers this service, call the membership services department.

Know the industry norms when setting your payment schedules. While 30 days is the norm in most industries, in others, 45- or 60-day payment cycles are typical. Learn your customers' payment practices, too. If they pay only once a month, for instance, make sure your invoice gets to them in plenty of time to hit that payment cycle. Also keep on top of industry trends and economic ups and downs that could affect customers' ability to pay.

Promptness is key not only in sending out invoices but also in following up. If payment is due in 30 days, don't wait until the 60th day to call the customer. By the same token, however, don't be overeager and call on the 31st day. Being too demanding can annoy customers, possibly costing you a valuable client. Knowledge of industry norms plus your customers' payment cycles will guide you in striking a middle ground.

Constant communication trains customers to pay bills promptly and leads to an efficient, professional relationship between you and them. Usually, a polite telephone call to ask about a late payment will get the ball rolling, or at least tell you when you can expect payment. If any problems exist that need to be resolved before payment can be issued, your phone call will let you know what they are so you can start clearing them up. It could be something as simple as a missing packing slip or as major as a damaged shipment.

The first 15 to 20 seconds of the call are crucial. Project good body language over the phone. Be professional and firm, not wimpy. Use a pleasant voice that conveys authority, and respect the other person's dignity. Remember the old saying: You catch more flies with honey than with vinegar.

REMINDER!

Invoice #: _____

You are past due
on your payment

Amount Now Due: $ _____

DATE: _____

Thank you for your prompt attention.

SECOND REMINDER!

Invoice #: _____

In reviewing your account, we have
determined that the above invoice
has not been paid and is now
seriously past due.

Amount Now Due: $ _____

DATE: _____

Thank you for your prompt attention.

FINAL REMINDER!

Invoice #: _____

We have not yet received payment for the above
mentioned invoice. Unless payment is received
within 10 days, we will be forced to initiate legal
collection proceedings. If you have made payment,
please contact us immediately.

Amount Now Due: $ _____ **DATE:** _____

Sample collection reminders. Remember to keep reminders friendly but firm.

What if payment still is not made after an initial phone call? Don't let things slide. Statistics show that the longer a debt goes unpaid, the more difficult it will be to collect and the greater chance that it will remain unpaid forever.

Most experts recommend making additional phone calls rather than sending a series of past-due notices or collection letters. Letters are easier to ignore, while phone calls tend to get better results.

If several phone calls fail to generate any response, a personal visit may be in order. Try to set up an appointment ahead of time. If this isn't possible, leave a message stating what date and time you will visit.

Make sure to bring all the proper documentation with you so you can prove exactly what is owed. At this point, you are unlikely to get full payment, so see if you can get the customer to commit to a payment plan. Make sure, however, that you put it in writing.

If the customer refuses to meet with you to discuss the issue or won't commit to a payment plan, you may be facing a bad debt situation and need to take further action. There are two options: using the services of an attorney or a collection agency. Your lawyer can advise you on what is best to do.

If you decide to go with a collection agency, ask friends or business owners for referrals, or look in the Yellow Pages to find collectors who handle your type of claim. To make sure the agencies are reputable, contact the Better Business Bureau or the Securities Division of your Secretary of State's office. Since all collection companies must be bonded with the state, this office should have them on file.

For more information, you can also contact the American Collectors Association. Most reputable collection firms are members of this international organization.

Many collection agencies take their fee as a cut of the collected money, so there is no upfront cost to you. Shop around to find an agency with a reasonable rate.

Also compare the cost of using a collection agency to the cost of using your lawyer. You may be able to recover more of the money using one option or the other, depending on the total amount of the debt and the hourly rate or percentage the lawyer or agency charges.

ACCEPTING CHECKS

Bounced checks can cut heavily into a small business's profit. Yet, a business that doesn't accept personal checks can't expect to stay competitive. How can you keep bad checks out of your cash register? Here are some steps to establishing a check-acceptance policy that works.

Start with the basics. Since laws regarding the information needed to

Bright Idea

Require employees to sign their initials on checks they accept. No one wants to have their initials on a check that might bounce, so employees will be extra careful about following your check acceptance policy.

cash checks vary greatly among states (and even within states), begin by contacting your local police department. They can familiarize you with the laws and regulations governing checks in your state. Some police departments conduct seminars instructing businesses on how to set up proper check-cashing policies.

While rules vary among states, here are some good general rules of thumb to follow. When accepting a check, always ask to see the customer's driver's license or similar identification card, preferably one with a photograph. Check the customer's physical characteristics against his identification. If you have reason to question his identity, ask the customer to write his signature on a separate piece of paper. Many people who pass bad checks have numerous false identifications and may forget which one they are using. Ask for the customer's home and work telephone numbers, so you can contact him in case the check bounces. Don't cash payroll checks, checks for more than the amount of purchase, or two-party checks.

Be observant. Desktop-publishing software, laser printers, and scanners have made it easier for people to alter, forge or duplicate checks. To avoid accepting a forged or counterfeit check, evaluate the document carefully. Smudge marks on the check could indicate the check was rubbed with moist fingers when it was illegally made. Smooth edges on checks are another sign of a possibly counterfeit document; authentic checks are perforated either on the top or left side of the check. Smudged handwriting or signs that the handwriting has been erased are other warning signs that you might be dealing with an illegal check.

Be especially cautious with new checks. A large majority of bad checks are written on new accounts. Many businesses will not accept checks that don't have a customer's name preprinted on them. If the check is written on a brand-new account (one with a check number, say, below 300), protect yourself by asking to see two forms of ID.

Establish a waiting period for refunds. Merchants can easily be stiffed when a customer makes a purchase by check and returns the merchandise the next day for a cash refund. When the check bounces, the merchant is out the cash paid for the refund. To avoid this scenario, many entrepreneurs require a five-to-seven-business-day grace period to allow checks to clear the bank before cash refunds are paid.

Consider getting electronic help. If you process a large volume of checks, you might benefit from the services of a check-verification company. By paying a monthly fee, ranging from $25 to $100 (depending on your company's size and volume of checks), you can tap into a company's database of individuals who write bad, stolen or forged checks. This is done by passing a customer's check through an electronic "check reader" at your checkout stand. If the check matches a name in the company's database, the check is refused.

Using a check reader is quick and efficient, notes Jalinna Jones of TeleCheck, a check-verification and check-guarantee company. "We can approve a check within 10 seconds," she claims, "which is generally as fast as or faster than a merchant getting acceptance for a credit card purchase."

Check-verification companies also offer a check-guarantee service. "If a check is approved by our company," Jones explains, "and it later turns out to be a bad check, we will reimburse the merchant for the value of the check. Our guarantee service reduces the risk of accepting bad checks."

Getting a handle on the bad checks that might pass through your business certainly has its benefits. "For small merchants," notes Jones, "one bad check can wipe out an entire day's profits."

Whatever check acceptance policy you develop, make sure your employees clearly understand the procedure to follow. Also be sure to post your check acceptance policy prominently where customers can see it. Specify any charges for bounced checks, what forms of ID are required, and what types of checks you will and will not accept. Posting signs helps pre-

---

CHECK IT OUT

For more information on preventing bad checks, consult these helpful resources:

◆ *Check Fraud Prevention Manual* provides information on how to detect fraudulent checks, how to adopt procedures to reduce your business's exposure to bad checks, and where to turn for help. Cost is $99 for members and $150 for nonmembers. Contact the American Bankers Association, 1120 Connecticut Ave. NW, Washington, DC 20036, or order through the association's customer service department at (800) 338-0626.

◆ *Common Sense Guide to Check Acceptance* offers guidelines to follow when cashing or accepting checks. This free brochure is available by sending a self-addressed stamped envelope to Check Technologies, P.O. Box 659595, San Antonio, TX 78265.

vent disgruntlement when customers wait in line, only to find at the register that you can't accept their check.

What if you do receive a bad check? In most cases, after a check bounces, the bank allows you another attempt to deposit it. After that, the responsibility for collecting the money falls to you.

Contact the customer, either by phone or mail. (Again, consult your local police on the proper procedure; some states require that a registered letter be sent and a specific amount of time elapse before other action can be taken.) Keep your cool; there's nothing gained by being angry or hostile about the situation. Most people bounce checks by accident. Explain the situation, and request immediate payment plus reimbursement for any bank charges you have incurred.

If the person still refuses to pay, or you cannot get ahold of them, you have several options. The first, and probably the easiest, is to hold the check for a short time (up to six months) from the date it was written. Although the bank will not allow the check to be deposited a third time, they will cash the check if there are sufficient funds. Call the debtor's bank periodically to see if the funds are there. When they are, cash the check immediately.

Another option is going to the police. Since through your check acceptance procedure you collected all the information needed to prosecute, you should be able to complete the proper paperwork. However, the hassle of hiring a lawyer, identifying suspects and going to court may be more effort than you want to expend for a $200 check. In that case, your best bet is to use a collection agency. (For more details on this, see the "Payment Due" section earlier in this chapter.)

ACCEPTING CREDIT CARDS

Why should a small-business owner accept credit cards? There are dozens of reasons. First and foremost, research shows that credit cards increase the probability, speed and size of customer purchases. Many people prefer not to carry cash, especially when traveling. Others prefer to pay with credit cards because they know that it will be easier to return or exchange the merchandise.

Accepting credit cards has several advantages for business owners as well. It gives you the chance to increase sales by enabling customers to make impulse buys even when they don't have cash in their wallets or sufficient funds in their checking accounts. Accepting credit cards can improve your cash flow because in most cases you receive the money within a few days instead of waiting for a check to clear or an invoice to come due. Finally, credit cards provide a guarantee that you will be paid, without the risks involved in accepting personal checks.

Merchant Status

To accept major credit cards from customers, your business must establish merchant status with each of the credit card companies whose cards you want to accept. You'll probably want to start by applying for merchant status with American Express or Discover. For these cards, all you need to do is contact American Express or Discover directly and fill out an application.

However, chances are you'll want to accept Visa and MasterCard, too, since these cards are used more frequently. You cannot apply directly to Visa or MasterCard; because they are simply bank associations, you have to establish a merchant account through one of several thousand banks that set up such accounts, called "acquiring banks."

The first thing you need to understand about accepting credit cards, ex-

A PRIVATE AFFAIR

MasterCard, Visa and American Express all have their place. But there's another option you may not have considered: issuing a private-label credit card with your company's name on it.

In addition to all the usual advantages of credit cards, a private-label credit card program allows businesses to focus on who their customers are. For example, your program can gather data about customer purchases, buying patterns, income and demographics.

Small businesses can save money and eliminate hassles by using an outside administrator that specializes in private-label credit cards. A number of banks have entered this arena; ask your banker if he or she administers such programs. If not, the banker may be able to recommend a private-label credit card administration company.

Administration companies can do everything from setting up the operation to developing specialized marketing programs, designing the credit cards, training employees and developing lists of potential customers. Fees vary depending on the number of services provided and the size of your customer base.

Before choosing an administration company, talk to other business owners who use private-label credit card programs to see if they're happy with the service and if the administration company does a good job handling customer applications, payments and the like. Weigh the cost of any program against the benefits you expect to get from it.

Dollar Stretcher

Even after you have obtained merchant status, keep looking for ways to lower your fee. Your bank can suggest some options. Also ask other merchants who process transactions similar to yours how much they are paying. If you find a better deal, let your bank know, and see if they will match it.

plains Debra Rossi at Wells Fargo Bank, is that the bank views this as an extension of credit. "When we give you the ability to accept credit cards, we are giving you the use of the funds before we get them. By the time the money arrives in the card-holder's account, it could be another 30 days," Rossi says. There is also the real concern that if your company goes out of business before merchandise is shipped to customers, the bank will have to absorb losses.

While requirements vary among banks, in general a business does not have to be a minimum size in terms of sales, says Steven Citarella, vice president of credit policy for First Data Merchant Services Corp., an independent credit processing service. However, some banks do have minimum requirements for how long you should have been in business. This doesn't mean a start-up can't get merchant status; it simply means you may have to look a little harder to find a bank that will work with you.

While being considered a "risky business"—typically a start-up, mail order or homebased business—is one reason a bank may deny your merchant status request, the most common reason for denial is simply poor credit. Approaching a bank for a merchant account is like applying for a loan. You must be prepared with a solid presentation that will persuade the bank to open an account for you.

You will need to provide bank and trade references, estimate what kind of credit card volume you expect to have and what you think the average transaction size will be. Bring your business plan and financial statements, along with copies of advertisements, marketing pieces and your catalog if you have one. If possible, invite your banker to visit your store or operation.

Banks will evaluate your product or service to see if there might be potential for a lot of returns or customer disputes. Called "charge-backs," these refunds are very expensive for banks to process. They are more common among mail order companies and are one reason why these businesses typically have a hard time securing merchant status.

In your initial presentation, provide a reasonable estimate of how many charge-backs you will receive, then show your bank why you don't expect them to exceed your estimates. Testimonials from satisfied customers or product samples can help convince the bank your customers will be satisfied with their purchases. Another way to reduce the bank's fear is to demonstrate that your product is priced at a fair market value.

Rossi at Wells Fargo says the bank's goal is to find out if your business is profitable and if it will be around for a long time to come. "We approve a lot of start-up businesses, and in those cases, we rely on the personal financial picture of the business principals," she says. "We look at [their personal] tax returns and at where they got the money to start the business. We also look to see if you're a customer at Wells Fargo and at your relationship with Wells."

As Rossi's comment suggests, the best place to begin when trying to get merchant status is by approaching the bank that already holds your business accounts. If your bank turns you down, ask around for recommendations from other business owners who accept plastic. You could look in the Yellow Pages for other businesses in the same category as yours (home-based, retail, mail order). Call them to ask where they have their merchant accounts and whether they are satisfied with the way their accounts are handled. When approaching a bank with which you have no relationship, you may be able to sweeten the deal by offering to switch your other accounts to that bank as well.

If banks turn you down, another option is to consider independent credit card processing companies, which can be found in the Yellow Pages. While independents often give the best rates because they have lower overhead, their application process tends to be more time-consuming, and start-up fees are sometimes higher.

You can also go through an independent sales organization (ISO). These are field representatives from out-of-town banks who, for a commission, help businesses find banks willing to grant them merchant status. Your bank may be able to recommend an ISO, or look in the Yellow Pages under "Credit Cards." An ISO can match your needs with those of the banks he or she represents, without requiring you to go through the application process with all of them.

Beware!

To help protect against credit card fraud, follow these procedures every time a credit purchase is made:

♦ Check the signature on the charge slip against the one on the back of the card. This may seem basic, but you'd be surprised at how often it is neglected.

♦ Verify the card's expiration date.

♦ Check the frequently updated bulletin listing canceled card numbers.

Money Matters

Enticing your bank with promising sales figures can also boost your case since the bank makes money when you do. Every time you accept a credit card for payment, the bank or card company deducts a percentage of the sale—called a "merchant discount fee"—and then credits your account with the rest of the sale amount.

Here are some other fees you can expect to pay. All of them are negotiable except for the discount fee:

◆ Start-up fees of $50 to $200

◆ Equipment costs of $250 to $1,000, depending on whether you decide to lease or purchase a handheld terminal or go electronic

◆ Monthly statement fees of $4 to $20

◆ Transaction fees of 5 to 50 cents per purchase

◆ The discount rate—the actual percentage you are charged per

FOR MAIL ORDER ONLY

It's ironic: While mail order businesses perhaps more than any other venture rely on credit cards as a means of payment, mail order companies also typically find it more difficult to get merchant status. Why? The credit card industry has been burned by mail order "con artists." Even in legitimate mail order businesses, the percentage of charge-backs is much higher than in other types of businesses.

If you have a phone-intensive or mail order business and are having difficulty securing merchant status, try one of these tactics:

◆ Set a limit on the volume of transactions you will process each month until the account is established.

◆ Offer to pay a higher discount fee for the first six months as a "loss reserve."

◆ Offer to let the bank hold on to your share of deposits for a few extra days to give it time to screen any unusual transactions.

◆ Consider putting up a cash deposit to protect the bank against large numbers of charge-backs.

◆ If you make special arrangements like these, be sure to get a written agreement specifying how long they will be in effect.

transaction based on projected card sales volume, the degree of risk and a few other factors (the percentage ranges from 1.5 percent to 3 percent; the higher your sales, the lower your rate)

◆ Charge-back fees of up to $30 per return transaction

◆ Miscellaneous fees, including a per-transaction communication cost of 5 to 12 cents for connection to the processor, a postage fee for sending statements, and a supply fee for charge slips

There may also be some charges from the telephone company to set up a phone line for the authorization and processing equipment. Before you sign on with any bank, consider the costs carefully to make sure the anticipated sales are worth the costs.

Beware!

Don't ask another merchant to deposit your sales slips for you, and never let another business deposit slips through your account. This practice is called "laundering" sales slips, and not only is it prohibited by Visa and MasterCard, but it is also illegal in some states. Honest business owners have been wiped out by scam artists who ask them to deposit their sales slips, then rack up thousands of dollars in phony sales, which later turn into charge-backs.

Getting Equipped

Once your business has been approved for credit, you will receive a start-up kit and personal instructions in how to use the system. You don't need fancy equipment to process credit card sales. You can start with a phone and a simple imprinter that costs less than $30. However, you'll get a better discount rate (and get your money credited to your account faster) if you process credit card sales electronically.

Although it's a little more expensive initially, purchasing or leasing a terminal that allows you to swipe the customer's card through for instant authorization of the sale (and immediate crediting of your merchant account) can save you money in the long run. Many cash registers can also be adapted to process credit cards. Also, using your personal computer as opposed to a terminal to obtain authorization can cut your cost per transaction even more.

Once you've got merchant account status, make the most of it. Both the credit card industries and individual banks hold seminars and users' conferences covering innovations in the industry, fraud detection techniques and other helpful subjects. Check with your credit card company's representatives for details . . . and keep on top of ways to get more from your customers' credit cards.

ACCEPTING DEBIT CARDS

In addition to credit cards and checks, there's a new form of payment that more and more small businesses are accepting these days. ATM or debit cards have become the latest consumer currency. Consumers like the cards because they allow them to avoid the hassle of writing checks, offset the need to stock a wallet with wads of cash, and ensure security, thanks to a customer-activated secret personal identification number (PIN).

Many merchants, too, prefer accepting debit cards over credit cards or checks. In fact, debit cards can even be better than traditional cash. Debit is less expensive than a credit card or check, and is not vulnerable to employee theft like cash is. Debit is also a guaranteed transaction: Money is immediately debited from the customer's account and deposited into yours—giving you instant access to funds. Finally, debit gives you access to consumers who don't have credit cards.

Getting Online

Installing a debit system in your business can be as easy as walking into your local bank, filling out an application requesting debit acceptance capabilities, and clearing some counter space next to your cash register for a debit terminal and printer (some banks can interface directly with your cash register).

Smart Tip

If you accept debit cards, be sure you educate customers about it. Many cardholders still don't understand they can use their cards at a merchant's POS terminal just as they would at an ATM. Stickers and signs by the cash register help, as does placing the PIN-pad terminal in an easily accessible location. Training your clerks to ask customers "Will you be using your ATM card today?" also encourages debit card use.

You can purchase equipment for as little as $200 to $500 or check out monthly leasing options. You may find that you already have most of the necessary equipment. Some merchants' existing credit terminals can simply be reprogrammed to accept debit cards as well. If your terminals don't already have printers, however, you'll need to install them, since federal regulations require merchants to provide receipts for debit card transactions.

Thanks to emerging technology, more electronic devices that accept both credit and debit cards are becoming available on the market. Some are even integrated with the cash register. Because the debit PIN-pad terminal needs to be within easy reach the customer and clerk, however, smaller businesses may opt for a stand-alone POS debit system. When you buy the service from a bank or other payment service provider, look for a system that accepts both credit and debit cards. A joint system takes up less counter space and is usually less confusing for clerks and customers to handle.

Another consideration is where your POS takes place. Restaurant merchants, for example, may choose to collect the bill from patrons while they are still seated at their tables. In this case, you'll need the capability to take the PIN pad to each table for customers to key in their PIN. Such technology is available through most major financial institutions that provide debit equipment.

Beware, however, that not all banks are experienced in debit card services. Although sticking with your current financial institution when setting up a debit card system may have its advantages, make sure your bank understands debit before signing on with them.

Once you find a bank to service your debit needs, you will most likely be required to fill out a simple one-page application. Applying for debit is not like requesting merchant credit card status, which is an extension of credit, and thus represents a risk for the bank. Since debit cards are typically a guaranteed transaction, the credit of the applicant merchant is not evaluated as stringently.

Once you've set up your POS terminal, the fee you pay for its use depends on which debit network you're connected to. Unlike the fee charged for credit card use, banks typically don't charge merchants a percentage of each debit card sale. Instead, the bank might charge merchants somewhere between 10 and 25 cents for each transaction.

While there's no doubt the cost per debit transaction adds up, it's still significantly less than some other options. For example, check processing typically runs from 18 to 50 cents per check, not taking into account the costs of bounced checks. Cash handling can also be expensive.

Entrepreneurs who accept debit cards say they like the safety and security of this method. The bottom line: Debit offers your customers another way to pay . . . and the easier you make it for customers to buy, the more sales your business will ring up.

GLOSSARY

Charge-back: when a customer purchases an item using a credit card, then returns it

Debit card: a card (often the customer's ATM card) that can be used to debit money directly from the customer's checking account

Discount rate: the actual percentage the merchant is charged per credit card transaction by the credit card company or bank; the discount rate is based on sales volume, risk and other factors

Independent sales organization: representatives from out-of-town banks who, for a commission, match businesses with banks that will grant them merchant status

Laundering: the practice of depositing one merchant's sales slips through another merchant's account; it is illegal in many states and prohibited by both Visa and MasterCard

Merchant account: an account that allows a merchant to accept payment from customers via credit card; may be granted through banks or directly from a credit card company

Private-label credit card: a credit card a merchant issues with his or her business's name on it

CHAPTER 21

IT'S IN
THE MAIL

Setting up mailing
and shipping
accounts

Mail is one of the lifelines of your business, and, depending on your business, it can also be one of your biggest costs. That's why it's so important to figure out the most efficient, convenient and economical ways to send mail. This chapter covers everything you need to know—from postage metering and sorting to overnight services—to deliver that letter, the sooner the better.

MAILING EQUIPMENT

There are a variety of mailing machines that can help you save time—so you can spend it on more important things, like growing your business.

Postage Meters

Buying your own postage meter saves a small business time and money—no more licking and sticking envelopes and stamps. With today's electronic mailing machines, you don't even have to stand in line at the post office to get your meter reset.

Under a recent change called decertification, the U.S. Postal Service (USPS) is calling in all its mechanical meters and declaring them obsolete. Electronic postage meters, which were required as of December 1997, can be reset either with a phone call or via computer instead of visiting the post office. Mailing equipment manufacturers offer this service free or for a nominal fee.

Electronic postage meters consist of a base through which envelopes are guided for stamping, which can be rented, leased, or bought from a mailing equipment manufacturer; and a meter, which must be leased from a mailing equipment manufacturer. The more automated and faster the machine, and the more features it incorporates, the more it costs to rent, lease or own.

The primary difference between bases is how letters are fed through the machines. The least expensive models require you to feed letters, one at a time, through a roller. More expensive models offer semiautomatic or fully automated letter feeding.

Options for the base include stackers, which stack your mail, and sealers, which automatically wet and seal each envelope as it passes through the base.

The USPS recently introduced Classification Reform, which changed the rates of postal discounts to various customers, depending on how intricate your automation is. If your mail is bar-coded, metered with an "indicia" (the red stamp imprinted by the meter's tiny printer), or sorted and bundled in quantities, you probably qualify for significant discounts under the new system.

Even the smallest office can benefit from a meter to determine exact postage and print out a stamp, and a scale to weigh mail. The USPS estimates accurate weighing can save customers up to 20 percent on mailings.

An efficient, automated mailing machine can also save hours of time if you handle direct mail or large mailings. Mail that's presorted and bar-coded bypasses many of the post office handling steps and is delivered 24 hours sooner than mail lacking automated preparation, according to the USPS. (And if you don't think a day makes a difference, consider the results of a study by market research firm The Gallup Organization and mailing equipment manufacturer Pitney Bowes Mailing Systems. Their study found that 11 percent of executives surveyed at large and midsized companies said the net income of their businesses would jump 5 percent if they received payments one day sooner!)

The latest mailing systems are multifunctional, handling everything from printing, folding, stapling, inserting, sealing, labeling, weighing and stamping to sorting, stacking and putting on a wrapper or binder. Many interact with a computer so you can track exactly how, when and to whom orders are sent out. Some PC-based systems can be programmed to simultaneously handle different sized paper—checks, invoices, brochures—without stopping the machine to reset the equipment.

Smart Tip

At press time, the USPS was in the process of implementing the Information Based Indicia Program, which will enable entrepreneurs to generate postage using their computers. Once the program is operational, several companies are expecting to launch electronic postage products that enable users to purchase postage off the Internet and print it out in the form of bar codes or "indicias," using special software.

PUSHING THE ENVELOPE

Looking for ways to prune postal bloat? The Direct Marketing Association offers this checklist of cost-cutting ideas:

1. *Fine-tune your mailing list.*

   ◆ Stop mailing to duplicate names.

   ◆ Eliminate nonresponders and marginal prospects. There are many mailing list software programs that can help you keep your mailing lists current.

2. *Be sure you're using accurate addresses.*

   ◆ Check for correct ZIP codes, especially when using addresses supplied by customers.

   ◆ Watch for mail shipped to wrong suite or apartment numbers.

   ◆ Check for missing directionals such as "N." for "North."

3. *Take advantage of postal discounts and services.*

   ◆ Use the USPS' National Change of Address list to keep your mailing list current.

   ◆ Print "Address Correction Requested" on the face of your mail. The Postal Service will tell you if the recipient files a change of address.

   ◆ Investigate commingling your mail with that of other small mailers to take advantage of discounts available mainly to large mailers. Contact your local mailing service for more information.

   ◆ Print your bar-coded ZIP +4 on Business Reply Mail. The Postal Service charges much less for cards using the nine-digit zips.

   ◆ Stockpile mail to build up larger volumes.

The most popular mailing equipment combines meters with electronic scales (see the following "Postal Scales" section for more); other machines have additional capabilities such as automatic feed and envelope-sealing functions. Speeds can vary from 25 to 200 envelopes a minute.

Besides faster delivery time and the ease of resetting by telephone or computer, metered mail machines offer other benefits:

◆ **Postal accounting:** Tracking and controlling money spent on direct mail, letters, parcel post, priority and express mail is easier. Because there is one dispenser with precise postage, accounting is streamlined and you know exactly how much postage remains in the meter.

◆ **Parcel post dating:** If your third-class letters and packages are metered, the stamp date requires the post office to expedite those items on the date received, thereby providing better service on less expensive classes of mail.

Dollar Stretcher

If rising postage costs are putting the squeeze on your new business, try shrinking your mailings. Many direct-mail and catalog companies are saving by reducing their mailings' dimensions. Keep your mailings within the size of the USPS' letter classification of 6¹/₈ inches by 11¹/₂ inches, with thickness no more than one-quarter inch.

◆ **Postmark ads:** Postage meters not only print stamps on your mail, they can print an advertising message, too. Postmark ads can include your company logo and name, giving your company extra advertising exposure.

Postal Scales

Besides postage meters, the second crucial piece of mailing equipment most businesses need is a postal scale. Scales are sold in 5-, 10-, 30-, 100- and 200-pound capacities and can be purchased as stand-alone units or combined with a postage meter.

A postal scale ensures that you're not paying more than you need to for your outgoing mail. What to look for when buying? Both electronic and manual versions are available. Because manual scales require you to read the postage amount, they increase the chance of human error. Electronic scales are more expensive, but their digital readouts reduce errors and ensure you get the most value from your scale.

Depending on the type, size and weight of letters and packages you'll be mailing, you may wish to look for a machine that lets you compare rates between various carriers, such as Federal Express and the U.S. Postal Service. You may also want a feature that automatically converts a ZIP code to the proper zone for calculating zone-dependent rates for carriers such as United Parcel Service.

Consider ease of use, especially if a number of people will be using the scale. Some models have easy-to-read keypads and user prompts. Consider the size of the weighing platform and maximum weight the machine can handle to make sure it can accommodate the types of packages you'll be sending. For shipments that exceed the scale's weighing capacity, look for a scale that will allow you to manually enter the weight for rate calculation.

If you need your scale to interface with a postage meter, you'll want to make sure the model you choose is compatible with your metering equipment.

Questions to ask the dealer:

◆ What adjustments will need to be made to the scale if postage rates change? What charges are involved?

◆ Does the scale offer alternative pricing options based on various postal classifications?

◆ Does the scale have a password feature to help guard against unauthorized uses?

◆ What are its size and weight limitations?

◆ How should the machine be maintained?

◆ What type of maintenance agreement is offered?

◆ Does the scale offer rates for foreign mailings?

◆ Does the scale offer rates for Federal Express and UPS?

Letter-Folding Machines

When you're preparing a promotional mailing, you may find yourself dealing with hundreds or thousands of letters or brochures. Folding letters yourself can be time-consuming; it's also unnecessary, thanks to today's letter-folding machines.

When buying a letter-folding machine, consider the volume the machine is capable of processing. Low-end equipment processes a few hundred pieces per hour; high-end equipment is capable of operating at speeds from 1,500 to 4,000 sheets per hour.

Also consider the types of fold the equipment can provide. Some possibilities are c-fold (standard letter), z-fold (accordion fold), double fold, single folds, right-angle folds and brochure folds.

Sheets are fed either through a friction feeder or a vacuum feeder. Friction feeders have a rubber wheel that pulls the sheets through; frequent use can cause this kind of feeder to wear out. Friction feeders can also smudge a newly printed document. Vacuum feeders, while sturdier and more effective for handling coated papers, can be substantially more expensive and are only available on high-volume machines.

You may also want to buy a model that includes a batch counter or a to-

CHANGE OF ADDRESS

Sick of standing in line at the post office? Try going online to the post office instead. At the USPS' Web site (www.usps.gov), you'll find dozens of time- and money-saving services.

Click on the Post Office icon from the home page, and you can look up ZIP codes for addresses nationwide. Or keep tabs on packages by using the site's Express Mail tracking feature.

There's also a "postage calculator" that helps you find the most cost-effective method of mailing letters and packages. Just enter the article's weight plus ZIP codes of the origin and destination, and up pops the price for shipping it by various methods.

Want shipping supplies sent to your door? Click on "Business," then "Shipping Supplies," to order Express or Priority Mail envelopes, labels, boxes and tags after registering your business address and credit card number.

While you can't order stamps online yet, you do have the option to view the latest kinds and call the toll-free number to order them via phone.

www. usps.gov

tal counter. Batch counters keep the machine from folding too many sheets together. Total counters tell you how many sheets have already been folded. You'll find a memory setting useful if you typically produce the same types of jobs on a regular basis. The memory setting allows you to enter the instructions for processing a particular type of job once, then call up that job whenever you need to apply the same parameters.

You should also check to see how the equipment handles paper jams. Better-designed machines can release rollers, giving you easier access to the problematic areas. Finally, you may want to consider a model with an inserter, which automatically inserts your documents into envelopes.

Questions to ask the dealer:

◆ How many pieces can it process per hour?

◆ Does the machine offer friction or vacuum feed?

◆ What types of folds is the machine capable of?

◆ How many sheets can it fold at once?

◆ How effective is it at handling stapled sheets? (Many cannot handle this automatically and will require hand feeding.)

◆ What counter features are available?

◆ What types and sizes of paper can it handle?

◆ How should the machine be maintained?

◆ What type of maintenance agreement is offered?

◆ Does it have an automatic feeder?

◆ Does it have a memory setting?

◆ How are paper jams handled?

Letter-Opening Machines

Letter-opening machines can greatly speed up the opening of mail. Some can process up to 600 envelopes per minute.

What to look for when buying? There are two types of letter openers: chadders and slitters. Chadders open envelopes by cutting one-eighth of an inch from the end. Slitters, while quite a bit more expensive (up to $1,000 or more), cut through the top seam of the envelope and reduce the risk of damaging the contents of the envelope.

Most models can handle standard #10 envelopes. More expensive models will accommodate different sizes and thicknesses of incoming mail. An automated feeder will send your mail through the machine; joggers will help settle the contents of the envelope so they don't get cut; counters let you count the number of pieces being processed.

Another feature you may find helpful is an automatic date-and-time stamp to help you keep track of when mail arrives. Because letter-openers are usually quite reliable, maintenance contracts are usually not required.

Questions to ask the dealer:

◆ Does the opener use a chadder or a slitter?

◆ What sizes of envelopes can the machine handle?

◆ Does it have an automatic feeder? A jogger? A counter?

◆ Can incoming mail be time-and-date stamped?

Lease Or Buy?

Mailing equipment can be rented, leased or purchased outright. You may prefer to lease to conserve working capital, then upgrade equipment as your business grows. Renting is the easiest method because if you need to cut costs at any time, you simply hand the equipment back and walk away. If you are leasing, you are obligated to make all the payments specified in the lease. However, leasing offers advantages, including lower rates than renting and the ability to roll the lease over for upgraded equipment.

If a mailing equipment salesperson sells you on leased equipment that ends up being too sophisticated for your needs, some suppliers will purchase the competitor's lease and give you their own equipment. When shopping around for equipment, ask if there are any special promotions available before you sign.

Basic machines lease from about $25 to $35 per month; more sophisticated machines for $60 and up. Anything more expensive than that is usually best suited to large corporations. The average lease is for five years and can include maintenance and free postage refills; the average rental agreement is for one year.

Bright Idea

Presorting bulk mail saves money but takes time. Speed up the process by using mail consolidation companies— firms that presort mail and deliver it to bulk-mail centers around the country. To find such companies, look in the Yellow Pages under "Mailing Services."

Carefully read the contracts you are offered, and, if renting, make sure there is no mention of the word "lease." Also, always ask what options you have if you need to get out of a lease.

Make sure the company is postal-certified with the USPS. Salespeople should be knowledgeable about their industry and the latest USPS regulations and rates, and ask you questions about your mailing process—how many boxes, how frequently you ship—so the equipment they recommend fits both your business and budget.

When shopping for mailing equipment, allow the salespeople enough time to make their pitch. The right mailing equipment can save you money, but only if you give the salesperson enough time to analyze your needs.

SENDING MAIL

Sending your mail under the appropriate classification can save your business hundreds—or even thousands—of dollars each year, depending on how much and how frequently you mail. The post office divides mail into six classifications:

1. Express Mail
2. Priority Mail
3. First-Class Mail
4. Periodicals
5. Standard Mail (A)
6. Standard Mail (B)

Express Mail offers next-day service. (For more on this, see the following section on "Overnight Mail.") Priority Mail can be used when the speed of Express Mail isn't necessary, but preferential handling is still desired. Priority mail offers faster delivery at the least expensive rate. The maximum weight for Priority Mail is 70 pounds.

Your local post office can supply you with Priority Mail stickers, labels, envelopes and boxes at no extra charge. The 2-pound flat-rate envelope is typically convenient to use. The rate of postage is the same as that charged for a 2-pound piece of priority mail, regardless of weight. A presort discount is available for large mailings. Priority Mail can be insured, registered, certified or sent c.o.d. for additional charges.

First-class mail is used for sending letters, postcards, greeting cards, checks and money orders. If your first-class item weighs more than 11 ounces, use Priority Mail. Additional services such as certificates of mailing, certified, registered and c.o.d. can also be purchased for first-class mail.

All first-class mail receives prompt handling and transportation. You can expect overnight delivery to local cities and within two days to local states. Delivery to outlying areas typically takes three days.

A periodical rate is available to publishers or registered news agents approved for periodicals mailing privileges. Other rates must be paid for magazines and newspapers mailed by the general public.

Standard mail (a) is used primarily by retailers, catalogers and other advertisers to promote their products and services. This is the type of mail you'd be using if, for example, you were sending out a direct-mail piece to 1,000 potential customers.

To qualify for standard mail (a) rates, you buy a standard rate permit from the post office. There is an annual fee for this (about $85), and other fees may be charged depending on the degree to which you are automating your mail. Standard mail (a) is available in two subclasses: regular (also called "bulk rate") and nonprofit. Standard rate (b) is for parcels weighing 1 pound or more.

For a mailing to get standard mail (a) rates, you must be mailing a minimum 200 pieces or 50 pounds per mailing; the pieces must each weigh less than 16 ounces. There are a variety of discounts available. Essentially, the more work you do in advance in terms of sorting, bundling and labeling, the lower postal rate you'll pay. At the minimum, nonautomated level, you'll need to presort your mail by ZIP code, mark it with "Bulk Rate" and pack it in trays. The more automated you get, the lower your per-piece mailing cost gets. The post office has specific guidelines for automation, including bar-coding, standards for address accuracy and requirements for automation compatibility.

To find out more about mail classifications and how to prepare your mail the least expensive way, visit the USPS' Web site at http://ribbs.usps.gov or go to one of the USPS' Postal Service Business Centers. These centers can advise you on preparing and designing mailings, discounts for presorting and saturation mailings, bar coding, ZIP +4 strategies and other ways to cut your mailing costs. Some also sponsor educational seminars for business owners.

The USPS will also bring your mailing list up to their standards and add the ZIP +4 extension to all complete addresses once at no cost. To find out where the closest Business Center is, contact your local post office.

Mailing equipment manufacturers or distributors (look in the Business-to-Business Yellow Pages under "Mailing Equipment") often sponsor educational seminars on mailing as well. "We hold regular seminars for our salespeople and customers so they can keep up to date on the latest government edicts and plan for future needs and budgeting," says Ed Lomasney, sales manager for Neopost, a national mailing equipment manufacturer.

OVERNIGHT MAIL

When your California company's proposal has to be in your New York client's hands, pronto, how do you get it there? Well, there are a variety of ways.

The biggest players in the field are DHL Worldwide Express, Federal Express, UPS and the U.S. Postal Service. Each will come right to the doorsteps of even the smallest homebased businesses.

When deciding on an express mail carrier, first think about the services you need. Will you be sending one package per week or 15 per day? Domestically or internationally? Do you want it delivered the same day, the next day, or in two or three days? Will you be shipping by air or ground?

When choosing an international courier, first ask the company for a list of countries they deliver to. Also remember that courier services overseas differ from domestic services in two ways. First, your package may be turned over to a foreign delivery service once it reaches the country to which it's being sent. Second, customs regulations require documentation for clearance of your export shipments.

Beware!

Liability is an important consideration when choosing an air courier. Each courier sets a predetermined maximum dollar amount that you will be paid if a package is lost. If you regularly send packages worth more than the courier's limit, look into acquiring additional insurance.

Whether domestic or international, ask about a courier's hours and days of service and if there are extra charges for deliveries on Saturdays. Companies may allow you to set up daily pickup times or may provide pickup on an as-needed basis. Typically, you get volume discounts based on how much mail you send. Most companies also offer a range of delivery times—for example, "next business day, a.m." or "next business day, p.m." Some may even offer same-day delivery for an extra fee. Other services that may be offered include management reports and acknowledgement cards.

Courier services are highly competitive and are eager to acquire new business. As a small-business owner, you have clout with courier services, so don't hesitate to ask questions and negotiate for special rates and services. Once you know what your express mail needs are likely to be, compare them against what the different courier services offer.

GLOSSARY

Batch counter: feature on a letter-folding machine that keeps the machine from folding too many sheets together

Chadder: type of letter-opening machine that cuts one-eighth inch from the end of the envelope

Friction feeder: feeder on a letter-folding machine that pulls sheets through using a rubber wheel

Jogger: mechanism on a letter-opening machine that helps settle contents of envelopes so they don't get cut

Sealer: part of a postage meter's base that seals mail

Slitter: type of letter-opening machine that slits the seam of the envelope

Stacker: part of a postage meter's base that stacks mail

Total counter: feature on a letter-folding machine that tells you how many sheets have been folded

Vacuum feeder: feeder on a letter-folding machine that pulls sheets through using vacuum technology

CHAPTER 22

PEOPLE WHO NEED PEOPLE

Hiring your first employee

To hire or not to hire? That is the question in the mind of the new entrepreneur. You see, hiring even one employee changes everything. Suddenly, you need payroll procedures, rules regarding hours, and a policy for vacation pay. You're hit with a multitude of legal requirements and management duties you'd never have to deal with if you worked solo.

To decide whether you need employees or not, take a closer look at your ultimate goals. Do you want to create the next Starbucks, or do you simply want to work on your own terms without a boss looking over your shoulder? If your goals are modest, then adding a staff may not be the best alternative.

If you do need employees, there are plenty of ways to meet your staffing needs—without driving yourself nuts. From temporaries and independent contractors to employee leasing, the following chapter takes a closer look at the do's and don'ts of staffing your business. Read it over, and you'll have a better idea whether to hire—or not to hire—is the right solution for you.

HOW TO HIRE

The employees you hire can make or break your business. While you may be tempted to hire the first person who walks in the door just to get it over with, doing so can be a fatal error. A small company can't afford to carry dead wood on staff, so start smart by taking time to figure out your staffing needs before you even begin looking for job candidates.

Job Analysis

Begin by understanding the requirements of the job being filled. What kind of personality, experience and education are needed? To determine these attributes, sit down and do a job analysis covering the following areas:

JOB ANALYSIS

Date: _____

Prepared By: _____

Title: _____

Department: _____

JOB RESPONSIBILITIES

Job Title:	Reporting To:

Major Responsibilities:

Minor Responsibilities:

EDUCATION/EXPERIENCE REQUIRED

GOALS/OBJECTIVES OF POSITION

KNOWLEDGE/SKILLS REQUIRED

RELATIONSHIPS

Number of People Supervised:	Reporting To:

PHYSICAL REQUIREMENTS

SPECIAL PROBLEMS/HAZARDS

♦ The physical/mental tasks involved (ranging from judging, planning and managing to cleaning, lifting and welding)

♦ How the job will be done (the methods and equipment used)

♦ The reason the job exists (including an explanation of job goals and how they relate to other positions in the company)

♦ The qualifications needed (training, knowledge, skills and personality traits)

Smart Tip

It's easy to hire employees who are just like you, but it's often a big mistake. Especially with your first employee, try to find someone who compensates for your strengths and weaknesses. While personal compatibility is important, hiring a carbon copy of yourself could leave your firm ill-prepared for future challenges.

If you are having trouble developing a list, one good way to get information for a job analysis is to talk to employees and supervisors at other companies that have similar positions.

Job Description

Use the job analysis to write a job description and a job specification. Drawing from these concepts, you can then create your recruitment materials, such as a classified ad.

The job description is basically an outline of how the job fits into the company. It should point out in broad terms the job's goals, responsibilities and duties. First, write down the job title and whom that person will report to. Next, develop a job statement or summary describing the position's major and minor duties. Finally, define how the job relates to other positions in the company. Which are subordinate and which are of equal responsibility and authority?

For a one-person business hiring its first employee, these steps may seem unnecessary, but remember, you're laying the foundations for your personnel policy, which will be essential as your company grows. Keeping detailed records from the time you hire your first employee will make things a lot easier when you hire your 50th.

The job specification describes the personal requirements you expect from the employee. Like the job description, it also includes the job title, whom the person reports to, and a summary of the position. However, it also lists any educational requirements, desired experience, and specialized skills or knowledge required. Include salary range and benefits. Finish by listing any physical or other special requirements associated with the job, as well as any occupational hazards.

Writing the job description and job specifications will also help you determine whether you need a part- or full-time employee, whether the person should be permanent or temporary, and whether you could use an independent contractor to fill the position (more on all these options later).

Writing The Ad

Use the job specification and description to write an ad that will attract candidates to your company. The best way to avoid wasting time on interviews with people who don't meet your needs is to write an ad that will lure qualified candidates and discourage others. Consider this example:

> *Interior designer seeks inside/outside sales-person. Flooring, drapes (extensive measuring), furniture, etc. In-home consultations. Excellent salary and commission. PREVIOUS EXPERIENCE A NECESSITY. San Francisco Bay Area. Send resume to G. Green at P.O. Box 5409, San Francisco, CA 90842-5409.*

This job description is designed to attract a flexible salesperson and eliminate those who lack the confidence to work on commission. The advertiser asks for expertise in "extensive measuring," the skill he has had the most difficulty finding.

The job location should be included to weed out applicants who don't live in the area or aren't willing to commute. Finally, the capitalized "PREVIOUS EXPERIENCE A NECESSITY" underscores that he will hire only candidates with previous experience.

To write a similarly targeted ad for your business, look at your job specifications and pull out the top four or five skills that are most essential to the job. Don't, however, list requirements other than educational or experience-related ones in the ad. Nor should you request specific personality traits (outgoing, detail-oriented) since people are likely to come in and imitate those characteristics when they don't really possess them. Instead, focus on telling the applicants about the excitement and challenge of the job, the salary, what they will get out of it and what it will be like working for you.

Finally, specify how employees should contact you. Depending on the type of job (professional or nonskilled), you may want to have the person send a cover letter and resume, or simply call to set up an appointment to come in and fill out an application.

JOB DESCRIPTION

Date: _____

Prepared By: _____

Title: _____

Department: _____

JOB DESCRIPTION

Job Title:	Reporting To:
Job Statement:	

MAJOR DUTIES

1.
2.
3.
4.
5.
6.
7.
9.
10.

MINOR DUTIES

1.
2.
3.
4.
5.
6.
7.
8.
9.
10.

RELATIONSHIPS

Number of People Supervised:
Person Assigning Work Assignments:

Recruiting Employees

The obvious first choice for recruiting employees is the classified ad section of your local newspaper. Place your ad in the Sunday or weekend edition of the largest-circulation local papers.

Beyond this, however, there are plenty of other places to recruit good employees. Here are some ideas:

◆ **Tap into your personal and professional network.** Tell everyone you know—friends, neighbors, professional associates, customers, vendors, colleagues from associations—that you have a job opening. Someone might know of the perfect candidate.

◆ **Contact school placement offices.** List your openings with trade and vocational schools, colleges and universities. Check with your local school board to see if high schools in your area have job training and placement programs.

◆ **Post notices at senior citizen centers.** Retirees who need extra income or a productive way to fill their time can make excellent employees.

WILLING AND ABLE

The Americans With Disabilities Act (ADA) of 1990 makes it illegal for employers with 15 or more employees to refuse to hire people with disabilities if making "reasonable accommodations" would enable the person to carry out the duties of the job. That could mean making physical changes to the workplace or reallocating certain responsibilities.

While the law is unclear on exactly how far an employer must go to accommodate a person with disabilities, what is clear is that it's the applicant's responsibility to tell the employer about the disability. Employers are not allowed to ask whether an applicant has a disability or a history of health problems. However, after the applicant has been given a written or verbal explanation of the job duties, you may then ask whether he or she can perform those duties or would need some type of accommodation.

For further clarification, see *Enforcement Guidance: Pre-employment Disability-Related Inquiries and Medical Examinations Under the Americans With Disabilities Act of 1990,* a free publication available from the Equal Employment Opportunity Commission's Publication Distribution Center in Washington, DC.

◆ **Use an employment agency.** Private and government-sponsored agencies can help with locating and screening applicants. Often their fees are more than justified by the amount of time and money you save.

◆ **List your opening with an appropriate job bank.** Many professional associations have job banks for their members. Contact groups related to your industry, even if they are outside your local area, and ask them to alert their members to your staffing needs.

> **Bright Idea**
>
> If relevant, ask employees to send samples of their work with their resumes or to bring them to the interview. Another technique: Ask them to complete a project similar to the actual work they'd be doing (and pay them for it). This gives you a strong indication of how they'd perform on the job . . . and gives them a clear picture of what you expect from them.

◆ **Use industry publications.** Trade association newsletters or industry publications often have classified ad sections where members can advertise jobs. This is an effective way to attract skilled people in your industry.

◆ **Go online.** There are a variety of online job banks and databases that allow employers to list openings. These databases can be searched by potential employees from all over the country. Often, you can even receive resumes online. This is an especially good way to search for tech-savvy employees.

Pre-Screening Candidates

Two important tools in pre-screening job candidates are the resume and the employment application. If you ask applicants to send in a resume, that will be the first tool you use to screen them. You will then have qualified candidates fill out an application when they come in for an interview. If you don't ask for a resume, you will probably want to have employees come in to fill out applications, then review the applications and call qualified candidates to set up an interview.

In either case, it's important to have an application form ready before you begin the interview process. You can buy generic application forms at most office-supply stores, or you can develop your own to meet your specific needs. Either way, make sure the application form conforms to Equal Employment Opportunity Commission (EEOC) guidelines regarding questions you can and cannot ask (see "Off Limits" in this chapter for more on this).

JOB APPLICATION

NAME/ADDRESS

Last:	First:	Middle Initial:	Social Security Number
Address:			
City:	State:	ZIP:	Telephone:

DESIRED EMPLOYMENT

Position:	Date You Can Start:	Desired Salary:
Are You Currently Employed?	If Employed, May We Inquire of Your Current Employer?	
Have You Applied to This Company Before?	If So, Where & When?	

EDUCATION

	Name & Location of School		
High School			
	Years Attended (Diploma/Degree)	Date Graduated	Grade Completed
University/College Undergraduate	Name & Location of School		
	Years Attended (Diploma/Degree)	Date Graduated	Grade Completed
University/College Graduate	Name & Location of School		
	Years Attended (Diploma/Degree)	Date Graduated	Grade Completed
Trade, Business or Correspondence School	Name & Location of School		
	Years Attended (Diploma/Degree)	Date Graduated	Grade Completed

EMPLOYMENT HISTORY

Employer:	Job Title:
Address:	Duties:
Phone:	Salary:
Date From: Date To:	Reason for Leaving:
Employer:	Job Title:
Address:	Duties:
Phone:	Salary:
Date From: Date To:	Reason for Leaving:
Employer:	Job Title:
Address:	Duties:
Phone:	Salary:
Date From: Date To:	Reason for Leaving:

JOB APPLICATION, CON'T.

REFERENCES

Name:	Occupation:
Address:	Relationship:
Phone Number:	Years Known:
Name:	Occupation:
Address:	Relationship:
Phone Number:	Years Known:
Name:	Occupation:
Address:	Relationship:
Phone Number:	Years Known:

PHYSICAL RECORD

Do you have any physical disabilities that prevent you from performing the work for which you are applying? If so, describe:

Have you ever been injured?	Provide Details:	
In case of emergency notify:	Name:	Address:	Phone:

ADDITIONAL AREAS OF EXPERTISE

Areas of specialized study, research or additional experience:

List the foreign languages you speak fluently:	Read:	Write:
U.S. Military Service:	Rank:	Present member in National Guard or Reserves:

_____   _____
Signature   *Date*

FOR INTERNAL USE ONLY

Interviewer:	Date:
Comments:	

Your application should ask for specific information such as name, address and phone number; educational background; work experience, including salary levels; awards or honors; whether the applicant can work full or part time as well as available hours; and any special skills relevant to the job (foreign languages, familiarity with software programs, etc.). Be sure to ask for names and phone numbers of former supervisors to check as references; if the candidate is currently employed, ask whether it is OK to contact his or her current place of employment. You may also want to ask for personal references.

Because many employers these days hesitate to give out information about an employee, you may want to have the applicant sign a waiver that states the employee authorizes former and/or current employers to disclose information about him or her.

When screening resumes, it helps to have your job description and specifications in front of you so you can keep the qualities and skills you're looking for clearly in mind. Since there is no standard form for resumes, evaluating them can be very subjective. However, there are certain criteria that you should expect to find in a resume.

It should contain the prospect's name, address, and telephone number at the top, and a brief summary of employment and educational experience, including dates. Many resumes include a "career objective" that describes what kind of job the prospect is pursuing; other applicants state their objectives in their cover letters. Additional information you may find on a resume or in a cover letter includes references, achievements and career-related affiliations.

Look for neatness and professionalism in the applicant's resume and cover letter. A resume riddled with typos raises some serious red flags. If a person can't be bothered to put their best foot forward during this crucial stage of the game, how can you expect them to do a good job if hired?

There are two basic types of resumes: the "functional" resume and the "chronological" resume. The chronological resume, which is what most of us are used to seeing, lists employment history in reverse chronological order, from most recent position to earliest. The functional resume does not list dates of employment; instead, it lists different skills or "functions" that the employee has performed.

Functional resumes have become more popular in recent years. In some cases, they are used by downsized executives who may be quite well-qualified and are simply trying to downplay long periods of unemployment. In other cases, however, they signal the applicant is a job-hopper or has something to hide.

Because it's easy for people to embellish resumes, it's a good idea to have candidates fill out a job application, by mail or in person, and then com-

OFF LIMITS

Equal Employment Opportunity Commission (EEOC) guidelines, as well as federal and state laws, prohibit asking certain questions of a job applicant, either on the application form or during the interview. What questions to sidestep? Basically, you can't ask about anything not directly related to the job, including:

◆ Age or date of birth (if interviewing a teenager, you can ask if he or she is 16 years old)

◆ Sex, race, creed, color, religion or national origin

◆ Disabilities of any kind

◆ Date and type of military discharge

◆ Marital status

◆ Maiden name (for female applicants)

◆ If a person is a citizen; however, you can ask if he or she has the legal right to work in the United States

Other questions to avoid:

◆ How many children do you have? How old are they? Who will care for them while you are at work?

◆ Have you ever been treated by a psychologist or psychiatrist?

◆ Have you ever been treated for drug addiction or alcoholism?

◆ Have you ever been arrested? (You may, however, ask if the person has been convicted if it is accompanied by a statement saying that a conviction will not necessarily disqualify an applicant for employment.)

◆ How many days were you sick last year?

◆ Have you ever filed for workers' compensation? Have you ever been injured on the job?

In doubt whether a question (or comment) is offensive or not? Play it safe and zip your lip. In today's lawsuit-happy environment, an offhanded remark could cost you plenty.

Bright Idea

Looking to fill an important position ... but dreading the hassle of hunting for candidates? Executive recruitment firms, also known as "headhunters" or search firms, can find qualified professional, managerial or technical candidates for you. Search firms typically charge a percentage of the executive's first-year salary.

pare it to the resume. Because the application requires information to be completed in chronological order, it gives you a more accurate picture of an applicant's real history.

Beyond functional and chronological resumes, there is something more important to be on the lookout for. That's what one consultant calls an "accomplishment" vs. a "responsibility" resume.

The responsibility resume is just that. It emphasizes the job description, saying things like "Managed three account executives; established budgets; developed departmental contests." An accomplishment resume, on the other hand, emphasizes accomplishments and results, such as "Cut costs by 50 percent" or "Met quota every month." Such a resume tells you the person is an achiever and has the bottom line firmly in mind.

When reading the resume, try to determine the person's career patterns. Look for steady progress and promotions in past jobs. Also look for stability in terms of length of employment. If a person changes jobs every year, they're probably not someone you want on your team. Look for people with three-to-four-year job stints.

At the same time, be aware of how economic conditions can affect a person's resume. During a climate of frequent corporate downsizing, for example, a series of lateral career moves may signal that a person is a survivor. It also shows that the person is interested in growing and taking on new responsibilities, even if there was no corresponding increase in pay or status.

By the same token, just because a resume or job application has a few gaps in it doesn't mean you should overlook it entirely. You could be making a big mistake. Stay focused on the skills or value the job applicant could bring to your company.

Interviewing Applicants

Once you've narrowed your stack of resumes down to 10 or so top candidates, it's time to start setting up interviews. If you dread this portion of the process, you're not alone. Fortunately, there are some ways to put both yourself and the candidates at ease—and make sure you get all the information you need to make a smart decision.

Start by preparing a list of basic interview questions in advance. While you won't read off this list like a robot, having it in front of you will ensure you cover all the bases and also make sure you ask all the candidates the same questions.

The initial few moments of an interview are the most crucial. As you meet the candidate and shake his or her hand, you'll gain a strong impression of his or her poise, confidence and enthusiasm (or lack thereof). Qualities to look for include good communication skills, a neat and clean appearance, and a friendly and enthusiastic manner.

Put the interviewee at ease with a bit of small talk on neutral topics. A good way to break the ice is by explaining the job and describing the company—its business, history and future plans.

Then, move on to the heart of the interview. You'll want to ask about several general areas, such as related experience, skills, educational background or training, and unrelated jobs. Open each area with a general, open-ended question, such as "Tell me about your last job."

Avoid questions that can be answered with a "yes" or "no" or that prompt obvious responses, such as "Are you detail-oriented?" Instead, ask questions that force the candidate to go into detail. The best questions are follow-up questions such as "How did that situation come about?" or "Why did you do that?" These queries force applicants to abandon pre-planned responses and dig deeper.

Here are some suggestions to get you started:

◆ If you could design the perfect job for yourself, what would you do? Why?

◆ What kind of supervisor gets the best work out of you?

◆ How would you describe your current supervisor?

◆ How do you structure your time?

◆ What are three things you like about your current job?

◆ What were your three biggest accomplishments in your last job? In your career?

◆ What can you do for our company that no one else can?

◆ What are your biggest strengths/weaknesses?

◆ How far do you think you can go in this company? Why?

◆ What do you expect to be doing in five years?

◆ What interests you most about this company? This position?

◆ Describe three situations where your work was criticized.

◆ Have you hired people before? If so, what did you look for?

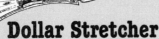

Dollar Stretcher

Whenever possible, look for employees you can cross-train into different job responsibilities. A welder with college courses in engineering and a secretary with human resources experience are workers one small business has successfully cross-trained. Cross-trained employees can fill in when others are absent, helping keep costs down.

Your candidate's responses will give you a window into his or her knowledge, attitude and sense of humor. Watch for signs of "sour grapes" about former employers. Also be alert for areas people seem reluctant to talk about. Probe a little deeper without sounding judgmental.

Pay attention to the candidate's nonverbal cues, too. Does she seem alert and interested, or does she slouch and yawn? Are his clothes wrinkled and stained, or clean and neat? A person who can't make an effort for the interview certainly won't make one on the job if hired.

Finally, leave time at the end of the interview for the applicant to ask questions—and pay attention to what he or she asks. This is the time when applicants can really show they've done their homework and researched your company . . . or, conversely, that all they care about is what they can get out of the job. Obviously, there's a big difference between the person who says "I notice that your biggest competitor's sales have doubled since they launched their Web site in January. Do you have any plans to develop a Web site of your own?" and the person who asks "How long is the lunch break?" Similarly, the candidate who can't come up with even one question may be demonstrating that they can't think on their feet.

End the interview by letting the candidate know what to expect next. How much longer will you be interviewing? When can they expect to hear from you? You're dealing with people's livelihoods, so the week you take to finish your interviews can seem like an eternity to them. Show some consideration by keeping them informed.

During the interview, jot down notes (without being obvious about it). After the interview, take five or 10 minutes to write down the applicant's outstanding qualities and evaluate his or her personality and skills against your job description and specifications.

Checking References

After preliminary interviews, you should be able to narrow the field to three or four top candidates. Now's the time to do a little detective work.

It's estimated that up to one-third of job applicants lie about their experiences and educational achievements on their resumes or job applications.

No matter how sterling the person seems in the interview process, a few phone calls upfront to check out their claims could save you a lot of hassle—and even legal battles—later on. Today, courts are increasingly holding employers liable for crimes employees commit on the job, such as drunk driving, when it is determined that the employer could have been expected to know about prior convictions for similar offenses.

Unfortunately, getting that information has become harder and harder to do. Fearful of reprisals from former employees, many firms have adopted policies that forbid releasing detailed information. Generally, the investigating party is referred to a personnel department, which supplies dates of employment, title and salary—period.

There are ways to dig deeper, however. Try to avoid the human resources department if at all possible. Instead, try calling the person's former supervisor directly. While the supervisor may be required to send you to personnel, sometimes you'll get lucky and get the person on a day he or she feels like talking.

Sometimes, too, a supervisor can tip you off without saying anything that will get him or her in trouble. Consider the supervisor who, when contacted by one potential employer, said, "I only give good references." When the employer asked, "What can you tell me about X?" the supervisor repeated, "I only give good references." Without saying anything, he said it all.

Depending on the position, you may also want to do education checks. You can call any college or university's admissions department to verify degrees and dates of attendance. Some universities require a written request or a signed waiver from the applicant before releasing this information.

If the person is going to be driving a company vehicle, you may want to do a motor vehicle check with the motor vehicle department. In fact, you may want to do this even if he or she will not be driving for you. Vehicle checks can uncover patterns of negligence or drug and alcohol problems.

If your company deals with property management, such as maintenance or cleaning, you may want to consider a criminal background check as well. Unfortunately, national criminal records and even state records are not coordinated. The only way to obtain records is to go to individual courthouses in each county. Although you can't run all over the state to check into a person's record, it's generally sufficient to investigate records in three counties—birthplace, current residence and residence preceding the current residence.

For certain positions, such as those that will give an employee access to your company's cash (a cashier or accounting clerk, for instance), a credit check may be a good idea as well. You can find credit reporting bureaus in any Yellow Pages. They will be able to provide you with a limited credit and payment history. While you shouldn't rely on this as the sole reason not to hire someone (credit reports are notorious for containing errors), a credit report can contribute to a total picture of irresponsible behavior. And if the person will have access to large sums of money at your company, hiring someone who is in serious debt is probably a bad idea.

Be aware, however, that if a credit check plays any role in your decision not to hire someone, you must inform them that they were turned down in part because of their credit report.

If all this seems too time-consuming to handle yourself, you can contract the job out to a third-party investigator. Look in the Yellow Pages for firms in your area that handle this task. The cost averages about $100—a small price to pay when you consider the damages it might save you.

After The Hire

Congratulations! You've hired your first employee. Now what?

As soon as you hire, call or write the applicants who didn't make the cut

---

FAMILY AFFAIR

Want to get good employees and tax savings, too? Consider putting your family members to work for you.

Hiring family, especially children, enables you to move family income out of a higher tax bracket into a lower one. It also enables you to transfer wealth to your kids without incurring federal gift or estate taxes.

Even preteen children can be put to work stuffing envelopes, filing or sorting mail. If their salary is reasonable, it is considered earned income and not subject to the "kiddie tax" rules that apply to kids under 14. And if your business is unincorporated, wages paid to a child under 18 are not subject to Social Security or FICA taxes. That means neither you nor your child has to pay these taxes. Finally, employed youngsters can make tax-deductible contributions to an individual retirement account.

Be sure to document the type of work the family member is doing, and pay them a comparable amount to what you'd pay another employee, or the IRS will think you're putting your family on the payroll just for the tax breaks. Keep careful records of time worked, and make sure the work is necessary to the business.

Your accountant can suggest other ways to take advantage of this tax situation without getting in hot water.

and tell them you'll keep their applications on file. That way, if the person you hired isn't the best—or is so good that business doubles—you won't have to start from scratch in hiring your second employee.

For each applicant you interviewed, create a file including your interview notes, the resume and the employment application. For the person you hire, that file will become the basis for his or her personnel file. Federal law requires that a job application be kept at least three years after a person is hired.

Even if you don't hire the applicant, keep the file. Under federal law, all recruitment materials, such as applications and resumes, must be kept for at least one year after the employment decision has been made.

In today's climate, where applicants sometimes sue an employer who decides not to hire them, it's a good idea to maintain all records related to a hire (or nonhire). Especially for higher-level positions where you narrow the field to two or three candidates, put a brief note or memo in each applicant's file explaining why he or she was or wasn't hired.

The hiring process doesn't end with making the selection. Your new employee's first day is critical. People are most motivated on their first day. Build on the momentum of that motivation by having a place set up for them to work, making them comfortable and making them feel welcome. Don't just dump them in an office and shut your door. Be prepared to spend some time with them, explaining job duties, getting them started on tasks or even taking them out to lunch. By doing so, you're building rapport and setting the stage for a long and happy working relationship.

ALTERNATIVES TO FULL-TIME EMPLOYEES

The traditional full-time employee isn't your only hiring option. In fact, more and more employers are turning to alternative arrangements, including temporary employees, part-timers, interns and leased employees. All these strategies can save you money, and some save you headaches, too. Here's a closer look at the options available.

Leasing Employees

If payroll paperwork, personnel hassles and employee manuals sound like too much work to deal with, consider an option that's growing in popularity: employee leasing.

Employee leasing—a means of managing your human resources without all the administrative hassles—first became popular in California in the early '80s, driven by the excessive cost of health-care benefits in the state. By combining the employees of several companies into one larger pool, employee leasing companies (also known as professional employer organizations, or PEOs) could offer business owners better rates on health care and workers' compensation coverage.

Today, there are more than 4 million leased employees in the United States, and the employee leasing industry is projected to continue growing at an annual rate of more than 30 percent over the next 10 years, according to the National Association of Professional Employer Organizations (NAPEO).

But today, employee leasing firms do a lot more than just offer better health-care rates. They manage everything from compliance with state and federal regulations to payroll, unemployment insurance, W-2 forms and claims processing—saving clients time and money. Some have even branched out to offer "extras" such as pension and employee assistance programs.

LOOK BEFORE YOU LEASE

How do you decide if an employee leasing company is for you? The National Association of Professional Employer Organizations (NAPEO) suggests you look for the following:

◆ Be sure their services fit your human resources needs. Is the company flexible enough to work with you?

◆ Check banking and credit references. Evidence that the company's payroll taxes and insurance premiums are up to date. Request to see a certificate of insurance.

◆ Ask for client and professional references, and call them.

◆ Investigate the company's administrative competence. What experience does it have?

◆ Understand how employees' benefits are funded. Do they fit your workers' needs? Find out who the third-party administrator or carrier is, and whether it is licensed if your state requires this.

◆ Make sure the leasing company is licensed or registered if required by your state.

◆ Review the agreement carefully and try to get a provision that permits you to cancel at short notice—say, 30 days.

For a list of NAPEO member organizations in your area, contact the NAPEO at (703) 836-0466 or write to 901 N. Pitt St., #150, Alexandria, VA 22314.

While many small-business owners confuse employee leasing companies with temporary help businesses, the two types of organizations are really quite different, explains Bruce Steinberg of the National Association of Temporary Services (NATS). "Generally speaking, temporary help companies recruit employees and assign them to client businesses to help with short-term work overload or special projects on an as-needed basis," Steinberg explains. With employee leasing companies, on the other hand, "a client business generally turns over all its personnel functions to an outside company, which administers these operations and leases the employees back to the client."

> **Smart Tip**
>
> Motivating independent contractors can be tough. How do you make them feel like part of your business? Communication is key. Send regular memos or hold in-person meetings with independent contractors to let them know what's going on in the company. Also include them in company social events, such as holiday parties or company picnics.

According to the NAPEO, leasing services are a contractual arrangement in which the leasing company is the employer of record for all or part of a client's work force. Employment responsibilities are typically shared between the PEO and the client, allowing the client to retain essential management control over the work performed by the employees.

Meanwhile, the PEO assumes responsibility for a wide range of employer obligations and risks, among them paying and reporting wages and employment taxes out of its own accounts, as well as retaining some rights to the direction and control of the leased employees.

The client, on the other hand, has one prime responsibility: writing one check to the PEO to cover the payroll, taxes, benefits and administrative fees. The PEO does the rest.

Who uses PEOs? According to the NAPEO, small businesses make up the primary market for leasing companies since—due to economies of scale—they typically pay higher premiums for employee benefits. If an employee hurts his or her back and files a workers' compensation claim, it could threaten the small business's existence. With another entity as the employer of record, however, these claims are no longer the small-business owner's problem. PEOs have also been known to help business owners avoid wrongful termination suits or negligent acts in the workplace, according to a NAPEO spokesperson.

Having to comply with a multitude of employment-related statutes, which is often beyond the means of smaller businesses, is another reason PEOs are so popular with entrepreneurs. According to the NAPEO, with a leasing company, you basically get the same type of human resources department you would get if you were a Fortune 500 firm.

Before hiring a professional employer organization, be sure to shop around since not all offer the same pricing structures or services. Fees may be based on a modest percentage of payroll (3 percent to 5 percent) or on a per-employee basis. When comparing fees, consider what you'd pay a full-time employee to handle the administrative chores the PEO will take off your hands. (For more information on what to look for, see "Look Before You Lease" in this chapter.)

Temporary Employees

If your business' staffing needs are seasonal—for example, you need extra workers during the holidays or during busy production periods—then temporary employees could be the answer. If the thought of a temp brings to mind a secretary, think again. The services and skills temporary help companies offer small businesses have expanded.

Today, some companies specialize in medical services; others find their niche in professional or technical fields, supplying everything from temporary engineers, editors and accountants to computer programmers, bankers, lab support staff and even attorneys.

With many temporary help companies now offering specialized employees, small-business owners have learned they don't have to settle for low skill levels or imperfect matches. Because most temporary help companies screen—and often train—their employees, entrepreneurs who choose this option stand a better chance of obtaining the quality employees they need.

In addition to pre-screened, pre-trained individuals, temporary help companies offer entrepreneurs a slew of other benefits. For one, they help keep your overhead low. For another, they save you time and money on recruiting efforts. You don't have to find, interview or relocate workers. Nor does the cost of health or unemployment benefits, worker's compensation insurance, profit-sharing, vacation time or other benefits come out of your budget since many temporary help companies provide these resources to their employees. (According to NATS, more than half the temporary work force receives holiday pay, while a substantial number also receive paid vacation days.)

How do you find the temporary help company that best suits your needs—from light secretarial to specialized technical support? First, look in the Yellow Pages under "Employment Contractors—Temporary Help." Call a few and ask some questions, including:

◆ Do they have insurance? Look for adequate liability and workers' compensation coverage to protect your company from a temporary worker's claim.

TEMPORARY TREATMENT

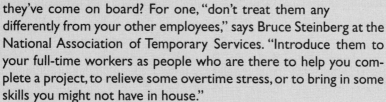

How do you make the most of your temporary workers once they've come on board? For one, "don't treat them any differently from your other employees," says Bruce Steinberg at the National Association of Temporary Services. "Introduce them to your full-time workers as people who are there to help you complete a project, to relieve some overtime stress, or to bring in some skills you might not have in house."

And don't expect temporary workers to be so well-trained that they know how to do all the little (but important) things, such as operating the copier or answering the phone. "Spend some time giving them a brief overview of these things, just as you would any new employee," advises Steinberg.

One strategy for building a better relationship with your temporary workers is to plan ahead as much as possible so you can use the same temporaries for an extended period of time—say, six months. Or try to get the same temporaries back when you need help again. This way, they'll be more productive, and you won't have to spend time retraining them.

◆ Do they check on the progress of their temporaries?

◆ How do they recruit their temporaries?

◆ How much training do they give temporaries? (According to the NATS, nearly half the temporary work force receives free skills training of some kind.)

◆ What benefits do they offer their temporaries?

◆ Should a temporary fail to work out, does the firm offer you any guarantees? Look for a firm that can provide a qualified temp right away.

◆ How quickly can they provide temporaries? (When you need one, you'll usually need one right away.)

Also ask the company to provide references. Contact references and ask their opinions of the temporary help company's quality level, reliability, reputation, service and training.

Before securing the services of a temporary help company, also consider your staffing needs. Do you need a part- or full-time temporary worker? What are your expectations? "The more clearly you define your needs, the

Beware!

Be sure you understand the precise legal relationship between your business and a leasing company. Some consider the leasing company the sole employer, effectively insulating the client from legal responsibility. Others consider the client and the leasing company joint employers, sharing legal responsibility. Have an attorney review your agreement to clarify any risks.

easier it is for the temporary help company to meet those needs," says Bruce Steinberg of the NATS.

"The company should also be able to work with you to help you define the skills you need," adds Steinberg, who notes that because temporary help companies are becoming true "staffing partners," you should expect them to work with you, not just sell you a service.

Defining the expected duration of your needs is also important, says Steinberg. While many entrepreneurs bring on a temporary worker for just that—temporary work—some may eventually find they'd like to hire the worker full time. Be aware that, at this point, some temporary help firms require a negotiated fee for "stealing" the employee away from them. Defining your needs upfront can help you avoid such penalties.

Because a growing number of entrepreneurs purposely use temporary workers part time to get a feel for whether they should hire them full time, many temporary help companies have begun offering an option: temporary-to-full-time programs, which allow the prospective employer and employee to evaluate each other. Temporary-to-full-time programs match a temporary worker who has expressed an interest in full-time work with an employer that has like interests. The client is encouraged to make a job offer to the employee within a predetermined time period, should the match seem like a good one. According to NATS, 76 percent of temporary workers decide to become temporary employees because "it's a way to get a full-time job."

Last, but not least, before contracting with a temporary help company, make sure it is a member of a trade association such as the NATS. According to Steinberg, "This means: 1) the company has agreed to abide by a code of ethics and good practices, 2) it is in the business for the long haul—meaning it has invested in its industry by becoming a member of its trade association, and 3) it has access to up-to-date information on trends that impact its business."

Part-Time Personnel

Another way to cut overhead and benefits costs while gaining flexibility is by hiring part-time workers. Under current law, you are not required to provide part-timers with medical benefits.

What are the other benefits to you? By using permanent part-timers, you can get more commitment than you'd get from a temp but more flexibility than you can expect from a nine-to-fiver. In some industries, such as fast food, retail and other businesses that are open long hours, part-timers are essential to fill the odd hours during which workers are needed.

A traditional source of part-time employees is students. These workers are typically flexible, willing to work odd hours, and do not require high wages. High school and college kids like employers who let them fit their work schedule to the changing demands of school.

Although students are ideal for many situations, there are some potential drawbacks to be aware of. For one thing, a student's academic or social demands may impinge on your scheduling needs. Some students feel that a manicure or tennis game is reason enough to change their work schedules. You'll need to be firm and set some standards for what is and is not acceptable.

Students aren't the only part-timers in town, however. One often overlooked source of employees is retired people. Often, seniors are looking for a way to earn some extra money or fill their days. Many of these people have years of valuable business experience that could be a boon to your company.

Frequently, seniors offer many of the advantages of other part-time employees without the flakiness that sometimes characterizes younger workers. They typically have an excellent work ethic and can add a note of stability to your organization. Plus, if you have a lot of customers who are seniors, they may prefer dealing with employees their own age.

Parents of young children, too, offer a qualified pool of potential part-time workers. Many stay-at-home moms or dads would welcome the chance to get out of the house for a few hours a day. Often, these workers are highly skilled and experienced.

Finally, one employee pool many employers swear by are people with disabilities. Workers from a local shelter or nonprofit organization can excel at assembling products or packaging goods. In most cases, the charity group will work with you to oversee and provide a job coach for the employees. To find disabled workers in your area, contact the local Association of Retarded Citizens office or the Easter Seals Society.

Bright Idea

Like the idea of part-time workers, but got a full-time slot to fill? Try job sharing—a strategy in which two part-timers share the same job. Susan works Mondays, Tuesdays and half of Wednesdays; Pam takes over Wednesday afternoon, Thursday and Friday. To make it work, hire people who are compatible in skills and abilities and keep lines of communication open.

The Intern Alternative

Some colleges encourage students to work, for a small stipend or even free, through internship programs. Student interns trade their time and talents in exchange for learning marketable job skills. Every year, colleges match millions of students with businesses of all sizes and types. Since they have an eye on future career prospects, the students are usually highly motivated.

Does your tiny one-person office have anything to offer an intern? Actually, small companies offer better learning experiences for interns since they typically have a greater variety of job tasks and offer a chance to work more closely with senior employees.

Routine secretarial or "gofer" work won't get you an intern in most cases. Colleges expect their interns to learn specialized professional skills. Hold up your end of the bargain by providing meaningful work. Can you delegate a direct-mail campaign? Have an intern help on photo shoots? Ask her to put together a client presentation?

Check with your local college or university to find out about internship programs. Usually, the school will send you an application, asking you to describe the job's responsibilities and your needs in terms of major, skill level and other qualifications. Then the school will send you resumes of students they think could work for you.

The best part of hiring interns? If you're lucky, you'll find a gem who'll stay with your company after the internship is over.

Outsourcing Options

One buzzword you're likely to hear more of these days is "outsourcing." Simply put, this refers to sending certain job functions outside of a company instead of handling them in-house. For instance, instead of hiring an in-house bookkeeper, you might outsource the job to an independent accountant who comes in once a month or does all the work off-site.

More and more companies large and small are turning to outsourcing as a way to cut payroll and overhead costs. Done right, outsourcing can mean you never need to hire an employee at all!

How to make it work? Make sure the company or individual you use can do the job. That means getting (and checking) references. Ask former or current clients about their satisfaction. Find out what industries and what type of workload the firm or individual is used to handling. Can you expect your deadlines to be met, or will your small business's projects get pushed aside if a bigger client has an emergency?

Make sure you feel comfortable with who will be doing the work and that you can discuss your concerns and needs openly. Ask to see samples of work if appropriate (for example, if you're using a graphic design firm).

If your outsourcing needs are handled by an individual, you're dealing with an independent contractor. The IRS has stringent rules regulating exactly who is and is not considered an independent contractor. The risk: If you consider a person an independent contractor and the IRS later reclassifies him or her as an employee, you could be liable for that person's Social Security taxes and a wide range of other costs and penalties.

For more on independent contractors, see "The Tax Man Cometh" chapter. If you're still in doubt, it always pays to consult your accountant. Making a mistake in this area could cost you big.

GLOSSARY

Cross-training: training employees to fill more than one position

Employee leasing company: company that administers personnel functions for clients and "leases" the client's employees back to them; also known as a professional employer organization (PEO)

Executive search firm: company that recruits executive, technical or professional job candidates for client companies; also called recruitment firm or headhunter

Job description: an outline of how a job fits into the company, listing broad goals and basic responsibilities

Job specification: more detailed than a job description, this describes the job but also lists specific education, experience, skills, knowledge, or physical requirements for performing the job

Outsourcing: practice of sending certain job functions outside of a company instead of having an in-house department or employee handle them; functions can be outsourced to a company or an individual

Temporary help company: company that recruits employees to work for client companies on a temporary basis

Waiver: form that typically accompanies or is part of an employment application; when signed by applicant, it authorizes former employers or schools to release information about the applicant

TREAT YOUR "CHILDREN" WELL

Developing an employee benefits plan

Once you've got great employees on board, how do you keep them? One way is by offering a good benefits package.

Many small-business owners mistakenly believe they cannot afford to offer benefits. But while going without benefits may boost your bottom line in the short run, that penny-wise philosophy could strangle your business's chance for long-term prosperity. "There are certain benefits good employees feel they must have," says Ray Silverstein, founder of PRO, President's Resource Organization, a small-business advisory network.

Heading the list of must-have benefits is medical insurance, but many job applicants also demand a retirement plan, disability insurance and more. Tell these applicants no benefits are offered and, often, top-flight candidates will head for the door.

The positive side to this coin: Offer the right benefits, and your business may just jump-start its growth. "Give employees the benefits they value, and they will be more satisfied, miss fewer workdays, be less likely to quit, and have a higher commitment to meeting the company's goals," says Joe Lineberry, a senior vice president at Aon Consulting, a human resources consulting firm that recently surveyed some 1,000 employees nationwide on what benefits programs mean to them. "The research shows that when employees feel their benefits needs are satisfied, they're more productive."

BENEFIT BASICS

The law requires employers to provide employees with certain benefits. You must:

◆ give employees time off to vote, serve on a jury or perform military service.

◆ comply with all workers' compensation requirements (see the following "Cover Your Assets" chapter).

◆ withhold FICA taxes from employees' paychecks and pay your own portion of FICA taxes, providing employees with minimum retirement and disability benefits.

◆ pay state and federal unemployment taxes, thus providing benefits for unemployed workers.

◆ contribute to state short-term disability programs in states where such programs exist.

◆ comply with the Family and Medical Leave Act (see "Family Matters," below).

You are not required to provide:

◆ retirement plans

◆ health plans (except in Hawaii)

◆ dental or vision plans

◆ life insurance plans

◆ paid vacations, holidays or sick leave

In reality, however, most companies do offer these benefits to stay competitive.

Most employers provide paid holidays for Christmas Day, New Year's, Memorial Day, Independence Day, Labor Day and Thanksgiving Day. Many

FAMILY MATTERS

The federal Family and Medical Leave Act (FMLA) requires employers to give workers up to 12 weeks off to attend to the birth or adoption of a baby or the serious health condition of the employee or an immediate family member.

After 12 weeks of unpaid leave, you must reinstate the employee in the same job or an equivalent one. The 12 weeks of leave does not have to be taken all at once; in some cases, employees can take it a day at a time.

In most states, only employers with 50 or more employees are subject to the FMLA. However, some states have family leave laws that place family leave requirements on businesses with as few as five employees. To find out your state's requirements, contact your state labor department.

employers also either allow employees to take time off without pay or use vacation days for religious holidays.

Most full-time employees will expect one to two weeks' paid vacation time per year. In explaining your vacation policy to employees, specify how far in advance requests for vacation time should be made, and whether in writing or verbally.

While no laws require employers to provide funeral leave, most do allow two to four days' leave for deaths of close family members. Companies that don't do this generally allow employees to use some other form of paid leave, such as sick days or vacation.

Legal Matters

Complications quickly arise as soon as a business begins offering bene-

---

ABOVE AND BEYOND

What does COBRA mean to you? No, it's not a poisonous snake coming back to bite you in the butt. The Consolidated Omnibus Budget Reconciliation Act (COBRA) extends health-insurance coverage to employees and dependents beyond the point at which such coverage traditionally ceases.

For employees, COBRA means an extension of up to 18 months of coverage under your plan even after they quit or are terminated by your company (provided the reason for termination isn't gross misconduct).

Employees' spouses can obtain COBRA coverage for up to 36 months after divorce or the death of the employee, and children can receive 36 additional months of coverage when they reach the age at which they are no longer classified as dependents.

The good news: Giving COBRA benefits shouldn't cost your company a penny. Employers are permitted by law to charge recipients 102 percent of the cost of extending the benefits (the extra 2 percent covers administrative costs).

The federal COBRA plan applies to all companies with more than 20 employees. However, many states have similar laws that pertain to much smaller companies, so even if your company is exempt from federal insurance laws, you may still have to extend benefits under certain circumstances. Contact the U.S. Department of Labor to determine whether your company must offer COBRA or similar benefits, and the rules for doing so.

fits, however. That's because key benefits such as health insurance and retirement plans fall under government scrutiny, and "it is very easy to make mistakes in setting up a benefits plan," says Kathleen Meagher, an attorney specializing in benefits at Landels Ripley & Diamond LLP.

And don't think nobody will notice: The IRS can discover in an audit that what you are doing does not comply with regulations. So can the U.S. Department of Labor, which has been beefing up its audit activities of late. Either way, a goof can be very expensive. "You can lose any tax benefits you have enjoyed, retroactively, and penalties can also be imposed," Meagher says.

Bright Idea

Want to get an idea what others in your industry are paying workers? The Bureau of Labor Statistics does Occupational Compensation Surveys for most regions of the country. The information is broken down by occupation and by various levels of experience within that occupation. The bureau also has information about benefits. To access the reports, visit http://stats.bls.gov:80/ocsdata.htm or by calling the Bureau of Labor Statistics' regional offices.

The biggest mistake? Leaving employees out of the plan. Examples range from exclusions of part-timers to failing to extend benefits to clerical and custodial staff. A rule of thumb is that if one employee gets a tax-advantaged benefit—meaning one paid for with pretax dollars—the same benefit must be extended to everyone. There are loopholes that may allow you to exclude some workers, but don't even think about trying this without expert advice.

Such complexities mean it's good advice never to go this route alone. You can cut costs by doing preliminary research yourself, but before setting up any benefits plan, consult with a lawyer or benefits consultant. An upfront investment of perhaps $1,000 could save you far more money down the road by helping you sidestep expensive potholes.

Expensive Errors

Providing benefits that meet employee needs and mesh with all the laws isn't cheap—benefits probably add 30 percent to 40 percent to base pay for most employees—and that makes it crucial to get the most from these dollars. But this is exactly where many small businesses fall short because, often, their approach to benefits is riddled with costly errors that can get them in trouble financially, with their insurers or even with their own employees. The most common mistakes:

1. **Absorbing the entire cost of employee benefits:** Fewer companies foot the whole benefits bill these days. According to a recent

survey of California companies by human resources management consulting firm William M. Mercer, 70 percent of employers require employee contributions toward health insurance, while 92 percent require employees to contribute toward the cost of insuring dependents.

The size of employee contributions varies from a few dollars per pay period to several hundred dollars monthly, but one plus of any co-payment plan is that it eliminates employees who don't need coverage. Many employees are covered under other policies—a parent's or spouse's, for instance—and if you offer insurance for free, they'll take it. But even small co-pay requirements will persuade many to skip it, saving you money.

Bright Idea

Peeved at payroll paperwork? Companies with as few as five employees can benefit from using a payroll service. First, get references, ask about services, and make sure the payroll service keeps abreast of federal and state payroll regulations. Rates depend on employees and frequency of payroll.

2. **Covering nonemployees:** Who would do this? Lots of business owners want to buy group-rate coverage for relatives or friends. The trouble: If there is a large claim, the insurer may investigate. And that investigation could result in disallowance of the claims, even cancellation of the whole policy. Whenever you want to cover somebody who might not qualify for the plan, tell the insurer or your benefits consultant the truth.

3. **Sloppy paperwork:** In small businesses, administering benefits is often assigned to an employee who wears 12 other hats. This employee really isn't familiar with the technicalities and misses a lot of important details. A common goof: Not enrolling new employees in plans during the open enrollment period. Most plans provide a fixed time period for open enrollment. Bringing an employee in later requires proof of insurability. Expensive litigation is sometimes the result. Make sure the employee overseeing this task stays current with the paperwork and knows that doing so is a top priority.

4. **Not telling employees what their benefits cost:** "Most employees don't appreciate their benefits, but that's because nobody ever tells them what the costs are," says PRO's Silverstein. Many experts suggest you annually provide employees with a benefits statement that spells out what they are getting and at what cost. A

simple rundown of the employee's individual benefits and what they cost the business is very powerful.

5. **Giving unwanted benefits:** A work force composed largely of young, single people doesn't need life insurance. How to know what benefits employees value? You can survey employees and have them rank benefits in terms of desirability. Typically, medical and financial benefits, such as retirement plans, will appeal to the broadest cross-section of workers.

If workers' needs vary widely, consider the increasingly popular "cafeteria plans," which give workers lengthy lists of possible benefits plus a fixed amount to spend.

Health Insurance

Health insurance is one of the most desirable benefits you can offer employees. There are several basic options for setting up a plan:

◆ **A traditional indemnity plan, or fee for service:** Employees choose their medical care provider; the insurance company either pays the provider directly or reimburses employees for covered amounts.

◆ **Managed care:** The two most common forms of managed care are the Health Maintenance Organization (HMO) and the Preferred Provider Organization (PPO). An HMO is essentially a prepaid health-care arrangement, where employees must use doctors employed by or under contract to the HMO and hospitals approved by the HMO. Under a PPO, the insurance company negotiates discounts with physicians and hospitals. Employees choose doctors from an approved list, then usually pay a set amount per office visit (typically $10 to $25); the insurance company pays the rest.

◆ **Self-insurance:** When you absorb all or a significant portion

Beware!

Beware the practice of "cherry-picking." Health insurance carriers often woo companies with younger, healthier employees away from their existing policies by promising substantially lower rates. All too often, however, those rates rise dramatically after the first year. Sticking with one carrier, rather than renegotiating your health insurance coverage every year, saves time and effort. In the end, that's money, too.

of a risk, you are essentially self-insuring. An outside company usually handles the paperwork, you pay the claims, and sometimes employees help pay premiums. The benefits include greater control of the plan design, customized reporting procedures and cash flow advantages. The drawback is that you are liable for claims, but you can limit liability with "stop loss" insurance—if a claim exceeds a certain dollar amount, the insurance company pays it.

◆ **Medical savings accounts (MSAs):** Congress recently approved a four-year test of MSAs, special savings accounts coupled with high-deductible insurance policies. Accounts are funded with employees' pretax dollars; disbursements are tax-free if used for approved medical expenses. Unused funds can accumulate indefinitely and earn tax-free interest. MSAs can be used by self-employed individuals or by employees of a company with 50 or fewer employees.

Cost Containment

Rising costs of health insurance have forced some small businesses to cut back on the benefits they offer. Carriers who write policies for small business tend to charge very high premiums. Often, they demand extensive medical information about each employee. If anyone in the group has a pre-existing condition, the carrier may refuse to write a policy. Or, if someone in the company becomes seriously ill, the carrier may cancel the policy the next time it comes up for renewal.

Further complicating matters, some states are mandating certain health-care benefits, so that if an employer offers a plan at all, they have to include certain types of coverage. Employers who can't afford to comply often have to cut out insurance altogether.

The good news: Many states are trying to ease the burden by passing laws that make it easier for small businesses to get health insurance and prohibit insurance carriers from discriminating against small firms. (MSAs, described above, are in part a response to the problems small businesses face.)

Until more laws are passed, what can a small business do? There are ways to cut costs without cutting into your employees' insurance plan. A growing number of small businesses band together with other entrepreneurs to enjoy economies of scale and gain more clout with insurance carriers.

Many trade associations offer health insurance plans for small-business owners and their employees at lower rates. Your business may have only five employees, but united with the other, say, 9,000 association members and their 65,000 employees, you've got substantial clout. The carrier issues a policy to the whole association; your business's coverage can't be terminated unless the carrier cancels the entire association.

Associations are able to negotiate lower rates and improved coverage because the carrier doesn't want to lose such a big chunk of business. This way, even the smallest one-person company can choose from the same menu of health-care options that big companies enjoy.

Beware!

As a boss, are you a saint ... or a Scrooge? Read Jim Miller's *Best Boss, Worst Boss* (Summit Group) to get an idea how you rate. Miller collected real-life stories (like the tightwad boss who charges employees 30 cents per personal call). Good bosses, by contrast, are generous, compassionate and empowering. Result? Happier, more productive and loyal employees.

Associations aren't the only route to take. In some states, business owners or groups have set up health-insurance networks among businesses that have nothing in common but their size and their location. Check with your local chamber of commerce to find out about such programs in your area.

Some entrepreneurs have been ripped off by unscrupulous organizations supposedly peddling "group" insurance plans at prices 20 percent to 40 percent below the going rate. The problem: These plans don't pay all policyholders' claims because they're not backed by sufficient cash reserves. Such plans often have lofty-sounding names that suggest a larger association of small employers.

How to protect yourself from a scam? Here are some tips:

1. **Compare prices.** If it sounds too good to be true, it probably is. Ask for references from other companies that have bought from the plan. How quick was the insurer in paying claims? How long has the reference dealt with the insurer? If it's less than a few months, that's not a good sign.

2. **Check the plan's underwriter.** The underwriter is the actual insurer. Many scam plans claim to be administrators for underwriters that really have nothing to do with them. Call the underwriter's headquarters and the insurance department of the state in which it's registered to see if it is really affiliated with the plan.

   To check the underwriter's integrity, ask your state's insurance department for it's A.M. Best rating, which grades companies according to their ability to pay claims. Also ask for its "claims-paying ability rating," which is monitored by services like Standard & Poor's. If the company is too new to be rated, be wary.

3. **Make sure the company follows state regulations.** Does the company claim it's exempt? Check with your state's insurance department.

4. **Ask the agent or administrator to show you what his or her commission, advance or administrative cost structure is.** Overly generous commissions can be a tip-off; some scam operations pay agents up to 500 percent commission.

5. **Get help.** Ask other business owners if they have dealt with the company. Contact the Better Business Bureau to see if there are any outstanding complaints. If you think you're dealing with a questionable company, contact your state insurance department or your nearest Labor Department Office of Investigations.

RETIREMENT PLANS

A big mistake some small-business owners make is thinking they can't afford to fund a retirement plan in lieu of putting profits back into the business. While 80 percent of big businesses offer retirement plans, only 20 percent of small companies have set up plans. Many small-business owners are at risk of having insufficient funds saved for retirement.

Don't ignore the value of investing early. If, starting at age 35, you invested $3,000 each year with a 14 percent annual return, you would have an annual retirement income of nearly $60,000 at age 65. But $5,000 invested at the same rate of return beginning at age 45 only results in $30,700 in annual retirement income. The benefit of retirement plans is that savings grow tax-free until you withdraw the funds—typically after age 59$1/2$. If you withdraw funds before that age, the withdrawn amount is fully taxable and also subject to a 10 percent penalty. The value of tax-free investing over time means it's best to start right away, even if you start with small increments.

Besides the long-term benefit of providing for your future, setting up a retirement plan also has the immediate gratification of cutting taxes.

Bright Idea

IRS Publication 560, *Retirement Plans for the Self-Employed*, describes rules for SEP-IRA, Keogh and SIMPLE plans. It's free; visit www.irs.ustreas.gov, or call (800) TAX-FORM.

Here's a closer look at a range of retirement plans for yourself and your employees.

Individual Retirement Account (IRA)

One of the greatest advantages of the IRA is its relative simplicity, although the Taxpayer Relief Act of 1997 has made this retirement vehicle a bit more complex. For the most part, however, the paperwork and tax reporting requirements are minimal, and you are not obligated to cover any of your employees, as you are required to do with the other types of retirement plans. You can set up or make annual contributions to an IRA any time up to the date your federal income tax return is due.

The biggest drawback to an IRA is that your maximum annual contribution is limited to the lesser of your earned income or $2,000. If you are not covered by an employer-provided retirement plan, you can make a tax deductible IRA contribution, regardless of income.

For joint filers, even if one spouse is covered by a retirement plan, the spouse who is not covered by a plan may make a deductible IRA contribution if the couple's adjusted gross income is $150,000 or less. The amount you can deduct is decreased in stages above that income level and is eliminated entirely for couples with income over $160,000. Previously, the IRA deduction for a working or nonworking individual whose spouse was covered by a retirement plan was decreased at $40,000 and eliminated at $50,000. Nonworking spouses and their partners can contribute up to $4,000 to IRAs ($2,000 each), provided the working spouse earns at least $4,000.

If you are covered by an employer-provided pension plan (such as if you start a business while still employed), you will be able to make tax-deductible contributions to an IRA if your adjusted gross income is $30,000 or less. That's up from $25,000 in 1997. For couples, the new income ceiling increases to $50,000, up from $40,000 in 1997. Under the 1997 Taxpayer Relief Act, the income limits will continue rising in later years, reaching $50,000 for single taxpayers in 2005 and $80,000 for married ones by 2007.

You also may wish to consider the Roth IRA, a new type of IRA created by the Taxpayer Relief Act of 1997. Unlike the rules for traditional IRAs, contributions to a Roth IRA are nondeductible, but withdrawals are tax-free (if certain conditions are met).

Joint filers can make the full contribution ($2,000) to a Roth IRA as long as their joint income is under $150,000. For those with income between $150,000 and $160,000, the contribution amount is decreased, until it is eliminated completely at $160,000.

Savings Incentive Match Plan For Employees (SIMPLE)

This is one of the most attractive options available to small-business owners with 100 or fewer employees. With a SIMPLE plan, you can decide whether to use a 401(k) or an IRA as your retirement plan.

A SIMPLE plan is just that—simple to administer. It doesn't come with a lot of paperwork or reporting requirements.

The employer must make contributions to the plan by either matching each participating employee's contribution dollar for dollar, up to 3 percent of the employee's pay, or by making an across-the-board 2 percent contribution for all employees, even if they don't participate in the plan, which can be expensive.

The maximum amount each employee can contribute to the plan is only $6,000 a year. This is one of the lowest contributions of all available plans. Therefore, the tax deduction for the contribution will not be as great as it could be with some of the other plans.

Simplified Employee Pension Plan (SEP)

As its name implies, this is the simplest type of retirement plan available. Essentially, this is a glorified IRA that allows you to contribute a set percentage up to a maximum amount each year. Paperwork is minimal, and you don't have to contribute every year. And regardless of the name, you don't need employees to set one up.

If you do have employees, well, that's the catch. Employees do not make any contributions to SEPs. Employers must pay the full cost of the plan, and whatever percentage you contribute for yourself must be applied to all eligible employees. The maximum contribution is 15 percent of an employee's salary or $24,000, whichever is less.

As your company grows, you may want to consider other types of retirement plans, such as Keogh or 401(k) plans.

Where To Go

With so many choices available, it's a good idea to talk to your accountant about what type of plan is best for you. Once you know what you want, where do you go to set up a retirement plan?

Banks, investment companies, full-service or discount brokers and inde-

Smart Tip

Taking time to thank your employees pays off in performance. Some ways to show appreciation: Send birthday cards to workers' homes. Write congratulatory notes for a job well done. Use food to boost morale—Popsicles on a hot day or hot chocolate in the winter. Small things make a big difference in making employees feel valued.

pendent financial advisors can all help you set up a plan that meets your needs. Many of these institutions also offer self-managed brokerage accounts where you can combine investments in mutual funds, stocks, bonds and certificates of deposit (CDs).

LOW-COST BENEFITS

In addition to the standard benefits discussed above, there are plenty of benefits that cost your company little or nothing but reap huge rewards in terms of employee satisfaction and loyalty. Consider these ideas:

♦ **Negotiate discounts with local merchants for your employees.** Hotels, restaurants and amusement parks may offer discounts on their various attractions, including lodging and food, through corporate customer programs. Warehouse stores, such as Sam's Club, give discounted memberships to employees of their corporate members. Movie theatres provide reduced-rate tickets for companies' employees. Don't forget to offer employees free or discounted prices on your own company products and services.

♦ **Ask a local dry cleaner for free pickup and delivery of your employees' clothes.** Or, ask a garage for free transportation to and from work for employees having their cars serviced there. Many businesses are willing to provide this service to capture— and keep—new customers.

♦ **Offer free lunch-time seminars to employees.** Financial planners, health-care workers, safety experts, attorneys and other professionals often offer their speaking services at no charge. Education is beneficial for both your employees and your business.

♦ **Offer supplemental insurance plans that are administered through payroll but are paid for by the employee.** Carriers of health, life, auto and accident insurance typically offer these plans at a lower rate to employers, so everybody benefits.

♦ **Offer a prepaid legal-services plan administered through payroll but paid for by the employee.** Like insurance, the purpose of the prepaid legal service is to provide protection against the emotional and financial stress of an employee's legal problems. Such services include phone consultations regarding personal or business-related legal matters, contract and document review, preparation of wills, legal representation in cases involving motor vehicle violations, trial defense services and IRS-audit legal services.

The employer deducts the monthly service fee from the paychecks of those employees who want to take advantage of the service. Typical fees range from $15 to $25 per month per employee and cover most routine and preventive legal services at no additional cost. More extensive legal services are provided at a lower rate when offered in this manner, saving employees money.

◆ **How about an interest-free computer-loan program?** Making it easier for employees to purchase computers for their personal use increases the technical productivity of employees on the job. The employee chooses the computer and peripherals based on the employer's parameters. (For example, the computer must be a Macintosh, and the total package may not exceed $3,000.) The company purchases the system, allows the employee to take it home, and deducts payments from the employee's paycheck. Although there is some initial capital outlay, it is recouped quickly. And any computer experience an employee can gain at home will likely enhance his or her proficiency in the workplace.

◆ **Let employees purchase excess inventory from your business at a significant discount via sample sales or employee auctions.** Arrange these purchases in conjunction with regularly scheduled companywide "yard sales" for employees to buy and sell their personal belongings.

One of the most appreciated, but most overlooked, employee benefits is membership in a credit union. There are some 6,000 well-established, state-chartered credit unions throughout the United States and Canada that accept start-up businesses as members—at no charge.

The benefits to your employees are threefold: They'll probably increase their savings rates (especially if you offer automatic payroll deduction), they'll have access to lower loan rates, and they'll typically pay lower fees—if any—for services.

Services credit unions frequently offer include:

◆ Automatic payroll deductions
◆ IRAs
◆ Savings certificates (often at higher yields than at banks or savings and loans)
◆ Personal and auto loans
◆ Lines of credit
◆ Checking accounts
◆ Christmas club accounts

Only state-chartered credit unions are allowed to add new companies to their membership rosters. To find a credit union that will accept your company, call your state's league of credit unions, or simply call a few local credit unions. You can also write to the National Credit Union Association, P.O. Box 431, Madison, WI 53701, or call (800) 356-9655, to receive a list of state leagues.

When comparing credit unions, get references and check them. Find out how communicative and flexible the credit union is. Examine the accessibility. Are there ATMs? Is there a location near your business? Consider the end users—your employees.

Once your company is approved, designate one person to be the primary liaison with the credit union. That person will maintain information about memberships, as well as enrollment forms and loan applications. Kick things off by asking a credit union representative to conduct on-site enrollment and perhaps return periodically for follow-up or new sign-ups.

EMPLOYEE POLICIES

Now that you have employees, you'll need to set policies on everything from pay rates to safety procedures. Many of these policies are regulated by federal and state laws. Here's what you need to know.

Paying Employees

There are many federal and state laws that regulate the paying of employees. The key one to be aware of is the Fair Labor Standards Act (FLSA), which covers most firms engaged in interstate commerce. The FLSA requires you to pay minimum wage and also requires you to pay overtime (time-and-a-half) to nonexempt employees who work more than 40 hours per week.

Not all employees or firms are covered. Exceptions include employees of retail stores and service establishments with annual gross sales or receipts less than $500,000; outside salespeople; and executive, administrative and professional personnel. However, companies not covered by the federal act are most likely subject to similar minimum-wage and overtime laws in their states.

Exempt And Nonexempt Employees

Under the FLSA, all employees are classified as either exempt or nonexempt. A nonexempt employee is entitled to a minimum wage and overtime pay as well as other protections set forth in the FLSA.

Exempt employees are not protected under these rules. However, if you wish to classify an employee as exempt, you must pay him or her a salary.

Anyone paid on an hourly basis is automatically considered nonexempt; however, there can be nonexempt employees who are paid a salary.

If salary isn't the determining factor, what makes an employee exempt? Exempt employees include:

1. **Executives:** Employees who have discretionary powers and perform managerial functions at least half the time.

2. **Administrative:** Employees who assist an executive or administrative official in carrying out his or her duties or do any of the following: 1) act in a staff or a functional capacity (such as a tax advisor), 2) perform special assignments, 3) perform office or nonphysical labor directly related to management policies, or 4) exercise discretion and independent judgment on a regular basis.

3. **Professional:** Employees in one of these categories: 1) a learned profession with a status that is recognized based on acquiring

MANUAL LABOR

Sooner or later, every entrepreneur needs to write a manual. An employee policy manual, a procedures manual or a safety manual are just a few of the more important ones.

Even if you only have one employee, it's not too soon to start putting policies in writing. Doing so now—before your staff grows—can prevent bickering, confusion and, worse, lawsuits later when Steve finds out you gave Joe five sick days and he only got four.

How to start? As with everything, begin by planning. Write a detailed outline of what you want to include.

As you write, focus on making sure the manual is easy to read and understand. Think of the simplest, shortest way to convey information. Use bullet points and numbered lists, where possible, for easier reading.

A lawyer or human resources consultant can be invaluable throughout the process. At the very least, you'll want your attorney to review the finished product for loopholes.

Finally, ensure all new employees receive a copy of the manual and read it. Include a page that employees must sign, date and return to you stating they have read and understood all the information in the manual and agree to abide by your company's policies. Maintain this in their personnel file.

knowledge through a lengthy course of study (such as a lawyer), 2) artistic professions, or 3) teachers.

There are other minor exemptions for homebased workers, workers with disabilities, apprentices and newspaper carriers.

Tip Credits

States sometimes set minimum wage laws either above or below the federal minimum wage. If your state minimum wage differs from the federal, you'll have to pay the higher of the two.

If your employees typically receive more than $30 per month in tips from customers, the federal minimum wage law lets you credit some of those tips toward your minimum wage obligations (within limits). The tip credit cannot exceed the value of the tips actually received.

In addition, the federal minimum wage, minus tip credit, cannot be less than the state minimum wage less any state tip credit. Many states have different tip credits than the federal one; again, the more favorable credit to the employee is the one you must go by.

Overtime Requirements

Nonexempt employees must be paid one-and-a-half times their normal rate for hours worked in excess of 40 per week. A workweek is defined as seven consecutive 24-hour periods. The workweek can start any day you want it to.

Entrepreneurs often assume overtime rules don't apply to salaried nonexempt employees. Make sure you don't make this error.

Again, states often have overtime laws of their own. However, the vast majority of state laws are the same as the federal system. If your state's overtime law is more generous to employees, that's the one you must follow.

WORKPLACE SAFETY

Why worry about safety? Because failing to do so could destroy your business. Besides the human loss, workplace accidents cost money and time. You could be liable for substantial penalties that could wipe out your business's cash flow. The Occupational Safety and Health Administration (OSHA) recently increased its minimum penalty for willful violations of safety rules that could result in death or serious physical harm from $10,000 to $70,000. So paying attention to safety is definitely worth your while.

OSHA Regulations

All employers, whether they have one employee or 1,000, are subject to federal OSHA requirements. However, in states where a federally certified plan has been adopted, the state plan governs. State standards must be at least as strict as the federal standards.

In some cases, businesses who use nonemployee workers, such as independent contractors, are also subject to OSHA. Workers are considered employees under OSHA if you:

◆ Control the actions of the employee

◆ Have the power to control the employee's actions

◆ Are able to fire the employee or modify employment conditions

Small employers (with 10 or fewer employees) are typically exempt from regularly scheduled OSHA inspections and don't have to report injuries or illnesses. However, that doesn't mean you're exempt from OSHA regulations.

Compliance With OSHA

The first step in complying with OSHA is to learn the published safety standards. The standards you must adhere to depend on the industry you're in.

Every business has to comply with general industry standards, which cover things like safety exits, ventilation, hazardous materials, personal protective equipment like goggles and gloves, sanitation, first aid and fire safety.

Under OSHA, you also have a general duty to "maintain a safe workplace," which covers all situations for which there are published standards. In other words, just because you complied with the standards that specifically apply to your industry, you aren't off the hook. You also need to keep abreast of possible hazards from new technology or rare situations the government may have thought of and published standards for.

Sound exhausting? Help is available. Start with your insurance carrier. Ask if an insurance company safety specialist can visit your business and make recommendations. Insurers are typically more than happy to do this since the safer your business is, the fewer accident claims you'll file.

The government can also help you set up a safety program. Both OSHA and state safety organizations conduct safety consultation programs. Check to see what programs your state safety department offers, too. You'll find local offices of government agencies, as well as state organizations, listed in the government pages of your phone book, usually under "Labor Department," "Department of Commerce" or a similar name.

Don't forget to tap into the resources of your chamber of commerce, industry trade association and other business groups. Many offer safety seminars and provide safety training literature free or for a nominal charge.

In addition, there are private consultants who can help small businesses set up safety programs that meet OSHA regulatory standards. Your lawyer may be able to recommend a good one in your area.

Put It In Writing

When you have a safety program in place, put it in writing with a safety manual (see "Manual Labor" in this chapter). Your safety manual should explain what to do in the event of a fire, explosion, natural disaster or any other catastrophe your business may face. Make sure you keep well-stocked fire extinguishers and first-aid kits at convenient locations throughout your building. Also make sure employees know where these are located and how to use them.

In addition to emergency procedures, your safety manual should explain proper procedures for performing any routine tasks that could be hazardous. Ask employees for input here; they are closest to the jobs and may know about dangerous situations that aren't obvious to you.

Finally, have an insurance professional, a government representative and an attorney review the finished manual. You're putting your company's commitment to safety on the line, so make sure you get it right.

Emphasize the importance of safety with regular meetings, inspections and incentive programs. These don't have to cost a lot (or anything). Try establishing a "Safe Employee of the Month" award or giving a certificate for a free dinner for winning suggestions on improving safety.

DISCRIMINATORY TREATMENT

Although sexual harassment is one of the hottest issues facing employers these days, it's not the only type of discrimination you need to be concerned about. Under the Civil Rights Act of 1991, employees who believe they were victims of job discrimination due to race, religion, sex or disability are entitled to a trial by jury.

While companies with fewer than 15 employees are exempt from federal discrimination laws, that doesn't mean they shouldn't worry about this issue. Most states have civil rights legislation that protects employees of small firms from discrimination. There is also the risk of lawsuits in a variety of forms. One attorney estimates the average legal fees for defense in a sexual harassment suit, regardless of the verdict, are upwards of $75,000.

Concerns over discrimination are more important than ever in today's increasingly diverse business world. If you run a small business, chances are you will be dealing with employees from many cultures, races and age groups. How can you keep things running harmoniously and protect your business from legal risk? The best policy is to make sure that everyone in your workplace understands what constitutes harassment or discrimination—and also understands the benefits of a diverse workplace.

Big companies may spend thousands on diversity training, but there are plenty of low-cost options available:

Beware!

Learn to spot some of the signs that sexual harassment may be occurring in your company. Increased absenteeism, drop-offs in productivity and lackluster performance are all signs that something may be wrong.

♦ Learn as much as you can from books on the subject and from exposure to people who are different from you.

♦ Investigate video series on managing diversity. Many are available for rental or purchase.

♦ Consider public programs. A growing number of Urban League, chamber of commerce, Small Business Administration and community college seminars and courses are bringing small-business owners together to learn about diversity issues

As the business owner, it's important to set a good example. Some ground rules to help keep you out of trouble:

♦ Don't touch employees without permission.

♦ Never date someone who works for you.

♦ Don't demean others or make suggestive comments. Watch your mouth; what seems humorous to some may offend others.

♦ Be sensitive to diversity of all kinds. Are employees in their 50s making condescending remarks about the "young upstarts" in their 20s? Two white women in their 40s might face a cultural conflict if one is from the Midwest and the other is from the West Coast, or if one has children and the other doesn't.

♦ If you decorate your office for the holiday season, don't include some religious symbols and leave out others. Many employers opt for a seasonal, rather than holiday, approach and use décor such as snowflakes and candles.

Put policies regarding discrimination and harassment in writing as part of your employee manual (see "Manual Labor" in this chapter). Outline the disciplinary action that will be taken and the process by which employees can make their complaints known.

Hold a brief orientation meeting to introduce employees to your new policy or reacquaint them with the one already in place. Spell out very plainly what is and isn't acceptable. Many employees are especially confused about what constitutes sexual harassment. You don't want your staff walking around scared to say hello to one another.

Even if an incident does arise, the good news for small-business owners:

Most complaints can be solved at the company level, before the issue comes close to a courtroom. To make this work, however, time is of the essence. Don't put off dealing with complaints, or the victim is likely to stew. Give both parties a chance to tell their side of the story. Often, the cause is a simple misunderstanding. To cover all your bases, you may want to have a neutral consultant or human resources professional from outside the company investigate the matter.

GLOSSARY

Americans With Disabilities Act (ADA): law passed in 1990 that prohibits employers with 15 or more employees to refuse to hire people with disabilities if making "reasonable accommodations" would enable the person to perform the job

Consolidated Omnibus Budget Reconciliation Act (COBRA): law requiring employers to extend health insurance coverage to employees and dependents beyond the point at which such coverage traditionally ceases (such as the termination or death of the covered employee)

Family and Medical Leave Act (FMLA): law requiring certain employers to give employees 12 weeks of unpaid leave for the birth or adoption of a baby or the serious illness of the employee or a close family member

Occupational Safety and Health Administration (OSHA): federal agency that regulates workplace safety

CHAPTER 24

COVER YOUR ASSETS

Getting
business
insurance

One of the most common mistakes start-up business owners face is failing to buy adequate insurance for their businesses. It's an easy error to make: Money is tight, and with so many things on your mind, protecting yourself against the possibility of some faraway disaster just doesn't seem that important. "Oh, I'll get insurance," you promise yourself, "one of these days." Soon, "one of these days" comes and goes, and you're still uninsured. Only now, your business has gotten much bigger, you've put a lot more into it, and you've got a lot more to lose. Everything, to be exact.

It doesn't take much. A fire, burglary, the illness of a key employee—any one of these could destroy everything you've worked so hard to build. When you think of all the time, effort and money you're investing in your business, doesn't it make sense to invest a little extra to protect it?

Following is a closer look at the types of business insurance available and what most entrepreneurs need, plus tips for keeping costs under control. (Health insurance is covered in Part 4 Chapter 23.)

BASIC INSURANCE NEEDS

The basic business insurance package consists of four fundamental coverages—general liability, workers' compensation, auto, and property/casualty—plus an added layer of protection over those, often called an umbrella policy.

Workers' Compensation

Workers' compensation, which covers medical and rehabilitation costs and lost wages for employees injured on the job, is required by law in all 50 states.

Workers' comp insurance consists of two components, with a third optional element. The first part covers medical bills and lost wages for the injured employee; the second encompasses the employer's liability, which covers the business owner should the spouse or children of a worker who's permanently disabled or killed decide to sue. The third and optional element of workers' compensation insurance is employment practices liability, which insures against lawsuits arising from claims of sexual harassment, discrimination and the like.

"Employment practices liability protects the unknowing corporation from the acts of the individual," says Todd Muller at the Independent Insurance Agents of America (IIAA), an industry association. "Whether you need it depends on the size of your business and how much control you have over the daily work of employees." This is something you may need to worry about as your company grows.

Muller says it is often hard for small companies to get workers' compensation insurance at reasonable rates. Consequently, some states have a risk-sharing pool for firms that can't buy from the private market. Typically state-run and similar to assigned risk pools for car insurance, these pools generally don't provide the types of discounts offered in the voluntary market, and thus are an "insurance of last resort."

Because insurance agents aren't always up to date on the latest requirements and laws regarding workers' comp, you should check with your state, as well as your agent, to find out exactly what coverage you need. Start at your state's department of insurance or insurance commissioner's office.

Generally, rates for workers' comp insurance are set by the state, and you purchase insurance from a private insurer. The minimum amount you need is also governed by state law. When you buy workers' comp, be sure to choose a company licensed to write insurance in your state and approved by the insurance department or commissioner.

If you are purchasing insurance for the first time, the rate will be based on your payroll and the average cost of insurance in your industry. You'll pay that rate for a number of years, after which an experience rating will kick in, allowing you to renegotiate premiums.

Dollar Stretcher

Ask your insurance agent about risk-reduction tactics that you can use to help save money. Altering your business practices—for instance, installing better locks or brighter lights to prevent crime—can cut your premiums (and your risk). You may even want to change your business operations to get rid of a high-risk activity.

Depending on the state you are located in, the business owner will be either automatically included or excluded from coverage; if you want something different, you'll need to make special arrangements. While excluding yourself can save you several hundred dollars, this can be penny-wise and pound-foolish. Review your policy before choosing this option because in most states if you opt out, no health benefits will be paid for any job-related injury or illness by your standard health insurance provider.

A better way to reduce premiums is by maintaining a good safety record. This could include following all the Occupational Health and Safety Administration guidelines related to your business, creating an employee safety manual or instituting a safety training program.

Another way to cut costs is to ensure that all jobs in your company are properly classified. Insurance agencies give jobs different classification ratings depending on the degree of risk of injury.

General Liability

Comprehensive general liability coverage insures a business against accidents and injury that might happen on its premises, as well as exposures related to its products.

For example, suppose a visiting salesperson slips on a banana peel while taking a tour of your office and breaks her ankle. General liability covers her claim against you. But let's say your company is a window-sash manufacturer, with hundreds of thousands of its window sashes installed in people's homes and businesses. If something goes wrong with them, general liability covers any claims related to the damage that results.

The catch is that the damage cannot be due to poor workmanship. This points up one difficulty with general liability insurance: It tends to have a lot of exclusions. Make sure you understand exactly what your policy covers . . . and what it doesn't.

You may want to purchase additional liability policies to cover specific concerns. For example, many consultants purchase "errors and omissions liability," which protects them in case they are sued for damages resulting from a mistake in their work. A com-

Beware!

If you operate a homebased business, don't assume your homeowner's policy provides sufficient property or liability coverage. You'll need to add an endorsement for higher coverage to your existing policy or buy a supplemental policy to cover business equipment. The good news: More and more insurance companies are developing policies especially for homebased business owners.

puter consultant who accidentally deletes a firm's customer list could be protected by this type of insurance, for example.

Companies with a board of directors may want to consider "directors and officers' liability" (D&O). This type of insurance protects top executives against personal financial responsibility due to actions taken by the company.

How much liability coverage do you need? Generally, experts say, $2 million to $3 million of liability insurance should be plenty. The good news is that liability insurance isn't priced on a dollar-for-dollar basis, so twice the coverage won't be twice the price.

The price you'll have to pay for comprehensive general liability insurance depends on the size of your business (measured either by square footage or by payroll) and the specific risks involved.

STAKING YOUR CLAIM

Though you hope it never happens, you may someday have to file an insurance claim. These tips should make it easier:

◆ **Report incidents immediately.** Notify your agent and carrier right away when anything happens—such as a fire, accident or theft—that could result in a claim.

◆ **Take steps to protect your property from further damage.** Most policies cover the cost of temporary repairs to protect against further damage, such as fixing a window to prevent looting.

◆ **If possible, save damaged parts.** A claims adjustor may want to examine them after equipment repairs have been made.

◆ **Get at least two repair estimates.** Your claims adjuster can tell you what kind of documentation the insurance company wants for bids on repairs.

◆ **Provide complete documentation.** The insurance company needs proof of loss. Certain claims require additional evidence. For example, a claim for business interruption will need financial data showing income before and after.

◆ **Communicate with your agent and claims adjuster.** Though your claim is against the insurance company, your agent should be kept informed so he or she can help your business if needed.

Auto Insurance

If your business provides employees with company cars, or if you have a delivery van, you need to think about auto insurance. The good news here is that auto insurance offers more of an opportunity to save money than most other types of business insurance. The primary strategy is to increase your deductible; then your premiums will decrease accordingly. Make sure,

---

POLICY POINTERS

Looking for some of the best small-business insurance resources on the Web? Check these out:

◆ *The Insurance Information Exchange (www.iix.com):* The Insurance Information Exchange contains links to hundreds of sites, including insurance publications, associations and company Web sites. Click on the "Insurance Business Professional" briefcase icon from the home page and then access "Insurance Links."

◆ *Independent Insurance Network (www.iiaa.iix.com):* If you're in the beginning stages of searching for small-business insurance, surf over to the Independent Insurance Network. From "Consumer Info" access the "Small Business Guide" navigation link near the bottom of the page, where you'll find The Consumer's Independent Guide to Small Business Insurance.

◆ *Insurance Information Institute (www.iii.org):* This site puts business insurance news, facts and figures at your fingertips. Begin by clicking on the "Consumer" icon. "What's New" gives recent developments in the insurance marketplace and timely insurance tips. For subjects such as insuring your homebased business and insuring your company against a catastrophe, check the Consumer Alerts department.

◆ *CIGNA (www.cigna.com):* Despite its bent toward larger companies, this user-friendly site contains a slew of informative and entertaining insurance-related resources.

◆ *CNA (www.cna.com):* While its technical language requires you to be well-versed in insurance lingo to fully comprehend it, this site has a Commercial Insurance for Small and Medium-Sized Businesses section that breaks down insurance coverage by industry.

however, that you can afford to pay the deductibles should an accident happen. For additional savings, remove the collision and comprehensive coverage from older vehicles in your fleet.

Pay attention to policy limits when purchasing auto coverage. Many states set minimum liability coverages, which may be well below what you need. "If you don't have enough coverage, the courts can take everything you have, then attach your future corporate income, thus possibly causing the company severe financial hardship or even bankruptcy," says Mike Fox, an account executive with Wausau Insurance Companies. "I recommend carrying at least $1 million in liability coverage."

> ## Bright Idea
>
> Keep detailed records of the value of your office or store's contents off-premises. Include photos of equipment plus copies of sales receipts, operating manuals and anything else that proves what you purchased and how much was paid. That way, in case of a fire, flood or other disaster, you can prove what was lost. It's also important to be able to prove your monthly income so you are properly reimbursed if you have to close down temporarily.

Property/Casualty Coverage

Most property insurance is written on an all-risks basis, as opposed to a named peril basis. The latter offers coverage for specific perils spelled out in the policy. If your loss comes from a peril not named, then it isn't covered.

> ## The Name's Bond . . .
>
> Sometimes confused with insurance, bonding is a guarantee of performance required for many businesses, either by law or by consumer demand. The most common businesses that bond employees are general contractors, temporary personnel agencies, janitorial companies and companies with government contracts. Bonding helps ensure that the job is performed and that the customer is protected against losses from theft or damage done by your employees.
>
> Although you still have to pay on claims if your employees are bonded, bonding has the side benefit of making your business more desirable to customers. They know that if they suffer a loss as the result of your work, they can recover the damages from the bonding company. The difference between a bond and insurance is that a bonding company ensures your payment by requiring security or collateral if a claim is made against you.

Dollar Stretcher

The IRS now allows self-employed businesspeople to deduct 40 percent of health insurance premium costs. For more information on specific IRS guidelines, request IRS Publication 533, *Self-Employment Tax*, and IRS Publication 502, *Medical and Dental Expenses*, by calling (800) 829-3676.

Make sure you get all-risks coverage. Then go the extra step and carefully review the policy's exclusions. All policies cover loss by fire, but what about such crises as hailstorms and explosions? Depending on your geographic location and the nature of your business, you may want to buy coverage for all these risks.

Whenever possible, you should buy *replacement cost insurance*, which will pay you enough to replace your property at today's prices, regardless of the cost when you bought the items. It's protection from inflation. (Be sure your total replacements do not exceed the policy cap.)

For example, if you have a 30,000-square-foot building that costs $50 per square foot to replace, the total tab will be $1.5 million. But if your policy has a maximum replacement of $1 million, you're going to come up short. To protect yourself, experts recommend buying replacement insurance with an inflation guard. This adjusts the cap on the policy to allow for inflation. If that's not possible, then be sure to review the limits of your policy from time to time to ensure you're still adequately covered.

Umbrella Coverage

In addition to these four basic "food groups," many insurance agents recommend an additional layer of protection, called an *umbrella policy*. This protects you for payments in excess of your existing coverage or for liabilities not covered in your other policies.

Business Interruption Coverage

When a hurricane or earthquake puts your business out of commission for days—or months—your property insurance has got it covered. But while property insurance pays for the cost of repairs or rebuilding, who pays for all the income you're losing while your business is unable to function?

For that, you'll need business interruption coverage. Many entrepreneurs neglect to consider this important type of coverage, which can provide enough to meet your overhead and other expenses during the time your business is out of commission. Premiums for these policies are based on your company's income.

Life Insurance

Many banks require a life insurance policy on the business owner before lending any money. Such policies typically take the form of term life insurance, purchased yearly, which covers the cost of the loan in the event of the borrower's death; the bank is the beneficiary.

Term insurance is less costly than permanent insurance at first, although the payments increase each year. Permanent insurance builds equity and should be considered once the business has more cash to spend.

The life insurance policy should provide for the families of the owners and key management. If the owner dies, the creditors are likely to take everything, and the owner's family will be left without the income or assets of the business to rely on.

Another type of life insurance that can be beneficial for a small business is "key person" insurance. If the business is a limited partnership or has a few

READ ALL ABOUT IT

Want to know more about insurance? Check out these books and publications:

- ◆ *Insurance for Business Owners, Insuring Your Business* and *Insuring Your Business Against a Catastrophe.* These brochures are available free from the Insurance Information Institute (III), 110 William St., New York, NY 10038. Send a self-addressed, stamped envelope; indicate on the envelope which brochures you want.

- ◆ *Insuring Your Business* by Sean Mooney. This book is published by III Press and is available through its publications department. Call (800) 331-9146, fax (212) 732-1916, or e-mail beverly@iii.org. Cost: $22.50 plus $2.50 shipping and handling.

- ◆ *Employer's Workers' Compensation Cost Control Handbook* is published by the National Foundation for Unemployment Compensation & Workers' Compensation, 1331 Pennsylvania Ave. NW, 1500 N. Tower, Washington, DC 20004-1703, (202) 682-1517. Cost: $30 (includes shipping and handling).

- ◆ *Reducing Your Costs: Facts About Self-Insuring Your Health Benefits.* This booklet was written by James A. Kinder, CEO of the Self-Insurance Institute of America Inc. It is available for $5 for nonmembers through Self-Insurers' Publishing Corp., P.O. Box 15466, Santa Ana, CA 92735, (714) 261-2553, fax: (714) 261-2594.

key stockholders, the buy-sell agreement should specifically authorize this type of insurance to fund a buyback by the surviving leadership. Without a provision for insurance to buy capital, the buy-sell agreement may be rendered meaningless.

The company is the beneficiary of the key person policy. When the key person dies, creating the obligation to pay, say, $100,000 for his or her stock, the cash with which to make that purchase is created at the same time. If you don't have the cash to buy the stock back from the surviving family, you could find yourself with new business partners you never bargained for—and lose control of your business.

In addition to the owners or key stockholders, any member of the company who is vital to operations should also be insured.

Disability Insurance

It's every businessperson's worst nightmare—a serious accident or long-term illness that can lay you up for months, or even longer. Disability insurance, sometimes called "income insurance," can guarantee a fixed

---

PACKAGE DEAL

If figuring out what insurance you need makes your head spin, calm down; chances are, you won't have to consider the whole menu. Most property and casualty companies now offer special small-business insurance policies.

A standard package policy combines liability; fire, wind and vehicle damage; burglary; and other common coverages. That's enough for most small stores and offices, such as an accounting firm or a gift store. Some common qualifiers for a package policy are that your business occupy less than 15,000 square feet and that the combined value of your building, operation and inventory be less than $3 million.

Basic package policies typically cover buildings, machinery, equipment and furnishings. That should protect computers, phones, desks, inventory and the like against loss due to robbery and employee theft, in addition to the usual risks such as fire. A good policy pays full replacement cost on lost items.

A package policy also covers business interruption, and some even offer you liability shelter. You may also be covered against personal liability. To find out more about package policies, ask your insurance agent; then shop around and compare.

BUSINESS INSURANCE PLANNING WORK SHEET

Types Of Insurance	Required (Yes/No)	Yearly Cost	Cost Per Payment
1. General liability insurance			
2. Product liability insurance			
3. Errors and omissions liability insurance			
4. Malpractice liability insurance			
5. Automotive liability insurance			
6. Fire and theft insurance			
7. Business interruption insurance			
8. Overhead expense insurance			
9. Personal disability			
10. Key-person insurance			
11. Shareholders' or partners' insurance			
12. Credit extension insurance			
13. Term life insurance			
14. Health insurance			
15. Group insurance			
16. Workers' compensation insurance			
17. Survivor-income life insurance			
18. Care, custody and control insurance			
19. Consequential losses insurance			
20. Boiler and machinery insurance			
21. Profit insurance			
22. Money and securities insurance			
23. Glass insurance			
24. Electronic equipment insurance			
25. Power interruption insurance			
26. Rain insurance			
27. Temperature damage insurance			
28. Transportation insurance			
29. Fidelity bonds			
30. Surety bonds			
31. Title insurance			
32. Water damage insurance			
Total Annual Cost		$	$

amount of income—usually 60 percent of your average earned income—while you're receiving treatment or are recuperating and unable to work. Because you are your business's most vital asset, many experts recommend buying disability insurance for yourself and key employees from day one.

There are two basic types of disability coverage: short term (anywhere from 12 weeks to a year) and long term (more than a year). An important element of disability coverage is the waiting period before benefits are paid. For short-term disability, the waiting period is generally seven to 14 days. For long-term disability, it can be anywhere from 30 days to a year. If being unable to work for a limited period of time would not seriously jeopardize your business, you can decrease your premiums by choosing a longer waiting period.

Another optional add-on is "business overhead" insurance, which pays for ongoing business expenses, such as office rental, loan payments and employee salaries if the business owner is disabled and unable to generate income.

CHOOSING AN INSURANCE AGENT

Given all the factors that go into business insurance, deciding what you need typically requires the assistance of a qualified insurance agent.

Type Of Agent

Selecting the right agent is almost as important, and sometimes as difficult, as choosing the types of coverage you need. The most fundamental question regarding agents is whether to select a direct writer—that is, someone who represents just one insurance company—or a broker, who represents many companies.

Some entrepreneurs feel they are more likely to get their money's worth with a broker because he or she shops all kinds of insurance companies for them. Others feel brokers are more efficient because they compare the different policies and give their opinions, instead of the entrepreneur having to talk to several direct writers to evaluate each of their policies. Another drawback to direct writers: If the insurance company drops your coverage, you lose your agent, too, and all his or her accumulated knowledge about your business.

Still, some people prefer direct writers. Why? An agent who writes insurance for just one company has more clout there than an agent who writes for many. So when something goes wrong, an agent who works for the company has a better chance of getting you what you need. Finally, direct writers often specialize in certain kinds of business and can bring a lot of industry expertise to the table.

Finding An Agent

To find an insurance agent, begin by asking a few of your peers whom they recommend. If you want more names, a trade association in your state may have a list of recommended agencies, or may even offer some forms of group coverage with attractive rates (see the "Cost Containment" section in Chapter 23 for more).

Once you've got a short list of agencies to consider, start looking for one you can develop a long-term relationship with. As your business grows and becomes more complicated, you'll want to work with someone who understands your problems. You don't want to spend a lot of time teaching the agent the ins and outs of your business or industry.

Find out how long the agency has been in business. An agency with a track record will likely be around to help you in the future. If the agency is new, ask about the principals; have they been in the industry long enough that you feel comfortable with their knowledge and stability?

One important area to investigate is loss-control service (which includes everything from fire-safety programs to reducing employees' exposures to injuries). The best way to reduce your premiums over the long haul is to minimize claims, and the best way to do that is through loss-control services. Look for a broker who will review and analyze which of the carriers offer the best loss-control services.

Another consideration is the size of the agency. The trend in insurance is consolidation. If you're looking for a long-term relationship, you want to avoid an agency that is going to get bought out. One way to get a handle on whether the agency you are considering is a likely acquirer (or acquiree) is by looking at the agency's owner. If he or she is older and is not grooming a successor, there's more chance the agency will get bought out than that it will be doing the buying.

Verify the level of claims service each agency provides. When a claim arises, you don't want the agent telling you to call some 800 number. If that's their idea of claims service, keep looking. An agency that gets involved in the claims process and works with the adjuster can have a positive impact on your settlement, while having an agency that doesn't get involved tends to minimize your settlement.

You want an agency that will stay on top of your coverage and be on the spot to adjust it as your business changes. Of course, it's always difficult to separate promises from what happens after the sale is closed. However, you might ask would-be agents how often they will be in touch. Even for the most basic business situation, the agent should still meet with you at least twice a year. For more complex situations, the agent should call you monthly.

You also want to make sure the company your agent selects or represents is highly rated. While there are a number of rating agencies, the most pro-lific is A.M. Best, which rates the financial strength of insurance companies from A++ to F, according to their ability to pay claims and their size. (You can find their rating book, *Best Rating Guide*, at your local library.) Look for a carrier rated no lower than A-.

Also make sure the agent you choose is licensed by the state. The best way to find out is by calling your state insurance department, listed in the telephone book. If you can't find a number there, call the Insurance Infor-mation Institute hotline at (800) 942-4242.

Ask for references, and check them. This is the best way to predict how an agent will work with you.

Last, but not least, listen to your gut. Does the agent listen to you and in-corporate your concerns into the insurance plan? Does he or she act as a part-ner or just a vendor? A vendor simply sells you insurance. Your goal is to find an agent who functions as a partner, helping you analyze risks and decide the best course of action. Of course, partnership is a two-way street. The more information you provide your agent, the more he or she can do for you.

INSURANCE COSTS

As with most other things, when it comes to insurance, you get what you pay for. Don't pay to insure against minor losses, but don't ignore real per-ils just because coverage carries hefty premiums.

You can lower your premiums if you take a higher deductible. Many agents recommend taking higher deductibles on property insurance and putting the money you save toward additional liability coverage instead.

How much can you afford for a deductible or uninsured risk? Look at your cash flow. If you can pay for a loss out of cash on hand, consider not insuring it.

You can also save money on insurance by obtaining it through a trade group or association. Many associations offer insurance tailored to your in-dustry needs—everything from disability and health to liability and prop-erty coverage.

You can also help keep insurance costs down by practicing these good insurance habits:

◆ Review your needs and coverage once a year. If your circum-stances or assets have changed, you may need to adjust your in-surance coverage.

◆ Ask your insurance agent for risk-reduction assistance. He or she should be able to visit your premises and identify improvements that would create a safer facility.

◆ Check out new insurance products. Ask your agent to keep you up to date on new types of coverage you may want to consider.

◆ Take time to shop for the best, most appropriate coverage. A few hours invested upfront can save thousands of dollars in premiums or claims down the road.

GLOSSARY

Bonding: a guarantee of performance required either by law or consumer demand for many businesses, most typically general contractors, temporary personnel agencies, janitorial companies and businesses with government contracts

Broker: an insurance agent who represents many different insurance companies

Business interruption insurance: pays for the cost of repair or rebuilding business, as well as income lost while business is out of commission

Direct writer: an insurance agent who represents one insurance company

Disability insurance: pays a fixed percentage of average earnings should the insured be unable to continue working due to disability

Employment practices liability insurance: an optional part of workers' compensation coverage, this protects the corporation from being sued for acts of individual employees (such as in a sexual harassment case)

Errors and omissions liability coverage: protects professionals, such as consultants or accountants, from damages resulting from an error or omission in their work

General liability coverage: insures the business against accidents and injuries that happen on its premises, as well as exposure to risk related to its products

Key person insurance: life insurance policy taken out on "key people" in the company, where the beneficiary is the company; proceeds used to buy out the deceased's shares or ownership interest in the company

Package policy: insurance policy that combines several standard coverages, such as liability, burglary and vehicle, in one package

Property/casualty coverage: protects physical property and equipment of the business against loss from theft, fire or other perils; "all-risks coverage" covers against all risks; "named peril coverage" covers only against specific perils named in the policy

Replacement cost insurance: covers cost of replacing property at current prices

Umbrella coverage: protects you for payments in excess of your existing coverage or for liabilities not covered in your other policies

Workers' compensation insurance: covers medical and rehabilitation costs and lost wages for employees injured at work; required by law in all states

Part Five:
You'd Better Shop Around

CHAPTER 25

STUFF

Business equipment basics

Stuff. Comedian George Carlin once built an entire routine around America's continuing fascination with, well, stuff. While some may fantasize of cars, jewelry and the like, business owners entertain visions of an entirely different sort. Their stuff of choice? Any and all pieces of equipment that promise to keep their businesses humming—from computers and fax machines to copiers.

What types of equipment do you actually need? It will vary depending on the demands of your business. In general, however, there are several basic pieces of equipment most new business owners need. (These are discussed in more detail throughout Part 5.)

◆ Computer

◆ Software

◆ Modem

◆ Fax machine

◆ Copier

◆ Phone

◆ Answering machine/voice mail

◆ Cellular phone

◆ Pager

◆ Postage meter

◆ Calculator

Look over the list and consider which items you can't live without, which would be nice to have, and which (if any) you don't need. When equipping a start-up business, you must tread a fine line. On one end of the

Smart Tip

To get the most from your equipment vendors, it's important to lay the proper groundwork and let them know you're a valuable customer. One way to do that is to make sure you send in the service registration card that comes with the product. Contact the vendor before problems arise to ask for all the relevant telephone and fax numbers so you know what to do if disaster strikes. Maintain contact with the vendor by asking questions as they come up and giving the vendor any comments or ideas that might improve the product. This identifies you as an active user and builds your relationship with the vendor.

spectrum are entrepreneurs who rush out and buy every big-ticket, bells-and-whistles item they see, convinced that they need it for their business. Feeling a compulsion to buy the latest technological tools simply because they're cutting edge, these entrepreneurs often end up spending way beyond their budget, only to find that the items they bought sit idle or aren't compatible.

At the other end of the spectrum is the entrepreneur who tries to make do with the bare bones. In an effort to save a few dollars, these business owners sacrifice efficiency and productivity, chugging along with a prehistoric computer, a one-line phone or a modem that crawls at a snail's pace. In short, they're penny-wise and pound-foolish.

Today's business climate is so fast-paced, clients won't do business with you if you can't keep up. Assess each item, and determine how it could benefit your business. Would you use a copier often enough to make it worth the cost? Will a fax machine pay for itself in a matter of weeks? A critical purchase may justify spending some extra money.

COST CUTTERS

Equipping your business can be a costly proposition. Fortunately, there are several different avenues you can take to keep the expenses to a minimum.

Financing Plan

If you're buying expensive equipment, consider having the manufacturers "lend" you money by selling the equipment to you over a period of time.

There are two types of credit contracts commonly used to finance equipment purchases: the *conditional sales contract*, in which the purchaser does not receive title to the equipment until it is paid for; and the *chattel-mortgage contract*, in which the equipment becomes the property of the purchaser on delivery, but the seller holds a mortgage claim against it until the contract amount is fully paid.

There are also lenders who will finance 60 percent to 80 percent of a new equipment purchase, while you pay down the balance as a down payment. The loan is repaid in monthly installments, usually over one to five years or the usable life of the equipment. (Make sure the financing period does not extend past the usable life of the equipment; you don't want to be paying for something you can no longer use.)

By using your equipment suppliers to finance the purchase, you reduce the amount of money you need upfront.

When Lease Is More

Another way to keep equipment costs down is to lease instead of buy. These days, just about anything can be leased—from computers and heavy machinery to complete offices. The kind of business you're in and the type of equipment you're considering are major factors in determining whether to lease or buy. If you are starting a one-person business and only need one computer, for instance, it probably makes more sense to buy. On the other hand, if you are opening an office that will have several employees and require a dozen computers, you may want to look into leasing.

According to the Equipment Leasing Association of America (ELA), approximately 80 percent of U.S. companies lease some or all of their equipment, and there are thousands of equipment-leasing firms nationwide catering to that demand. "[Leasing is] an excellent hedge against obsolescence," explains Suzanne Jackson of the ELA, "especially if you're leasing something like computer equipment and want to update it constantly."

Other leasing advantages include: lower monthly payments than you would have with a loan, getting a fixed financing rate instead of a floating rate, tax advantages, conserving working capital and avoiding cash-devouring down payments, and gaining immediate access to the most up-to-date business tools. The equipment also shows up on your income statement as a lease expense rather than a purchase. If you purchase it, your balance sheet becomes less liquid.

Leasing also has its downside, however. "A disadvantage of leasing is you [may] pay a higher price over the long term," says Bill Matyastik, director of the rental division of Business Interiors, which sells office furniture and

Bright Idea

Want to keep equipment costs *way* down? Consider launching from a business incubator, where services, facilities and equipment are shared among several businesses. (For more on incubators, see Part 4 Chapter 17).

PACKAGE DEAL

As you put together an equipment leasing package, consider these issues:

1. What equipment do you need and for how long?

2. Do you want to bundle service, supplies, training and the equipment lease itself into one contract?

3. Have you anticipated your company's future needs so you can acquire adequate equipment?

4. What is the total payment cost?

Also ask the following questions about each leasing source you investigate:

1. Who will you be dealing with—is there a separate company financing the lease? This is not desirable.

2. How long has the company been in business? As a general rule, deal only with financing sources that have been operating at least as many years as the term of your proposed lease.

3. Do you understand the terms and conditions during and at the end of the lease?

4. Is casualty insurance (required to cover damage to the equipment) included?

5. Who pays the personal property tax?

6. What are the options regarding upgrading and trading in equipment?

7. Who is responsible for repairs?

systems. Another drawback is that leasing commits you to retaining a piece of equipment for a certain time period, which can be problematic if your business is in flux.

Every lease decision is unique, so it's important to study the lease agreement carefully. Compare the costs of leasing to the current interest rate, examining the terms to see if they're favorable. What is the lease costing you? What are your savings? Compare those numbers to the cost of purchasing the same piece of equipment, and you'll quickly see which is the more profitable route.

Because they tend to have little or no credit history, start-ups often find it difficult or even impossible to lease equipment, says Matyastik. However, some companies will consider your personal rather than business credit history during the approval process.

If you decide to lease, make sure you get a closed-end lease without a balloon payment at the end. With a closed-end lease, nothing is owed when the lease period ends. When the lease period terminates, you just turn the equipment in and walk away. With an open-end lease, it's not that simple. If you turn in the equipment at the end of the lease and it's worth less than the value established in the lease contract, then you're responsible for paying the difference. If you do consider an open-end lease, make sure you are not open to additional charges such as wear and tear.

Finally, balloon payments require you to pay small monthly payments with a large payment (the balloon) at the end. While this allows you to conserve your cash flow as you're making those smaller monthly payments, the bad news is the final balloon payment may be more than the equipment is worth.

There are many different avenues through which you can secure an equipment lease:

◆ Banks and bank-affiliated firms that will finance an equipment lease may be difficult to locate, but once found, banks may offer some distinct advantages, including lower costs and better customer service. Find out whether the bank will keep and service the lease transaction after it's set up.

◆ Equipment dealers and distributors can help you arrange financing through an independent leasing company.

◆ Independent leasing companies range in size and scope, offering many financing options.

◆ Captive leasing companies are subsidiaries of equipment manufacturers or other firms.

◆ Broker/packagers represent a small percentage of the leasing market. Much like mortgage or real estate brokers, they charge a fee to act as an intermediary between financial resources and lessees.

For more information on leasing, the ELA in Arlington, Virginia, and the Business Technology Association in Kansas City, Missouri, offer member directories that cost $100 and $90, respectively. *The Leasing Sourcebook*, published by Bibliotechnology Systems and Publishing Co., is a directory of companies leasing equipment. You can also check your local Yellow Pages for leasing companies.

LEASING VS. PURCHASING EQUIPMENT WORK SHEET

Answer the following questions to help determine whether it is better to lease or purchase equipment for your business in terms of:

☑ Cost   ☑ Cash Availability
☑ Tax Benefits ☑ Obsolecence

Cost	Lease	Purchase
What is the required down payment for the lease or loan?		
What is the length of the lease or loan?		
What is the monthly payment of the lease or loan?		
Are there balloon payments associated with the lease or loan?		
What is the amount of the balloon payment?		
What is the cost of an extended warranty if purchasing one?		
What is the total cost of the lease or loan (including maintenance and warranties) over its lifetime?		

Cash Availability		
Is there sufficient cash flow to handle the monthly lease or loan payments? (Answer yes or no.)		
Are maintenance costs included in the lease or loan? (Answer yes or no.)		
What are the maintenance costs associated with the item?		
What are the insurance costs included in the lease or loan if any?		
What are the estimated insurance costs associated with the item?		
If business is seasonal, does the lease or the loan fit periods of sufficient cash flow better?		

Tax Benefits		
Can the item be depreciated for tax purposes in a lease or loan?		
What is the depreciable life of the item?		
What is the estimated depreciable expense of the item over its depreciable life?		
What is the amount of other tax benefits associated with this item?		

Obsolescence		
What is the operable lifetime of the item?		
What is the total cost of the item spread over this lifetime? (Divide cost by lifetime.)		
What is the technological lifetime of the item?		
Will the item need to be replaced due to technological advancement?		
What is the total cost of the item spread over the technological lifetime? (Divide cost by lifetime.)		

WISE BUYS

If your calculations show that buying makes more sense for you, you've still got some decisions to make. First and foremost, where to buy?

Buying New Equipment

The same piece of new equipment that costs $400 at one store can cost $1,000 at another. It all depends on where you go. Here are some of the most common sources for buying new equipment, with a look at the pros and cons of each.

Dollar Stretcher

If you purchase all your equipment from a single supplier, you may be able to negotiate volume discounts, free shipping and other extras. Be aware, though, that purchasing from a single vendor also limits your options; for example, the merchant you choose for your computer system may not offer the brand of printer you want.

♦ **Superstores:** Office or electronics superstores usually offer rock-bottom prices because they buy from manufacturers in volume. On the downside, remember that you won't get delivery or installation from a superstore. For service, you'll probably have to call the manufacturer. Nor can you expect a lot of qualified help choosing the right equipment since superstores are unlikely to be staffed by expert employees. If you know exactly what you need, however, or have a knowledgeable friend or associate who can help you, the superstore could be the option for you.

♦ **Specialty stores:** Small electronics stores or office equipment retailers are likely to offer more assistance in putting together a package of products. Salespeople will be more knowledgeable than at superstores, and service will be more personal. Some even offer service plans. On the downside, prices go up accordingly.

♦ **Dealer direct sales:** Check your Yellow Pages for companies that sell direct to consumers. Many manufacturers choose this option as a way of maintaining their service-oriented reputation. On the plus side, you will get assistance from highly knowledgeable salespeople who can help you put together the right system of products. You may also get delivery, installation and training at no extra cost. Many entrepreneurs swear by this method of buying. The downside: Since you're dealing with one manufacturer, you won't get to compare brands.

No matter what source you buy from, however, be sure to investigate the type of service and support you'll get before you whip out your wallet. A tempting price may seem like a compelling reason to forego solid service when you buy, but it won't seem like such a good deal when the equipment grinds to a halt in the middle of an urgent project . . . and the vendor is nowhere to be found.

Before you buy, prioritize what's important to your company; then get the answers to these questions:

- ◆ How long does the warranty last?

- ◆ Does the vendor offer a money-back guarantee? Many computer peripherals, for instance, come with 30-day money-back guarantees. Use this time to make sure the item works with the rest of your system.

- ◆ Does the vendor charge a restocking fee? Even when a company offers a money-back guarantee on a piece of equipment, it may charge you a restocking fee of up to 15 percent of the product's cost to return it.

LEMON ALERT

Whether you are buying used equipment from an individual or a business, take these steps to make sure you don't get stuck with a lemon.

- ◆ *Know the market.* Do some research before you make an offer on a piece of equipment. Read the classifieds to learn the going rates for the items you want. Notice how quickly items move: Is it a seller's market, or do you see the same ads run again and again?

- ◆ *Try before you buy.* Just as you would with new equipment, it's essential to "test drive" used equipment. Run diagnostic tests; make sure all the parts are working; ask about any problems. (Often, the item is still worth buying even with the cost of repairs.)

- ◆ *Bring a buddy.* If you're a novice, it helps to take a more experienced friend or colleague with you when you test the equipment. He or she can ask questions you may not think of and pinpoint problems you might miss.

- ◆ *Don't feel comfortable?* Don't buy. Never let anyone talk you into a purchase or make you feel guilty. If you don't feel good about it, walk away.

◆ What fees, if any, does the vendor charge for technical support?

◆ How easy is it to reach technical support? Try calling before you buy the product to see how long you're put on hold and whether or not the company returns phone calls.

Dollar Stretcher

Before calling a vendor or supplier, call the toll-free directory at (800) 555-1212 to see if they have a toll-free number.

◆ What hours is technical support available? Be aware of time zones. If you're in California and your East Coast vendor shuts down at 5 p.m., you could be out an afternoon's work if your computer breaks down after 2 p.m. California time.

◆ How quickly can the vendor fix problems? What are the costs for different repairs and time frames (on-site repair, 24-hour turn-around, etc.)?

◆ Does the vendor offer any value-added services?

Buying Used Equipment

If new equipment is out of your price range, buying used equipment can be an excellent cost cutter. There are several sources for buying used; one little-known avenue is an asset remarketing company.

Asset remarketers work with equipment leasing companies to resell repossessed office equipment through a network of dealers and wholesalers—and sometimes directly to business owners. The prices are a fraction of the cost of buying or leasing brand-new equipment.

Buying repossessed equipment through an asset remarketer is also simpler than going to a bankruptcy auction. As in most auctions, the asset remarketing company accepts bids—but that's where the similarities end. Asset remarketers keep equipment in warehouses, which buyers visit at their convenience as they would a discount office equipment retailer. Often, the remarketer has a price sheet showing the equipment's original price and its approximate resale value. Use this price sheet as a guideline in making your offer.

Leasing companies and asset remarketers must resell equipment at a fair market price, so three bids are usually required. There is no set deadline, but these companies are eager to move their equipment out of storage and into the highest bidder's hands, so if you see something you want, move fast. If you want to buy, make an offer to the asset remarketing firm, which then sends it to the leasing company's asset recovery manager. Some asset remarketers may require a small $100 deposit when the leasing company accepts the bid; you will then need to pay with cash, certified funds or cashier's check within a few days.

While finding asset remarketing companies is as easy as calling a local repossession company in the Yellow Pages, be careful to find a reputable one. While some states regulate asset remarketing or repossession firms, there are unscrupulous remarketers in many states who hang out their shingle, pocket consumers' deposits, then disappear. The safest way to find an honest asset remarketer is to call a leasing company's asset recovery manager and ask for the name of a local firm. Some leasing companies prefer to sell to end users directly, and they may ask for a description of the equipment you want to purchase.

In addition to asset remarketers or leasing companies, you can also buy used equipment from individuals (look in the local classifieds) or check your Yellow Pages for used equipment retailers, such as the Aaron Rents & Sells nationwide chain. The resale of used equipment is becoming more common, so in most cities, you will have several sources to choose from.

GLOSSARY

Asset remarketers, asset remarketing companies: firms that work with equipment leasing companies to resell repossessed office equipment through a network of dealers and wholesalers as well as directly to business owners

Balloon payments: lease arrangement that requires small monthly payments with a large payment (the balloon) at the end of the lease

Chattel-mortgage contract: type of credit contract used for equipment purchase in which the equipment becomes the property of the purchaser on delivery, but the seller holds a mortgage claim against it until the contract amount is fully paid

Closed-end lease: type of equipment lease in which no money is owed when the lease period ends; the lessee simply turns in the equipment and walks away

Conditional sales contract: type of credit contract used for equipment purchase in which the purchaser does not receive title to the equipment until it is paid for

Open-end lease: type of equipment lease in which if the value of the equipment at the end of the lease is less than the value established in the lease contract, the lessee must pay the difference

CHAPTER 26

PHONEY BUSINESS

What kind of phone
system do you need?

C alling all entrepreneurs! It's time to focus on an essential feature of any new business: your phone system. Perhaps the most basic piece of business equipment, the phone is your company's link to the outside world. And, for better or worse, most customers' first impression of your business will be conveyed over the phone. That's why a professional phone setup is so crucial to any company, whether it's a one-person business or a multisite operation.

Today's small-business owner faces a dizzying array of phone choices. It seems you can't open a newspaper, turn on the television or pick up a magazine without being bombarded with ads for some fantastic new phone plan that will save you big money or a nifty new phone gadget that does everything but slice and dice. This chapter will help you cut through the hype by outlining the basic phone systems and services small businesses are likely to need, including voice mail, long-distance services and toll-free numbers. (Part 5 Chapter 27 discusses cellular communications, including cellular phones and pagers.)

PHONE FEATURES

Although every new business is different, today's phone systems are flexible enough to meet just about every business owner's needs. The challenge is to identify those needs and take the time to find out how telephones can fill them.

A practical approach to telephone shopping begins with the size of your company. If you are a one-person show, a simple "feature phone" is probably adequate. A feature phone contains all its features directly in the unit. Most home phones are feature phones. Other features, such as call waiting, are actually services offered by the local phone company.

Here are the primary built-in features available in phones:

◆ **Multiline system:** A multiline phone allows you to switch back and forth between lines while on one phone.

◆ **Automatic redial:** The phone redials the last number called, or it may dial and redial a number at regular intervals until it gets through.

◆ **Speakerphone:** A speakerphone allows you to hear the other person's voice without using the receiver. It's useful if you're put on hold and want to move around. Some speakerphones simply allow you to hear the person on the other end; others allow you to talk into the speaker and carry on a hands-free conversation. This is useful if you want to have several people in your office talk to one person on the other end of the line.

◆ **Programmable memory:** You can store frequently called numbers and dial them automatically by pushing a single button. This is helpful if you frequently call long distance.

The hardware in your phone system, of course, is only as smart as the computer within. That's where services come in. Services are provided either by the local and long-distance phone companies or by an on-site host computer. They can be as simple as call waiting, or can include voice mail, caller ID, automatic call distribution, call forwarding, conferencing and call accounting.

One of the biggest trends in small offices is the cordless phone (see "Cutting the Cord" in this chapter). Once considered a poolside toy, the cordless telephone is now a serious business tool. The newest models use digital technology, virtually eliminating former complaints about static and limited range. Digital technology also means greater security since digital phones have a microchip that encrypts signals and scrambles them to help protect against eavesdropping.

Today's cordless phones handle from two to six lines. Many new cordless phones also use tapeless voice mail technology, often incorporating a time and date stamp to record when each message was received. Most can also be plugged into a wall jack. There are also combination cordless/cellular

Smart Tip

As a rule of thumb, you should have one outside line for every five employees, depending on the type of business you're in and your call volume. Still not sure if you need more phone lines? Get a "busy study": For a small fee, your local phone company will track the number of times callers receive a busy signal on your telephone.

phones that are charged at landline rates in your home and switch to cellular service when away from the base unit.

As business telecommunications continue to improve and prices continue to fall, a number of innovations are trickling down to the small-business level. For example, automatic call distribution (ACD), already a staple at Fortune 500 companies, is now making life easier for the small-business owner as well. Callers are automatically routed when they key in the desired extension; they are offered a menu of options ("if you want Sales, press '1', if you want Technical Support, press '2' . . . "), and, if they have to wait, their call is queued up on a first-come, first-served basis. ACD also generates reports with details such as the number, time, date and origin of each call.

Some options that can help you cut telephone costs include toll restriction, which limits outgoing phone calls to specified areas; least-cost routing, which finds the least expensive phone line for calling out; and WATS, which most people know as a volume discount service for long-distance phone calls.

SECONDHAND PHONES

Buying a used phone system can shave 30 percent to 50 percent off the price of a new one. To make sure you're getting a good deal, however, keep these points in mind:

- ◆ *Your needs:* Do you need basic phone service or state-of-the-art technology? How will your needs change? Be sure the system can grow with your company.

- ◆ *The age of the system:* Optimally, look for a system that is no more than 5 to 7 years old.

- ◆ *Brand name:* Choose a system from a manufacturer you recognize or can at least check out.

- ◆ *Warranty:* It's reasonable to expect a one-year warranty on a used system.

- ◆ *Installation and training:* Be sure these are included in the price.

- ◆ *Trade-in value:* You may be able to negotiate a commitment for a certain trade-in value if you buy your next system from the same company.

Making The Right Choice

Instead of looking for phones on a feature-by-feature basis, you should study the system as a whole. Investigate the manufacturer and the distributor since they are the ones with whom you will have a long-term working relationship.

Make sure the company is reputable before laying down any money. How long has the company been in business? Find out the history of the manufacturer. Does it introduce a new product every few years, meaning your system will soon be obsolete? Does telecommunications make up a large portion of its business? Factor in the value of intangibles, such as service, upgrading and product diversity. Look for manufacturers with multiple distributors: That way, if the manufacturer goes out of business, you can still get a maintenance contract from one of its distributors.

Beware!

The way you put callers on hold can make or break your business. Never put someone on hold without asking "Can you please hold for a moment?" Don't leave someone on hold longer than 20 seconds; if it looks like you'll be longer, check back and ask if the person would like to leave a voice mail message or if you can take a message.

Questions to ask the distributor include: How much inventory does it have of each product? What is the extent of its technical staff? Always ask for customer references, too.

It's often tempting to go with the big, well-known phone companies, but they aren't your only options. Meet with at least three or four vendors before making your decision. Explain your needs, and ask what they recommend. Have them put the services and prices in writing; that way, when Vendor A gives you a package price, you can show it to Vendor B and ask what he or she can do for you.

When it comes to small-business telecommunications, knowledge is power. Gather as much information as you can about telephone systems and services——it could give you the edge you've been looking for.

Long-Distance Services

In addition to setting up your physical phone system, you'll also need to decide on services. The good news here: Phone companies are courting small business like never before. Perhaps the biggest change in this arena was the Telecommunications Act of 1996. This deregulation bill was enacted to increase competition between local and long-distance telephone companies by forcing the Baby Bells to open local markets to long-distance phone companies, and vice versa. The act also gave cable companies the opportunity to expand into phone services. No wonder there are more companies than ever vying for your business.

Today's telephone services can make your phone a multidimensional marketing tool. Yet many small-business owners fail to use long-distance services to their full potential. If you think of long-distance services as just another utility, like electricity or gas, you're missing out on some big opportunities. Assets like 800 numbers, fax and data transmission, bill management, language translation or frequent-caller perks can all be used to your advantage. As you weigh the offerings from different vendors, try to strike a balance between good value and services that will pay off for your business.

Just as you wouldn't buy a new car without kicking a few tires first, you shouldn't sign up with a long-distance carrier without doing some homework. Start by analyzing your needs. Do you use the Internet? Is cellular communication important to you? Do you call internationally? How much do you expect to spend on local vs. long-distance calls? Do you use a calling card frequently?

The basic cost of long-distance calls depends primarily on how many calls you make, for how long and to where. Nearly every vendor offers volume discounts of anywhere from 5 percent to 20 percent; the challenge is choosing from a host of discount plans for certain types of calls. Some carriers offer discounts to the countries you call most frequently—a boon for companies that do business internationally. Others offer flat rates; for example, you can call anywhere in the United States for 15 cents a minute.

Virtually all phone companies also offer custom billing, which enables you to choose how you want calls broken down on your invoices—by account, location, duration, employee and more. Custom billing is a godsend for many small businesses, enabling them to decipher call patterns. Using this information, you can better manage calls, schedule staff and figure out where costs can be cut.

Fax machines can be installed on existing phone lines; however, if you expect to do a lot of faxing, consider installing a dedicated line. (For more on fax machines, see Part 5 Chapter 31) Look for vendors that will consoli-

Bright Idea

Is your head spinning from comparing the costs of different long-distance companies? The Telecommunications Research & Action Center's (TRAC) Web site (www. trac. org) has a handy checklist to help you pin down your needs. You can also order TRAC's Long Distance Comparison Chart for Business ($7), which gives an unbiased look at the leading long-distance companies and their services.

CUTTING THE CORD

Considering a cordless phone? Deciding what features you need before you shop can save money. Here's a list of the most popular features and some terms you should know:

◆ *Auto scan channel-hopping:* This feature automatically scans various frequencies for the channel with the greatest clarity.

◆ *Call log:* This stores the last few numbers dialed on the handset so the user can scroll through if necessary.

◆ *Call waiting ID:* If you want to know who's on call waiting, the screen identifies the caller's phone number and, on some models, the caller's name.

◆ *Channels:* Cordless phones using the 900 MHz radio band automatically monitor a variety of transmission channels and select the clearest one. Lots of channels means your phone has a greater chance of switching to a clearer one if you encounter interference.

◆ *Digital security codes:* These help prevent unauthorized use of your phone line and protect against false rings from other cordless phones in the area.

◆ *Memory telephone number:* This allows you to store phone numbers in memory.

◆ *Out-of-range alert:* This sounds a beep that lets you know you've walked out of frequency range when using the phone, and you need to move closer to the base unit.

◆ *Page find:* Some phones have a one-way paging system to help you locate the phone if you misplace it.

◆ *Range:* If your work area is small, a short range may be fine. If you often wander more than 1,000 feet from your desk, look for a long-range phone.

◆ *Standby time:* This is the number of minutes, hours or days the phone can function away from the base unit without being recharged.

◆ *Time and date stamp:* Some phones display this on screen; others use a digitized voice.

Dollar Stretcher

Want to save money and make paying your phone bills easier? Look into the "single package" services some carriers now offer. These packages bundle all your telecommunication needs (local, long-distance, paging, cellular, Internet) into one account.

date all your phone expenses, including fax charges, into one bill for maximum discounts. Also make sure your carrier will consolidate long-distance charges if you have more than one location.

In addition to comparing costs, look for a long-distance company that is sensitive to your needs. Is the company flexible and willing to work with you? One way to test the waters is to do a little long-distance shopping; switch carriers on a monthly basis to see which you prefer. Don't switch around for too long, though. While it could result in some good deals, you might miss out on significant long-term discounts.

The best way to choose a long-distance company is to know your requirements upfront, then find the company that matches them. When you understand the many services phone companies offer, you can use your telephone service to add value to your operations rather than simply shopping for the best deal.

Toll-Free Numbers

If you think toll-free numbers are just for the big guys, think again. The cost of maintaining a toll-free number has come way down since this service was first offered in 1967. In fact, toll-free numbers are becoming so commonplace, the country has run out of 800 numbers and has had to add new toll-free codes, such as 888. There are even international toll-free numbers.

It goes without saying that toll-free numbers are a big business builder for companies with a lot of phone orders. But they can also improve customer service for any business by providing toll-free access to information or technical support, and can give traveling employees a convenient way to call the office.

Technological advances have made it possible to integrate toll-free number service into your existing phone lines and equipment. Most long-distance and local phone companies offer toll-

Beware!

Choose your toll-free number carefully. If it's one digit away from L.L. Bean's mail order number, for instance, you could be in for an unpleasant surprise when your bill comes at the end of the month.

Smart Tip

Is talking on the phone getting to be a pain in the neck? Switch to a headset. Headsets typically cost $120 to $450, but headset manufacturer Hello Direct says if you normally spend four hours a day on the phone, the increased productivity will make up the cost of the set in just 12 days.

If your workplace is noisy, you may need a unit that covers both ears. If you don't like the feeling of a band around your head, buy a model that wraps around your ear. Can't sit still? Look for a cordless unit.

free service at extremely competitive rates. Setup costs, if they exist, are nominal, and most carriers are willing to negotiate on this point. Small businesses typically pay less than $20 per month in fixed costs (again, a negotiable point) and then on a per-minute basis for actual use.

Since most toll-free carriers offer standard services and comparable levels of quality, the differentiating factor for most consumers is price. Complicated pricing structures can make it difficult to determine the best deal. Be ready to spend some time contacting several carriers and analyzing their plans. Keep in mind that the first price you hear from a company is not necessarily the final price you'll be offered. Businesses, even smaller ones, have negotiating power with toll-free carriers, so don't accept the first rate you are quoted.

One area ripe for price negotiation is in the multitude of add-on features designed to accommodate varying business needs. These include call routing, identification, coding and management features. Ask each carrier what it offers, and don't be afraid to ask for free installation or other discounts for these services. You may be surprised at how quickly these services will be given away if it means capturing your business.

Your regular long-distance usage can also be a bargaining tool. Though you can purchase a stand-alone toll-free plan, you may get better rates with an integrated plan that combines your toll-free and regular long-distance service.

You may also get a better deal by committing to stay with a particular carrier for a specified time period. One- and two-year terms may provide excellent rates; three-year terms are probably too long for serious consideration.

If you do business internationally, ask about the availability of toll-free service in the countries you'll be doing business with. Another feature to ask about: call reports showing where your toll-free calls come from. This can be an invaluable marketing tool.

Once you've negotiated your arrangement, review it regularly. Evaluate your usage and rates on an annual basis; then check with several carriers to make sure you're still getting the best deal.

Voice Mail

Every small business needs some way to take messages when people are out of the office. If you're a one-person operation, an answering machine could be the answer to your needs. You should expect to pay between $40 and $150 for an answering machine, depending on the features and quality.

However, as an alternative to answering machines, more and more business owners are now using voice mail systems, which offer greater flexibility and more features. Answering machines can't take calls that come in while you're on the line; voice mail can. Voice mail also has features such as multiple mailboxes, pager notification and remote access. Perhaps most important, voice mail can create the illusion that your start-up is a much larger company.

Voice mail options fall into two basic categories: services you can subscribe to and systems you can purchase.

Subscribing To Voice Mail

A variety of independent voice mail services are available to choose from. When you subscribe to an independent voice mail service, the company typically assigns you one phone number for customers to call. You use an-

---

Mail Call

The biggest mistake most businesspeople make when buying a voice mail system is failing to consider their real needs. Before you go shopping, answer these questions:

◆ Which systems are compatible with your current phone system?

◆ How many of your employees need mailboxes?

◆ How many recordings will you need to make?

◆ Will your messages be picked up in person or from an outside location?

◆ How fast is your business growing?

◆ Which voice processing features do you need?

◆ What kind of phone traffic patterns do you expect?

◆ Which categories of people will call most often: customers or suppliers?

other, private number to access your messages. Most companies can have your voice mail service up and running within 24 hours. Some voice mail services also offer toll-free packages, either with per-minute charges or at a flat rate.

The cost of subscriber services can add up quickly, however. While basic service may be as little as $10 per month, each option you add increases the cost.

To save money, consider using the voice mail services offered through your local phone company. Monthly fees for adding voice mail to your existing phone number range from $6 to $20, depending on your location.

> ## Smart Tip
>
> Use voice mail to eliminate annoying games of phone tag. If you're calling with a simple question, leave a voice mail message specifying exactly what information you need ("I need to know by what date you want the XYZ shipment"). Chances are the person can leave the answer on your voice mail, so you can take care of business even if you don't connect in person.

Some phone companies may also charge a one-time setup fee, ranging from $10 to $65.

One drawback of using phone company services is that they can't always offer what you need. If you require a lot of custom features, you may be better off using an independent service.

Regardless of whether you use your phone company or an independent service, subscribing means you won't have to worry about buying your own equipment, repairing and maintaining it, or replacing it when it becomes outdated. Representatives are generally available around the clock to answer your questions, and as new technology becomes available, you'll have access to it.

Finally, if you're trying to conserve cash during the crucial start-up phase, using a service could be the way to go. You'll be paying a monthly fee, instead of paying for equipment upfront, so costs will be spread out over a period of time.

Buying A Voice Mail System

With all the advantages of subscribing to a voice mail service, why buy your own? Perhaps the biggest reason is flexibility. If your business is phone-intensive, owning your own system allows you to customize it to fit your needs. Just one of these personalized call processing systems can replace up to 10,000 customer service workers to provide sales information, take orders, set up appointments, route calls and record messages into users' mailboxes.

John Jainschigg, editor of *Teleconnect,* a communications magazine, estimates there are some 50 to 100 different voice mail systems you can buy,
most of which work with a personal computer. Some come complete with
a monitor and keyboard; others come with software only and connect to
your existing computer, as well as your current phone system. Incoming
information is stored in the computer and can be picked up at any time by
mailbox owners, who can then record a follow-up message if necessary,
change their message, or simply make a note of the message. Some voice
mail systems can even be programmed to fax messages to mailbox owners
on the road.

Outgoing information, from you to your customers, can easily and quickly
be changed—daily if necessary—so your callers can receive specific information without talking to a live person. By following a series of voice prompts,
called a menu or option list, callers can be transferred directly to the receiver's
mailbox without waiting for an operator to assist them.

Other options allow callers to punch in certain numbers and receive instructions for placing orders, asking for service or checking on deliveries.
Some voice mail systems have a broadcasting feature that lets you send one
message to several people at once.

In addition to all these functions, some voice mail systems can also:

◆ automatically fax documents to callers

◆ provide private passwords for confidential messages

◆ copy messages, then reroute them to another mailbox

◆ pause while replaying a message

◆ save messages for later or off-site retrieval

◆ announce a caller's name before
transferring a call

Beware!

Being directed by a nonhuman
through an irritatingly lengthy phone
menu when all you want to do is ask
one simple question can turn off even
the most patient caller. However, today's voice mail systems are much
more caller-friendly and can be programmed to reflect the way you do
business. Some new models allow
callers to short-circuit confusing lists of
choices and go directly to a single
source.

Disconnecting your best customer in midsentence could
cause him to disconnect you
from his vendor list. The time
to experiment with your phone
system is before you're in the
middle of an important call.
Learn what your system can do
and practice using its features
until it becomes automatic.

What To Look For

Prices for voice mail systems range from $1,000 to $4,000 for entry-level systems up to $5,000 to $25,000 for more advanced systems.

In most cases, obtaining voice mail does not require the purchase of an entirely new phone system. Voice mail can typically be connected to a current phone system for a relatively modest sum. However, since you are in start-up mode anyway, you may want to consider voice mail systems that come as complete units built in to a phone system.

A more limited but still effective voice mail system can be set up by buying interactive voice response (IVR) software, which is loaded into your computer and connects to your phone system. These systems are basically databases callers tap into, using a touch-tone phone to access various menu options.

Most banks and credit card companies use IVR systems—the caller punches in an account number and follows a series of menu commands and prompts. They're useful for order entry, credit authorizations, reservations, catalog sales, appointment centers and customer service.

It's important to choose a system that's compatible with your phone system and can be integrated with it. If your systems aren't integrated, voice mail could cut off callers instead of connecting them. Your phone system's manufacturer can give you a list of recommended voice mail vendors.

Also make sure the system can grow with your business. Voice mail systems come standard with a set number of ports and mailboxes. A port is a connection between the phone system and the voice mail system. Each port can receive and send out one transmission, or message. The more ports you want on your system, the higher the price.

Most entry-level systems have two or four ports, but many allow you to add more ports as your business grows. A two-port system is considered sufficient for companies with one to 25 employees; a four-port system should be sufficient for up to 50 users.

Your computer's operating system is another consideration if you are buying voice mail to work with your existing computer. Windows, for example, is not designed to be mission-critical, which means it can seize up at any time. If your computer's operating system crashes, so will your voice mail.

To minimize this risk, it's best to use

Bright Idea

If telecommunications are a big part of your business, check out *Teleconnect* magazine. This monthly publication covers news and trends in the telecommunications industry, from hardware to applications. Subscriptions are $15 per year. To order, call (888) 824-9795.

one computer for nothing but your voice mail system. If you can't afford to dedicate a computer just to voice mail, you'll be safest if you stick with typical computer uses such as word processing and spreadsheets. You could get into trouble, though, when using high-stress programs like graphics and page layout.

If you envision heavy computer use and can't afford a separate computer for voice mail, consider buying a stand-alone system. These are typically small boxes, about the size of a TV remote control, that plug into your phone and your wall. The features are similar to any computer-based voice mail system.

"Some of these little stand-alone boxes are awesome," says Jainschigg. But before you buy a stand-alone setup, make sure your phone system has the capacity to take advantage of all its features. For example, you may need call waiting or conferencing ability to use all the available features.

Take the time to talk to several manufacturers. Get price quotes in writing and compare. The right voice mail system can put your business one step ahead of the pack, so do your homework before you buy to make sure you get exactly what you need.

GLOSSARY

Feature phone: a phone that has all the features built into the physical phone itself; most home phones are feature phones

Centrex: short for "central exchange," the name of the telecommunications switching service available through most local phone companies

PBX: short for "private branch exchange"; also called a Hybrid system, a combination of single-line and multiline phones, with a stand-alone "brain" console that handles all the switching activity

Automatic call distribution (ACD): routes callers automatically when they key in the desired extension

Toll restriction: service that limits outgoing calls to certain specified areas

Least-cost routing: phone option that finds the least expensive line for calling out

WATS: volume discount service for long-distance calls

Interactive voice response (IVR) software: a low-cost voice mail system that connects to the phone system; this is essentially a database callers can tap into, using a touch-tone phone to access menu options

Port: a connection between the phone system and the voice mail system

CHAPTER 27

AIR TIME

Buying pagers and cellular phones

You're an hour away from your office, concluding your breakfast meeting with Mr. Jones, your most important client. Meanwhile, a potentially huge new customer calls your office and needs to speak with you immediately about your business proposal. But how will you know about this call and start working with this new client without offending Mr. Jones?

It's just such a scenario that leads more and more entrepreneurs to rely on cellular phones and pagers. These mobile communications devices can keep you connected wherever you are, without the hassles of searching for a pay phone and digging for your calling card or spare change.

Wireless technologies like pagers and cellular phones used to be a luxury for small-business owners. No more. Considering the sharp declines in pricing and the improved quality of recent years, wireless communications are a viable option for every small company.

"Wireless is coming to the masses," says Iain Gillott, director of wireless and broadband networking with technology research firm IDC/Link. "More and more people are buying it."

Here is a closer look at how wireless communications can work to your business's advantage.

PAGER POINTERS

While there's a perception that paging isn't necessary anymore because of the prevalence of cellular phones, there is still an important place for paging in many small businesses. Pagers are useful for companies with simple transmission needs—those that don't require in-depth communications but just want to stay in touch.

Many entrepreneurs also find pagers essential in situations where they

Smart Tip

There's nothing more annoying than the piercing tones of someone else's pager breaking the silence . . . and your concentration. If possible, when in public put your pager on "silent vibration" alert instead of using a ring or buzz. That way, you get the message, but no one else is disturbed. This is especially considerate when you're attending a meeting or public performance.

don't want the ringing phone to disturb them. If you are meeting with a client, for example, a ringing phone could be a rude interruption. A vibrating pager, on the other hand, unobtrusively alerts you that you're needed at the earliest opportunity.

Finally, pagers can be an excellent way to keep cellular costs down. Since most cellular services charge for both incoming and outgoing calls, giving out your pager number instead of your cell phone number gives you the option of choosing which calls you will return from your cell phone.

Today's pagers relay messages in a variety of ways:

◆ **Two-way paging:** One of the biggest complaints about paging is the inability to respond to urgent messages. Two-way paging eliminates that problem by allowing users to answer by hitting a button and sending back a simple alphanumeric message (see below) or a variety of pre-programmed messages. While coverage is limited in most markets except for major metropolitan areas, two-way paging is becoming more commonplace.

◆ **Voice paging:** Voice-paging service is also offered in limited areas. Voice paging works like a portable answering machine. Usually, callers access a toll-free number, enter a personal identification number and then leave a message that is forwarded to the voice pager. Pages are received in the caller's voice and can be listened to immediately or stored.

◆ **Alphanumeric:** These are the most commonly used types of pagers and are useful tools for small businesses. Alphanumeric pagers use a type of memory that stores both letters and numbers. Because of text capabilities that allow callers to relay simple messages, the need to call back for more details is often eliminated. When using an alphanumeric pager heavily, keep in mind it's easy to drain the battery in a few days.

◆ **Numeric:** Numeric pagers support numbers only. Even so, giving out your pager number to clients or placing it on business cards is an effective way to stay in the loop.

CALLING ALL CELL PHONES

Portable phone technology is changing so fast, it's hard to keep up. With new standards and more carriers, choosing what you need can be confusing. There are two basic types of cellular phone technology: analog and digital.

Analog cellular technology modulates radio signals to carry voices. The most popular trend in analog telephones is making them as small and as light as possible. Although these minuscule models are easy to carry, using them can be another story. You may find the small buttons difficult to use, and the pint-sized phones can sometimes be awkward to hold and speak into. Short battery life can also be a problem.

Digital technology sends data as zeroes and ones (bits), which allows more data to be sent during a call. As a result, users can benefit from a slew of services—including paging, voice mail and caller ID—in one phone. Digital service formerly suffered from complaints of hard-to-hear conversations. Today, however, carriers claim the problems have been ironed out, and digital service boasts better sound quality, longer battery life and more reliable service.

Within the digital phone arena, there are two standards. Time Division Multiple Access (TDMA) sends phone calls immediately over the air; many service providers already support this standard. Code Division Multiple Access (CDMA) breaks phone calls into coded bits and reassembles them at the other end. Support for CDMA phones is becoming more widespread. Carriers claim CDMA offers high sound quality, although its merits are less well-known.

Phone Features

Cellular phones come in a variety of configurations and varying degrees of portability and power.

◆ *Car-mounted* cellular phones are powerhouses, generating 3 watts of transmitting power.

◆ *Transportable* units can be used in or out of a car; they come with portable battery packs, giving a user 3 watts of transmission power while away from an automobile.

Beware!

Once you've chosen your cellular phone technology, you need to put a few policies in place—or you could find cell phones costing you more than they're worth. Explain to employees what portable phones should and should not be used for. Also discuss your expectations for response time. If employees start handing out pager and cellular numbers and messages go unreturned, customers are liable to become quite frustrated.

◆ *Portables* are what most people think of when they think of cellular phones these days. Small and lightweight, they generate just six-tenths (0.6) of a watt.

If you have a lower-powered phone, it may be tough making a call if you're in an area that's congested with cellular users or located in difficult terrain—like a metropolitan downtown area with many skyscrapers. However, portables can also be pumped up from their normal six-tenths of a watt to 3 watts by using a car adaptor, which boosts their power by drawing on the car's battery.

Dollar Stretcher

Because digital cellular phones offer caller ID, one way to reduce costs (and wasted time) is to screen your calls and let the unwanted ones go straight to voice mail.

When buying any cellular phone, consider these features:

◆ Battery performance

◆ Alphanumeric memory storage

◆ Automatic redial, memory dial

◆ Length of talk time and standby time

◆ Speed dialing

◆ Scratch pad (lets you store numbers during conversation)

◆ Ring volume range

◆ Rapid battery recharger and low-charge alerter

◆ Lighted keypad

◆ Custom menu programming

◆ Long-distance lockout

◆ Microphone jack and earpiece for privacy

◆ Voice activation for hands-free dialing

◆ Voice mail capability

◆ Ease of reading screen

◆ Paging indicator

◆ Retractable or built-in antenna

◆ Data links to interface with computer/fax machine

◆ Warranty

◆ Call forwarding; call waiting

◆ Theft lock

Shop Around

The place to begin exploring the options of mobile communications is with a large company that sells mobile-communications services. Consultants with these companies will discuss the benefits of each of their products, explain the options, and design a plan tailored for your start-up business.

Most large providers of cellular services do not charge for consultation—that service is part of the sales process. Most also have toll-free numbers, stores or sales representatives on call.

"Communications consultants [can be a big help] because there are so many different products and services available," says Pat Devlin, executive director of stores for Bell Atlantic NYNEX Mobile. "The best way for someone to familiarize themselves with the products is to call and talk to a professional, visit a store or have a salesperson call. Have someone show you the products, and talk to them about your needs. Also, talk to people in your field to see what they have done and what their experiences have been."

Phone Smarts

Do you really need that sleek cell phone ... or do you just want to look suave and successful? Now that cellular phones have become a status item, you may be tempted to tote one even if your business doesn't demand it.

The type of wireless communication you need depends on a variety of factors, including budget, work habits and travel expectations. If you're on a tight budget, paging is more affordable, with pricing plans starting at just a few dollars a month. Or, if you work in an environment where you can't be bothered with talking on the phone, a pager could do just fine.

If you own a business that relies heavily on customer service, on the other hand, a cellular phone could increase your response time. Sit down and think about how many times a day you are likely to use a phone away from the office. Could a pay phone do instead?

If you need a cell phone only occasionally—such as when traveling—you can rent one for as low as $5 a day plus phone service charges. Some airports have phone rental machines; your local phone company, cellular retail stores or the business center at your hotel can help you, too.

Cost Considerations

Buying a cellular phone—the actual equipment, that is—isn't expensive. In fact, many carriers offer phones free as part of a service package or offer such deep discounts on the phone as part of the service package that the phone is essentially free.

Where cellular phones get expensive is when it comes to usage. Costs can add up quickly, surprising unwary entrepreneurs with a monstrous bill at the end of the month. To protect yourself, here are some cost factors to be aware of before you sign up for a plan.

Rates for cellular usage depend on where you live and where the calls are made to. You will be charged one rate for calls inside your CGSA, or cellular geographic service area. Everything outside your CGSA is subject to additional "roaming charges." The charges and your geographic area depend on the package you choose and your cellular provider.

Costs also vary depending on what time calls are made. Peak times are the specified periods of time when communications are busiest and when the cellular charges are highest; off-peak hours are when rates are lower. Generally, nights and weekends are off-peak hours, while normal business hours usually carry heavier charges.

Local calls can cost up to $1 per minute; long-distance calls much more. Unlike regular phone service, you must also pay for incoming calls; in fact, you even pay for calls you don't answer. As for outgoing calls, charges begin from the time you dial the number, not when the call is answered. In addition to the cost of actual calls, monthly service charges alone can run $30.

Also factor in the cost of batteries when estimating your cellular phone expenses. Expect to pay $30 to $80 for an average replacement battery with a life of six to 30 hours. You may want to invest in a battery recharger. It can cost as much as $100, but at least it's a one-time purchase. Some phones have an internal charger that plugs into an outlet.

Rechargeable batteries may need to be recharged after an hour or less of talk time. Standby time—when the phone is active so you can receive calls, but not in actual use—eats up battery power, too.

Bright Idea

Something new to watch out for in the wireless realm: PCS (Personal Communications Services). While a relatively new player in the United States, PCS employs GSM (global standard mobile) digital technology that is standard in many other countries. Similar to digital cellular phones, PCS' merits include long-lasting batteries and myriad services. Several carriers across the country are expected to roll out their PCS services soon.

Signing Up

The good news is that competition among carriers continues to be fierce—meaning lower prices for you. Most carriers offer a slew of different plans and pricing schedules. There are different service plans available for different types of businesses, depending on your usage and location. For instance, on the East Coast, you can get service that includes a tri-state area or just one county in the service area. Pat Devlin at Bell Atlantic NYNEX Mobile says choosing the right plan could save a customer 25 percent or 30 percent on a bill.

When evaluating a carrier, be sure to ask about coverage areas, compare different plans and read the fine print. If you travel extensively, be sure your cellular service carrier has coverage in the areas you go to. And remember, not all areas are served by digital service, so you'll need a dual-mode phone that switches from digital to analog.

Beware!

Be wary of small ads in newspapers that offer used or "reconditioned" cellular phones. Cellular phones that are stolen are reported to a "negative list" so that the phone can't be used in other carriers' markets. Look for a warranty and a recognizable name, and ask questions of the people you are buying from—like how they service the phone or where to take it if something is wrong.

If you are buying equipment as part of a package that includes service, it's important that the unit comes with a loan or replacement option should the product fail or break. If the unit isn't part of a cellular package, it's imperative that the new equipment be bought from a reputable retailer.

Most carriers offer inducements to get you to sign up for service, such as a discount for the first two months, reduced rates if you use the phone often or a certain amount of free calls. If you're a first-time user, you may want to sign up for the least expensive plan until you establish a usage pattern, then upgrade as your needs increase. Be aware, however, that there are usually hefty termination fees if you want to get out of your phone contract early.

Finding the right combination of wireless communication tools takes a bit of doing, but the effort will be richly rewarded with increased accessibility, greater convenience and more business.

GLOSSARY

Cellular geographic service area (CGSA): the service area within which your cellular phone calls are not subject to roaming charges

Roaming charges: additional charges for cellular phone calls made outside of you service area, see also cellular geographic service area

Peak times: periods of time when cellular phone charges are highest (generally, normal business hours)

Off-peak times: periods of time when cellular phone charges are low (generally, nights and weekends)

CHAPTER 28

HIT THE ROAD

Should you
lease or
buy a car?

Does your business need a company vehicle for making deliveries, traveling to clients' offices, carrying equipment and more? Whether buying or leasing a vehicle is more advantageous for you depends on a variety of factors. And if you need several cars or vans for salespeople or delivery drivers, you may be eligible for fleet leasing programs that can save you big money. Here's a closer look at the different ways to get your business on the road.

THE LEASING OPTION

Vehicle leasing is a contract between a lessor (the dealer) and a lessee (the customer) for a new vehicle to be used for a specified time period and a specified payment. The title of the vehicle remains in the lessor's name as owner, but insurance, registration and other fees are paid by the lessee.

There are two types of leases: *open-end* and *closed-end* (see "Learning The Lingo" in this chapter). The former can last up to five years and offers lower monthly payments. However, if the assessed value of the car when you turn it in is less than the car's book value, you have to pay the difference (called a *residual*).

Although your monthly payments will probably be higher, the closed-end lease allows you to walk away clean. Providing the car has normal wear and tear and you're within the mileage limits imposed by the lease, you simply hand the car back to the dealer when the lease is up, with no residual payment. (Of course, you must pay for any damage the car may have incurred.)

You can also roll the closed-end lease over and drive off in another brand-new car. Dealers are partial to this type of lease because it keeps customers coming back, so they're likely to sweeten the deal if they think you'll be a lessee for the long term.

Beware!

Don't sign a lease that is longer than two years. The interest on a four- or five-year lease can make payments skyrocket.

How does leasing compare to buying? Leasing payments are generally lower than financing payments because you pay only for part of the depreciation of the vehicle during the time you lease it rather than for the price of the entire vehicle. However, at the end of, say, a two-year lease, the car could still be worth several thousand dollars, which means the dealer ends up with both your payments and a highly resaleable vehicle. You'll also have no vehicle to trade in should you decide to purchase rather than lease the next time around.

In addition to lower monthly payments, some dealers are attracting lessees with smaller or no down payments. At the same time, many leases now offer higher mileage caps, meaning you can drive more free miles.

It's usually easier to qualify for financing to lease a car than to buy one. And unlike buying, your leasing arrangement is not considered a loan and therefore is not a liability when seeking financing for your business.

Of course, paying cash for a car will net you a better price than either leasing or financing a purchase, but is that the best way to use your available capital? When you consider that the greatest benefit of leasing for the self-employed is the tax deduction for leasing payment interest, you may think twice about using your savings or stretching your credit line to buy a vehicle.

Leasing is a good option for you if:

◆ you like to drive brand-new models every two years. It's easy to roll over a lease from one new car to another.

◆ you'd rather keep your capital in the bank.

◆ you can live within the lease's mileage restriction. Calculate the average mileage you will drive on business each year, and negotiate a cap. Make sure you read the fine print for the exact figure.

◆ you prefer to drive a luxury car but have an economy budget. High-end vans, light trucks, sports cars and exotic imports can be within your grasp with no-down-payment leases. Plus, the net deductions when you lease luxury cars are generally greater than the deductions when you buy.

◆ you need to make a statement for image purposes. Like it or not, we are judged by the cars we drive; the more expensive-looking the car, the more success we are perceived to have achieved.

Arguments against leasing? Here are a few points to consider:

◆ Don't lease if you want to own the car at the end of the term. In addition to the payments you've already made, you'll be charged the residual value before you can take possession of the vehicle.

◆ Don't lease if vehicles take a beating in your line of business. Wear-and-tear charges can cripple your budget when you turn the car in.

◆ Don't lease if you plan to keep the car for more than four years; otherwise, you'll be paying for the same vehicle twice.

◆ Don't lease if you are not sure you can make the monthly payments. Terminating a lease early usually means being liable for the difference between the value of the car and the amount you've already paid. Ask what the penalties are before you sign.

◆ Don't sign a lease until you've talked to a finance company about insurance. If you damage the car, your own insurer may only pay its current cash value, and the lessor may expect you to pay the penalty for early termination. It's typical for the finance company to provide "gap protection" for free and pay the dealer the difference you owe. In addition, the dealer may require you to carry higher insurance.

◆ Don't lease if you plan to keep the car longer than the life of its warranty. You'll be responsible for repairs after the warranty runs out.

Sit down with your accountant and compare the tax benefits of leasing and buying. Leasing allows you to deduct some or all of your lease payments and interest, depending on how much you use the car for business. Keep in mind, however, that these deductions are subject to "inclusion amounts"—specific amounts that are added back to your taxable income according to IRS tables.

Still, if you're interested in a luxury car, you're probably better off

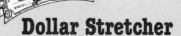

Dollar Stretcher

There's a growing market for leasing used vehicles, with warranties that cover the full term of the lease. Many of these cars are 2-year-old luxury vehicles still in their prime and coming off first-time leases—some with fewer than 25,000 miles on the odometer. Because leased vehicles are generally well-maintained and under three-year warranties, these cars and trucks are often a very good deal.

LEARNING THE LINGO

Here is a glossary of terms you may find when leasing a vehicle:

◆ *Lessee:* This is the party paying for the use of the vehicle.

◆ *Lessor:* This is the party funding the lease of the vehicle.

◆ *Additional insured:* In a lease, the vehicle belongs to the lessor, but the insurance is the responsibility of the lessee. The lessor must be named as "additional insured" on your insurance policy.

◆ *Business lease:* This is a lease agreement in which at least 50 percent of the vehicle's use is business-related (excluding commuting) to qualify for special tax treatment.

◆ *Capitalized cost:* This is the selling price of the vehicle plus any lessee costs, fees or taxes. It is used as a basis for calculating your monthly lease payments.

◆ *Capitalized cost reduction:* You can reduce the capitalized cost by paying a lump sum of money, receiving a rebate from the dealer, or getting a trade-in allowance for a vehicle. A capitalized cost reduction is often incorrectly called a down payment.

◆ *Mileage allowance:* This is the lessee's estimate of the mileage expected to be driven during the term of the vehicle's lease. Some leases impose penalties if you drive an average of more than 15,000 miles a year.

◆ *Closed-end lease:* Recommended for most people, this type of lease specifies the lessee is not accountable for the value of the vehicle at the end of the lease but is responsible for excess mileage and wear and tear. This lease generally gives the lessee an option to buy the car when the lease runs out.

◆ *Open-end lease:* Sometimes called a finance or equity lease, the open-end lease requires you to pay the difference between the estimated value and the market price of the car when the lease runs out, regardless of the mileage and condition of the car.

◆ *Residual value:* This is the estimated value of the leased vehicle at the end of the lease term.

◆ *Security deposit:* This deposit is usually refundable at the end of the lease.

leasing. The net deductions for leasing luxury cars are generally greater than the deductions when you buy.

Purchasing allows you to deduct the depreciation of the vehicle up to certain limits. You can save all your receipts—for gas, insurance and so on—and deduct those costs; or, if you own your business car, you can also use the simpler *standard mileage method*—which simply means deducting a standard amount per mile. You don't have this option with leased cars; however, in many cases, you get a bigger deduction by saving receipts, so you wouldn't want to use the standard mileage method anyway.

From a tax standpoint, the lease or buy decision generally comes down to the cost of the vehicle—the more expensive it is, the greater the tax advantages of leasing.

Smart Tip

The paperwork involved in fleet management can overwhelm first-time fleet owners. To help, many automotive gas companies have commercial programs that not only give you a discount on fuel for your fleet but also provide itemized reports and billing systems, organized by vehicle or credit card, that track mileage and expenses. Manufacturers may also offer such programs. Some companies charge for this service; others offer it free.

Fleet Leasing

Need more than one company vehicle? Good news: Leasing a small fleet of cars, minivans or pickups is easier and more advantageous than ever.

Retail leases are for consumers who want personal-use vehicles; commercial leases are generally for companies that need more than one car. Businesses that buy or lease 10 or more vehicles qualify as commercial fleet buyers and are given a fleet registration number (obtained through the dealer), entitling them to all available manufacturers' and dealers' fleet incentive programs.

While manufacturers have always offered attractive discount programs to commercial fleet buyers, there have rarely been such programs for the small fleet lessee requiring fewer than 10 cars. Nowadays, however, many dealers are beginning to offer their own programs to small-business owners and will work with you to get your business. In fact, some dealers can get you a fleet registration number even if you lease only a few cars.

"There are far fewer restrictions on what constitutes a commercial fleet these days, both at the manufacturing end and in dealerships, so the small-business person can get into fleet leasing much more easily," says Ed Bobit, editor and publisher of *Automotive Fleet*, a car and truck leasing management magazine. Manufacturers are also making it easier for small businesses to finance the leasing of their fleets, with flexible programs and special financing plans.

To decide whether fleet leasing is for you, sit down with your accountant and estimate what it will cost, taking into account monthly lease payments, insurance, gas, oil, maintenance and license fees. Will you need to hire someone to manage the fleet? If not, how will you keep tabs on regular tune-ups and administrative matters?

You may decide it is more economical to give your employees an allowance and have them lease their own cars. These and other questions should be put to your accountant before making a decision on fleet leasing. Always check to see what the penalties are for terminating a lease early, especially if your cash flow tends to fluctuate from month to month.

Fleet Factors

The typical considerations of leasing are multiplied when you lease several vehicles, so consider these possible pitfalls before you sign on the dotted line:

◆ **Higher insurance coverage:** Some dealers require you to increase your insurance coverage since they, not you, own the leased vehicles. Shop around for prices before you order your fleet because insurance can amount to a lot of money (see the "Cover Your Assets" chapter). As a business owner, you can probably get a blanket policy to cover both your business and your fleet.

◆ **Overextending your hard-earned bucks:** Six shiny new vehicles in your company parking lot may boost your ego, but do you really need them? It's easy to get carried away when ordering a fleet, so make sure you have analyzed your needs thoroughly before signing on the dotted line.

◆ **Neglecting to ask about mileage limits:** These can vary radically and can cost you as much as 15 to 20 cents for each mile you drive the car over the limit. If you cover 50,000 miles a year, it pays to buy rather than lease.

Bright Idea

Even if you decide leasing isn't for you, you can still benefit from leasing programs. When cars come off a lease, they are often sold at dealerships as used cars. They're in better shape than a car that's traded in. They've got low mileage, they're well-maintained, and the dealers know their history since they're the ones who leased them originally.

FULL DISCLOSURE

Confused by all the fine print on the leasing contract? You're not alone. The good news: Recent regulations issued by the Federal Reserve Board should simplify and clarify auto leases.

The new rules require leasing companies to use a revised disclosure format, which includes segregating certain disclosures that were previously scattered throughout the contract. To make comparison shopping easier, contracts must also disclose the total amount of payments. But that's not all: Leasing companies must also:

♦ make the disclosure of costs paid at the lease signing easier to understand,

♦ include strong warnings about possible penalties for excessive wear and tear or early lease termination,

♦ include a disclosure with any percentage rate indicating the limitations of the rate information, and

♦ include a mathematical progression that shows how the monthly payment is calculated and the relationship of terms such as "residual value" and "gross capitalized cost" (see "Learning The Lingo" in this chapter).

♦ **Failing to compare buying price with lease price**: Dealers may have vehicles on the lot they are anxious to get rid of and will give you a special deal if you buy rather than lease. Ask the fleet manager to work out the figures for buying vs. leasing so you can see the difference, and always get it in writing.

♦ **Putting down too much money**: Don't be talked into a down payment that's bigger than normal—first month's payment, a small deposit and license fees.

♦ **Forgetting state taxes**: Although some states, such as Nevada and Texas, have no state taxes, others, such as California, have high registration fees and taxes, which must be paid upfront when you lease a car.

♦ **Getting buried under the paperwork**: Operating a fleet of vehicles, however small, requires at the very least keeping track of mileage and expenses with a running report on each vehicle so you can budget your cash outlay.

Know Your Options

Once you've decided fleet leasing is for you, here are some additional questions to ask:

◆ Do you need minivans, pickups or passenger cars? Determine what each vehicle will be used for.

◆ Do you need to specially equip the vans and pickups?

◆ What options do you need on each vehicle? Air conditioning and radios are probably needed, but leave the fancy options off the price tag.

◆ How much trunk or cargo space is needed to accommodate your product?

◆ How many miles a year will you clock? Most leases allow you 12,000 to 15,000 miles annually before charging you by the mile.

◆ Can you lease different types of vehicles from a single manufacturer? Leasing your fleet from a single dealer is more efficient and economical, so shop around for a dealer who sells each of the types of vehicles you require rather than having to lease your compact pickup from one dealer and your full-sized van from another.

When visiting dealerships, ask to meet with the fleet manager. He or she will be much more knowledgeable about programs and special deals than regular floor salespeople.

Don't just shop around for vehicles; shop different lenders as well. Get a lease quote from the dealer first, then run it through your bank to check for lower interest rates.

There are several fleet financing companies that will discuss incentive programs, modified payments and your buying needs. To find them, ask your dealer to provide a business line of credit or to recommend a leasing company with whom the dealer already does business. Check out other lenders under "Leasing" in your Business-to-Business Yellow Pages. Ask your bank about its fleet leasing programs. Or use a buying service, which negotiates the deal and sets up the financing. You can find these in the Yellow Pages under "Automobile Brokers" or through auto clubs.

ROAD TEST

Whether they lease or buy, many people skip one crucial step in obtaining a business vehicle: taking the car out for a comprehensive test drive. Unless you get out in traffic with the car, you could be making a serious mistake. Performance and handling can only be judged on the road. Also check the following items:

◆ Can you reach all the controls without stretching?

◆ Are the seats comfortable?

◆ Is the seat adjustable to your preferred driving position?

◆ Is visibility good on all four sides?

◆ Are the seat belts comfortable?

◆ Do the positions of the brake and gas pedals cause you fatigue?

The test drive is an opportunity to check the car's handling and response. Use this nine-point checklist:

1. Is the acceleration responsive?
2. How quickly do the brakes respond?
3. Is there vibration at highway speeds?
4. Does the suspension provide a smooth ride?
5. Do the gears shift easily?
6. Is there loss of power when accelerating?
7. Is there a lot of cabin noise?
8. How is the steering control on curves?
9. Does the car have straight-line ability at highway speeds?

Don't play the car stereo or talk to the salesperson unnecessarily while taking your test drive. You need to be able to "listen" to the car and concentrate on its performance.

Most salespeople have a route already mapped out for test drives, but you should insist on driving in road conditions similar to those you encounter in your normal driving. Your route should include left and right turns, stops at traffic signals, merging traffic, hills and bumps. See if you can take a test drive alone; you'll pay more attention to the car's performance without the salesperson breathing down your neck.

Make sure the model you test drive is the same as the one you want to buy. If you want to test drive a sedan and only a hatchback is available, come back when they have a sedan on the premises, or go somewhere else. If you can't decide what size engine you want, try them all and compare their power. If optional equipment you're considering, such as a moon roof, isn't on the test vehicle, have the salesperson show you another vehicle with the equipment so you can check out its operation. Try out various features, such as tailgates, van doors and convertible tops for convenience and ease of handling. If the convertible top is difficult to operate, you may be paying for a high-priced option you won't use. A van door or tailgate that's awkward or too small for easy loading and unloading will waste time while you're making deliveries.

Pull down the sun visor to make sure it doesn't block your view, and practice parallel parking—is the car easy to maneuver? When backing up, do you have good rear-view visibility? Do you have enough legroom? Check out the air conditioning and heater—are they too noisy? Don't hurry through your test drive. You're spending a lot of money, so take as much time as you need to really get a feel for the vehicle, and insist on both highway and local street driving.

During your test drive, ask as many questions as you feel are necessary to make an informed decision. Don't be intimidated by salespeople. If they're rude, walk out of the dealership.

Last, but not least, remember that you can haggle over prices whether you are buying or leasing, so don't accept the dealer's first offer. Keep working until you get the deal you want.

CHAPTER 29

GET WIRED

Demystifying the world of computers

By Ed Tittel,
author of more than 50 computer-related books,
including HTML for Dummies *(IDG Books Worldwide)*

In recent years computers have become one of the most important of all office tools; most business owners would agree that computers are second only to the telephone in their value. In fact, many of today's business tasks just can't be performed accurately, quickly or profitably enough without access to a computer. There's no longer any need to justify why a computer is a good idea. So now that you know you need a computer, the next step is to learn what kind of computer to buy, how to select what components you need and how to get the best of all possible deals.

Purchasing a computer, especially for those new to this frenetic marketplace, can be overwhelming and confusing. There are thousands of configurations to choose from, a wide range of features and abilities to ponder, and no consistent pricing or rating systems to help you through this maze. But the purchase of a computer can be simplified dramatically by sticking to two purchasing principles: 1) You get what you pay for, and 2) trust those best who you know best. Before you can put these fundamentals to work, however, you will need a usable foundation from which to proceed. That is, you must be armed with sufficient information about computer terminology and technology to permit you to separate hype from help.

KNOW THE PLAYERS ON THE FIELD

To begin with, you should be aware that there are several types of computers available for purchase. Two of the most popular and well-known are the PC and the Macintosh. While there are others types of computers for sale, these higher-end alternatives are more expensive (running upwards of $6,000) and are designed for special-purpose rather than general-office use.

In years past, there has been heated debate about which type of computer was best for everyday use. As few as three years ago, there were lots of good reasons to choose a Mac over a PC (and vice versa), but these preferences reflect personal taste and inclinations today more than they do technical considerations. Right now, either a Macintosh or a PC can handle all your business computing needs. Thus, sheer capability is no longer a distinguishing factor between the two types of machines.

Recent setbacks at Apple have caused significant ripples in the computer industry, making uncertainty the only sure thing about the Mac's future. If you're already familiar with the Mac, it may still be a good choice for you. But if you have no experience with computers, you should seriously consider a PC for two major reasons: First, as the dominant industry sector, PCs offer a larger selection and more price levels than do Macs; and second, savage competition in the large market for PC buyers fosters lower prices and much better deal-making potential.

Low- Or High-end System?

What type of system you purchase usually depends on two primary factors: purpose and cost. Your overall computing needs should help you determine how much computing power, capacity and capability you must buy. Don't be quick to assume that the most expensive model will suit your needs

How Suite It Is

A productivity suite is a single product that includes two or more software programs. Productivity suites are usually designed to give you all of the functionality and features you need in a single purchase. The most popular and well-known productivity suite is Microsoft Office, which contains Word (word processor), Excel (spreadsheet), Access (database), PowerPoint (presentation builder) and more. Other similar suites include Lotus' SmartSuite and Corel's WordPerfect Suite. Typically, the cost of a productivity suite is much less than purchasing each of these products separately, which probably explains why this kind of software is one of the most frequently purchased in the industry. It also explains why some system manufacturers will throw in a suite, or offer a discount on a suite, as an inducement to get your business. If the system you're considering doesn't include a productivity suite, ask about special pricing if one is purchased with a system or if the software can be included in the cost of the sale.

Beware!

Beware of extremely low prices, as-is deals and close-outs. Deals like these often hide problems you wouldn't want, even for free! Never buy a system that comes without at least a 90-day warranty, and pass on items that can't be returned for a refund (or store credit, at the minimum). If possible, pay with a credit card because even if the store gives you problems, if you can document that the merchandise was returned (a signed acceptance form from a shipper is a great testament), the credit card company will often permit you to refuse charges.

better than something less expensive. Nor should you ever forget that good deals on computers are always available to comparison shoppers. You needn't break the bank to buy solid, reliable and useful equipment.

You can determine your computing needs based on a variety of criteria, but software requirements and business processes are the most germane and the easiest to apply. Many buyers select what software they wish to use first and then purchase the computer that will support that software.

If this type of general speculation is a bit too ethereal, here are some specific characteristics and capabilities that should help you match your business needs to a high- or low-end computer system. A typical low-end computer is powerful enough for a single user to handle financial chores, create documents, manage reasonable amounts of data, and access the Internet or some other online service. A low-end system may not always be instantly responsive nor can it support intense use of several applications at once, but it gets the job done.

A typical high-end computer can support nearly any task you throw at it and will often be able to handle several such tasks simultaneously. A high-end system is quick and responsive. It is also more than capable of supporting business computing needs reliably and efficiently.

COMMON PIECES AND PARTS

When it comes to selecting a machine, you'll quickly realize that there are certain basic computer components that are always part of the package, no matter what level of performance or price you seek.

♦ **CPU:** The CPU, or central processing unit, is the brains of a computer. This component is a small computer chip where all the serious computation and processing occurs. Generally, purchasing the fastest processor available in your price range is a good strategy, and buying slightly more power than you need will add some time to the life of your system. The speed for most CPUs is rated in megahertz (MHz), which measures cycles per second, and provides a rough way to compare capabilities (and for CPUs of the same type, faster always means more powerful).

◆ **RAM:** RAM (random access memory), provides fast, temporary storage for the CPU. When it comes to RAM, more is better.

TAKE NOTE

A notebook computer is a small portable machine that offers most of the components, features and abilities found in a full-sized desktop computer. Notebook computers are invaluable to frequent travelers or to those who wish to take work home. The only drawback to notebook computers is their price, especially when compared to their upgradability. A typical notebook costs between 1.2 and 2 times as much as a similarly equipped desktop computer. However, unlike a desktop, a notebook rarely offers any useful or cost-effective upgrade options. The components used in a notebook are small to conserve space and weight, but the smaller a device, the more it costs. Typically, the only possible upgrade options for a notebook are memory and the hard drive.

Notebooks can use most of the external peripherals you already have for your desktop computer if you have the appropriate connection port or interface. Most notebooks are equipped with a PCMCIA or PC card slot, where credit-card-sized expansion cards can be inserted to add features, functions and devices.

When purchasing a notebook, look for 24MB to 40MB RAM, a 2GB hard drive, a 10-inch active-color display area or larger, a built-in pointing device, removable CD-ROM and floppy drives, and long battery life. Keep in mind, the more features you purchase in a notebook, the heavier it will be. Those ultralight notebooks are nice to carry but are often skimpy on features. If you aren't willing to carry 15 to 20 pounds, including the laptop, accessories and carrying case, you're not a good candidate for a notebook computer.

Most of the same manufacturers of desktop computers also sell notebook equivalents. The machines from Dell Computer and Toshiba are consistent award-winners and are known to be able to take the kind of beating that regular travel can dish out.

Don't purchase any computer system with less than 32 megabytes (MB).

♦ **Drive controller:** This device controls floppy and hard drives. There are two types of controllers: EIDE or SCSI. SCSI controllers are the standard for connecting devices such as scanners, optical drives and backup tape drives to computers.

♦ **Hard drive:** This is the storage device where a computer's operating system, applications and data files are kept. The hard drive is used for extended storage, unlike RAM, which is used for short-term data storage. Don't buy any drives smaller than 1 gigabyte (GB); 2GB to 4GB drives leave plenty of room to expand.

♦ **CD-ROM drive:** This device is used to read CD-ROMs (compact disk, read-only memory), which are disks that look just like the audio CDs you listen to in your stereo and are replacing floppy disks as the way that most software gets distributed these days. Instead of installing up to 20 floppy disks, you can put in just one CD—which can hold up to 650MB—and install an entire software program. Most drives operate at speeds of 8X or better

SIDEKICKS

Palmtops, PDAs (personal digital assistants), and PIMs (personal information managers) are the rage among techno-savvy entrepreneurs. These devices are often the size of a pocket calculator but deliver the features and abilities of a desktop computer. These gems function as electronic calendars, address books and scheduling tools. Several of them offer word processing, wireless fax, Internet access and more. Through an infrared or cable interface you can exchange data between a PDA and your desktop computer, allowing you to "take it with you."

These devices range from $300 to more than $1,000. Take the time to find a store with several display models before purchasing one. Some of the leading vendors in this category include Apple Newton, U.S. Robotics' Pilot and Philips' Velo 1. For an excellent review of these devices, visit www.cnet.com/Content/Reviews/Compare/Handheld/.

As long as you remember they're no substitute for a desktop computer, but rather a supplement to these machines, they're a great addition to your business's equipment team.

(meaning the drive spins 8 times faster than a standard audio CD player).

◆ **Monitor:** This television-like device is used to display visual information. A large monitor is the easiest to use over a long period of time, but a monitor can represent between one-fourth to one-half of a computer's overall cost. A 17-inch monitor suits most business situations admirably, and decent 17-inch models can be found for less than $500 these days.

◆ **Display card:** Display cards can speed up the intense processing required to show complex video images like those found in encyclopedia software such as Microsoft's Encarta, for movie clips, or in computer games like Doom. The prevailing standard for display cards is Super VGA (SVGA); never purchase anything but an SVGA card or better, and purchase no video card with less than 2MB of video RAM.

> ## Smart Tip
>
> Many computer components and peripherals come in either internal or external versions. Both offer the same functionality and features. When choosing between the two, keep this in mind: If a peripheral is used only with a single computer, an internal version may make more sense. But if a device will be shared among several machines, an external version will be more convenient.

◆ **Modem:** This device establishes communication links with other computers over telephone lines. You'll need a modem if you want to access the Internet, use an internal fax, or access a commercial online service like America Online. Modems are rated by transmission speed, which is measured in kilobits per second (Kbps). The slowest modem you should purchase is 33.6 Kbps since that's the type supported by most Internet service providers (ISPs) and online services. If you need more speed and can afford the added expense, you may want to move up to ISDN speeds instead (these digital services provide speeds of 64 or 128 Kbps, but monthly service costs more than a modem connection, and hardware costs more, too). For more information on ISPs and online services, see the following "Surf's Up" chapter.

◆ **Keyboard/Mouse:** A keyboard is used to type in (or input) data, while the mouse is what you use to select or move text, objects or icons on the computer screen. For instance, you'll usually launch an application by positioning the on-screen pointer (usually an arrow or a hand)—which represents a mouse's position on the desktop—onto the icon for that application, and then double-clicking your mouse. A mouse is often used in conjunction with the keyboard to jump from one location to another or to select commands or actions by pointing and clicking instead of using multiple keyboard strokes.

A typical low-end system might be configured as follows:

Bright Idea

Here are some Web sites that offer great information about purchasing a computer or obtaining more information: *Computer Shopper Online* (www. zdnet.com/cshopper/), NetBuyer (www.netbuyer. com/), BuyDirect. Com (www.buydirect.com/), ZD Net (www.zdnet.com/), and Yahoo's Retail Computer Companies(www.yahoo.com/Business_ and_Economy/Companies/Com puters/Retailers/).

◆ **CPU:** 200 MHz Pentium II PC or 200 MHz 604e Macintosh PowerPC

◆ **Memory:** 32MB

◆ **Hard drive:** 2GB

◆ **CD-ROM drive:** 8X or better (priced under $200, 12X and 16X drives are also becoming quite affordable)

◆ **Video card:** SVGA 2MB true-color (here "true color" means the device supports a 24-bit color depth, which makes its colors much more true to life than less capable hardware)

◆ **Monitor:** 17-inch (while 19-, 20- and 21-inch monitors are available, they're still quite pricey)

◆ **Modem:** 33.6 Kbps

Such a system will cost in the neighborhood of $2,000 to $2,200; by shopping for a slightly slower CPU, such as a 166 MHz Pentium II or a 166 MHz PowerPC, you might trim this price by $200 to $400. This system would be usable for two to three years before increased processing needs and bigger, more demanding operating systems begin to strain its capabilities.

A typical high-end system might be configured as follows:

◆ **CPU:** 300 MHz Pentium II PC or 300 MHz 604e Macintosh PowerPC

◆ **Memory:** 64MB to 128MB

◆ **Hard drive:** 4GB to 8GB

◆ **CD-ROM drive:** 12X to 16X

◆ **Video card:** SVGA 4MB true-color

- ◆ **Monitor:** 17-inch to 21-inch
- ◆ **Modem:** 56 Kbps or ISDN interface

Such a system will cost between $3,300 and $3,700, and should be usable for at least the next three to five years, if not longer.

THE OPERATING SYSTEM

Once you've decided on a computer type and the kind of hardware you want (low- or high-end), you must select an operating system (OS). An OS supplies the software that manages a computer's hardware and also allows the hardware and other software programs to interact and communicate, while providing you, the system's user, with access to the system. Without an operating system, a computer is just a pile of components that can't do anything useful.

If you've chosen to purchase a Macintosh, you really don't have a choice of operating systems: Macintosh System 8 is the only useful or manageable option. PC buyers, on the other hand, have several options

SECOND STRINGERS

Many software vendors, including companies like Microsoft (MS Works) and Claris (Claris Works) offer second-tier software suites in addition to their top-of-the-line packages. These so-called "integrated software packages" offer many of the same features as their high-end brethren—which include MS Office, Lotus SmartSuite and Corel's WordPerfect Office. But the second-tier suites fall far short of the flexibility, power and portability available from their more expensive counterparts.

As many computer buyers have realized too late, such second-tier alternatives are not anywhere near as good as the real thing. Unfortunately, these second-tier products are more often bundled for sale with PCs than the top-tier versions. Always ask your dealer if the suite you're getting with your machine is the best of its kind from the manufacturer; if it's not the top-of-the-line version, you'd be better off paying a bit more to replace that version with one that's likely to do you the most good. And because you're buying a system at the same time, this add-on shouldn't cost more than $200 or $300 (whereas buying one of these babies by itself, even with a trade-in or other promotional deal, is likely to cost $500 or more).

to choose from, including Windows 98, Windows NT, Solaris and OS/2. But only the Windows products are worth considering for first-time computer buyers.

The good news here is that you rarely need to purchase an OS if you buy a complete system. If you purchase a Mac, you will invariably receive a copy of the latest Mac OS in the bargain. If you purchase a PC, you'll probably be offered Windows 98 or Windows NT.

Bright Idea

It is a good idea to purchase all your software from a single manufacturer. This virtually guarantees compatibility between applications and helps ensure similarity in their operation and in the types of data they support. You'll be able to seamlessly move data from one software program to another—an ability you'll learn is not just convenient but downright essential.

OFFICE PRODUCTIVITY SOFTWARE

In a work environment, a computer is useless without the right software to support those activities and functions that your business needs. The following sections describe several types of software that are nearly universal on most business computers.

Word Processing

A word processing application is an absolute necessity for any office. A word processor is more than just a tool for typing words into documents like a typewriter; this tool offers innumerable added capabilities that include spell-checking, document formatting, numerous typefaces and font controls, graphics support, links to other applications (so that an Excel spreadsheet can feed into a Word table that gets automatically updated when the spreadsheet changes) and more. While there are numerous worthwhile contenders in the word processing category, those that are most worthy of consideration include Microsoft Word, Lotus Word Pro and Corel's WordPerfect. Cost: $60-$220.

Spreadsheets/Databases

For small to medium-sized organizations, a spreadsheet or database program may be used for simple data management, chart/graph creation, and mathematical calculations of all kinds. With a little experience, it is possible to use these products to create customized applications, such as a dynamic customer directory, a work-flow tool or a report generator. There are several worthwhile contenders in this category. In the databases category: Microsoft's

Access, Corel's Paradox and Lotus Approach; and in the spreadsheet category: Microsoft's Excel, Corel's Quattro Pro and Lotus 123. Cost: $80-$300.

Accounting

Accounting or financial software enables computer owners to manage their checkbooks, bank accounts, invoices, bills and even taxes—all electronically. The best benefit of using financial software is that the calculations are always correct (provided, of course, that the data was entered accurately). A computer can simplify the process of paying bills, sending invoices and tracking cash flow. Some products can interface with your bank so you can manage your accounts and pay bills online, use your printer to write checks, and even complete your tax return without requiring the services of a CPA. (See the "Bean-Counting 101" chapter for a list of popular programs.)

Presentation

Presentation software permits you to create graphical presentations that are most often displayed on a large computer monitor or projection system—right from a laptop or desktop computer. If you've ever been to any computer trade shows or training sessions, then you have probably seen several such presentations, some of which may have even incorporated full color, animation and other special effects that these packages can provide. Computer-based presentation tools permit you to communicate information to an audience with greater ease and ability than with slides or transparencies, and are easier to update and maintain. If your business requires you or your employees to make presentations to customers or the public, you will find this kind of software absolutely invaluable. The "Big Three" contenders in this category include Microsoft PowerPoint, Lotus Freelance Graphics and Corel's Presentations. Cost: $65-$275.

Contact Management

Contact management software is basically a powerful combination of an electronic calendar, a date book, an address book, a contact-tracking database and an electronic personal assistant. These software tools can keep track of

Dollar Stretcher

Some national chains advertise that they'll beat any local store price, so if you can find a good deal from a small shop, you can use this information to get a better price. And if you wait to shop until the end of the month or a quarter (March, June, September or December), you can sometimes catch salespeople when they'll do just about anything to make their quotas!

all the little bits of information that are so important to business life but that are also so easy to lose, misplace or forget. Contact management software can remind you about appointments, track attempts to reach customers, log your work hours, dial the telephone and more. These programs are so versatile that even your complex life can't begin to stress their abilities. Some of the most noteworthy entrants in this software category are Microsoft's Outlook, Symantec's ACT, GoldMine Software's GoldMine and NetManage's Ecco Pro. Cost: $75-$160.

This is one software category where personal taste and proclivities play an enormous role. Many of these manufacturers offer trial copies, and it's a good idea to "test drive" one before buying. Don't be afraid to play the field until you find something you really like. For most entrepreneurs, this is the one program you'll use the most, so compatibility with your needs and personal style is paramount.

Virus Protection

A computer virus is a software program that can cause serious damage to a computer's hardware and data files. Catching a virus is rare, but even a single infected file can render a computer unusable. Virus protection, scanning and cleaning software is widely available and offers protection against this menace. Most modern virus programs handle networks with aplomb and scan e-mail attachments and Internet downloads with ease. While floppies have historically been the primary sources of virus infection, today's users are much more likely to "catch something" from their e-mail or the Internet. There is a large field of contenders in the anti-virus category, but the best-known products include Symantec's Norton Anti-Virus, McAfee's Virus Scan and Dr. Solomon's Anti-Virus. Cost: around $70.

File Backup

Backup software enables you to make copies of an entire file system or just the important data files. These copies can be used to restore your precious data in the event of a drive failure or a virus infection. A backup is the only way to ensure that your data is protected from loss or damage. Backup software requires a storage device to save or copy data to. This can be a tape drive, a writable optical drive, a DAT drive, or even a removable hard drive. Be sure to ask your hardware vendor about the options for a backup device when you purchase your machine. The two biggest players in this category are Seagate's Backup Exec and Cheyenne Backup. Cost: $100-$300.

Remember two things about backups: 1) If you don't back up, you can't restore; and 2) always store a copy of your data off site (even if you just take a tape or a disk home with you at night)—if the place burns down and your backups go up in smoke, they're no good to you.

PERIPHERAL DEVICES

With a basic computer system, you can accomplish most office tasks. But there are lots of additional ways to improve and expand the capabilities of your computer, simply by adding more devices. Such extra or add-on devices are often called peripherals.

Printers

You need a printer to produce hard copies of your computer documents and other work. There are several types of printers to choose from, including dot matrix, inkjet and laser printers.

- **Dot matrix printers** have all but disappeared from the marketplace since they offer little by way of print quality or graphics capabilities. If you can even find a dot matrix printer for sale, it should only be considered if you have some special need that cannot be satisfied with one of the other two types.

- An **inkjet printer** creates images on paper by squirting microscopic beads of ink onto the paper. One drawback: It is often easy to smear and smudge newly printed pages. Most inkjets offer print speeds between four and nine pages per minute, can deliver print quality at a maximum of 600 dots per inch (300 dpi is far more common), and can print in color as well as monochrome (black type). With a price tag of $200 to $500, inkjets are an excellent low-end system component.

- **Laser printers** create images on paper through a complex light-ink attraction process, which results in a fused image that won't smear. Laser printers deliver print speeds of four to 20 pages per minute or more, with a quality range between 600 and 2400 dpi. Most laser printers print in black only, but color models are available for 1.5 to 3 times the price of a monochrome unit. Basic business-use laser printers range between $350 to $1,000 and should suffice for both low- and high-end applications.

> ## Smart Tip
>
> Dots per inch, or dpi, describes a printer's detail rendering. A newspaper is around 150 to 200 dpi, while most magazines are 600 to 1200 dpi. Unless your documents will be used as "camera ready" art, a 600 dpi printer will satisfy most business needs. Higher-resolution printers cost more, so if you only need high-quality output occasionally, it is much more economical to outsource the work.

Some entrepreneurs prefer a laser printer for documents but find a color inkjet comes in handy for charts, graphs, letterhead and other applications where color adds value to what they're trying to communicate. That explains why many small businesses often wind up buying both kinds of printers.

When shopping for a printer, remember that a higher output rate (more pages per minute, in other words) and print quality result in a higher cost. Take the time to compare the features of several models before making a decision. For instance, Hewlett Packard, Epson and Canon offer numerous printer models. When buying a printer, keep the following points in mind:

◆ **Compatibility:** Make sure the printer you buy will work with your computer and operating system. It's much easier to start on the right path than to have to return something because it won't work (this is one reason why it's a good idea to purchase name-brand printers like those from Hewlett Packard—they work with nearly everything).

◆ **Paper-handling:** Make sure the printer can handle enough paper, of the right kinds for the jobs you want it to perform. If you want to print envelopes or labels, make sure the printer you choose can handle them. If you need to print large documents or numbers of copies, make sure the printer has a big enough paper tray so you can avoid having to stop to add paper in the middle of a job.

◆ **Special features:** Not every printer can handle 11 x 17 paper, print double-sided, or collate, staple or provide other special functions. Such advanced features can add significantly to the cost of a printer, so make sure you don't pay for any functions you don't really need.

Multimedia

Multimedia describes any electronic device that adds motion or sound to a computer. Multimedia is no longer just for fun and video games. Many training and communication software packages use multimedia to enhance the information they deliver. A basic multimedia setup includes a CD-ROM drive, a sound card, speakers and a cheap microphone. A high-end multimedia setup can add surround-sound speakers, a more powerful microphone, video capture and processing cards, and more. With a multimedia setup, you can conduct audio or video conferences and presentations or audiovisual online training.

If you need multimedia capabilities, it is much cheaper if you buy them as part of a fully equipped system. But if you must add these capabilities to an existing system, keep an eye out for prepackaged multimedia bundles, which will often include everything you need, at a price that's 25 percent to 40 percent less than the cost of buying the elements individually. When selecting multimedia devices, here are a few manufacturers to consider: Creative Labs, Advanced Gravis and Diamond Multimedia.

Scanners

A scanner can read or capture printed images so they can be used or manipulated within a computer. Scanners are most often used for two basic purposes: for OCR text or to grab images. OCR, or optical character recognition, is a technology that "reads" text from a printed page and converts it into an editable electronic document. OCR can save countless hours of retyping. Grabbing images using a scanner simply creates a graphics file without requiring you to recreate a picture using a graphics program.

> **Smart Tip**
>
> Looking for a single device, a software product or even a whole computer? You can find multiple resellers at a Web site called ComputerESP. This search tool can look by name, vendor or product type and will provide you with feature information, current prices, and links to online vendors that have the product in stock. Visit it at www.computeresp.com/.

Scanners range in price as widely as printers do. A quality scanner will cost you more than $500 and will support a direct-capture capability of 300 dpi; through the use of special hardware and software, this can be bumped up to 2400 dpi. For most everyday uses, except when creating artwork for printing or publication, 300 dpi is plenty of resolution. If you are going to print any of your scanned images, the upgrade to 2400 dpi may be worth the extra $600 to $2,000.

The best scanner manufacturers just happen to be the best printer vendors—namely, Hewlett Packard, Epson and Canon.

UNSUNG NECESSITIES

Even after you've purchased all the hardware and software for a computer, there may still be a few more items left over that you may not have considered, or might just have overlooked. Without some of these items, you won't be able to use your computer to its fullest potential; without others, you and your computer may someday find yourselves in deep, deep trouble. That's why this list is worth serious perusal and profound consideration.

- ◆ **Surge protector:** For the bargain price of $15, a surge protector not only provides multiple outlets instead of the two that are standard on wall outlets, but these devices also offer vital protection from power surges and lightning strikes.

♦ **UPS:** An uninterruptible power supply is a rechargeable battery-powered device that provides a few minutes of power to enable a graceful system shutdown in case of power outages or allows you to ride out power surges, dips and brownouts. These types of devices range from $125 to more than $800; if you need your computer up and running as much as possible, you definitely need one of these.

♦ **Computer desk and/or printer stand:** A computer can be placed on any sturdy desk, but most desks and tables do not offer the best ergonomic positioning for optimal use. Be sure your work area is properly oriented so your arms, back and neck are not forced into unnatural positions. A printer stand will save desk space and keep your printer out of the way of more important devices or materials. Cost: $150 or more.

COMPUTER EQUIPMENT COMPARISON		
Item	**Low-end Cost**	**High-end Cost**
Computer	$2,200	$3,500
Modem	Included	$200 for ISDN
Communication line cost	$30 per month plus $75 installation for phone line	$100 per month plus $200 installation for ISDN
ISP cost	$30 per month plus $25 setup	$100 per month plus $50 setup
Printer	$300 (inkjet)	$600 (laser)
Computer desk	Use current one	$250
Printer stand	Use desk	$75
Multimedia	Not included	$200-$1,000
UPS	$15 surge protector	$250
OS and software	$1,000	$2,000
Scanner	Not included	$600
Misc. supplies: cable, diskettes, etc.	$60	$200
Total	**$3,675**	**$8,125**

◆ **Mouse and wrist pad:** These and other comfort devices may seem a bit frivolous, but they can protect your equipment and reduce the stress on your joints and muscles. It's best to buy a mouse pad with a wrist rest built in and also purchase a wrist rest for your keyboard. Once you start using these items, you'll never want to be without them again. Cost: $25.

◆ **Insurance:** Normal homeowner's or office insurance does not cover computers or related software, equipment and supplies. But these items are subject to loss and damage and should be protected. Expect to pay between $5 and $20 per $1,000 worth of equipment and software annually. Be sure to select a deductible that's as high as you can handle, but no higher. Don't try to do without this essential form of coverage.

WHERE TO BUY?

Where you buy a computer is important. Usually, that decision boils down to a choice between what's least expensive or where you'll get the best service. Local computer stores offer the easiest access to post-sale service, but their prices are higher. Online and mail or phone order operations offer the lowest prices, but they can be difficult to press for service after the sale. Thus there is no clear factor that makes one of these vendors more preferable than another; only you can decide whether price or support is more important to you.

Nevertheless, here are some general principles to keep in mind when selecting a computer vendor:

◆ **Stick with those you know.** Look for companies you're already familiar with or whose reputations are outstanding. Stay away from fly-by-night or no-name companies.

◆ **Ask for references.** Contact other customers to get a feel for a vendor's business practices.

◆ **Check with the Better Business Bureau.** Find out if the vendor has a large file of complaints or a small one.

◆ **How long have they been in business?** Start-ups may offer the best prices, but they may not stick around long enough to prove themselves or to give you much support, either.

◆ **Always get it in writing.** Never make any deal or purchase anything until you get a written summary of the specifics and the system's features and its exact price (this includes fax and e-mail capabilities).

◆ **Compare all warranties and guarantees.** Read the vendor's "post sale" documents to determine how much the vendor promises and what you can return to them at their cost.

◆ **Get service details.** Find out what you must go through to obtain service and support, including costs, turnaround time, whether cross-shipping is available (in which they send you a replacement at the same time you send the original unit), etc.

◆ **Ask about an extended warranty or a repair/service policy.** Many vendors contract their post-sales support to national companies like GTE or VanStar. While an extended policy may cost you extra, if you buy such a policy, it will cost less than if you purchase one separately, and it may make the difference between a system that's dead for weeks and one that's revived in short order.

Even if you ultimately choose a long-distance outfit instead of a local reseller, use the showroom floor of a local reseller to "test drive" your choices. Most large computer superstores have dozens of models on display. Take an afternoon and a notepad, and drive a few systems around the block to determine what you like. Computer chain stores vary by region, but they include well-known names such as CompUSA, Circuit City and Best Buy.

There are a huge number of mail order system vendors to choose from, but three of the most reputable companies in this category include:

◆ Dell Computer (has won major customer satisfaction awards for the past three years)

OLD IS NEW AGAIN

Many of the larger computer vendors operate factory outlet stores (or online classified ads) where you can purchase reconditioned equipment at prices that are significantly lower than retail. Reconditioned equipment is a machine that may have been a floor model, an overstock from one of the vendor's showrooms or another dealer, an item damaged in shipping, or a customer return, which creates a computer that may not legally be sold as new. Vendors inspect, test and fix these devices, then package them for sale as reconditioned. Most reconditioned equipment is just as good as new but is often granted a more limited warranty of 30 to 90 days rather than the one to three years that is typical of new equipment. Some vendors who sell reconditioned machines include Micron Electronics and Dell Computer.

- ◆ Micron Electronics (offers excellent value at competitive prices)
- ◆ Internet Shopping Network (best for do-it-yourselfers who don't mind deciding on every last component they want in their machines)

You can locate other resellers, including mail order and phone-only vendors, through *Computer Shopper* magazine, which is available at most newsstands or on the Internet at www.zdnet.com/cshopper/contactus/knowus.html.

UPGRADING YOUR COMPUTER

The ability to upgrade and improve a computer system will be a key factor in ensuring that the machine you purchase today will have some reasonable value over the next three or four years. The development of new and faster technology in the computer world is exceptionally quick and ever increasing. There's no part of a computer that's immune to the relentless forward march of technology.

When purchasing a new computer, your goal should be to purchase the most powerful and full-featured system you can reasonably afford but to make sure that there's sufficient room to expand, add and upgrade that system when money and availability of options permit and need dictates that more is not just better, but downright necessary.

Here are some common upgrade strategies:

- ◆ **CPU:** A CPU can be upgraded by replacing one chip with another; however, it is normally possible to upgrade only within the same CPU type, not across generations. Speeding up your CPU will let you run software programs more quickly and will allow you to run more applications at the same time.

- ◆ **Memory:** The most common computer upgrade is to add more memory. For memory-hungry environments like Windows, adding more memory is often the best thing you can do for your machine. More RAM makes programs run faster, gives the operating system more room to work in, and will let you run more programs at the same time.

- ◆ **Storage:** Adding more storage most often means installing a new hard drive. Just remember that more storage makes adequate backups increasingly important. Adding more storage space will let you add more programs and upgrade your OS, where it's not unusual for such software to consume tens to hundreds of megabytes.

The most common reason to upgrade a machine is to improve its performance. Every component within a computer can contribute to or detract from a system's overall performance. Locating, identifying and replacing whichever component drags down performance the most results in the most noticeable improvement.

The cost of upgrading a computer varies greatly, depending on which components must be exchanged or added. The latest version of most computer devices can cost anywhere from two to 10 times more than its immediate predecessor. Upgrading a computer is not usually extremely difficult, but it does require a bit of know-how. You may find that paying $75 an hour for a professional to install your upgrades is worth the headache, time, and, best of all, the guarantee that it will work. Most computer retail stores will install hardware, even if purchased elsewhere (many will replace old equipment for free if you purchase the new pieces from them).

There are lots of choices to make when purchasing a computer. Fortunately, there is ample information both online and in books and magazines that you can use to educate yourself about every component and software product you might be considering. If you take the time to research and even test drive your choices, you can greatly improve the odds that your final decision will result in long-term satisfaction with your computer purchase.

CHAPTER 30

SURF'S UP

Making the Internet work for you

No entrepreneur starting up today can afford to ignore the power of the Internet. While it's easy to feel intimidated by the size of this information medium, small-business owners have more to gain than anyone else from learning to harness its power.

The Internet gives small businesses access to information, contacts and networking opportunities previously enjoyed only by large corporations. It can help even the tiniest homebased company do business on a global scale. It can streamline communications with customers, vendors and suppliers, speeding your response time and slashing your costs. And all you need is a computer, phone line and modem. Don't you owe it to yourself to find out exactly what the Internet can do for you?

BENEFITS OF GOING ONLINE

When you're a busy entrepreneur, it's easy to become isolated . . . and it's sometimes hard to find the time to get together with other business owners to share ideas and advice. Through the Internet, you can do all this quickly and easily. By logging onto the Internet or an online service with a modem hooked up to a computer, you can bounce ideas off people in your field and share experiences with others who may have valuable advice.

Online services and many Web sites have bulletin boards, or forums, geared to any number of special interests, such as homebased business owners, women entrepreneurs and more. The forums let you communicate with other subscribers by posting messages, participating in live conferences, or sending e-mail.

In addition to networking, you can access a vast amount of information from the government, trade associations, other companies and more. You can access databases of market research or customer mailing lists. You can visit magazines' or newspapers' Web sites to find archives of business articles. You can even download software online onto your own computer.

Online services offer daily business news from the major newspapers and wire services, so you can always be on top of what's happening in your industry. And instead of subscribing to dozens of publications or trekking to the library to do research, it's all at your fingertips, any time you want.

UNDERSTANDING THE INTERNET

Dollar Stretcher

For more information about the Internet, what it is and how to use it, see *The Whole Internet User's Guide and Catalog.* You can find it in most major bookstores, or order directly from the publisher at O'Reilly & Associates, 103-A Morris St., Sebastopol, CA 95472, (800) 998-9938.

The Internet is a worldwide system of interconnected computer networks, including academic, commercial, military and government networks. The World Wide Web is one of those networks; commercial online services, such as America online and CompuServe, belong to another.

The Web is the most popular part of the Internet, mostly because it features a graphic, point-and-click interface that allows users to easily access hundreds of thousands of Web sites. You travel the Web using a Web browser—software that navigates the various sites. Popular browsers include Netscape Navigator and Microsoft Internet Explorer. Once you're on the Web, you can search for specific topics using search engines—the online equivalent of a reference librarian. Search engines, including Lycos, WebCrawler, Yahoo!, Infoseek and Excite, let you find information by keywords or by concept. If you want to visit a specific Web site, you simply type in its address, or "URL," such as www.companyname.com.

Beware!

Internet service providers don't always live up to their promises. Make sure you're thoroughly satisfied with a provider before you plaster your Internet address all over your business cards and product literature.

How do you access the Internet in the first place? There are two different ways. One is to get an account through a major online service. Each online service provides its own news information service, message boards, file databases and conference capabilities. Commercial online services also offer connections, or "gateways," that let you jump directly from the service to the Internet. The second option is to bypass the online service and set up a direct connection to the Internet through an Internet service provider (ISP).

Rates for both ISPs and online services are constantly dropping, and most are very competitive with each other. For a list of major online services with contact numbers and Web addresses, see "Appendix A"; to find an ISP, also see "Appendix A" or look in the Yellow Pages or order *Boardwatch Magazine's Directory of Internet Service Providers* (also available online at www.boardwatch.com).

What is the difference between accessing the Internet through an online

INSIDE ISPS

With some 4,500 Internet service providers operating today, it's no wonder more and more of them are offering additional services to stay competitive. Here are a few of the services some ISPs provide:

◆ Web-site hosting: Typically, you get 10MB to 20MB storage for about $50 a month—usually enough space for a basic Web site with limited graphics.

◆ If you'd like the ability to process credit cards online, some ISPs will set up and manage this service for you; costs generally range from $400 to $500 per month.

◆ A few ISPs are gearing their services toward the small-business market, with specialized services for entrepreneurs and Internet packages aimed at specific industries, such as accounting.

◆ Some ISPs are bundling Internet and local phone services together, offering both Internet access and local calling service in one affordable package.

When selecting an ISP, don't rely solely on friends' recommendations or sign up with the first company that gives you some kind of freebie. Contact a variety of local and national providers and let them know what services you require, as well as what others are charging, so you can negotiate a fair price. Ask about the provider's standard rates, additional charges for access to certain portions of the Internet, local toll charges, support of varying modem rates, the average number of busy signals and the extent of customer service. Also ask if they offer service guarantees for reliable Internet access or for their Web-hosting services.

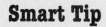

Smart Tip

If you don't have an unlimited-use plan, fees for online connect time can add up if you're not careful. To minimize costs, write your messages offline, upload them to the service and capture messages online, then disconnect and read them offline.

service or an ISP? Think of it as the difference between taking a guided tour of Europe in an air-conditioned bus and taking a trip to Europe with nothing but a backpack. With the guided tour, you've got someone to hold your hand, show you what's important and help you find the sights you want to see. You can also break away from the group if you like for some unguided sightseeing (that is, surfing the Web). With the solo journey, however, you're on your own. Chances are you'll see some nifty things you wouldn't have seen on the guided tour. But you may also get lost once or twice, struggle with the language and spend more time getting where you need to go.

If you like exploring on your own and are fairly tech-savvy, you may prefer going the ISP route. (For more on what ISPs can offer, see "Inside ISPs" in this chapter.) If you are a first-time Internet user, however, signing up with an online service could be a good way to get your feet wet.

Even if you are comfortable with technology, online services offer one major advantage over ISPs: convenience. As a busy entrepreneur, your goal when going online is to find what you need as quickly and easily as possible. And, in most cases, an online service is still the most convenient way of doing this. Online services provide:

◆ **easy access to content.** With a wide array of sites across the globe, the Web provides more content than any online service, with new sites appearing online daily. But it can be difficult to find that content, even if you're experienced and have a good Web browser.

   While online services can't compete with the World Wide Web in terms of sheer quantity of content, they are continually adding original content, including a wide range of references and technical support for a variety of products. More important, that content is much better organized and easier to find than it is on the Web. In fact, online services even help organize information from the Web by providing links to Web sites.

◆ **a feeling of community.** For entrepreneurs, who often work in isolation, one of the biggest differences between commercial services and the Web is that online services create a sense of community with bulletin boards, forums and chat rooms where members can congregate to chat, network or share information.

Rules Of The Road

Before you go online, there are a few dangers you should be aware of. First, realize it's more difficult to communicate with people online than in person, or even over the phone. None of the nonverbal communication conveyed by your body language or tone of voice is transmitted over the wire. Something you meant as a joke can easily appear quite harsh. That's why you'll often see signs such as ":-)," which is a smiley face turned sideways, or ";-)," which is a wink, indicating that a particular posting is a joke.

It's important to use good judgment when dealing with people in a forum. "You don't know who you're talking to, so everyone should exercise caution," says Paul G. Guti, president and CEO of Paul Guti Enterprises Inc., an international marketing firm. You have no idea how many people could be reading your messages, so don't say anything you wouldn't want the whole world to see.

Also remember that online services require a certain amount of reciprocity. Don't just ask for help every time you sign on; it's important to respond to people's requests as well.

Internet service providers do not have chat rooms or databases. Although you can access these directly on some Web sites, those on online services are often easier to use.

When you post a message on a bulletin board, you're putting it up for any subscriber to see. People often post messages to ask questions, provide comments or answer someone else's question.

Occasionally, people who frequent bulletin boards schedule live conferences. Here, several subscribers can talk to each other in "real time" about a particular topic, just as they would in a conference call on the telephone. There are also "chat rooms," where subscribers can send messages in real time.

Most online services provide free e-mail as part of the service. E-mail is a great way for busy business owners to keep in touch with each other. No more dealing with time zone differences or playing phone tag; you simply send a message, and your recipient responds when it's convenient for them.

◆ **downloadable software.** Another big draw of online services is their vast libraries of freeware and shareware, which you can easily find using keywords. True, you can also use a Web browser to access millions of files scattered across thousands of sites, but it takes more effort to find them. With online services, you can access programs from the services' own software libraries or directly from the World Wide Web.

◆ **technical support.** If you're looking for technical support, stick with an online service.

Good Connections

Although it's touted as an instantaneous source of information, the Internet often suffers from "rush hour traffic." As more and more users crowd online, access and download times may crawl to a halt. If your computer's slow speeds are due to heavy traffic (meaning you're logging on at the same time as tons of other users), you may just have to hang up and try again later.

Even when online traffic is light, sites with lots of graphics or sound and video clips may be slow to download. To get what you need quickly, make sure your modem's up to speed. A modem's speed is measured in kilobits per second (Kbps). The recommended speed today is 36.6 Kbps or higher. Currently, manufacturers are transitioning to 56 Kbps as the new standard, so if you are buying a new modem, buy one at that speed or higher.

A faster modem costs more, but you'll find it rapidly pays for itself by drastically shortening your connect time. This not only cuts phone costs, but frees up your time to do more important things—like running your business.

If you're seeking even higher speeds, another option is upgrading to ISDN technology, which offers data transfer speeds of 128 Kbps. In addition to an ISDN modem, you'll also need an ISDN line instead of a standard phone line.

If Internet access via phone line is like an LP record, then Internet access via ISDN lines is a CD. Like CDs, however, it's also more expensive, and ISDN service is not available in all areas. To find out if it's offered in your region, contact your local phone company. Because the technology is fairly new, phone companies are still learning how to support it, so expect some delays in getting up and running. To make sure you'll really be able to use all that horsepower, check with your ISP; not all of them support ISDN.

Smart Tip

Want more information on ISDN? Access www.ascend.com/1097.html for an explanation of ISDN, its advantages over analog solutions and more.

Dollar Stretcher

Want free software? Just dial into one of the many 24-hour online software stores that let you download freeware and low-cost shareware. You'll find sources through your ISP or online bulletin boards. (Be sure you have virus protection software in place before using any software downloaded from the Internet.)

Another technology currently being tested nationwide is the cable modem. As the name implies, these modems run over cable TV lines. Eventually, they will make ISDN look downright slow, as they will be able to receive data at speeds of up to 10 Mbps (megabits per second) and upload data at speeds of 640 Kbps. However, cable modems are still only in the testing stages, so it remains to be seen if they will be a lasting technology or just a flash in the pan.

Another technology under development, ADSL promises speeds similar to the cable modem. Offering speeds of between 1.6 Mbps and 8 Mbps downstream and 640 Kbps upstream, ADSL's big advantage is that it can be used over the same copper wire you use for your phone. Unfortunately, the widespread application of this technology is being held up by litigation by the local phone companies.

The rate at which your modem processes data depends not only on the modem, but also on the type of line you are using and the software you have. Make sure all the parts work together to give you the fastest, most convenient Internet access.

GLOSSARY

ADSL: high-speed line that transmits data at up to 8 Mbps downstream and 640 Kbps upstream

Bulletin board: online site where subscribers can post messages for others to read; see also forum

Cable modems: modems that transmit data over cable TV lines at speeds up to 10 Mbps downstream and 640 Kbps upstream

Chat room: online forum where users can "talk" in real time by typing in messages

Forum: online site where subscribers can post messages for others to read; see also bulletin board

Freeware: software that can be downloaded free from the Internet; see also shareware

Internet: a worldwide system of linked or interconnected computer networks comprised of academic, commercial, government and military networks; the World Wide Web is one of those networks, as are commercial online services

Internet service provider (ISP): company that provides subscribers with direct connection to the Internet

ISDN (Integrated Services Digital Network): ISDN lines and modems offer data transmission at speeds of 128 Kbps

Online service: company that provides subscribers with proprietary content and additional services in addition to Internet access

Search engine: software that helps you find information by keyword or concept; search engines are free to use as long as you have access to the Web

Shareware: software that can be downloaded free from the Internet; see also freeware

Web browser: software that lets you travel the World Wide Web

Web site: a collection of pages that live on the Web; "Web site" usually refers to a constellation of separate pages accessed through a main title or contents page

World Wide Web: a graphical user interface within the Net that allows the use of text and graphics

CHAPTER 31

WISE BUYS

Shopping for copiers and fax machines

Acomputer isn't all you need to power up your new business. If you're like most entrepreneurs, you'll find that a fax machine and copier are smart investments as well. Or, if you want to get the features of several machines packed into one, check out multifunction machines that give you more for your money. Here's a closer look at the features and factors to consider when you're shopping for fax machines, copiers or multifunction devices.

CHOOSING A COPIER

If you're planning to make do without a copier because you think you can't afford one, stop and think about the cost of your time. Simply count how often you'll have to run to the copy shop "just to make a few copies," and you'll realize not having a copier could cost your business more than you can afford.

Of small businesses with fewer than 100 employees, nearly 20 percent make between 1,000 and 2,500 copies per month, according to market research firm BIS Strategic Decisions. The majority (42 percent) average between one and 249 copies a month, and the rest fall somewhere in between. No matter where you are on that scale, it may be a good idea to consider a copier of your own.

Just a few years ago, the average personal copier cost $10,000 or more and was housed in a huge console. Today, copiers are far more compact—and far more affordable. They're small enough to sit on a desktop and are designed for easier maintenance.

If you're like most small-business owners, you'll be choosing among three types of copiers:

Personal copiers, defined as compact (or mini) copiers for home and private use, handle anything from single sheets (where the user must manually feed in one blank page at a time) to 10 copies per minute (cpm).

A bit higher on the scale are *desktop* copiers. Even the plainest desktop copiers have a speed of 10 cpm, which is considered the minimum for a business copier.

The more powerful *midvolume* copiers are typically floor consoles, too large to sit on a desk or table. You'll need extra room if you add sorter equipment or special paper trays.

To decide which type of copier is right for your business, start by figuring out your monthly copy volume. The number of documents you copy each month determines how much a copier will cost you over the long term. While today's copiers may have low price tags, the cost of running them can be surprisingly high. And using a copier for a heavier volume than it's designed for will probably cause problems.

If you make 500 or fewer copies per month, you can get by with a personal copier. Personal copiers cost less than traditional desktop or floor models. You can get a low-end, no-frills personal copier for between $500 and $1,000. They also require less maintenance since most are made with replaceable cartridges containing all the parts that need servicing on a regular copier. After a few thousand copies, you simply take out the old cartridge and put in a new one. Since you don't have to worry about servicing, you can buy a personal copier anywhere you want, without the extra time and hassle of working with authorized dealers.

Make sure you will be making under 500 copies per month, though. The handy replaceable toner cartridges found in personal copiers are more expensive than traditional copier parts because they have to be replaced after a relatively low number of copies. Overuse of the copier will quickly cancel out any savings you might expect.

If your monthly copy count is 500 or greater, it's time to move up to desktop models. Most desktop copiers start at 10 cpm and go as high as 20 to 25 cpm. Their recommended copy volume per month ranges from 800 to 20,000 copies. Standard features vary widely, but usually include a selection of copy sizes (including legal-sized and 11-by-17-inch documents), reduction/enlargement capabilities, a paper tray, and the ability to make up to 99

Beware!

When evaluating a copier's speed and efficiency, don't forget to consider its ability to produce continuous-run copies. If you do a lot of high-volume copying, look for a machine that can copy several hundred sheets at once. If the continuous-run number is low, you'll have to reset the machine constantly to make additional copies—a time-consuming hassle.

copies of one original at a time. Expect to pay about $2,000 to $3,000 for a desktop copier.

If you make 10,000 to 50,000 copies per month, you probably need a midvolume copier (although some desktop models can handle up to 20,000 copies per month). Retail prices for midvolume copiers range from $5,000 to $11,000 or more.

The good news about copier prices: In most cases, "street" or actual prices are substantially less than the suggested retail cost. When considering the cost of a copier, however, remember that buying the copier is only the first step. You also need to take operating costs into account. When you add up the cost of paper, toner and replacement parts, 500 copies per month may cost, say, 4 cents a page—which tacks another $240 per year onto the copier's price.

Feature Factors

Once you've pinpointed your copy volume, determine what your primary copying needs are. Factors to consider:

◆ How much money do you have to spend?

◆ How fast do you want your machine to work?

◆ Do you use only letter-sized paper, or also legal- and odd-sized paper?

◆ Do you require reduction/enlargement features?

◆ Do you need to copy lengthy documents, such as books and manuals?

◆ Are the documents you copy printed on both sides?

◆ Must you have all the bells and whistles, such as color reproduction, collation and stapling?

Desktop and personal copiers usually lack the document-handling accessories found in larger copiers. They probably won't have a sorter, double-sided copying capacity, or automatic

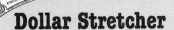

Dollar Stretcher

Since desktop copiers are inexpensive compared to midvolume models, you probably won't be able to lease one. In some cases, though, you may be able to work out an arrangement where you pay per copy rather than buying the machine outright. In other words, the company charges you 3 or 4 cents per page, which covers everything but the price of paper. This option is usually available only with higher copy volumes—say, 5,000 to 10,000 per month—but it's something to consider when you've outgrown your 500-copies-permonth machine.

paper feed. Some may not even have paper trays; others have trays that can hold from 50 to 250 sheets. Here are some common copier features; be aware that many are found only on midvolume copiers and above:

1. **Paper trays:** Make sure they hold enough sheets to work efficiently.

2. **Sorters:** This feature sorts documents and collates and slots them into different shelves as they are printed. You can buy a machine with a single sorter bin, then add on higher-capacity bins later on.

3. **Feeders:** This feature can feed a single sheet or a stack of documents into the copier automatically. The feeders of most midvolume copiers can handle a stack of up to 50 sheets at once.

4. **Stapler:** Automatic stapling should be a prerequisite if you make many sets of documents. However, check out the price since staplers can be expensive if not included in the standard model.

5. **Folding, stapling and binding:** If you are in the mail order business, you may want a combination of these three features. Such copiers will fold your fliers or newsletters, then staple or heatbind them.

6. **Double-sided copying:** Many small-business owners save paper by using both sides of a single sheet. If this is the custom in your office, you'll want to buy a copier with double-sided copying capability.

Smart Tip

When considering copy volume, entrepreneurs should look not only at the number of copies made but also at the flow of work. If you make an estimated 20,000 copies a month, does that total consist of hundreds of small jobs, or is it primarily a large monthly report that requires a single long run every four weeks? If you tend to run a few large jobs, you'll save time and money with a faster, higher-volume copier that staples and sorts the copies.

Some small businesses may need a low-volume or midvolume copier in addition to a high-volume copier. If you or your staff have to line up to use the copy machine, consider getting an additional copier with top volume capacity and centralizing certain jobs in a production center.

7. **Reducing and enlarging:** To reduce or enlarge on some midvolume machines, you must push a button until you find the size needed; other copiers automatically calculate the best percentage of reduction or enlargement based on the original document's size.

8. **Automatic tray switching:** If expense is not a concern and you're looking at higher-end copiers with extra features, this is a nice time-saver that automatically switches from an empty tray to a full one.

9. **Bypass:** This is useful for making a single copy on paper that is different from that already loaded into the paper tray. A drawback of the bypass feature is that you must feed documents in one page at a time.

10. **Book copying:** Use this to copy the left, the right or both pages of a bound original, such as a magazine or book.

11. **Copy-editing:** An advanced, external option, this allows you to automatically block out portions of a document using an electronic pen.

Since these extra features can get expensive, you may want to consider a copier that allows you to incorporate them as add-ons at a later date.

Service First

As anyone who's ever used one knows, a copier is very service-intensive. Just because a copier breaks down doesn't necessarily mean it's an inferior machine. Most problems are related to paper passing through an extremely narrow slot. Paper thickness varies with paper vendor, quality, age and even office humidity levels. With different types of paper constantly passing through the slots at high speeds, jams occur. The rollers also wear down and become hardened with use. If they aren't cleaned or replaced at the right time, the machine will stop functioning.

"No other piece of office equipment needs such tender, loving care as the photocopier," says John Derrick, editor of *What to Buy for Business* consumer guides. "Copiers rely on a large number of moving parts. Though manufacturing processes have improved substantially over the past decade, the fundamental technology has remained remarkably constant, so who you buy from can be as important as what you buy."

Today's copiers don't have as many problems as in the past, but they still need routine maintenance. That means a dealer's service, support and warranties should be as much a concern to you as the machine's price, reputation and reliability.

Ask whether the dealer offers a backup copier if yours needs repairing;

ask for customer referrals, and check whether they are satisfied with the service; ask what the service maintenance schedule is and how much an extended service warranty costs.

The replacement part copiers most frequently need is a toner cartridge. Before falling in love with a particular copier, ask how many copies its average toner cartridge will make before you have to replace it. Other parts that will eventually need replacing are the drum and the developer units. Some warranties offer free replacements on these parts during the regular maintenance and service schedule.

Smart Tip

The proliferation of computers might make a typewriter seem about as relevant to your business as a quill pen and a powdered wig. In reality, typewriters are useful for entrepreneurs who often deal with preprinted forms. You can get a good electric typewriter for $100 to $200. Don't go overboard—as long as the machine prints clearly, it's fulfilling its purpose.

Buying from a dealer does cost more (about 10 percent to 20 percent) than buying through "alternative channels" (computer superstores, mail order companies or consumer retailers/discounters). However, when you're talking copiers, the extra cost is usually worth it because you get service and support as part of the deal.

Payment Plans

Copy machines can be rented, leased or bought outright. The decision depends on the size of your business and how you manage capital expenses. If you have copying seasonal highs and lows, consider buying copies, not copiers. A cost-per-copy purchase plan, where you are charged only for actual usage of the machine, affords companies a break during slow periods.

Renting enables a business to obtain the machine, maintenance and supplies for a monthly rate. However, since most rental agreements may be canceled any time, the dealer usually builds a higher cost into the fee.

Leasing is usually a good deal as long as you lease over a period of 36 months or more. Leasing minimizes your cash outlay, and the payments may be tax-deductible.

If you're buying just one copier, the best option is probably purchasing outright, either in one payment or through financing. But make sure you get a good warranty contract.

FAX FACTS

Aside from your phone, the most important communication device in your office is likely to be your fax machine. Faster and more efficient than the mail, faxes can also keep your phone bill low. Consumers are clamoring for lower-cost, more efficient models, and manufacturers have complied. Today's fax machines boast amazing technological advances at prices that won't break the bank.

Today, you can find affordable fax machines that are small enough to fit in the most cramped quarters. The latest models use plain paper, so you don't have to deal with costly (and curly) thermal fax paper anymore. And many machines combine a copier function with their faxing capabilities.

There are a few hundred plain paper fax machines on the market, ranging from simple to sophisticated. Some can transmit documents to you in a confidential electronic file you can access while on the road. Others can be integrated into your computer and used as printers.

Most plain-paper fax machines use the same paper you buy for your copier and laser printer. That means you can save money by buying paper in bulk. And because plain-paper faxes are becoming so popular, prices for these machines are plummeting lower by the day.

DECISIONS, DECISIONS

Stuck trying to decide between an entry-level fax machine or one with all the bells and whistles? The four most important factors to consider are paper tray capacity, document feeding capacity, print quality and transmission speed. Also ask yourself these questions:

◆ Can I afford a second phone line for my fax if necessary?

◆ Do I need to transmit documents, charts and graphics in color?

◆ Is my company expanding so fast that it will soon outgrow the basic, low-end fax machine?

◆ How many faxes do I want to send at night to save on phone costs?

◆ What are the maintenance considerations?

◆ What features are essential to running my business?

◆ What other features are nice to have but not essential?

◆ Is this model expandable?

◆ How much memory do I need?

Just The Fax

There are four methods of transmitting messages via fax. Each has advantages and disadvantages.

Dollar Stretcher

When assessing a fax machine, don't just consider cost of the machine itself. Also take into account how often the cartridges need to be replaced and how costly they are, how expensive the paper is, and how fast the machine transmits. A cheaper machine could end up costing you more in the end if it runs up higher phone bills while sending faxes.

1. **Thermal transfer:** These machines are the least expensive, but they have higher maintenance costs and require special paper. Average cost per page: 5 to 6 cents.

2. **Inkjet:** These machines are affordable, but image quality isn't the best. Print can fade, too, and cartridges need more frequent replacement. However, if you only need to read a document once and chuck it, this could be your best bet. Average cost per page: 5 cents.

3. **Laser:** These machines feature top-quality images but are more expensive. Cartridges last longer, however. Average cost per page: 3 cents.

4. **LED (light-emitting diode):** These machines are similar in print quality and cost to laser faxes, have fewer moving parts, but are slower. Average cost per page: 2 to 3 cents.

Here are some features to look for on fax machines:

◆ **Memory:** This feature electronically stores incoming documents in a memory chip until you've refilled the paper tray; it also holds outgoing letters for later transmission. Most memory systems are measured in megabytes; the standard is 1MB. Many machines offer an upgrade option to expand memory by an additional 1MB or 2MB.

◆ **Scan and quick scan:** With scanning and the speedier quick scan options, your document is stored in the fax machine's memory in seconds so you don't need to leave it in the machine during transmission. This saves waiting time and increases privacy.

◆ **Convenience copying and printing:** Even older fax machines have a "copy" key to make copies of documents. It's provided as a convenience, so don't expect top quality; same with convenience printing.

◆ **Dual access:** A welcome feature for busy offices, dual access scans your documents and stores them in memory for sending while the machine is receiving. As soon as the incoming fax is received, the machine automatically sends your outgoing letter.

◆ **Delayed transmission:** This allows you to store documents in memory and program the fax machine to relay them at night, when phone charges are less expensive.

◆ **Broadcasting:** If you regularly send sales reports or other documents, this is a time-saving feature. It stores a document in memory, then sends it to multiple pre-programmed locations. A similar feature, called "polling," allows your fax machine to call other machines and request pre-programmed documents to be sent at various times; this prevents several faxes coming in at the same time.

◆ **Junk mail block:** If you're receiving unwanted messages, you can program the fax machine's memory to block specific phone numbers.

◆ **Reduction/enlargement:** This helps cut down on the number of pages you need to send or enlarges small print.

◆ **Autodial:** Like many phone systems, autodial provides pre-programming of frequently called phone numbers, so you can punch in one number instead of several. These are also referred to as speed-dial numbers.

◆ **Auto redial:** A time-saver, this feature tells the fax machine to keep trying until the fax goes through.

◆ **Auto phone/fax switch:** If you have only one phone line in your office, a fax machine with this feature will automatically switch incoming fax calls over to the fax machine to receive documents. Some machines supply a distinctive ring so you know whether to pick up the handset to answer or not.

Smart Tip

Make the most of your fax correspondence with these fax etiquette tips:

◆ Since faxes may be read by others, never fax anything you don't want the public to read.

◆ When sending an unsolicited fax, keep it to one page.

◆ Sending a lengthy document? Consider a method other than fax machines, such as overnight mail. You don't want to tie up the recipient's machine for a long time.

◆ **Remote retrieval:** This feature allows you to dial in from another fax machine to receive faxes stored in memory. You can also use your laptop's modem to receive the faxes into your computer, or use a phone to instruct your office fax machine to send the faxes to a different fax machine.

◆ **Cover page:** Once programmed with a company name, phone number and logo, this feature automatically prints and faxes a dated cover page with every document you send.

The Computer Connection

The future of faxing is here, and it's PC connectivity. PC or local area network (LAN) interfaces send and receive faxes, scan documents, and print through the PC or a LAN terminal. The interface allows users to transmit directly to the computer when a hard copy is not required. In turn, documents created on the computer can be sent to the fax machine for transmission. An interface can reduce fax labor time and unnecessary supply expenditures.

The main benefit of sending documents through your fax machine via your PC instead of simply through the machine itself is the cost savings on long-distance charges since phone connections via your PC are usually based on local phone charges. Another advantage is speed. Most new fax machines transmit at a 14.4 baud rate; by hooking up to your PC with its 36.6 Kbps or faster modem, your fax machine will double its speed and thus reduce phone bills. You also eliminate the need to print documents, then feed them through a fax machine.

With a PC interface, fax machines are turning into multifunction machines (though they should not be confused with multifunction devices, which are printer-based). Prices for the new high-tech fax machines vary widely, ranging from the mid-$200s to the high $2,000s. The greater the number of features, the greater the price. If the PC interface is not a standard feature but an option, it can add as much as $300 to $750 to your purchase price.

MULTIFUNCTION MACHINES

Are you starting up in a small or homebased office, where a fax machine, printer, scanner and copier will be a tight squeeze on your desk? If so, you may want to consider buying one electronic helper that can do the job of four, five or six.

Multifunction machines (MFMs) combine several essential tools in a single unit, measuring an average of 18 inches wide, 18 inches deep and

Beware!

Multifunction machines may sound great, but there are some drawbacks:

◆ Most MFMs print only in black and white—a disadvantage for business owners who want to produce their own full-color fliers, brochures and ads.

◆ If you need crisp, clear copies, check the print quality carefully; some machines offer "convenience" copying only.

◆ Most important, ask the dealer about rapid-response repair time. If the MFM crashes, your entire office could be paralyzed until it's up and running again.

12 inches tall. Most MFMs copy, scan, fax, print and provide electronic filing cabinets.

Initially built with laser printers, which kept prices high, MFMs have begun to use less expensive inkjet print technology, bringing them within the budget of small-business owners.

Additional jobs MFMs can perform include remote fax storage and retrieval, multitasking (performing two or three tasks simultaneously, such as printing while faxing), auto-dialing, fax broadcasting and telephony. Features on some models include distinctive ringing, battery backup, junk fax block, reduction/enlargement, collation, two-sided printing and document feeders that handle up to 99 sheets of paper. Some MFMs can even store voice-mail messages if the unit is busy with another function. Other MFM features are PC faxing, printing and scanning, which work in conjunction with your PC and require Microsoft Windows.

PC faxing uses a PC interface device to transmit faxes directly from your computer, without having to print documents out first and feed them manually into a fax machine. You can also store received faxes in your computer and keep them only long enough to read, instead of printing them out and wasting paper. Additional optional memory cards can increase the number of pages your fax can store. Just make sure the software you'll need is compatible with your computer.

Scanning allows you to copy text, graphics, logos or line art from paper into your computer. However, the scanned text cannot be edited—it must be retyped if you want to change it. More convenient is PC scanning, which allows users to scan both graphics and text into the computer, then edit the text directly without retyping it.

An MFM with dual-fax capabilities works as a plain-paper fax, sending and receiving documents in the usual manner by feeding documents into the machine. It can also send PC faxes directly from the computer to the receiver's PC fax or standard fax machine, and to a local area network (LAN) to which several computers are connected. Sending to a LAN allows several recipients to view a document at the same time from their individual workstations. The software for this feature is usually optional.

Another innovation is a basic "hub" MFM unit to which you can add printing, copying and scanning options as needed. On many MFMs, these additional functions require nothing more than connecting them to your PC via software, an interface, or a PC Card.

Most MFMs save you money by using the same toner and drum units to perform all functions. And if your utility bill is getting out of hand, you'll probably find you use less power with a single MFM than with separate printers, copiers, scanners and fax machines.

Before buying an MFM, ask for a detailed demonstration of all its functions, and remember that street prices can lop several hundred dollars off a manufacturer's list price.

GLOSSARY

Desktop copier: copier small enough to fit on a desktop, with a capacity of 10 copies per minute (cpm), copy volume per month is typically 800 to 20,000 copies; see also personal copier

Midvolume copier: usually floor consoles, midvolume copiers handle 10,000 to 50,000 copies per month

Multifunction machine: equipment that combines several features in a single unit, typically printing, faxing, scanning and storing documents; some also have telephone features and can be connected to a PC

Personal copier: copier small enough to fit on a desktop, with capacity from single sheet to 10 cpm; copy volume per month is 500 or under; see also desktop copier

Plain-paper fax machine: prints on standard paper as opposed to thermal paper; see also thermal fax machine

Thermal fax machine: prints using heat transfer on special thermal paper; see also plain paper fax machine

Go . . .

All systems are go and you're ready to launch your new business. To make sure the launch is successful, Part 6, "Strut Your Stuff," shows you how to spread the word about your company. Find out how to create a marketing and advertising campaign that works . . . without spending a fortune. From direct mail and print ads to radio and catalogs, we share smart strategies to make your business the talk of the town. You'll also learn about the single best way to promote your business: public relations. From special events to community projects to media coverage, we show you dozens of ways to get your business noticed—most of them virtually free!

The Web is the latest and greatest way to promote a business, but it can be tricky for the newcomer to navigate. Find out smart ways to net publicity online—from Web sites and newsgroups to hot links and more.

If the idea of selling scares you, you're not alone. That's why we provide everything you need to know to sell like a pro. Learn how to get over your fear of cold calls, techniques for overcoming objections, how to spot hot prospects and how to close the sale. Once you've made the sale, the game isn't over: You've got to keep the customer coming back. Our secrets to great customer service will give you the edge you need to win repeat business . . . over and over again.

If you're doing everything right, you'll be dealing with a bundle of money. In Part 7, "By The Books," we show you the strategies to make the most of your money. Whether or not you're a math whiz, you'll want to read our bookkeeping basics, which contain everything you need to know to keep track of your finances. You'll learn the accounting methods that can make a difference come tax time, what records to keep and why, and whether to computerize or do it by hand. Check out our step-by-step look at creating financial statements, income statements, cash flow statements and other important indicators that help you measure your money. Then learn ways to manage your finances, including secrets to pricing your product or service; how to get short-term capital infusions when you're low on cash; how to determine your overhead, profit margin and more. We also show you how to stay out of trouble when the tax man comes calling. Get the inside scoop on payroll taxes, personal vs. corporate tax returns, and what to file when. Learn what you can deduct...and what you can't.

To keep you on the path to success, our final chapter takes a closer look at success and failure factors. Find out what causes businesses to succeed or fail, and how you can learn from mistakes along the way to make your business better than ever!

Part Six:
Strut
Your
Stuff

CHAPTER 32

TO MARKET, TO MARKET

Advertising and marketing your business

You may know how to build the perfect product or provide excellent service, but do you know how to market and advertise your business? If not, all your expertise won't help keep your business afloat. Without marketing, no one will know your business exists—and if customers don't know you're there, you won't make any sales.

Advertising doesn't have to mean multimillion-dollar TV commercials. There are plenty of ways to market your business that are affordable or even free. All it takes is a little marketing savvy...which you'll have plenty of after reading this chapter.

CREATING A MARKETING PLAN

Every start-up venture needs a business plan, yet many entrepreneurs don't realize a marketing plan is equally vital.

Unlike a business plan, the marketing plan focuses on the customers. A marketing plan includes numbers, facts and objectives, but it is not primarily numerical; it is strategic. It is your plan of action—what you will sell, to whom you will sell it and how often, at what price, and how you will get the product to the buyer. Here's a closer look at putting together a marketing plan that works.

Step One: Define your product. The first part of the marketing plan defines your product or service and its features and benefits in detail, then shows how it is different from the competition's. The more clearly and succinctly you describe your product in your marketing plan, the better you'll communicate with your target customer.

Markets and products have become extremely fragmented. There are hundreds of special-interest magazines, for example, each targeted to a very specific market segment. It's the same with restaurants, cars and retail

clothing stores, just to name a few industries. Positioning your product
competitively requires an understanding of this fragmented market. Not
only must you be able to describe your
product, you must also be able to describe your competitor's product and
show why yours is better.

Positioning your product involves
two steps. First, analyze your product's features, and decide how they differentiate your product from its competitors. Second, decide what type of
buyer is most likely to purchase your product.

Pricing and placement are critical to competitive positioning. In today's
marketing culture, pricing cannot be separated from the product.

Take grocery stores, for example. The full-service supermarket is still the
most popular form of grocery distribution. But today, busy families want
faster service and more convenience, even if it means higher prices. As a result, convenience stores, home delivery services, personal shoppers and
takeout restaurants have proliferated. At the same time, warehouse grocery
retailing has also increased. Warehouse stores cater to customers who prefer low prices to convenience.

Service, distribution and price are the essential elements of the products
offered by supermarket, convenience and warehouse stores. To develop a
successful marketing plan, you need to analyze how these same elements fit
into your business. What are you selling—convenience? Quality? Discount
pricing? You can't offer it all. Knowing what your customers want helps you
decide what to offer.

Step Two: Describe your target customer. Developing a profile of your
target customer is the second step in an effective marketing plan. You can
describe customers in terms of demographics—age, sex, family composition, earnings and geographical location—as well as lifestyle. Ask: Are my
customers conservative or innovative? Leaders or followers? Timid or aggressive? Traditional or modern? Introverted or extroverted? How often do
they purchase what I offer? How much of it at a time? Are there peak buying periods or times of the year when people won't buy my product or service? (Part 2 Chapters 6 and 7 explain in detail how to define your target
customer.)

Step Three: Create a communication strategy. Your target customer
must not only know your product exists but must also have a favorable impression of its benefits. Communication includes everything from logo design and advertising to public relations and promotions.

Find out what your target customers read and listen to. You need to know this to get their attention. In addition to where to place your message, consider how frequently customers need to receive it.

This part of the marking plan should spell out your promotional objectives. What do you want to achieve? Do you want people to recognize your company name? Know where you're located? How much money can you spend to get your message across? What media are available, and which will work best? Finally, how will you evaluate the results?

Ask yourself the right questions and analyze your answers, and you'll come up with a marketing plan that will help you achieve your goals.

Market Planning Checklist

Before you launch a marketing campaign, answer the following questions about your business and your product or service.

❏ Have you analyzed the total market for your product or service? Do you know which features of your product or service will appeal to different market segments?

❏ In forming your marketing message, have you described how your product or service will benefit your clients?

❏ Have you prepared a pricing schedule? What kinds of discounts do you offer, and to whom do you offer them?

❏ Have you prepared a sales forecast?

❏ Which media will you use in your marketing campaign?

❏ Do your marketing materials mention any optional accessories or added services that consumers might want to purchase?

❏ If you offer a product, have you prepared clear operating-and-assembly instructions if required? What kind of warranty do you provide? What type of customer service or support do you offer after the sale?

❏ Do you have product liability insurance?

❏ Is your packaging likely to appeal to your target market?

❏ If your product is one you can patent, have you done so?

❏ How will you distribute your product?

Setting An Advertising Budget

You'll need to devote a percentage of projected gross sales to your annual advertising budget. A good rule of thumb is to devote 2 percent to 5 percent of anticipated gross sales to this need.

There are two primary methods of determining your advertising budget more specifically. First is the *cost method*, which theorizes that an advertiser can't afford to spend more than he or she has. For instance, using the cost method to determine the advertising budget, and devoting 5 percent of gross sales, a business projecting $300,000 in gross sales in a given year would have $15,000 for that year, or about $1,250 per month, to spend on

Go For The Pros

Can you create your own advertising copywriting and design? If you have a background in marketing and advertising, the answer is yes. If not, however, you're better off hiring a professional. No matter how creative you are, a commercial artist or graphic designer can vastly improve almost any ad created by an entrepreneur.

However, since no one knows your business better than you, it's a good idea to develop your own rough draft first. Think about the key benefits you want to get across, what makes your company different and better than the rest, and the major advantages of doing business with you. Then put pencil to paper and draw a rough sketch.

If you're reluctant to spend the money on a copywriter and graphic designer, don't be. Printing, distributing and placing your advertising and marketing materials is going to be costly in itself. If the materials you're paying to have printed aren't well-written, eye-catching and effective, you're wasting your money.

Graphic design and copywriting is one area of business where it's possible to get good work at substantial savings. Plenty of freelance, one-person graphic design and copywriting businesses exist, many of them quite reasonably priced. Ask friends, other business owners, or your chamber of commerce for referrals. Many copywriters and designers will cut you a price break on the first project in hopes of winning your business in the future.

Or consider approaching a college or art school. Many talented students will work for reduced rates (or even for free) for the chance to add your ad to their portfolios.

advertising. (Since businesses typically advertise more heavily when they first open, the same business could allocate more—about $2,500—for its grand opening.)

This may not seem like much money, and for some companies it won't be enough. These companies base their advertising budgets on the amount of money they need to attract the customer or sell the product. This is called the *task method*. A company using the task method typically determines how much money is needed based on past experience. Of course, as a start-up you won't have experience to go on. In this case, you'll have to base the figures on your business plan and market survey, which should estimate the costs you'll incur.

WHERE TO ADVERTISE

Once you know your target customers, it'll be easier to determine which media will work well for you. Much of this is just common sense, based on your product, method of sales and audience.

Sure, it would be great if you could afford to buy a full-page color ad in *Time* magazine or a 60-second commercial during the Super Bowl. But in addition to being beyond your budget, such ads aren't even the most effective way to go for a small company.

POSITIONING POWER

The right image packs a powerful marketing punch. To make it work for you, follow these steps:

1. Create a positioning statement for your company. In one or two sentences, describe what distinguishes you from your competition.

2. Test your positioning statement. Does it appeal to your target audience? Refine it until it speaks directly to their wants and needs.

3. Use the positioning statement in every written communication to customers.

4. Create image marketing materials that communicate your positioning. Don't skimp.

5. Include your team in the image marketing plan. Help employees understand how to communicate your positioning to customers.

ADVERTISING CHECKLIST

Overview

❏ Have you defined your advertising objectives and written them down?

❏ What exactly do you want to communicate to your potential customers?

❏ How will you measure the effectiveness of your ad?

❏ Are you communicating buyer benefits?

❏ Have you strategized an advertising campaign?

❏ Is the timing right?

❏ Do you have a planned advertising budget?

❏ Are you prepared for a successful response?

❏ Have you asked suppliers about cooperative programs?

❏ Have you made sure that employees (if any) are informed of your goals?

❏ Have all appropriate employees reviewed your advertising and approved of it?

❏ What is your lead time for ad placement? Some newspapers require only a few days; some magazines require two months or longer.

Specifics

❏ Does your ad present a central idea or theme?

❏ Does your message require a response?

❏ Have you told customers where and how to reach you?

❏ Is your ad clear and concise?

❏ Is your ad consistent with your desired business image?

Files

❏ Are you keeping files on all aspects of each ad?

❏ Where did the ad run? What were the results? (Number of sales? Sales increases?)

❏ Have you reflected/brainstormed/evaluated?

❏ What variables (weather, competition, etc.) have you targeted for further study?

Competitors And Customers

❏ Are you watching competitors? (If advertisers repeat ads, try to determine why.)

❏ Are you listening to your customers? What do they want? What's important to them?

❏ What media are most cost-effective to reach your customers?

Small companies succeed by finding a niche, not by targeting every Tom, Dick and Harry. (Remember the defining your market chapter in Part 2?) Similarly, you need to target your advertising focus as narrowly as possible to the media that will reach your customers. Your customers' location, age, income, interests and other information will guide you to the right media.

For example, if you run a business selling model train supplies nationwide by mail order, it makes sense to advertise in one of the many national magazines, newsletters or circulars catering to this hobby rather than advertising in, say, *The New York Times*. On the other hand, if you sell model trains from a hobby shop rather than via mail order, the vast majority of your customers will be drawn from the local area. Therefore, advertising in national hobbyist magazines would net you only a few customers. In this case, it makes more sense to advertise in newspapers or magazines or do commercials on cable TV or radio shows targeting the local area.

Like any aspect of running a business, marketing involves a measure of trial and error. As your business grows, however, you'll quickly learn which advertising media are most cost-effective and draw the most customers. Here's a closer look at the different types of advertising methods and tips for succeeding with each.

PRINT ADVERTISING

The print ad is the basic unit of advertising, the fountainhead from which all other forms of advertising spring. Knowing the principles of creating print ads will help you get results in any other advertising media you

THE SMALL STUFF

Should you use your limited advertising budget to create larger, more visible ads that restrict you to advertising less frequently or smaller, less visible ads that you can then afford to run more frequently?

The answer: smaller ads more frequently. The reason is that most people—even those who are likely candidates for your product—typically don't respond to ads the first time they see them. Prospects may have to notice an ad a number of times and develop a level of comfort with it (especially if the product or service is new to them) before they take action. The more often prospects see your ad, the more comfortable they will become and the better the chance they will respond to it.

use. Print ads have helped launch some of the most successful products and services we know. And there's no reason they can't work for you, too—if you observe a few hard-and-fast rules.

Most print ads out there are poorly conceived and, as a result, perform badly. If an ad lacks a strong motivating message, especially in the crowded marketplace of a newspaper or magazine, it becomes a costly lesson—one the business will be lucky to survive. The good news? With so many bad ads out there, if you can put together a good one, you're way ahead of the game.

Whether you are developing an ad yourself or having someone else craft it for you, make sure it follows the five fundamentals of successful ads.

1. **It should attract attention.** That sounds obvious, but nothing else matters unless you can do this. And that means having a truly arresting headline and visual element.

2. **It should appeal to the reader's self-interest or announce news.** An ad that takes the "you" point of view and tells readers how they will benefit from your product or service piques and keeps their interest. And if, in addition, it has news value ("Announcing a bold new breakthrough in moisturizers that can make your skin look years younger"), your ad has a better than fighting chance.

3. **It should communicate your company's unique advantage.** In other words, why should the prospect pick your firm over a competitor's?

4. **It should prove your advantage.** The most convincing way to do that is through testimonials and statistics.

5. **It should motivate readers to take action.** This is usually accomplished by making a special offer that "piggybacks" your main sales thrust. Such offers include a free trial, a discount or a bonus.

An ad does not have to do a "hard sell," as long as it is an all-out attempt to attract, communicate with and motivate the reader. That process starts with the single most important element of any ad: the headline.

Smart Tip

Sometimes, the story of your business can make an interesting "hook" for a print ad or brochure. The social worker who started a maid service could use a headline like "Why I gave up social work to rid the world of dust balls." If your story's intriguing enough, it could get readers hooked.

Golden Opportunity

It's a publication absolutely everyone gets, refers to and saves on their bookshelves for a year or more. It's the Yellow Pages—but, for too many entrepreneurs, it's an opportunity they fail to fully take advantage of.

Look at most Yellow Pages ads and what do you see? A sea of sameness. Most businesses still use their name as the major focus of the ad. They rely on rubber-stamped cliches like "prompt, courteous service" and "friendly staff." Even when they do identify specific product or service benefits, the descriptions are virtually identical to neighboring ads.

Like any ad, your Yellow Pages ad should have a strong benefit headline, a call to action, and compelling supporting copy highlighting the elements that make your product or service different and special. Here are ways some typical small businesses could improve their ads. The ideas could be adapted to many businesses.

◆ *TV repair:* Try a headline that leads in with "Check these possible fix-it-yourself solutions before you call us." Besides intriguing the reader with information that might save them money, the company ingratiates itself by unselfishly suggesting ways to avoid a service call. If the problem is more serious (as it usually is), this shop is likely to get the nod.

◆ *Tire store:* How about a headline like: "Do your tires show any of these warning signs?" Here the ad lists some of the characteristics of a worn tire, with the implication that it might be time to buy new ones.

◆ *Plumber:* One thing you almost never see in the Yellow Pages is a strong testimonial as an ad headline. Imagine a headline for a plumber that reads "Your company really came to the rescue when I needed you." This would be followed by the customer's name in small print, then a list of reasons why the prospect should choose your service over others.

If your Yellow Pages ad is too small to accommodate a major headline plus all the details of your product or service, get rid of some details. Use terms like "full-service dealer" or "wide name-brand selection" instead of a full list of your wares.

Headlines That Work

Some of the biggest flops in advertising contained convincing copy that never got read because the ads lacked a great headline or visual element to hook the reader.

David Ogilvy, founding partner of legendary ad agency Ogilvy & Mather, said that on the average, five times as many people read the headlines of ads as read the body copy. Headlines that work best, according to Ogilvy, are those that promise the reader a benefit—more miles per gallon, freedom from pimples or fewer cavities.

Flip through a magazine or newspaper and see what you notice about the ads. Typically, it's the headlines. Then notice how many of those headlines promise a benefit of some kind.

However, expressing a benefit isn't enough if the way you communicate it is dull and hackneyed. Your headline should be unusual or arresting enough to get interest. Some examples of headlines that got noticed:

◆ "When doctors feel rotten, this is what they do."

◆ "Why some foods explode in your stomach."

◆ "How a fool stunt made me a star salesman."

John Caples, a member of the Copywriters Hall of Fame and author of *Tested Advertising Methods* (Prentice Hall), recommends beginning headlines with such words or phrases as "new," "now," "at last," "warning" or "advice" to pique interest. He also suggests using one- or two-word headlines, and giving readers a test in the headline to get them involved (such as "Do you have an iron deficiency? Take this simple test to find out.").

Whatever you do, don't use your company name as the headline for your ad. This is one of the most common mistakes small companies make. Would *you* read an ad whose most eye-catching element was "Brockman Financial Services"? We thought not.

Ads That Stand Out

Imagine scanning a convention half full of people dressed in formal attire and suddenly noticing that one brazen attendee is wearing overalls and a red flannel shirt. Is it safe to say your eyes would be riveted to that individual? Your first reaction might be "How dare he?" but you'd also probably be curious enough to walk over and find out what this audacious character is all about.

Bright Idea

The most persuasive words in advertising: "free," "you," "now," "new," "win," "easy," "introducing," "save," "money," "today," "guarantee," "health," "safety" and "discovery."

Such nonconformity can have the same riveting effect in advertising. Imagine scanning a newspaper page full of well-groomed little ads and then noticing that one of them—drawn in pencil, let's say—stands out from the crowd. All of a sudden, the other little ads become invisible, and the scribbled one grabs all the attention. That ad has accomplished the single most difficult task small-business advertising faces—simply getting noticed.

Ideally, your advertising should reflect your company in both look and message. An ad represents you and what you have to offer. If it's generic, it won't have the power to grab attention or persuade prospects to take action.

THE GOOD WORD

Third-party praise—whether from a customer, an industry organization or a publication—is one of the most effective tools you can use to give your ad, commercial or direct-mail package added credibility. This can take a variety of forms:

◆ If your business has received some kind of prize, mention in the press or other honor, don't hesitate to put it in your advertising. "Rated #1 by 'Dog Groomers' Monthly" or "Voted 'Best Value' by *The Chagrin Falls Gazette*" are good ways to establish your product or service's benefit in customers' eyes.

◆ Testimonials from individual customers carry weight, too. "Wanda's Party Planners gave my son the best birthday ever!—Jane Smith, Wichita, Kansas," attracts customers' attention. How to get testimonials? If a customer says something nice about your business, don't let the compliment slide—ask, then and there, if you can use the testimonial in your sales materials. (You may want to get this in writing, just to be on the safe side.) Most customers will be happy to comply.

◆ Even if your company hasn't gotten recognition, perhaps you use a part, process or ingredient from one of your suppliers that has received praise. For example, you could say "Made with the flame retardant rated #1 by the American Fire Safety Council." This tells your customers you think highly enough of them to provide them with such a great product or ingredient.

◆ If you're a member of the Better Business Bureau, that's an implied endorsement, too. Be sure to post your BBB plaque prominently on your store or office wall or use the logo on your letterhead.

A small ad that exhibits something a little unexpected often steals the thunder of much larger, more traditional ads that surround it. But what can you say in a small space that gets noticed and makes an impression? Here are a few ideas that could work with a variety of products or services.

◆ **For a restaurant:** Use a large but short headline that can't help but arouse curiosity, such as "Oh, my God!" This would then be followed by an explanation that this is usually the reaction when one of Francisco's Super-Subs (or whatever large-serving entrée) is placed in front of a customer.

◆ **For a bed and breakfast inn:** Try a cut-out with the big headline "Tape to your mirror tonight!" Below the headline is a box of copy that reads: "Just a reminder that you should call and make reservations this morning if the two of you want to spend an unforgettable weekend at Martha's Inn in Nantucket."

◆ **For a beauty salon:** Use small ad with the headline "Can we have your autograph?" in quotes. Follow with copy that reads: "Be ready to draw the attention of admirers when you leave Noreen's Cut 'n' Curl—for people are sure to recognize you as the goddess you are."

◆ **For a carpet cleaner:** Try a small ad that shows a blowup of a dust mite with the headline "They're hiding in your carpet." The body copy then explains that these bugs are invisible to the naked eye but are accumulating by the thousands in your uncleaned carpet.

Ad Placement

There are two principal publication categories to consider for print advertising. The first, newspapers, has a positive and a negative side. On the plus side, you can get your ad in very quickly. That enables you to run an ad, for example, capitalizing on some market turn of events that saves your prospects money if they act fast and buy from you. This could be very exciting news for them, and that's perfect because they're in a "newsy" frame of mind when they read the newspaper.

On the downside, newspapers usually have a shelf life of just 24 hours. Therefore, if you run your ad on Monday, you can't depend on anyone discovering that ad on Tuesday. As the saying goes, "Nobody wants to read yesterday's news."

If your budget allows for multiple insertions—that is, running your ad more than once—do so. Regular exposure of the ad builds recognition and credibility. If some of your prospects see but don't respond to your first insertion, they may well respond to your second or third. If you have confidence in your ad's message, don't panic if the initial response is less than you wanted. More insertions may bring a better response.

The second type of publication is magazines, for which there are specialty categories of every kind. This allows you to target any of hundreds of special-interest groups. Another advantage of magazines, especially monthlies, is that they have a longer shelf life; they're often browsed through for months after publication. So your ad might have an audience for up to six months after its initial insertion. Moreover, readers spend more time per sitting with a magazine than a newspaper, so there's more chance they'll run across your ad.

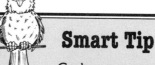

Smart Tip

Can't come up with ideas for your ad? Try a brainstorming session. Jot down words or phrases related to your product or service and its benefits. Then see what associations they trigger. Write down all the ideas you can think of without censoring anything. From those associations— whether words, phrases or visual images—come ideas that make good ads.

One researcher found the following about magazine ads:

◆ A two-page spread attracts about one-quarter more readers than a one-page ad.

◆ A full-page ad attracts one-third more readers than a half-page ad.

◆ Positioning in the front or back of the magazine doesn't matter in terms of noticeability.

◆ People respond better to illustrations or photos showing the product in use than to those that show it just sitting there.

◆ Ads with people in them attract more attention than those without.

When advertising in any print medium, contact the publication first and ask for a media kit. This contains rate information for various sizes of ads, as well as demographic information about the publication's readership— age, income and other details—to help you decide if this is where your buyers are. The media kit also indicates specifications for the format in which you will have to deliver your ad to the publication.

RADIO AND TV ADVERTISING

Many entrepreneurs believe that TV and radio advertising is beyond their means. But while national TV advertising is out of the entrepreneur's price range, advertising on local stations and, especially, on cable television can be surprisingly affordable. Armed with the right information, the small-business owner may find that TV and radio advertising can, in fact, deliver more customers than any other type of ad campaign. The key is to have a clear understanding of the market so the money spent on broadcast advertising isn't wasted.

LIGHTS, CAMERA, ACTION!

Advertising on cable TV is one thing—but have you ever thought about hosting your own show on cable television? It's easier than you think—and could make you and your business a household name!

You could never afford to run a 30-minute commercial for your business. But on public access, you can put on a 30-minute show promoting you and your business. For instance, the owner of an antiques shop could host a weekly show on restoring, finding and pricing antiques. A car-repair specialist could host a weekly car-care show. The possibilities are endless.

The Federal Communications Commission requires cable systems in the 100 largest markets to provide free public access channels. Call your local cable station, and request their public access guidelines. They'll require a commitment for a specific number of shows and will want to know your format.

There are three basic show formats that work for different businesses:

1. Interview shows work well for any industry that can draw on a large number of experts.

2. Demonstration shows work for labor-intensive businesses such as plumbing or car repair.

3. Live call-in shows are effective for professional advisors such as consultants or accountants.

Be creative. Even if your business doesn't lend itself to a show, you can benefit from public access by providing your products or services as prizes on someone else's show.

Rehearse before you go on the air, and be sure to promote your show. Put a sign in your window; sponsor store specials on items featured on the show; mention the show in your print ads or fliers. Offer to send free information or coupons to any viewer who writes or calls. This way, you build a mailing list of interested customers.

"A lot of advertising decisions are made more from the heart than from the head," says William Witcher, author of *You Can Spend Less and Sell More* (Mark Publishing), a guide to low-cost advertising. Witcher warns entrepreneurs not to get so swept up in the idea of advertising on television or radio that they neglect to do the necessary research.

Sitting down and coming up with a well-thought-out advertising plan is crucial, Witcher says. "Don't feel that you can simply throw a bunch of dollars into the advertising mill and create miracles."

Planning is especially essential for the businessperson approaching broadcast advertising for the first time. When you're first starting out, it's important to educate yourself about the media, and the only way you can do that is to talk to a lot of people. This includes advertising representatives from TV and radio stations, other business owners, and your customers.

Experts suggest an entrepreneur take the following steps before diving into broadcast advertising:

> ## Dollar Stretcher
>
> Get your ad on the radio—for free—by bartering your products or services for air time. Called "trade-out," this practice is common in the industry. Radio stations need everything from janitorial services and graphic designers to products they can give away as on-air prizes, so whatever you sell, you're likely to find a ready market.

◆ **Establish your target market by asking yourself who your customers are and, therefore, who you want to reach with your advertising.** This may seem obvious, but many advertisers don't have any idea who they're selling to.

◆ **Set a rough budget for broadcast advertising.** Come up with an amount that won't strain your business but will allow you to give broadcast advertising a good try. Many stations suggest running ads for at least three months. This can easily cost several thousand dollars for a TV campaign. Radio generally costs a little less, although rates vary widely depending on the size of the market, the station's penetration, and the audience of the show on which you want to advertise.

◆ **Contact sales managers at TV and radio stations in your area and arrange to have a salesperson visit you.** Ask salespeople for a list of available spots on shows during hours that reach your target audience.

◆ **Talk to other businesspeople in your area about their experiences with broadcast advertising.** While salespeople from TV and radio stations can be very help-ful, they are, after all, trying to sell you something. It's your re-sponsibility to be a smart con-sumer.

Dollar Stretcher

Considering advertising on cable? Look into a "cable co-op" where several companies collaborate on an ad package that promotes all their services or products.

◆ **Ask about the "audience de-livery" of the available spots.** Using published guides (Arbi-tron or Nielsen), ask the sales-person to help you calculate the CPM (cost per thousand) of reaching your target audience. Remember, you are buying an audience, not just time on a show, and you can calculate pretty exactly how much it's going to cost you to reach every single member of that audience.

◆ **Inquire about the production of your commercial.** As a general rule, TV stations charge you to produce your commercial (prices range from about $200 to $1,500), while radio stations will put your ad together for free. However, some independent TV sta-tions will include production for free if you enter into an agree-ment to advertise for at least three months. And with a similar contract, some radio stations will provide a well-known personal-ity to be the "voice" of your business at no extra cost.

Compare the various proposals. Look at the CPMs and negotiate the most attractive deal based on which outlet offers the most cost-effective way of reaching your audience. Buying time well in advance can help lower the cost. For TV ads, stick with 30-second spots, which are standard in the industry. And keep in mind that the published rates offered by TV and ra-dio stations are often negotiable. Generally, rates vary widely during the first quarter of the year, and sometimes during the third quarter or late in the fourth quarter, traditionally slow seasons for many businesses. But ex-pect to pay full rates during the rest of the year or during popular shows or prime time.

Getting Help

Once you've gone through all these steps, you should have a good idea of what is involved in broadcast advertising. But learning to be a smart con-sumer in the TV and radio market isn't always easy. If you're worried about making the right choice on your own, consider hiring a consultant or an advertising agency to guide you.

Advertising agency owner Gene Murray says that for most small businesses, radio is probably the best solution. Television is more expensive and often reaches a broader audience than a small company needs.

When approaching radio stations, learn their demographics and look closely at how they match your target market. Murray says sorting out demographics is one area where hiring an ad agency or consultant can really help. "If the businessperson tries to do it on their own, they may get confused because every radio station in the country says they're number one in a certain time spot or with a certain audience," says Murray.

Many business owners find that even local TV stations cover such a broad geographical area that they reach a lot of people who will probably never visit their stores. Unless you offer an unusual product or service that will draw people from far away, advertising on a TV station with a 250-mile radius may mean paying for 240 worthless miles. That's why radio can be the best option for your advertising needs if you only need to reach a small geographical area.

Another option that can help an advertiser pinpoint a small geographical area is cable television. With stations featuring all news, sports, music, weather and other specialized topics, cable lets you microtarget the groups that fit your ideal customer profile.

For example, a business owner looking to reach upscale members of the community might try advertising on Cable News Network (CNN). A sport-

ADDED DIMENSION

Add dimension to your sales letters—literally—by attaching some type of small item to the letter. Make it something that ties in to the letter's headline or subject. For example:

◆ A plumber could stick a minipacket of aspirin to a letter with a headline reading "Pipes giving you a headache? Take two of these, and call us in the morning."

◆ Child's plastic play scissors attached to the letter could be combined with a "Cut your costs ..." message.

◆ Or try a packet of coffee with a headline like "Sit down, have a cup of coffee on us, and learn how you can profit from stocking Steve's Safety Bolts."

A 3-D item inside gives your direct-mail package bulk. Recipients are curious and more likely to open the letter. Once they see what's inside, they'll read on to find out the connection between the item and the words.

ing goods store might make a big splash by advertising locally during the national broadcast of "Monday Night Football," often carried by ESPN.

Cable allows an advertiser to target specific towns, without wasting money covering viewers who are too far away to use the company's product or service. And cable is very inexpensive as well. A prime 30-second spot on cable that only reaches viewers in a city of about 36,000 households would cost under $50.

DIRECT MAIL

Direct mail encompasses a wide variety of marketing materials, including brochures, catalogs, postcards, newsletters and sales letters. Major corporations already know direct-mail advertising is one of the most effective and profitable ways to reach out to new and existing clients.

What's the advantage? Unlike other forms of advertising, in which you're never sure just who is getting your message, direct mail lets you communicate one-on-one with your target audience. That allows you to control who receives your message, when it is delivered, what is in the envelope, and how many people you reach.

To create an effective direct-mail campaign, start by getting your name on as many mailing lists as possible. Junk mail isn't junk when you're trying to learn about direct mail. Obtain free information every chance you get, especially from companies that offer products or services similar to yours. Take note of your reaction to each piece of mail, and save the ones that communicate most effectively, whether they come from large or small companies.

The most effective direct-mail inserts often use key words, colors and formats that can be adapted into your own mailer. Make sure the colors you use promote the appropriate image. Neon colors, for example, can attract attention for party planner or gift basket businesses. On the other hand, ivory and gray are usually the colors of choice for lawyers, financial planners and other business services.

To involve the reader in the ordering process, many mailers enclose stickers that say Yes or No to be pasted on the order form. Companies such as Publishers' Clearinghouse take this technique further by asking recipients to find hidden stickers throughout the mailing and paste them on the sweepstakes entry. It also asks customers to choose their prizes, which gets them even more involved.

Next, read up on the subject. A wealth of printed information is available to help educate yourself about direct mail. *Do-It-Yourself Direct Marketing: Secrets for Small Business* (John Wiley & Sons), by Mark S. Bacon, is a comprehensive manual that touches on all aspects of direct mail. *The National*

Directory of Mailing Lists (Oxbridge Communications) covers most mailing lists available for rental, including small and highly targeted offerings. Two of the better-known publications are *DM News,* a weekly trade paper, and *Direct Magazine,* a monthly.

The Direct Marketing Association (DMA), in New York City, is a national trade organization for direct marketers. For a catalog that highlights many of the direct marketing industry's books, a free brochure that lists a variety of direct marketing institutes and seminars across the country, or more information about joining, call the DMA at (212) 768-7227. You can also visit the group's Web site at www.the-dma.org.

ALL WRAPPED UP

While direct mail can mean everything from a postcard to a catalog, many business owners get the best response from sending out a direct-mail "package." In addition to the sales letter and brochure (see the "Sales Letters" and "Brochures" sections later in this chapter), this typically includes three other elements:

1. **The outside envelope:** There are two schools of thought on this. One school swears that "teaser" copy on the envelope can get recipients to open it. On the other hand, some people throw away anything that looks like junk mail. The opposite strategy is to trick readers into opening your mail by sending direct mail that looks like personal letters. Software programs can print addresses so they look like handwriting. Put only your address, not your company name, on the return address to arouse the recipient's curiosity.

2. **A response form:** The form should be easy to fill out. Be sure to include your phone number in case the prospect wants to ask a question or order by phone.

3. **A reply envelope:** Enclosing postage-paid reply envelopes helps get orders. Even if you can't afford postage-paid envelopes, include a pre-addressed reply envelope. If the prospect has to put the mailing down and search for an envelope, they may have time to have second thoughts.

DIRECT HITS

Try these attention-getting direct-mail ideas to power up your business:

1. **Reactivation voucher:** Mail a $20 no-strings-attached voucher to any customer you haven't seen in six months or longer. Few can turn it down . . . and even fewer will spend only $20.

2. **Magalog:** If you have a catalog, give it more value by enhancing it with problem-solving editorial content. This creates a combination magazine and catalog.

3. **$2 bill:** Send a $2 bill with a questionnaire asking about product/service preferences.

4. **We've missed you:** Send a card to clients you haven't seen in a year telling them they're missed. Include a discount coupon.

5. **Birthday call:** Record all customers' birth dates, and make sure that they get a special call or card from you.

Mailing Lists

No matter what type of direct mail you send out, you'll need a mailing list. The basic way to build a mailing list is by capturing name and address information for everyone who buys or shows interest in your product. If you sell by mail, you'll already have this information. If not, you can get it off customers' checks. Hold a drawing and ask customers to fill out an entry card or drop their business cards in a bowl. Or simply put a mailing list book next to your cash registers where customers can sign up to receive mailers and advance notices of sales. You can also gather names by placing a classified or display ad in print, then compiling the names of people who respond to your ad.

The list you develop using your own customers' names is called your "house list." Of course, when you're first starting out, your house list is likely to be skimpy. To augment it, one way to go is rent a mailing list. There are two ways to rent a mailing list—approaching the

Dollar Stretcher

Keep your house mailing list up-to-date by cleaning it regularly. To do this, send out mailers with the notation "Address Correction Requested." The post office won't charge you for sending you the new addresses of your customers when the cards are returned.

Bright Idea

A growing number of list publishers sell lists on CD-ROM. Since these lists may not be updated as regularly as other list sources, be sure to ask how current the list is before you buy.

company you want to rent from directly or using a list broker.

Any company that mails merchandise or information to its customers—magazine publishers, manufacturers, catalog companies, etc.—usually has a list manager, who handles inquiries and orders for the mailing list. If, for example, you know that subscribers to *Modern Photography* magazine are likely to be good prospects for your product, then you can rent their subscriber list directly. Another good source is local newsletters or group membership lists. Many organizations will let you use their member lists; these can be very cost-effective.

If you aren't sure whose list you want, call a mailing list broker. List brokers know all the lists available and can advise you on what type of list would work best for your business. Many can also custom-create lists based on your requirements. You can find brokers in the Yellow Pages under "Mailing Lists" and "Mailing Services," and in the classified sections of mail order trade magazines. The DMA can also refer you to brokers. Another source is the bimonthly directory *Standard Rate and Data Service Direct Marketing List Source,* available in most public libraries.

Some list companies let you sample a list before making a purchase. Rental costs typically range from $50 to $80 per thousand names. This is for a one-time use only. (List owners typically "seed" their lists with their own names and addresses, so they can tell if you use the list more than once.) Lists will typically be shipped on computer disks so you can easily use them with your computer; others send pre-printed names on mailing labels.

Most experts agree renting fewer than 5,000 names isn't worthwhile, primarily because a larger mailing doesn't cost much more per piece than a smaller mailing, and the returns are higher. Start with about 5,000 names for your first mailing, and consider it a test.

If your response is less than 1 percent or 2 percent, something is wrong. Either the market isn't right for your product, your mailer isn't attention-grabbing enough, or your prices are too

Smart Tip

Even if you do most of your business by mail or over the phone, customers like to see who they're doing business with. Put your photo on your brochures or mailings. It conveys friendliness and builds confidence in your company.

high. If you get a response of 2 percent or higher, then you're on the right track.

Once you develop a complete mailer, continue to test your enclosures by adding or eliminating one important element at a time and keeping track of any upward or downward changes in response.

Brochures

For many businesses, especially service companies, a brochure is the building block of all other marketing materials. A brochure is an information piece that doubles as an image maker. The look and feel of the brochure can not only describe the benefits of your product or service but also convey your legitimacy and professionalism. A brochure can make your small company look just as substantial as a more established rival, making it a great equalizer.

The good news is that a brochure doesn't have to be expensive. It can be almost as cheap to produce as a flier, as long as it's well-written and well-designed. A brochure can be as uncomplicated as a piece of folded paper—the same piece of letter-sized paper that would otherwise be a flier. By folding it twice, as you would a letter, then turning it upright so it opens like a book, you have the basis for a brochure.

The magic of the brochure format is that it allows for a more dramatic presentation of the material than does a flier. Think of your brochure cover as the stage curtain, creating anticipation of the excitement that lies inside. An eye-catching headline on the cover is like the master of ceremonies, piquing the prospect's interest about what's behind the "curtain." Inside, you first need to pay off the promise, or claim, in the cover headline with another headline, then use the remaining space for elaboration.

The principles of writing successful brochures are basically the same as those for writing print ads (see the "Print Advertising" section in this chapter). However, since brochures offer more room than most ads, there is a tendency to get long-winded and wordy. Keep your brochure brief, with enough information to interest readers but not so much repetition that they get bored.

The sample at the right shows a "before and after" makeover of a brochure for a company called My Right Hand that provides business support services. The first step in boosting this brochure's appeal was coming up with a tempting headline for the cover. The goal is to arouse the interest of potential clients—the harried sole proprietor who needs help with the detailed paperwork involved in running a business alone. The revised headline "HOW TO FREE YOUR BUSINESS FROM PAPERWORK PURGATORY" accomplishes that goal.

In this or any other headline, it's important to go beyond the ordinary.

BEFORE:

The flier format, while imparting the basic message, is a bit "down-scale" for a somewhat sophisticated service.

We know what this headline is trying to say, but technically, paperwork is part of "your business."

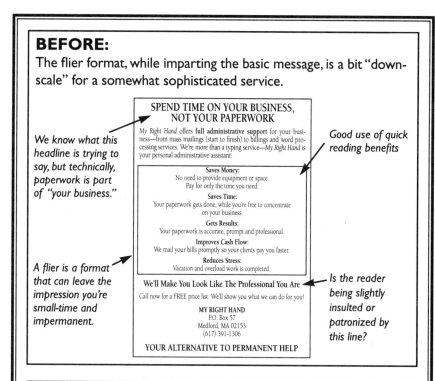

Good use of quick reading benefits

SPEND TIME ON YOUR BUSINESS,
NOT YOUR PAPERWORK

My Right Hand offers **full administrative support** for your business—from mass mailings (start to finish) to billings and word processing services. We're more than a typing service—My Right Hand is your personal administrative assistant.

Saves Money:
No need to provide equipment or space.
Pay for only the time you need.

Saves Time:
Your paperwork gets done, while you're free to concentrate on your business.

Gets Results:
Your paperwork is accurate, prompt and professional.

Improves Cash Flow:
We mail your bills promptly so your clients pay you faster.

Reduces Stress:
Vacation and overload work is completed.

We'll Make You Look Like The Professional You Are

Call now for a FREE price list. We'll show you what we can do for you!

MY RIGHT HAND
P.O. Box 57
Medford, MA 02153
(617) 391-1306

YOUR ALTERNATIVE TO PERMANENT HELP

A flier is a format that can leave the impression you're small-time and impermanent.

Is the reader being slightly insulted or patronized by this line?

AFTER:

A brochure gives you a more polished image. It says you're seasoned, sophisticated, professional.

A brochure adds a lot to your image, without costing much more than a flier.

A brochure allows you to manage the information in a way that gives each element special importance.

Give your headline an unexpected word or phrase that expresses the idea in a memorable fashion. Adding the word "purgatory" gives this headline extra drama and emotion, and puts the worst face on paperwork.

When the prospect flips the page, he or she finds a short-story-length headline that builds on the cover: *"PAPERWORK. It ties you up. It slows you down. It ticks you off. All good reasons to delegate it to us . . . a service you'll feel confident calling MY RIGHT HAND."*

This headline pushes the prospect's buttons (i.e., sensitivities) by emphasizing that paperwork is a grind, a bore and a frustration. The buzzword "delegate" is used because delegation is recognized as essential to entrepreneurial success when a business has grown too big for one person to handle. And, since confidence and trust are key in giving your business papers to an unknown company, the headline also emphasizes the company's trustworthiness by using the word "confident."

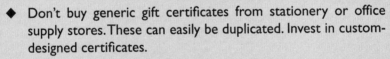

GIFTS THAT KEEP ON GIVING

Do you offer customers gift certificates? Many entrepreneurs don't, not realizing how this can boost sales. Here are some suggestions to make the most of this sales tool and also prevent fraud:

◆ Don't buy generic gift certificates from stationery or office supply stores. These can easily be duplicated. Invest in custom-designed certificates.

◆ Avoid cash refunds. State on the certificate that if more than $5 in change is due, it will be issued in the form of another gift certificate.

◆ Keep a log. Record the number, date of sale and dollar amount of each gift certificate sold. Be sure to note when the certificate is redeemed.

◆ Use security features like an embossed logo or watermark to prevent photocopying.

Properly used, certificates are like money in the bank for your business since customers often don't redeem them till months later.

The overall look of a brochure is key to making a good impression. Here are some tips to make sure yours is inviting to the eye:

1. Have the descriptive copy typeset in a fairly large size. There's no bigger turnoff for a prospect than squinting at fly-speck-sized printing.

2. Use light-colored paper. This, too, makes the brochure easier to read.

3. Break up the copy with subheads. This makes the overall brochure less formidable to read.

4. Add something unexpected visually. One good idea is to have an illustrator create a cartoon to use on the cover.

5. Use the back of your brochure for a "business biography." This is a good place to talk about how your company got started, how it has succeeded and where it is today.

6. Always use testimonials, endorsements or other credibility-raising elements.

Spend a little extra. It's worth it to have your brochure printed on card stock or quality heavyweight paper. A key part of the impression it makes is the way it feels in the customer's hand.

Sales Letters

Whether you send it out solo or as part of a direct-mail package (see "All Wrapped Up" in this chapter), a sales letter can be one of your most effective marketing tools, allowing you to speak one-on-one to prospects and customers. What makes a good sales letter? There are three key rules:

1. **Start with a hook.** Begin your letter with a provocative thought or idea that "hooks" readers and makes them want to keep reading.

2. **Give them the facts fast.** Quickly list the top two or three benefits of doing business with your company.

3. **End persuasively.** Close the letter with a strong argument that compels readers to respond.

How long should a sales letter be? The standard answer is "long enough to do the job." And yes, it takes longer to persuade a prospective customer to buy than to merely get him to inquire further. But in today's high-tech age, people have become impatient with anything that takes much longer than an eye blink to read.

Does this mean the sales letter is dying out? No; people will still read

A Little Surgery Can...

This company's old letter is a good first start. It's persuasive and has immediacy. All it needs is some additional structure and a little nipping and tucking to make it work even harder.

BEFORE

It's not too late
to lower your
property tax.

1. **Dec. 26 Deadline:** The town of Plainville just mailed the Fiscal 1991 Real Estate Tax Bills. You still have until December 26 to contest your assessed valuation and get an abatement which would lower your taxes.

2. **Get an expert:** Property owners can obtain abatements on their own; however, the adjustment is usually nominal. For substantial reduction of property taxes, the services of a professional CPA and real estate tax expert is advised to substantiate your case.

3. **No-risk contingent fee:** My firm, Property Tax Associates, only gets paid if I successfully reduce your property tax. I know what method is currently being used in Plainville to assess your property. I know how similar properties are assessed. And, I can evaluate whether your assessment is taking advantage of the full depreciation deductions to which you are entitled and apply declining value multipliers. In a word, I am a property tax abatement expert and have successfully lowered the property taxes of my clients by thousands of dollars.

4. **Free evaluation:** I know the Plainville real estate market and can quickly evaluate your current assessment and tax situation, at no obligation to you. I will not take your case if I do not believe I can substantially reduce your real estate taxes. My fee is based on a percentage of your actual tax reduction. So it is in my interest as well to make sure your taxes are lowered to the full limit of the law.

5. **You must act quickly:** State law limits the number of days an abatement application can be filed. Call me at (508) 429-2527 for an appointment now so there will be enough time to properly and legally substantiate your tax reduction request.

Property Tax Associates
Rocco Beatrice, CPA, MST, MBA
156 Mitchell Road
Holliston, MA 01746
(508) 429-2527

Suggested Operations:

A. Headline transplant: The old headline telegraphs a strong benefit—but may work better as a subhead, beneath the new headline.

B. Personalization implant: Who are you talking to? With no salutation, this letter doesn't draw readers in.

C. Pace lift: The old letter opens a little slowly and dully. That can be a turnoff to the impatient, indifferent reader.

D. Paragraph liposuction: The old letter has a few oversized paragraphs that look formidable to read. That immediately disinvites the reader.

A letter with potential ...

. . . Make A Letter Better

AFTER

Will you OVERPAY Your Property Tax Again This Year?

It's not too late to lower it if you act by the <u>December 26th deadline</u>.

Mr. George Wagner
R-B Electronics
1313 Azure Blvd.
Plainview, MA 01746

Dear Mr. Wagner,

Will you be "nailed" again this year?

Amazingly, six out of every 10 property owners overpay on their property taxes . . . and you could be one of them.

But if you act by December 26th—the deadline for contesting your assessed valuation—you can get an abatement that will lower your taxes.

Why you should call Property Tax Associates:

1. **Get a larger abatement.** You can expect a much larger cut than you could obtain on your own because of our special understanding and knowledge of the abatement process.

2. **Pay only if you get a reduction.** You don't pay us unless we successfully reduce your tax. And our fee is based on a percentage, so it is in our interest to get your taxes reduced as low as possible.

3. **Get a free evaluation.** It costs you nothing to learn if you have a chance for an abatement. We know the Plainview real estate market and can quickly evaluate your assessment and tax situation, without obligation.

We've helped many owners like you save thousands on their property taxes. And we can do the same for you.

MAKE NO MISTAKE: The city will not reduce your tax automatically. You must apply by December 26th for a reduction—or overpay again. Call me at (508) 429-2527 today so there is enough time to evaluate and prepare your request.

Sincerely,

Rocco Beatrice
Certified Public Accountant

Suggested Operations:

A. Headline transplant:
The new headline pushes an emotional "hot button" that gets prospects riled up—and ready to act.

B. Personalization implant:
A letter with opening personalization enables you to bond one-to-one with the reader. That connection is the same that any sales rep hopes to achieve. And a letter is a sales rep.

C. Pace lift:
The new letter opens with a provocative, one-sentence "hook," then quickly hops from point to point.

D. Paragraph liposuction:
The new letter keeps paragraphs lean, mean and easy to read.

Potential released

sales letters. However, they don't like it when you make them work at it—so keep it lean and mean.

Equal in importance to your message (some would say more important) is the look of your letter. It should be visually inviting. As soon as prospective customers pull your letter out of the envelope, and before they even read one word of your sales message, they instantly have a positive or negative reaction based on the overall look of the letter. If it's crammed with words, readers will have a negative impression right away.

To have the best chance of being read, your letter should be open and airy-looking with short paragraphs—including some that are one sentence or even one word long. (A one-word paragraph? Here's how: Write something like "I have one word for suppliers who say they can't offer you a one-year guarantee." Follow that with a one-word paragraph, such as "Baloney!" or any similar word you want to use. It's a real attention-getter.)

Strip your sales message down to the essentials so readers can breeze through it. This may mean hacking out words and phrases you've slaved over. But each extra bit you take out increases your chances of actually getting a response.

Last, but not least, be sure to use "you." This is a good rule of thumb in any form of advertising, but especially in a sales letter where you're, in a sense, talking to the prospect face-to-face. Always talk about your product or service in terms of its benefit to the reader, such as "You'll save more than 50 percent." Sounds obvious, but it's easy to lapse into the impersonal "we" mode, as in "We offer our customers discounts of over 50 percent."

Postcards

The humble postcard has the power to beat all other direct marketing formats when it comes to generating sales leads. Why is the postcard so effective? It's much less costly to prepare and mail than other direct-mail efforts, but that's not its greatest strength. It can be mailed out practically overnight, but that's not its greatest strength, either.

The real power of a postcard is that it takes only a flip of the wrist for recipients to get your message. They read their name on it, then flip it over to see what's on the other side. Simple, but incredibly powerful. Why? Because a huge percentage of direct mail never even gets opened. That's the key word—"opened." A postcard never has to overcome that obstacle. Even a folded flier has to be opened and unfolded, while all a postcard requires is a flick of the wrist.

More than letters, postcards convey a sense of urgency, making them an ideal way to notify customers of a limited-time offer or special sale. Don't restrict yourself to the standard 4-by-6 inch postcard format, either. Postcards can be as big as a letter-sized piece of paper, and many really benefit from that

BEFORE: This postcard has the basics—for a business card. But it's supposed to grab attention as an advertisement, and it doesn't.

What makes this company special? What makes it worth remembering? There's no telling from this card.

AFTER: This approach catches your eye with the cartoon, the contrasting panels and the proposition.

This headline makes an attractive offer from a memorably named mechanic.

The relevant cartoon makes your message interesting and more palatable.

extra size. Although this costs more (but still not as much as a full direct-mail package), it gives you more room to dramatize your offer. If you do use a larger size, you can make it a picture postcard, with just a large visual on the front and words on the back, next to the recipient's name and address.

Consider the "before and after" makeover on a postcard for SWD Truck Repair (see page 467). Like many service businesses, SWD's services are not an impulse purchase—meaning buyers usually don't leap for the phone right after getting the promotional mailer.

What's a great way to get more attention in the nanosecond of time it takes the recipient to turn the postcard over? First, the company needs a catchier nickname to use for the purposes of advertising. In this case, "The Truck Doctor" fits the bill perfectly. Nicknames can work for many types of service businesses. Some examples:

◆ For a wedding planner: The Marriage Maestro.

◆ For an auto mechanic: The Car Medic.

◆ For a fax machine repair service: The Fax Fixer.

◆ For a party planning service: The Party Smarty.

◆ For a carpenter: The Wood Wizard.

You get the idea. Next, add an eye-catching graphic on the front of the postcard, along with a provocative headline or teaser that conveys the company's benefit. In this example, the illustration shows a struggling truck, and the headline urges "CALL FOR A FREE CHECKUP AT THE TRUCK DOCTOR." It's a nice play on words that offers a benefit few can resist—a free service. Cartoons with copy balloons are an excellent way to cut through the advertising clutter and grab the reader's attention.

Fliers

A hybrid of the postcard and brochure, fliers give you more room to get your message across than a postcard but are cheaper (and easier to design) than a brochure.

Fliers are ideal for certain situations, such as for posting on a bulletin board, sticking under car windshield wipers in a parking lot or stuffing in mailboxes. They're also a good tool to enclose in a sales letter if, for example, you want to notify recipients about a short-term sale or upcoming special event.

Because fliers' primary benefit is that they convey information quickly, make sure yours is easy to read and stands out. Try bright colors to grab the viewer's eye, and use large type so information can be seen from a distance. Keep type brief and to the point. A crowded flier won't get anyone's attention.

While fliers are indeed a useful addition to a marketing campaign, don't

use them as your only direct-mail tool, or your business could come off looking amateurish.

Catalogs

For mail order entrepreneurs, a catalog is the backbone of their businesses. But even if selling by mail is only a small part of what your business is about, you'd be surprised to find out how much you can benefit from a catalog.

If you're picturing the hefty *Spiegel* catalog or a glossy magazine like those sent by Pottery Barn, don't despair. A catalog can be as basic as a four-page, black-and-white fold-over and still be successful. Here are six tips to ensure yours is, too:

1. **Keep it simple.** Don't try to reinvent the wheel. Catalogs look the way they do for a reason. Almost every format you can imagine has been tested numerous times, and the formula you see most often are the overall winners. Choose a size from one of the most common catalog sizes.

2. **Borrow from the best.** The surest way to plot your catalog layout is to study other catalogs—at least 50 or 60, black and white as well as color. You will then have a collection of the best ideas from the best designers and copywriters money can buy. Study the catalogs, and note any useful ideas.

3. **Start a clip file.** Collect useful layout ideas, and divide your clippings into categories with a folder for each of them. Make folders for front covers, back covers and order forms. Then make folders to suit your special interest.

4. **Sketch a basic layout.** Once you gather ideas, you will probably notice the layouts follow a few general patterns. Some use lots of words and only a few illustrations; others use lots of illustrations and few words. Choose one or two basic layouts, and substitute your products for theirs. Examine your clip files for ideas and adjust those ideas to fit your products. For a craftsy product, handwritten copy and illustrations may work; for something high-tech, a slicker look works best. Sketch your ideas, and jot down copy. Next, weed out the bad ideas, and improve on the good ones.

5. **Find the perfect printer.** Shop around—you'll be amazed at the range of prices printers quote you for the same job. If you live in a small town, call large printers in nearby metropolitan areas since they often offer substantial savings and give quotes over the phone. Get at least four bids on any print job you plan to run; get up to 20 on a big one.

    The printers will want to know the physical dimensions of your catalog, the number of

Smart Tip

Trial sizes and sampling work. Have employees pass out product samples in front of your store; if you provide a service, offer a free trial period or consultation.

pages to be printed, the kind of paper you want (stay with the cheapest newsprint to start with), and the number of catalogs you want.

The more catalogs you print, the cheaper your cost per unit. In addition to the catalogs you mail out, you need to include a fresh catalog with each order shipped, give away catalogs to be used as a form of advertising, and have extras to

Beware!

Don't launch a direct-mail campaign (especially a catalog) until you're sure you can handle the orders you might receive. If fulfillment systems aren't in place and orders don't get sent out, you'll lose credibility—and future business.

send when someone expresses interest. If you plan to mail 10,000 catalogs, print 20,000; then distribute the excess over the next few months to get new customers.

6.   **Put it all together.** You can spend tens of thousands of dollars on a mail order catalog—but why should you, when you can produce an attention-getting book so cheaply? Do as much as you can yourself—product drawings, photos, copy. Today's technology, from "idiot-proof" cameras to simple desktop publishing programs, makes catalog production and layout simpler than ever.

But the key to catalog success isn't the technology—it's understanding your customers. Show them why they should buy from you and no one else. Target them with the right mailing lists. And remember, the more you do yourself, the more you save.

Need more help? The Direct Marketing Association can refer you to catalog consultants in your area.

Newsletters

Publishing a company newsletter is a great way to get the word out about your business . . . and keep past customers coming back. Most people actually look at newsletters rather than pitching them into the trash with the rest of the ads.

"The primary benefit of a customer newsletter is keeping your existing customers informed about what you're doing," says Elaine Floyd, author of *Marketing With Newsletters* (EF Communications). Newsletters are also a good way to reach new customers because, if done correctly, they come off as more informative and with less sales hype than most items consumers receive in the mail. In addition to telling readers about your product or ser-

Premium Prospects

Whether you call them premiums, advertising specialties or flat-out bribes, free gifts are a marketing gimmick that works with all demographic groups. Studies show 40 percent of people remember an advertiser's name up to six months after receiving a free gift. Thirty-one percent still use the item up to a year later.

Premiums can be used to generate leads, build name awareness, thank customers, increase store traffic, introduce new products, motivate customers and create an unconscious obligation to buy. Premiums can be used at trade shows, open houses, special events and grand openings.

Classic premiums include T-shirts, baseball caps, jackets, headbands, writing instruments, desk and office accessories, scratch pads and mugs. Mouse pads and screen savers are some of the more recent premiums gaining in popularity.

How to make a premium work for you? Research it first. Make sure the item is matched with your target audience. Also make sure the item is good quality. A cheap premium that breaks or doesn't work in the first place makes a negative impression—just the opposite of what you want.

When choosing a premium, ask five questions:

1. How many people do I want to reach?

2. How much money do I have to spend?

3. What message do I want to print?

4. What gift will be most useful to my prospects?

5. Is this gift unique and desirable? Would I want it?

You can find specialty advertising firms listed in the Yellow Pages. Ask to see their catalogs; compare sample quality and prices.

While the free gift is being offered, focus your marketing and advertising efforts on it. There's no more powerful word in advertising than "free," so put the power of freebies to work for you.

vice, newsletters inform them about developments in your industry or theirs and share information that affects them. "People might not think they need your product or service," says Floyd. "Reading an informative newsletter helps convince them they do."

The businesses that benefit most from newsletters are those that have to educate customers about the advantages of using their product or service. If you own a candy shop, for example, you might not have enough pertinent information for customers to justify a newsletter. On the other hand, a computer consultant could do a real service by publishing a newsletter about the latest software and hardware.

Your newsletter doesn't have to be all information. Including a coupon, special offer or other call to action helps get people to buy. Also, always give upcoming sales or promotions a prominent place in your newsletter. "The promotional aspects of your newsletter should be woven in with the informational," advises Floyd. If you're reporting on your industry, talk about your company's place within the industry. If you're talking about a trend in the economy—the rise of dual-income households, let's say—then tie in the fact that using your company's service helps free up valuable time.

Floyd recommends using the following formula, which she calls RISE, to be sure your newsletter covers all the bases:

◆ **Recognition:** Your newsletter should tell people who you are, what you do and where they can find you. If consumers have to read through two pages of text to find the name of your company, you're not increasing your name recognition. Use your company logo on the newsletter.

◆ **Image:** Your newsletter is an extension of your company's image. If it's interesting and professional-looking, customers will think well of your business. If it's not, they may doubt your credibility. With desktop publishing programs, Floyd says most people can create their own professional-looking newsletter or have it done fairly cheaply by a freelancer.

◆ **Specifics:** Give your readers specific reasons why they should choose your product or service. Vague assertions like "We're the best" don't work nearly as well as matter-of-fact details about exactly what you can do for them.

◆ **Enactment:** Make the reader take action—whether by picking up the phone, mailing in a reply card or coming down to your store.

Strapped for things to write about—or don't have time to write it yourself? Try asking your industry trade association for news services that provide copy in return for a monthly subscription fee. This also ensures the articles are professionally written.

If you can't find a news service, use a clippings service to get story ideas. Though clippings from other publications can't be reprinted without the writer's permission, they can give you ideas for similar articles of your own and keep you updated on hot industry topics.

Tap clients for copy by featuring a "Client of the Month," showing how your product or service solved a problem they were facing. Or team with related businesses; for example, an interior designer could have guest columns written by florists or furniture store owners.

Easy ways to get clients to contribute? Conduct a survey—and print the results. Start a "Letters to the Editor" column. Add a "Q&A" column, where customers can pose problems and other customers can write in with solutions.

Keep your writing style simple, and make sure you get help proofreading if your spelling skills aren't up to snuff. A newsletter full of typos or grammatical errors shows clients you're a careless amateur.

Newsletters can be monthly, quarterly or semimonthly, depending on your budget, available time and how fast-paced your industry is. Quarterly publications are generally sufficient to get your name in front of customers; then increase frequency if needed. The key is to be consistent, so don't take on more than you can handle.

Renting a mailing list isn't generally a good idea for newsletters, says Floyd. "Your newsletter will be better received if the reader knows about you or needs your product," she says. Floyd recommends sending newsletters only to current customers, qualified leads and referrals. When someone gives you a business card, send him or her a newsletter. Then you or a salesperson can call the person later, using the newsletter as a starting point to ask about products or services they might need.

CLASSIFIED ADS

Classified ads don't draw the huge response of a display ad, but they still provide the most economical way to get your business into the public eye. And since they demand neither the eye-catching design of a display ad nor the clever wording of a direct-mail campaign, almost anyone can write them.

What should your ad say? The Newspaper Association of America recommends you simply list your product or service's main benefit to the customer. Does it make people money? Improve their self-image? Use a catchy statement, such as "Feel good now!" to create an impact. Since not every reader is looking for the same benefit, list as many as you can afford. The more readers know about your business, the more they will trust you.

COUPON CUTTERS

If you want to attract and keep customers, you need to offer an incentive. A coupon for a free sample or service, or a discount on your normal prices, can be just the nudge a customer needs to try your new business. Coupons help you reach many goals: introducing a new product or service, increasing repeat business, beating the competition and more.

One of the most powerful ways to use coupons is through direct mail. This method is especially good for occasions such as grand openings or new product/service introductions. How to make the most of your direct-mail coupon campaign? Keep these tips in mind:

◆ Coupons can be offered as a "thank you for buying from us" or a "stop by and try us" message.

◆ A coupon can be a single item for a one-shot promotion or used in combination with other offers.

◆ The value must be substantial enough to make it worthwhile. Better to err on the side of giving too big a discount than to seem cheap.

◆ Use coupon promotions sparingly. They wear themselves out if overused.

◆ Be clear. State exactly what the offer is, how long it lasts and the terms of redemption.

◆ Color-code your coupons if a variety of groups will receive them. For example, if you're mailing to six ZIP codes, color-code them differently so you know how many were redeemed from each area.

The newest way to distribute coupons: on the Internet. Design your Web page so people can e-mail you to receive coupons. This way, you can add them to your mailing list even before the coupons are redeemed. Or consider using a Web coupon service, which offers coupons in booklets by mail or online for consumers to download and print out themselves.

Experts also recommend using white space to make your classified ad stand out from the competition. White space works especially well in newspapers, which sell ads for pennies a word or by the line. If you place just a few words in each line—the first line listing a benefit, the second the name of your company, the third your address, for example—you have a striking, centered ad surrounded by white space.

These brief ads work best when they offer a commonly sold product or service such as tax preparation or catering. Listing the benefits of each isn't essential because the public knows what to expect. White space in classifieds is also effective when you offer a catalog or another form of literature describing your product. In this case, you might place the main benefit in an opening line that is designed to grab the reader's attention, and below the benefit list how to send for the information, noting its price if any. For example, "Play Backgammon Like a Pro" would be a good benefit line in an ad offering free information about a booklet that shows backgammon players how to improve their game.

Ads that use white space are less common in magazines since these ads are often twice as costly as a typical newspaper classified. However, they are often more effective as well—even more so than in a newspaper because few other white space ads will be competing for the attention of the readers.

Before placing a classified ad, write or call the publications that interest you and ask for an advertising kit (also called a media or press kit). Ad kits often include guidelines in the form of booklets, pamphlets or newsletters, which help you construct your ad and give you tips on choosing the main benefit, consolidating words or determining whether the tone should be boldly stated or instead employ a conservative description and a list of benefits. Most ad kits also list demographic information about the readers.

Finally, repeat your ad as often as possible, so long as it brings in enough money to justify its expense. Repeating ads helps customers gain familiarity with your product or service and helps break down sales resistance. Once the ad stops pulling in new accounts, it's time to develop a new ad. A classified that uses fewer words will cost less to run, so it doesn't have to pull as well to justify itself. But sometimes adding more words can help your sales, too. It doesn't hurt to experiment.

How much profit do you need to make on classifieds? Unless you run a one-product, one-sale business, you

Beware!

Don't mess with success. Once you find an advertising idea that works for you, stick with it. Repetition is key to getting your message across.

can build a profitable operation through classifieds just by breaking even, or even by coming in a little under the money since many of those buyers will become repeat customers.

Co-op Advertising

How can a small retailer or distributor maintain a high profile without spending lots of money? One answer is co-op advertising.

Co-op advertising is a cooperative advertising effort between suppliers and retailers—such as between a soda company and a convenience store that advertises the company's products.

Both retailers and suppliers benefit: retailers because co-op advertising increases the amount of money they can spend on ads, and suppliers through increased local exposure and better sales.

Although each manufacturer or supplier that uses co-op advertising sets up its own individual program, all co-op programs run on the same basic premise. The retailer or distributor builds a fund (called accrual) based on the amount of purchases made from the supplier. Then, when the retailer or distributor places ads featuring that supplier's products, the supplier reimburses all or part of the cost of the ad, up to the amount accrued.

To start using co-op advertising, begin by asking your suppliers what co-op programs they offer. Follow their rules carefully to be sure you get reimbursed. Some suppliers require that ads feature only their products, not any other supplier's. Others simply ask that no competing products be included.

Though procedures may vary, there are three basic steps to filing a claim for reimbursement. First, show "proof of performance." For print ads, this is just a copy of the ad exactly as it was printed. If you buy TV or radio ads, you'll need a copy of the script with station affadavits of dates and times aired.

Next, document the cost of the advertising—usually with copies of applicable invoices from the publication or station where you ran the ad. Third, fill out and submit a claim form, which you can get from the supplier.

Other steps to make the most of co-op advertising:

◆ Keep careful records of how much you've purchased from each supplier.

◆ If you try something unusual, such as a sales video or a catalog, get prior approval from each vendor before proceeding.

◆ If you're preparing your own ads, work with an advertising professional to prepare an ad you think will appeal to the manufacturer. Keep in mind the image the manufacturer presents in its own ads.

◆ Make sure your company's name stands out in the ad. Your goal is not so much to sell the supplier's product but to get customers into your store.

◆ If there's no established co-op program, pitch your ad campaign to the vendor anyway.

◆ Expect vendors to help out. After all, you're bringing them business. If your vendor doesn't offer co-op money, look for someone who does.

◆ Be sure to follow up. Money goes only to those who submit claims.

MEASURING ADVERTISING EFFECTIVENESS

Just as important as creating a strong marketing plan is following through on the results. How will you know which ads are working if you don't analyze the results? Check the effectiveness of your advertising programs regularly by using one or more of the following tests:

1. Run the same ad in two different publications with a different identifying mark on each. Ask customers to clip the ad and bring it in for a discount or free sample. Or, if you're running an ad that asks customers to order by mail, put a code in your company address such as "Dept. SI." By looking at the marks on the clipped ads or the addresses on the mail-in orders, you'll be able to tell which ad pulled better.

2. Offer a product at slightly different prices in different magazines. This has the added benefit of showing whether consumers will buy your product at a higher price.

3. Advertise an item in one ad only. Don't have any signs or otherwise promote the item in your store or business. Then count the calls, sales or special requests for that item. If you get calls, you'll know the ad is working.

4. Stop running an ad that you regularly run. See if dropping the ad affects sales.

5. Check sales results whenever you place an ad for the first time.

Checks like these will give you some idea how your advertising and marketing program is working. Be aware, however, that you can't expect immediate results from an ad. Especially with small ads—the type most entrepreneurs are likely to be running—you need to give the reader a "getting to know you" period during which he gets to feel comfortable with your business.

One study showed that an ad from a new company has to be noticed by a prospect a total of nine times before that prospect becomes a customer. The bad news: Two out of every three times you expose a prospect to your marketing message, it's ignored. That means you have to expose a customer to your message an average of 27 times before he or she will buy.

Evaluate an ad's cost-effectiveness, too. Consider the CPM. A cheaper ad is no bargain if it doesn't reach many of your prospects.

GLOSSARY

CPM (cost per thousand): figure that tells you how much it costs to reach 1,000 potential customers with a given form of advertising

Direct mail: any form of advertising material that is mailed directly to potential customers, including catalogs, brochures, letters, fliers, postcards and newsletters

House list: the mailing list a business develops in-house, comprised of names and addresses collected from current or potential customers

List broker: company that rents mailing lists of potential customers to other businesses

Premium: any free giveaway to customers (also called ad specialties); common premiums include key chains, T-shirts, pens and desk accessories

Trade-out: term used in radio industry to refer to bartering products or services for air time

CHAPTER 33

SPREAD THE WORD

How to promote your business

Paid advertising isn't the only way to spread the word about your business. In fact, one of the best ways to get your business noticed doesn't have to cost you a dime. We're talking about public relations.

Public relations is a broad category, spanning everything from press releases and networking at chamber of commerce meetings to sponsoring contests or holding gala special events. This chapter will show you the basics of public relations, and give you plenty of ideas to get started. And ideas are what it's all about because when it comes to public relations, you're limited only by your own imagination.

GETTING PUBLICITY

Just what is public relations? And how does it differ from advertising? Public relations is the opposite of advertising. In advertising, you pay to have your message placed in a newspaper, TV or radio spot. In public relations, the article that features your company is not paid for. The reporter, whether broadcast or print, writes about or films your company as a result of information he or she received and researched.

Publicity is more effective than advertising for several reasons. First, publicity is far more cost-effective than advertising. Even if it isn't free, your only expenses are generally phone calls and mailings to the media.

Second, publicity has greater longevity than advertising. An article about your business will be remembered far longer than an ad.

Publicity also reaches a far wider audience than advertising generally does. Sometimes, your story might even be picked up by the national media, spreading the word about your business all over the country.

Finally, and most important, publicity has greater credibility with the public than does advertising. Readers feel that if an objective third party—the magazine, newspaper or radio reporter—is featuring your company, you must be doing something worthwhile.

Why do some companies succeed in generating publicity while others don't? It's been proved time and time again that no matter how large or small your business is, the key to securing publicity is identifying your target market and developing a well-thought-out public relations campaign. To get your company noticed, follow these steps. You'll notice that many are similar or identical to steps you went through when developing your marketing plan in the last chapter.

1. **Write your positioning statement.** This sums up in a few sentences what makes your business different from the competition.

2. **List your objectives.** What do you hope to achieve for your company through the publicity plan you put into action? List your top five goals in order of priority. Be specific, and always set deadlines.

   Using a clothing boutique as an example, some goals may be to:

   ◆ increase your store traffic, which will translate into increased sales.

   ◆ create a high profile for your store within the community.

3. **Identify your target customers.** Are they male or female? What age range? What are their lifestyles, incomes and buying habits? Where do they live?

4. **Identify your target media.** List newspapers and TV and radio programs in your area that would be appropriate outlets. Make a complete list of the media you want to target, then call them and ask who you should contact regarding your area of business. Identify the specific reporter or producer who covers your area so you can contact them directly. Your local library will have media reference books that list contact names and numbers. Make your own media directory, listing names, addresses, and telephone and fax numbers. Separate TV, radio and print

Smart Tip

Find out the time frame in which the media you are interested in work. Magazines, for instance, typically work several months in advance, so if you want to get a story about your business in the December issue, you may need to send in your idea in June.

sources. Know the "beats" covered by different reporters so you can be sure you are pitching your ideas to the appropriate person.

5.   **Develop story angles.** Keeping in mind the media you are approaching, make a list of story ideas you can pitch to them. Develop story angles you would want to read about in the newspaper or see on television. Plan a 45-minute brainstorming session with your spouse, a business associate or your employees to come up with fresh ideas.

   If you own a toy store, for example, one angle could be to donate toys to the local hospital's pediatric wing. If you own a clothing

---

YOU'RE THE EXPERT

As an entrepreneur, it's your responsibility to get your business noticed—which means you've got to toot your own horn. You need to do whatever it takes to let others know you exist and that you are an expert source of information or advice about your industry.

Being regarded as an industry expert can do wonders for your business. How can you get your expertise known?

◆   Start by making sure you know everything you can about your business, product and industry.

◆   Contact experts in the field and ask them how they became experts.

◆   Talk to as many groups as possible. (If public speaking strikes fear in your heart, you'd better get over it. This is one skill you're going to need as an entrepreneur.) Volunteer to talk to key organizations, service clubs, business groups . . . whoever might be interested in what you have to say. Do it free of charge, of course, and keep it fun, interesting and timely.

◆   Contact industry trade publications and volunteer to write articles, opinion pieces or columns. (If you can't do that, write a letter to the editor.)

◆   Offer seminars or demonstrations related to your business (a caterer could explain how to cook Thai food, for instance).

◆   Host (or guest on) a local radio or TV talk show.

Do all this and, by the time you contact media people and present yourself as an expert, you'll have plenty of credentials.

Meet The Press

Think of a press release as your ticket to publicity—one that can get your company coverage in all kinds of publications or on TV and radio stations. Editors and reporters get hundreds of press releases a day. How to make yours stand out?

First, be sure you have a good reason for sending a press release. A grand opening, a new product, a record-setting sales year, a new location or a special event are all good reasons.

Second, make sure your press release is appropriately targeted for the publication or broadcast you're sending it to. The editor of *Motorcycle World* is not going to be interested in the new baby pacifier you've invented.

To ensure readability, your press release should follow the standard format: typed, double-spaced, on white letterhead with a contact person's name, title, company, address and phone number in the upper right-hand corner. Below this information, put a brief, eye-catching headline in bold type. A dateline—for example, "Los Angeles, California, April 10, 1998—" follows, leading into the first sentence of the release.

Limit your press releases to one or two pages, at most. It should be just long enough to cover the six basic elements: who, what, when, where, why and how. The answers to these six questions should be mentioned in order of their importance to the story.

Don't embellish or hype the information. Remember, you are not writing the article; you are merely presenting the information and showing why it is relevant to that publication. Pay close attention to grammar and spelling. Competition for publicity is intense, and a press release full of typos or errors is more likely to get tossed aside.

Some business owners use gimmicks to get their press releases noticed. But if your release is well-written and relevant, you don't need singing telegrams to get your message across.

If you have the money to invest, you may want to try sending out a press kit. This consists of a folder containing a cover letter, press release, your business card, and photos of your product or location. You can also include any other information that will convince reporters your business is newsworthy: articles other publications have written about your business, product reviews, or information on the company and its principals. If you do send out a press kit, make sure all graphic elements tie in with your company's logo and image.

store, you could alert the local media to a fashion trend in your area. What's flying out of your store so fast you can't keep it in stock? If it's shirts featuring the American flag, you could talk to the media about the return of patriotism. Then arrange for a reporter to speak with some of your customers about why they purchased that particular shirt. Suggest the newspaper send a photographer to take pictures of your customers wearing the shirts.

Bright Idea

Sending out publicity photos with your press release or kit? Make them fun, different and exciting. Editors and reporters see thousands of dull, sitting-at-the-desk photos every year. Come up with a creative way to showcase something photogenic about your business . . . and make it stand out from the pack.

6. **Make the pitch.** Put your thoughts on paper, and send them to the reporter in a "pitch letter." Start with a question or an interesting fact that relates your business to the target medium's audience. For instance, if you were writing for a magazine aimed at older people, you could start off "Did you know over half of women age 50 and older have not begun saving for retirement?" Then lead into your pitch: "As a Certified Financial Planner, I can offer your readers 10 tips to start them on the road to a financially comfortable retirement. . . ." Make your letter no longer than one page; include your telephone number so the reporter can contact you.

    If appropriate, include a press release with your letter (see "Meet The Press" in this chapter). Be sure to include your positioning statement in any correspondence or press releases you send.

7. **Follow up.** Following up is the key to securing coverage. Wait four to six days after you've sent the information, then follow up your pitch letter with a telephone call. If you leave a message on voice mail and the reporter does not call you back, call again until you get him or her on the phone. Do not leave a second message within five days of the first. If the reporter requests additional information, send it immediately and follow up to confirm receipt.

Talking To The Media

Once you reach the reporter on the telephone, remember that he or she is extremely busy and probably on deadline. Be courteous, and ask if he or she has time to talk. If not, offer to call back at a more convenient time. If the reporter can talk to you, keep your initial pitch to 20 seconds; afterward, offer to send written information to support your story ideas.

The following tips will boost your chances of success:

◆ If a reporter rejects your story idea, ask if he or she can recommend someone else who might be interested.

◆ Know exactly what you're going to say before you telephone the reporter. Have it written down in front of you—it's easier, and you'll feel more confident.

◆ Everyone likes a compliment. If you've read a story you particularly enjoyed by the reporter you're contacting, let him or her know. This will also show that you're familiar with the reporter's work.

◆ Be persistent. Remember, not everyone will be interested. If your story idea is turned down, try to find out why and use that information to improve your next pitch. Just keep going, and don't give up. You will succeed eventually.

◆ Don't be a pest. You can be persistent without being annoying. Use your instincts: If the reporter sounds rushed, offer to call back.

◆ Be helpful and become a resource by providing reporters with information. Remember, they need your story ideas: There's only so much they can come up with on their own.

◆ Always remember that assistants get promoted. Be nice to everyone you speak with, no matter how low they are on the totem pole. After you establish a connection, keep in touch; you never know where people will end up.

◆ Say thank you. When you succeed in getting publicity for your business, always write a thank-you note to the reporter who worked on it with you. You'd be surprised how much a note means.

Plan your publicity efforts just as carefully as you plan the rest of your business. You'll be glad you made the effort when you see your company featured in the news—and when you see the results in your bottom line.

Bright Idea

Capitalize on old-fashioned publicity stunts. No, you don't have to swallow goldfish or sit atop a telephone pole, but consider the landscaping company whose precision lawnmowing team shows off its fancy footwork while marching in local parades.

SPECIAL EVENTS

Ever since the first Wild West Show was staged to sell "Doctor Winthrop's Miracle Elixir," businesspeople have understood the value of promotional events. Even the most obscure product or service takes on new cachet when accompanied by a dash of showmanship. From "fun runs" to fashion shows, contests to concerts, businesses have learned it pays to be associated with special events.

In fact, special events are one of the fastest-growing areas of marketing today. And while large corporations shell out billions each year to host events, small companies, too, can use promotions to reach their market in a way no conventional method could.

> **Bright Idea**
>
> Whenever possible, tie your business to a current event or trend. Does your product or service somehow relate to the Olympics, the presidential election, the environment, the hot movie of the moment? Whether you're planning a special event or just sending out a press release, you can gain publicity by association.

No matter how spectacular an event is, however, it can't stand alone. You can use advertising or public relations without doing a special event, but you need both advertising and public relations to make your event work. How do you put together the right mix to make your event successful?

First, you must know what you want to accomplish. The desired outcome of event marketing is no different from that of any other marketing effort: You want to draw attention to your product or service, create greater awareness of it and increase sales.

While the number of special event ideas is infinite, some general categories exist. Following are some of the most popular:

1. **Grand openings:** You're excited about opening your new business. Everyone else will be, too . . . right? Wrong. You have to create the excitement, and a knockout grand opening celebration is the way to do it. From start to finish, your event has to scream "We're here. We're open. We're ready to go. We're better than, different from and more eager to serve you than our competitors. We want to get to know you and have you do business with us."

    A grand opening is one of the best reasons to stage a special event. No one thinks twice about why you're blowing your own horn. What you do want them to think about is what a great time they had at your event.

    That means no run-of-the-mill, garden-variety ribbon-cutting. Be original. If you own an electronics store, open your doors via remote control. If you're opening a yarn store, unravel a huge knitted ribbon. If you sell sporting goods, reel in both ends of an enormous bow until the ribbon is untied. Whatever your specialty, do something unusual, entertaining and memorable.

Also give thought to what other activities go along with your grand opening. Design a terrific invitation, do plenty of publicizing, provide quality refreshments and entertainment, select a giveaway that promotes your business (and draws people into the store to get it), and incorporate some way of tracking who attended your event (contest entry forms, coupons, free newsletter subscriptions, birthday club sign-ups and so on).

2. **Entertainment and novelty attractions:** Time, space and popular appeal are three things to consider if and when you host or sponsor a one-time special attraction. If space permits and a beach motif fits your business, having a huge sand castle built in your parking lot might draw attention and business for the entire time it takes to construct it.

    Just keep in mind that the novelties and entertainment shouldn't last so long or be so distracting that no one finds the time or inclination to do business with you. Think of these events as the appetizer, with your product or service as the main course.

3. **Holidays and seasons:** Some of the most common and easily developed special events are based on holidays or times of year. For example, during the Christmas season, Santa's Workshop can be found in thousands of communities, not just the North Pole. Or kick off the summer season with a "Beach Boys" music marathon.

    Again, when planning an event tied to a holiday or season, make originality your motto. If the average December temperature in your city is a balmy 76 degrees, then don't dredge up icicles and fake snow for the store. Take a cue from your locale: Put antlers on pink flamingos and dress Santa in shorts and sunglasses.

4. **Celebrity appearances:** Working with celebrities is like buying a volatile stock—high risk but high return. If you're will-

Bright Idea

Get publicity by giving an award to a member of your community. An environmental consultant could present an award for the most environmentally sound business; a house painting service could honor the most colorful or prettiest house in town.

ing to go out on a limb, you may harvest the sweetest fruit. Many celebrities are affable, cooperative and generous if they are treated professionally and supplied with all the necessary details in advance.

The key to using a celebrity to promote your business is knowing what kind of "personality" is appropriate for your company and marketing goals. Think about whom you want to attract, what kind of media coverage you want to generate, and what kind of lasting impression you want to create.

Whether you are seeking soap stars, sports stars or movie stars, it's usually best to contact their agents first. If you don't know who a star's agent is, contact a talent agency or the organization the celebrity works for.

Unless you know celebrities personally, you must consider the arrangement a commercial venture for them. There are literally hundreds of details to work out and opportunities at every turn for something to go wrong unless you are experienced in dealing with celebrities or have contacted a reputable talent or public relations agency to help you.

Celebrities don't have to be nationally known names, either. Think about local celebrities in your community who might be willing to be part of your special event. A politician, well-known businessperson or community leader can be an excellent addition to your big day.

5. **Co-sponsoring:** You can partner with complementary businesses to host an event, or you can take part as a sponsor of an established charity or public cause. Sporting events, fairs and festivals have proved to be popular event choices with good track records for achieving companies' marketing goals. Keep in mind not every event is right for every business. As with any marketing strategy, your event must be suited to your customers' needs.

Think about how your company can benefit an event. If you're a florist, for instance, you could provide flowers for a wide range of charity lun-

Beware!

Before sponsoring a contest or giving away a prize, make sure you contact the Federal Trade Commission (FTC), a lawyer specializing in games and promotions, or your secretary of state's office to check out the FTC guidelines governing different types of promotions.

SOCIAL GRACES

Does your business use recycled paper products or donate to a homeless shelter? A growing number of consumers consider such factors when deciding whether to patronize your business.

If you think getting involved in social causes would work for your business, here are some things to consider. First and foremost, customers can smell "phony" social responsibility a mile away, so unless you're really committed to a cause, don't try to exploit customers' concerns to make a profit.

Business consultant David Calabria suggests these steps to making social responsibility work for you—and your community.

1. *Set goals.* What do you want to achieve? What do you want your company to achieve? Do you want to enter a new market? Introduce a product? Enhance your business's image?

2. *Decide what cause you want to align yourself with.* This may be your toughest decision, considering all the options out there: children, the environment, senior citizens, homeless people, people with disabilities . . . the list goes on. Calabria suggests considering a cause that fits in with your products or services; for example, a manufacturer of women's clothing could get involved in funding breast cancer research.

3. *Choose a nonprofit or other organization to partner with.* Get to know the group, and make sure it's sound, upstanding, geographically convenient and willing to cooperate.

4. *Design a program, and propose it to the nonprofit group.* Besides laying out what you plan to accomplish, also include tangible indicators that will measure the program's success.

5. *Negotiate an agreement with the organization.*

6. *Involve employees.* Unless you get employees involved from the beginning, they won't be able to communicate the real caring involved in the campaign to customers.

7. *Involve customers.* Don't just do something good and tell your customers about it later. Get customers involved, too. A sporting goods store could have customers bring in used equipment for a children's shelter, then give them a 15 percent discount on new purchases.

cheons or galas. A health-food retailer could provide free energy bars to participants in a local 10K race. Whatever you do, be sure to promote it with press releases, a sign in your window or a mention in the event's program.

6. **Anniversary celebrations:** This is one special event most people can relate to. Staying in business for a number of years is something to be proud of, so why not share the achievement with others? Throw a party and invite current, past and prospective customers to enjoy your anniversary, too.

Beware!

It's not what you say; it's how you say it. If your speaking voice sounds like Elmer Fudd's, here's how to improve: Breathe. Enunciate. Pace yourself, speaking neither too fast nor too slowly. Nervous? 'Fess up—admitting your insecurity puts the listeners on your side. Finally, remember practice makes perfect.

7. **Games and contests:** From naming a mascot to guessing the number of jelly beans in a jar, contests are a proven means of attracting attention. But they pay off big only when they are properly promoted and ethically managed. So be sure your prizes are first-rate and that you get the word out in a timely and professional manner.

Let people know how and when they can participate. Think through all the ramifications of judging, selecting and awarding a prize. Check out the need for special permits or licenses well before staging any contest (it never hurts to get a legal opinion just to be on the safe side). Above all, deliver on your promises.

Networking

The ability to network is one of the most crucial skills any start-up entrepreneur can have. How else will you meet the clients and contacts necessary to grow your business?

But many people are put off by the idea of networking, thinking it requires a phony, glad-handing personality that oozes insincerity. Nothing could be further from the truth.

Think a moment. What does a good networker do? How does he or she act? What is his or her basic attitude? You will probably be surprised at how much you instinctively know about the subject.

You may decide, for example, that a good networker should be outgoing, sincere, friendly, supportive, a good listener or someone who follows up and stays in touch. To determine other skills an effective networker needs, simply ask yourself "How do I like to be treated? What kinds of people do I trust and consider good friends?"

Now that you have an idea of what attributes a good networker must have, take an objective look at your own interactive abilities. Do you consider yourself shy and regard networking groups as threatening? Do you tend to do all the talking in a conversation? Do you give other people referrals and ideas without a thought to your own personal gain? Can people count on your word?

Many people go to networking events, but very few know how to net-

THE MEET MARKET

To make the most of any networking situation, heed the following do's and don'ts:

♦ **Don't spend too much time with one person, or you defeat the purpose of networking.** Your objective is to take advantage of the entire room. If you spend three minutes with a prospect, that gives you a possibility of 20 contacts per hour. Spending five minutes with each person reduces that to 12 contacts and so on.

♦ **Do give others the chance to sell, too.** At a networking event, everyone wants to sell. You may have to play buyer to get a chance to be a seller. You must be able to wear both hats.

♦ **Do know the kinds of problems you can solve rather than a bunch of boring facts about your product or service.** Talk in terms of how you—not just your product or service—benefit customers.

♦ **Don't be negative.** Never complain about or bad-mouth a person or business. You never know whether the prospect you're talking to has some connection, interest or affiliation with the people, company or product you're slamming.

♦ **Don't forget your manners.** "Please" and "thank you" go a long way toward creating a good impression.

♦ **Do be prepared.** When people ask you what you do, be ready to describe your business in one short, interesting sentence that intrigues and enlightens.

work effectively. Networking is more than just getting out and meeting people. Networking is a structured plan to get to know people who will do business with you or introduce you to those who will.

The best way to succeed at networking is to make a plan, commit to it, learn networking skills and execute your plan. To make the best plan, ask yourself: What do I want to achieve? How many leads (prospects) do I want per month? Where do my customers and prospects go to network? What business organizations would benefit me? How can I build my image and my

IMAGE POWER

Throughout this book, we've touched on various aspects of developing a corporate image. Your business cards, logo, signage and letterhead all tie into that image. So do your marketing materials and ads. It's equally important to keep your image in mind when planning a publicity campaign.

Any events or causes you participate in should be in keeping with your business image. If your company is in a fun, creative industry, like a toy store, you can get zany and silly with special events like a balloon-popping race or pot-bellied pig races. On the other hand, if you're in a serious industry like medical transcription or accounting, it makes more sense to take part in more serious events like a 10K walk or a blood drive.

The publications and broadcast stations you target with your publicity must fit your image, too. A company that makes clothes targeted at teenage skateboarders would prefer publicity in a cutting-edge lifestyle magazine rather than in a mainstream publication aimed at middle-aged moms. Think about how the publication or broadcast will affect your image, and make sure the results will be positive.

Don't forget the most important parts of your public image: yourself and your employees. Your marketing materials and corporate sponsorships can tout your socially responsible, kind-hearted company ... but if your employees are rude and uncaring toward customers, all your efforts to promote that image will be in vain.

Make sure your employees understand the image you are trying to convey to customers and how they contribute to creating that image. Show them by example how you want them to behave whenever they're in the public eye.

business's image? What would I like to volunteer to do in the community?

Make a five-year networking plan listing your five best customers, five targeted prime prospects and five targeted organizations. Next, set goals for involvement in each organization, how much time you'll need to commit to each organization and prospect, and what kinds of results you expect.

Now that you have a plan, get committed. Tell yourself that you will devote enough time and effort to make it work. Half the battle of networking is getting out there and in the swim.

> ## Bright Idea
>
> Always be alert to networking opportunities. Don't rule out traffic school, Little League games, aerobics class and other nonbusiness events as chances to share your story. Leisure activities provide a natural setting for networking and encourage relationship-building.

The other half of the battle is learning to network effectively. Typically, ineffective networkers attend several networking groups but visit with the same friends each time. Obviously, this behavior defeats the entire purpose of networking. If you stick with familiar faces, you never meet anyone new. And since most people stay within their circle of friends, newcomers view the organization as a group of cliques. This is one reason people fear going to new organizations by themselves—they are afraid no one will notice them.

The trick with networking is to become proactive. This means taking control of the situation instead of just reacting to it. Networking requires going beyond your comfort zone and challenging yourself. Try these tips:

> ## Smart Tip
>
> After you finish talking to someone at a networking event, take a few seconds to jot down pertinent information on the back of their business card. This can be anything from their business's biggest problem to the college their daughter attends—whatever will give you a "hook" to follow up on when you call them later on.

1. **Set a goal to meet five (or more) new people at each event.** Whenever you attend a group, whether a party, mixer or industry luncheon, make a point of heading straight for people you don't know. Greet the newcomers (they'll love you for it!). If you don't make this goal a habit, you'll naturally gravitate toward the same old acquaintances.

2. Try one or two new groups per month. You can attend almost

any organization's meetings a few times before you must join. This is another way to stretch yourself and make a new set of contacts. Determine what business organizations and activities you'd best fit into. It may be the chamber of commerce, the arts council, a museum society, a civic organization, a baseball league, a computer club or the PTA. Attend every function you can that synergizes your goals and customer/prospect interaction.

> ## Smart Tip
>
> How do you join an organization and reap maximum benefits? Easy: Meet with the organization's leader, and share how you'd like to get involved. Get known by those who count in the organization. Find other doers in the group. Ask others for information and advice. Never miss meetings.

3. **Carry your business cards with you everywhere.** You never know when you might meet a key contact, and if you don't have your cards with you, you lose out. Take your cards to church, the gym, parties, the grocery store, even on walks with the dog.

4. **Don't make a beeline for your seat.** Frequently, you'll see people at networking groups sitting at the dinner table staring into space—half an hour before the meal is due to start. Why are they sitting alone? Take full advantage of the valuable networking time before you have to sit down. Once the meeting starts, you won't be able to mingle.

5. **Don't sit by people you know.** Mealtime is a prime time for meeting new people. You may be in that seat for several hours, so don't limit your opportunities by sitting with your friends. This is a wonderful chance to get to know new people on either side of you. Sure, it's more comfortable to hobnob with familiar faces. But remember, you are spending precious time and money to attend this event. Get your money's worth; you can talk to your friends some other time.

6. **Get active.** People remember and do business with leaders. Don't just warm a chair; join a committee or become a board member. If you don't have time for that, volunteer to help with hospitality at the door or checking people in. This gives you a reason to talk to others, gets you involved in the inner workings of the group, and provides more visibility.

7. **Be friendly and approachable.** Pretend you are hosting the event. Make people feel welcome. Find out what brought them

there and see if there is any way you can help them. Introduce them to others, make business suggestions or give them a referral. Not only will you probably make a friend, but putting others at ease eliminates self-consciousness. A side benefit: What goes around comes around. If you make the effort to help others, you'll soon find people helping you.

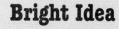

Bright Idea

When considering media that can publicize your business, don't forget the "hidden" media in your community. These can include free publications for singles and seniors, for tourists, for local companies' employees, and for social or charitable organizations like the Junior League.

8. **Set a goal for what you expect from each meeting.** Your goals can vary from meeting to meeting. Examples might be: learning from the speaker's topic, looking for new prospects, discovering industry trends or connecting with peers. If you work out of your home, you may find your purpose is simply to get out and talk to people face to face. Focusing your mind on your goal before you even walk into the event keeps you on target.

9. **Be willing to give to receive.** Networking is a two-way street. Don't expect new contacts to shower you with referrals and business unless you are equally generous. Follow up on your contacts; keep in touch; always share information or leads that might benefit them. You'll be paid back tenfold for your thoughtfulness.

GLOSSARY

Positioning statement: statement that sums up, in one or two sentences, what differentiates your business from others

Pitch letter: an introductory letter sent to members of the media in an effort to get publicity for a business; sometimes this is a cover letter accompanying a press release

Press kit: packet (typically a folder) containing a cover letter, press release, photos and additional information about a business; sent to members of the media to get publicity for the business

Press release: standard written notice sent to the media in an effort to get publicity for your business

CHAPTER 34

NET WORKS

Setting up
your company
Web site

Sometimes it seems as if the World Wide Web is all you hear about these days. In fact, there's so much information floating around about the Internet, it can be hard to know where to start when promoting your business online.

The Internet can be used to do everything from getting publicity to actually selling your products and services. Some methods of publicizing your business are virtually free, others require a more substantial investment, but all will get results when used in the right way. The following chapter takes a closer look at the do's and don'ts of promoting your business online.

DO YOU NEED A WEB SITE?

Should you go online? Many experts believe small businesses have the most to gain by going online. "The Internet is leveling the playing field for small businesses that compete against big companies," says Stephen Fickas, an associate professor of computer and information science at the University of Oregon in Eugene. "The wide-open opportunities available online today are like those found last century in the Wild West."

But don't build a Web site just because it's the trendy thing to do. "The key question is, Are your customers and potential customers online?" says Jill Ellsworth, co-author of *New Internet Business Book* (John Wiley & Sons). "If your target audience is online, you should be, too." If your customers aren't online, spending time and money to establish a Web site could be a big waste.

Just as with any other marketing strategy, successfully going online requires a plan of attack. You can't just slap up a Web site and expect orders to come pouring in. Start by asking yourself what you want your online presence to achieve.

Setting up a Web site is no guarantee of instant riches. Very few companies have seen substantial sales online. Then why put up a Web page? Because even if your page is little more than an electronic billboard for your company, it's still a powerful tool for building a business. Web sites can serve a number of goals: advertising, selling, building prospect lists and more.

Setting up a Web site offers several advantages over other modes of marketing:

◆ You can change content quickly, easily and at virtually no cost.

◆ You can provide customers with essentially an infinite amount of product information.

◆ You don't have to worry about printing or postage costs.

Another advantage is that on the Web, the clock no longer matters. "Your business can be open 24 hours a day, seven days a week," says Gail Houck, a consultant and Web strategist.

What's more, Houck says, a Web site done right is a great way to build customer loyalty. Many Web-savvy companies use online technology to provide low-cost, detailed customer assistance tips, plus constantly updated information on their products or services. When a customer can get answers to questions at any hour of day or night, his or her loyalty to your company will be stronger.

GETTING ONLINE

There are a number of ways to do business online—from starting a "store" on the World Wide Web to using e-mail to entice customers to shop. "Some of these online tactics are very low-cost but still get you a lot of mileage," says Marcia Yudkin, author of *Marketing Online* (Plume/Penguin).

"The cheapest way to get a foothold in the Net is to make your online presence known by using forums," advises Yudkin. The major online services offer hundreds of forums—essentially electronic bulletin boards—where users are welcome to ask questions, give ad-

> **Smart Tip**
>
> If you don't respond to customers' e-mail messages within a day or two, you're liable to lose them as customers. If a large volume of e-mail bogs you down, ask your e-mail provider if it supports "auto-responding." This feature sends everyone an automatic reply that answers commonly asked questions, thanks them for e-mailing, or posts whatever information you want to include.

vice or spout opinions. Many thousands of users visit these boards daily, meaning creative marketers can find a large audience.

Yudkin suggests a strategy she uses herself to sell books, tapes and seminars: Regularly visit relevant forums, and when you spot a user question that relates to your expertise, post a helpful reply. Along the way, mention your business' services or products—and, very often, you'll find users come to your Web site ready to buy.

Keep stoking that urge to buy through clever use of e-mail. Because the

E-Mail Etiquette

To make sure your e-mail messages are received in the manner you intended, you must put as much thought into them as you do any other form of communication. Online communication is rife with opportunities for misunderstandings. Because you can't use gestures and vocal inflections or see other people's body language and facial expressions, you need to be extra careful to make sure you get your message across. Here are some tips:

◆ Don't type in all uppercase letters. This is the online equivalent of shouting.

◆ Carefully check your spelling and grammar. If your e-mail program doesn't have a spelling checker, create your messages in a word processing program that does. Your communications represent your business, and a message full of misspellings suggests your work is equally sloppy.

◆ Write every message as if the whole world will see it. It's easy for customers or employees to forward messages to others (accidentally or on purpose).

◆ Use a "signature file" to create and save signature information—your name, your company's name, address and telephone number—so you don't have to retype it every time.

◆ Make your messages as concise as possible, and stick to a single subject. Long messages take time to transfer to your recipients' computers.

◆ Use the "subject line" on all your e-mail messages so recipients can see at a glance what you are writing about.

◆ Keep it simple. Learn to write short, succinct messages so you don't waste people's time.

Bright Idea

Provide a "guest book" at your site so that customers can sign in, type their comments and indicate whether they want to be contacted for special sales.

Internet is not the place for a "hard sell" approach (see "Spam-Free Zone" in this chapter), Yudkin avoids overt selling in her forum posts. However, she often urges users to contact her directly to get her list of FAQs—"Frequently Asked Questions"—about her areas of expertise. Users who send a message to her e-mail address automatically receive by return e-mail her FAQ list, which provides plenty of useful information as well as plugs for her products.

"E-mail is a great tool for getting out information about what you do at little cost," Yudkin says. How little? Yudkin spends $25 per month to operate several automatic e-mail accounts.

You can also profitably use e-mail to contact customers and prospects, and most businesses would gain by doing so, says Steve Jones, a consultant and communications professor. "Ask for e-mail addresses from customers. Build a list, and use it to send out discount coupons, spec sheets, anything you otherwise would mail or fax," Jones says. "The cost is small, and delivery is instantaneous. The results of creatively using e-mail can be substantial."

SETTING UP A WEB SITE

Before you set up a Web site, you need to find a place to put it. You can either put your Web site up through an Internet access provider (IAP), such as America Online or Earthlink, or through a Web-hosting service.

Most IAPs provide some type of free space for members' Web sites. There are drawbacks to this free space, however. For one thing, most IAPs require that advertisements for their service appear on your pages. But the biggest hitch is that selling at sites erected on free space is generally prohibited. (Find out for sure by checking the provider's "terms of service," or TOS, which should be prominently flagged on the welcoming screen.)

Other negatives to setting up with an IAP: You can't have your own domain name (such as www.yourcompany-name.com), and you generally are not furnished with reports detailing the number of "hits" (when your site is viewed or accessed) or your visitors' domain names, which help you track who is coming to your Web site. None of this means you have to rule out the

Smart Tip

Choose your Web site address carefully. Make sure it's easy to remember and spell.

Smart Tip

If you want to get noticed online offer to provide content to others. Electronic newsletters and magazines always need new information. One of the best ways to create an online presence is to e-mail sites and volunteer content on a regular basis.

space for business; you can still erect a site that offers plenty of information about your products and services.

If you do want to sell online, however, or if you want more space than an IAP provides, then you'll need to sign up with a Web-hosting service, which provides site storage and management. There are hundreds of these available, with prices ranging from a bare-bones $10 per month for storage space alone to $75 or more per month for storage space, free access to your site, and Web-page authoring software.

Use your favorite search engine to find Web-hosting options; then investigate each service before you sign up. Ask about their rates, years in business, the different modem rates they support, security features and the amount of backups they perform. If you're going to sell products, see if the service provider offers features like electronic ordering blanks to notify you of orders. Also ask about the kinds of tracking reports provided; most Website hosts furnish weekly and even daily reports.

Always ask any potential Web-hosting service for the e-mail addresses of current customers. Contact a dozen or so and ask for feedback: How reliable is the server? How fast is it? Does tech support promptly handle problems? If their customers are unhappy with the Web-hosting service, your customers probably won't stick around, either.

If you just want a relatively simple Web site that is a source of information about your business's products or services and you don't care about a domain name or tracking reports, the IAP route may be for you. However, if you want a more sophisticated Web site and you want to sell your products and services on it, then a Web-hosting service may be your best bet.

Selling Online

When setting up a Web site to sell, the two most important factors to consider are organization and security. If your site will comprise many pages, it is a good idea to draw an organizational chart of your entire site beforehand to ensure that all pages are linked to your home page (the first page of your site).

Start by studying Web sites that sell

Bright Idea

To learn about credit card transactions, security and other online sales information, visit the Wilson Internet Services site at www.wilson.web.com/.

products or services similar to yours. What do you like—and dislike—about them? How easy is it to place an order? How fast does information download? Can you quickly find what you need?

The old adage that you only have one chance to make a good first impression is absolutely true on the Web. Companies selling their products or services must make sure that visitors can easily move around their Web site, that pages load as quickly as possible, and that there is an e-mail address or phone number for those with questions or comments. Once those pieces are in place, the second most important factor is security, especially if companies are going to conduct electronic credit card transactions over the Web.

Buying online is still a relatively new concept, and many potential buyers are concerned about security. They will not furnish credit card infor-

SELLING SMARTS

To learn more about selling online, visit these Web sites:

◆ *The Common Gateway Interface* (CGI) (http://hoohoo. ncsa.uiuc.edu/cgi/) is a site that introduces newcomers to CGI—the programs that allow a form to be sent to a Web server computer for processing and the results to be sent back to the page from which the form was sent. Here, you can download sample CGI programs from which you can create your own CGI programs.

◆ *LinkExchange* (www.linkexchange.com/index.html) is a free service that helps Web sites advertise each other. When you join, you agree to display advertising banners on your site; in return, your advertising appears at other members' sites.

◆ *Wilson Internet Services* (www.wilsonweb.com/) contains many articles about the best ways to sell goods and services online and to market your site. Articles cover a variety of sales and marketing topics. The site also provides "Web Marketing Today," a free electronic newsletter.

◆ *PerlShop Shopping Cart Script* (www.arpanet.com/Perl-Shop/ perlshop.html) is a free CGI shopping-cart script. To use this script, you must display a PerlShop logo on the main page of your catalog. You must also provide a link to the PerlShop home page. PerlShop runs on computers using UNIX or Windows operating systems.

mation unless they know that a site is completely safe from intruders. When they send electronic order forms, buyers don't want hackers grabbing their account numbers to do a little shopping of their own.

To show your customers that you are thinking about their welfare, you need to offer them choices. They should be able to call a toll-free number, send a check to your street address or fax you an order-form page that they printed from your site. You can also use special programs to conduct online transactions safely.

Here's a closer look at various ways to sell online:

1. **Phone, fax or mail:** The simplest way to sell online is to have customers call, fax or mail in their orders, just as they would with a paper catalog. Simply create an illustrated online catalog with product information and prices. In a prominent place on each page of your site, include your telephone number, mailing address and e-mail address so that customers can contact you—either to place an order or to ask a question.

2. **Selling electronically:** A slightly more complex way to run a sales site is to have your customers send you e-mail to place an order, as well as to ask questions and make comments. You or the person setting up your Web site will need to add a *Mailto* command to a HyperText Markup Language (HTML) statement in each page at your site. Using HTML form tags, or commands, you can also create order forms that your customers can fill in and send electronically to your e-mail address by using the *Mailto* command or by clicking on a button.

    Online forms usually require Common Gateway Interface (CGI) programming and a knowledge of the HTML forms tags. Be sure to get permission from your Web-site host, and be aware that because order forms and CGI programs use extra computer and storage resources, you may have to pay more for your Internet connection.

3. **Shopping-cart programs:** The most expensive method for operating a secure sales site is using a shopping-cart program, which is also known as an electronic catalog system.

Dollar Stretcher

Looking for an easy, inexpensive way to market your new Web site? Call your local phone company. Several regional phone companies are beginning to list businesses' World Wide Web and e-mail addresses in their telephone directories. Or, you can add a line to your existing Yellow Pages advertising.

SPAM-FREE ZONE

The Internet is its own community, with its own set of rules—rules that entrepreneurs must understand to market effectively online. The primary rule: Don't "spam" or send "junk e-mail." (Spamming is the indiscriminate sending of messages to Usenet newsgroups; junk e-mail is the term for sending unsolicited messages to multiple e-mail boxes.)

Online users are leery of what they call "crass commercial advertising." How can you advertise without offending? Jason Catlett, president of Junkbusters Corp., which monitors junk e-mail, junk mail and junk telemarketing, believes the key is staying within the bounds of "good behavior."

"The basic rules are: Don't spam, and don't post commercial messages to newsgroups that have rules against these types of messages," Catlett explains. "Most newsgroups—especially those that are moderated—post a message containing regulations for those visiting and using the group."

Catlett says the best way to market on the Web is by getting people to come to your Web site, instead of sending your message to them. Another option is offering to e-mail information or product updates to people who request it. This way, you avoid bombarding people with unsolicited messages. And always offer users the option of discontinuing the messages. Advertisers who offend too many people on the Net run the risk that action will be taken against them, so be sure to mind your manners.

Want more details on what to do and what not to do? The Internet Engineering Task Force's Responsible Use of the Network Working Group is an organization of volunteers that helps set Internet standards and guidelines. Its 13-page guide includes policy statements from several organizations that oversee the Internet community. Called Requests for Comments (RFC) #1855, *Netiquette Guidelines* is an etiquette guide for all Internet users. Visit www.dtcc.edu/cs/rfc1855.html to get a copy.

As a customer shops, a shopping-cart program accumulates information: a unique customer identification to prevent all the current orders from overlapping, customer address information for automatic computation of shipping charges and taxes, and a record and availability of each piece of selected merchandise.

When the computer signals that the order is complete, the program totals the order, takes credit card information, verifies the credit card, and writes the order to a file for later processing.

This type of program provides many features, which may include automatic credit card checks, security options such as encryption (turning the credit card information into coded characters that cannot be read by outsiders), sophisticated searches, sales-tax and shipping calculations, and online help for visitors.

Most shopping-cart programs cost hundreds or thousands of dollars to license. You can find shopping-cart programs by searching online using your favorite search engine.

Whatever system you use for online selling, the important thing is to use common sense. Make sure your order form is easy for customers to use and that you provide alternate ways to place an order for those who are wary about putting their credit-card numbers on the Internet.

Setting Up The Site

Should you have a Web site set up for you or do it yourself? Designing a Web page used to require hours of laborious wrestling with HTML. But new Web-authoring tools are easier to use. With many programs, building a Web site involves little more than pointing and clicking a mouse.

Visit your local software store, or search online, and you'll find a multitude of Web-authoring programs. If you're a beginner, look for a software program that comes with an assortment of templates. This way, all you have to do is tweak them a little, and you're done.

Even though setting up a Web site is fairly easy, many busy business owners have other things to do with their time or simply prefer getting professional help. If that's the case, you have literally hundreds of companies to choose from. But these days, with everybody and his uncle hanging out a shingle and calling themselves Web page designers, you've got to be careful.

"There are people doing this as a business and people just having a good time," cautions Susan Estrada, author of *Connecting to the Internet* (O'Reilly & Associates). "Select the ones doing it as a business, and make

> ### Smart Tip
>
> Want to set up a Web site ... fast? BusinessWeb, a service offered by CompuServe, claims it gives entrepreneurs all the tools they need to build a Web site in as little as two hours—and costs are minimal. Visit http://businessweb.csi.com, and you'll be walked through the seven-step process.

sure the group you're working with is somewhat stable."

Before selecting a company to do your site, take a look at other sites they've created. Make sure both graphics and text live up to your expectations. It's a good idea to sketch a rough outline of what you want, says Estrada, so you can find out if the developer can handle it.

Setting up a Web site is just the first step. Because the Internet relies on a constant supply of new content, you'll

Dollar Stretcher

Seeking free art for your Web site? Search the Web for free art by graphic artists who are eager to get their work in the public eye. Many will let you download graphics and even animated images for free.

need to update your Web site regularly so visitors have a reason to keep coming back. Make sure the Web designer you use is either willing to update your site for you or can show you how to do it yourself.

ATTRACTING VISITORS TO YOUR SITE

The greatest Web site in the world does you no good if no one visits it. And attracting visitors is getting tougher by the day. With literally thousands of new Web sites created every day, the competition is tough. Here are some ideas for getting visitors to your site:

1. **Promote your Web site through all your marketing materials.** Put your Web site address on your business cards, brochures, letterhead, product packaging, on promotional items, in your ads and anywhere else you can think of.

2. **Get listed with the major search engines.** InfoSeek, Excite, AltaVista, Yahoo!, HotBot and Lycos are the most popular search engines. Visit their Web sites for instructions on getting your site's address, or URL, listed with them. That way, when online users do a search for "tennis rackets," your sporting goods shop's Web site will come up.

   In addition to the big-name search engines, there are hundreds of smaller search engines on the Web. Search online for companies that will do the legwork involved in getting your business listed with these engines.

3. **Enroll in free link exchange programs.** These programs will display your company's banner on other sites if you make space for third-party banners on yours. Just as with search engines,

there are many link exchange programs. Search online to find them.

4. **Set up links to related sites.** A "link" allows visitors to your site to click on a Web site address and instantly link to another company's Web site. To get the ball rolling, simply e-mail related sites asking if they would be interested in putting up links to each other's sites. For example, a florist could put up a link to a local bridalwear shop's site.

KEEPING VISITORS AT YOUR SITE

You've gotten customers to visit your site. Now, how do you keep them there? "A lot of companies just stick their [product] information on the Web and then wonder why people aren't buying," says Rosalind Resnick, co-author of *The Internet Business Guide: Riding the Information Superhighway to Profit* (Sams Publishing). Here's her advice on setting up a site that tempts users to stay.

◆ **Hit 'em hard.** Put all your company's key information, including your e-mail address or toll-free number, on the first screen. That way, potential customers won't have to wait until all your information loads to get an idea of what your company is all about.

◆ **Make connections.** If possible, hyperlink your e-mail address; this means visitors can simply click to open a message blank and send you a note.

◆ **Have fun.** People who surf the Internet are looking for fun. You don't have to be wild and wacky (unless you want to). Just make sure you offer original content presented in an entertaining way.

◆ **Don't overdose on graphics.** Since not everyone has high-speed modems, go easy on the art. If it takes too long to download, users will get antsy.

◆ **Add value.** Offering something useful customers can do adds tremendous value to your site. For example, customers can track their own packages at the Federal Express site, or concoct a recipe for a new drink at the Stolichnoya vodka site. While it doesn't have to be quite so elaborate, offering users the ability to download forms, play games or create something useful or fun will keep them coming back.

◆ **Keep it simple.** Don't build a site that's more than three or four levels deep. Internet users love to surf, but they get bored when they have to sift through loads of information to find what they're looking for.

◆ **Provide a map.** Use icons and button bars to create clear navigational paths. A well-designed site should have a button at the bottom of each subpage that transports the visitor back to the site's home page.

◆ **Stage a contest.** Nothing is more compelling than giving something away. Have all contestants fill out a registration form so you can find out who's coming to your site.

◆ **Make payment a snap.** If you're setting up an online storefront, give customers an easy way to pay you. Consider including an online order form, toll-free ordering number or fax line.

GLOSSARY

FAQ (Frequently Asked Questions): many Web sites feature lists of FAQs about the business, product or service that users can read

Junk e-mail: unsolicited e-mail, typically advertising-related

Link: allows visitors to one site to click on a URL in the text and instantly link to another Web site

Shopping-cart program: method of operating a secure site for selling products online; also called electronic catalog system

Spam: (v.) the indiscriminate sending of messages (usually advertising-related) to online user groups; (n.) a message so sent

URL (Universal Resource Locator): a Web site's address

Also see the glossary for Part 5 Chapter 30.

CHAPTER 35

SHOW & SELL

Effective selling techniques

No matter what business you're in, if you're an entrepreneur, you're in sales. "But I hate to sell," you groan. You're not alone. Many people are intimidated by selling—either because they're not sure how to proceed or they think they don't have the "right" personality to sell.

Well, guess what? Anyone can sell—anyone, that is, who can learn to connect with the customer, listen to his or her needs and offer the right solutions. In fact, as your business's founder, you're better positioned than anyone else to sell your products and services. Even if you have a team of crack salespeople, there's no one else who has the same passion for, understanding of and enthusiasm about your product as you do. And once you finish reading this chapter, you'll have plenty of sales skills as well.

UNDERSTANDING YOUR UNIQUE SELLING POSITION

Before you can begin to sell your product or service to anyone else, you have to sell yourself on it. This is especially important when your product or service is similar to those around you. Very few businesses are one-of-a-kind. Just look around you: How many clothing retailers, hardware stores, air conditioning installers or electricians are truly unique?

The key to effective selling in this situation is what advertising and marketing professionals call a "unique selling proposition" (USP). Unless you can pinpoint what makes your business unique in a world of homogeneous competitors, you cannot target your sales efforts successfully.

Pinpointing your USP requires some hard soul-searching and creativity. One way to start is to analyze how other companies use their USPs to their advantage. This requires careful analysis of other companies' ads and marketing messages. If you analyze what they *say* they sell, not just their product or service characteristics, you can learn a great deal about how companies distinguish themselves from competitors.

For example, Charles Revson, founder of Revlon, always used to say he sold *hope,* not makeup. Some airlines sell friendly service, while others sell on-time service. Neiman Marcus sells luxury, while Wal-Mart sells bargains.

Each of these is an example of a company that has found a USP "peg" on which to hang its marketing strategy. A business can peg its USP around *product* characteristics, *price* structure, *placement* strategy (location and distribution) or *promotional* strategy. These are what marketers call the "four

MAKING TIME

Many new business owners fall into a common cycle: They have so much work to do, there is no time for marketing and sales. A few months go by, and work slows down—so you begin marketing heavily, doing everything you can think of until work rolls in again. Then you stop marketing, focus on work . . . and repeat the whole cycle all over again.

No matter how busy you are, you must always make time for marketing and sales, or you'll find yourself trapped on this economic roller coaster. Consider this: In the fastest-growing small companies in the United States, the company presidents spend an average of 40 percent of their time each week on advertising and marketing. As the owner of a start-up, you should expect marketing to consume 60 percent of your time or more.

Kim Gordon, president of marketing consulting firm National Marketing Federation Inc., says a well-rounded sales and marketing program reaches out to prospects in three stages of readiness—cold, warm and hot. Cold prospects are companies or people you've targeted, but that have little or no information about you. Warm prospects are those you've familiarized with your products and services. With a little legwork, they'll eventually turn into hot prospects—a category that also includes current customers and referrals.

To get off the economic roller coaster, focus on all prospects in all three stages. Don't neglect the warm prospects, or they'll soon cool off again. Adopt an overall marketing strategy that combines sales tactics with the marketing strategies discussed throughout Part 6.

Bright Idea

Condition prospects to say yes by asking questions they will agree with. "It's a great day, isn't it?" or "You got an early start today, didn't you?" Little questions like these help start customers on a momentum that builds trust. Subconsciously, because they are agreeing with you, they begin to trust you.

P's" of marketing. They are manipulated to give a business a market position that sets it apart from the competition.

Sometimes a company focuses on one particular "peg," which also drives the strategy in other areas. A classic example is Hanes L'Eggs hosiery. Back in an era when hosiery was sold primarily in department stores, Hanes opened a new distribution channel for hosiery sales. The idea: Since hosiery was a consumer staple, why not sell it where other staples were sold—in grocery stores?

That placement strategy then drove the company's selection of product packaging (a plastic egg) so the pantyhose did not seem incongruent in the supermarket. And because the product did not have to be pressed and wrapped in tissue and boxes, it could be priced lower than other brands.

Here's how to uncover your USP and use it to power up your sales:

1. **Put yourself in your customers' shoes.** Too often, entrepreneurs fall in love with their product or service and forget that it is the customer's needs, not their own, that they must satisfy. Step back from your daily operations and carefully scrutinize what your customers really want. Suppose you own a pizza parlor. Sure, customers come into your pizza place for food. But is food all they want? What could make them come back again and again and ignore your competition? The answer might be quality, convenience, reliability, friendliness, cleanliness, courtesy or customer service.

    Remember, price is never the only reason people buy. If your competition is beating you on pricing because they are larger, you have to find another sales feature that addresses customers' needs and then build your sales and promotional efforts around that unique feature.

Smart Tip

Want to know the best way to get through to a prospect? Send a letter, then follow it up with a phone call. Next best is a referral. Then comes a cold call, then a personal visit. Least effective is a single direct-mail piece.

2. **Know what motivates your customers' behavior and buying decisions.** Effective marketing requires you to be an amateur psychologist. You need to know what drives and motivates customers. Go beyond the traditional customer demographics, such as age, gender, race, income and geographic location that most businesses collect to analyze their sales trends. For our pizza shop example, it is not enough to know that 75 percent of your customers are in the 18-to-25 age range. You need to look at their motives for buying pizza—convenience, taste, peer pressure and so on.

   Perhaps one of the best marketing tips I ever heard was from an entrepreneur who sold training products. He told me cosmetics and liquor companies are great examples of businesses that know the value of psychologically oriented promotion. People buy these products based on their desires (for pretty women, luxury, glamour and so on), not on their needs.

3. **Uncover the real reasons customers buy your product instead of a competitor's.** As your business grows, you'll be able to ask your best source of information: your customers. For example, the pizza entrepreneur could ask them why they like his pizza over others, plus ask them to rate the importance of the features he offers, such as taste, size, ingredients, atmosphere and service. You'll be surprised how honest people are when you ask how you can improve your service.

   Since your business is just starting out, you won't have a lot of customers to ask yet, so "shop" your competition instead. Many retailers routinely drop into competitors' stores to see what and how they are selling. If you're really brave, try cornering a few of your competitors' customers after they leave the premises and asking what they like and dislike about the competitors' products and services.

Once you have gone through this three-step market intelligence process, you need to take the next—and hard-

Smart Tip

Sell to the people most likely to buy. Your best prospects have a keen interest in your product or service and the money to purchase it. If you're selling fax machines, don't try to sell to people who have never bought one. Sell to those who already have one or those you know are interested in buying one. Show them how yours is superior.

est—step: clearing your mind of any preconceived ideas about your product or service and being brutally honest. What features of your business jump out at you as something that sets you apart? What can you promote that will make customers want to patronize your business? How can you position your business to highlight your USP?

Don't get discouraged. Successful business ownership is not about having a unique product or service; it's about making your product stand out—even in a market filled with similar items.

COLD-CALLING

The aspect of selling that strikes the greatest fear in people's hearts is usually cold calls. A good way to make cold calls more appealing is to stop thinking of them as "cold" calls. Try thinking of them as "introductory" calls instead. All you're trying to do is introduce yourself and your business to the prospect.

It's important to understand the purpose of introductory calls so you have a realistic attitude about this type of business development activity. Phone prospecting takes longer to pay off than other types of marketing efforts, so go into it knowing you're exploring a new frontier, and it's going to take some time to get results.

Just as with any marketing method, you should never make introductory calls without a predetermined plan. First, always use a targeted list of prospects when making your calls. If your product is household cleaning services, why call a random neighborhood if you have no knowledge of income levels, number of household wage earners, or number of children? If you sell nutritional products to hospitals, why call nurses or doctors if a third-party pharmacy makes all the buying decisions? Get the right list of prospects.

You can obtain the information about prospects from the list broker who provides you with the list; if you are working from your house list, you should already have the information. If for some reason you don't, try an introductory call like the following: "We provide mobile pet grooming for dogs and cats. Would that be a service your customers would want to know about, Mr./Ms. Veterinarian?"

Bright Idea

Got cold-call phobia? Psych yourself up with a numbers game: If every sale brings you $200 profit and it takes an average of 10 calls to make one sale, then each "no" is worth $20. Or try the "immersion" technique: Make 100 cold calls without worrying about the results. When it's over, you'll have learned a great deal about selling . . . and your fear of cold calls will be history.

Next, determine the best time frames for calling. If you are selling financial services to upper-income CEOs or entrepreneurs, wouldn't it be nice to know when their corporate fiscal years end? Perhaps most of their investment purchases are made two to four weeks prior to that year-end close-out. That's when they know how much extra income needs to be sheltered in a pension plan.

Sometimes timing is your ace in the hole. Granted, follow-up calls throughout the year may make that one important sale possible, but knowing when to instigate the first call is a priceless piece of information.

Third, plan by preparing a "sales script" ahead of time. Write down what you are going to say, what responses the prospect is likely to have and how you will reply to them. No, you're not going to follow this word for word, but if you're nervous about making calls, it helps to have something in front of you. Chances are, after you get beyond the opening sentences you'll be able to "wing it" just fine.

VOICE MAIL VICTORIES

When making cold calls, always leave voice mail messages if possible instead of leaving messages with a secretary. No one can transmit your enthusiasm for your products or services the way you can. Here are some tips to make the most of voice mail:

◆ *State your business.* Clearly tell prospects who you are and why they should be interested in talking to you. "Hello, my name is Jane Smith, and I'm with the Smith Co. We're the people who conduct one-day Sales Power seminars all over the country. Our seminar is coming to your area, and I'd like to tell you about it."

◆ *Offer good news.* After identifying yourself and your business, say "I have some really good news I'd like to share with you."

◆ *Be courteous.* Use the phrase "I'd appreciate the courtesy of a return call at (number)." Be careful of your tone of voice, however, so that you don't sound condescending.

◆ *Follow up with a fax.* Send a fax that says "Mr. Wilson, please check your voice mail for an important message." Or leave a voice mail message saying "I'm faxing you the information; if it is of interest to you, please give me a call."

◆ *Always leave your phone number—twice.* Repeat your number near the end of the message. Practice writing it down as you talk so you don't go too quickly.

If preparation for cold-calling is easy, but actually making calls is painful for you, here are seven easy steps to get you on the phone fast.

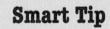

Smart Tip

Trying to scare up business? If your product is necessary but not very appealing or exciting, one way to motivate customers to action is by describing the consequences of not using your product. For products that increase security, safety or health, fear can be an effective business-boosting tool.

1. **Personalize each call by preparing mentally.** Your mindset must be aligned with your language, or the conversation will not ring true. Work on developing a warm, but not sugarcoated, telephone voice that has that "Don't I know you?" or "Gee, you sound so familiar" ring to it.

2. **Perfect your phone style alone before making any calls.** If you are self-conscious about calling, you need to feel safe to act uninhibited. Try this: Gather a tape recorder, a mirror, a sales journal of incoming and outgoing phone scripts, a pen and a legal-sized pad. Either write or select a favorite phone dialogue, then talk to yourself in the mirror. Do you look relaxed, or are your facial expressions rigid? Our exteriors reflect our inner selves. If you look like you're in knots, your voice will sound strained as well.

Beware!

Never, ever waste a buyer's time. Whenever you call on a prospect, whether in person or by phone, be organized and prepared with facts, figures, demonstrations and answers.

Push the "record" button on your tape recorder, and pretend you're talking to a new prospect. Play back the tape, and listen to your conversation. Ask yourself how you could improve your delivery. If your voice seems unnatural and the dialogue contrived, don't despair. As you practice and participate in real phone experiences, you will improve. Mastering the art of cold-calling is no different than improving your golf swing or skiing techniques.

3. **Create familiarity all around you.** Use family photos, framed testimonial letters, motivational quotes, or whatever gets you in a positive, enthusiastic mood. If you like, play some music that inspires you.

4. **Use your imagination.** Pretend you're a prospective customer calling a bookstore to see if they have a book in stock. If it helps, record how you sound to get the feel of your inquiring phone voice. It's always easier to imagine you're a customer in need of information than a salesperson trying to force your way into the customer's time.

   The inquiry call is good practice because the tone of the conversation is "Can you help me?" or "I need some information." Try to convey that same attitude when you use the phone to contact future customers.

> ## Smart Tip
>
> Sell benefits, not features. The biggest mistake entrepreneurs make is in focusing on what their product or service *is* (its features). Rather, it's what it *does* (its benefits) that's important. A health-food product contains nutrients that are good for the body. That's what it *is*. What the product does is make the customer thinner, more energetic, and able to accomplish more with less sleep. Always concentrate on how your product will benefit your customer.

5. **Watch your tone of voice.** You don't want to sound sheepish and embarrassed, nor do you want to be arrogant. The ideal tone is warm, businesslike, curious and straight to the point. A good option is a cut-to-the-chase statement or question such as: "I've got a problem. We are offering a two-for-one special during the next 30 days on all our coffee drinks, just to get people into the store. I need to know if you have ever stopped in while shopping at the mall, and, if not, why not? We've got the greatest ice-blended mochas in town."

6. **Make your goal a fast "50 in 150"—that is, 50 calls in 150 minutes.** Three minutes per call is all you need. With so many voice-mail systems intercepting calls today, this should be easy. Never give people the impression you have time to chat. Chatting is not prospecting. You are on a mission. Get to the point, then move to the next prospect.

7. **Take five after 15.** After 15 calls, take a five-minute break—stretch, eat an apple, sip a soda, turn on some tunes, and pat yourself on the back because you are making it happen. Then grab the phone for 15 more calls.

Following Up

Your initial cold call typically will not result in a sale, or even in an appointment to make a sales presentation. One study shows it takes an average of seven contacts, impressions or follow-ups to make a sale.

Think of each follow-up contact as a chance to get closer to the prospect and change his or her mind about meeting with you. Plan your follow-up contacts carefully, and be flexible and creative. How do you start the follow-up call? Here are some lead-in lines:

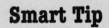

Smart Tip

Tips for better cold calls: Stand up when you talk on the phone. It puts power and confidence in your voice. Smile when you say hello. It makes you sound relaxed and confident. Prospects can't see these telephone tricks, but they'll hear and feel the difference in your tone—and in your persuasive powers.

- ◆ "I thought of a few things that might help you decide . . ."

- ◆ "Something new recently happened that I thought you might want to know about . . ."

- ◆ "There has been a change in the status of . . ."

- ◆ "I was thinking about you, and wanted to tell you about . . ."

Here are some other sales tools you can use in follow-up situations:

- ◆ **A personal note:** A handwritten note on your company note cards is far more effective than a typed business letter.

- ◆ **An endorsement from a mutual friend:** A friend is far more influential than you are.

- ◆ **An article about your company:** Something in print can work wonders. You can even send articles about the prospect's company or, better yet, about a personal interest of the prospect's. "Thought you might be interested in . . ."

- ◆ **An invitation to visit your facility:** Bring the prospect to your home turf.

- ◆ **A meal:** Meetings in a nonbusiness environment are powerful and help you build personal relationships that lead to sales.

Making Sales Presentations

Your cold calls and follow-up efforts have paid off, and you've made an appointment to visit a prospect in person and make a sales presentation.

GET ORGANIZED

No matter how dedicated you are, your follow-up won't get results unless you track your efforts. A good follow-up tracking system includes three components:

1. *A computer:* Check out the many contact management and sales follow-up programs available. There's sure to be one that fits your work style. When you've got all the information on computer, your mind is free for more important things ... like thinking of new, creative ways to follow up.

2. *Business card file:* When you meet new prospects, write personal and business information about them on the back of their business cards. Transfer this information to your computer ASAP.

3. *Daily planner:* Use whatever organizer or calendar system you prefer to keep your appointments and notes in when you're on the move.

How can you make sure it's a success? From the very beginning of a presentation, four elements determine whether a sale will be made or not:

1. **Rapport:** putting yourself on the same side of the fence as the prospect

2. **Need:** determining what factors will motivate the prospect to listen with the intent to purchase

3. **Importance:** the weight the prospect assigns to a product, feature, benefit, price or time frame

4. **Confidence:** your ability to project credibility, to remove doubt, and to gain the prospect's belief that the risk of purchase will be less than the reward of ownership

Here is a closer look at the steps you can take to make your sales presentation a success.

Before The Presentation

1. **Know your customer's business.** Potential clients expect you to know their business, customers and competition as well as you know your own product or service. Study your customer's industry. Know its problems and trends. Find out who the company's biggest competitors are. Some research tools include the com-

pany's annual report, brochures, newsletters and catalogs; trade publications; chamber of commerce directories; and the Internet.

2.   **Write out your sales presentation.** Making a sales presentation isn't something you do on the fly. Always use a written presentation. The basic structure of any successful sales presentation includes five key points: Build rapport with your prospect, introduce the business topic, ask questions to better understand your prospect's needs, summarize your key selling points, and close the sale. Think about the three major selling points of your product or ser-

---

PRESENTATION PERFECT

Want to improve your sales presentation skills? Use these strategies to hone your speaking abilities:

◆ *Tag-team sell for evaluation purposes.* Have a colleague go on sales calls with you once a week to listen to your presentation. Create a review form for them to fill out immediately after your performance. (Include your strengths as well as your weaknesses.) Read it right away, and talk about what you can do to improve.

◆ *Record your telephone sales conversations.* Use them as a self-monitor of your ability to present a clear and confident message. Play them back. If you can't stand your voice, change your pitch.

◆ *Read a chapter from a sales book aloud, recording it on audiotape.* Play it in your car. You'll learn about sales and about how you present your pitch. Would you buy from yourself? If not, record another version with style and emotion.

◆ *Videotape the first five minutes of your sales presentation.* Ask a friend or colleague to be the prospect. Watch the video together, and rate your performance. Repeat the process once a week for two months. Work to eliminate your two worst habits; at the same time, work to enhance your two best strengths.

Above all, be yourself. Don't put on an act. Your personality will shine if you believe in what you are saying. Being genuine will win the prospect's confidence ... and the sale.

vice. Develop leading questions to probe your customer's reactions and needs.

3. **Make sure you're talking to the right person.** This seems elementary, but many salespeople neglect to do it. Then, at the last minute, the buyer wriggles off the hook by saying he or she needs a boss's, spouse's or partner's approval. When you are setting the appointment, always ask "Are you the one I should be talking to, or are there others who will be making the buying decision?"

> **Bright Idea**
>
> Offer a first-time incentive to help clinch the sale. If prospects like your product or service, they'll be inclined to make a decision now rather than wait a few days or put off the decision indefinitely. First-time incentives might include: "10 percent off with your purchase today" or "With today's purchase, you'll receive one free hour of consultation."

In The Customer's Office

1. **Build rapport.** Before discussing business, build rapport with your prospect. To accomplish this, do some homework. Find out if you have a colleague in common. Has the prospect's company been in the news lately? Is he or she interested in sports? Get a little insight into the company and the individual so you can make the rapport genuine.

2. **Ask questions.** Don't jump into a canned sales spiel. The most effective way to sell is to ask the prospect questions and see where he or she leads you. (Of course, your questions are carefully structured to elicit the prospect's needs—ones that your product just happens to be able to fill.)

    Ask questions that require more than a yes or no response, and that deal with more than just costs, price, procedures and the technical aspects of the prospect's business. Most important, ask questions that will reveal the prospect's motivation to purchase, his or her problems and needs, and decision-making processes. Don't be afraid to ask a client why he or she feels a certain way. That's how you'll get to understand your customers.

3. **Take notes.** Don't rely on your memory to remind you of what's important to your prospect. Ask upfront if it's all right for you to take notes during your sales presentation. (Prospects will be flat-

tered.) Write down key points you can refer to later during your presentation.

Be sure to write down objections. This shows your prospect you are truly listening to what he or she is saying. In this way, you can answer objections by showing how the customer will benefit from your product or service. It could be, for instance, by saving money, raising productivity, increasing employee motivation, or increasing the company's name recognition.

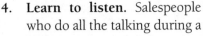

Beware!

What's the best way to talk yourself out of a sale? Overselling—pushing your features and benefits too hard—is a common problem for salespeople. The problem is that you aren't hearing the customer's needs. Shut up and listen. Then start asking questions. Keep asking questions until you can explain how your product or service meets the customer's needs.

4. **Learn to listen.** Salespeople who do all the talking during a presentation not only bore the prospect but also generally lose the sale. A good rule of thumb is to listen 70 percent of the time and talk 30 percent of the time. Don't interrupt. It's tempting to step in and tell the prospect something you think is vitally important. Before you speak, ask yourself if what you are about to say is really necessary.

    When you do speak, focus on asking questions. Pretend you're Barbara Walters interviewing a movie star: Ask questions, then shut up. You can improve your listening skills by taking notes, observing your prospect's body language, not jumping to conclusions and concentrating on what your prospect is saying.

5. **Answer objections with "feel," "felt" and "found."** Don't argue when a prospect says "I'm not interested," "I just bought one," or "I don't have time right now." Simply say "I understand how you feel. A lot of my present customers felt the same way. But when they found out how much time they saved by using our product, they were amazed." Then ask for an appointment. Prospects like to hear about other people who have been in a similar situation.

6. **Probe deeper.** If a prospect tells you "We're looking for cost-savings and efficiency," will you immediately tell him how your product meets his need for cost-savings and efficiency? A really smart salesperson won't—he or she will ask more questions and

probe deeper: "I understand why that is important. Can you give me a specific example?" Asking the prospect for more information—and listening to the answers—enables you to better position your product and shows you understand the client's needs.

7. **Find the "hot button."** A customer may have a long list of needs, but there is usually one "hot button" that will get the person to buy your product or service. The key to the hot button is that it's an emotional, not practical, need—a need for recognition, love or reinforcement. Suppose you're selling health-club memberships. For a prospect who is planning a trip to Hawaii in two months, the hot button is likely to be losing a few pounds and looking good in a bikini. For a prospect who just found out he has high blood pressure, the hot button could be the health benefits of exercise. For a busy young mother, the hot button may be the chance to get away from the kids for a few hours a week and reduce stress.

8. **Eliminate objections.** When a prospect raises an objection, don't immediately jump in with a response. Instead, show empathy by saying "Let's explore your concerns." Ask for more details about the objection. You need to isolate the true objection so you can handle it. Here are some ways to do that:

THE PRICE ISN'T RIGHT

How do you overcome that most common objection, "Your price is too high"? Lawrence L. Steinmetz, author of *How to Sell at a Price Higher Than Your Competitors* (Horizon Publications), says you need to learn how to acknowledge that your price is higher than competitors'—then use that as a selling tool.

Showing that customers get more services, better warranties or higher-quality products for the extra cost makes the higher price seem less imposing. Telling them why the competition's services or products don't measure up differentiates you from the competition and convinces customers you're worth the extra money.

Whatever you do, don't be too willing to negotiate or slash prices. "When you ask a customer 'Is that too much?' you are encouraging him or her to beat you up," says Steinmetz.

With the right ammunition, you can turn price problems into selling points.

◆ **Offer a choice.** "Is it the delivery time or the financing you are concerned about?"

◆ **Get to the heart of the matter.** "When you say you want to think about it, what specifically did you want to think about?"

◆ **Work toward a solution.** Every sale should be a win-win deal, so you may need to compromise: "I'll waive the delivery charge if you agree to the purchase."

As you get more experience making sales calls, you'll become familiar with different objections. Maintain a list of common objections and ways you have successfully dealt with them.

TEAMWORK

The right sales team—whether they are in-house employees or outside sales representatives—makes a big difference in how quickly your company grows. How to make sure you're hiring the right people? Try these tips:

◆ Don't rely solely on resumes. Good salespeople sell themselves so well, they don't even need resumes.

◆ Try placing a classified ad that says "Send resume to (address) or call (number)." Don't even look at the resumes; just interview the people who call. These are the people who won't be afraid to pick up the phone and make cold calls.

◆ In the first phone contact, if the applicant doesn't ask for an appointment, stop right there. If the person doesn't ask for an interview now, he or she won't ask for orders later.

◆ Does the person sound like someone you want to spend time with? If you don't want to, neither will your customers.

◆ When they first call, tell them you're busy and will call them back. Then don't. If they don't call you back, they lack the persistence you need in a salesperson.

◆ Does the applicant listen? If they're too busy talking to listen to you, they'll be too busy to listen to your customers.

◆ At the end of the phone call, say you plan to talk to several candidates and will get back to them. Wait until one says "You don't need to talk to more people. I'm the one you want." That's the kind of person you need.

9. **Close the sale.** There's no magic to closing the sale. If you've followed all the previous steps, all you should have to do is ask for the customer's order. However, some salespeople make the mistake of simply not asking for the final decision. It's as if they forget what their goal is!

    For some people, "closing" sounds too negative. If you're one of them, try changing your thinking to something more positive, such as "deciding." As you talk with the customer, build in the close by having fun with it. Say something like "So how many do you want? We have it in a rainbow of colors; do you want them all?" Ask them several times in a fun, nonthreatening way; you're leading them to make the decision.

> **Bright Idea**
>
> How to boost sales? Offer a 100 percent guarantee. This minimizes customer objections and shows you believe in your product or service. Product guarantees should be unconditional, with no hidden clauses like "guaranteed for 30 days." Use guarantees for services, too: "Satisfaction guaranteed. You'll be thrilled with our service, or we'll redo it at our expense."

After The Sale

1. **Follow up.** What you do after the sale is as crucial as what you do to get it. "Nearly 85 percent of all sales are produced by word-of-mouth referrals," says sales guru Brian Tracy. "In other words, they're the result of someone telling a friend or associate to buy a product or service because the customer was satisfied."

    Concentrate on developing future and referral business with each satisfied customer. Write thank-you notes, call the customer after the sale to make sure he or she is satisfied, and maintain a schedule of future communications. Be in front of that client, and always show attention and responsiveness. (For more on retaining customers, see Chapter 36.)

2. **Ask for feedback.** Ask customers what you need to do to maintain and increase their business. Many customers have minor complaints but will never say anything. They just won't buy from you again. If you ask their opinions, on the other hand, they'll be glad to tell you—and, in most cases, will give you a chance to solve the problem.

Speaking Effectively

The difference between good and great salespeople is the way they deliver their messages. You can have the greatest sales pitch in the world, but if you deliver it with no enthusiasm, sincerity or belief, you'll lose the sale.

Here are some suggestions to improve your speaking skills and power up your presentations:

◆ **Speak clearly.** If the prospect doesn't understand you, you won't get the sale.

◆ **Lean forward.** Leaning into the presentation gives the prospect a sense of urgency.

◆ **Don't fidget.** Knuckle-cracking, hair-twirling and similar nervous habits detract from your presentation.

PASS IT ON

Referrals are among a salesperson's best weapons. Yet many salespeople fail to take advantage of this powerful marketing tool. Here are secrets to getting and making the most of referrals:

◆ Ask for specific referrals. Many salespeople ask for referrals by saying "Do you know anyone else who might be interested in my product?" The prospect replies "Not off the top of my head, but I'll let you know if I think of anyone." And that's where it ends.

More effective is to ask for a specific referral that deals with a need your business addresses. For instance, ask "Steve, at your last Rotary Club meeting, did you talk to anyone who was thinking about moving or selling a home?"

◆ Gather as much information about the referral as possible. Use this to prepare for the cold call.

◆ Ask your customer for permission to use his or her name when contacting the referral.

◆ Ask your customer to help you get an appointment with the referral.

◆ Contact the referral as soon as possible.

◆ Inform your customer about the outcome of the referral. People like to know when they have been of help.

◆ Prospect for referrals just as you would for sales leads.

◆ **Don't "um," "ah" or "er."** These vocal tics are so irritating, they make the prospect focus on the flaws rather than the message. Best cure? Practice, practice, practice.

◆ **Be animated.** Act as if the greatest thing in the world just happened to you.

◆ **Vary your voice.** Don't drone on in a monotone. Go from high to low tones. Punch the critical words. Whisper some of the key information as if it's a secret. Get the prospect to lean into your words. Make him or her feel special for receiving this message.

◆ **Look prospects in the eye.** Eye contact signals credibility and trustworthiness.

◆ **Follow the prospect's lead.** Keep your tone similar to his or hers. If the prospect is stuffy and conservative, don't get too wild.

◆ **Relax.** High anxiety makes prospects nervous. Why do salespeople get nervous? Either they're unprepared or they need the money from the sale. Calm down. Never let them see you sweat.

CHAPTER 36

KEEP 'EM COMING BACK

Offering superior customer service

To the ordinary entrepreneur, closing and finalizing the sale is the completion of serving the customer's needs. But for the pro, this is only the beginning. Closing the sale sets the stage for a relationship which, if properly managed by you, the entrepreneur, can be mutually profitable for years to come.

Remember the "80/20 rule" discussed in an earlier chapter? It states that 80 percent of your business comes from 20 percent of your customers. Repeat customers are the backbone of every successful business. So now that you know how to land customers, it's time to learn how to keep them.

BUILDING CUSTOMER RELATIONSHIPS

It's tempting to concentrate on making new sales or pursuing bigger accounts. But attention to your existing customers, no matter how small they are, is equally essential to keep your business thriving. The secret to repeat business is following up in a way that has a positive effect on the customer.

Effective follow-up begins immediately after the sale, when you call the customer to say "thank you" and find out if he or she is pleased with your product or service. Beyond this, there are several effective ways to follow up that ensure your business is always in the customer's mind.

1. **Let customers know what you are doing for them.** This can be in the form of a newsletter mailed to existing customers (see Part 6 Chapter 32), or it can be more informal, such as a phone call. Whichever method you use, the key is to dramatically point out to customers what excellent service you are giving them. If you never mention all the things you are doing for them, customers may not notice. You aren't being cocky when

you talk to customers about all the work you have done to please them. Just make a phone call and let them know they don't have to worry because you handled the paperwork, called the attorney or double-checked on the shipment—one less thing they have to do.

2. **Write old customers personal, handwritten notes frequently.** "I was just sitting at my desk and your name popped into my head. Are you still having a great time flying all over the country? Let me know if you need another set of luggage. I can stop by with our latest models any time." Or, if you run into an old customer at an event, follow up with a note: "It was great seeing you at the CDC Christmas party. I'll call you early in the New Year to schedule a lunch."

3. **Keep it personal.** Voice mail and e-mail make it easy to communicate, but the personal touch is lost. Don't count these as a legitimate follow-up. If you're having trouble getting through, leave a voice mail message that you want to talk to the person directly or will stop by his or her office at a designated time.

4. **Remember special occasions.** Send regular customers birthday cards, anniversary cards, holiday cards . . . you name it. Gifts are excellent follow-up tools, too. You don't have to spend a fortune to show you care; use your creativity to come up with interesting gift ideas that tie into your business, the customer's business or his or her recent purchase.

5. **Pass on information.** If you read an article, see a new book, or hear about an organization that a customer might be interested in, drop a note or make a quick call to let them know.

6. **Consider follow-up calls as business development calls.** When you talk to or visit old clients or customers, you'll often find they have referrals to give you, which can lead to new business.

With all that your existing customers can do for you, there's simply no reason not to stay in regular contact with them. Use your imagination, and you'll think of plenty of other ideas that can help you develop a lasting relationship.

Bright Idea

To ensure you don't drop the ball on follow-up, check out one of the many contact management or sales software programs on the market. These little wonders can remind you of everything from a big client's birthday to an important sales call.

Customer Service

There are plenty of things you, the entrepreneur, can do to ensure good customer service. And when you're a one-person business, it's easy to stay on top of what your customers want. But as you add employees, whether it's one person or 100, you are adding more links to the customer service chain—and creating more potential for poor service along the way.

That's why creating a customer service policy and adhering to it is so important. Here are some steps you can take to ensure that your clients receive excellent service, every step of the way.

1. Put your customer service policy in writing. These principles should come from you, but every employee should know what the rules are and be ready to live up to them.

2. Establish support systems that give employees clear instructions for gaining and maintaining service superiority. These systems will help you out-service any competitor by giving more to customers and anticipating problems before they arise.

3. Develop a measurement of superb customer service, and reward employees who practice it consistently.

4. Be certain that your passion for customer service runs rampant throughout your company. Employees should see how good service relates to your profits and to their future with the company.

5. Be genuinely committed to providing more customer service excellence than anyone else in your industry. This commitment must be so powerful that every one of your customers can sense it.

6. Share information with people on the front lines. Meet regularly to talk about improving service. Solicit ideas from employees— they are the ones who are dealing with the customers most often.

7. Act on the knowledge that what customers value most are attention, dependability, promptness and competence. They love being treated as individuals and being referred to by name. (Don't you?)

Bright Idea

Make it easy for customers to contact you—by phone, fax or e-mail—to share ideas, frustrations and suggestions.

Interacting With Customers

Principles of customer service are all very well, but you need to put those principles into action with everything you do and say. There are certain "magic words" that customers want to hear from you and your staff. Make sure all your employees understand the importance of these key words:

1. **"How can I help?"** Customers want the opportunity to explain in detail what they want and need. Too often, business owners feel the desire or the obligation to guess what customers need rather than carefully listening first. By asking how you can help, you begin the dialogue on a positive note (you are "helping," not "selling"). And by using an open-ended question, you invite discussion.

2. **"I can solve that problem."** Most customers, especially business-to-business customers, are looking to buy solutions. They appreciate direct answers in a language they can understand.

Go To The Source

Excellent customer service is more than what you say or do for the customer; it also means giving customers a chance to make their feelings known. Here are some suggestions for finding out what your customers want, need and care about:

1. *Attend trade shows and industry events that are important to your customers.* You'll find out what the competition is doing and what kinds of products and services customers are looking for.

2. *Nurture a human bond, as well as a business one, with customers and prospects.* Take them out to lunch, dinner, the ballgame or the opera. In the relaxed atmosphere of socializing, you'll learn the secrets that will allow you to go above and beyond your competition.

3. *Keep alert for trends; then respond to them.* Read industry trade publications; be active in trade organizations; pay attention to what your customers are doing.

4. *Ask for feedback.* Survey your customers regularly to find out how you're doing. Send postage-paid questionnaire cards or letters; call them by phone; set up focus groups. Ask for suggestions, then fix the trouble areas revealed.

Whatever you do, don't rest on your laurels. Regularly evaluate your product or service to be sure it is still priced, packaged and delivered right.

3. **"I don't know, but I'll find out."** When confronted with a truly difficult question that requires research on your part, admit it. Few things ruin your credibility faster than trying to answer a question when you are unsure of all the facts. Savvy buyers may test you with a question they know you can't answer, and then just sit quietly while you struggle to fake an answer. An honest reply enhances your integrity.

COMPLAINT DEPARTMENT

Studies show that the vast majority of unsatisfied customers will never tell you they're unsatisfied. They simply leave quietly, then tell everyone they know not to do business with you. So when a customer does complain, don't think of it as a nuisance—think of it as a golden opportunity to change that customer's mind and retain his or her business.

Even the best product or service meets with complaints or problems now and then. Here's how to handle them for positive results:

◆ Let customers vent their feelings. Encourage them to get their frustrations out in the open.

◆ Never argue with a customer.

◆ Never tell a customer "You do not have a problem." Those are fighting words.

◆ Share your point of view as politely as you can.

◆ Take responsibility for the problem. Don't make excuses. If an employee was sick or a third-party supplier let you down, that's not the customer's concern.

◆ Immediately take action to remedy the situation. Promising a solution, then delaying it only makes matters worse.

◆ Empower your front-line employees to be flexible in resolving complaints. Give employees some leeway in deciding when to bend the rules. If you don't feel comfortable doing this, make sure they have you or another manager handle the situation.

◆ Imagine you're the one with the complaint. How would you want the situation to be handled?

4. **"I will take responsibility."**
Tell your customer you realize
it's your responsibility to ensure
a satisfactory outcome to the
transaction. Assure the customer you know what she expects and will deliver the
product or service at the agreed-
upon price. There will be no unexpected changes or expenses
required to solve the problem.

> **Bright Idea**
>
> Create external in-
> centives to keep customers
> coming back. Offer customers
> free merchandise or services af-
> ter they buy a certain amount.
> This gets them in the habit of
> buying again and again.

5. **"I will keep you updated."** Even if your business is a cash-and-carry operation, it probably requires scheduling and coordinating numerous events. Assure your customers they will be advised of the status of these events. The longer your lead time, the more important this is. The vendors customers trust the most are those that keep them apprised of the situation, whether the news is good or bad.

6. **"I will deliver on time."** A due date that has been agreed upon is a promise that must be kept. "Close" doesn't count. Monday means Monday. The first week in July means the first week in July, even though it contains a national holiday. Your clients are waiting to hear you say "I deliver on time." The supplier who consistently does so is a rarity and well-remembered.

7. **"It'll be just what you ordered."** It will not be "similar to," and it will not be "better than" what was ordered. It will be exactly what was ordered. Even if you believe a substitute would be in the client's best interest, that's a topic for discussion, not something you decide on your own. Your customer may not know (or be at liberty to explain) all the ramifications of the purchase.

8. **"The job will be complete."** Assure the customer there will be no waiting for a final piece or a last document. Never say you will be finished "except for . . ."

9. **"I appreciate your business."** This means more than a simple "Thanks for the order." Genuine appreciation involves follow-up calls, offering to answer questions, making sure everything is performing satisfactorily, and ascertaining that the original problem has been solved.

Neglecting any of these steps conveys the impression that you were interested in the person only until the sale was made. This leaves the buyer feeling deceived and used, and creates ill will and negative advertising for your company. Sincerely proving you care about your customers leads to recommendations . . . and repeat sales.

Going Above And Beyond

These days, simply providing adequate customer service isn't enough. You need to go above and beyond the call of duty to provide customer service that truly stands out. How to do this?

Begin by thinking about your own experiences as a customer—what you've liked and disliked in certain situations. Recall the times you were delighted by extra efforts taken to accommodate your needs or were outraged by rudeness or negligence. This will give you greater insight into what makes for extraordinary customer service.

To put yourself in the customer's shoes, try visiting a wide range of businesses your customers are likely to frequent. This could include your direct competitors, as well as companies that sell related products and services. Observe how customers are treated, in addition to the kinds of services that seem to be important to them. Then adapt your business accordingly.

Going above and beyond is especially important when a customer has complained or if there is a problem with a purchase. Suppose an order is delayed. What can you do?

◆ Call the customer personally with updates on the status of the order and expected arrival time.

◆ Hand-deliver the merchandise when it arrives.

◆ Take 20 percent or 30 percent off the cost.

◆ Send a note apologizing for the delay . . . tucked inside a gift basket full of goodies. These are all ways of showing the customer you're on his side.

Going above and beyond doesn't always mean offering deep discounts or giving away products. With a little ingenuity and effort, you can show customers they're important at any time. Suppose you've just received the newest samples and colors for your home furnishings line. Why not invite your best customers to a private showing, complete with music, appetizers, and a coupon good for one free hour of consultation?

Smart Tip

When it comes to customer service, department store chain Nordstrom is a superstar. The Nordstrom service manual is eloquent in its simplicity: "Use your good judgment in all situations. There will be no additional rules."

Emergency orders and last-minute changes should be accommodated whenever possible, especially for important occasions such as a wedding or a big trade show. Customers remember these events . . . and they'll remember your flexibility and prompt response to their needs, too.

Being accessible also wins loyalty. One entrepreneur who runs a computer chip company has installed a customer service line on every employee's telephone, from the mail room clerk on up. This means every caller gets through to a real person who can help him or her, instead of getting lost in a voice mail maze.

Smart Tip

When customers are happy with your service, ask them for a testimonial letter. Get permission to use quotes from the letters in your print ads and brochures. Also ask if you can give past customers' phone numbers to certain qualified prospects so they can get a solid recommendation about your business firsthand.

Customer loyalty is hard to win and easy to lose. But by going above and beyond with your customer service, you'll soon see your sales going above and beyond those of your competitors.

Part Seven:

By The Books

CHAPTER 37

BEAN-COUNTING 101

The basics of bookkeeping

By J. Tol Broome Jr., a freelance
business writer and banker
with 14 years of experience
in commercial lending

S o you say you would rather wrestle an alligator with one hand tied behind your back than get bogged down in numbers? Well, you aren't alone. Many small-business owners would rather focus on making and selling their products than on keeping their books and records in order. However, bookkeeping is just as important as production and marketing. Many a great business idea has failed due to a poor bookkeeping system.

Simply put, a business's bookkeeping system tracks the money coming in vs. the money going out. And, ultimately, you won't be able to keep your doors open if you have more dollars going out than coming in.

Aside from every business owner's inherent desire to stay in business, there are two other key reasons to set up a good bookkeeping system:

1. It is legally required.

2. Bookkeeping records are an excellent business management tool.

Of course, staying out of jail is a good thing. And a good basic accounting system will provide useful financial information that will enable you to run your business proactively rather than reactively when it comes to important financial decisions.

THE BOOKKEEPING ADVANTAGE

As a new business owner, you are in an enviable position in setting up a bookkeeping system for your venture. You are not bound to the "we've always done it that way" mentality that bogs down many businesses. For your new endeavor, you have the advantage of being able to develop the bookkeeping system that is most compatible with your business type, as well as your financial management skills.

Beware!

All businesses are subject to laws governing the payment of federal and state withholding taxes. Here are three rules that must never be violated in your business:

1. Make sure you have current withholding tax tables.

2. *Always* make your payroll deposits on time.

3. Stay up-to-date and accurate with payroll record-keeping reporting requirements.

While many businesses still operate using a manual (checkbook and receipts) bookkeeping system, it is not a good idea for a new business to use this type of system. It is far more efficient to go with an automated system, and there are now many bookkeeping software packages on the market that won't break your wallet. For a financially complex business such as a manufacturing concern, you can buy industry-specific software, but there also are many generic programs available that would suffice for most new businesses (see "It All Adds Up" in this chapter).

A good accounting system meets three criteria. First, it is accurate; the numbers must be right. Automation will help ensure accuracy, but it won't guarantee it. Bookkeeping numbers should be checked and rechecked to maintain accuracy.

Second, a good accounting system is relevant. The system provides information that is required *and* needed. The law requires that certain pieces of financial information be tracked for tax reporting purposes. Obviously, these items (which comprise a basic income statement and balance sheet) must be measured and tracked. However, it is equally important to include information that you will need to run your business successfully.

Third, a good accounting system is user-friendly. It should not require a CPA to operate and interpret it. Most of the Windows-based bookkeeping software packages are pretty user-friendly. They include tutorials and help screens that walk you through the programs. Find one with which you are comfortable, even if it doesn't have some of the bells and whistles of more complicated programs.

BASIC ACCOUNTING PRINCIPLES

Most businesses typically use one of two basic accounting methods in their bookkeeping systems: cash basis and accrual basis. While most businesses use the accrual basis, the most appropriate method for your company depends on your sales volume, whether or not you sell on credit, and your business structure.

The cash method is the most simple in that the books are kept based on the actual flow of cash in and out of the business. Income is recorded when it is received, and expenses are reported when they are actually paid. The cash method is used by many sole proprietors and businesses with no inventory.

From a tax standpoint, it is sometimes advantageous for a new business to use the cash method of accounting. That way, recording income can be put off until the next tax year, while expenses are counted right away.

With the accrual method, income and expenses are recorded as they occur, regardless of whether or not cash has actually changed hands. An excellent example is a sale on credit. The sale is entered into the books when the invoice is generated rather than when the cash is collected. Likewise, an expense occurs when materials are ordered or when a workday has been logged in by an employee, not when the check is actually written. The downside of this method is that you pay income taxes on revenue before you've actually received it.

It All Adds Up

In the not-too-distant past, to set up an automated bookkeeping system, you had to spend countless hours yourself or hire a programmer to customize an accounting system for your business. And since most new business owners did not have the time to do it themselves or the financial resources to hire a programmer, cumbersome manual systems were used or the bookkeeping function was completely outsourced to an accountant or bookkeeping service.

Fortunately, those days are over. In today's market, new business owners will find a number of very affordable and full-featured accounting software packages from which to choose. These popular accounting packages not only allow business owners to track and manage every aspect of their companies' finances, but they also reduce accounting expenses by saving accounting firms time and effort in producing companies' year-end tax return and/or financial statements.

Here are some of the most popular "canned" accounting software packages: Inuit's Quickbooks Pro, Peachtree's Complete Accounting, Bestware's M.Y.O.B. Accounting, and Accpac's Simply Accounting. They range in price from $49 to $199. Regardless of which package you buy, it will be one of the most beneficial purchases you make in starting your small business.

Should you use the cash or accrual method? The accrual method is required if your annual sales exceed $5 million and your venture is structured as a corporation. In addition, businesses with inventory must also use this method. It also is highly recommended for any business that sells on credit, as it more accurately matches income and expenses during a given time period. The cash method may be appropriate for a small, cash-based business or a small service company. You should consult your accountant when deciding on an accounting method.

ACCOUNTING SYSTEM COMPONENTS

Every accounting system has several key components. Even if you choose to farm out all your bookkeeping to an outside accountant, you will need to understand the basic elements of an accounting system. While some may vary depending on the type of business, these components typically consist of the chart of accounts, general ledger, accounts receivable, inventory, fixed-asset accounting, accounts payable and payroll.

Chart Of Accounts

The first step in setting up an accounting system for your new business is deciding what you want to track. A chart of accounts is simply a list of your accounts and is kept by every business to record and follow specific entries (see the sample chart of accounts in this chapter). Whether you decide to use a manual system or a software program, you can customize the chart of accounts to your business.

Account numbers are used as an easy account identification system. For most businesses, a three-number system will suffice; however, a four-number system is sometimes used for more complex ventures.

The chart of accounts is the fuel for your accounting system. After the chart of accounts, you establish a general ledger system, which is the engine that actually runs your accounting system on a daily basis.

General Ledger

Every account that is on your chart of accounts will be included in your general ledger, which should be set up in the same order as the chart of accounts. While the general ledger does

Smart Tip

The chart of accounts is the foundation on which you will build your accounting system. Take care to set up your chart of accounts right the first time. Keep your account descriptions as concise as possible. And leave plenty of room in your numbering system to add accounts in the future.

SAMPLE CHART OF ACCOUNTS

BALANCE SHEET (1-500)	Account #
Assets (1-300)	
Cash (1-50)	
Petty Cash on Hand	11
Cash in Bank—General Bank Account	21
Cash in Bank—Payroll Bank Account	31
Receivables From Others (51-100)	
Notes Receivable	51
Accounts Receivable—Customers	61
Accounts Receivable—Others	71
Inventories (101-150)	
Finished Goods for Sale	101
Work in Process	111
Raw Materials	121
Prepaid Expenses (151-200)	
Advertising	151
Insurance	161
Rent	181
Property and Equipment (201-250)	
Land	201
Buildings	211
Buildings—Allowance for Depreciation	212
Automobiles and Trucks	216
Automobiles and Trucks—	
Allowance for Depreciation	217
Furniture and Office Equipment	221
Furniture and Office Equipment—	
Allowance for Depreciation	222
Machinery	226
Machinery—Allowance for Depreciation	227
Leasehold Improvements	246
Leasehold Improvements—	
Allowance for Amortization	247
Miscellaneous Assets (251-300)	
Organization Expenses (Start-up Costs)	251
Franchise Rights	271
Liabilities (301-450)	
Notes and Amounts Payable to Others (301-350)	
Notes Payable—Short Term	301

SAMPLE CHART OF ACCOUNTS, CON'T.

Current Maturities of Long-Term Debt	302
Accounts Payable (Trade Bills Due)	311
Sales Tax Payable	321
FICA Tax Withheld	331
Federal Income Taxes Withheld	332
State Income Taxes Withheld	333

Expenses Owed to Others (351-400)

Accrued Wages	351
Accrued Interest	361
Accrued FUTA	371
Accrued State Unemployment Tax	372
Accrued Federal Income Taxes	391
Accrued State Income Taxes	392

Long-Term Obligations (401-450)

Notes Payable—Long Term	401
Mortgages Payable	411
Deferred Taxes	421

Stockholders' Equity (451-500)

Paid in Capital (Owners' Investment in Business)	451
Capital Stock (Stock Issued)	461
Owner Draws (Cash Taken Out by Owners Other Than Salary)	481
Retained Earnings (Cumulative Profits Not Expended)	491

INCOME STATEMENT (501-999)	**Account #**

Sales and Other Income (501-550)

Sales of Merchandise	501
Sales Returns and Allowances	502
Cash Discounts Allowed (To Customers)	503
Miscellaneous Income	541

Cost of Goods Sold (551-600)

Cost of Merchandise Sold	551
Freight Expense	561

Business Operating Expenses (601-700)

Wages	601
Supplies	611
Rental of Equipment	
Repairs to Equipment	631
Truck Maintenance	641

SAMPLE CHART OF ACCOUNTS, CON'T.

Selling Expenses (701-750)

Advertising	701
Automobile Expenses—Sales Force	711
Commissions	721
Entertainment	731

Administrative Expenses (751-800)

Salaries	751
Office Supplies	761
Postage	762
Telephone	763
Dues and Subscriptions	764
Insurance	771
Automobile Expenses	781
Professional Services (Attorney and CPA)	786
Bad Debts (Uncollectible Accounts Receivable)	791
Interest	796

Miscellaneous Expenses (801-850)

Building Expenses (851-900)

Rent	851
Building Repairs	861
Utilities	871

Depreciation (901-950)

Buildings	911
Automobiles	916
Furniture and Office Equipment	921
Machinery	926
Leasehold Improvements	946

Taxes (951-999)

FICA	951
FUTA	952
Real Estate Taxes	961
Federal Income Taxes	991
State Income Taxes	992

Source: American Institute of Certified Public Accountants

not include every single accounting entry in a given period, it does reflect a summary of all transactions made.

If your new business will be a small, cash-based business, you can set up much of your general ledger out of your checkbook. The checkbook includes several pieces of information vital to the general ledger—cumulative cash balance, date of the entry, amount of the entry and purpose of the entry. However, if you plan to sell and buy on account as most businesses do, a checkbook alone will not suffice as a log for general ledger transactions. And even for a cash-based business, a checkbook cannot be your sole source for establishing a balance sheet.

An important component of any general ledger is source documents. Two examples of source documents are copies of invoices to customers and from suppliers. Source documents are critical in that they provide an audit trail in case you or someone else has to go back and study financial transactions made in your business. For instance, a customer might claim that he never received an invoice from you. Your source document will prove otherwise. And your source documents are a required component for your accountant at tax time. Other examples of source documents include canceled checks, utility bills, payroll tax records and loan statements.

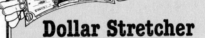

Dollar Stretcher

Managing your accounts payable effectively can significantly enhance your cash flow. Following are three tips for your accounts payable system that will improve your business's cash flow:

1. **Take discounts whenever feasible:** Saving 1 percent or 2 percent on an order can be significant.

2. **If discounts aren't offered, don't pay early:** There's no need to drain your cash flow unnecessarily.

3. **Keep your suppliers informed:** If you do fall behind, keep your lines of communication open with your suppliers. You can ill afford to get put on c.o.d.

All general ledger entries are double entries. And that makes sense, because for every financial transaction in your business, the money (or commitment to pay) goes from one place to another. For instance, when you write your payroll checks, the money flows out of your payroll account (cash) into the hands of your employees (an expense). When you sell goods on account, you record a sale (income) but must have a journal entry to make sure you collect that account later (an account receivable).

The system used in recording entries on a general ledger is called a system of debits and credits. In fact, if you can gain even a basic understanding of debits and credits, you will be well on your way to understanding your entire accounting system.

As outlined above, for every debit, there should be an equal and offsetting credit. It is when the debits and credits are not equal or do not offset

SAMPLE GENERAL LEDGER ENTRIES

While the bookkeeping process for your business can be rather intricate, single debit and credit entries are really quite basic. Remember that for every entry, there is an equal and offsetting co-entry. Also keep in mind that the different types of accounts have both debits and credits depending on whether the account is increased or decreased (see the chart on page 546). Here are five examples of equal and offsetting general ledger entries for a sock manufacturing business:

1. Purchasing a delivery truck	Debit	Credit
Cash (Asset)		$20,000
Fixed Asset (Asset)	$20,000	
2. Purchasing yarn on account to make the socks		
Accounts Payable (Liability)		$25,000
Inventory (Asset)	$25,000	
3. Selling a sock order to a customer on account		
Accounts Receivable (Asset)	$10,000	
Sales (Income)		$10,000
4. Collecting the account receivable from the same customer		
Accounts Receivable (Asset)		$10,000
Cash (Asset)	$10,000	
5. Funding payroll at the end of the month		
Payroll Expense (Expense)	$20,000	
Cash (Asset)		$20,000

that your books don't balance. A key advantage of any automated bookkeeping system is that it will police your debit-and-credit entries as they are made, making it far more difficult not to balance. It won't take many 3 a.m. error-finding sessions in a manual system to persuade you to automate your bookkeeping system!

All debits and credits either increase or decrease an account balance. These basic relationships are summarized as follows:

Account Type	Debit	Credit
Asset	Increases	Decreases
Liability	Decreases	Increases
Stockholder's Equity	Decreases	Increases
Income	Decreases	Increases
Expense	Increases	Decreases

In a general ledger, debits always go on the left and credits always go on the right. (For sample general ledger entries, see the chart in this chapter.)

While many double entries are made directly to the general ledger, it is necessary to maintain subledgers for a number of accounts in which there is regular activity. The information is then taken in a summary format from the subledgers and transferred to the general ledger. Subledgers showing cash receipts and cash disbursements are pretty easy to follow. However, some subledgers, such as accounts receivable, inventory, fixed assets, accounts payable and payroll can prove to be a challenge in their daily maintenance.

Accounts Receivable

If you plan to sell goods or services on account in your business, you will need a method of tracking who owes you how much and when it is due. This is where the accounts receivable subledger comes in. If you will be selling to a number of different customers, then an automated system is a must.

A good bookkeeping software system will allow you to set up subledgers for each customer. So when a sale is made on account, you can track it specifically to the customer. This is essential to ensure that billing and collection are done in a timely manner.

Inventory

Unless you are starting a service business, a good inventory-control feature will be an essential part of your bookkeeping system. If you are going to be manufacturing products, you will have to track raw materials, work-in-process and finished goods, and separate subledgers should be established for each of these inventory categories. Even if you are a wholesaler or retailer, you will be selling many different types of inventory and will need an effective system to track each inventory item offered for sale.

Another key reason to track inventory very closely is the direct relationship to cost of goods sold. Since nearly all businesses that stock inventory are required to use the accrual method for accounting, good inventory records are a must for accurately tracking the material cost associated with each item sold.

From a management standpoint, tracking inventory is also important. An effective and up-to-date inventory-control system will provide you with the following critical information:

♦ Which items sell well, and which items are slow moving

♦ When to order more raw materials or more items

♦ Where in the warehouse the inventory is stored when it comes time to ship it

♦ Number of days in the production process for each item

♦ The typical order of key customers

♦ Minimum inventory level needed to meet daily orders

(For more information on inventory-control systems, see the "Taking Stock" chapter.)

Fixed Assets

Fixed assets are items that are for long-term use, generally five years or more. They are not bought and sold in the normal course of business operation. Fixed assets include vehicles,

---

Bright Idea

If you will be selling on credit in your new business, your accounts receivable accounting system will be vital. Here are five key components of a good accounts receivable system:

1. **Verify accounts receivable balances:** You will use source documents such as invoices to keep your balances accurate.

2. **Send accurate and timely invoices:** You won't get paid until you send an accurate invoice.

3. **Generate accounts receivable reports:** This will help you to determine which customers are past due and to track credit limits.

4. **Post the paid invoices:** It's important to track who pays you when.

5. **Match your records:** Your customer records totals must match your general ledger and subledgers.

---

land, buildings, leasehold improvements, machinery and equipment.

In an accrual system of accounting, fixed assets are not recorded when they are purchased, but rather they are expensed over a period of time that coincides with the useful life (the amount of time the asset is expected to last) of the item. This process is known as depreciation. Most businesses that own fixed assets keep subledgers for each asset category as well as for each depreciation schedule.

In most cases, depreciation is easy to compute. The cost of the asset is divided by its useful life. For instance, a $60,000 piece of equipment with a five-year useful life would be depreciated at a rate of $12,000 per year. This is known as straight-line depreciation.

There are other more complicated methods of fixed-asset depreciation that allow for accelerated depreciation on the front end, which is advantageous from a tax standpoint. You should seek the advice of your CPA before setting up depreciation schedules for fixed-asset purchases.

Accounts Payable

The accounts payable subledger is similar to that used to track accounts receivable. The difference is that accounts payable occur when you purchase inventory or other assets on credit from a supplier.

It is important to track accounts payable in a timely manner to ensure that you know how much you owe each supplier and when payment is due. Many a good supplier relationship has been damaged due to a sloppy accounts payable system. Also, if your suppliers offer discounts for payment within 10 days of invoice, a good automated accounts payable system will alert you when to pay to maximize the discounts earned.

Payroll

Payroll accounting can be quite a challenge for the new business owner. There are many federal and state laws regulating what you have to track related to payroll (see the "The Tax Man Cometh" chapter). Failure to do so could result in heavy fines—or worse.

Many small-business owners use outside payroll services. These companies guarantee compliance with all applicable laws. This keeps the small-business owner out of trouble with the law and saves valuable time that can be devoted to something else in the business.

However, if you choose to do your own payroll, it is highly recommended that you purchase an automated payroll system. Even if the rest of your books are done manually, an automated payroll system will save valuable time and help considerably with compliance. There's not a lot of margin for error when dealing with the federal government!

COST ACCOUNTING

Cost accounting is the process of allocating all costs associated with generating a sale, both direct and indirect. Direct costs include materials, direct labor (the total wages paid to the workers who made the product), foreman/plant manager salaries and freight. Indirect costs include all other costs associated with keeping your doors open.

AGING OF
ACCOUNTS RECEIVABLE

REPORTING PERIOD

FROM: _____   TO: _____

DATE	INVOICE NUMBER	ACCOUNT	ACCOUNT NUMBER	DESCRIPTION	AMOUNT 30 DAYS	AMOUNT 60 DAYS	AMOUNT 90+ DAYS	TOTAL

Aging Of
Accounts Payable

REPORTING PERIOD

FROM: _____ TO: _____

DATE	INVOICE NUMBER	ACCOUNT	ACCOUNT NUMBER	DESCRIPTION	AMOUNT 30 DAYS	60 DAYS	TOTAL

PETTY CASH
JOURNAL

REPORTING PERIOD

FROM: _____ TO: _____ BALANCE [_____]

DATE	VOUCHER NUMBER	ACCOUNT	ACCOUNT NUMBER	PAYEE	APPROVED BY	TOTAL	BALANCE

AUDITED BY:

_____

APPROVED BY:

_____

TOTAL VOUCHER AMOUNT [_____]
TOTAL RECEIPTS [_____]
CASH ON HAND [_____]
OVERAGE/SHORTAGE [_____]
PETTY CASH REIMBURSEMENT [_____]
BALANCE FORWARD [_____]

As profit margins have shrunk in many businesses, particularly manufacturing ventures, cost accounting has become an increasingly valuable tool. By knowing the total costs associated with the production of a product, you can determine which inventory items are the most profitable to make. This will enable you to focus your sales effort on those items rather than on ones that offer little or no bottom-line enhancement.

> **Bright Idea**
>
> The Web site of the American Institute of Certified Public Accountants (www.aicpa.org) provides links to news updates, accounting-related software, state CPA societies and answers to frequently asked tax questions.

To set up an effective cost accounting system, you should seek input from your CPA. Cost accounting can get fairly complicated, and the money you might spend for a CPA will be more than made up in the expertise he or she will provide in customizing a cost accounting system for your business.

UNDER CONTROL

Do you know any small-business owners who have suffered significant losses due to employee theft or embezzlement? They probably did not have an effective internal-control system in place. Many successful ventures have been set back or even put out of business by an unscrupulous employee or financial service provider. And it is often someone who the business owner least suspected of wrongdoing.

When setting up a bookkeeping system, you need to focus a good deal of effort on instituting a sound system of policies and procedures governing internal control. Here are 10 areas where you need internal control:

1. **You need a written policy that clearly spells out your internal-control system.** Make sure all employees read this policy. Having a policy not only spells out the procedures to be followed, but it lets your employees know you are serious about internal controls.

2. **On a regular basis, review the internal-control policy to ensure it is up-to-date.** When changes are made, hold meetings with employees to discuss the changes and to maintain a focus on this vital area.

3. **Make sure all employees take at least one week's vacation each year.** This is often the time during which embezzlement is discovered.

FOR THE RECORD

As you set up your bookkeeping system, you will need procedures for keeping financial records. The IRS requires that you keep records for certain periods of time. And with some records, it just makes good sense to keep them so you can access them later.

Make sure these records are kept in a safe place. Whether you store them on site or at a remote location (such as a self-storage unit), make sure you use a fireproof cabinet or safe.

Another recommendation is to minimize paper buildup by storing as much as possible on computer disks or CD-ROMs. Here is a list of what you need to save and for how long you must save it as recommended by accounting firm Price Waterhouse:

Record Type	How Long?
Income tax reports, protests, court briefs, appeals	Indefinitely
Annual financial statements	Indefinitely
Monthly financial statements	3 years
Books of account, such as the general ledger	Indefinitely
Subledgers	3 years
Canceled, payroll and dividend checks	6 years
Income tax payment checks	Indefinitely
Bank reconciliations, voided checks, check stubs and check register tapes	6 years
Sales records such as invoices, monthly statements, remittance advisories, bills of lading and customers' purchase orders	6 years
Purchase records, including purchase orders and payment vouchers	6 years
Travel and entertainment records	6 years
Documents substantiating fixed-asset additions and depreciation policies	Indefinitely
Personnel and payroll records	6 years
Corporate documents, retirement and pension records, labor contracts, and license, patents, trademarks and registration applications	Indefinitely

MAKE NO MISTAKE

Following are four pitfalls to avoid when setting up a bookkeeping system:

1. **Competency:** To run a small business effectively, you must become familiar with your bookkeeping system, as well as the financial reports it will generate. Even if you hire an internal bookkeeper on day one, it is critical that you understand the numbers. Don't make the mistake of focusing all your efforts on marketing and production/operations while leaving the financial facet in someone else's hands.

    Successful entrepreneurs are proficient in all aspects of their ventures, including the numbers. Most community colleges offer basic accounting and finance courses. If numbers aren't your thing, sign up for one. It will be well worth the time investment.

2. **Computerization:** Don't let your lack of computer skills keep you from automating your bookkeeping system. If you aren't computer-literate, community colleges also offer a host of classes that provide training both in general computer use as well as specific software programs.

    You've got to think long term here. Just because a manual system might suffice in the early stages of your operation doesn't mean that you should ignore automation. Think about what will be needed three to five years down the road. Converting from a manual to an automated system is no fun—you can avoid this costly time drain by going automated upfront.

3. **Consistency:** When deciding on a software package for your bookkeeping system, don't just consider the price. The important issues to consider when buying bookkeeping software are: a) the track record of the software manufacturer, b) the track record of the software system itself, and c) the amount of technical assistance provided by the manufacturer.

4. **Compatibility:** Before you make a final bookkeeping software decision, check to see if the system is compatible with the other software programs you plan to use in your venture. Imagine the frustration you would experience if the spreadsheets you create in Microsoft Excel, say for payroll-tracking, cannot be exported into your bookkeeping system.

4. **Cross-train others in the company to handle daily bookkeeping duties.** If someone who is stealing from you is out sick or on vacation, you'll have a hard time catching him if you allow the work to go unprocessed until his or her return.

5. **Perform background checks before hiring new employees.** This may sound obvious, but dishonest employees often are hired by unsuspecting employers who failed to check references before making the offer.

6. **Use dual control.** You are asking for trouble if you have the same person running the accounts payable system, making journal entries, printing and signing checks and reconciling the checkbook.

7. **Have your CPA or outside bookkeeper perform unannounced spot audits.** You may be uncomfortable performing these audits yourself, but if your policy calls for periodic audits, the CPA looks like the bad guy.

8. **Be careful who you hire as an outside financial service provider.** There are countless stories of entrepreneurs being ripped off by supposedly trusted professional service providers such as accountants and attorneys. Don't relinquish total control of your cash to an outside bookkeeper. And if he or she seems reluctant to share information with you when you ask for it, this could be a sign of deceptive financial advisory practices.

9. **Backup your computer information regularly.** This is an important function for all aspects of your business. If you begin to suspect an employee of stealing, the ability to study past transactions will be vital in finding out if your suspicions are justified.

10. **In the early stages of your business, you may be able to monitor much of the cash-control procedures yourself.** However, as your business grows, you will be forced to delegate certain internal-control functions. When you do, make sure you choose qualified, well-trained employees who have proved to be trustworthy. And make sure your policy clearly stipulates who is authorized to perform internal control tasks such as processing invoices and signing checks.

FINANCIAL STATEMENTS

One of the primary benefits of a good bookkeeping system is the generation of timely and useful financial statements. Most automated software packages offer the capability of producing monthly financial statements.

This information includes a balance sheet, an income statement, a reconciliation of net worth and a cash flow statement. These monthly reports provide invaluable information on the historical measures you need to make the financial decisions that will positively impact your business tomorrow.

Refer to the next chapter for a look at these financial statements in detail and how you can use them for effective short- and long-term financial planning.

GLOSSARY

Accounts payable: a company liability that represents amounts due for goods or services purchased on credit

Accounts receivable: a company asset that represents amounts owed for goods or services sold on credit

Asset: tangible or intangible object of value to its owner

Chart of accounts: the list of accounts that will be tracked within the general ledger

Cost accounting: the process of allocating all direct and indirect expenses associated with the production and/or sale of a produc

Credit: the right-side entries in a double-entry accounting system

Debit: the left-side entries in a double-entry accounting system

Depreciation: allocation of the cost resulting from the purchase of a fixed asset over the entire period of its use

Double-entry accounting: a system of accounting in which the total of all left-side entries is equal to and offset by the total of all right-side entries

Expense: money spent for goods or services

Fixed assets: assets that are not bought and sold in the normal course of business, but that are purchased for long-term use in the production or sales process

General ledger: the main records of the assets, liabilities, owner's equity, income and expenses of an organization

Income: money received for goods or services produced or as a return on investment

Internal control: a system that is designed to minimize the risk of financial loss due to incompetence or dishonesty of an employee or outside bookkeeper

Inventory: the assets produced by a manufacturing business or the assets bought and sold for profit by a wholesaling or retailing business

Liability: an obligation to another party

Owner's equity: excess of total assets minus total liabilities

CHAPTER 38

MAKING A STATEMENT

How to create
financial statements

By J. Tol Broome Jr.,
a freelance business writer and banker
with 14 years of experience in commercial lending

In the last chapter, we explored the key facets of establishing a good bookkeeping system for your new business. And while a well-organized bookkeeping system is vital, even more critical is what you do with it to establish your methods for financial management and control.

Think of your new bookkeeping system as the body of a car. A car body can be engineered, painted and finished to look sleek and powerful. However, the car body won't get anywhere without an engine. Your financial management system is the engine that will make your car achieve peak performance.

You may be wondering what exactly is meant by the term "financial management." It is the process you use to put your numbers to work to make your business more successful. With a good financial management system, you will know not only how your business is doing financially, but why. And you will be able to use it to make decisions to improve the operation of your business.

Why is financial management important? Because a good financial management system enables you to accomplish important big picture and daily financial objectives. A good financial management system helps you become a better macromanager by enabling you to:

1. manage proactively rather than reactively.

2. borrow money more easily; not only can you plan ahead for financing needs, but sharing your budget with your banker will help in the loan approval process.

3. provide financial planning information for investors.

4. make your operation more profitable and efficient.

5. access a great decision-making tool for key financial considerations.

Financial planning and control help you become a better micromanager by enabling you to:

1. avoid investing too much money in fixed assets.

2. maintain short-term working capital needs to support accounts receivable and inventory more efficiently.

3. set sales goals; you need to be growth-oriented, not just an "order taker."

4. improve gross profit margin by pricing your services more effectively or by reducing supplier prices, direct labor, etc., that affect cost of goods sold.

5. operate your business more efficiently by keeping selling and general and administrative expenses down more effectively.

6. perform tax planning.

7. plan ahead for employee benefits.

8. perform sensitivity analysis with the different financial variables involved.

Smart Tip

All new businesses should produce an annual year-end financial statement. These statements should be prepared by your CPA, who will offer you three basic choices of financial statement quality:

1. **Compilation:** This is the least expensive option. Here, the CPA takes management's information and compiles it into the proper financial statement format.

2. **Review:** In addition to putting management's information into the proper format, the CPA performs a limited review of the information.

3. **Audit:** This option is the most costly but offers the highest quality. Audited financial statements are prepared in accordance with generally accepted accounting principles and are the type preferred by most lenders and investors.

CREATING FINANCIAL STATEMENTS

The first step in developing a financial management system is the creation of financial statements. To manage proactively, you should plan to generate financial statements on a monthly basis. Your financial statements should include an income statement, a balance sheet and a cash flow statement (see Figures 38-1, 38-2 and 38-3, respectively).

A good automated accounting software package will create the monthly financial statements for you. If your bookkeeping system is manual, you still can use an internal or external bookkeeper to provide you with monthly financial statements.

Income Statement

Simply put, the income statement measures all your revenue sources vs. all your business expenses for a given period. Let's consider an apparel manufacturer as an example in outlining the major components of the income statement:

◆ **Sales:** This is the gross revenues generated from the sale of clothing less returns (cancellations) and allowances (reduction in price for discounts taken by customers).

◆ **Cost of goods sold:** This is the direct cost associated with manufacturing the clothing. These costs include materials used, direct labor, plant manager salaries, freight and other costs associated with operating a plant (i.e., utilities, equipment repairs, etc.).

◆ **Gross profit:** The gross profit represents the amount of direct profit associated with the actual manufacturing of the clothing. It is calculated as sales less the cost of goods sold.

◆ **Operating expenses:** These are the selling, general and administrative expenses that are necessary to run the business. Examples include office salaries, insurance, advertising, sales commissions and rent. (See the schedule of operating expenses on the following page for a more detailed list of operating expenses.)

◆ **Depreciation:** Depreciation is usually included in operating expenses and/or cost of goods sold, but it is worthy of special mention due to its unusual nature. Depreciation results when a company purchases a fixed asset and expenses it over the entire period of its planned use, not just in the year purchased. The IRS requires certain depreciation schedules to be followed for tax reasons. Depreciation is a noncash expense in that the cash flows out when the asset is purchased, but the cost is taken over a period of years depending on the type of asset.

Whether depreciation is included in cost of goods sold or in operating expenses depends on the type of asset being depreciated. Depreciation is listed with cost of goods sold if the expense associated with the fixed asset is used in the direct production of inventory. Examples include the purchase of production equipment and machinery or a building that houses a production plant.

Depreciation is listed with operating expenses if the cost is associated with fixed assets used for selling, general or administra-

FIGURE 38-1

INCOME STATEMENT
ABC CLOTHING INC.

	Year 1	Year 2
Sales	$1,000,000	$1,500,000
Cost of Goods Sold	−750,000	−1,050,000
Gross Profit	250,000	450,000
Operating Expenses	−200,000	−275,000
Operating Profit	50,000	175,000
Other Income & Expenses	3,000	5,000
Net Profit Before Taxes	53,000	180,000
Income Taxes	−15,900	−54,000
Net Profit After Taxes	**$37,100**	**$126,000**

SCHEDULE OF OPERATING EXPENSES
ABC CLOTHING INC.

	Year 1	Year 2
Advertising	$5,000	$15,000
Auto Expenses	3,000	7,500
Bank Charges	750	1,200
Depreciation	30,000	30,000
Dues & Subscriptions	500	750
Employee Benefits	5,000	10,000
Insurance	6,000	10,000
Interest	17,800	15,000
Office Expenses	2,500	4,000
Officers' Salaries	40,000	60,000
Payroll Taxes	6,000	9,000
Professional Fees	4,000	7,500
Rent	24,000	24,000
Repairs & Maintenance	2,000	2,500
Salaries & Wages	40,000	60,000
Security	2,250	2,250
Supplies	2,000	3,000
Taxes & Licenses	1,000	1,500
Telephone	4,800	6,000
Utilities	2,400	2,400
Other	1,000	3,400
Total Operating Expenses	**$200,000**	**$275,000**

tive purposes. Examples include vehicles for salespeople or an office computer and phone system.

◆ **Operating profit:** This is the amount of profit earned during the normal course of operations. It is computed by subtracting operating expenses from gross profit.

◆ **Other income and expenses:** Other income and expenses represent those items that do not occur during the normal course of operation. For instance, a clothing maker does not normally earn income from rental property or interest on investments, so these income sources are accounted for separately. Interest expense on debt is also included in this category. A net figure is computed by subtracting other expenses from other income.

◆ **Net profit before taxes:** This represents the amount of income earned by the business before paying taxes. It is computed by adding other income (or subtracting if other expenses exceed other income) to the operating profit.

◆ **Income taxes:** This is the total amount of state and federal income taxes paid.

◆ **Net profit after taxes:** This is the "bottom line" earnings of the business. It is computed by subtracting taxes paid from net profit before taxes.

Balance Sheet

The balance sheet provides a snapshot of the business's assets, liabilities and owner's equity for a given time. Again, using an apparel manufacturer as an example, here are the key components of the balance sheet:

◆ **Current assets:** These are the assets in a business that can be converted to cash in one year or less. They include cash, stocks and other liquid investments; accounts receivable; inventory; and prepaid expenses. For a clothing manufacturer, inventory would include raw materials (yarn, thread, etc.), work-in-progress (started but not finished), and finished goods (shirts and pants ready to sell to customers). Accounts receivable represent the amount of money owed to the business by customers who have purchased on account.

◆ **Fixed assets:** These are the tangible assets of a business that will not be converted to cash within a year during the normal course of operation. Fixed assets are for long-term use and include land, buildings, leasehold improvements, equipment, machinery and vehicles.

FIGURE 38-2

BALANCE SHEET
ABC CLOTHING INC.

	Year 1	Year 2
Assets:		
Current Assets:		
Cash	$10,000	$20,000
Accounts Receivable	82,000	144,000
Inventory	185,000	230,000
Prepaid Expenses	5,000	5,000
Total Current Assets	$282,000	$399,000
Fixed Assets:		
Land	0	0
Buildings	0	0
Equipment	150,000	120,000
Accumulated Depreciation	−30,000	−30,000
Total Fixed Assets	120,000	90,000
Intangibles	0	0
Other Assets	10,000	11,000
Total Assets	**$412,000**	**$500,000**
Liabilities & Equity:		
Current Liabilities:		
Notes Payable—Short Term	$60,000	$42,400
Current Maturities—Long-Term Debt	30,000	30,000
Accounts Payable	82,000	86,000
Accrued Expenses	7,900	13,500
Taxes Payable	0	0
Stockholder Loans	0	0
Total Current Liabilities	179,900	171,900
Long-Term Debt	120,000	90,000
Total Liabilities	$299,900	$261,900
Stockholders' Equity:		
Common Stock	$75,000	$75,000
Paid-in-capital	0	0
Retained Earnings	37,100	163,100
Total Stockholders' Equity	112,100	238,100
Total Liabilities & Equity	**$412,000**	**$500,000**

◆ **Intangible assets:** These are assets that you can't touch or see but that have value. Intangible assets include franchise rights, goodwill, noncompete agreements, patents and many other items.

◆ **Other assets:** There are many assets that can be classified as other assets, and most business balance sheets have an other assets category as a "catch-all." Some of the most common other assets include cash value of life insurance, long-term investment property, and compensation due from employees.

◆ **Current liabilities:** These are the obligations of the business that are due within one year. Current liabilities include notes payable on lines of credit or other short-term loans, current maturities of long-term debt, accounts payable to trade creditors, accrued expenses and taxes (an accrual is an expense such as the payroll that is due to employees for hours worked but has not been paid), and amounts due to stockholders.

◆ **Long-term debt:** These are the obligations of the business that are not due for at least one year. Long-term liabilities typically consist of all bank debt or stockholder loans payable outside of the following 12-month period.

◆ **Stockholders' equity:** This figure represents the total amount invested by the stockholders plus the accumulated profit of the business. Components include common stock, paid-in-capital (amounts invested not involving a stock purchase), and retained earnings (cumulative earnings since inception of the business less dividends paid to stockholders).

Cash Flow Statement

The cash flow statement is designed to convert the accrual basis of accounting used to prepare the income statement and balance sheet back to a cash basis. This may sound redundant, but it is necessary. The accrual basis of accounting generally is preferred for the income statement and balance sheet because it more accurately matches revenue sources to the expenses incurred generating those specific sources. How-

Bright Idea

Many small-business owners make the mistake of preparing financial statements only at year-end when the IRS requires it. The consequence is reactive financial planning. If you want to be a proactive financial manager, generate monthly financial statements, and use them to make the key financial decisions that affect the daily success of your business.

ever, it also is important to analyze the actual level of cash flowing into and out of the business.

Like the income statement, the statement of cash flow measures financial activity over a period of time. And the cash flow statement also tracks the effects of changes in balance sheet accounts.

The cash flow statement is one of the most useful financial management tools you will have to run your business. The cash flow statement is divided into four categories:

◆ **Net cash flow from operating activities:** Operating activities are the daily internal activities of a business that either require cash or generate it. They include cash collections from customers; cash paid to suppliers and employees; cash paid for operating expenses, interest and taxes; and cash revenue from interest dividends.

◆ **Net cash flow from investing activities:** Investing activities are discretionary investments made by management. These primarily consist of the purchases (or sale) of equipment.

◆ **Net cash flow from financing activities:** Financing activities are those external sources and uses of cash that affect cash flow. These include sales of common stock, changes in short- or long-term loans, and dividends paid.

◆ **Net change in cash and marketable securities:** The results of the first three calculations are used to determine the total increase or decrease in cash and marketable securities caused by fluctuations in operating, investing and financing cash flow. This number is then checked against the change in cash reflected on the balance sheet from period to period to verify that the calculation has been done correctly.

CASH FLOW ANALYSIS

The cash flow statement enables you to track cash as it flows in and out of your business and reveals to you the causes of cash flow shortfalls and surpluses. The operating activities are the daily occurrences that are essential to any business operation. If these are positive, then it indicates to the owner that the business is self-sufficient in funding its daily operational cash flows internally. If the number is negative, then it indicates that outside funds were needed to sustain the operation of the business.

Investing activities generally use cash because most businesses are more likely to acquire new equipment and machinery than to sell old fixed as-

FIGURE 38-3
CASH FLOW STATEMENT
ABC CLOTHING INC.

	Year 1	Year 2
Cash Flow From Operating Activities*:		
Cash Received From Customers	$918,000	$1,438,000
Interest Received	3,000	5,000
Cash Paid To Suppliers For Inventory	(853,000)	(1,091,000)
Cash Paid To Employees	(80,000)	(120,000)
Cash Paid For Other Operating Expenses	(69,300)	(104,400)
Interest Paid	(17,800)	(15,000)
Taxes Paid	(15,900)	(54,000)
Net Cash Provided (Used) By Operating Activities	($115,000)	$58,600
Cash Flow From Investing Activities:		
Additions To Property, Plant And Equipment	(150,0000)	0
Increase/Decrease In Other Assets	(10,000)	(1,000)
Other Investing Activities	0	0
Net Cash Provided (Used) By Investing Activities	($160,000)	($1,000)
Cash Flow From Financing Activities:		
Sales Of Common Stock	$75,000	0
Increase (Decrease) In Short-Term Loans (Includes Current Maturities Of Long-Term Debt)	90,000	(17,600)
Additions To Long-Term Loans	120,000	0
Reductions Of Long-Term Loans	0	(30,000)
Dividends Paid	0	0
Net Cash Provided (Used) By Financing Activities	285,000	(47,600)
Increase (Decrease) In Cash	**$10,000**	**$10,000**

* Calculations Are As Follow:

Cash Collections From Customers =	Sales	— Increase In Accounts Receivable
		+ Decrease In Accounts Receivable
		+ Increase In Deferred Revenue
		— Decrease In Deferred Revenue

Cash Paid To Suppliers =	Cost Of Goods Sold	+ Increase In Inventory
		— Decrease In Inventory
		— Increase In Accounts Payable
		+ Decrease In Accounts Payable

| Cash Paid To Employees = | Salary Expense | — Increase In Accrued Salaries Payable |
| | | + Decrease In Accrued Salaries Payable |

Cash Paid To Other Operating Expenses =	Other Operating Expenses	— Depreciation And Amortization
		+ Increase In Prepaid Expenses
		— Decrease In Prepaid Expenses
		— Increase In Accrued Operating Expenses
		+ Decrease In Accrued Operating Expenses

| Cash Revenue From Interest = | Interest Revenue | — Increase In Interest Receivable |
| | | + Decrease In Interest Receivable |

| Cash Paid For Interest = | Interest Expenses | — Increase In Accrued Interest Payable |
| | | + Decrease In Accrued InterestPayable |

Cash Paid For Taxes =	Tax Expenses	— Increase In Deferred Tax Liability
		+ Decrease In Deferred Tax Liability
		— Decrease In Deferred Tax Asset
		+ Increase In Deferred Tax Asset
		— Increase In Accrued Taxes Payable
		+ Decrease In Accrued Taxes Payable
		— Decrease In Prepaid Tax
		+ Increase In Prepaid Tax

sets. When a company does need cash to fund investing activities in a given year, it must come either from an internal operating cash flow surplus or from financing activity increases or from cash reserves built up in prior years.

Financing activities represent the external sources of funds available to

BALANCE BOOSTERS

A common problem for small-business owners is the struggle to maintain adequate cash flow levels. And increasing sales isn't always the answer. Here are six tips that enhance your bank balance regardless of whether sales are on the rise:

1. *Practice good inventory management.* Don't try to be all things to all people, particularly if you are a wholesaler or retailer. Keeping slow-moving inventory in stock "just in case" someone asks costs money.

2. *Concentrate on higher margin items.* Focus your efforts on selling those items that generate the most profit rather than on the items that sell the fastest.

3. *Take full advantage of trade terms.* Wait until the day a bill or invoice is due to pay it. Your cash flow will be enhanced, and your valued supplier relationships will not be harmed because you will still be paying on time.

4. *Shop for lower priced suppliers.* Before you get started, check with a number of different suppliers to see which one offers the best price and terms.

5. *Control operating expenses better.* Utilities expenses can be lowered by minimizing the use of electricity and by adjusting the thermostat upward or downward a few degrees during the summer and winter months. Insurance and telephone service providers should be comparison shopped on a regular basis. Keep a close eye on employee downtime and overtime. And shop for the best lease rates.

6. *Extend bank loans on longer terms.* Many banks are more than willing to extend the term on a loan to businesses in search of cash flow relief. For instance, by extending the term on a $20,000 loan (at 9 percent interest) from two years to three, a business realizes annual cash flow enhancement of $3,336.

the business. Financing activities typically will be a provider of funds when a company has shortfalls in operating or investing activities. The reverse is often true when operating activities are a source of excess cash flow, as the overflow often is used to reduce debt.

The increase/decrease in cash figure at the bottom of the cash flow statement represents the net result of operating, investing and financing activities. If a business ever runs out of cash, it can't survive, so this is a key number.

Our hypothetical clothing business in the sample financial statements, ABC Clothing Inc., provides a good example. In Year 1, the growth in accounts receivable and inventory required $115,000 in cash to fund operating activities. The purchase of $150,000 in equipment also drained cash flow. ABC funded these needs with the sale of common stock of $75,000 and loans totaling $210,000. The outcome was that the company increased its cash resources by $10,000.

Year 2 was a different story. Because the company had a net income of $126,000, there was a good deal more cash ($58,600) flowing in from customers than flowing out to suppliers, employees, other operating expenses, interest and taxes. This enabled ABC to reduce its overall outside debt by $47,600 and to increase its cash balance by $10,000.

When you start your business, you will be able to use the cash flow statement not only to analyze your sources and uses of cash from year to year but also from month to month if you set up your accounting system to produce monthly statements. You will find the cash flow statement to be an invaluable tool in understanding the hows and whys of cash flowing into and out of your business.

As a new business owner, you will need accurate and timely financial information to help you manage your business effectively. Your financial statements will also be critical budgeting tools as you seek to achieve financial milestones in your business.

GLOSSARY

Accrued expenses: expenses that have been accounted for on the income statement but that have not yet been paid

Balance sheet: a "snapshot" of the assets, liabilities and owners' equity of a business for a given period

Cash flow statement: the financial statement that reflects all inflows and outflows of cash resulting from operating, investing and financing activities during a specific time period

Common stock: shares of stock that make up the total ownership of a corporation

Cost of goods sold: the cost that a business incurs to produce a product for sale to its customers

Current maturities of long-term debt: the portion of long-term debt that is due in one year or less

Income statement: a financial statement that charts revenues and expenses over a period of time

Intangible assets: assets of a business such as patents, franchise rights and goodwill that do not physically exist but that have value to the business

Long-term debt: the portion of external debt (usually from banks) that is due after one year

Notes payable: short-term notes of less than one year either under lines of credit or with a stated repayment date

Operating expenses: the selling and general and administrative expenses incurred by a business

Paid-in-capital: the additional amount paid for common stock over and above the value upon issuance

Retained earnings: the cumulative amount of after-tax earnings less dividends paid that the owner draws over the life of a business

Sales: the gross amount of revenue generated by a business

CHAPTER 39

WATCH YOUR PENNIES

Effectively managing your finances

By J. Tol Broome Jr.,
a freelance business writer and banker
with 14 years of experience in commercial lending

Now that you have the framework for establishing a bookkeeping system and for creating financial statements, what's next? In this chapter, we will explore how to analyze the data that results from an effective financial management and control system. Additionally, we will consider the key elements of a good budgeting system.

The financial analysis tools we will discuss are computing gross profit margin and markup, in addition to break-even, working capital and financial ratio analyses. In the section on budgeting, we will look at when, what and how to budget, as well as how to perform a sensitivity analysis.

GROSS PROFIT MARGIN AND MARKUP

One of the most important financial concepts you will need to learn in running your new business is the computation of gross profit. And the tool that you use to maintain gross profit is markup.

The gross profit on a product sold is computed as:

Sales - Cost of Goods Sold = Gross Profit

To understand gross profit, it is important to know the distinction between variable and fixed costs. Variable costs are those that change based on the amount of product being made and are incurred as a direct result of producing the product. Variable costs include:

◆ Materials used

◆ Direct labor

◆ Packaging

◆ Freight

◆ Plant supervisor salaries

◆ Utilities for a plant or warehouse

◆ Depreciation expense on production equipment and machinery

Fixed costs generally are more static in nature. They include:

◆ Office expenses such as supplies, utilities and a telephone for the office

◆ Salaries and wages of office staff, salespeople and officers and owners

◆ Payroll taxes and employee benefits

◆ Advertising, promotional and other sales expenses

◆ Insurance

◆ Auto expenses for salespeople

◆ Professional fees

◆ Rent

Variable expenses are recorded as cost of goods sold. Fixed expenses are counted as operating expenses (sometimes called selling and general and administrative expenses).

Gross Profit Margin

While the gross profit is a dollar amount, the gross profit margin is expressed as a percentage. It is equally important to track since it allows you to keep an eye on profitability trends. This is critical because many businesses have gotten into financial trouble with an increasing gross profit that coincided with a declining gross profit margin. The gross profit margin is computed as follows:

Gross Profit/Sales = Gross Profit Margin

There are two key ways for you to improve your gross profit margin. First, you can increase your prices. Second, you can decrease the costs to produce your goods. Of course, both are easier said than done.

An increase in prices can cause sales to drop. If sales drop too far, you may not generate enough gross profit dollars to cover operating expenses. Price increases require a careful reading of inflation rates, competitive factors and basic supply and demand for the product you are producing.

The second method of increasing gross profit margin is to lower the variable costs to produce your product. This can be accomplished by decreasing material costs or making the product more efficiently. Volume discounts are a good way to reduce material costs. The more material you buy from a supplier, the more likely they are to offer you discounts. Another way to reduce material costs is to find a less costly supplier. However,

How Do You Rate?

Ratio analysis is a financial management tool that enables you to compare the trends in your financial performance, as well as provides some measurements to compare your performance against others in your industry. Comparing ratios from year to year highlights areas in which you are performing well, as well as areas that need tweaking. Most industry trade groups can provide you with industry averages for key ratios that will provide a benchmark against which you can compare your company.

Financial ratios can be divided into four subcategories: profitability, liquidity, activity and leverage. Here are 15 financial ratios that you can use to manage your new business. (See Figure 39-6 for sample financial ratios for ABC Clothing.)

1. **Profitability Ratios**

   Gross Profit/Sales = Gross Profit Margin

   Operating Profit/Sales = Operating Profit Margin

   Net Profit/Sales = Net Profit Margin

   Net Profit/Owner's Equity = Return on Equity

   Net Profit/Total Assets = Return on Assets

2. **Liquidity Ratios**

   Current Assets/Current Liabilities = Current Ratio

   (Current Assets - Inventory)/Current Liabilities = Quick Ratio

   Working Capital/Sales = Working Capital Ratio

3. **Activity Ratios**

   (Accounts Receivable x 365)/Sales = Accounts Receivable Days

   (Inventory x 365)/Cost of Goods Sold = Inventory Days

   (Accounts Payable x 365)/Purchases = Accounts Payable Days

   Sales/Total Assets = Sales to Assets

4. **Leverage Ratios**

   Total Liabilities/Owner's Equity = Debt to Equity

   Total Liabilities/Total Assets = Debt Ratio

   (Net Income + Depreciation)/Current Maturities of
     Long-term Debt = Debt Coverage Ratio

Smart Tip

As you start your business, it will be important to track external financial trends to ensure you are headed in the right direction. It also will be critical to compare your company's performance to others in your industry. If you are a member of a trade association, the group should offer comparative industry data. Information may also be available from your CPA or banker.

you might sacrifice quality if the goods purchased are not made as well.

Whether you are starting a manufacturing, wholesaling, retailing or service business, you should always be on the lookout for ways to deliver your product or service more efficiently. However, you also must balance efficiency and quality issues to ensure that they do not get out of balance.

Let's look at the gross profit of ABC Clothing Inc. (see Figure 38-1 on page 561) as an example of the computation of gross profit margin. In Year 1, sales were $1 million and the gross profit was $250,000, resulting in a gross profit margin of 25 percent ($250,000/$1 million). In Year 2, sales were $1.5 million and the gross profit was $450,000, resulting in a gross profit margin of 30 percent ($450,000/$1.5 million).

It is apparent that ABC Clothing not only earned more gross profit dollars in Year 2 but also a higher gross profit margin. The company either raised prices, lowered variable material costs from suppliers, or found a way to produce its clothing more efficiently (which usually means fewer labor hours per product produced).

Computing Markup

ABC Clothing did a better job in Year 2 of managing its markup on the clothing products it manufactured. Many business owners often get confused when relating markup to gross profit margin. They are first cousins in that both computations deal with the same variables. The difference is that gross profit margin is figured as a percentage of the selling price, while markup is figured as a percentage of the seller's cost.

Markup is computed as follows:

(Selling Price - Cost to Produce)/Cost to Produce = Markup Percentage

Let's compute markup for ABC Clothing for Year 1:

($1 million - $750,000)/$750,000 = 33.3%

Now, let's compute markup for ABC Clothing for Year 2:

($1.5 million - $1.05 million)/$1.05 million = 42.9%

While computing markup for an entire year for a business is very simple, using this valuable markup tool daily to work up price quotes is a bit more

Figure 39-1

Markup Computation For ABC Clothing Price Quote

	Hours/ Dozen	Cost/ Hour	Cost/ Dozen	Number Of Dozens	Total Cost
Labor	1.00	$7.00		100	$700.00
Supervision	0.05	$20.00		100	$100.00
Total Labor Cost					$800.00
Fabric			$35.00	100	$3,500.00
Sewing Thread			$2.50	100	$250.00
Buttons			$2.50	100	$250.00
Total Materials Cost			$40.00	100	$4,000.00
Total Labor And Materials Costs					$4,800.00
Desired Markup					0.429
Price Quote To Customer					$6,859.20

complicated. However, it is even more vital. Computing markup on last year's numbers helps you understand where you have been and gives you a benchmark for success. But computing markup on individual jobs will affect your business going forward and can often make the difference in running a profitable operation.

In bidding individual jobs you must carefully estimate the variable costs associated with each job. And the calculation is different in that you typically seek a desired markup with a known cost to arrive at the price quote. Here is the computation to find a price quote using markup:

$$\text{(Desired Markup x Total Variable Costs)}$$
$$+ \text{ Total Variable Costs} = \text{Price Quote}$$

Let's again use ABC Clothing as an example. ABC has been asked to quote on a job to produce 100 dozen shirts. Based on prior experience, the owner estimates that the job will require 100 labor hours of direct labor and five hours of supervision from the plant manager. The total material costs based on quotes from suppliers (fabric, sewing thread, buttons, etc.) will be $40 per dozen. If ABC Clothing seeks a markup of 42.9 percent on all orders in Year 2, it would use a markup table (see Figure 39-1) to calculate the price quote.

What if you're a new business owner and don't have any experience to base an estimate on? Then you need to research material costs by getting quotes from suppliers as well as study the labor rates in the area. You should also research industry manufacturing prices. Armed with this information, you will have a well-educated "guess" to base your job quote on.

How you use markup to set prices will depend on the type of business you are starting. If you are launching a manufacturing, wholesale or retail operation, you will be able to compute markup using the above formulas to factor in all the variables in the cost of producing or generating the items you will be selling. Markup can also be used to bid one job or to set prices for an entire product line.

If you are starting a service business, however, markup is more difficult to calculate, particularly for new business owners. With most service businesses, the key variable cost associated with delivering the service to your customers will be you and your employees' time. In computing proper markup for a ser-

Bright Idea

When you set up your computerized bookkeeping system to create automatic monthly financial statements, make sure you also automate your business's financial ratios. There's no sense in having to compute them manually when the information is available off your PC. Reviewing financial ratios monthly will help you keep an eye on your business's financial trends.

vice business, you must pay close attention to the time spent to provide the service to customers, as well as to market prices of the services provided. In starting a service business, you will need to research the going rate paid to employees and the market prices for the services you will be providing.

For instance, if you are starting a temporary help agency, you will need to know what rate is typically paid to employees in this industry, as well as the market rate charged to your customers for temporary labor. This will enable you to compute the proper markup in setting your price to ensure that you will be profitable.

(See Figure 39-1 for how the price quote was calculated for ABC Clothing, then go to Figures 39-2 and 39-3 for price-quote work sheets you can use in your own business.)

BREAK-EVEN ANALYSIS

One useful tool in tracking your business's cash flow will be break-even analysis. It is a fairly simple calculation and can prove very helpful in deciding whether to make an equipment purchase or just to know how close you are to your break-even level. Here are

Beware!

Here are 10 signs that you might be experiencing embezzlement or employee theft in your business:

◆ Unwillingness of employees to take vacation

◆ Employees who refuse to delegate certain tasks

◆ A lack of dual control for tasks involving cash

◆ Ledgers and subledgers that don't balance

◆ Financial statements that don't balance

◆ Lack of audit trails

◆ Regular complaints from customers that inventory shipments aren't complete

◆ Unwillingness of a bookkeeper or accountant to share information

◆ Erratic behavior by an employee

◆ Unexpected bouncing of checks

the variables needed to compute a break-even sales analysis:

◆ Gross profit margin

◆ Operating expenses (less depreciation)

◆ Total of monthly debt payments for the year (annual debt service)

Since we are dealing with cash flow and depreciation is a noncash expense, it is subtracted from the operating expenses. The break-even calculation for sales is:

FIGURE 39-2

PRICE QUOTE WORK SHEET
FOR A SERVICE BUSINESS

	Hours/ Unit	Cost/ Hour	Cost/ Unit	Number Of Units	Total Cost
Labor #1		$			$
Labor #2		$			$
Supervision		$			$
Total Labor Cost[1]					$
Other Variable Costs			$		$
Total Labor And Other Variable Costs[2]					$
Desired Markup[3]					%
Price Quote To Customer[4]					$

[1] Depending on the type of service business, there may be many more labor contributions. All should be considered.

[2] Derived by adding together Total Labor Costs And Other Variable Costs.

[3] Stated as a percentage markup on the costs to provide the service. In most service businesses, this will range from 25% (0.25) to 100% (1.0).

[4] Price Quote computed as follows:
Total Labor Costs + Other Variable Costs + ([Total Labor Costs +Other Variable Costs] × Desired Markup)

FIGURE 39-3

PRICE QUOTE WORK SHEET
FOR A NONSERVICE BUSINESS

	Hours/ Unit	Cost/ Hour	Cost/ Unit	Number Of Units	Total Cost
Labor		$			$
Supervision		$			$
Total Labor Cost[1]					$
Materials Item #1			$		$
Materials Item #2			$		$
Materials Item #3			$		$
Total Materials Cost[2]			$		$
Other Variable Production Costs			$		$
Total Labor, Materials And Other Variable Production Costs[3]					$
Desired Markup[4]					%
Price Quote To Customer[5]					$

[1] *Depending on the type of company, there may be many more labor contributions. All should be considered.*

[2] *Depending on the type of company, there may be many types of materials used to produce a product. All should be considered.*

[3] *Derived by adding together Total Labor Costs, Total Materials Costs And Other Variable Production Costs.*

[4] *Stated as a percentage markup on production costs. In some businesses, this may be as low as 5% (.05); in others it might be 100% (1.0) or higher.*

[5] *Price Quote computed as follows:*
   Total Labor Costs + Total Materials Costs + Other Variable Production Costs + ([Total Labor Costs + Total Materials Costs + Other Variable Production Costs] × Desired Markup)

(Operating Expenses + Annual Debt Service)/Gross Profit Margin = Break-even Sales

Let's use ABC Clothing as an example and compute this company's break-even sales for Years 1 and 2:

	Year 1	Year 2
Gross Profit Margin	25.0%	30.0%
Operating Expenses (less depreciation)	$170,000	$245,000
Annual Current Maturities of Long-term Debt*	$30,000	$30,000

This represents the principal portion of annual debt service; the interest portion of annual debt service is already included in operating expenses.

Break-even Sales for Year 1: ($170,000 + $30,000)/.25 = $800,000

Break-even Sales for Year 2: ($245,000 + $30,000)/.30 = $916,667

It is apparent from these calculations that ABC Clothing was well ahead of break-even sales both in Year 1 ($1 million sales) and Year 2 ($1.5 million). Break-even analysis also can be used to calculate break-even sales needed for the other variables in the equation. Let's say the owner of ABC Clothing was confident he could generate sales of $750,000, and the company's operating expenses are $170,000 with $30,000 in annual current maturities of long-term debt. The break-even gross margin needed would be calculated as follows:

($170,000 + $30,000)/$750,000 = 26.7%

Now let's use ABC Clothing to determine the break-even operating expenses. If we know that the gross profit margin is 25 percent, the sales are $750,000 and the current maturities of long-term debt are $30,000, we can calculate the break-even operating expenses as follows:

(.25 x $750,000) - $30,000 = $157,500

WORKING CAPITAL ANALYSIS

Working capital is one of the most difficult financial concepts to understand for the small-business owner. In fact, the term means a lot of different things to a lot of different people. By definition, working capital is the amount by which current assets exceed current liabilities. However, if you simply run this calculation each period to try to analyze working capital,

WHERE CREDIT IS DUE

When you book a credit sale in your business, you must collect from the customer to realize your profit. Many a solid business has suffered a severe setback or even been put under by its failure to collect accounts receivable.

It is vital that you stay on top of your A/R if you sell on credit. Here are four tips that will help you maintain high-quality accounts receivable:

1. *Check out references upfront.* Find out how your prospective customer has paid other suppliers before selling on credit. Ask for supplier and bank references and follow up on them.

2. *Set credit limits, and monitor them.* Establish credit limits for each customer. Set up a system to regularly compare balances owed and credit limits.

3. *Process invoices immediately.* Send out invoices as soon as goods are shipped. Falling behind on sending invoices will result in slower collection of accounts receivable, which costs you cash flow.

4. *Don't resell to habitually slow-paying accounts.* If you find that a certain customer stays way behind in payment to you, stop selling to that company. Habitual slow pay is a sign of financial instability, and you can ill afford to write off an account of any significant size during the early years of your business.

you won't accomplish much in figuring out what your working capital needs are and how to meet them.

A useful tool for the small-business owner is the operating cycle. The operating cycle analyzes the accounts receivable, inventory and accounts payable cycles in terms of days. In other words, accounts receivable are analyzed by the average number of days it takes to collect an account. Inventory is analyzed by the average number of days it takes to turn over the sale of a product (from the point it comes in your door to the point it is converted to cash or an account receivable). Accounts payable are analyzed by the average number of days it takes to pay a supplier invoice.

Most businesses cannot finance the operating cycle (accounts receivable days + inventory days) with accounts payable financing alone. Consequently, working capital financing is needed. This shortfall is typically covered by the net profits generated internally or by externally borrowed funds or by a combination of the two.

FIGURE 39-4
OPERATING CYCLE*
ABC CLOTHING INC.

	Year 1	Year 2
Accounts Receivable Days	30	35
Inventory Days	90	80
Operating Cycle	120	115
Accounts Payable Days	−32	−29
Days To Be Financed	88	86
Purchases	$935,000	$1,095,000
$ Per Day Accounts Receivable	$2,740	$4,110
$ Per Day Inventory	$2,055	$2,877
$ Per Day Accounts Payable	$2,562	$3,000

*Calculations are as Follow:
Accounts Receivable Days = (Accounts Receivable x 365)/Sales
Inventory Days = (Inventory x 365)/Cost of Goods Sold
Accounts Payable Days = (Accounts Payable x 365)/Purchases
Purchases = Cost of Goods Sold + Ending Inventory − Beginning Inventory
$ Per Day Accounts Receivable = 1/365 x Sales
$ Per Day Inventory = 1/365 x Cost of Goods Sold
$ Per Day Accounts Payable = 1/365 x Purchases

Operating Cycle Work Sheet

	Year 1	Year 2
Accounts Receivable Days	_____	_____
Inventory Days	_____	_____
Operating Cycle	_____	_____
Accounts Payable Days	_____	_____
Days To Be Financed	_____	_____
Purchases	$ _____	$ _____
$ Per Day Accounts Receivable	$ _____	$ _____
$ Per Day Inventory	$ _____	$ _____
$ Per Day Accounts Payable	$ _____	$ _____

*Calculations are as Follow:

Accounts Receivable Days = (Accounts Receivable x 365)/Sales

Inventory Days = (Inventory x 365)/Cost of Goods Sold

Accounts Payable Days = (Accounts Payable x 365)/Purchases

Purchases = Cost of Goods Sold + Ending Inventory - Beginning Inventory

$ Per Day Accounts Receivable = 1/365 x Sales

$ Per Day Inventory = 1/365 x Cost of Goods Sold

$ Per Day Accounts Payable = 1/365 x Purchases

Most businesses need short-term working capital at some point in their operations. For instance, retailers must find working capital to fund seasonal inventory buildup between September and November for Christmas sales. But even a business that is not seasonal occasionally experiences peak months when orders are unusually high. This creates a need for working capital to fund the resulting inventory and accounts receivable buildup.

STOCKING UP

If your business will produce or sell inventory, your inventory management system will be crucial to your business' success. Keeping too much inventory on hand will cost you cash flow and will increase the risk of obsolescence. Conversely, an inventory level that is too lean can cost you sales.

Here are five suggestions to help you better manage your inventory:

1. **Pay attention to seasonality.** Depending on the type of business you are starting, you may have certain inventory items that sell only during certain times of the year. Order early in anticipation of the peak season. Then, make sure you sell the stock down so that you don't get stuck holding onto it for a year.

2. **Rely on suppliers.** If you can find suppliers who are well-stocked and can ship quickly, you can essentially let them stock your inventory for you. "Just in time" inventory management can save valuable working capital that could be invested in other areas of your business.

3. **Stock what sells.** This may seem obvious, but too many business owners try to be all things to all people when it comes to inventory management. When you see what sells, focus your purchasing efforts on those items.

4. **Mark down stale items.** Once you're up and running, you will find that certain items sell better than others. Mark down the items that don't sell, and then don't replace them.

5. **Watch waste.** Keep a close eye on waste. If production mistakes aren't caught early, you can ruin a whole batch of inventory, which can be extremely costly.

Some small businesses have enough cash reserves to fund seasonal working capital needs. However, this is very rare for a new business. If your new venture experiences a need for short-term working capital during its first few years of operation, you will have several potential sources of funding. The important thing is to plan ahead. If you get caught off guard, you might miss out on the one big order that could have put your business over the hump.

Here are the five most common sources of short-term working capital financing:

◆ **Equity:** If your business is in its first year of operation and has not yet become profitable, then you might have to rely on equity funds for short-term working capital needs. These funds might be injected from your own personal resources or from a family member, friend or third-party investor.

◆ **Trade Creditors:** If you have a particularly good relationship established with your trade creditors, you might be able to solicit their help in providing short-term working capital. If you have paid on time in the past, a trade creditor may be willing to extend terms to enable you to meet a big order. For instance, if you receive a big order that you can fulfill, ship out and collect in 60 days, you could obtain 60-day terms from your supplier if 30-day terms are normally given. The trade creditor will want proof of the order and may want to file a lien on it as security, but if it enables you to proceed, that shouldn't be a problem.

◆ **Factoring:** Factoring is another resource for short-term working capital financing. Once you have filled an order, a factoring company buys your account receivable and then handles the collection. This type of financing is more expensive than conventional bank financing but is often used by new businesses.

◆ **Line of credit:** Lines of credit are not often given by banks to new businesses. However, if your new business is well-capitalized by equity and you have good collateral, your business might qualify for one. A line of credit allows you to borrow funds for short-term needs when they arise. The funds are repaid once you collect the accounts receivable that resulted from the short-term sales peak. Lines of credit typically are made for one year at a time and are expected to be paid off for 30 to 60 consecutive days sometime during the year to ensure that the funds are used for short-term needs only.

◆ **Short-term loan:** While your new business may not qualify for a line of credit from a bank, you might have success in obtaining a

FIGURE 39-5
FINANCIAL BUDGET AND INCOME STATEMENT WORK SHEET

	Month 1	Month 2	Month 3	Month 4	Month 5	Month 6	Month 7	Month 8	Month 9	Month 10	Month 11	Month 12	Year 1
Sales													
Cost of Goods Sold													
Gross Profit													
Operating Expenses:													
Advertising													
Auto Expenses													
Bank Charges													
Depreciation													
Dues & Subscriptions													
Employee Benefits													
Insurance													
Interest													
Office Expense													
Officers' Salaries													
Payroll Taxes													
Professional Fees													
Rent													
Repairs & Maintenance													
Salaries & Wages													
Security													
Supplies													
Taxes & Licenses													
Telephone													
Utilities													
Other													
Total Operating Expenses													
Net Profit Before Taxes													
Income Taxes													
Net Profit After Taxes													

BALANCE SHEET WORK SHEET

	Month 1	Month 2	Month 3	Month 4	Month 5	Month 6	Month 7	Month 8	Month 9	Month 10	Month 11	Month 12	Year 1
Assets:													
Cash													
Investments													
Accounts Receivable													
Inventory													
Prepaid Expenses													
Other Current Assets													
Land													
Buildings													
Equipment													
Less: Accumulated Depreciation													
Long-Term Investments													
Intangibles													
Other Assets													
Total Assets													
Liabilities & Equity:													
Notes Payable—Short Term													
Current Maturities—Long-Term Debt													
Accounts Payable													
Accrued Expenses													
Taxes Payable													
Stockholder Loans													
Other Current Liabilities													
Bonds Payable													
Long-Term Debt													
Common Stock													
Paid-in-capital													
Treasury Stock													
Retained Earnings													
Total Liabilities & Equity													

CASH FLOW WORK SHEET

	Month 1	Month 2	Month 3	Month 4	Month 5	Month 6	Month 7	Month 8	Month 9	Month 10	Month 11	Month 12	Year 1
Cash Available:													
Net Income After Taxes													
Depreciation													
Amortization													
Decrease in A/R													
Decrease in Inventory													
Increase in Accounts Payable													
Increase in Notes Payable-ST													
Increase in Long-Term Debt													
Decrease in Other Assets													
Increase in Other Liabilities													
Total Cash Available													
Cash Disbursements:													
Owners' Draw/Dividends													
Increase in A/R													
Increase in Inventory													
Decrease in Accounts Payable													
Capital Expenditures													
Decrease in Notes Payable-ST													
Current Maturities Long-Term Debt													
Increase in Other Assets													
Decrease in Other Liabilities													
Total Cash Disbursements													
Monthly Cash Flow													
Cumulative Cash Flow													

one-time short-term loan (less than a year) to finance your temporary working capital needs. If you have established a good banking relationship with a banker, he or she might be willing to provide a short-term note for one order or for a seasonal inventory and/or accounts receivable buildup.

In addition to analyzing the average number of days it takes to make a product (inventory days) and collect on an account (account receivable days) vs. the number of days financed by accounts payable, the operating cycle analysis provides one other important analysis.

From the operating cycle, a computation can be made of the dollars required to support one day of accounts receivable and inventory and the dollars provided by a day of accounts payable. Let's consider ABC Clothing's operating cycle (see Figure 39-4). Had the company maintained accounts receivable at Year 1 levels in Year 2, it would have freed up $20,500 in cash flow ($4,110 x 5 days). Likewise, the 10-day improvement in inventory management in Year 2 enhanced cash flow by $28,770 ($2,877 x 10 days).

You can see that working capital has a direct impact on cash flow in a business. Since cash flow is the name of the game for all business owners, a good understanding of working capital is imperative to make any venture successful.

Building A Financial Budget

For many small-business owners, the process of budgeting is limited to figuring out where to get the cash to meet next week's payroll. There are so many financial fires to put out in a given week that it's hard to find the time to do any short- or long-range financial planning. But failing to plan financially might mean that you are unknowingly planning to fail.

Business budgeting is one of the most powerful financial tools available to any small-business owner. Put simply, maintaining a good short- and long-range financial plan enables you to control your cash flow instead of having it control you.

The most effective financial budget includes both a short-range month-to-month plan for at least a calendar year and a quarter-to-quarter long-range plan you use for financial statement reporting. It should be prepared during the two months preceding the fiscal year-end to allow ample time for sufficient information-gathering.

The long-range plan should cover a period of at least three years (some go up to five years) on a quarterly basis, or even an annual basis. The long-term budget should be updated when the short-range plan is prepared.

While some owners prefer to leave the one-year budget unchanged for the year for which it provides projections, others adjust the budget during the year based on certain financial occurrences, such as an unplanned equipment purchase or a larger-than-expected upward sales trend. Using the budget as an ongoing planning tool during a given year certainly is recommended. However, here is a word to the wise: Financial budgeting is vital, but it is important to avoid getting so caught up in the budget process that you forget to keep doing business.

What Do You Budget?

Many financial budgets provide a plan only for the income statement; however, it is important to budget both the income statement and balance sheet. This enables you to consider potential cash flow needs for your entire operation, not just as they pertain to income and expenses. For instance, if you had already been in business for a couple of years and were adding a new product line, you would need to consider the impact of inventory purchases on cash flow.

Budgeting the income statement only also doesn't allow a full analysis of potential capital expenditures on your financial picture. For instance, if you are planning to purchase real estate for your operation, you need to budget the effect the debt service will have on cash flow. In the future, a budget can also help you determine the potential effects of expanding your facilities and the resulting higher rent payments or debt service.

How Do You Budget?

In the start-up phase, you will have to make reasonable assumptions about your business in establishing your budget. You will need to ask questions such as:

◆ How much can be sold in year one?

◆ How much will sales grow in the following years?

◆ How will the products and/or services you are selling be priced?

◆ How much will it cost to produce your product? How much inventory will you need?

◆ What will your operating expenses be?

◆ How many employees will you need? How much will you pay them? How much will you pay yourself? What benefits will you offer? What will your payroll and unemployment taxes be?

◆ What will the income tax rate be? Will your business be an S corporation or a C corporation?

◆ What will your facilities needs be? How much will it cost you in rent or debt service for these facilities?

FIGURE 39-6

COMPARATIVE FINANCIAL RATIOS
ABC CLOTHING INC.

	Year 1	Year 2
Profitability Ratios:		
Gross Profit Margin	25.0%	30.0%
Operating Profit Margin	5.0%	11.7%
Net Profit Margin	3.7%	8.4%
Return on Equity	33.1%	52.9%
Return on Assets	9.0%	25.2%
Liquidity Ratios:		
Current	1.57	2.32
Quick	0.54	0.98
Working Capital To Sales	0.10	0.15
Activity Ratios:		
Accounts Receivable Days	30	35
Inventory Days	90	85
Accounts Payable Days	32	29
Sales to Assets	2.43	3.00
Leverage Ratios:		
Debt to Equity	2.68	1.10
Debt Ratio	0.73	0.52
Debt Coverage	2.24	5.20

◆ What equipment will be needed to start the business? How much will it cost? Will there be additional equipment needs in subsequent years?

◆ What payment terms will you offer customers if you will sell on credit? What payment terms will your suppliers give you?

◆ How much will you need to borrow? What will the collateral be? What will the interest rate be?

As for the actual preparation of the budget, you can create it manually or with the budgeting function that comes with most bookkeeping software packages. You can also purchase separate budgeting software such as Quicken or WinFast.

Yes, this seems like a lot of information to forecast. But it is not as cumbersome as it looks. (See Figure 39-5 for a sample financial budget; you should find a similar format in any budgeting software.)

The first step is to set up a plan for the following year on a month-to-month basis. Starting with the first month, establish specific budgeted dollar levels for each category of the budget. The sales numbers will be critical since they will be used to compute gross profit margin and will help determine operating expenses, as well as the accounts receivable and inventory levels necessary to support the business. In determining how much of your product or service you can sell, study the market in which you will operate, your competition, potential demand that you might already have seen, and economic conditions. For cost of goods sold, you will need to calculate the actual costs associated with producing each item on a percentage basis.

For operating expenses, consider items such as advertising, auto, depreciation, insurance, etc. Then factor in a tax rate based on actual business tax rates that you can obtain from your accountant.

On the balance sheet, break down inventory by category. For instance, a clothing manufacturer has raw materials, work-in-process and finished goods. For inventory, accounts receivable and accounts payable, you will figure the total amounts based on a projected number of days on hand. (See Figure 39-4 for the calculations needed to compute these three key numbers for your budget.)

Consider each specific item in fixed assets broken out for real estate, equipment, investments, etc. If your new business requires a franchise fee or copyrights or patents, this will be reflected as an intangible asset.

On the liability side, break down each bank loan separately. Do the same for the stockholders' equity—common stock, preferred stock, paid-in-capital, treasury stock and retained earnings.

Do this for each month for the first 12 months. Then, prepare the quarter-to-quarter budgets for years two and three. For the first year's budget, you will want to consider seasonality factors. For example, most retailers experience heavy sales from October to December. If your business will be highly seasonal, you will have wide-ranging changes in cash flow needs. For this reason, you will want to consider seasonality in the budget rather than take your annual projected year-one sales level and divide by 12.

As for the process, you will need to prepare the income statement budgets first, then balance sheet, then cash flow. You will need to know the net income figure before you can prepare a pro forma balance sheet because the profit number must be plugged into retained earnings. And for the cash flow projection, you will need both income statement and balance sheet numbers.

No matter whether you will budget manually or using software, it is advisable to seek input from your CPA in preparing your initial budget. His or her role will depend on the internal resources available to you and your background in finance. You may want to hire your CPA to prepare the financial plan for you, or you may simply involve him or her in an advisory role. Regardless of the level of involvement, your CPA's input will prove invaluable in providing an independent review of your short- and long-term financial plan.

In future years, your monthly financial statements and accountant-prepared year-end statements will be very useful in preparing a budget.

Sensitivity Analysis

One other major benefit of maintaining a financial budget is the ability to perform a sensitivity analysis. Once you have a plan in place, you can make adjustments to it to consider the potential effects of certain variables on your operation. All you have to do is plug in the change and see how it affects your company's financial performance.

Here's how it works: Let's say you have budgeted a 10 percent sales growth for the coming year. You can easily adjust the sales growth number to 5 percent or 15 percent in the budget to see how it affects your business's performance. You can perform a sensitivity analysis for any other financial variable as well. The most common items for which sensitivity analysis is done are:

◆ Sales

◆ Cost of goods sold and gross profit

◆ Operating expenses

◆ Interest rates

◆ Accounts receivable days

◆ Inventory days

◆ Accounts payable days on hand

◆ Major fixed asset purchases or reductions

◆ Acquisitions or closings

To be an effective and proactive small-business owner, you will need to learn to generate and understand the financial management tools discussed in this chapter. Even if you don't consider yourself a "numbers person," you will find that regular analysis of your financial data will be vital as you start and grow your business.

GLOSSARY

Financial budget: a projection of future financial performance

Gross profit margin: the percentage of gross profit realized on goods sold after subtracting cost of goods sold from sales

Markup: the percentage above the cost of producing a product that is charged to the customer

Ratio analysis: the use of certain financial ratios to compare the performance of a business to years past and to industry peers

Sensitivity analysis: the process in preparing a financial budget of changing certain financial variables to determine their potential impact on the company's future performance

CHAPTER 40

THE TAX MAN COMETH

What you need to know about taxes

By Joan Szabo, a freelance writer
who has covered tax issues for more than 11 years

When it comes to taxes, there's no way to get around the fact that you have to pay them regularly. Federal, state and local taxes combined can take a big chunk out of your company's money, leaving you with less cash to operate your business.

That's why it's important to stay abreast of your business's tax situation and work with a qualified accountant to understand all that's required of you by federal and state governments. The task is by no means simple. New business owners face a host of tax requirements and ever-changing rules.

If you miss deadlines or fail to comply with specific rules, you may be hit with large penalties, and, in the worst-case scenario, be forced to close up shop. You'll also want to pay close attention to tax planning, which will help you find legitimate ways to trim your overall tax liability. Your goal is to take the deductions to which you're entitled and to defer taxes as long as you possibly can.

While a knowledgeable accountant specializing in small-business tax issues will keep you out of potential tax quagmires, you'll be on more solid footing if you spend time acquiring your own working knowledge and understanding of the tax laws.

First Things First

One of the first steps you will take as a small-business owner is to obtain a taxpayer identification number so the IRS can process your returns. There are two types of identification numbers: a Social Security number and an Employer Identification Number (EIN).

The EIN is used to identify the tax accounts of sole proprietors, corporations, partnerships and other entities. You need an EIN if you have employees or operate your business as a corporation or partnership. Be sure to include your taxpayer ID on all returns or other documents you send to the IRS.

You can get an EIN either through the mail or by telephone. If you apply by mail, be sure to send in Form SS-4 (*Application for Employer Identification Number*) at least four or five weeks before you need the EIN. If you apply by phone by calling (800) TAX-FORM, the IRS will give you one immediately. The latter is the recommended way to go.

Ins And Outs Of Payroll Taxes

If you do any hiring, your employees must complete Form I-9 and Form W-4. Form I-9 provides verification that each new employee is legally eligible to work in the United States. This form can be obtained from Immigration and Naturalization Service (INS) offices; keep this form in your files in the event an IRS inspector wants to see it.

Form W-4 indicates the employee's filing status and withholding allowances. These allowances are used to determine how much federal income tax to withhold from an employee's wages. The IRS can provide you with a tax table to determine the withholding amounts for your employees. To receive a copy of this table, call the IRS and ask for Circular E and the supplement to Circular E.

You must also withhold Social Security and Medicare taxes—these are known as FICA (Federal Insurance Contributions Act) taxes. The FICA tax actually consists of two taxes: a 6.2 percent Social Security tax and 1.45 percent Medicare tax. To calculate the tax you need to withhold for each employee, multiply an employee's gross wages for a pay period by the tax rates. In addition, as an employer, you're required to pay a matching amount of FICA taxes on each of your employees.

Here's how it works: If an employee has gross wages of $1,000 every two weeks, you must withhold $62 ($1,000 x 6.2%) in Social Security taxes and $14.50 ($1,000 x 1.45%) in Medicare taxes, or $76.50. As an employer you owe a matching amount as well, so the total amount in FICA taxes to be paid is $153. The maximum amount of wages per person currently subject to Social Security tax is $68,400. There is no limit on the amount of wages subject to the Medicare tax.

You can mail or deliver federal payroll taxes with deposit coupons to an authorized financial institution or a Federal Reserve Bank for your area. The form to use is 8109, *Federal Tax Deposit Coupon*. On each coupon show the deposit amount, the type of tax, the period for which you are making a deposit and your phone number. You typically send

Beware!

If you withhold taxes but don't deposit or pay them to the IRS, you face a penalty on the unpaid tax, plus interest. If you deposit the taxes late, you will also be hit with a penalty.

Smart Tip

Consider using a payroll tax service to take care of all payroll tax requirements. The fees charged by services are relatively reasonable. In addition, these firms specialize in this area and know the ins and outs of all the rules and regulations. With a service you don't have to worry about making mistakes or being tardy with payments.

in these coupons monthly, depending on the size of your business. Approximately five to six weeks after you receive your EIN, the IRS will send you the coupon book.

In addition to making your monthly payroll deposits, you are required to file Form 941, *Employer's Quarterly Federal Tax Return*. This is a form that provides the government with information on the federal income taxes you withheld from your employees' pay as well as the FICA taxes you withheld and paid.

Another tax you have to pay is FUTA (Federal Unemployment Tax Act) taxes, which are used to compensate workers who lose their jobs. You report and pay FUTA tax separately from FICA and withheld income taxes.

You pay FUTA tax on your payroll if during the current or prior calendar year you meet one of two tests: You paid total wages of $1,500 to your employees in any calendar quarter, or you have at least one employee working on any given day in each of 20 different calendar weeks.

The FUTA tax is figured on the first $7,000 in wages paid to each employee annually. The gross FUTA tax rate is 6.2 percent. However, you are given a credit of up to 5.4 percent for the state unemployment tax you pay, effectively reducing the tax rate. As an employer, you pay FUTA tax only from your own funds. Employees do not have this tax withheld from their pay. You generally deposit FUTA taxes quarterly. In addition, you must file an annual return for your FUTA taxes using Form 940 (*Employer's Annual Federal Unemployment Tax Return*), which must be filed by January 31 of the following year.

Federal payroll taxes aren't your only concern. States and localities have their own taxes, which will most likely affect you. Most states (nine don't) have a personal income tax, which means you are also required to withhold this tax from your employee's wages. The same is true if you do business in a city or locality with an income tax. When applying for an EIN from your state, which you'll need to do business there, ask about the procedures and forms for withholding and depositing state income taxes. The place to start is with your state department of revenue.

At the end of the tax year, you must furnish copies of Form W-2 (*Wage and Tax Statement*) to each employee who worked for you during the year.

Be sure to give the forms to your employees by January 31 of the year after the calendar year covered by the form. Form W-2 provides information on how much money each employee earned and the amount of federal, state and FICA taxes you withheld. You'll want to send copies of W-2s to the Social Security Administration as well.

DECLARATION OF INDEPENDENTS

You may decide your business can't afford to hire too many full-time employees, and you'd like to use the services of an independent contractor. With an independent contractor, you don't have to deduct and withhold the person's income tax, Social Security and Medicare tax.

Beware!

The IRS has begun requiring any business paying more than $50,000 annually in payroll taxes or other federal taxes to pay them through the Electronic Federal Tax Payment System (EFTPS). Don't risk being charged a penalty. It's your responsibility to do your homework and check with the IRS before you pay your taxes to determine if you're required to pay them electronically.

While independent contractors mean lower payroll costs, be advised that the IRS scrutinizes this whole area very carefully. It wants to make sure your workers are properly classified and paying the government the necessary income and payroll taxes that are due.

To stay out of hot water with the IRS, be sure the workers you classify as independent contractors meet the IRS definition of an independent contractor. The IRS has a 20-point test its auditors use to determine the proper classification. Here are some of the major points:

- ◆ **Who has control?** A worker is an employee if the person for whom he works has the right to direct and control him in the way he works, both as to the final results and as to the details of when, where and how the work is to be done. The employer need not actually exercise control; it is sufficient that he has the right to do so.

- ◆ **Right to fire:** An employee can be fired by an employer. An independent contractor cannot be fired so long as he or she produces a result that meets the specifications of the contract.

- ◆ **Training:** An employee may be trained to perform services in a particular manner. Independent contractors ordinarily use their own methods and receive no training from the employer.

TAX TALK

Employee benefits such as health insurance and pension plan contributions provide attractive tax deductions. With a qualified pension plan, you not only receive a tax deduction for the contributions you make on behalf of your employees, but the money you contribute to your own retirement account is also deductible and is allowed to grow tax-deferred until withdrawn. (A qualified plan meets the requirements of the Employee Retirement Income Security Act [ERISA] and the Internal Revenue Code.)

There are a number of different plans available, ranging from a Savings Incentive Match Plan for Employees (SIMPLE) to a traditional 401(k) plan (see the "Treat Your 'Children' Well" chapter). The pension design may be slightly different, but they all offer important tax benefits for business owners. So take the time to see which plan will work best for you.

As far as health insurance is concerned, if your business is incorporated and you work for it as an employee, you can deduct all costs for your own insurance as well as for the coverage for your employees. For self-employed individuals, the Taxpayer Relief Act of 1997 makes the health insurance deduction more attractive. The deduction is phased in gradually over a number of years. In 1998 and 1999, 45 percent of these health insurance expenses are deductible. By 2007, they become100 percent deductible.

Self-Employed Health Insurance Deduction	
For taxable years beginning in:	Deductible %
1998-1999	45
2000-2001	50
2002	60
2003-2005	80
2006	90
2007 and thereafter	100

◆ **Set hours of work:** Workers for whom you set specific hours of work are more likely to be employees. Independent contractors, on the other hand, usually establish their own work hours.

Beware!

Once you've selected to file either on a calendar- or fiscal-year basis, you have to get permission from the IRS to change it. To do so, you must file Form 1128 and pay a fee.

To stay on the right side of the IRS, it is best to document the relationship you have with any independent contractors in a written contract. This can be a simple agreement that spells out the duties of the independent contractor. The agreement should state that the independent contractor, not the employer, is responsible for withholding any necessary taxes. In addition, have the independent contractor submit invoices. Also, be sure you file Form 1099 at year-end. By law, you are required to file and give someone Form 1099 if you pay that person more than $600 a year.

If the IRS finds you have misclassified an employee as an independent contractor, you'll pay back taxes plus any accrued interest and penalties. Even worse, if the IRS determines your misclassification was "willful," you'll be assessed additional penalties and run the risk that the IRS will go back to any open years and examine your tax returns to see if a pattern exists.

Be advised that there is some relief being offered. According to Ralph Anderson, a CPA and small-business tax specialist with accounting firm M.R. Weiser, if a business realizes it is in violation of the law regarding independent contractors, it can inform the IRS of the problem and then properly classify the workers without being hit with an IRS assessment for prior year taxes.

SELECTING YOUR TAX YEAR

When you launch your business, you'll have to decide what tax year to use. The tax year is the annual accounting period used to keep your records and report your income and expenses. There are two accounting periods: a calendar year and a fiscal year .

A calendar year is 12 consecutive months starting January 1 and ending December 31. Most sole proprietors, partnerships, limited liability companies and S corporations use the calendar year as their tax year. If you operate a business as a sole proprietorship, the IRS says the tax year for your business must be the same as your individual tax year.

A fiscal tax year is 12 consecutive months ending on the last day of any month other than December. For business owners who start a company during the year and have substantial expenses or losses, it may be smart to select a fiscal year that goes beyond the end of the first calendar year. This way, as much income as possible is offset by start-up expenses and losses.

FILING YOUR TAX RETURN

Your federal tax filing obligations and due dates generally are based on the legal structure you've selected for your business and whether you use a calendar or fiscal year.

◆ **Sole proprietorships:** If you are a sole proprietor, every year you must file Schedule C (*Profit or Loss From Business*) with your Form 1040 (*U.S. Individual Income Tax Return*) to report your business income and deductions. You also must file Schedule SE (*Self-Employment Tax*) with your 1040. If you are a calendar-year taxpayer, your tax filing date is April 15. Fiscal-year taxpayers must file their returns no later than the 15th day of the fourth month after the end of their tax year.

In addition to your annual tax return, many self-employed individuals such as sole proprietors and partners make quarterly estimated tax payments to cover their income and Social Security tax liability. If your adjusted gross income last year was less than $150,000, your estimated tax payments must be at least 90 percent of your current year's tax liability or 100 percent of the prior year's liability, whichever is less.

According to the Taxpayer Relief Act of 1997, estimated tax payments must be made for income not subject to withholding if you owe at least $1,000 in federal taxes for the year. The federal government allows you to pay estimated taxes in four

Bright Idea

The IRS offers STEP (Small Business Tax Education Program), a cooperative effort with local organizations to provide business tax education to small-business owners. Instructors teach you the tax advantages and disadvantages of the various forms of business organization, what records to keep and how to keep them, how to use federal tax deposit coupons and more. The costs for the program vary—some are free. To find out more, call (800) 829-1040.

equal amounts throughout the year on the 15th of April, June, September and January.

◆ **Partnerships and limited liability companies (LLCs):** Companies set up with these structures must file Form 1065 (*U.S. Partnership Return of Income*). The partnership must furnish copies of Schedule K-1 (*Partner's Share of Income, Credits, Deductions*), which is part of Form 1065, to the partners or LLC members by the filing date for Form 1065. The due dates are the same as those for sole proprietors.

◆ **Corporations:** If your business is structured as a standard corporation, you must file Form 1120 (*U.S. Corporation Income Tax Return*). For calendar-year taxpayers, the due date for the return is March 15. For fiscal-year corporations, the return must be filed by the 15th day of the third month after the end of corporation's tax year.

◆ **S corporations:** Owners of these companies must file Form 1120S (*U.S. Income Tax Return for an S Corporation*). Like partnerships and LLCs, shareholders must receive a copy of Schedule K-1, which is part of Form 1120S. The due dates are the same as those for standard corporations.

SALES TAXES

Sales taxes vary by state and are imposed at the retail level. It's important to know the rules in the states and localities where you operate your business because if you are a retailer you must collect state sales tax on each sale you make, says Anderson.

While many states and localities exempt service businesses from sales taxes, some have recently begun to change their laws in this area and are applying the sales tax to some services. If you are a service business, contact your state revenue and/or local revenue offices for information on the laws in your area.

Before you open your doors, be sure to register to collect sales tax by applying for a sales permit for each separate place of business you have in the state. A license or permit is important because in some states it is a criminal offense to undertake sales without one. In addition, if you fail to collect sales tax, you can be held liable for the uncollected amount.

If you are an out-of-state retailer, such as a mail order seller, who ships and sells goods in another state, be careful. In the past, many retailers have not collected sales taxes on the sale of these goods. Anderson advises you to be sure you or your accountant knows the state sales tax requirements where you do business. Says Anderson, "Just because you don't have a physical location in a state doesn't always mean you don't have to collect the sales tax."

Many states require business owners to make an advance deposit against future taxes. Some states will accept a surety bond from your insurance company in lieu of the deposit.

It's possible for retailers to defer paying sales taxes on merchandise they purchase from suppliers. Once the merchandise is sold, however, the taxes are due. The retailer adds the sales taxes (where applicable) to the purchase. To defer sales taxes, you need a reseller permit or certificate. For more details on obtaining a permit, contact your state tax department.

TAX-DEDUCTIBLE BUSINESS EXPENSES

According to the IRS, the operating costs of running your business are deductible if they are "ordinary and necessary." The IRS defines "ordinary" as expenses that are common and accepted in your field of business. "Necessary expenses" are those that are appropriate and helpful for your business. Following are some of the business expenses you may be able to deduct:

IN THE RED?

If you find after you've tallied up all your business deductions and subtracted them from your income that you're in the red for the year, don't despair. There's something called the net operating loss deduction that will help. It allows you to offset one year's losses against another year's income.

The IRS lets you carry this operating loss back two years and use it to offset the income of those previous two years. Doing so may result in a refund. If you still have some losses left after carrying them back, you can carry them forward for up to 20 years. If you don't want to use the two-year carryback period, you can elect to deduct the net operating loss over the next 20 years. However, once you make that election you can't reverse it. Remember, if there is any unused loss after 20 years, you may no longer apply it to any income.

Dollar Stretcher

To help you wade through all the tax laws and regulations, the IRS offers these free publications: *Tax Guide for Small Business* (Publication No. 334), *Business Expenses* (Publication No. 535), *Travel, Entertainment, Gift and Car Expenses* (Publication No. 463), *Circular E, Employer's Tax Guide* (Publication No. 15), and *Employer's Supplemental Tax Guide* (Publication No. 15-A).

To order copies of these publications, call (800) TAX-FORM or download them from the IRS Web site at irs.ustreas.gov.

Equipment Purchases

If you buy equipment for your business, you will be able to deduct a portion of the cost of that equipment in the year you placed the equipment in service. In 1998, the amount you can deduct is $18,500. The limit continues to increase incrementally each year until it reaches $25,000 by 2003. Under current law, the deduction cannot exceed the taxable income derived from your business. If your equipment purchases are more than $200,000, the $18,500 limit is reduced dollar for dollar by the amount that exceeds $200,000.

Business Expenses

Common business expenses for which you can take a deduction include advertising expenses, employee benefit programs, insurance, legal and professional services, telephone and utilities costs, rent, office supplies, employees wages, membership dues to professional associations, and business publication subscriptions.

Auto Expenses

For a car you own and use in your business, the IRS allows you to either deduct your actual business-related expenses or claim the standard mileage rate, which is a specified amount of money you can deduct for each business mile you drive. The rate is generally adjusted each year by the IRS. To calculate your deduction, multiply your business miles by the standard mileage rate for the year.

If you use the standard mileage rate, the IRS says you must use it in the first year the car is available for use in your business. Later, you can use either the standard mileage rate or actual expenses method. However, if you use two or more cars for business at the same time, you cannot take the standard mileage rate for these cars. For tax purposes, be sure to keep a log of your business miles as well the costs of business-related parking fees and tolls because you can deduct these expenses.

With the actual cost method, the IRS allows you to deduct various expenses, including depreciation, gas, insurance, cleaning, leasing fees, routine maintenance, tires and personal property taxes. If you use the actual cost method, keep records of your car's costs during the year and multiply those expenses by the percentage of total car mileage driven for business purposes.

While using the standard mileage rate is easier for record-keeping, you may receive a larger deduction using the actual cost method. If you qualify to use both methods, the IRS recommends figuring your deduction both ways to see which gives you a larger deduction, as long as you have kept detailed records to substantiate the actual cost method.

Meal And Entertainment Expenses

To earn a deduction for business meals and entertainment expenses, you must discuss business during, immediately before or immediately after the event. Your deduction is limited to 50 percent of the cost of qualified expenses, and you must have receipts for any cost of $75 or more. If you have an individual entertainment expense of less than $75, you can record the necessary information in an expense account book and not worry about keeping receipts. The information to record is the reason for the expense, amount spent, date, location and people entertained.

START ME UP

The expenses you incur when launching a new business can run into a lot of money. But how do you treat them when it comes time to do your taxes? For the most part, it is not possible to claim these start-up expenses as business deductions.

But you can amortize start-up costs over a time frame of at least 60 months as long as the expenses actually bring forth a real live operational business. Amortization allows you to deduct costs evenly over a period of time.

If you spent time looking for a business but did not purchase one, however, the expenses you incurred during the search are deductible and don't have to be spread out over five years.

The kind of costs you can amortize include advertising expenses, any wages you paid, and professional fees. In addition, you can also amortize expenses associated with investigating the potential of starting the business, such as market or product research and site selection.

Travel Expenses

You can deduct ordinary and necessary travel expenses you incur while traveling on business. Your records should show the amount of each expense for items such as transportation, meals and lodging. Be sure to record the date of departure and return for each trip, the number of days you spent on business, the name of the city, and the business reason for the travel or the business benefits you expect to achieve. Keep track of your cleaning and laundry expenses while traveling because these are deductible as well.

Home Office

If you use a portion of your home exclusively and regularly for business, you may be able to claim the home office deduction on your annual tax return. To claim the deduction, the part of the home you use for your office must be your principal place of business, or you must use it to personally meet with clients. Keep in mind that you can't claim the deduction if you have an outside office as well.

The Taxpayer Relief Act of 1997 liberalizes this deduction. Starting in 1999, business owners who keep records, schedule appointments and perform other administrative or management activities from their home offices qualify for a deduction as long as they don't have any other fixed place of business where they do a large amount of administrative or management work. This holds true even if they don't see clients or customers in their home offices. The change overturns a 1993 Supreme Court ruling, which stated that no deduction could be taken if the home office was used merely for administrative or management functions. The IRS scrutinizes this deduction very carefully, so be sure to follow the rules and keep good records. (For more on home offices, see Entrepreneur's business start-up guide No. 1815, *Starting & Running a Homebased Business*.)

TAX PLANNING

As you operate your business, be on the lookout for ways to reduce your federal and state tax liability. Small-business owners typically have a lot of ups and downs from one year to the next. If you make a lot of money one year and have to pay taxes on all that profit, your business won't have the reserves needed to tide you over in some other year when business may not be as good.

That's why it's important to defer or reduce taxes whenever possible. This is a good way to cut business costs without affecting the quality of your product or service.

Throughout the year, periodically review your tax situation with the help of your accountant. If your income is increasing, look for deductions to help reduce your taxes. For example, if you're a cash-basis taxpayer, think about doing some needed business repairs or stocking up on office supplies before the end of the year. Cash-basis taxpayers can also defer income into the next year by waiting until the end of December to mail invoices.

For businesses using the accrual method, you can establish a bonus plan for your employees and take a deduction for its cost. You can start the plan in the current tax year and take the deduction for it, yet not actually pay the bonuses until the following year. By law, you have two and a half months after your fiscal year-end to pay the bonuses to employees, as long as they don't own more than 50 percent of the business.

Both cash and accrual taxpayers can make charitable donations before the end of the year, and take deductions for them. Beware, if you donate $250 or more, a canceled check is no longer considered adequate documentation, so make sure the charity gives you written substantiation of the contribution amount or a description of the property given.

Tax planning is a year-long endeavor. Be sure you know what deductions are available to you, and keep good records to support them. This way, you can reap tax savings, which you can use to successfully operate and grow your business.

GLOSSARY

Accrual method of accounting: transactions occur when the sale takes place, even if the money for it hasn't been collected; in addition, expenses are deducted when they are incurred, even if they haven't been paid for

Basis: refers to the amount paid for property or equipment

Calendar year: a year that ends December 31

Capital expenses: costs that are not currently deductible and are added to the basis of property

Cash method of accounting: income is recorded when it is received and expenses are recorded when they are paid

Depreciate: the ability to write off each year the cost of equipment, vehicles or other fixed assets

Fiscal year: a 12-month period ending on the last day of any month other than December

Standard mileage rate: a fixed rate that the IRS allows for business auto expenses instead of deducting actual expenses

Tax deferral: shifting income to a later year

CHAPTER 41

IF AT FIRST YOU DON'T SUCCEED . . .

Learning from your failures

What's the key to business success? Is it adequate capital? A good business plan? A slick advertising campaign? All these factors play crucial roles, of course, but surprisingly, many prosperous entrepreneurs say that previous business failures, more than anything else, helped them attain their current successes.

The old adage "Learn from your mistakes" may be a cliché, but thousands of successful business owners have done just that. Instead of letting business failure frustrate them, these entrepreneurs profited from the painful experience, garnering some valuable lessons they couldn't have learned any other way.

The following chapter will help give you a new perspective on the inevitable failures that accompany business ownership—from the customer who rejects your sales proposal to the bank that says no to your loan application. Read on . . . and learn how you, too, can profit from failure.

BUSINESS FAILURE

Behind every successful person lurk the remains of past failures. Consider the historic examples of Abraham Lincoln, who suffered defeat in four elections before being voted president; Babe Ruth, who struck out 1,330 times en route to hitting 714 homers, including a record 60 in the 1927 baseball season; and, more recently, Tom Monaghan, who failed in business twice before launching Domino's Pizza.

Failure hurts, traumatizes and can destroy, but it also challenges, motivates and humbles us, cutting through the illusion that success is easy. At a "failure conference" at the University of Michigan, Ann Arbor, several years ago, Warren Avis, founder of Avis Rent-a-Car, shared some of the business blunders that cost him bundles over the years.

"Failure has a tremendous impact from which you can derive strength if you analyze [the experience] and try to understand why you have failed," said Avis. "You cannot avoid failure, but you must quit feeling sorry for yourself and get up and try again."

As Avis' comments illustrate, there is a big difference between failure and being a failure. The true failure simply gives up; the savvy entrepreneur tries again, learns from his or her mistakes, and ultimately succeeds.

Causes Of Failure

Experts and entrepreneurs have pinpointed several common causes of entrepreneurial failure:

◆ Unsound ideas (a toy that's dangerous to children or a service the market doesn't need) are likely to fail early on. They illustrate the need for more time spent at the drawing board.

◆ Poor planning (lack of capital or a poorly positioned product or service) can cripple or doom a viable concept early in the game, driving home the importance of a thoroughly researched and well-formulated business plan.

◆ A product whose market is not ready for it or is already long gone (a great spacesuit or a better buggy whip) proves the importance of timing and placement.

WORDS FROM THE WISE

Here's Avis Rent-a-Car founder Warren Avis' advice about failure, gained over years of business experience:

◆ There's no such thing as the perfect deal. Look for what is wrong with it.

◆ Despite popular opinion to the contrary, the first solution to a problem is usually not the best. Force yourself to list at least four other solutions; 80 percent of the time, one of them will be better than your original solution.

◆ If properly put together, groups make better decisions than individuals. Take advantage of the talents others possess, especially the oddball who sees things a bit differently.

◆ Expect the unexpected—more often than not, it happens. Be prepared for the worst.

◆ Never say never.

◆ Ironically, success can often lead to failure. An entrepreneur who has never experienced failure may believe he or she is infallible, which can prevent him or her from planning for worst-case scenarios.

◆ Success can also lead to failure when an entrepreneur gets orders for a product that he or she lacks the money, manpower or production capacity to fill. Many entrepreneurs don't realize that when your sales increase, you need more money—not less—to keep up with demand.

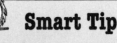

Smart Tip

For maximum business success, be disciplined about relaxing. It sounds contradictory, but it works. Schedule in time for sleep, exercise and R&R. Then, keep those appointments as diligently as you would keep an appointment with an important customer. If you give 150 percent to your business and have nothing left for yourself, your business will suffer in the end.

◆ Personnel difficulties. If partners or key employees disagree on the business's goals or the methods used to achieve them, power struggles may erupt that can ultimately destroy the business.

◆ Inadequate capitalization. This is the most common cause of business failure, but, typically, it is precipitated by one of the causes above.

Failing To Succeed

Many experts and entrepreneurs believe some degree of failure is essential to long-term success. "The more you fail, the more you succeed," contends Jack Matson, author of *Using Intelligent Fast Failure* (Penn State).

To develop "intelligent failure"—the type that Matson says later forms building blocks to success—the first step is to get over the fear of failure. After all, you're constantly dealing with failure in everything you do. If one thing doesn't work, that means it has failed, so you simply try something else—both in your personal life and in your business.

Consider job seekers, for example, who schedule dozens of interviews knowing that most of them will result in rejection; inventors, who must often try hundreds of ideas to find one that works; and salespeople, who know the vast majority of cold calls will not lead to a sale. (In fact, every business begins with what could be termed a failure—an unmet need, a problem awaiting a solution.)

Look for the partial successes in any failure; these can become corner-

Beware!

Want to know what warning signs to look out for? Mark Rice, professor of entrepreneurship at Rensselaer Polytechnic University in Troy, New York, says most failures stem from one of three causes: failure to market adequately; lack of capital; or internal problems hiring, retaining and training good people. The last two often stem from too-rapid growth.

stones for future efforts. Matson suggests a technique he calls "straffing" (Success Through Rapid Accelerated Failures). He encourages entrepreneurs to generate lots of different ideas simultaneously, and try them out quickly to find out which ones work. "The usual approach is what I call 'slow, stupid failure,'" Matson explains. "You try your first idea and fail; try the second idea and fail; try the third idea and fail . . . and then give up." Instead, he proposes "fast, intelligent failure," in which you try out many ideas at the same time. This greatly accelerates the learning process and compresses failure time, allowing you to progress more rapidly toward a solution. Each idea will possess some positive elements that can be combined with the positive elements of other discarded ideas to form a new solution.

Such creativity is crucial to the successful entrepreneur. Business owners need to develop new ways of looking at the same problems or situations. To illustrate this point, audiences at the University of Michigan failure conference were asked to build the tallest structure they could, using notched ice cream sticks handed out by assistants. The results offered some insight into different ways of learning from failure creatively:

◆ Some participants persisted in building the same type of structure despite repeated collapses, while others altered their designs, trying out different approaches. Typically, people who tried different options were able to build higher structures.

◆ Some participants peeked at what their neighbors were building and borrowed or stole ideas. This can be a great way to

Beware!

How do you know if perseverance is smart—or foolhardy? The key is a healthy adaptation of the "if at first you don't succeed" adage. Yes, you should try and try again—but you should try differently or try something else. If you find yourself repeating the same mistakes over and over again, it's time to move on.

leapfrog technology. There's no sense in reinventing the wheel each time.

♦ Other people worked in groups to pool resources. Groups can capitalize on each other's ideas and share in the success (or the blame if the venture is a flop).

Learning From Failure

The best way to protect yourself against business failure is by going back to the basics: a good business plan, a solid marketing plan, an experienced management team and adequate capitalization. Even with all those factors in place, however, there are inevitably surprises and errors along the way.

BOUNCING BACK

It's got to be among the 10 most dreaded words in the English language. "No" means rejection, plain and simple. Whether it's the loss of an account, distribution or financing, it hurts.

But successful entrepreneurs quickly find ways to combat rejection. They look at it objectively and learn from the experience. Those who are able to overcome rejection tend to share certain traits: determination, open-mindedness and a belief in themselves. Self-confidence keeps you bouncing back, no matter how much rejection comes your way.

One secret to handling rejection is so simple, many entrepreneurs never think of it: Just ask why. If you ask for an explanation of why your service isn't good enough, often rejection becomes a positive tool to help you open the next door.

For example, a polite response that gets results could be something like "If you don't mind my asking, could you tell me why you're unable to distribute my product? If I knew the reason, maybe we could find a comfortable middle ground for both of us. I'd like to find a way to work with you."

Customers love to be asked for help and to give advice, which helps build rapport and set the foundation for long-term relationships. And it's the long term that's important. Be patient; just because someone said no now doesn't mean they'll feel the same way six months down the road.

Businesses aren't built overnight, but, as entrepreneurs who've weathered difficult times will attest, the end result is well worth the struggle.

Stress Test

Problems and setbacks are made worse by stress. Yet since stress is an unavoidable part of owning your own business, you need to learn to deal with it. Here are some simple steps you can take to lessen your stress—and run a better business.

1. *Identify the "stress factors" in your life.* Be as specific as you can—not just "lack of time" or "Monday mornings"—but who or what bothers you and how much on a scale of, say, 1 to 10. Often, just the act of recognizing something as stressful releases a lot of tension.

2. *Make a schedule, and stick to it.* Have you ever said "Just thinking about all the things I have to do makes me tired"? Stress builds when we keep reviewing what we have to do without doing it. Make lists of everything you need to start, finish, remember or worry about. Once you write it down, you can dump it from your mind.

3. *Delegate.* You may not have employees yet, but why not call in a freelancer or temp to help out, especially during crunch times? You can even ask a family member to help with paperwork, filing, mailing or other simple but time-consuming tasks.

4. *Cultivate a relaxing workplace.* Make sure you have adequate lighting, a comfortable desk and good ventilation. Work near a window, or make sure you get outside at least once a day, even if it's just for a five-minute walk down the block. Tidy up your office; this not only makes you feel less panicked psychologically, but it also helps by making it easier to find things.

5. *Sleep and eat right.* Make sure you get seven to eight hours' sleep per night. Eliminate fast-food meals from your diet. Drink coffee in moderation—two cups per day, max.

6. *Get physical.* Exercise is crucial in combating stress. Try doing workouts that are the opposite of your work. In other words, if you're around people all day, go for a solitary run. If you work isolated at home in a one-person office, take an aerobics class where you can enjoy socializing as well as stretching.

Beware!

It's hard to be objective when analyzing your own mistakes. Get outside help if possible. Try setting up an informal "advisory board" including your lawyer, accountant, banker and colleagues. Ask them where you went wrong and how you can make it right. These people can act as a sounding board, helping you make smarter decisions in the future.

The key is learning from those errors as you go along so that small failures don't balloon into big ones.

To learn from experience, including past mistakes, we need accurate perceptions and honest self-appraisal. While denial may heal the wounds failure inflicts on our egos, the successful entrepreneur spends quite a lot of time analyzing his or her mistakes and finding innovative ways to profit from them.

Should failures, setbacks, mistakes or whatever you want to call them occur, the important thing to do is put them in the best possible perspective—and thereby learn the most useful lesson possible. Try not to look at failure from too negative a perspective, lest it become a life sentence . . . or, at least, a large and long-lasting rut.

Work to get out from under your failures and into your best frame of mind, to where problems yield solutions. At that point, even the very worst mistakes can be the best learning experiences. Always ask yourself "What is the lesson in this setback? What is the opportunity?" You can often assign several causes for any one failure, and you should be as clear in identifying them as you can. Observe, adjust and, when necessary, move on.

Moving on is key. Don't beat yourself up about setbacks or the past: Use them to change the future. Failure is something entrepreneurs must have a high tolerance for since it is an almost inevitable step along the way to success.

There's also danger in failing to persevere despite momentarily daunting odds. Although perseverance must be based on a rational view of reality, that reality must be balanced with a courageous sense of vision. Even Alexander Graham Bell's telephone was rejected

Smart Tip

Attitude adjustment is key to dealing with stress. Sure, bad things happen, but often, there is a difference between reality and your perception of it. Psychologists call the internal response to a problem "self-talk," and many say it causes most of our stress. When tension hits, ask yourself "Is this really a crisis, or am I making a mountain out of a molehill?"

several times before it went on to revolutionize communication. The lesson to be learned here is the value of daring and persistence.

For those who listen, setbacks are good teachers. (Those who don't listen are doomed to repeat their mistakes rather than learning from them.) Besides honing business skills, setbacks can call forth an inner resiliency. Those who fail are more likely to see the big picture, take the lesson to be learned from the failure, and try to incorporate that lesson into their daily lives as well as their business lives. As a result, they are less likely to be disturbed by the daily pressures. They know not to sweat the small stuff but to concentrate on solving the big problems.

Do entrepreneurs learn more from setbacks than from successes? "Success is a reward for hard work—not a teacher," says one entrepreneur. "It is the hard lessons I've learned along the way that led to my success."

APPENDIX A
BUSINESS RESOURCES

ACCOUNTING AND TAXES

Associations

♦ American Accounting Association, 5717 Bessie Dr., Sarasota, FL 34233, (941) 921-7747, www.aaa-edu.org

♦ American Institute of Certified Public Accountants, Harborside Financial Center, 201 Plaza 3, Jersey City, NJ 07311-3881, (201) 938-3447, www.aicpa.org

♦ CCH Inc., 4025 W. Peterson Ave., Chicago, IL 60646, (312) 583-8500, www.cch.com

♦ Financial Executives Institute, 10 Madison Ave., P.O. Box 1938, Morristown, NJ 07962-1938, (201) 898-4600, fax: (201) 898-4649

♦ Independent Accountants International, 9200 S. Dateland Blvd., #510, Miami, FL 33156, (305) 670-0580

♦ Institute of Certified Management Accountants, 10 Paragon Dr., Montvale, NJ 07645, (201) 573-6300

♦ Institute of Chartered Financial Analysts, P.O. Box 3668, Charlottesville, VA 22908, (804) 977-6600, fax: (804) 977-1103

♦ International Credit Association, P.O. Box 419057, St. Louis, MO 63141-1757, (314) 991-3030, www.ica-credit.org

Books

♦ *Accounting and Recordkeeping Made Easy for the Self-Employed*, Jack Fox, John Wiley & Sons

♦ *Accounting for the New Business*, Christopher R. Malberg, Adams Media, 260 Center St., Holbrook, MA 02343, (800) 872-5627

♦ *Bottom Line Basics: Understand and Control Business Finances*, Robert J. Low, The Oasis Press, 300 N. Valley Dr., Grants Pass, OR 97526

♦ *Day-to-Day Business Accounting*, Arlen K. Mose, John Jackson and Gary Downs, Prentice Hall

♦ *Finance and Accounting for Non-Financial Managers*, Steven A. Finkler, Prentice Hall

♦ *The McGraw Hill 36 Hour Accounting Course*, Robert L. Dixon and Harold E. Arnett, McGraw-Hill

♦ *Simplified Small Business Accounting*, Daniel Sitarz, Nova Publishing, 1103 W. College St., Carbondale, IL 62901

♦ *The Vest Pocket CPA*, Nicky A. Dauber, Joel G. Siegel and Jae K. Shim, Prentice Hall

Magazines And Publications

♦ *Accounting Office Management & Administration*, 29 W. 35th St., 5th Fl., New York, NY 10001, (212) 244-0360

♦ *Accounting Periods and Methods* (IRS publication #538)

♦ *Institute of Management Accountants*, 10 Paragon Dr., Montvale, NJ 07645, (201) 573-9000

♦ *Starting a Business and Keeping Records* (IRS publication #583)

♦ *Taxes: The Tax Magazine*, CCH Inc., 4025 W. Peterson Ave., Chicago, IL 60646, (773) 583-8500, www.cch.com

♦ *The Tax Adviser*, Harborside Financial Center, #201, Plaza 3, Jersey City, NJ 07311-3881, (800) 862-4272, (201) 938-3447, www.aicpa.org

♦ *Your Tax Questions Answered*, 100 Merrick Rd., #200 E., Rockville Centre, NY 11570, (800) 350-1007

ADVERTISING AND MARKETING

Associations

♦ American Advertising Federation, 1101 Vermont Ave. NW, #500, Washington, DC 20005, (202) 898-0090, www.aaf.org

♦ American Marketing Association, 250 S. Wacker Dr., #200, Chicago, IL 60606, (312) 648-0536, www.ama.org

♦ Association of National Advertisers, 155 E. 44th St., New York, NY 10017-4270, (212) 697-5950

- ◆ Direct Marketing Association, 1120 Ave. of the Americas; 13th Fl., New York, NY 10036, (212) 768-7227
- ◆ Marketing Research Association, 2189 Silas Deane Hwy., #5, Rocky Hill, CT 06067, (860) 257-4008, www.mra-net.org
- ◆ Outdoor Advertising Association of America, 12 E. 49th St., 22nd Fl., New York, NY 10017, (212) 688-3667, www.oaaa.org
- ◆ Radio Advertising Bureau, 304 Park Ave. S., 7th Fl., New York, NY 10010, (212) 254-4800

Books

- ◆ *The Advertising Handbook for Small Business: Make a Big Impact With a Small Budget,* Dell Dennison, Self-Counsel Press, 1704 N. State St., Bellingham, WA 98225-4605, (800) 663-3007, (360) 676-4530
- ◆ *Advertising on the Internet,* Robin Zeff and Bradley Aronson, John Wiley & Sons, www.wiley.com
- ◆ *The Building Blocks of Business Writing,* Jack Swenson, Crisp Publications, (800) 442-7477
- ◆ *The Complete Idiots Guide to Marketing Basics,* Sarah White, Alpha Books
- ◆ *Getting Business to Come to You: Everything You Need to Know to Do Your Own Advertising, Public Relations, Direct Mail and Sales Promotion,* Paul and Sarah Edwards and Laura Clampitt Douglas, J.P. Tarcher
- ◆ *Growing Your Home-Based Business: A Complete Guide to Proven Sales & Marketing Strategies,* Kim T. Gordon, Prentice Hall Trade
- ◆ *Guerrilla Advertising: Cost-Effective Techniques for Small-Business Success,* Jay Conrad Levinson, Houghton Mifflin
- ◆ *Guerrilla Marketing for the Home-Based Business,* Jay Conrad Levinson and Seth Godin, Houghton Mifflin
- ◆ *How to Say It: Choice Words, Phrases, Sentences & Paragraphs for Every Situation,* Rosalie Maggio, Prentice Hall
- ◆ *Online Marketing Handbook: How to Promote, Advertise and Sell Your Products and Services on the Internet,* Daniel S. Janal, Van Nostrand Reinhold
- ◆ *Selling the Invisible: A Field Guide to Modern Marketing,* Harry Beckwith, Warner Books
- ◆ *Six Steps to Free Publicity: And Dozens of Other Ways to Win Free Media Attention for Your Business,* Marcia Yudkin, Plume

◆ *Successful Sales & Marketing: Smart Ways to Boost Your Bottom Line* (business guide No.1809), Entrepreneur Media Inc., (800) 421-2300, www.smallbizbooks.com

Magazines And Publications

◆ *Adcrafter*, 1249 Washington Blvd., Detroit, MI 48226, (313) 962-7225, www.adcraft.org

◆ *Advertising Age*, 220 E. 42nd St., New York, NY 10017, (212) 210-0100, www.adage.com

◆ *Advertising Communications Times*, 121 Chestnut St., Philadelphia, PA 19106, (215) 629-1666

◆ *Adweek*, 1515 Broadway, New York, NY 10036-8986, (212) 536-5336, www.adweek.com

◆ *American Advertising*, 1101 Vermont Ave. N.W., #500, Washington, DC 20005, (202) 898-0089, www.aaf.org

◆ *American Demographics*, P.O. Box 68, Ithaca, NY 14851, (607) 273-6343, www.demographics.com

◆ *Business Marketing*, 740 N. Rush St., Chicago, IL 60611, (312) 649-5200, www.net626.com

◆ *Cowles Business Media* (publishes *Catalog Age, Promo* and *Marketing Tools*), P.O. Box 4294, Stamford, CT 06907-0949, (203) 358-4334, www.mediacentral.com

◆ *Direct Magazine*, 11 Riverbend Dr. S., P.O. Box 4949, Stamford, CT 06907-0949, (203) 358-9900

◆ *Direct Marketing News*, 100 Sixth Ave., New York, NY 10013, (212) 741-2095

◆ *Journal of Marketing Research*, 250 S. Wacker Dr., #200, Chicago, IL 60606, (312) 648-0536, www.ama.org

◆ *Quirk's Marketing Research Review*, 8030 Cedar Ave. S., #229, Bloomington, MN 55425, (612) 854-5101, www.quirks.com

◆ *Tradeshow Week*, 5700 Wilshire Blvd., #120, Los Angeles, CA 90036, (213) 965-5300, www.tradeshowweek.com

CREDIT SERVICES

◆ Dun & Bradstreet (provides business credit-reporting services), (800) 234-3867

◆ Equifax (provides credit-reporting services), (800) 685-1111

- Experian (TRW) (provides credit-reporting services), (800) 682-7654
- First Data Merchant Services Corp. (provides credit-processing services), 265 Broadhollow Rd., Melville, NY 11747, (576) 843-6000
- Telecheck (provides check-guarantee services), 5251 Westheimer, Houston, TX 77056, (800) TELE-CHECK
- TransUnion (provides credit-reporting services), (800) 916-8800

CUSTOMER SERVICE

Books

- *Delivering Knock Your Socks Off Service*, Kristen Anderson and Ron Zenke, Amacom
- *Knock Your Socks Off Answers: Solving Customer Nightmares & Soothing Nightmare Customers*, Kristen Anderson and Ron Zenke, Amacom
- *Positively Outrageous Service*, T. Scott Gross, Warner Books
- *Raving Fans: A Revolutionary Approach to Customer Service*, Ken Blanchard and Sheldon Bowles, William Morrow & Co.

EQUIPMENT

Cellular Phones

- Motorola, 600 N. Hwy. 45, Libertyville, IL 60048, (800) 331-6456, www.startac.com
- Oki Telecom, 437 Old Peachtree Rd., Suwanee, GA 30174, (800) 554-3112, (770) 995-9800, www.oki.com
- Panasonic Telecommunications Systems Co., 2 Panasonic Wy., Secaucus, NJ 07094, (800) 414-4408, (201) 348-9090, www.panasonic.com
- Uniden America, 4700 Amon Carter Blvd., Ft. Worth, TX 76155, (800) 235-3874, www.uniden.com

Computers

- Apple Computer, 1 Infinite Loop, Cupertino, CA 95014, (800) 776-2333, (408) 996-1010, www.apple.com
- Compaq Computer, P.O. Box 692000, Houston, TX 77269-2000, (800) 345-1518, (281) 370-0670, www.compaq.com

◆ Hewlett Packard, Home Products Division, 5301 Stevens Creek Blvd., Santa Clara, CA 95052-8059, (800) 752-0900, (650) 857-1501, www.hp.com

◆ IBM, Product Support Center, 3039 Cornwallis Rd., Bldg. 201, Dept. BMGB, Research Triangle, NC 27709, (800) 426-4968, (770) 858-5890, www.ibm.com

Copiers/Fax Machines

◆ Canon USA, 1 Canon Plaza, Lake Success, NY 11042, (800) 828-4040, (516) 488-6700, www.usa.canon.com

◆ Sharp Electronics, 1 Sharp Plaza, Mahwah, NJ 07430, (800) 237-4277, www.sharp.usa.com

◆ Xerox, 100 Clinton Ave. S., Rochester, NY 14644, (800) ASK-XEROX, www.xerox.com

Mailing Equipment

◆ Neopost, 30955 Huntwood Ave., Hayward, CA 94544-7084, (510) 387-3232, www.neopost.com

◆ Pitney Bowes, 1 Elmcroft Rd., 63-09, Stamford, CT 06926-0700, www.pitneybowes.com

Software

◆ Eudora (e-mail software), P.O. Box 120, Dept. 505, Buffalo, NY 14207, (800) 238-3672, (619) 587-1121, www.eudora.com

◆ Intuit (Quicken and Quickbooks), P.O. Box 3014, Menlo Park, CA 94026, (800) 446-8848, (415) 322-0573, www.quicken.com

◆ Lotus (SmartSuite, Approach, 1-2-3 Organizer), 55 Cambridge Pkwy., Cambridge, MA 02142, (800) 343-5414, (617) 577-8500, www.lotus.com

◆ Microsoft (Windows, Word, Excel, Office, Access, Front Page, Publisher), 1 Microsoft Wy., Redmond, WA 98052-6399, (800) 426-9400, (206) 882-8080, www.microsoft.com

◆ Symantec (Norton Utilities, Norton Antivirus), 10201 Torre Ave., Cupertino, CA 95014-2132, (800) 441-7234, (408) 253-9604, www.symantec.com

FRANCHISES AND BUSINESS OPPORTUNITIES

Association

♦ American Association of Franchisees and Dealers, P.O. Box 81887, San Diego, CA 92138-1887, (800) 733-9858

Books

♦ Franchising & Expanding Your Business (business guide No.1808), Entrepreneur Media Inc., (800) 421-2300, www.smallbizbooks.com

♦ *Franchise Opportunities Handbook*, U.S. Government Printing Office, Superintendent of Documents, Washington, DC 20402, (202) 512-1800

♦ *Franchising and Licensing: Two Ways to Build Your Business*, Andrew J. Sherman, Amacom

♦ *Franchising in the U.S.: Two Ways to Build Your Business*, Michael Coltman, Self-Counsel Press, 1704 N. State St., Bellingham, WA 98225-4605, (800) 663-3007, (360) 676-4530, www.self-counsel.com

♦ *Home Businesses You Can Buy: The Definitive Guide to Exploring Franchises, Multi-Level Marketing and Business Opportunities, Plus How to Avoid Scams*, Paul and Sarah Edwards and Walter Zooi, Putnam

♦ *How to Franchise Your Business*, Mac O. Lewis, Pilot Books, P.O. Box 2102, Greenport, NY 11944, (800) 79-PILOT, www.pilotbooks.com

♦ *The Insider's Guide to Franchising*, Bryce Webster, Amacom

♦ *Understanding Franchise Contracts*, David Hjelmfelt, Pilot Books, P.O. Box 2102, Greenport, NY 11944, (800) 79-PILOT, www.pilotbooks.com

Magazines And Publications

♦ *Business Start-Ups*, Entrepreneur Media Inc., 2392 Morse Ave., Irvine, CA 92614, (714) 261-2325, www.entrepreneurmag.com/bizstarts.hts

♦ *Entrepreneur's Franchise Special*, Entrepreneur Media Inc., 2392 Morse Ave., Irvine, CA 92614, (714) 261-2325

GENERAL SMALL-BUSINESS RESOURCES

Associations

♦ American Management Association, 160 Broadway, New York, NY 10019, (212) 586-8100

♦ Center for Entrepreneurial Management Inc., 180 Varick St., 17th Fl., New York, NY 10014, (212) 633-0060

♦ The Edward Lowe Foundation (provides business information and educational seminars for small companies), P.O. Box 8, Cassopolis, MI 49031, (800) 357-LOWE, (616) 445-4200, www.lowe.org

♦ Equipment Leasing Association of America, 1300 N. 17th St., #1010, Arlington, VA 22209, (703) 527-8655

♦ Executive Suite Association (provides executive-suite location assistance), 438 E. Wilson Bridge Rd., #200, Worthington, OH 43085-2382, (800) 237-4741, (614) 431-8295, fax: (614) 431-8258

♦ Independent Insurance Agents of America, 127 S. Payton St., Alexandria, VA 22314, (800) 221-7917

♦ The National Association for the Self-Employed, P.O. Box 612067, Dallas, TX 75261-2067, (800) 232-6273

♦ National Association of Professional Employee Organizations, 901 N. Pitt St., #150, Alexandria, VA 22314, (703) 836-0466

♦ The National Management Association, 2210 Arbor Blvd., Dayton, OH 45439, (937) 294-0421

♦ National Resource Center for Consumers of Legal Services, P.O. Box 340, Gloucester, VA 23061, (804) 693-9330

♦ Small Business Service Bureau (provides business insurance for small companies), 544 Main St., P.O. Box 15014, Worcester, MA 01615-0014, (508) 756-3513

♦ Society of Industrial and Office Realtors, 700 11th St. NW, #510, Washington, DC 20001-4511, (202) 737-1150, fax: (202) 737-8796, www.sior.com\par

Books

♦ *The Employer's Legal Handbook*, Fred Steingold, Nolo Press, 950 Parker St., Berkeley, CA 94710, (800) 992-6656, (510) 549-1976

♦ *The Entrepreneur Small Business Problem Solver: An Encyclopedic Reference and Guide*, William Cohen, John Wiley & Sons, www.wiley.com

♦ *For Entrepreneurs Only: Success Strategies for Anyone Starting or Growing a Business*, Wilson L. Harrell, Career Press, P.O. Box 687, Franklin Lakes, NJ 07417-1322, (800) 227-3371, (201) 848-0130

♦ *Generation E <Entrepreneur>: The Do-It-Yourself Business Guide for Twenty-somethings and Other Non-Corporate Types*, Joel and Lee Naftali and Joel Ross, Ten Speed Press

♦ *Golden Entrepreneuring: The Mature Person's Guide to Starting a Successful Business*, James B. Arkebauer, McGraw-Hill

♦ *The Home Office and Small Business Answer Book: Solutions to the Most Frequently Asked Questions About Starting and Running Home Offices and Small Businesses*, Janet Attard, Henry Holt

♦ *How to Build a Successful One-Person Business: A Common-Sense Guide to Starting and Growing a Company*, Veltisezar B. Bautista, Bookhaus

♦ *How to Make Millions With Your Ideas: An Entrepreneur's Guide*, Dan S. Kennedy, Plume

♦ *Interviewing and Selecting High Performers*, Richard H. Beatty, John Wiley & Sons, www.wiley.com

♦ *The Portable MBA in Entrepreneurship*, William D. Bygrave, John Wiley & Sons, www.wiley.com

♦ *Running a One Person Business*, Claude Whitmyer and Salli Rasberry, Ten Speed Press

♦ *Secrets of Self-Employment: Surviving and Thriving on the Ups and Downs of Being Your Own Boss*, Paul and Sarah Edwards, Putnam

♦ *The Small Business Encyclopedia: An Entrepreneur's Complete Guide to Success* (business guide No. 3500), Entrepreneur Media Inc., (800) 421-2300, www.smallbizbooks.com

♦ *Small Time Operator: How to Start Your Own Small Business, Keep Your Books, Pay Your Taxes and Stay Out Of Trouble!*, Bernard Kamaroff, Bell Springs Publishing, P.O. Box 1240, Willits, CA 95490, (800) 515-8050, (707) 459-6372

♦ *Streetwise Hiring Top Performers*, Bob Adams and Peter Veruki, Adams Media, 260 Center St., Holbrook, MA 02343, (800) 872-5627

♦ *Visionary Business: An Entrepreneur's Guide to Success*, Marc Allen, New World Library

Magazines And Publications

♦ *Barron's The Dow Jones Business and Financial Weekly*, 200 Liberty St., New York, NY 10281, (800) 544-0422

◆ *The Business Owner*, 16 Fox Ln., Locust Valley, NY 11560, (516) 671-8100

◆ *Business Week*, 1221 Ave. of the Americas, 39th Fl., New York, NY 10020, (800) 635-1200

◆ *Entrepreneur's Home Office*, Entrepreneur Media Inc., 2392 Morse Ave., Irvine, CA 92614, (714) 261-2325, www.entrepreneurmag.com

◆ *Entrepreneur Magazine*, Entrepreneur Media Inc., 2392 Morse Ave., Irvine, CA 92614, (714) 261-2325, www.entrepreneurmag.com

◆ *Entrepreneurial Edge*, The Edward Lowe Foundation, P.O. Box 8, Cassopolis, MI 49031, (800) 357-LOWE, (616) 445-4200, www.edgeonline.com

◆ *Entrepreneurial Manager*, 180 Varick St., New York, NY 10014-4692, (212) 633-0060

◆ *Entrepreneurial Manager's Newsletter*, 180 Varick St., 17th Fl., New York, NY 10014, (212) 633-0060

◆ *Journal of Small Business Management*, West Virginia University, College of Business, Bureau of Business and Economic Research, P.O. Box 6025, Morgantown, WV 26506-6025, (304) 293-5837

◆ *The Pricing Advisor*, 3277 Roswell Rd., #620, Atlanta, GA 30305, (404) 252-5708

◆ *The Wall Street Journal*, (800) 568-7625

HOMEBASED BUSINESS RESOURCES

Associations

◆ American Association of Home-Based Businesses, P.O. Box 10023, Rockville, MD 20849, (800) 447-9710, www.aahbb.org

◆ American Home Business Association, 60 Art St., Greenwich, CT 06820, (203) 531-8552

◆ Home Business Institute Inc., P.O. Box 301, White Plains, NY 10605-0301, (888) 342-5424, (914) 946-6600, www.hbiweb.com

◆ Mother's Home Business Network, P.O. Box 423, East Meadow, NY 11554, (516) 997-7394, www.homeworkingmom.com

◆ National Association of Home Based Businesses, 10451 Mill Run Cir., Owings Mills, MD 21117, (410) 363-3698, www.usahomebusiness.com

Books

♦ *The Home Based Business Occupational Handbook*, National Association of Home Based Businesses, 10451 Mill Run Cir., Owings Mills, MD 21117, (410) 363-3698, www.usahomebusiness.com

♦ *Home Business Big Business: How to Launch Your Home Business and Make It a Success*, Mel Cook, MacMillan

♦ *The Home Team: How Couples Can Make a Life and a Living by Working at Home*, Scott Gregory and Shirley Silvk Gregory, Panda Publishing, www.bookhome.com

♦ *The Kitchen Table Millionaire*, Patrick Cochrane, Prima Publishing, 3875 Atherton Rd., Rocklin, CA 95765, (800) 632-8676, (916) 632-4400

♦ *On Your Own: A Guide to Working Happily, Productively & Successfully From Home*, Lionel L. Fisher, Prentice Hall Trade

♦ *The Perfect Business: How to Make a Million From Home With No Payroll, No Employee Headaches, No Debts and No Sleepless Nights!*, Michael Leboeuf, Fireside

♦ *Start and Run a Profitable Home-Based Business*, Edna Sheedy, Self-Counsel Press, 1704 N. State St., Bellingham, WA 98225-4605, (800) 663-3007, (360) 676-4530

♦ *Starting & Running Your Homebased Business: A Complete Guide to Homebased Success* (business guide #1815), Entrepreneur Media Inc., (800) 421-2300, www.smallbizbooks.com

♦ *Working From Home: Everything You Need to Know About Living and Working Under the Same Roof*, Paul and Sarah Edwards, Putnam

INVENTORS AND IDEA PROTECTION

Associations

♦ Affiliated Inventors Foundation Inc., 1405 Potter Dr., #107, Colorado Springs, CO 80909, (800) 525-5885, (719) 380-1234

♦ American Society of Inventors, P.O. Box 58426, Philadelphia, PA 19102, (215) 546-6601

♦ Innovation Assessment Center, Washington State University, P.O. Box 644851, Pullman, WA 99164-4851, (509) 335-1576, www.sbdc.wsu.edu

♦ Invention Services International (sponsors the Invention Convention Trade Show), (800) 458-5624

- The Inventors Assistance League International Inc., 403 S. Central Ave., Ste. A, Glendale, CA 91204, (818) 246-6540, www.inventions.org
- National Inventors Foundation, 345 W. Cypress St., Glendale, CA 91204, (818) 246-6542

Books

- *Bringing Your Product to Market: How to Turn Your Idea Into a Booming Business* (business guide No. 1813), Entrepreneur Media Inc., (800) 421-2300, www.smallbizbooks.com
- *The Complete Idiots Guide to New Product Development*, Edwin E. Bobrow, Alpha Books
- *How to License Your Million Dollar Idea: Everything You Need to Know to Make Money From Your New Product Idea*, Harvey Reese, John Wiley & Sons, www.wiley.com
- *Inventors/Entrepreneurs Bookshop*, P.O. Box 1020, Ft. Jones, CA 96032, (800) 339-3127, (916) 468-2957
- *Inventors Guidebook—A Step-by-Step Guide to Success*, Melvin L. Fuller, M&N Associates
- *The Inventor's Notebook*, Fred E. Grissom, David Pressman and Stephen Elias, Nolo Press, 950 Parker St., Berkeley, CA 94710, (800) 992-6656, (510) 549-1976
- *Patents, Trademarks & Copyrights: Practical Strategies for Protecting Your Ideas and Inventions*, David G. Rosenbaum and Richard L. Strohm, Career Press, P.O. Box 687, Franklin Lakes, NJ 07417-1322, (800) 227-3371, (201) 848-0130

ONLINE SERVICES AND THE INTERNET

Books

- *Cyberwriting: How to Promote Your Product or Service Online (Without Being Flamed)*, Joe Vitale, Amacom
- *The Internet Business Book*, Jill H. and Matthew V. Ellsworth, John Wiley & Sons, www.wiley.com
- *Net Guide: Your Complete Guide to the Internet & Online Services*, Michael Wolff, Dell Publishing, www.amazon.com/exe/obidos/ISBN=044022 3903/sisoftwareA

- *Online Law: The SBA's Legal Guide to Doing Business on the Internet,* Andrew R. Basile Jr. and Geoffrey Gilbert, Addison-Wesley
- *Rules of the Net: On-Line Operating Instructions for Human Beings,* Gerald Van Der Leun and Thomas Mandel, Hyperion
- *Today's Nontraditional Workplace,* Alice Brendin, John Wiley & Sons, (800) 225-5945, www.wiley.com
- *The Virtual Office Survival Handbook: What Telecommuters and Entrepreneurs Need to Succeed in Today's Nontraditional Workplace,* Alice Brendin, John Wiley & Sons, www.wiley.com
- *The Whole Internet User's Guide and Catalog,* O'Reilly & Associates, 103-A Morris St., Sebastopol, CA 95472, (800) 998-9938, www.oreilly.com
- *World Wide Web Marketing: Integrating the Internet Into Your Marketing Strategy,* Jim Sterne, John Wiley & Sons, www.amazon.com/exec/obidos/ISBN=0471128430/sisoftwareA/

Internet Resources

- Accounting Software Directory, www.cpanews4u.com/actgsof2.htm
- *Boardwatch Magazine* (provides Internet service information and Internet service provider directories), 8500 W. Bowles Ave., #210, Littleton, CO 80123, (800) 933-6038, www.boardwatch.com
- Dow Jones Interactive Publishing, Dow Jones & Co., Customer Service, P.O. Box 300, Princeton, NJ 08543-0300, (800) 369-7466, ip.dowjones.com
- InterNIC (Web site domain name registration), Network Solutions Inc., Attn: InterNIC Registration Services, 505 Huntmar Park Dr., Herdon, VA 20170, (703) 742-4777, http://rs.internic.net/index.html
- Knight-Ridder Information Services Inc., 2440 El Camino Real, Mountain View, CA 94040, (800) 334-2564, www.krinfo.com
- Petry Interactive (Internet advertising service), 1290 Ave. of the Americas, 7th Fl., New York, NY 10104, (212) 603-5701, www.petrynetwork.com
- Submit It! (free service that promotes your Web site to online directories and search engines), www.submit-it.com
- Small Business Showcase (Internet advertising service), The National Association for the Self-Employed, P.O. Box 612067, Dallas, TX 75261-2067, (800) 232-6273

- Accounting Software Suppliers, www.accounting.org/actgsupp.html
- Business Advisor (a division of the Small Business Administration), www.business.gov

Internet Service Providers

- AT&T Worldnet Service, AT&T Customer Service, P.O. Box 563, Morrisville, NC 27560, (800) 967-5353, www.att.com
- Earthlink Network, 3100 New York Dr., #201, Pasadena, CA 91107, (800) 395-8425, www.earthlink.com
- MCI Internet, Customer Relations, 1925 Boyrum St., Iowa City, IA 52240, (800) 950-5555, www.mci2000.com

Online Services

- America Online, 8619 Westwood Center Dr., Vienna, VA 22182, (800) 827-6364, (703) 448-8700, www.aol.com
- CompuServe, 5000 Arlington Centre Blvd., Columbus, OH 43220, (800) 848-8990, www.compuserve.com
- Delphi Internet Services, 1030 Massachusetts Ave., Cambridge, MA 02138, (800) 544-4005, (617) 441-4801, www.delphi.com
- IBM Internet Services, 231 Martingale Rd., Schaumberg, IL 60173, (800) 722-1425, www.ibm.net
- Microsoft Network Online Service, Attn: MSN Customer Service, 1 Microsoft Wy., Redmond, WA 98052, (800) 386-5550, (206) 936-7329, www.microsoft.com
- Netscape Communications Corp., 501 E. Middlefield Rd., Mountain View, CA 94043, www.netscape.com
- Prodigy, 445 Hamilton Ave., White Plains, NY 10601, (800) 776-3449, www.prodigy.com

Web Browsers

- Microsoft Internet Explorer, 1 Microsoft Wy., Redmond, WA 98052, (800) 386-5550, (206) 936-7329, www.microsoft.com
- Netscape Communicator, Netscape Communications, 501 E. Middlefield Rd., Mountain View, CA 94043, (800) 638-7483, www.netscape.com

Web Search Engines

- Alta Vista, www.altavista.com

- Excite, www.excite.com
- HotBot, www.hotbot.com
- Infoseek, www.infoseek.com
- Lycos, www.lycos.com
- WebCrawler, www.webcrawler.com
- Yahoo!, www.yahoo.com

Start-Up Assistance

Associations

- America's Community Bankers, 900 19th St. N.W., #400, Washington, DC 20006, (202) 857-3100
- American Bankers Association, 1120 Connecticut Ave., Washington, DC 20037, (202) 663-5000
- American League of Financial Institutions, 900 19th St. N.W., #400, Washington, DC 20006, (202) 628-5624
- Association of Small Business Development Centers, 3108 Columbia Pike, #300, Arlington, VA 22204, (703) 271-8700
- Bancard Services Trust Co. (a financial services help line), 22121 Clarendon St., #624, Woodland Hills, CA 91354, (818) 999-3333
- Commercial Finance Association, 225 W. 34th St., #1815, New York, NY 10122-4272, (201) 938-3447, www.aicpa.org
- Independent Bankers Association of America, 1 Thomas Cir. N.W., #950, Washington, DC 20005, (202) 659-8111
- National Association of Small Business Investment Companies, 666 11th St. N.W., #750, Washington, DC 20001, (202) 628-5005, www.nasbic.org
- National Business Incubation Association (provides incubator-location assistance), 20 E. Circle Dr., #190, Athens, OH 45701-3751, (614) 593-4331, fax: (614) 593-1996, www.nbia.org
- National Venture Capital Association, 1655 N. Ft. Myers Dr., #700, Arlington, VA 22209, (703) 351-5269
- Service Corps of Retired Executives (national office), 409 Third St. S.W., 6th Fl., Washington, DC 20024, (202) 205-6762, www.scn.org/civic/score-online

Books

♦ *Creating a Successful Business Plan: A Step-by-Step Guide to Building Your Plan* (business guide No.1800), Entrepreneur Media Inc., (800) 421-2300, www.smallbizbooks.com

♦ *Easy Financials for your Home-Based Business: The Friendly Guide to Successful Management Systems for Busy Home Entrepreneurs,* Norm Ray, Rayve Productions, P.O. Box 726, Windsor, CA 95492, (800) 852-4890

♦ *The Fast Forward MBA in Finance,* John A. Tracey, John Wiley & Sons, www.wiley.com

♦ *Financing Your Small Business: How to Raise the Money You Need* (business guide No.1806), Entrepreneur Media Inc., (800) 421-2300, www.smallbizbooks.com

♦ *Guerrilla Financing: Alternative Techniques to Finance Any Small Business,* Bruce Jon Blechman and Jay Conrad Levinson, Houghton Mifflin

♦ *Money—Smart Secrets for the Self-Employed,* Linda Stern, Random House

♦ *Understanding Financial Statements,* Lyn M. Fraser, Prentice Hall

♦ *Venture Capital: Where to Find It,* National Association of Small Business Investment Companies Directory, P.O. Box 2039, Merrifield, VA 22116, (202) 628-5055

Magazines and Publications

♦ *Bankers Digest,* 7515 Greenville Ave., #901, Dallas, TX 75231, (214) 373-4544

♦ *Business Credit,* 8815 Centre Park Dr., #200, Columbia, MD 21045-2158, (410) 740-5560, www.nacm.org

♦ *Business Start-ups,* Entrepreneur Media Inc., 2392 Morse Ave., Irvine, CA 92614, www.entrepreneurmag.com

♦ *Corporate Finance,* 1328 Broadway, New York, NY 10001, (212) 594-5030, www.financialworld.com

♦ *Corporate Financing Week,* 488 Madison Ave., New York, NY 10022, (212) 303-3300

♦ *Credit,* American Financial Services Association, 919 18th St N.W., 3rd Fl., Washington, DC 20006, (202) 296-5544, www.americanfinsvcs.org

♦ *D&B Reports,* 299 Park Ave., New York, NY 10171-0102, (908) 665-5430

♦ *The Independent Banker,* 518 Lincoln Rd., P.O. Box 267, Sauk Centre, MN 56378, (612) 352-6546

◆ *The Secured Lender,* 225 W. 34th St., #1815, New York, NY 10122, (212) 594-3490, www.cfa.com

◆ *TMA Journal,* 7315 Wisconsin Ave., #600, Bethesda, MD 20814, (301) 907-2862, www.tma-net.org

APPENDIX B
GOVERNMENT LISTINGS

GOVERNMENT AGENCIES

◆ Copyright Clearance Center, 222 Rosewood Dr., Danvers, MA 01923, (508) 750-8400, www.copyright.com

◆ Copyright Office, Library of Congress, 101 Independence Ave., Washington, DC 20559, (202) 707-3000, www.loc.gov/copyright

◆ Department of Agriculture, 1400 and Independence Aves. S.W., Washington, DC 20250, (202) 720-7420, www.fas.usda.gov

◆ Department of Commerce, 14th St. and Constitution Ave. N.W., Washington, DC 20230, (202) 482-2000, www.doc.gov

◆ Department of Energy, 1000 Independence Ave. S.W., Washington, DC 20585, (202) 586-5000, www.doe.gov

◆ Department of Interior, 1849 C St. N.W., Washington, DC 20240, (202) 208-3100, www.doi.gov

◆ Department of Labor, 200 Constitution Ave. N.W., Rm. S-1004, Washington, DC 20210, (202) 219-6666, www.dol.gov

◆ Department of Treasury, Main Treasury Bldg., 1500 Pennsylvania Ave. N.W., Washington, DC 20220, (202) 622-2000, www.treas.gov

◆ Export-Import Bank of the United States, 811 Vermont Ave. N.W., Washington, DC 20571, (202) 565-3946, www.exim.gov

◆ Internal Revenue Service, 1111 Constitution Ave. N.W., Washington, DC 20224, (202) 622-5000, www.irs.ustreas.gov

◆ Patent and Trademark Office, Washington, DC 20231, (800) 786-9199, www.uspto.gov

◆ Printing Office, Superintendent of Documents, Washington, DC 20402, (202) 512-1800, www.access.gpo.gov\su_docs

◆ Securities and Exchange Commission, 450 Fifth St. N.W., Washington, DC 20549, (202) 942-8088, www.sec.gov

◆ Small Business Administration, 409 Third St. S.W., Washington, DC 20416, (800) 827-5722, www.sba.gov

STATE COMMERCE AND ECONOMIC DEVELOPMENT DEPARTMENTS

◆ Alabama: Alabama Development Office, 401 Adams Ave., Montgomery, AL 36130, (334) 242-0400, www.ado.state.al.us

◆ Alaska: Alaska State Dept. of Commerce and Economic Development, State Office Bldg., P.O. Box 110800, Juneau, AK 99811-0800, (907) 465-2500, www.state.ak.us/local/akdir.htm#doc

◆ Arizona: Arizona State Dept. of Commerce Business Assistance Center, 3800 N. Central Ave., Phoenix, AZ 85012, (602) 280-1480, www.commerce.state.az.us/fr_abc.shtml

◆ Arkansas: Arkansas Economic Development Commission, Minority and Small Business Development Division, 1 State Capitol Mall, Little Rock, AR 72201, (501) 682-1060, www.aedc.state.ar.us

◆ California: California Trade and Commerce Agency, Office of Small Business, 801 K St., #1700, Sacramento, CA 95814, (916) 324-5068, www.commerce.ca.gov/

◆ Colorado: Colorado Office of Business Development, 1625 Broadway, #1710, Denver, CO 80202, (303) 892-3840

◆ Connecticut: Connecticut Economic Resource Center, 805 Brook St., Bldg. 4, Rocky Hill, CT 06067, (860) 571-7136, www.cerc.com

◆ Delaware: Delaware Economic Development Office, 99 Kings Hwy., Dover, DE 19901, (302) 739-4271, www.state.de.us

◆ District of Columbia: Office of Economic Development, 441 Fourth St. NW, #140, Washington, DC 20001, (202) 727-6365

◆ Florida: Enterprise Florida, 390 N. Orange, #1300, Orlando, FL 32801, (407) 316-4600

◆ Georgia: Georgia Dept. of Community Affairs, 60 Executive Park S., Atlanta, GA 30329-2231, (404) 679-4940, www.dca.state.ga.us

◆ Hawaii: Business Action Center, 1130 N. Nimitz Hwy., Second Level, Ste. A-254, Honolulu, HI 96817, (808) 586-2545, www.hawaii.gov

◆ Idaho: Idaho State Dept. of Commerce, P.O. Box 83720, Boise, ID 83720-0093, (208) 334-2470, www.idoc.state.id.us

◆ Illinois: Illinois Dept. of Commerce and Community Affairs, 100 W. Randolph St., #3-400, Chicago, IL 60601, (312) 814-7179, www.commerce.state.il.us

◆ Indiana: Indiana State Dept. of Commerce, 1 N. Capitol, #700, Indianapolis, IN 46204-2288, (317) 232-8782

◆ Iowa: Iowa Dept. of Economic Development, 200 E. Grand Ave, Des Moines, IA 50309, (515) 281-3251

◆ Kansas: Kansas Dept. of Commerce and Housing, Business Development Dept., 700 S.W., Harrison St., #1300, Topeka, KS 66603, (785) 296-5298, www.kansascommerce.com

◆ Kentucky: Kentucky Dept. of Economic Development, Business Information Clearinghouse, 22nd Fl., Capitol Plaza Tower, Frankfort, KY 40601, (800) 626-2250, www.state.ky.us/edc/bic.htm

◆ Louisiana: Louisiana Dept. of Economic Development, P.O. Box 94185, Baton Rouge, LA 70804-9185, (504) 342-5388, www.lded.state.la.us

◆ Maine: Business Answers, Dept. of Economic and Community Development, 33 Stone St., 59 Statehouse Station, Augusta, ME 04333, (207) 287-2656

◆ Maryland: Maryland Dept. of Business and Economic Development, Division of Regional Development, 217 E. Redwood St., 10th Fl., Baltimore, MD 21202, (410) 767-0095, www.mdbusiness.state.md.us

◆ Massachusetts: Massachusetts Office of Business Development, 1 Ashburton Pl., 21st Fl., Boston, MA 02108, (617) 727-3221, www.magnet.state.ma.us/mobd/

◆ Michigan: Michigan Jobs Commission, Customer Assistance, 201 N. Washington Square, Victor Office Center, 4th Fl., Lansing, MI 48913, (517) 373-9808, www.mjc.state.mi.us/mjc

◆ Minnesota: Minnesota Small Business Assistance Office, 500 Metro Square, 121 Seventh Pl. E., St. Paul, MN 55101, (800) 657-3858, (612) 282-2103, www.dted.state.mn.us

◆ Mississippi: Mississippi Dept. of Economic and Community Development, Division of Existing Industry and Business, New

Business, P.O. Box 849, Jackson, MS 39205-0849, (601) 359-3593, www.decd.state.ms.us

◆ Missouri: Missouri Dept. of Economic Development, P.O. Box 118, Jefferson City, MO 65102, (573) 751-4982, www.ecodev.state.mo.us/mbac

◆ Montana: Dept. of Commerce, Economic Development Division, 1424 Ninth Ave., Helena, MT 59620, (406) 444-3814, http://com/mt.gov

◆ Nebraska: Dept. of Economic Development, P.O. Box 94666, Lincoln, NE 68509-4666, (402) 471-3782, www.ded.state.ne.us

◆ Nevada: Nevada State Dept. of Business and Industry, Business Advocacy Center, 2501 E. Sahara Ave., #100, Las Vegas, NV 89104, (702) 486-4335, www.state.nv.us

◆ New Hampshire: New Hampshire Office of Business and Industrial Development, P.O. Box 1856, Concord, NH 03302-1856, (603) 271-2591, http://ded.state.nh.us

◆ New Jersey: Dept. of Commerce and Economic Development, 20 State St., CN 820, Trenton, NJ 08625, (609) 292-2444, www.nj.com/business/

◆ New Mexico: New Mexico Economic Development Dept., P.O. Box 20003-5003, Santa Fe, NM 87504, (505) 827-0300, www.edd.state.nm.us

◆ New York: Division for Small Business, Empire State Development, 1 Commerce Plaza, Albany, NY 12245, (518) 473-0499, www.empire.state.ny.us

◆ North Carolina: Small Business and Technology Development Center, 333 Fayetteville Street Mall, #1150, Raleigh, NC 27601-1742, (919) 715-7272, www.sbrdc.org

◆ North Dakota: Center for Innovation, P.O. Box 8372, Grand Forks, ND 58202, (701) 777-3132, www.und.nodak.edu/dept/cibd/welcome.htm

◆ Ohio: Ohio One-Stop Business Center, 77 S. High St., 28th Fl., Columbus, OH 43216, (614) 644-8748

◆ Oklahoma: Department of Commerce, P.O. Box 26980, Oklahoma City, OK 73126-0980, (405) 843-9770, www.odoc.state.ok.us

◆ Oregon: Oregon Economic Development Dept., 775 Summer St. N.E., Salem, OR 97310, (503) 986-0123, www.econ.state.or.us

◆ Pennsylvania: Pennsylvania Small Business Resource Center, Rm. 374, Forum Bldg., Harrisburg, PA 17120, (717) 783-5700, www.dced.state.pa.us/

◆ Rhode Island: Rhode Island Economic Development Corporation, 1 W. Exchange St., Providence, RI 02903, (401) 277-2601, www.riedc.com

◆ South Carolina: Enterprise Inc., 1105 Belleview Ave., Columbia, SC 29201, (803) 252-8806,

◆ South Dakota: Governor's Office of Economic Development, 711 E. Wells Ave., Pierre, SD 57501-3369, (605) 773-5032, www.state.sd.us

◆ Tennessee: Small Business Office, Dept. of Economic and Community Development, 320 Sixth Ave. N., 7th Fl., Rachel Jackson Bldg., Nashville, TN 37243-0405, (615) 741-2626, www.state.tn.us/ecd/

◆ Texas: Texas Dept. of Economic Development, Small Business Division, P.O. Box 12728, Austin, TX 78711, (512) 936-0100, www.tded.state.tx.us

◆ Utah: Utah Dept. of Community and Economic Development, 324 S. State St., #500, Salt Lake City, UT 84111, (801) 538-8800, www.ce.ex.state.ut.us

◆ Vermont: Vermont Agency of Commerce and Community Development, 109 State St., Montpelier, VT 05609-0501, (802) 828-3211, www.state.vt.us/dea/economic/develp.htm

◆ Virginia: Dept. of Business Assistance, Small Business Development Center Network, 901 E. Byrd St., #1400, Richmond, VA 23219, (804) 371-8253, www.vdba.org

◆ Washington: Business Assistance Division, Community Trade and Economic Development, 906 Columbia St. S.W., P.O. Box 48300, Olympia, WA 98504-8300, (360) 753-4900, www.wa.gov/cted

◆ West Virginia: West Virginia Development Office, 950 Kanawha Blvd., Charleston, WV 25301, (304) 558-2960, www.wvdo.org/sbdc

◆ Wisconsin: Department of Commerce, 201 Washington Ave., Madison, WI 53703, (608) 266-9467, http://badger.state.wi.us/agencies/commerce

◆ Wyoming: Wyoming Division of Economic and Community Development, 1st Fl. E., Herschler Bldg., Cheyenne, WY 82002, (307) 777-7284, www.state.wy.us/

SMALL BUSINESS DEVELOPMENT CENTERS

The following state Small Business Development Centers (SBDCs) can direct you to the SBDC in your region of interest. You can access all state SBDC Web sites at www.smallbiz.suny.edu/sbdcnet.htm.

◆ Alabama: Alabama Small Business Development Center, University of Alabama, Box 870397, Tuscaloosa, AL 35487, (205) 348-7011

◆ Alaska: UAA Small Business Development Center, 430 W. Seventh Ave., #110, Anchorage, AK 99501, (907) 274-7232

◆ Arizona: Arizona Small Business Development Center, 2411 W. 14th St., #132, Tempe, AZ 85281, (602) 731-8720

◆ Arkansas: Arkansas Small Business Development Center, 100 S. Main, #401, Little Rock, AR 72201, (501) 324-9043

◆ California: California Small Business Development Center, Office of Small Business, 801 K St., #1700, Sacramento, CA 95814, (916) 324-5068

◆ Colorado: Colorado Business Assistance Center, 1625 Broadway, #805, Denver, CO 80202, (800) 333-7798, (303) 592-5720

◆ Connecticut: Connecticut Small Business Development Center, University of Connecticut, 2 Bourn Pl., U-94, Storrs, CT 06269-5094, (860) 486-4135

◆ Delaware: Delaware Small Business Development Center, University of Delaware, 102 MBNA America Hall, Newark, DE 19716, (302) 831-2747

◆ District of Columbia: Small Business Development Center, Howard University, School of Business, Rm. 128, 2600 Sixth St. N.W., Washington, DC 20059, (202) 806-1550

◆ Florida: Florida Small Business Development Center, 19 W. Garden St., #302, Pensacola, FL 32501, (850) 470-4980

◆ Georgia: Business Outreach Services, Small Business Development Center, Chicopee Complex, University of Georgia, 1180 E. Broad St., Athens, GA 30602-5412, (706) 542-6762

◆ Guam: Pacific Islands Small Business Development Center Network, P.O. Box 5061, Mangiloa, Guam 96923, (671) 735-2590

◆ Hawaii: University of Hawaii at Hilo, Small Business Development Center Network, 200 W. Kawili St., Hilo, HI 96720-4091, (808) 933-3515

◆ Idaho: Idaho Small Business Development Center, Boise State

University, 1910 University Dr., Boise, ID 83725-1655, (208) 385-1640

◆ Illinois: Illinois Greater North Pulaski Small Business Development Center, 4054 W. North Ave., Chicago, IL 60639, (773) 384-2262, (800) 252-2923 (in Illinois)

◆ Indiana: Indiana Small Business Development Center, 1 N. Capitol, #420, Indianapolis, IN 46204, (317) 264-6871

◆ Iowa: Iowa Small Business Development Center, 137 Lynn Ave., Ames, IA 50014, (515) 292-6351

◆ Kansas: Small Business Development Center, 1501 S. Joplin, Pittsburg, KS 66762, (316) 235-4920

◆ Kentucky: Kentucky Small Business Development Center, 225 Gatton College of Business and Economics, Lexington, KY 40506, (606) 257-7668

◆ Louisiana: Louisiana Small Business Development Center, College of Business Administration, Northeast Louisiana University, Monroe, LA 71209-6435, (318) 342-5506

◆ Maine: University of Southern Maine, 96 Falmouth St., P.O. Box 9300, Portland, ME 04104-9300, (207) 780-4420

◆ Maryland: Maryland Small Business Development Center, 7100 E. Baltimore Ave., #401, College Park, MD 20740-3627, (301) 403-8300

◆ Massachusetts: Massachusetts Small Business Development Center, University of Massachusetts, P.O. Box 34935, Amherst, MA 01003, (413) 545-6301

◆ Michigan: Michigan Small Business Development Center, 2727 Second Ave., #107, Detroit, MI 48201, (313) 964-1798

◆ Minnesota: Minnesota Small Business Development Center, Dept. of Trade and Economic Development, 500 Metro Square, 121 Seventh Pl. E., St. Paul, MN 55101-2146, (612) 297-5773

◆ Mississippi: Mississippi Small Business Development Center, University of Mississippi, 216 Old Chemistry Bldg., University, MS 38677, (601) 232-5001, (800) 725-7232 (in Mississippi)

◆ Missouri: Missouri Small Business Development Center, 1205 University Ave., #300, Columbia, MO 65211, (573) 882-0344

◆ Montana: Small Business Development Center, Department of Commerce, 1424 Ninth Ave., Helena, MT 59620, (406) 444-4780

◆ Nebraska: Nebraska Business Development Center, College of Business Administration, University of Nebraska at Omaha, Rm. 407, Omaha, NE 68182-0248, (402) 554-2521

◆ Nevada: Nevada Small Business Development Center, University of Nevada at Reno, College of Business Administration/032, Reno, NV 89557-0100, (702) 784-1717

◆ New Hampshire: New Hampshire Small Business Development Center, 100 Elm St., 12th Fl., Manchester, NH 03101, (603) 624-2000

◆ New Jersey: New Jersey Small Business Development Center, 49 Bleeker St., Newark, NJ 07102-1993, (973) 353-5950

◆ New Mexico: New Mexico Small Business Development Center, Santa Fe Community College, 6401 S. Richards Ave., Santa Fe, NM 87505, (800) 281-SBDC, (505) 438-1362

◆ New York: New York Small Business Development Center, SUNY Plaza, S-523, Albany, NY 12246, (518) 443-5398, (800) 732-SBDC (in New York state)

◆ North Carolina: North Carolina Small Business and Technology Development Center, 333 Fayetteville Street Mall, #1150, Raleigh, NC 27601, (919) 715-7272, (800) 258-0862 (in North Carolina)

◆ North Dakota: North Dakota Small Business Development Center, University of North Dakota, P.O. Box 7308, Grand Forks, ND 58202, (701) 777-3700 (no Web site available)

◆ Ohio: Ohio Small Business Development Center, P.O. Box 1001, Columbus, OH 43261-1001, (614) 466-2480

◆ Oklahoma: Oklahoma Small Business Development Center, Stn. A, P.O. Box 2584, Durant, OK 74701, (405) 924-0277

◆ Oregon: Oregon Small Business Development Center Network, 44 W. Broadway, #501, Eugene, OR 97401-3021, (541) 726-2250

◆ Pennsylvania: Pennsylvania Small Business Development Center, University of Pennsylvania, Vance Hall, 3733 Spruce St., 4th Fl., Philadelphia, PA 19104, (215) 898-1219

◆ Rhode Island: Rhode Island Small Business Development Center, Bryant College, 1150 Douglas Pike, Smithfield, RI 02917, (401) 232-6111

◆ South Carolina: South Carolina Small Business Development Center, College of Business Administration, Rm. 652, University of South Carolina, Columbia, SC 29208, (803) 777-4907

◆ South Dakota: South Dakota Small Business Development Center, University of South Dakota, School of Business, 414 E. Clark St., Vermillion, SD 57069-2390, (605) 677-5498

◆ Tennessee: Tennessee Small Business Development Center, University of Memphis, South Campus, Bldg. No. 1, Memphis, TN 38152, (901) 678-2500

◆ Texas: Texas Small Business Development Center, 1100 Louisiana, #500, Houston, TX 77002, (713) 752-8400

◆ Utah: Utah Small Business Development Center, 1623 S. State St., Salt Lake City, UT 84115, (801) 957-3840

◆ Vermont: Vermont Small Business Development Center, 60 Main St., #103, Burlington, VT 05401, (802) 658-9228

◆ Virginia: Virginia Small Business Development Center, P.O. Box 446, Richmond, VA 23218-0446, (804) 371-8258

◆ Washington: Washington Small Business Development Center, Washington State University, P.O. Box 644851, Pullman, WA 99164-4851, (509) 335-1576

◆ West Virginia: West Virginia Small Business Development Center, 950 Kanawha Blvd. E., #200, Charleston, WV 25301, (304) 558-2960

◆ Wisconsin: University of Wisconsin at Whitewater, Small Business Development Center, Carlson 2000, Whitewater, WI 53190, (414) 472-3217

◆ Wyoming: Wyoming Small Business Development Center, 111 W. Second St., #502, Casper, WY 82601, (307) 234-6683

SBA DISTRICT OFFICES

The Small Business Administration has several types of field offices. Of these, the district offices offer the fullest range of services to small businesses.

◆ Alabama: 2121 Eighth Ave. N., #200, Birmingham, AL 35203-2398, (205) 731-1344

◆ Alaska: 222 W. Eighth Ave., Rm. A36, Anchorage, AK 99513-7559, (907) 271-4022

◆ Arizona: 2828 N. Central Ave., #800, Phoenix, AZ 85004-1093, (602) 640-2316

- Arkansas: 2120 Riverfront Dr., #100, Little Rock, AR 72202, (501) 324-5871

- California: 2719 N. Air Fresno Dr., #107, Fresno, CA 93727-1547, (209) 487-5189

  330 N. Brand Blvd., #1200, Glendale, CA 91203-2304, (818) 552-3210

  550 W. C St., #550, San Diego, CA 92101, (619) 557-7252

  455 Market St., 6th Fl., San Francisco, CA 94105-1988, (415) 744-6801

  660 J St., Rm. 215, Sacramento, CA 95814-2413, (916) 498-6410

  200 W. Santa Ana Blvd., #700, Santa Ana, CA 92701, (714) 550-7420

- Colorado: 721 19th St., #426, Denver, CO 80202-2599, (303) 844-3984

- Connecticut: 330 Main St., 2nd Fl., Hartford, CT 06106, (860) 240-4700

- Delaware: 824 N. Market St., #610, Wilmington, DE 19801-3011, (302) 573-6294

- District of Columbia: 1110 Vermont Ave. N.W., #900, Washington, DC 20005, (202) 606-4000

- Florida: 1320 S. Dixie Hwy., #350, Coral Gables, FL 33146-2911, (305) 536-5521

  7825 Baymeadows Wy., #100-B, Jacksonville, FL 32256-7504, (904) 443-1900

- Georgia: 1720 Peachtree Rd. N.W., 6th Fl., Atlanta, GA 30309, (404) 347-4749

- Hawaii: 300 Ala Moana Blvd., Rm. 2314, Honolulu, HI 96850-4981, (808) 541-2990

- Idaho: 1020 Main St., #290, Boise, ID 83702-5745, (208) 334-1696

- Illinois: 500 W. Madison St., #1250, Chicago, IL 60661-2511, (312) 353-4508

  511 W. Capitol Ave., #302, Springfield, IL 62704, (217) 492-4416

- Indiana: 429 N. Pennsylvania, #100, Indianapolis, IN 46204-1873, (317) 226-7272

- Iowa: Mail Code 0736, 215 Fourth Ave. S.E., #200, The Lattner Bldg., Cedar Rapids, IA 52401-1806, (319) 362-6405

210 Walnut St., Rm. 749, Des Moines, IA 50309-2186, (515) 284-4422

◆ Kansas: 100 E. English St., #510, Wichita, KS 67202, (316) 269-6616

◆ Kentucky: 600 Dr. Martin Luther King Jr. Pl., Rm. 188, Louisville, KY 40202, (502) 582-5971

◆ Louisiana: 365 Canal St., #2250, New Orleans, LA 70130, (504) 589-6685

◆ Maine: 40 Western Ave., Rm. 512, Augusta, ME 04330, (207) 622-8378

◆ Maryland: 10 S. Howard St., #6220, Baltimore, MD 21201-2525, (410) 962-4392

◆ Massachusetts: 10 Causeway St., Rm. 265, Boston, MA 02222-1093, (617) 565-5590

◆ Michigan: 477 Michigan Ave., Rm. 515, Detroit, MI 48226, (313) 226-6075

◆ Minnesota: 100 N. Sixth St., #610, Buder Square, Minneapolis, MN 55403-1563, (612) 370-2324

◆ Mississippi: 101 W. Capitol St., #400, Jackson, MS 39201, (601) 965-4378

◆ Missouri: 323 W. Eighth St., #501, Kansas City, MO 64105, (816) 374-6708

815 Olive St., Rm. 242, St. Louis, MO 63101, (314) 539-6600

◆ Montana: 301 S. Park Ave., Rm. 334, Helena, MT 59626-0054, (406) 441-1081

◆ Nebraska: 11145 Mill Valley Rd., Omaha, NE 68154, (402) 221-4691

◆ Nevada: 301 E. Stewart Ave., Rm. 301, Las Vegas, NV 89101, (702) 388-6611

◆ New Hampshire: 143 N. Main St., #202, Concord, NH 03302-1248, (603) 225-1400

◆ New Jersey: 2 Gateway Center, 4th Fl., Newark, NJ 07102, (201) 645-2434

◆ New Mexico: 625 Silver S.W., #320, Albuquerque, NM 87102, (505) 766-1870

◆ New York: 111 W. Huron St., Rm. 1311, Buffalo, NY 14202, (716) 551-4301

26 Federal Plaza, #31-00, New York, NY 10278, (212) 264-2454

100 S. Clinton St., #1071, Syracuse, NY 13260, (315) 448-0423

◆ North Carolina: 200 N. College St., Ste. A-2015, Charlotte, NC 28202-2137, (704) 344-6563

◆ North Dakota: 657 Second Ave. N., Rm. 219, Fargo, ND 58108-3086, (701) 239-5131

◆ Ohio: 1111 Superior Ave., #630, Cleveland, OH 44114-2507, (216) 522-4180

1111 Nationwide Plaza, #1400, Columbus, OH 43215-2542, (614) 469-6860

◆ Oklahoma: 210 Park Ave., #1300, Oklahoma City, OK 73102, (405) 231-5521

◆ Oregon: 1515 S.W. Fifth Ave., #1050, Portland, OR 97201-6695, (503) 326-2682

◆ Pennsylvania: 475 Allendale Rd., #201, King of Prussia, PA 19406, (610) 962-3800

1000 Liberty Ave., Rm. 1128, Pittsburgh, PA 15222-4004, (412) 644-2780

◆ Puerto Rico: 252 Ponce de Leon Blvd., Rm. 201, Hato Rey, PR 00918, (787) 766-5572

◆ Rhode Island: 380 Westminster Mall, 5th Fl., Providence, RI 02903, (401) 528-4561

◆ South Carolina: 1835 Assembly St., Rm. 358, Columbia, SC 29201, (803) 765-5377

◆ South Dakota: 110 S. Phillips Ave., #200, Sioux Falls, SD 57102-1109, (605) 330-4231

◆ Tennessee: 50 Vantage Wy., #201, Nashville, TN 37228-1500, (615) 736-5881

◆ Texas: 4300 Amon Carter Blvd., #114, Ft. Worth, TX 76155, (817) 885-6500

10737 Gateway W., #320, El Paso, TX 79935, (915) 540-5676

9301 Southwest Hwy., #550, Houston, TX 77074-1591, (713) 773-6500

222 E. Van Buren St., Rm. 500, Harlingen, TX 78550-6855, (210) 427-8533

1611 10th St., #200, Lubbock, TX 79401-2693, (806) 743-7462

727 E. Durango Blvd., Rm. A-527, San Antonio, TX 78206-1204, (210) 472-5900

◆ Utah: 125 S. State St., Rm. 2229, Salt Lake City, UT 84138-1195, (801) 524-5804

◆ Vermont: 87 State St., Rm. 205, Montpelier, VT 05602, (802) 828-4422

◆ Virginia: 1504 Santa Rosa Rd., #200, Richmond, VA 23229, (804) 771-2400

◆ Washington: 1200 Sixth Ave., Rm. 1700, Seattle, WA 98101-1128, (206) 553-7310

W. 601 First Ave., 10th Fl., Spokane, WA 99204-0317, (509) 353-2810

◆ West Virginia: 168 W. Main St., 5th Fl., Clarksburg, WV 26301, (304) 623-5631

◆ Wisconsin: 212 E. Washington Ave., Rm. 213, Madison, WI 53703, (608) 264-5261

◆ Wyoming: 100 E. B St., Rm. 4001, Casper, WY 82602-2839, (307) 261-6500

APPENDIX C

SMALL-BUSINESS-FRIENDLY BANKS

L ooking for a little extra expansion capital? You couldn't have picked a better time. According to a recent report by the U.S. Small Business Administration's Office of Advocacy, bankers are lending money to small business like never before.

According to Jere Glover, chief counsel for the Office of Advocacy, which compiles and publishes the Micro-Business-Friendly Banks in the United States report, there are a number of reasons for the lending increase. "A lot has to do with an increase in lending to women," he says. "More women are starting businesses, and bankers are beginning to realize they are good loan risks."

The SBA's LowDoc program, which encourages banks to make small loans with reduced paperwork, is at the center of another change, adds Glover. It showed bankers that it's cost-effective to make such microloans (which are less than $100,000). Now banks are taking the initiative and making these loans on their own.

The latest study used three new criteria to rank the top microbusiness-friendly banks. Consequently, a broader view of the lending climate is presented.

"The old ranking system favored very small banks. Now we're using four factors that give a more balanced view," explains Glover. As a result of the new evaluation criteria, 20 larger banks were included in the latest study.

The four variables measured are: 1) microbusiness loans-to-assets ratio, 2) microbusiness loan-to-total-business-loan ratio, 3) dollar volume of microbusiness loans, and 4) total number of microbusiness loans.

Armed with the study's information, says Glover, you can find the banks in your community that have made microloans in the past—and will be more likely to do so in the future.

The following ranking lists the SBA's top two microbusiness-friendly banks in each state (where there were two). The listing also includes banks whose microloans-to-assets ratio was 40 percent or higher.

Alabama

Bankers Trust of Madison, 2200 Clinton Ave., Madison, AL 35804, (205) 533-5422

CB&T Bank of Russell County, P.O. Box 2400, Phenix City, AL 36838-2400, (334) 297-7000

Alaska

First National Bank, 646 W. Fourth Ave., Anchorage, AK 99501, (907) 276-6300

Arizona

Bank of Casa Grande Valley, 1300 E. Florence Blvd., Casa Grande, AZ 85222, (520) 836-4666

Mohave State Bank, 1771 McCulloch Blvd., Lake Havasu City, AZ 86405, (520) 855-0000

Arkansas

Caddo First National Bank, P.O. Box 47, Glenwood, AR 71943, (501) 356-3196

Fidelity National Bank, 330 W. Broadway, West Memphis, AR 72301, (501) 735-8700

California

First Mountain Bank, P.O. Box 6868, Big Bear Lake, CA 92315, (909) 866-5861

Wells Fargo Bank N.A., 1 Montgomery St., San Francisco, CA 94104, (800) 869-3557

Colorado

Cheyenne Mountain Bank, 1580 E. Cheyenne Mtn. Blvd., Colorado Springs, CO 80906, (719) 579-9150

The Bank of Grand Junction, 2415 F Rd., Grand Junction, CO 81505, (970) 241-9000

Connecticut

Bank of Southington, 130 N. Main St., Southington, CT 06489, (860) 620-5000

Maritime Bank & Trust Co., P.O. Box 920, Essex, CT 06426, (860) 767-1166

Delaware

Citibank Delaware, 1 Penns Wy., New Castle, DE 19720, (800) 341-4727

PNC Bank, Delaware, 222 Delaware Ave., Wilmington, DE 19801, (302) 429-2107

Florida

First National Bank of Southwest Florida, 2724 Del Prado Blvd., Cape Coral, FL 33904, (941) 772-2220

Transatlantic Bank, 102 N.W. 37th Ave., Coral Gables, FL 33125, (305) 643-0200

Georgia

Coastal Bank, P.O. Box 529, Hinesville, GA 31310, (912) 368-2265

First National Bank of Alma, P.O. Box 2028, Alma, GA 31510, (912) 632-7262

Hawaii

City Bank, 201 Merchant St., Honolulu, HI 96813, (808) 546-2411

Idaho

Panhandle State Bank, P.O. Box 967, Sandpoint, ID 83864, (208) 263-0505

Farmers National Bank of Buhl, P.O. Box 392, Buhl, ID 83316, (208) 543-4352

Illinois

Bank of Bourbonnais, 1 Heritage Plaza, Bourbonnais, IL 60914, (815) 933-0570

First National Bank of Wheaton, 1151 E. Butterfield Rd., Wheaton, IL 60187, (630) 260-2200

Indiana

Farmers State Bank, P.O. Box 455, Mentone, IN 46539, (219) 353-7521

First Community Bank & Trust, 210 E. Harriman, Bargersville, IN 46106, (317) 422-5171

Iowa

Clear Lake Bank & Trust Co., 322 Main Ave., Clear Lake, IA 50428, (515) 357-7121

Solon State Bank, P.O. Box 129, 126 S. Market St., Solon, IA 52333, (319) 644-3405

Kansas

The Kaw Valley State Bank and Trust Co., 1110 N. Kansas Ave., Topeka, KS 66608, (913) 232-6062

First National Bank of Wamego, P.O. Box 226, Wamego, KS 66547, (913) 456-2221

Kentucky

The Bank of Mt. Vernon, P.O. Box 157, Mt. Vernon, KY 40456, (606) 256-5141

First Southern National Bank, P.O. Box 27, Hustonville, KY 40437, (606) 346-4921

Louisiana

First Guaranty Bank, P.O. Box 2009, Hammond, LA 70404, (504) 345-7685

South Louisiana Bank, 1362 W. Tunnel Blvd., Houma, LA 70360, (504) 868-2463

Maine

United Bank, 145 Exchange St., Bangor, ME 04401, (207) 942-5263

Katahdin Trust Co., P.O. Box I, Patten, ME 04765, (207) 528-2211

Maryland

Home Bank, P.O. Box 10, Newark, MD 21841, (410) 632-2151

Peoples Bank of Kent County, Maryland, P.O. Box 210, 100 Spring St., Chestertown, MD 21620, (410) 778-3500

Massachusetts

Luzo Community Bank, 1724 Acushnet Ave., New Bedford, MA 02746, (508) 999-9980

Bank of Western Massachusetts, 29 State St., Springfield, MA 01103, (413) 781-2265

Michigan

MFC First National Bank, 1205 Ludington St., Escanaba, MI 49829, (906) 786-5010

MFC First National Bank, M&M Plaza, Menominee, MI 49858, (906) 863-5523

Minnesota

First State Bank of Excelsior, 19765 Hwy. 7, Shorewood, MN 55331, (612) 474-2307

State Bank of Delano, P.O. Box 530, Delano, MN 55328, (612) 972-2935

Mississippi

First Bank, P.O. Box 808, McComb, MS 39648, (601) 684-2231

Pike County National Bank, P.O. Box 1666, 350 Rawls Dr., McComb, MS 39648, (601) 684-7575

Missouri

First City National Bank, 500 E. Battlefield, Springfield, MO 65808, (417) 887-8044

Central Bank of Kansas City, 2301 Independence Blvd., Kansas City, MO 64124, (816) 483-1210

Montana

Bitterroot Valley Bank, LoLo Shopping Center, P.O. Box 9, LoLo, MT 59847, (406) 273-2400

Mountain West Bank of Helena, 1225 Cedar St., Helena, MT 59601, (406) 449-2265

First Security Bank of West Yellowstone, P.O. Box 550, West Yellowstone, MT 59758, (406) 646-7646

Nebraska

Ashland State Bank, 2433 Silver St., Ashland, NE 68003, (402) 341-5123

Dakota County State Bank, 2024 Dakota Ave., South Sioux City, NE 68776, (402) 494-4215

Nevada

First National Bank of Ely, 595 Aultman St., Ely, NV 89301, (702) 289-4441

U.S. Bank of Nevada, 5190 Neil Rd., #130, Reno, NV 89502, (702) 689-2062

New Hampshire

The First Colebrook Bank, 147 Main St., P.O. Box 88, Colebrook, NH 03576, (603) 237-5551

First National Bank of Portsmouth, 1500 Lafayette Rd., Portsmouth, NH 03801, (603) 433-2952

New Jersey

Burlington County Bank, 1660 Beverly Rd., Burlington, NJ 08016, (609) 387-2265

Panasia Bank, 183 Main St., Ft. Lee, NJ 07024, (201) 947-6666

New Mexico

Centinel Bank of Taos, P.O. Box 828, Taos, NM 87571, (505) 758-6700

First National Bank of Tucumcari, P.O. Box 1107, Tucumcari, NM 88401, (505) 461-3602

New York

Solvay Bank, 1537 Milton Ave., Solvay, NY 13209, (315) 468-1661

Bank of Richmondville, P.O. Box 40, Cobleskill, NY 12043, (518) 234-4397

North Carolina

Yadkin Valley Bank & Trust Co., 110 W. Market St., Elkin, NC 28621, (910) 526-6300

Triangle Bank, 4300 Glenwood Ave., Raleigh, NC 27612, (919) 881-0455

North Dakota

Kirkwood Bank & Trust Co., 919 S. Seventh St., Bismarck, ND 58504, (701) 258-6550

First Western Bank & Trust, 900 S. Broadway, Minot, ND 58701, (701) 852-3711

Ohio

Citizens Banking Co., P.O. Box 247, Salineville, OH 43945, (330) 532-4123

First Bank of Marietta, 320 Front St., Marietta, OH 45750, (614) 373-4904

Oklahoma

First Bank of Hennessey, 101 N. Main, P.O. Box 724, Hennessey, OK 73742, (405) 853-2530

Bank of Cushing & Trust Co., P.O. Box 951, Cushing, OK 74023, (918) 225-2010

Oregon

Valley Commercial Bank, P.O. Box 766, Forest Grove, OR 97116, (503) 359-4495

Inland Empire Bank, 101 E. Main, P.O. Box 1170, Hermiston, OR 97838-3170, (541) 564-4216

Pennsylvania
First Columbia Bank & Trust Co., 11 W. Main St., Bloomsburg, PA 17815, (717) 784-1660

First National Bank of Leesport, 133 N. Centre Ave., P.O. Box C, Leesport, PA 19533-0905, (610) 926-2161

Rhode Island
Washington Trust Co., 23 Broad St., Westerly, RI 02891, (401) 348-1227

South Carolina
Enterprise Bank of South Carolina, 206 E. Broadway, Ehrhardt, SC 29081, (803) 267-3191

Palmetto State Bank, P.O. Box 158, Hampton, SC 29924, (803) 943-2671

South Dakota
American State Bank, P.O. Box 2530, Rapid City, SD 57709, (605) 348-3322

First Western Bank, 648 Mt. Rushmore Rd., Custer, SD 57730, (605) 673-2215

Tennessee
Volunteer Bank & Trust Co., 728 Broad St., Chattanooga, TN 37402, (423) 265-5099

Bank First, 330 N. Cedar Bluff Rd., Knoxville, TN 37923, (423) 595-2760

Texas
First Commercial Bank, P.O. Box 1960, Seguin, TX 78155-8960, (210) 379-8390

Midland American Bank, 401 W. Texas, #100, Midland, TX 79701, (915) 687-3013

Utah
Cache Valley Bank, 101 N. Main, Logan, UT 84321, (801) 753-3020

Advanta Financial Corp., 11850 S. Election Rd., Salt Lake City, UT 84020, (801) 523-0858

Vermont
Union Bank, 20 Main St., P.O. Box 667, Morrisville, VT 05661, (802) 888-6600

Citizens Savings Bank & Trust, P.O. Box 219, Saint Johnsbury, VT 05819, (802) 748-3131

Virginia

Benchmark Community Bank, 100 S. Broad St., Kenbridge, VA 23944, (804) 676-8444

Virginia Community Bank, P.O. Box 888, Louisa, VA 23093, (540) 967-2111

Washington

Pend Oreille Bank, P.O. Box 1530, Newport, WA 99156, (509) 447-5641

National Bank of Tukwila, 505 Industry Dr., Tukwila, WA 98188, (206) 575-1445

Washington, DC

Century National Bank, 1875 Eye St. N.W., Washington, DC 20006, (202) 496-4000

Franklin National Bank of Washington DC, 1722 Eye St. N.W., Washington, DC 20006, (202) 429-9888

West Virginia

Traders Bank, 303 Main St., Spencer, WV 25276, (304) 927-3340

Calhoun County Bank, P.O. Box 430, Grantsville, WV 26147, (304) 354-6116

Wisconsin

Stephenson National Bank & Trust Co., P.O. Box 137, Marinette, WI 54143-0137, (715) 732-1650

First National Bank Fox Valley, 161 Main St., Menasha, WI 54952, (414) 729-6900

Wyoming

Western Bank of Cheyenne, P.O. Box 127, 1525 E. Pershing Blvd., Cheyenne, WY 82001, (307) 637-7333

First Interstate Bank of Commerce, 4 S. Main St., Sheridan, WY 82801, (307) 674-7411

INDEX

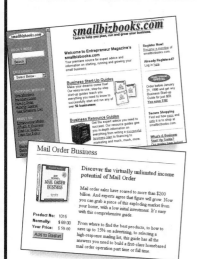

FREE ADVICE

When was the last time you got **free** advice that was worth something?

free issue!

Entrepreneur Magazine, the leading small business authority, is loaded with <u>free advice</u>—advice that could be worth millions to you. Every issue gives you detailed, practical knowledge on how <u>to start a business</u> and run it success-fully. Entrepreneur is the perfect resource to keep small business owners up-to-date, on track, and growing their business.

Get your **free issue** of Entrepreneur today!

Call 800-274-6229 Dept. 5HBJ4,
or fill out and mail the back of this card.

Entrepreneur MAGAZINE.

BREAK OUT

Business Start-Ups helps you **break** out of the 9–5 life!

free issue!

<u>Do you want</u> to get out of the 9–5 routine and take control of your life? <u>Business Start-Ups</u> shows you the franchise and business opportunities that will give you the future you dream of. Every issue answers your questions, <u>highlights hot trends</u>, spotlights new ideas, and provides the inspiration and real-life information you need to succeed.

Get your **free issue** of Business Start-Ups today!

Call 800-274-8333 Dept. 5HDJ2,
or fill out and mail the back of this card.

Business Start-Ups.

MILLION DOLLAR SECRETS

Exercise your right to make it **big**.

Get into the small business authority—
now at **80% off** the newsstand price!

free issue!

Yes! Start my one year subscription and
bill me for just $9.99. I get a full year of Entrepreneu
and save 80% off the newsstand rate. If I choose no
to subscribe, the free issue is mine to keep.

Name ☐ Mr. ☐ Mrs. _____
(please print)

Address _____

City_____ State _____ Zip_____

☐ **BILL ME**   ☐ **PAYMENT ENCLOSED**

Guaranteed. Or your money back. Every subscription to Entrepreneur comes with a 100% satisfaction guarantee: your money back
whenever you like, for whatever reason, on all unmailed issues! Offer good in U.S. and possessions only. Please allow 4–6 weeks for mailing o
first issue. Canadian and foreign: $39.97. U.S. funds only.

5H

Mail this coupon to **Entrepreneur** MAGAZINE P.O. Box 50368, Boulder, CO 80321-0368

OPPORTUNITY KNOCKS!!!

save 72%!

free issue!

Please enter my subscription to Business
Start-Ups for one year. I will receive 12 issues for
only $9.99. That's a savings of 72% off the news-
stand price. The free issue is mine to keep, even if
I choose not to subscribe.

Name ☐ Mr. ☐ Mrs. _____
(please print)

Address _____

City_____ State _____ Zip_____

☐ **BILL ME**   ☐ **PAYMENT ENCLOSED**

Guaranteed. Or your money back. Every subscription to Business Start-Ups comes with a 100% satisfaction guarantee: your money bac
whenever you like, for whatever reason, on all unmailed issues! Offer good in U.S. and possessions only. Please allow 4–6 weeks for mailing
first issue. Canadian and foreign: $34.97. U.S. funds only.

5H

Mail this coupon to **Business Start-Ups** P.O. Box 50347, Boulder, CO 80321-0347